# THE ESSENTIAL
# WAYNE DYER
## COLLECTION

# ALSO BY WAYNE DYER

# THE ESSENTIAL
# WAYNE DYER
## COLLECTION

*Includes the all-time international bestsellers*
## THE POWER OF INTENTION
## INSPIRATION AND
## EXCUSES BEGONE!

**HAY HOUSE, INC.**
Carlsbad, California • New York City
London • Sydney • Johannesburg
Vancouver • Hong Kong • New Delhi

*Published and distributed in the United States by:* Hay House, Inc.: www.hay house.com® • *Published and distributed in Australia by:* Hay House Australia Pty. Ltd.: www.hayhouse.com.au • *Published and distributed in the United Kingdom by:* Hay House UK, Ltd.: www.hayhouse.co.uk • *Published and distributed in the Republic of South Africa by:* Hay House SA (Pty), Ltd.: www.hayhouse.co.za • *Distributed in Canada by:* Raincoast: www.raincoast.com • *Published in India by:* Hay House Publishers India: www.hayhouse.co.in

*Cover design:* Aeshna Roy

The poems on pages 94 and 100 are from the Penguin publication *I Heard God Laughing, Rendering of Hafiz,* copyright 1996 & 2006 Daniel Ladinsky and used with his permission.

Page 525: ©1982 by Stephen Mitchell. Reprinted from *The Selected Poetry of Rainer Maria Rilke,* edited and translated by Stephen Mitchell, Random House.

**Library of Congress Control Number:** 2013942840


**Hardcover ISBN:** 978-1-4019-4422-3


16  15  14  13    5  4  3  2
1st edition, September 2013
2nd edition, October 2013


Printed in the United States of America

# CONTENTS

**Part III: The *Excuses Begone!* Paradigm Shift**

# THE
# POWER OF
# INTENTION

\* \* \*

For my daughter Skye Dyer.
Your singing voice is a perfect vibrational match
to your angelic soul.
I love you!

\* \* \*

# PREFACE

The book that you're now holding in your hands, and all of the information it contains, was once a formless idea residing in the invisible domain of the field of intention. This book, *The Power of Intention,* was intended into the material world by applying all of the principles written about here. I managed to make my own vibrational energy match up to the all-creating Source, and allowed these words and ideas to flow through me directly to you. You're holding in your hands evidence that anything we can conceive of in our minds—while staying in harmony with the universal all-creating Source—can and must come to pass.

If you'd like to know how this book might impact you and how you might think, feel, and co-create after reading and applying its messages, I encourage you to read the final chapter, *A Portrait of a Person Connected to the Field of Intention,* before beginning this journey. You and everyone else, as well as all of life, emanated from the universal all-creating field of intention. Live from that perspective, and you will come to know and apply the power of intention. You have an endless stream of green lights before you!

— Dr. Wayne W. Dyer
Maui, Hawaii

〜 ✳ 〜 ✳ 〜

3

"*Every beauty which is seen here below by persons of perception resembles more than anything else that celestial source from which we all come . . .*"

— Michelangelo

"*Self-realization means that we have been consciously connected with our source of being. Once we have made this connection, then nothing can go wrong. . . .*"

— Swami Paramananda

# PART I

# THE
# ESSENTIALS
# OF
# INTENTION

*"Beside the river stands the holy tree of life.
There doth my father dwell, and my home is in him.
The heavenly father and I are one."*

— The Essene Gospel of Peace

# CHAPTER ONE

# Viewing Intention from a New Perspective

*"In the universe there is an immeasurable, indescribable force which shamans call intent, and absolutely everything that exists in the entire cosmos is attached to intent by a connecting link."*

— Carlos Castaneda

During the past several years, I've been so strongly attracted to studying *intention* that I've read hundreds of books by psychological, sociological, and spiritual writers; ancient and modern scholars; and academic researchers. My research reveals a fairly common definition of *intention* as a strong purpose or aim, accompanied by a determination to produce a desired result. People driven by intention are described as having a strong will that won't permit anything to interfere with achieving their inner desire. I imagine a sort of pit-bull kind of resolve or determination. If you're one of those people with a never-give-up attitude combined with an internal picture that propels you toward fulfilling your dreams, you fit this description of someone with intention. You are, most likely, a super-achiever and probably proud of your ability to recognize and take advantage of opportunities that arise.

For many years I've held a similar belief about intention. In fact, I've written and spoken often about the power of intention being just what I've described above. Over the past quarter of a century, however, I've felt a shift in my thinking from a purely psychological or personal-growth emphasis, toward a spiritual orientation where healing, creating miracles, manifesting, and making a connection to divine intelligence are genuine possibilities.

This hasn't been a deliberate attempt to disengage from my academic and professional background, but rather a natural evolution that's been unfolding as I began to make more conscious contact with Spirit. My writing now emphasizes a belief that we can find spiritual solutions to problems by living at higher levels and calling upon faster energies. In my mind, intention is now something much greater than a determined ego or individual will. It's something almost totally opposite. Perhaps this comes from shedding many levels of ego in my own life, but I also feel the strong influence of two sentences I read in a book by Carlos Castaneda. In my writing life, I've often come across something in a book that starts a thought germinating in me that ultimately compels me to write a new book. At any rate, I read these two sentences in Castaneda's final book, *The Active Side of Infinity*, while I was waiting to have a cardiac procedure to open one clogged artery leading into my heart that had caused a mild heart attack.

Castaneda's words were: "Intent is a force that exists in the universe. When sorcerers (those who live of the Source) beckon intent, it comes to them and sets up the path for attainment, which means that sorcerers always accomplish what they set out to do."

When I read those two sentences, I was stunned by the insight and clarity it gave me about the power of intention. Imagine that intention is not something *you do,* but rather a force that exists in the universe as an invisible field of energy! I had never considered intention in this way before reading Castaneda's words.

I wrote those two sentences down, and then I had them printed on a card and laminated. I carried the laminated card with me into the catheter lab for my minor surgical procedure, and as soon as I could, I began talking about the power of intention to everyone who would listen. I made intention a part of every speech I gave. I immersed myself in this idea to use it, not only for my own healing, but to help others use the power of intention to carry them where they're fully equipped to go. I had experienced *satori*, or instant awakening, and was intent on offering this insight to others. It had become clear to me that accessing the power of intention relieved so much of the seemingly impossible work of striving to fulfill desires by sheer force of will.

Since that defining moment, I've thought of the power of intention in virtually all of my waking hours—and books, articles, conversations, telephone calls, items arriving in my mailbox, and arbitrary works I might be looking at in a bookstore all seemed to conspire to keep me on this path. So here it is: *The Power of Intention*. I hope this book will help you view intention in a new way and make use of it in a manner that leads you to define yourself as Patanjali suggested more than 20 centuries ago: "Dormant forces, faculties, and talents come alive, and you discover yourself to be a greater person by far than you ever dreamed yourself to be."

Patanjali's two words, "dormant forces," kick-started me in the direction of writing about intention. Patanjali was referring to forces that *appear to be* either nonexistent or dead, *and* he was referring to the powerful energy a person feels when inspired. If you've ever felt inspired by a purpose or calling, you know the feeling of Spirit working through you. *Inspired* is our word for *in-spirited*. I've thought long and hard about the idea of being able to access seemingly dormant forces to assist me at key times in my life to achieve an inner burning desire. What are these forces? Where are they located? Who gets to use them? Who is denied access? And why? Questions like these have propelled me to research and write this book and subsequently arrive at a totally new perspective of intention.

At this point, as I'm writing about my excitement of realizing a long-obscured truth, I *know* that intention is a force that we all have within us. Intention is a field of energy that flows invisibly beyond the reach of our normal, everyday habitual patterns. It's there even before our actual conception. We have the means to attract this energy to us and experience life in an exciting new way.

### Where Is This Field Called Intention?

Some prominent researchers believe that our intelligence, creativity, and imagination interact with the energy field of intention rather than being thoughts or elements in our brain. The brilliant scientist David Bohm, writing in *Wholeness and the Implicate Order*, suggested that all ordering influence and information is present in an invisible domain or higher reality and can be called upon in times of need. I found thousands of examples of these kinds of conclusions in the research and reading I did. If scientific evidence appeals to you, I suggest that you read *The Field: The Quest for the Secret Force of the Universe* by Lynne McTaggart. Her book is filled with studies supporting the existence of a higher, faster energy dimension or field of intention that can be tapped in to and used by everyone.

The answer to *Where is this field?* is: *There's no place that it's not,* because everything in the universe has intention built into it. This is true for all life forms, whether it be a wildebeest, a rosebush, or a mountain. A mosquito has intent built into its creation and life experience. A tiny acorn with no apparent power to think or make plans for its future contains intention from the invisible field. If you cut the acorn open, you won't see a giant oak tree, but you know it's there. An apple blossom in the springtime appears to be a pretty little flower, yet it has intent built into it and will manifest in the summer as an apple. Intention doesn't err. The acorn never turns into a pumpkin, or the apple blossom into an orange. Every aspect of nature, without exception, has intention built into it, and as far as we can tell, nothing in nature questions its path of intent. Nature simply progresses in harmony from the field of intention. We, too, are *intended* from the energy of this field.

There is what some call a *future-pull* in the DNA that's present at conception in each of us. In the moment of our conception, when an infinitely tiny drop of human protoplasm combines with an egg, life in physical form begins, and intention directs the growth process. Our body structure, the shape of our physical features, our development, including our aging, are intended in that one moment of conception. The sagging skin, the wrinkles, and even our death are all there. But wait, what exactly happens at the moment of conception? Where did this life, born of intention, begin?

As we examine that seed/egg dance attempting to discover its origin, moving backwards toward Creation, we first find molecules, then atoms, then electrons, then subatomic particles, and then sub-subatomic particles. Ultimately, were we to put these tiny quantum subatomic particles into a particle accelerator and collide them, trying to put our finger on the source of life, we'd discover what Einstein and his scientific compatriots discovered: There's no particle at the source; particles do not create more particles. The Source, which is intention, is pure, unbounded energy vibrating so fast that it defies measurement and observation. It's invisible, without form or boundaries. So, at our Source, we are formless energy, and in that formless vibrating spiritual field of energy, intention resides. On a lighter note, *I know* it's there, since somehow it managed to get into a drop of sperm and an ovarian egg and determine that my hair will no longer grow on my head after 25 years . . . and in 50 years, it will grow in my nose and ears, and all I (the observer) can do is watch it and snip it away!

This field of intent can't be described with words, for the words emanate from the field, just as do the questions. That placeless place is intention, and it handles everything for us. It grows my fingernails, it beats my heart, it digests my food, it writes my books, and it does this for everyone and everything in the universe. This reminds me of an ancient Chinese story I love, told by Chuang Tzu:

*There once was a one-legged dragon called Hui.*
*"How on earth do you manage those legs?" he asked*
*a centipede. "I can hardly manage one!"*
*"Matter of fact," said the centipede, "I do not*
*manage my legs."*

There's a field, invisible and formless, that manages it all. The intention of this universe is manifested in zillions of ways in the physical world, and every part of you, including your soul, your thoughts, your emotions, and of course the physical body that you occupy, are a part of this intent. So, if intention determines everything in the universe and is omnipresent, meaning there's no place that it's not, then why do so many of us feel disconnected from it so frequently? And even more important, if intention determines everything, then why do so many of us lack so much of what we'd like to have?

### The Meaning of Omnipresent Intention

Try imagining a force that's everywhere. There's no place that you can go where it isn't. It can't be divided and is present in everything you see or touch. Now extend your awareness of this infinite field of energy beyond the world of form and boundaries. This infinite invisible force is everywhere, so it's in both the physical and the nonphysical. Your physical body is one part of your totality emanating from this energy. At the instant of conception, *intention* sets in motion how your physical form will appear and how your growing and aging process will unfold. It also sets in motion your nonphysical aspects, including your emotions, thoughts, and disposition. In this instance, *intention is infinite potential activating your physical and nonphysical appearance on Earth.* You've formed out of the omnipresent to become present in time and space. Because it's omnipresent, this energy field of intent is accessible to you after your physical arrival here on Earth! The only way you deactivate this *dormant force* is by believing that you're separate from it.

Activating intention means rejoining your Source and becoming a modern-day sorcerer. Being a sorcerer means attaining the level of awareness where previously inconceivable things are available. As Carlos Castaneda explained, "The task of sorcerers was to face infinity" (*intention*), "and they plunged into it daily, as a fisherman plunges into the sea." Intention is a power that's present everywhere as a field of energy; it isn't limited to physical development. It's the source of nonphysical development, too. This field of intention is here, now, and available to you. When you activate it, you'll begin to feel purpose in your life, and you'll be guided by your infinite self. Here's how a poet and a spiritual teacher describes what I'm calling intention:

> *O Lord, thou art on the sandbanks*
> *As well as in the midst of the current;*
> *I bow to thee.*
> *Thou art in the little pebbles*
> *As well as in the calm expanse of the sea;*
> *I bow to thee.*
> *O all-pervading Lord,*
> *Thou art in the barren soil*
> *And in the crowded places;*
> *I bow to thee.*

— from *Veda XVI* by Sukla Yajur

As *you* make your metaphorical bow to this power, recognize that you're bowing to yourself. The all-pervading energy of intention pulses through you toward your potential for a purposeful life.

### How You Came to Experience Yourself as Disconnected from Intention

If there's an omnipresent power of intention that's not only within me, but in everything and everyone, then we're connected by this all-pervading Source to everything and everyone, and to what

13

we'd like to be, what we'd like to have, what we want to achieve, and to everything in the universe that will assist us. All that's required is realigning ourselves and activating intention. But how did we get disconnected in the first place? How did we lose our natural ability to connect? Lions, fish, and birds don't get disconnected. The animal, vegetable, and mineral worlds are always connected to their Source. They don't question their intention. We humans, however, with our capability for presumably higher brain functions, have something we refer to as *ego,* which is an idea that we construct about who and what we are.

Ego is made of six primary ingredients that account for how we experience ourselves as disconnected. By allowing ego to determine your life path, you deactivate the power of intention. Briefly, here are the six ego beliefs. I've written more extensively about them in several of my previous books, most notably *Your Sacred Self.*

1. *I am what I have.* My possessions define me.

2. *I am what I do.* My achievements define me.

3. *I am what others think of me.* My reputation defines me.

4. *I am separate from everyone.* My body defines me as alone.

5. *I am separate from all that is missing in my life.* My life space is disconnected from my desires.

6. *I am separate from God.* My life depends on God's assessment of my worthiness.

No matter how hard you try, intention can't be accessed through ego, so take some time to recognize and readjust any or all of these six beliefs. When the supremacy of ego is weakened in your life, you can seek intention and maximize your potential.

## *Holding on to the Trolley Strap*

This is a practice I find exceedingly helpful when I want to activate intention. You may find that it works for you, too. (See Chapter 3 for an entire chapter describing ways to access intention.)

One of my earliest memories is my mother taking her three boys on the streetcar on the east side of Detroit to Waterworks Park. I was two or three years old, and I recall looking up from the seat and seeing the hand straps hanging down. The grown-ups were able to hold on to the straps, but all I could do was imagine what it would be like to be so tall as to grab those straps way above my head. I actually pretended that I was light enough to float up to the hanging handles. I then imagined feeling safe and the trolley taking me where it was destined to go, at whatever speed it chose, picking up other passengers to go along on this glorious adventure of streetcar riding.

In my adult life, I use the image of the trolley strap to remind myself to get back to intention. I imagine a strap hanging down about three to four feet above my head, higher than I'm capable of reaching or jumping up to grab. The strap is attached to the trolley, only now the trolley symbolizes a flowing power of intention. I've either let go of it or it's just out of my reach temporarily. In moments of stress, anxiety, worry, or even physical discomfort, I close my eyes and imagine my arm reaching up, and then I see myself float up to the trolley strap. As I grab the strap, I have an enormous feeling of relief and comfort. What I've done is eliminate ego thoughts and allow myself to reach intention, and I trust this power to take me to my destination, stopping when necessary, and picking up companions along the way.

In some of my earlier works, I've called this process the *pathway to mastery*. The four pathways may be helpful to you here as steps toward activating intention.

### Four Steps to Intention

Activating your power of intention is a process of connecting with your natural self and letting go of total ego identification. The process takes place in four stages:

**1. Discipline** is the first stage. Learning a new task requires training your body to perform as your thoughts desire. So, eliminating ego identification doesn't mean disconnecting from your relationship with your body, but rather, training your body to activate those desires. You do that with practice, exercise, nontoxic habits, healthy foods, and so on.

**2. Wisdom** is the second stage. Wisdom combined with discipline fosters your ability to focus and be patient as you harmonize your thoughts, your intellect, and your feelings with the work of your body. We send children off to school telling them: *Be disciplined* and *Use your head,* and call this education, but it falls short of mastery.

**3. Love** is the third stage. After disciplining the body with wisdom, and intellectually studying a task, this process of mastery involves loving what you do and doing what you love. In the world of sales, I call it falling in love with what you're offering, and then selling your love or enthusiasm to potential customers. When learning to play tennis, it involves practicing all of the strokes while studying strategies for playing the game. It also involves enjoying the feeling of hitting the ball and of being on the tennis court— and everything else about the game.

**4. Surrender** is the fourth stage. This is the place of intention. This is where your body and your mind aren't running the show and you move into intent. "In the universe there is an immeasurable, indescribable force which shamans call intent, and absolutely everything that exists in the entire cosmos is attached to intent by a connecting link," is the way Carlos Castaneda describes it. You relax, grab the trolley strap, and allow yourself to be carried by the same power that turns acorns into trees, blossoms into apples, and microscopic dots into humans. So grab that trolley strap and create your own unique connecting link. *Absolutely everything in the entire cosmos* includes you and your disciplined, wise, loving self, and all of your thoughts and feelings. When you surrender, you lighten up and can consult with your infinite soul. Then the power of intention becomes available to take you wherever you feel destined to go.

All of this talk of intention and surrender may cause you to question where your free will fits in. You might be inclined to conclude that free will is nonexistent or that you become whatever your program dictates. So, let's take a look at your will and how it fits into this new view of intention. As you read the next two sections, please keep an open mind, even if what you read conflicts with what you've believed all your life!

### Intention and Your Free Will Are Paradoxical

A paradox is a seemingly absurd or contradictory statement, even if well founded. *Intention* and *free will* certainly qualify as being paradoxical. They conflict with many a preconceived notion of what's reasonable or possible. How can you possess free will and also have intention shaping your body and your potential? You can fuse this dichotomy by choosing to believe in the infinity of intention *and* in your capacity to exercise free will. You know how to think rationally about the rules of cause and effect, so try your intellect on this.

Obviously, it's impossible to have two infinites, for then neither would be infinite; each would be limited by the other. You can't divide *infinite* into parts. Essentially, infinite is unity, continuity, or oneness, like the air in your home. Where does the air in your kitchen stop and the air in your living room begin? Where does the air inside your home stop and the air outside start? How about the air you breathe in and out? Air may be the closest we can come to understanding the infinite, universal, omnipresent Spirit. Some-how, you must travel in thought beyond the idea of your individual existence to the idea of a unity of universal being, and then beyond this to the idea of a universal energy. When you think of part of a whole being in one place and part in another, you've lost the idea of unity. And (keeping an open mind as I beseeched you earlier), get this! At any moment in time, all Spirit is concentrated at the point where you focus your attention. Therefore, *you* can consolidate all creative energy at a given moment in time. *This is your free will at work.*

Your mind and your thoughts are also thoughts of the divine mind. Universal Spirit is in your thoughts *and* in your free will. When you shift your thoughts from Spirit to ego, you seem to lose contact with the power of intention. Your free will can either move *with* Universal Spirit and its unfolding, or *away* from it toward ego dominance. As it moves away from Spirit, life appears to be a struggle. Slower energies flow through you, and you may feel hopeless, helpless, and lost. You can use your free will to rejoin higher, faster energies. The truth is that *we* do not create anything alone; we are all creatures with God. Our free will combines and redistributes what's already created. *You choose!* Free will means that you have the choice to connect to Spirit or not!

So, the answer to the questions, *Do I have a free will?* and *Is intention working with me as an all-pervasive universal force?* is *Yes.* Can you live with this paradox? If you think about it, you live with paradox in every moment of your existence. At the exact same instant that you're a body with beginnings and ends, with boundaries, and a definition in time and space, you're also an invisible, formless, unlimited, thinking and feeling being. A ghost in the machine, if you will. Which are you? Matter or essence? Physical or metaphysical? Form or spirit? The answer is *both,* even though they appear to be opposites. Do you have a free will, and are you a part of the destiny of intention? *Yes.* Fuse the dichotomy. Blend the opposites, and live with both of these beliefs. Begin the process of allowing Spirit to work with you, and link up to the field of intention.

## *At Intention, Spirit Will Work for You!*

With your free will consciously deciding to reconnect to the power of intention, you're altering its direction. You'll begin to feel pleasant recognition and reverence for the unity of Spirit and yourself as an individual concentration of it. I silently repeat the word *intent* or *intention* to help me get my ego and my self-absorption out of the picture. I think often of this quote from Castaneda's *Power of Silence:* "Having lost hope of ever returning to the source of everything, the average man seeks solace in his selfishness." For me, personally, I attempt to return to the source of everything on a daily basis, and I refuse to be the "average man" that Castaneda describes.

Many years ago I decided to give up drinking alcohol. I wanted to experience continuous sobriety to improve my ability to do the work that I felt was burning inside of me. I felt called upon to teach self-reliance through my writing and speaking. Several teachers had told me that complete sobriety was a prerequisite for the work I was called to do. In the early stages of this dramatic life change, a power seemed to help me when I was tempted to return to my old habits of having a few beers each evening. On one occasion, in my state of wavering, I actually went out to purchase a six-pack but forgot to bring money with me. I *never* forget to take cash with me!

In the few minutes it took me to return home and retrieve the cash, I reevaluated the free will that would allow me to buy beer, and chose to stay with my intention. I found, as the first weeks passed, that these kinds of events started occurring with regularity. I'd be guided by circumstances that led me away from situations where drinking was a temptation. A telephone call might distract me from a tempting situation; a family minicrisis would erupt and deter me from a potential slip. Today, a couple of decades later, it's clear to me that a firm handle on that trolley strap I described earlier allows me to be whisked along my path to destinations invoked eons ago by intention. And I also see that my free will is a paradoxical partner of the power of intention.

My awareness of intention as a power for me to reconnect to, rather than something my ego must accomplish, has made a huge difference in my life's work. The simple awareness that my writing and speaking are manifested from the field of intention has been of immeasurable benefit to me. I'm awed by the creative energy when I get my self-importance and ego identification out of the way.. Before taking the microphone, I send ego to the lobby or tell it to have a seat in the audience. I repeat the word *intent* to myself and feel myself floating up to this energy field of intention. I surrender and allow, and I find myself completely at ease, remembering tiny details in the midst of my speech, never losing my way, and experiencing the unique connection that's occurring with the audience. Fatigue dissolves, hunger disappears—even the need to pee vanishes! Everything that's necessary for delivering the message seems almost effortlessly available.

### Combining Free Will with Intention

In mathematics, two angles that are said to *coincide* fit together perfectly. The word *coincidence* does not describe luck or mistakes. It describes that which *fits together perfectly.* By combining free will with intention, you harmonize with the universal mind. Rather than operating in your own mind outside of this force called intention, your goal may very well be, as you read this book, to work at being in harmony at all times with intention. When life appears to be working against you, when your luck is down, when the supposedly wrong people show up, or when you slip up and return to old, self-defeating habits, recognize the signs that you're out of harmony with intention. You can and will reconnect in a way that will bring you into alignment with your own purpose.

For example, when I write, I open myself to the possibilities of universal Spirit and my own individual thoughts collaborating with fate to produce a helpful, insightful book. But as I reconsidered my account of leaving alcohol behind me, I wanted *another* example to put in this chapter of how intention collaborates with life circumstances to produce what we need.

Recently my 19-year-old daughter, Sommer, told me that she'd quit her temporary job as a restaurant hostess and wasn't sure what she wanted to do before resuming her college studies. I asked her what made her feel most purposeful and happy, and she said it was teaching horseback riding to young children, but she refused to return to the old barn where she'd worked a year before because she felt unappreciated, overworked, and underpaid.

I was in Maui writing this first chapter on a new perspective on intention when we had this telephone conversation. I launched into my intention-as-a-force-in-the-universe spiel and told my daughter that she needed to realign her thoughts, and so on. "Open up to receiving the assistance you desire," I told her. "Trust in intention. It exists for you. Stay alert, and be willing to accept any guidance that comes your way. Stay in vibrational harmony with the all-providing Source."

The next day, at the very moment I was searching for that additional example of intention to put into this chapter, the telephone rang, and it was Sommer, bubbling with enthusiasm. "You're not going to believe this, Dad. On second thought, I'm sure you'll believe it. Remember yesterday how you told me to be open to intention? I was skeptical, even thinking, *That's my weird dad,* but I decided to try it. Then I saw a sign on a telephone pole that said *Horseback-Riding Lessons* and there was a telephone number. I wrote the number down and just called it. The woman who answered told me that she needed to hire someone she could trust to do trail rides with young kids. She pays exactly double what I was making at the restaurant. I'm going out to see her tomorrow. Isn't that cool?!"

Cool? Hell yes, it's cool! Here I am writing a book, looking for a good example, and it arrives in the form of help I was attempting to offer the day before to my daughter. Two for the price of one!

## Merging Your Individual Thoughts with the Universal Mind

Our individual thoughts create a prototype in the universal mind of intention. You and your power of intention are not separate. So, when you form a thought within you that's commensurate with Spirit, you form a spiritual prototype that connects you to intention and sets into motion the manifestation of your desires. Whatever you wish to accomplish is an existing fact, already present in Spirit. Eliminate from your mind thoughts of conditions, limitations, or the possibility of it not manifesting. If left undisturbed in your mind and in the mind of intention simultaneously, it will germinate into reality in the physical world.

In simpler words, "All things whatsoever ye pray and ask for, believe that ye have received them, and ye shall receive them" [Mark 11:24]. In this scriptural quotation, you are told to believe that your desire has already been fulfilled, and then it will be accomplished. Know that your thought or prayer is already here. Remove all doubt so that you create a harmonious thought with universal mind or intention. When you know this beyond doubt, it will be realized in the future. This is the power of intention at work.

I'll close this section with words from Aldous Huxley, one of my favorite authors: "The spiritual journey does not consist in arriving at a new destination where a person gains what he did not have, or becomes what he is not. It consists in the dissipation of one's own ignorance concerning one's self and life, and the gradual growth of that understanding which begins the spiritual awakening. The finding of God is a coming to one's self."

\* \* \*

In this first chapter, I've asked you to stop doubting the existence of a universal, omnipresent force I've called intention, and told you that you can link to and be carried to your destination on the energy of intention. Here are my suggestions for putting this to work in your life.

## Five Suggestions for Implementing the Ideas in This Chapter

1. *Whenever you feel out of sorts, lost, or even in a sour mood, visualize the trolley strap hanging down from the field of intention three or four feet above your head.* Imagine floating up and allowing the trolley to carry you to your built-in intention. This is a tool for implementing surrender in your life.

2. *Say the word __intent__ or __intention__ repeatedly when you're in a state of anxiety or when everything around you seems to have conspired to keep you from your mission.* This is a reminder to be peaceful and calm. Intention is spirit, and spirit is silently blissful.

3. *Tell yourself that you have a life mission and a silent partner who's accessible at any moment you choose.* When ego defines you by what you have or do, or compares you to others, use your power of free will to terminate those thoughts. Say to yourself, "I'm here on purpose, I can accomplish anything I desire, and I do it by being in harmony with the all-pervading creative force in the universe." This will become an automatic way of responding to life. Synchronistic results will begin to happen.

4. *Act as if anything you desire is already here.* Believe that all that you seek you've already received, that it exists in spirit, and know you shall have your desires filled. One of my ten secrets for success and inner peace is to *treat yourself as if you already are what you'd like to become.*

5. *Copy this ancient Hasidic saying and carry it with you for a year.* It's a reminder of the power of intention and how it can work for you every day in every way.

*When you walk across the fields with your mind pure and holy, then from all the stones, and all growing things, and all animals, the sparks of their soul come out and cling to you, and then they are purified and become a holy fire in you.*

\* \* \*

In the next chapter, I describe how this field of intention might look were you able to see it, and what the *faces of intention* look like. I'll close this chapter with another quotation from Carlos Castaneda's teacher, don Juan Matus: ". . . the spirit reveals itself to everyone with the same intensity and consistency, but only warriors are consistently attuned to such revelations."

Readers and warriors alike, proceed in the spirit of free will to access the power of intention.

〜 \* 〜 \* 〜

# CHAPTER TWO

# THE
# SEVEN FACES
# OF INTENTION

*"Four thousand volumes of metaphysics
will not teach us what the soul is."*

— Voltaire

## *Moving from Thinking about*
## *Intention to Knowing Intention*

Yesterday, while writing this book here on Maui, I experienced a *knowing* that I'll attempt to explain to you. A woman from Japan was pulled from the surf, her body bloated from an excessive intake of seawater. I knelt over her, with others, attempting to get her heartbeat going with CPR, while many of her friends from Japan cried out in anguish as the futile attempts at resuscitation proceeded. Suddenly I felt a quiet awareness of this woman's spirit hovering above our lifesaving attempts. As I watched the rescue scene on the beach, I felt the presence of blissfully peaceful

25

energy, and in some unfathomable way I knew that she wasn't going to be revived and that she was no longer connected to the body that so many well-meaning people, including myself, were trying to bring back to life.

This quiet knowing led me to stand up, put my hands together, and say a silent prayer for her. We were from different parts of this world and didn't even share a common language, yet I felt connected to her. I felt peaceful, with a knowing that her spirit and mine were somehow connected in the mystery of the transient/ephemeral nature of our physical lives.

As I walked away, the pain of death wasn't dominating my thoughts. Instead, I knew and felt that the departure of this woman's spirit from what was now a lifeless, bloated body was inexplicably all a part of perfect divine order. I couldn't prove it. I had no scientific evidence. I didn't think it—I *knew* it. This is an example of what I mean by *silent knowledge*. I still feel her presence as I write this, 24 hours later. In *Power of Silence*, Carlos Castaneda describes silent knowledge as "something that all of us have. Something that has complete mastery, complete knowledge of everything. But it cannot think, therefore it cannot speak of what it knows. . . . Man has given up silent knowledge for the world of reason. The more he clings to the world of reason, the more ephemeral intent becomes."

Since intention is being presented in this book as an invisible energy field that is inherent in all physical form, intention, then, is a part of the inexplicable, nonmaterial world of Spirit. Spirit eludes our attempts to explain and define it because it's a dimension beyond beginnings and ends, beyond boundaries, beyond symbols, and beyond form itself. Consequently, written and spoken words, our symbols for communicating our experiences in this world, can't really explain Spirit the way they do the physical world.

I agree with Voltaire's statement at the beginning of this chapter and readily admit that I can't definitively teach anyone what Spirit is or use words that give a precise picture of what it looks like. What I *can* do is describe a way that I conceptualize intention—

if it were somehow possible to remove the veil that keeps the field of intention from our sensory perception and reasoning mind. I'll give you my concept of what I refer to as the *seven faces of intention*. These points represent my imagined picture of what the power of intention looks like.

Intention is something that I believe we can feel, connect with, know, and trust. It's an inner awareness that we explicitly feel, and yet at the same time cannot truly describe with words. I use this concept to help guide me toward the power of intention that's the source of creation, and activate it in my daily life. It's my hope that you too will begin to recognize what you personally need to do to begin activating intention in your life.

The descriptions that follow are distilled from my experience with master teachers, my professional work with others over the past 30 years, the veritable library of metaphysical books I've read and studied, and my personal evolution. I'm attempting to convey my personal knowing of the extraordinary benefits of linking to intention. Hopefully *you* will feel inspired by the *silent knowing* of the power of intention and go on to create an increasingly enchanted experience for yourself and everyone else in your life.

Silent knowledge starts when you invite the power of intention to play an active part in your life. This is a private and very personal choice that needn't be explained or defended. When you make this inner choice, silent knowledge will gradually become a part of your normal, everyday awareness. Opening to the power of intention, you begin *knowing* that conception, birth, and death are all natural aspects of the energy field of creation. Clinging to attempts to think or reason your way to intention is futile. By banishing doubt and trusting your intuitive feelings, you clear a space for the power of intention to flow through. This may sound like hocus-pocus, but I prefer to think of it as emptying my mind and entering the heart of mystery. Here, I set aside rational thoughts and open to the magic and excitement of an illuminating new awareness.

A great teacher in my life named J. Krishnamurti once observed: "To be empty, completely empty, is not a fearsome thing; it is absolutely essential for the mind to be unoccupied; to be empty, unenforced, for then only can it move into unknown depths."

Take a moment right now to put this book down and allow yourself to trust and gently experience an awareness of your non-physical self. First, close your eyes and empty your mind of rational thoughts and the multitudinous ever-changing chatter that goes on. Next, hit the delete button every time doubt appears. Finally, open to the emptiness. Then you can begin to discover how to silently know the power of intention. (In the following chapter, I'll discuss in more depth other ways to access and reconnect to intention.)

But now, I'll describe what I think our view might be if we could be outside of ourselves, floating above our body, like the spirit of the Japanese lady on the beach yesterday. From this perspective, I imagine myself looking at the faces of intention through eyes that are capable of seeing higher vibrations.

### The Seven Faces of Intention

**1. The face of creativity.** The first of the seven faces of intention is the creative expression of the power of intention that designed us, got us here, and created an environment that's compatible with our needs. The power of intention has to be creative or nothing would come into existence. It seems to me that this is an irrefutable truth about intention/spirit, because its purpose is to bring life into existence in a suitable environment. Why do I conclude that the life-giving power of intention *intends* us to have life, and have it in increasing abundance? Because, if the opposite were true, life as we know it couldn't come into form.

The very fact that we can breathe and experience life is proof to me that the nature of the life-giving Spirit is creative at its core. This may seem obvious to you, or in fact it may appear confusing, or even irrelevant. But what *is* clear is: You are here in your physical body; there was a time when you were an embryo, before that a seed, and before that formless energy. That formless energy contained intention, which brought you from *no where* to *now here*.

At the very highest levels of awareness, intention started you on a path toward your destiny. The face of creativity intends you toward continued creativity to create and co-create anything that you direct your power of intention toward. Creative energy is a part of you; it originates in the life-giving Spirit that *intends* you.

**2. The face of kindness.** Any power that has, as its inherent nature, the need to create and convert energy into physical form must also be a kindly power. Again, I'm deducing this from the opposite. If the all-giving power of intention had at its core the desire to be unkind, malevolent, or hurtful, then creation itself would be impossible. The moment unkind energy became form, the life-giving Spirit would be destroyed. Instead, the power of intention has a face of kindness. It is kind energy intending what it's creating to flourish and grow, and to be happy and fulfilled. Our existence is proof to me of the kindness of intention. Choosing to be kind is a choice to have the power of intention active in your life.

The positive effect of kindness on the immune system and on the increased production of serotonin in the brain has been proven in research studies. Serotonin is a naturally occurring substance in the body that makes us feel more comfortable, peaceful, and even blissful. In fact, the role of most antidepressants is to stimulate the production of serotonin chemically, helping to ease depression. Research has shown that a simple act of kindness directed toward another improves the functioning of the immune system and stimulates the production of serotonin in both the recipient of the kindness and the person extending the kindness. Even more amazing is that persons observing the act of kindness have similar beneficial results. Imagine this! Kindness extended, received, or observed beneficially impacts the physical health and feelings of everyone involved! Both the face of kindness and the face of creativity are smiling here.

When you're unkind, you're blocking the face of kindness. You're moving away from the power of intention. No matter whether you call it God, Spirit, Source, or intention, be aware that unkind thoughts weaken, and kind thoughts strengthen, your connection. Creativity and kindness are two of the seven faces of intention.

**3. The face of love.** The third of the seven faces of intention is the face of love. That there's a life-giving nature inherent in the power of intention is an irrefutable conclusion. What would we name this quality that encourages, enhances, and supports all of life, if not love? It's the prime moving power of the Universal Spirit of intent. As Ralph Waldo Emerson put it: "Love is our highest word and the synonym for God."

The energy field of intention is pure love resulting in a nurturing and totally cooperative environment. Judgment, anger, hate, fear, or prejudice won't thrive here. So, were we able to actually see this field, we'd see creativity and kindness in an endless field of love. We entered the physical world of boundaries and beginnings through the universal force field of pure love. This face of intention that is an expression of love wishes only for us to flourish and grow, and become all that we're capable of becoming. When we're not in harmony with the energy of love, we've moved away from intention and weakened our ability to activate intention through the expression of love. For example, if you aren't doing what you love and loving what you do, your power of intention is weakened. You attract into your life more of the dissatisfaction that isn't the face of love. Consequently, more of what you don't love will appear in your life.

Thoughts and emotions are pure energy; some higher and faster than others. When higher energies occupy the same field as lower energies, the lower energies convert to higher energies. A simple example of this is a darkened room that has lower energy than a room bathed in light. Since light moves faster than non-light, when a candle is brought into a dark room, the darkness not only dissolves and disappears, but it seems magically converted into light. The same is true of love, which is a higher/faster energy than the energy of hate.

St. Francis, in his famous prayer, beseeches God: "Where there is hatred, let me sow love." What he is seeking is the power to dissolve and ultimately convert hate to the energy of love. Hate converts to love when the energy of love is in its presence. This is true for you, too. Hate, directed toward yourself or others, can be converted to the life-giving, love-granting life force of intention. Pierre Teilhard de Chardin put it this way: "The conclusion is always the same: Love is the most powerful and still the most unknown energy of the world."

**4. The face of beauty.** The fourth of my seven faces of intention is the face of beauty. What else could a creative, kind, and loving expression be, other than beautiful? Why would the organizing intelligence of intention ever elect to manifest into form anything that's repugnant to itself? Obviously, it wouldn't. So we can conclude that the nature of intention has an eternal interaction of love and beauty, and add the expression of beauty to the face of a creative, kind, loving power of intention.

John Keats, the brilliant young romantic poet, concludes his *Ode on a Grecian Urn* with: "'Beauty is truth, truth beauty,' that is all/ Ye know on earth, and all ye need to know." Obviously truth exists in the creation of everything. It's true that it shows up here in form. It's now here in a form that's an expression of the invisible creative power. So, I agree with Keats that we need to *silently know* that truth and beauty are one and the same. Out of the truth of the originating spirit in an expression of the power of intention comes truth as beauty. This *knowing* leads to valuable insights in relation to exercising your individual will, imagination, and intuition.

In order to grasp the significance of beauty as one of the faces of intention, remember this: *Beautiful thoughts build a beautiful soul.* As you become receptive to seeing and feeling beauty around you, you're becoming attuned to the creative power of intention within everything in the natural world, including yourself. By choosing to see beauty in everything, even a person who was born into poverty and ignorance will be able to experience the power of intention. Seeking beauty in the worst of circumstances with individual intent connects one to the power of intention. It works. It has to work. The face of beauty is always present, even where others see non-beauty.

I was deeply honored to be on a panel with Viktor Frankl in 1978 in Vienna, Austria. I strongly recollect that he shared with me and the audience his assertion that it's the ability to see beauty in all of life's circumstances that gives our lives meaning. In his book *Man's Search for Meaning,* he describes a bowl of filthy water with a fish head floating in it, given to him by his Nazi captors in a concentration camp during WWII. He trained himself to see beauty in this meal, rather than focus on the horror of it. He attributed his ability to see beauty anywhere as a vital factor in surviving those horrific camps. He reminds us that if we focus on what's ugly, we attract more ugliness into our thoughts, and then into our emotions, and ultimately into our lives. By choosing to hang on to one's corner of freedom even in the worst situations, we can process our world with the energy of appreciation and beauty, and create an opportunity to transcend our circumstances.

I love the way Mother Teresa described this quality when she was asked, "What do you do every day in the streets of Calcutta at your mission?" She responded, "Every day I see Jesus Christ in all of his distressing disguises."

**5. The face of expansion.** The elemental nature of life is to increase and seek more and more expression. If we could sharply focus on the faces of intention, we'd be startled. I imagine that one of the faces we'd see is a continuously expanding expression of the power of intention. The nature of this creative spirit is always operating so as to expand. Spirit is a forming power. It has the principle of increase, meaning that life continues to expand toward more life. Life as we know it originates from formless intention. Therefore, one of the faces of intention looks like something that's eternally evolving. It might look like a tiny speck in a continuous state of duplicating itself, and then enlarging itself, and then moving forward, all the while continuing its expansion and expression.

This is precisely what's happening in our physical world. This fifth face of intention takes the form of what is expressing it. It can be no other way, for if this ever-expanding force disliked itself or felt unconnected, it could only destroy itself. But it doesn't work that way. The power of intention manifests as an expression of expanding creativity, kindness, love, and beauty. By establishing your personal relation to this face of intention, you expand your life through the power of intention, which was, is, and always will be, a component of this originating intention. The power of intention is the power to expand and increase all aspects of your life. No exceptions! It's the nature of intention to be in a state of increased expression, so it's true for you, too.

The only proviso to this forward movement of intention is to cooperate with it everywhere and allow this spirit of increase to express itself through you and for you, and for everyone you encounter. Then you will have no worry or anxiety. Trust the face of expansion and do what you do because you're loving what you do and doing what you love. Know that expansive, beneficial results are the only possibilities.

**6. The face of unlimited abundance.** This sixth face of intention is an expression of something that has no boundaries, is everywhere at once, and is endlessly abundant. It's not just huge, it never stops. This marvelous gift of abundance is what you were created from. Thus you too share this in the expression of your life. You're actually fulfilling the law of abundance. These gifts are given freely and fully to you just as the air, the sun, the water, and the atmosphere are provided in unlimited abundance for you.

From the time of your earliest memories, you probably were taught to think in terms of limitations. *My property starts here. Yours over there.* So we build fences to mark our boundaries. But ancient explorers gave us an awareness of the world as potentially endless. Even more ancient astronomers pushed back our beliefs about an immense dome-shaped ceiling covering the earth. We've learned about galaxies that are measured in the distance light travels in a year. Science books that are only two years old are outdated. Athletic records that supposedly demonstrated the limits of our physical prowess are shattered with amazing regularity.

What all this means is that there are no limits to our potential as people, as collective entities, and as individuals. This is largely true because we emanate from the unlimited abundance of intention. If the face of the power of intention is unlimited abundance, then we can know that our potential for manifestation and attracting anything into our lives is the same. The face of abundance has absolutely no limits. Imagine the vastness of the resources from which all objects are created. Then consider the one resource that stands above all others. This would be your mind and the collective mind of humankind. Where does your mind begin and end? What are its boundaries? Where is it located? More important, where is it not located? Is it born with you, or is it present before your conception? Does it die with you? What color is it? What shape? The answers are in the phrase *unlimited abundance.* You were created from this very same unlimited abundance. The power of intention is everywhere. It is what allows everything to manifest, to increase, and to supply infinitely.

Know that you're connected to this life force and that you share it with everyone and all that you perceive to be missing. Open to the expression of the face of unlimited abundance, and you'll be co-creating your life as you'd like it to be. As is so often true, the poets can express in a few short words what seems so difficult for us to grasp. Here is Walt Whitman speaking to us in *Song of Myself.* As you read these lines, substitute *the face of endless abundance* for *God* to gain a flavor of what the power of intention is.

> *I hear and behold God in every object, yet understand*
> *God not in the least . . .*
> *I see something of God each hour of the twenty-four,*
> *and each moment then,*
> *In the faces of men and women I see God, and*
> *in my own face in the glass;*
> *I find letters from God dropt in the street,*
> *and every one is signed by God's name,*
> *And I leave them where they are, for I know*
> *that whereso'er I go*
> *Others will punctually come forever and ever.*

You don't have to have an intellectual understanding. It's enough to *silently know* and proceed to live with your awareness of this face of endless abundance.

**7. The face of receptivity.** This is how I imagine the seventh face, the receptive face of intention. It's simply receptive to all. No one and no thing is rejected by the receptive face of intention. It welcomes everyone and every living thing, without judgment—never granting the power of intention to some and withholding it from others. The receptive face of intention means to me that all of nature is waiting to be called into action. We only need to be willing to recognize and receive. Intention can't respond to you if you fail to recognize it. If you see chance and coincidence governing your life and the world, then the universal mind of intention will appear to you as nothing but an amalgamation of forces devoid of any order or power.

Simply put, to be unreceptive is to deny yourself access to the power of intention. In order to utilize the all-inclusive receptivity of intention, you must produce within yourself an intelligence equal in affinity to the universal mind itself. You must not only become receptive to having guidance available to you to manifest your human intentions, but you must be receptive to giving this energy back to the world. As I've said many times in speeches and earlier writings, your job is not to say *how*, it's to say *yes! Yes, I'm willing. Yes, I know that the power of intention is universal. It's denied to no one.*

The face of receptivity smiles on me, as what I need flows to me from the Source, and the Source is receptive to my tapping in to it to co-create books, speeches, videos, audios, and anything else that I've been fortunate enough to have on my résumé. By being receptive, I'm in harmony with the power of intention of the universal creative force. This works in so many different ways. You'll see the right people magically appearing in your life; your body healing; and if it's something that you want, you'll even discover yourself becoming a better dancer, card player, or athlete! The field of intention allows everything to emanate into form, and its unlimited potential is built into all that has manifested even before its initial birth pangs were being expressed.

* * *

In this chapter, you've read about my concept of the seven faces of intention. They're creative, kind, loving, beautiful, ever-expanding, endlessly abundant, and receptive to all, and you can connect to this alluring field of intention. Here are five suggestions you can implement now to put into practice the essential messages in this chapter.

## Five Suggestions for Implementing the Ideas in this Chapter

1. *Visualize the power of intention.* Invite *your* visualization of the field of energy, which is the power of intention, to appear in your mind. Be receptive to what appears as you visualize your concept of this field of energy. Even though you know it's invisible, close your eyes and see what images you receive. Recite the seven words that represent the seven faces of intention: *creative, kind, loving, beautiful, expanding, abundant,* and *receptive.* Memorize these seven words and use them to bring you to harmony with the power of intention as you visualize it. Remind yourself that when you feel or behave inconsistently with these seven faces of intention, you've disconnected from the power of intention. Allow the seven words to decorate your visualization of the power of intention, and notice the shift in your perspective as you regain your connection to it.

2. *Be reflective.* A mirror reflects without distortion or judgment. Consider being like a mirror, and reflect what comes into your life without judgment or opinions. Be unattached to all who come into your life by not demanding that they

stay, go, or appear, at your whim. Discontinue judging yourself or others for being too fat, too tall, too ugly—too anything! Just as the power of intention accepts and reflects you without judgment or attachment, try to be the same with what appears in your life. Be like a mirror!

3. *Expect beauty.* This suggestion includes expecting kindness and love along with beauty to be in your life by deeply loving yourself, your surroundings, and by showing reverence for all of life. There's always something beautiful to be experienced wherever you are. Right now, look around you and select beauty as your focus. This is so different from habitually being alert for ways to feel hurt, angry, or offended. Expecting beauty helps you perceive the power of intention in your life.

4. *Meditate on appreciation.* Cherish the energy that you share with all living beings now and in the future, and even those that have lived before you. Feel the surge of that life force that allows you to think, sleep, move about, digest, and even meditate. The power of intention responds to your appreciation of it. The life force that's in your body is key to what you desire. As you appreciate your life force as representative of the power of intention, a wave of determination and knowing surges through you. The wisdom of your soul as it responds to your meditation on appreciation assumes command and knows every step that must be taken.

5. *Banish doubt.* When doubt is banished, abundance flourishes and anything is possible. We all tend to use our thoughts to create the world we choose. If you doubt your ability to create the life you intend, then you're refusing the power of intention. Even when nothing seems to indicate that you're accomplishing what you desire in your life, refuse to entertain doubt. Remember, the trolley strap of intention is waiting for you to float up and be carried along.

Shakespeare declared, "Our doubts are traitors, and make us lose the good we oft might win by fearing to attempt." And Ramana Maharshi observed, "Doubts arise because of an absence of surrender."

You may well choose to doubt what others say to you or what you experience with your senses, but banish doubt when it comes to knowing that a universal force of intention designed you and got you here! Don't doubt your creation from a field of energy that's always available to you.

\* \* \*

In the following chapter, I offer what may seem to you to be unusual methods for polishing the connecting link between you and this enthralling energy field we're calling intention.

～ \* ～ \* ～

# CHAPTER THREE

# CONNECTING

# TO

# INTENTION

*"The law of floatation was not discovered
by contemplating the sinking of things,
but by contemplating the floating of things
which floated naturally, and then intelligently
asking why they did so."*

— Thomas Troward

E xamine this observation by the great mental-science practitioner of the early 20th century, Thomas Troward. In the
early days of shipbuilding, ships were made of wood, and
the reasoning was that wood floats in water and iron sinks. Yet
today, ships all over the world are built of iron. As people began
studying the law of flotation, it was discovered that *anything*
could float if it's lighter than the mass of liquid it displaces. So
today, we're able to make iron float by the very same law that
makes it sink. Keep this example in mind as you read and apply
the contents of this chapter on connecting to all that you're
intended to become.

The key word here is *contemplating,* or what you're placing your thoughts on, as you begin utilizing the enormous potential and power of intention. You must be able to connect to intention, and you can't access and work with intention if you're contemplating the impossibility of being able to intend and manifest. You can't discover the law of co-creation if you're contemplating what's missing. You can't discover the power of awakening if you're contemplating things that are still asleep. The secret to manifesting anything that you desire is your willingness and ability to realign yourself so that your inner world is in harmony with the power of intention. Every single modern advance that you see and take for granted was created (and creating is what we're doing here in this book) by someone contemplating what they intended to manifest.

*The way to establish a relationship with Spirit and access the power of this creating principle is to continuously contemplate yourself as being surrounded by the conditions you wish to produce.* I encourage you to emphasize this idea by underlining the previous sentence both in this book and in your mind. Dwell on the idea of a supreme infinite power producing the results that you desire. This power is the creative power of the universe. It's responsible for everything coming into focus. By trusting it to provide the form and the conditions for its manifestation, you establish a relationship to intention that allows you to be connected for as long as you practice this kind of personal intent.

The Wright brothers didn't contemplate the *staying on the ground of things.* Alexander Graham Bell didn't contemplate the *noncommunication of things,* Thomas Edison didn't contemplate the *darkness of things.* In order to float an idea into your reality, you must be willing to do a somersault into the inconceivable and land on your feet, contemplating what you want instead of what you don't have. You'll then start floating your desires instead of sinking them. The law of manifestation is like the law of flotation, and you must contemplate it working *for you* instead of contemplating it not working. This is accomplished by establishing a strong connecting link between you and the invisible, formless field of energy—the power of intention.

*Entering into the Spirit of Intention*

Whatever you intend to create in your life involves generating the same life-giving quality that brings everything into existence. The spirit of anything, the quality that allows it to come into the world of form, is true as a general principle, so why not activate it within you? The power of intention simply awaits your ability to make the connection.

We've already established that intention isn't a material substance with measurable physical qualities. As an example of this, think of artists. Their creations aren't merely a function of the quality of the paint, brush, canvas, or any other combination of materials they use. To understand and grasp the creation of a masterpiece, we have to take into account the thoughts and feelings of the artist. We must know and enter into the movement of the creative mind of the artist in order to understand the creation process. The artist creates something out of nothing! Without the thoughts and feelings of the artist, there would be no art. It's their particular creative mind in contemplation that links to intention to give birth to what we call an artistic creation. This is how the power of intention worked in creating you, someone new, entirely unique, someone out of nothing. Reproducing this in yourself means encountering the creative impulse and knowing that the power of intention is reaching for the realization of all that it *feels,* and that it is expressing itself as you.

What you're feeling is a function of how you're thinking, what you're contemplating, and how your inner speech is being formulated. If you could tap in to the *feeling* of the power of intention, you'd sense that it is ever-increasing, and confident in itself because it's a formative power so infallible that it never misses its mark. It's always increasing and creating. The forward movement of spirit is a given. The power of intention yearns toward fuller expressions of life, just as the artist's feelings pour out in a fuller expression of his or her ideas and thoughts. Feelings are clues about your destiny and potential, and they're seeking the full expression of life through you.

How do you enter into the spirit of intention, which is all about feelings expressing life? You can nurture it by your continual ongoing expectation of the infallible spiritual law of increase being a part of your life. We saw it through our imaginary capacity to see higher vibrations, and we heard it in the voice given to it by spiritual masters throughout the ages. It's everywhere. It wants to express life. It's pure love in action. It's confident. And guess what? You are it, but you've forgotten. You need to simply trust your ability to cheerfully rely upon Spirit to express itself through and for you. Your task is to contemplate the energies of life, love, beauty, and kindness. Every action that's in harmony with this originating principle of intention gives expression to your own power of intention.

### Your Will and Your Imagination

There's no disputing the existence of your free will. You're a being with a mind capable of making choices. Indeed, you're in a continuous state of deliberate choice-making during your life. This isn't about free will versus predetermined destiny, but look carefully at how you've chosen to rely on your ability to will yourself toward whatever you desire. Intention, in this book, isn't about having a strong desire and backing it up with a pit-bull kind of determination. Having a strong will and being filled with resolve to accomplish inner goals is asking ego to be the guiding force in your life. *I will do this thing, I will never be stupid, I will never give up.* These are admirable traits, but they won't reconnect you to intention. Your willpower is so much less effective than your imagination, which is your link to the power of intention. Imagination is the movement of the universal mind within you. Your imagination creates the inner picture that allows you to *participate* in the act of creation. It's the invisible connecting link to manifesting your own destiny.

Try to imagine willing yourself to do something that your imagination doesn't want you to do. Your will is the ego part of you that believes you're separate from others, separate from what you'd like to accomplish or have, and separate from God. It also believes that you are your acquisitions, achievements, and accolades. This *ego will* wants you to constantly acquire evidence of your importance. It pushes you toward proving your superiority and acquiring things you're willing to chase after with hyperdedication and resolve. On the other hand, your imagination is the concept of Spirit within you. It's the God within you. Read William Blake's description of imagination. Blake believed that with imagination, we have the power to be anything we desire to be.

> *I rest not from my great task!*
> *To open the Eternal Worlds,*
>  *to open the immortal Eyes of Man*
> *Inwards into the Worlds of Thought;*
> *Into eternity, ever expanding*
> *In the Bosom of God,*
> *The Human Imagination*

— from *Jerusalem* by William Blake

Now go back to the idea of willing yourself to do something when your imagination says no. An example of a fire walk comes to my mind. You can stare at those hot coals and will yourself to walk across them, and if you rely exclusively on your willpower, you'll end up with severe burns and blisters. But if you imagine yourself divinely protected—in Blake's words, *in the Bosom of God,* and can see yourself in your imagination able to be something beyond your body, you can accomplish the fire walk unscathed. As you imagine yourself impervious to the heat of the red-hot coals, you begin to feel yourself as something beyond your body. You visualize yourself as stronger than the fire. Your inner picture of purity and protection lets you will yourself to walk across the coals. It's your imagination that allows you to be safe. Without it, you'd be scorched!

I recall imagining myself being able to complete my first marathon run of 26-plus miles. It wasn't my will that got me through those three and a half hours of continuous running. It was my inner imagination. I tuned in to it and then allowed my body to be pushed to its limit through my will. Without that image, no amount of will would have been sufficient for me to complete that endeavor.

And so it is with everything. Willing yourself to be happy, successful, wealthy, number one, famous, the top salesperson, or the richest person in your community are ideas born of the ego and its obsessive self-absorption. In the name of this willpower, people run roughshod over anyone who gets in their way; cheating, stealing, and deceiving to accomplish their personal intention. Yet these kinds of practices will ultimately lead to disaster. You may achieve the physical goal of your individual intention. However, your imagination, that inner place where you do all of your living, won't allow you to feel peaceful.

I've used this power of imagination over my will in the production of all of my life's work. For instance, I see myself as having already completed this book. This *thinking from the end* causes me to behave as if all that I'd like to create is already here. My credo is: *Imagine myself to be and I shall be,* and it's an image that I keep with me at all times. I don't complete a book because I have a strong will to do so. That would mean I believe that it's me, the body named Wayne Dyer, that's doing all of this, whereas my imagination has no physical boundaries and no name called Wayne Dyer. My imagination is my very own "chip off of the old block" of intention. It provides what I need, it allows me to sit here and write, it guides my pen in my hand, and fills in all the blanks. I, Wayne Dyer, am not willing this book into reality. My picture of it is so clear and precise that it manifests itself. In ancient times, a divine being named Hermes wrote:

> *That which* IS *is manifested;*
> *That which has been or shall be, is unmanifested,*
>   *but not dead;*
> *For soul, the eternal activity of God, animates all things.*

These are significant words to ponder as you think about reconnecting to intention and gaining the power to create anything that's in your imagination. You, your body, and your ego do not intend, do not create, do not animate anything into life. Set your ego aside. By all means, have an aim in life and be full of determination, but rid yourself of the illusion that you're the one who's going to manifest your heart's desire through your will. It's your *imagination* that I want you to focus on throughout the reading of this book, and view all of your determined goals and activities as functions of your imagination working, guiding, encouraging, and even pushing you in the direction that intention had for you while you were still in an *unmanifested* state. You're looking for a vibrational match-up of your imagination and the Source of all Creation.

Your imagination allows you the fabulous luxury of *thinking from the end.* There's no stopping anyone who can think from the end. You create the means and surmount limitations in connection with your desires. In imagination, dwell on the end, fully confident that it's there in the material world and that you can use the ingredients of the all-creative Source to make it tangible. Since the Source of everything proceeds with grace, and its alluring seven faces, then you too shall use this method and only this method, to co-create all that you were intended to be. Become indifferent to doubt and to the call of your will. Remain confident that through continued reliance on your imagination, your assumptions are materializing into reality. Reconnecting to intention involves expressing the same seven faces that the all-creating Source uses to bring the unmanifest into the manifest. If imagination works for God, then surely it works for you, too. Through imagination, God imagines everything into reality. This is your new strategy as well.

### Applying the Seven Faces for Connecting to Intention

Having been in the business of human development for most of my life, the question I most frequently hear is: "How do I go about getting what I want?" At this juncture of my life, as I sit here writing this book, my response is: "If you become what you think about, and what you think about is getting what you want, then you'll stay in a state of wanting. So, the answer to how to get what you want is to reframe the question to: *How do I go about getting what I intend to create?*" My answer to that question is in the remaining pages of this chapter, but my short answer is this: "You get what you intend to create by being in harmony with the power of intention, which is responsible for all of creation." Become just like intention and you'll co-create all that you contemplate. When you become one with intention, you're transcending the ego-mind and becoming the universal all-creative mind. John Randolph Price writes in *A Spiritual Philosophy for the New World*: "Until you transcend the ego, you can do nothing but add to the insanity of the world. That statement should delight you rather than create despair, for it removes the burden from your shoulders."

Begin to remove that ego burden from your shoulders and reconnect to intention. When you lay your ego aside and return to that from which you originally emanated, you'll begin to immediately see the power of intention working with, for, and through you in a multitude of ways. Here are those seven faces revisited to help you to begin to make them a part of your life.

**1. Be creative.** Being creative means trusting your own purpose and having an attitude of unbending intent in your daily thoughts and activities. Staying creative means giving form to your personal intentions. A way to start giving them form is to literally put them in writing. For instance, in my writing space here on Maui, I've written out my intentions, and here are a few of them that stare at me each day as I write:

- *My intention is for all of my activities to be directed by Spirit.*

- *My intention is to love and radiate my love to my writing and any who might read these words.*

- *My intention is to trust in what comes through me and to be a vehicle of Spirit, judging none of it.*

- *My intention is to recognize the Spirit as my Source and to detach from my ego.*

- *My intention is to do all that I can to elevate the collective consciousness to be more closely in rapport with the Spirit of the originating supreme power of intention.*

To express your creativity and put your own intentions into the world of the manifest, I recommend that you practice *Japa*, a technique first offered by the ancient Vedas. Japa meditation is the repetition of the sound of the names of God while simultaneously focusing on what you intend to manifest. Repeating the sound within the name of God while asking for what you want generates creative energy to manifest your desires. And your desires are the movement of the universal mind within you. Now, you may be skeptical about the feasibility of such an undertaking. Well, I ask you to open yourself to this idea of Japa as an expression of your creative link to intention. I won't describe the method in depth here because I've written about it in a small book with an accompanying CD by Hay House called *Getting in the Gap: Making Conscious Contact with God Through Meditation.* For now, just know that I consider meditating and practicing Japa essential in the quest to realign yourself with the power of intention. That power is Creation, and you need to be in your own unique state of creativity to collaborate with the power of intention. Meditation and Japa are surefire ways to do so.

**2. Be kind.** A fundamental attribute of the supreme originating power is kindness. All that's manifested is brought here to thrive. It takes a kindly power to want what it creates to thrive and multiply. Were this not the case, then all that's created would be destroyed by the same power that created it. In order to reconnect to intention, you must be on the same kindness wavelength as intention itself. Make an effort to live in cheerful kindness. It's a much higher energy than sadness or malevolence, and it makes the manifestation of your desires possible. *It's through giving that we receive;* it's through acts of kindness directed toward others that our immune systems are strengthened and even our serotonin levels increased!

Low energy thoughts that weaken us fall in the realm of shame, anger, hatred, judgment, and fear. Each of these inner thoughts weakens us and inhibits us from attracting into our lives what we desire. If we become what we think about, and what we think about is what's wrong with the world and how angry and ashamed and fearful we are, it stands to reason that we'll act on those unkind thoughts and become what we're thinking about. When you think, feel, and act kindly, you give yourself the opportunity to be like the power of intention. When you're thinking and acting otherwise, you've left the field of intention, and you've assured yourself of feeling cheated by the all-creative Spirit of intent.

— *Kindness toward yourself.* Think of yourself like this: There's a universal intelligence subsisting throughout nature inherent in every one of its manifestations. You are one of those manifestations. You are a piece of this universal intelligence—a slice of God, if you will. Be good to God, since all that God created was good. Be good to yourself. You are God manifested, and that's reason enough to treat yourself kindly. Remind yourself that you want to be kind to yourself in all the choices that you make about your daily life. Treat yourself with kindness when you eat, exercise, play, work, love, and everything else. Treating yourself kindly will hasten your ability to connect to intention.

— *Kindness toward others.* A basic tenet of getting along and being happy, as well as enlisting the assistance of others toward achieving all that you want to attract, is that people want to help you and do things for you. When you're kind to others, you receive kindness in return. A boss who's unkind gets very little cooperation from his employees. Being unkind with children makes them want to get even rather than help you out. Kindness given is kindness returned. If you wish to connect to intention and become someone who achieves all of your objectives in life, you're going to need the assistance of a multitude of folks. By practicing extending kindness everywhere, you'll find support showing up in ways that you could never have predicted.

This idea of extending kindness is particularly relevant in how you deal with people who are helpless, elderly, mentally challenged, poor, disabled, and so on. These people are all part of God's perfection. They, too, have a divine purpose, and since all of us are connected to each other through Spirit, their purpose and intent is also connected to you. Here's a brief story that will touch you at the heart level. It suggests that those whom we meet who are less than able to care for themselves may have come here to teach us something about the perfection of intention. Read it and know that this kind of thinking, feeling, and behavior empowers you to connect to intention through matching its kindness with your own.

*In Brooklyn, New York, Chush is a school that caters to learning-disabled children. Some children remain in Chush for their entire school career, while others can be mainstreamed into conventional schools. At a Chush fundraiser dinner, the father of a Chush child delivered a speech that would never be forgotten by all who attended. After extolling the school and its dedicated staff, he cried out, "Where is the perfection in my son, Shaya? Everything God does is done with perfection. But my child cannot understand things as other children do. My child cannot remember facts and figures as other children do. Where is God's perfection?" The audience was shocked by the question, pained by the father's anguish, and stilled by the piercing query.*

*"I believe," the father answered, "that when God brings a child like this into the world, the perfection that he seeks is in the way people react to this child." He then told the following story about his son, Shaya.*

One afternoon Shaya and his father walked past a park where some boys Shaya knew were playing baseball. Shaya asked, "Do you think they'll let me play?" Shaya's father knew that his son was not at all athletic and that most boys would not want him on their team. But Shaya's father understood that if his son was chosen to play, it would give him a sense of belonging. Shaya's father approached one of the boys on the field and asked if Shaya could play. The boy looked around for guidance from his teammates. Getting none, he took matters into his own hands and said, "We're losing by six runs, and the game is in the eighth inning. I guess he can be on our team, and we'll try to put him up to bat in the ninth inning."

Shaya's father was ecstatic as Shaya smiled broadly. Shaya was told to put on a glove and go out to play in center field. In the bottom of the eighth inning, Shaya's team scored a few runs but was still behind by three. In the bottom of the ninth inning, Shaya's team scored again, and now had two outs and the bases loaded, with the potential winning run on base, Shaya was scheduled to be up. Would the team actually let Shaya bat at this juncture and give away their chance to win the game?

Surprisingly, Shaya was given the bat. Everyone knew that it was all but impossible because Shaya didn't even know how to hold the bat properly, let alone hit with it. However, as Shaya stepped up to the plate, the pitcher moved a few steps to lob the ball in softly so Shaya could at least be able to make contact. The first pitch came in, and Shaya swung clumsily and missed. One of Shaya's teammates came up to Shaya, and together they held the bat and faced the pitcher waiting for the next pitch. The pitcher again took a few steps forward to toss the ball softly toward Shaya. As the pitch came in, Shaya and his teammate swung the bat, and together they hit a slow ground ball to the pitcher. The pitcher picked up the soft grounder and could easily have thrown the ball to the first baseman. Shaya would have been out and that would have ended the game. Instead, the *pitcher took the ball and threw it on a high arc to right field far beyond the reach of the first baseman. Everyone started yelling, "Shaya, run to first. Run to first." Never in his life had Shaya run to first. He scampered down the baseline wide-eyed and startled. By the time he reached first base, the right-fielder had the ball. He could have thrown the ball to the second baseman who would tag out Shaya, who was still running.*

*But the right-fielder understood what the pitcher's intentions were, so he threw the ball high and far over the third baseman's head. Everyone yelled, "Run to second, run to second." Shaya ran toward second base as the runners ahead of him deliriously circled the bases toward home. As Shaya reached second base, the opposing shortstop ran to him, turned him in the direction of third base, and shouted, "Run to third." As Shaya rounded third, the boys from both teams ran behind him screaming, "Shaya, run home." Shaya ran home, stepped on home plate, and all 18 boys lifted him on their shoulders and made him the hero, as he had just hit a "grand slam" and won the game for his team.*

*"That day," said the father softly with tears now rolling down his face, "those 18 boys reached their level of God's perfection."*

If you don't feel a tug in your heart and a tear in your eye after reading this story, then it's unlikely that you'll ever know the magic of connecting back to the kindness of the supreme all-originating Source.

— *Kindness toward all of life.* In the ancient teachings of Patanjali, we're reminded that all living creatures are impacted dramatically by those who remain steadfast in the absence of thoughts of harm directed outward. Practice kindness toward all animals, tiny and huge, the entire kingdom of life on Earth such as the forests, the deserts, the beaches, and all that has the essence of life pulsating within it. You can't reconnect to your Source and know the power of intention in your life without the assistance of the environment. You're connected to this environment. Without gravity, you can't walk. Without the water, you can't live a day. Without the forests, the sky, the atmosphere, the vegetation, the minerals—all of it—your desire to manifest and reach intention is meaningless.

Extend thoughts of kindness everywhere. Practice kindness toward Earth by picking up a piece of litter that's on your path, or saying a silent prayer of gratitude for the existence of rain, the color of flowers, or even the paper you hold in your hand that was donated by a tree. The universe responds in kind to what you elect to radiate outward. If you say with kindness in your voice and in your heart, "How may I serve you?" the universe's response will be, "How may I serve you as well?" It's attractor energy. It's this spirit of cooperation with all of life that emerges from the essence of intention. And this spirit of kindness is one that you must learn to match if connecting back to intention is your desire. My daughter Sommer has written from her experience about how small acts of kindness go a long way:

> I was getting off the turnpike one rainy afternoon and pulled up to the tollbooth while fumbling through my purse. The woman smiled at me and said, "The car before you has paid your toll." I told her I was traveling alone and extended my money. She replied, "Yes, the man instructed me to tell the next person who came to my booth to have a brighter day." That small act of kindness did give me a brighter day. I felt so moved by someone I would never know. I began to wonder how I could brighten someone else's day. I called my best friend and told her about my paid toll. She said she'd never thought of doing that, but it was a great idea. She goes to the University of Kentucky and decided to pay for the person behind her every day on her way to school as she exits the toll road. I laughed at her sincerity. "You think I'm kidding," she said, "but like you said, it's only 50 cents." As we hung up, I wondered if the man who paid my toll even fathomed that his thoughtfulness would travel to Kentucky.

*I had an opportunity to extend kindness at the supermarket one day when I had my cart filled to the top with food that my roommate and I would share over the next two weeks. The woman behind me had an antsy toddler and not nearly as much in her cart as I had. I said to her, "Why don't you go first? You don't have as much as I do." The woman looked at me as if I'd just sprouted extra limbs or something. She replied, "Thank you so much. I haven't seen many people around here be thoughtful of another person. We've moved here from Virginia and are considering moving back because we're questioning whether this is the right place to raise our three children." Then she told me that she was about ready to give up and move back home, even though it would create a huge financial strain on her family. She said, "I'd promised myself if I didn't see a sign by the end of today, I was going to demand that we move back to Virginia. You are my sign."*

*She thanked me again, smiling as she left the store. I was flabbergasted, realizing that such a small gesture had impacted a whole family. The clerk said as she was checking me out, "You know what, girl? You just made my day." I walked out smiling, wondering how many people my act of kindness would affect.*

*The other day I was getting a breakfast sandwich and coffee and thought my co-workers might like some doughnuts. The four guys I work with at the stables live in the little apartments at the front of the barns. None of them has a car, but they share a bike. I explained to them that the doughnuts were for them. The look of gratitude on each of their faces was rewarding in an immeasurable way. I haven't worked there all that long, and I think that those 12 small doughnuts helped break the ice a little bit. My small act of kindness turned into something huge as the week went on. We started looking out for one another more carefully and working as a team.*

**3. Be love.** Ponder these words thoughtfully: *God is love,* "and he that dwelleth in love dwelleth in me, and I in him." That is God talking, so to speak. Keeping in mind the central theme of this chapter, and in fact, this entire book, that you must learn to be like the energy that allowed you to be in the first place, then being in a state of love is absolutely necessary for you to reconnect to intention. You were intended out of love, you must be love in order to intend. Volumes have been written about love, and still we have as many definitions for this word as we have people to offer them. For the purposes of this chapter, I'd like you to think about love in the following two ways.

— *Love is cooperation rather than competition.* What I'd like you to be able to experience right here in physical form on planet Earth is the essence of the spiritual plane. If this were possible, it would mean that your very life is a manifestation of love. Were this to be true for you, you'd see all of life living together in harmony and cooperating with each other. You'd sense that the power of intention that originates all life cooperates with all other life forms to ensure growth and survival. You'd note that we all share the same life force, and the same invisible intelligence that beats my heart and your heart, beats the heart of everyone on the planet.

— *Love is the force behind the will of God.* I'm not suggesting the kind of love that we define as affection or sentiment. Nor is this kind of love a feeling that seeks to please and press favors on others. Imagine a kind of love that is the power of intention, the very energy that is the cause behind all of creation. It's the spiritual vibration that carries divine intentions from formless to concrete expression. It creates new form, changes matter, vivifies all things, and holds the cosmos together beyond time and space. It's in every one of us. It is what God is.

I recommend that you pour your love into your immediate environment and hold to this practice on an hourly basis if possible. Remove all unloving thoughts from your mind, and practice kindness in all of your thoughts, words, and actions. Cultivate this love in your immediate circle of acquaintances and family, and ultimately it will expand to your community and globally as well. Extend this love deliberately to those you feel have harmed you in any way or caused you to experience suffering. The more you can extend this love, the closer you come to being love, and it's in the beingness of love that intention is reached and manifestation flourishes.

**4. Be beauty.** Emily Dickinson wrote: "Beauty is not caused. It is . . . " As you awaken to your divine nature, you'll begin to appreciate beauty in everything you see, touch, and experience. Beauty and truth are synonymous as you read earlier in John Keats's famous observation in *Ode on a Grecian Urn:* "Beauty is truth, truth beauty." This means, of course, that the creative Spirit brings things into the world of boundaries to thrive and flourish and expand. And it wouldn't do so were it not infatuated with the beauty of every manifested creature, including you. Thus, to come back into conscious contact with your Source so as to regain the power of your Source is to look for and experience beauty in all of your undertakings. Life, truth, beauty. These are all symbols for the same thing, an aspect of the God-force.

When you lose this awareness, you lose the possibility of connecting to intention. You were brought into this world from that which perceived you as an expression of beauty. It couldn't have done so if it thought you to be otherwise, for if it has the power to create; it also possesses the power not to do so. The choice to do so is predicated on the supposition that you're an expression of loving beauty. This is true for everything and everyone that emanates from the power of intention.

Here's a favorite story of mine that illustrates appreciating beauty where once you didn't. It was told by Swami Chidvilasananda, better known as Gurumayi, in her beautiful book, *Kindle My Heart.*

> *"There was a man who did not like his in-laws because he felt they took up more space in the house than they should. He went to a teacher who lived nearby, as he had*

*heard a lot about him, and he said, 'Please do something! I cannot bear my in-laws anymore. I love my wife, but my in-laws—never! They take up so much space in the house; somehow I feel they are always in my way.'*

*The teacher asked him, 'Do you have some chickens?'*

*'Yes, I do,' he said.*

*'Then put all your chickens inside the house.'*

*He did what the teacher said and then went back to him.*

*The teacher asked, 'Problem solved?'*

*He said, 'No! It's worse.'*

*'Do you have any sheep?'*

*'Yes.'*

*'Bring all the sheep inside.' He did so and returned to the teacher. 'Problem solved?'*

*'No! It's getting worse'*

*'Do you have a dog?'*

*'Yes, I have several.'*

*'Take all those dogs into the house.'*

*Finally, the man ran back to the teacher and said, 'I came to you for help, but you are making my life worse than ever!'*

*The teacher said to him, 'Now send all the chickens, sheep, and dogs back outside.'*

*The man went home and emptied the house of all the animals. There was so much space! He went back to the teacher. 'Thank you! Thank you!' he said. 'You have solved all my problems.'"*

**5. Be ever-expansive.** The next time you see a garden full of flowers, observe the flowers that are alive, and compare them to the flowers that you believe are dead. What's the difference? The dried-up, *dead* flowers are no longer growing, while the alive flowers are indeed still growing. The all-emerging universal force that intended you into beingness and commences all life is always growing, and perpetually expanding. As with all seven of these faces of intention, by reason of its universality, it must have a common nature with yours. By being in an ever-expanding state and growing intellectually, emotionally, and spiritually, you're identifying with the universal mind.

By staying in a state of readiness in which you're not attached to what you used to think or be, and by thinking from the end and staying open to receiving divine guidance, you abide by the law of growth and are receptive to the power of intention.

**6. Be abundant.** Intention is endlessly abundant. There's no scarcity in the universal invisible world of Spirit. The cosmos itself is without end. How could there be an end to the universe? What would be at the end? A wall? So how thick is the wall? And what's on the other side of it? As you contemplate connecting to intention, know in your heart that any attitude you have that reflects a scarcity consciousness will hold you back. A reminder here is in order. You must match intention's attributes with your own in order to capitalize on those powers in your life.

Abundance is what God's kingdom is about. Imagine God thinking, *I can't produce any more oxygen today, I'm just too tired; this universe is big enough already, I think I'll erect that wall and bring this expansion thing to a halt.* Impossible! You emerged from a consciousness that was and is unlimited. So what's to prevent you from rejoining that limitless awareness in your mind and holding on to these pictures regardless of what goes before you? What prevents you is the conditioning you've been exposed to during your life, which you can change today—in the next few minutes if you so desire.

When you shift to an abundance mind-set, you repeat to yourself over and over again that you're unlimited because you emanated from the inexhaustible supply of intention. As this picture solidifies, you begin to act on this attitude of unbending intent. There's no other possibility. We become what we think about, and as Emerson reminded us: "The ancestor to every action is a thought." As these thoughts of plentitude and excessive sufficiency become your way of thinking, the all-creating force to which you're always connected will begin to work with you, in harmony with your thoughts, just as it worked with you in harmony with your thoughts of scarcity. If you think you can't manifest abundance into your life, you'll see intention agreeing with you, and *assisting* you in the fulfillment of meager expectations!

* * *

I seem to have arrived into this world fully connected to the abundance attributes of the spiritual world from which I emanated. As a child growing up in foster homes, with poverty consciousness all around me, I was the "richest" kid in the orphanage, so to speak. I always thought I could have money jingling in my pocket. I pictured it there, and I consequently acted on that picture. I'd collect soda-pop bottles, shovel snow, bag groceries, cut lawns, carry out people's ashes from their coal furnaces, clean up yards, paint fences, babysit, deliver newspapers, and on and on. And always, the universal force of abundance worked *with* me in providing opportunities. A snowstorm was a giant blessing for me. So too were discarded bottles by the side of the road, and little old ladies who needed help carrying their groceries to their automobiles.

Today, over a half century later, I still have that abundance mentality. I've never been without several jobs at one time throughout many economic slumps over my lifetime. I made large amounts of money as a schoolteacher by starting a driver-education business after school hours. I began a lecture series in Port Washington, New York, on Monday evenings for 30 or so local residents to supplement my income as a professor at St. John's University, and that Monday-night series became an audience of over a thousand people in the high school auditorium. Each lecture was tape-recorded by a staff member, and those tapes led to the outline for my first book to the public, which was called *Your Erroneous Zones*.

One of the attendees was the wife of a literary agent in New York City who encouraged him to contact me about writing a book. That man, Arthur Pine, became like a father to me and helped me meet key publishing people in New York. And the same story of unlimited thinking goes on and on. I saw the book *from the end* becoming a tool for everyone in the country, and proceeded to go to every large city in America to tell people about it.

The universal Spirit has always worked with me in bringing my thoughts of unlimited abundance into my life. The right people would magically appear. The right break would come along. The help I needed would seemingly manifest out of nowhere. And in a sense, I'm still collecting pop bottles, shoveling snow, and carrying out groceries for little old ladies today. My vision hasn't changed, although the playing field is enlarged. It's all about having an inner picture of abundance, thinking in unlimited ways, being open to the guidance that intention provides when you're in a state of rapport with it—and then being in a state of ecstatic gratitude and awe for how this whole thing works. Every time I see a coin on the street, I stop, pick it up, put it into my pocket, and say out loud, "Thank you, God, for this symbol of abundance that keeps flowing into my life." Never once have I asked, "Why only a penny, God? You know I need a lot more than that."

Today, I arise at 4 A.M. with a knowing that my writing will complete what I've already envisioned in the contemplations of my imagination. The writing flows, and letters arrive from intention's manifest abundance urging me to read a particular book, or to talk to a unique individual, and I know that it's all working in perfect, abundant unity. The phone rings, and just what I need to hear is resonating in my ear. I get up to get a glass of water, and my eyes fall on a book that's been on my shelf for 20 years, but this time I'm compelled to pick it up. I open it, and I'm once again being directed by spirit's willingness to assist and guide me as long as I stay in harmony with it. It goes on and on, and I'm reminded of Jelaluddin Rumi's poetic words from 800 years ago: "Sell your cleverness, and purchase bewilderment."

**7. Be receptive.** The universal mind is ready to respond to anyone who recognizes their true relationship to it. It will reproduce whatever conception of itself you impress upon it. In other words, it's receptive to all who remain in harmony with it and stay in a relationship of reverence for it. The issue becomes a question of your receptivity to the power of intention. Stay connected and know you'll receive all that this power is capable of offering. Take it on by yourself as separate from the universal mind (an impossibility, but nevertheless, a strong belief of the ego), and you remain eternally disconnected.

The nature of the universal mind is peaceful. It isn't receptive to force or violence. It works in its own time and rhythm, allowing everything to emanate by and by. It's in no hurry because it's outside of time. It's always in the eternal now. Try getting down on your hands and knees and hurrying along a tiny tomato plant sprout. Universal Spirit is at work peacefully, and your attempts to rush it or tug new life into full creative flower will destroy the entire process. Being receptive means allowing your "senior partner" to handle your life for you. *I accept the guidance and assistance of the same force that created me, I let go of my ego, and I trust in this wisdom to move at its own peaceful pace. I make no demands on it.* This is how the all-creating field of intention creates. This is how you must think in order to reconnect to your Source. You practice meditation because it allows you to receive the inner knowing of making conscious contact with God. By being peaceful, quiet, and receptive, you pattern yourself in the image of God, and you regain the power of your Source.

That is what this chapter, and indeed this entire book, is all about. That is, tapping in to the essence of originating Spirit, emulating the attributes of the creative force of intention, and manifesting into your life anything that you desire that's consistent with the universal mind—which is creativity, kindness, love, beauty, expansion, abundance, and peaceful receptivity.

\* \* \*

A beautiful woman born in India in 1923 named Shri Mataji Nirmala Devi arrived here on Earth in a fully realized state and lived in the ashram of Mahatma Gandhi, who often consulted her on spiritual questions. She's spent her life working for peace, and discovered a simple method through which all people can receive their self-realization. She teaches Sahaja Yoga, and has never charged for this instruction. She emphasizes the following points, which are a perfect summary on this chapter on connecting to intention:

- *You cannot know the meaning of your life until you are connected to the power that created you.*

- *You are not this body, you are not this mind, you are the Spirit . . . this is the greatest truth.*

- *You have to know your Spirit . . . for without knowing your Spirit, you cannot know the truth.*

- *Meditation is the only way you can grow. There is no other way out. Because when you meditate, you are in silence. You are in thoughtless awareness. Then the growth of awareness takes place.*

Connect to the power that created you, know that you are that power, commune with that power intimately, and meditate to allow that *growth of awareness* to take place. A great summary indeed, from a fully realized being, no less.

## Five Suggestions for Implementing the Ideas of this Chapter

1. *To realize your desires, match them with your inner speech.* Keep all inner talk focused on good reports and good results. Your inner speech mirrors your imagination, and your imagination is your connecting link to Spirit. If your inner speech is in conflict with your desires, your inner voice will win. So, if you match desires with inner speech, those desires will ultimately be realized.

2. *Think from the end.* That is, assume within yourself the feeling of the wish being fulfilled, and keep this vision regardless of the obstacles that emerge. Eventually you'll act on this *end thinking,* and the Spirit of Creation will collaborate with you.

3. *To reach a state of impeccability, you need to practice unbending intent.* This will match you up with the unbending intent of the all-creative universal mind. For example, if I set out to write a book, I keep a solid picture of the completed book in my mind, and I refuse to let that intention disappear. There's nothing that can keep me from that intention being fulfilled. Some say that I have great discipline, but I know otherwise. My unbending intent won't allow for anything but its completion to be expressed. I'm pushed, prodded, and propelled, and finally almost mystically attracted to my writing space. All waking and sleeping thoughts are focused on this picture, and I never lack for being in a state of awe at how it all comes together.

4. *Copy the seven faces of intention on three-by-five cards.* Have them laminated and place them in crucial locations that you must look at each day. They'll serve as reminders for you to stay in fellowship with the originating Spirit. You want a relationship of camaraderie to exist with intention. The seven reminders strategically placed around your living and working environment will do just that for you.

5. *Always keep the thought of God's abundance in mind. If any other thought comes, replace it with that of God's abundance.* Remind yourself every day that the universe can't be miserly; it can't be wanting. It holds nothing but abundance, or as St. Paul stated so perfectly, "God is able to provide you with every blessing in abundance." Repeat these ideas on abundance until they radiate as your inner truth.

This concludes the steps for connecting to intention. But before you make this somersault into the inconceivable, I urge you to examine any and all self-imposed obstacles that need to be challenged and eradicated as you work anew at living and breathing this power of intention that was placed in your heart before a heart was even formed. As William Penn put it: "Those people who are not governed by God will be ruled by tyrants." Remember as you read on, that those tyrants are often the self-imposed roadblocks of your lower self at work.

~ * ~ * ~

# CHAPTER FOUR

## OBSTACLES TO CONNECTING TO INTENTION

*"... does a firm persuasion that a thing is so, make it so?*
*He replied, 'All poets believe that it does.*
*And in ages of imagination, this firm persuasion*
*    removed mountains;*
*But many are not capable of a firm persuasion of anything.'"*
— from *The Marriage of Heaven and Hell* by William Blake

William Blake's passage from *The Marriage of Heaven and Hell* is the basis of this chapter about overcoming obstacles to the unlimited power of intention. Blake is telling us that poets have an inexhaustible imagination and consequently an unlimited ability to make something so. He also reminds us that many aren't capable of such a firm persuasion.

In the previous chapter, I gave you suggestions for making positive connections to intention. I deliberately arranged the chapters this way so that you'd read about what you're capable of before examining barriers you've erected that keep you from the bliss of your intention. In the past, as a practicing counselor and therapist, I've encouraged clients to first consider what they want to

manifest in their lives and hold that thought firmly in their imagination. Only after this was solidified would I have them examine
and consider the obstacles. Often my clients were unaware of the
obstructions even when they were self-imposed. Learning to identify ways in which you're creating your own obstacles is tremen-
dously enlightening if you're willing to explore this area of your life.
You may discover the obstacles that keep you from *a firm persuasion of anything.*

I'm devoting this chapter to three areas that may be unrecog-
nized obstacles to your connection to the power of intention. You'll
be examining *your inner speech, your level of energy,* and *your self-
importance.* These three categories can create almost insurmountable blocks to connecting to intention when they're mismatched.
Taken one at a time, you'll have the opportunity to become aware
of these blockages and explore ways of overcoming them.

There's a game show that has aired on television for several
decades now (in syndication). It's called *The Match Game.* The
object of this game is to match up your thoughts and potential
responses with that of someone on your team, usually a partner or
family member. A question or statement is given to one partner, and
several possible responses are offered. The more matches made,
in competition with two other couples, the more points received.
The winner is the one with the most matches.

I'd like to play the match game with you. In my version, I'm asking you to match up with the universal Spirit of intention. As we
go through the three categories of obstacles that hinder your connection to intention, I'll describe the areas that don't match, and
offer suggestions for creating a match. Remember that your ability to activate the power of intention in *your* life depends on your
matching up with the creative Source of *all* life. Match up with that
Source, and you win the prize of being like the Source—and the
power of intention. Fail to match up . . . and the power of intention eludes you.

### *Your Inner Speech—Match or No Match?*

We can go all the way back to the Old Testament to find a reminder about our inner dialogue. For instance, *as a man thinketh, so is he.* Generally, we apply this idea of becoming what we think to our positive thoughts—that is, think positively and you'll produce positive results. But thinking also creates stumbling blocks that produce negative results. Below are four ways of thinking that can prevent you from reaching for and connecting to the universal, creative Spirit of intention.

**1. Thinking about what's missing in your life.** To match up with intention, you first have to catch yourself in that moment you're thinking about *what's missing.* Then shift to intention. Not *what I find missing in my life,* but to *what I absolutely intend to manifest and attract into my life*—with no doubts, no waffling, and no explaining! Here are some suggestions to help you break the habit of focusing your thoughts on what's missing. Play a version of the match game, and match up with the *all-creating force:*

**No match:** I don't have enough money.
**Match:**     I intend to attract unlimited abundance into my life.

**No match:** My partner is grouchy and boring.
**Match:**     I intend to focus my thoughts on what I love about my partner.

**No match:** I'm not as attractive as I'd like to be.
**Match:**     I'm perfect in the eyes of God, a divine manifestation of the process of creation.

**No match:** I don't have enough vitality and energy.
**Match:**     I'm a part of the ebb and flow of the limitless Source of all life.

This isn't a game of empty affirmations. It's a way of *matching* yourself to the power of intention and recognizing that what you think about, expands. If you spend your time thinking about what's missing, then that's what expands in your life. Monitor your inner dialogue, and match your thoughts to what you want and intend to create.

**2. Thinking about the circumstances of your life.** If you don't like some of the circumstances of your life, by all means don't think about them. This may sound like a paradox to you, in this match game, you want to match up with the Spirit of creation. You must train your imagination (which is the universal mind running through you) to shift from what you don't want to what you do want. All of that mental energy you spend complaining about *what is*— to anyone who will listen—is a magnet for attracting *more of what is* into your life. You, and only you, can overcome this impediment because you've put it on your path to intention. Simply change your inner speech to what you intend the new circumstances of your life to be. Practice *thinking from the end* by playing the match game, and by realigning yourself with the field of intention.

Here are some examples of a **no match** versus a **match** for the inner dialogue relating to the circumstances of your life:

**No match:** I hate this place we're living in; it gives me the creeps.
**Match:** I can see our new home in my mind, and I intend to be living in it within six months.

**No match:** When I see myself in the mirror, I despise the fact that I'm nearsighted and out of shape.
**Match:** I'm placing this drawing of how I intend to look right here on my mirror.

**No match:** I dislike the work I'm doing and the fact that I'm not appreciated.
**Match:** I'll act upon my inner intuitive impulses to create the work or job of my dreams.

**No match:** I hate the fact that I'm sick so often and always seem to be getting colds.

**Match:** I am divine health. I intend to act in healthy ways and attract the power to strengthen my immune system in every way I can.

You must learn to assume responsibility for the circumstances of your life without any accompanying guilt. The circumstances of your life aren't the way they are because of karmic debt or because you're being punished. The circumstances of your life, including your health, are yours. Somehow they showed up in your life, so just assume that you participated in all of it. Your inner speech is uniquely your own creation, and it's responsible for attracting more of the circumstances that you don't want. Link up with intention, use your inner speech to stay focused on what you intend to create, and you'll find yourself regaining the power of your Source.

**3. Thinking about what has always been.** When your inner speech focuses on the way things have always been, you act upon your thoughts of what has always been, and the universal all-creating force continues to deliver what has always been. Why? Because your imagination is a part of that which imagined you into existence. It's the force of creation, and you're using it to work against you with your inner speech.

Imagine the absolute Spirit thinking like this: *I can't create life anymore because things haven't worked for me in the past. There have been so many mistakes in the past, and I can't stop thinking about them!* How much creating do you think would occur if Spirit imagined in this way? How can you possibly connect to the power of intention if your thoughts, which are responsible for your intending, focus on all that's gone before, which you abhor? The answer is obvious, and so is the solution. Make a shift and catch yourself when you're focusing on *what always has been*, and move your inner speech to *what you intend to manifest*. You'll get points in this match game by being on the same team as the absolute Spirit.

**No match:** I've always been poor; I was raised on shortages and scarcity.
**Match:** I intend to attract wealth and prosperity in unlimited abundance.

**No match:** We've always fought in this relationship.
**Match:** I'll work at being peaceful and not allowing anyone to bring me down.

**No match:** My children have never shown me any respect.
**Match:** I intend to teach my children to respect all of life, and I'll treat them in the same way.

**No match:** I can't help feeling this way; it's my nature. I've always been this way.
**Match:** I'm a divine creation, capable of thinking like my Creator. I intend to substitute love and kindness for feelings of inadequacy. It's my choice.

The **match** items reflect a rapport with the originating Spirit. The **no match** statements represent interference that you've constructed to keep you from matching up with intention. Any thought that takes you backward is an impediment to manifesting desires. The highest functioning people understand that if you don't have a story, you don't have to live up to it. Get rid of any parts of your story that keep you focused on *what has always been.*

**4. Thinking about what "they" want for you.** There's probably a long list of people, most of them relatives, who have strong ideas about what you should be doing, how you should be thinking and worshiping, where you should be living, how you should be scheduling your life, and how much of your time you should be spending with them—especially on special occasions and holidays! Our definition of friendship thankfully excludes the manipulation and guilt that we so often put up with in our families.

Inner dialogue that commiserates about the manipulative expectations of others ensures that this kind of conduct continues to flow into your life. If your thoughts are on what others expect of you—even though you despise their expectations—you'll continue to act on and attract more of what they want and expect for you. Removing the obstacle means that you decide to shift your inner speech to what you intend to create and attract into your life. You must do this with unswerving intent, and a commitment to not giving mental energy to what others feel about how you live your life. This can be a tough assignment at first, but you'll welcome the shift when you do it.

Practice catching yourself when you have a thought of what others want for you, and ask yourself, *Does this expectation match up with my own?* If not, simply laugh at the absurdity of being upset or frustrated over the expectations of others about how you should be running your life. This is a way to match up and become impervious to the criticisms of others, and simultaneously put a stop to the insidious practice of continuing to attract into your life something you don't want. But the big payoff is that these critics realize that their judgments and critiques are pointless, so they simply desist. A three-for-one bonus, achieved by shifting your attention *away* from what others want or expect for you *to* how you want to live your life.

Here are a few examples of how to win at the match game:

**No match:** I'm so annoyed with my family. They just don't understand me and they never have.

**Match:** I love my family; they don't see things my way, but I don't expect them to. I'm totally focused on my own intentions, and I send them love.

**No match:** I make myself sick trying to please everyone else.

**Match:** I'm on purpose and doing what I signed up to do in this lifetime.

**No match:** I feel so unappreciated by those I serve that it sometimes makes me cry.

**Match:** I do what I do because it's my purpose and my destiny to do so.

**No match:** No matter what I do or say, it seems as if I can't win.

**Match:** I do what my heart tells me to do with love, kindness, and beauty.

### *Your Level of Energy—Match or No Match?*

A scientist will tell you that energy is measured by speed and the size of the wave being created. The size of the wave is measured from low to high, and slow to fast. Anything else that we attribute to the conditions we see in our world is a judgment imposed upon those pulsating frequencies. That being said, I'd like to introduce a judgment of my own here: *Higher energy is better than lower energy.* Why? Because this is a book written by a man who stands for healing, love, kindness, health, abundance, beauty, compassion, and similar expressions; and these expressions are associated with higher and faster energies.

The impact of higher and faster frequencies on lower and slower frequencies can be measured, and it's in this regard that you can make a huge impact on eradicating the energy factors in your life that are obstructing your connection to intention. The purpose of moving up the frequency ladder is to change your vibratory level of energy so that you're at the higher and faster frequencies where your energy level matches up with the highest frequencies of all: the energy of the all-creating Spirit of intention itself. It was Albert Einstein who observed, "Nothing happens until something moves."

Everything in this universe is a movement of energy. Higher/faster energy dissolves and converts lower/slower energy. With this in mind, I'd like you to consider yourself and all of your thoughts in the context of being an *energy* system. That's right—

you're an *energy* system, not just a system of bones, fluids, and cells, but actually a multitude of energy systems encapsulating an inner energy system of thoughts, feelings, and emotions. This energy system that you are can be measured and calibrated. Every thought you have can be energetically calibrated, along with its impact on your body and your environment. The higher your energy, the more capable you are of nullifying and converting lower energies, which weaken you, and impacting in a positive way everyone in your immediate and even distant surroundings.

The objective in this section is to become aware of your own energy level and the actual frequencies of thought that you regularly employ in daily life. You can become proficient at raising your energy level and permanently obliterate energetic expressions that weaken or inhibit your connection to intention. Ultimately, your goal is to have a perfect match with the highest frequency of all. Here's a simple explanation of the five levels of energy that you work with, moving from the lowest and slowest frequencies to the highest and fastest.

**1. The material world.** Solid form is energy slowed down so that it's approximately commensurate with your sense perception of the world of boundaries. Everything that you see and touch is energy slowed down so that it appears to be coalesced mass. Your eyes and your fingers agree, and there you have the physical world.

**2. The sound world.** You seldom perceive sound waves with your eyes, but they can actually be felt. These invisible waves are also high/low and fast/slow. This *sound* level of energy is where you connect to the highest frequencies of Spirit through the practice of Japa meditation, or the repetition of the sound of God, as I've written about extensively in *Getting in the Gap.*

**3. The light world.** Light moves faster than the material world and faster than sound, yet there are no actual particles to form a substance called light. What you see as red is what your eye perceives a certain pulsating frequency to be, and what you perceive as violet is an even faster and higher frequency. When light is brought to darkness, darkness becomes light. The implications for this are startling. Low energy when faced with high energy experiences an automatic conversion.

**4. The thought world.** Your thoughts are an extremely high frequency of pulsation that moves beyond the speed of sound and even light. The frequency of thoughts can be measured, and the impact that they have on your body and your environment can be calculated. Once again, the same rules apply. Higher frequencies nullify lower; faster energies convert slower. A colleague I admire enormously, David Hawkins, M.D., has written a work, which I've referenced often, called *Power vs. Force.* In this remarkable book, Dr. Hawkins elaborates on the lower frequencies of thought and their accompanying emotions, and how they can be impacted and converted by exposure to higher and faster frequencies. I urge you to read his book, and I'll present some of those findings in the section on raising your energy levels. Every thought you have can be calculated to determine if it's strengthening or weakening your ability to reconnect to the highest and fastest energy in the universe.

**5. The Spirit world.** Here is the ultimate in energy. These frequencies are so supersonically rapid that the presence of disorder, disharmony, and even disease is impossible. These measurable energies consist of the seven faces of intention, written about throughout the pages of this book. They are the energies of creation. When you reproduce them in yourself, you reproduce the same creative quality of life that called you into existence. They are the qualities of creativity, kindness, love, beauty, expansion, peaceful abundance, and receptivity. These are the highest energies of the universal Spirit itself. You came into existence from this energy, and you can match up with it energetically as you remove the low-energy pulsations from your thoughts and feelings.

Consider these words of the Nobel Prize–winning physicist Max Planck as he accepted his award for his study of the atom: "As a man who has devoted his whole life to the most clear-headed science, to the study of matter, I can tell you as the result of my research about atoms this much: There is no matter as such! All matter originates and exists only by virtue of a force which brings the particles of an atom to vibration and holds this most minute solar system of the atom together. . . . We must assume behind this force the existence of a conscious and intelligent mind. This mind is the matrix of all matter." It is to this mind that I urge you to match up.

### *Raising Your Energy Level*

Every thought you have has an energy that will either strengthen or weaken you. It's obviously a good idea to eliminate the thoughts that weaken you, since these thoughts are obstacles to creating a winning *match* with the universal, supreme Source of intention. Take a moment to ponder the meaning behind Anthony de Mello's observation in *One Minute Wisdom*:

> *Why is everyone here so happy except me?*
> "Because they have learned to see goodness and beauty everywhere," said the Master.
>
> *Why don't I see goodness and beauty everywhere?*
> "Because you cannot see outside of you what you fail to see inside."

What you may fail to see inside is a result of how you choose to process everything and everyone in your world. You project onto the world what you see inside, and you fail to project into the world what you fail to see inside. If you knew that you were an expression of the universal Spirit of intention, that's what you'd see. You'd raise your energy level beyond any possibility of encumbrances to your connection to the power of intention. *It is only discord acting within your own feelings that will ever deprive you of every good thing that life holds for you!* If you understand this simple observation, you'll curb interferences to intention.

There's a vibratory action to your thoughts, your feelings, and your body. I'm asking you to increase those frequencies so they're high enough to allow you to connect to the power of intention. This may sound like an oversimplification, but I hope you'll try raising your energy level as a way to remove the obstacles that prevent you from experiencing the perfection you're a part of. *You cannot remedy anything by condemning it.* You only add to the destructive energy that's already permeating the atmosphere of your life. When you react to the lower energies you encounter with your own low energies, you're actually setting up a situation that attracts more of that lower energy. For example, if someone behaves in a hateful manner toward you and you respond by *hating them for hating you,* you're participating in a lower energy field, and impacting all who enter that field. If you're angry at those around you for being angry people, you're attempting to remedy the situation through condemnation.

Don't use weakening energies employed by those around you. Other people can't bring you down if you're operating at the higher energies. Why? Because higher and faster energies nullify and convert lower/slower energies, not the reverse. If you feel that the lower energies of those around you are bringing you down, it's because you're joining them at their energy levels.

Your unbending intention may be to be slim and healthy. You know that the universal all-creative Spirit brought you into existence in that microscopic dot of human cellular tissue not to be sickly, overweight, or unattractive . . . but to create love, be kind, and express beauty. This is what the power of intention intended for you to become. Now get this: *You cannot attract attractiveness into your life by hating anything about what you've allowed yourself to become.* Why? Because hatred creates a counter-force of hatred that disempowers your efforts. Here is how Dr. Hawkins describes it in *Power vs. Force:*

Simple kindness to one's self and all that lives is the most powerful transformational force of all. It produces no backlash, has no downside, and never leads to loss or despair. It increases one's own true power without exacting any toll. But to reach maximum power such kindness can permit no exceptions, nor can it be practiced with the expectation of some selfish reward. And its effect is as far reaching as it is subtle." [Note that *kindness* is one of the seven faces of intention.]

He adds further:

That which is injurious loses its capacity to harm when it is brought into the light, and we attract to us that which we emanate.

The lesson is clear in terms of removing lower energy obstacles. We must raise ourselves to the levels of energy where we *are* the light we seek, where we *are* the happiness we desire, where we *are* the love we feel is missing, where we *are* the unlimited abundance we crave. By being it, we attract it to us. By condemning its absence, we ensure that condemnation and discord will continue to flow into our lives.

If you're experiencing scarcity, anguish, depression, an absence of love, or any inability to attract what you desire, seriously look at how you've been attracting these circumstances into your life. Low energy is an attractor pattern. It shows up because you've sent for it, even if on a subconscious level. It's still yours and you own it. However, if you practice deliberately raising your energy level by being cognizant of your immediate environment, you'll move rather rapidly toward intention and remove all of those self-imposed roadblocks. The obstacles are in the low-energy spectrum.

### A Mini-Program for Raising Your Energy Vibrations

Here's a short list of suggestions for moving your energy field to a higher faster vibration. This will help you accomplish the twofold objective of removing the barriers and allowing the power of intention to work with and through you.

**Become conscious of your thoughts.** Every thought you have impacts you. By shifting in the middle of a weakening thought to one that strengthens, you raise your energy vibration and strengthen yourself and the immediate energy field. For example, in the midst of saying something to one of my teenage children that was intended to make her feel ashamed of her conduct, I stopped and reminded myself that there's no remedy in condemnation. I proceeded to extend love and understanding by asking her how she felt about her self-defeating behavior and what she'd like to do to correct it. The shift raised the energy level and led to a productive conversation.

Raising the energy level to a place where my daughter and I connected to the power of intention took place in a split second of my becoming aware of my low-energy thinking and making a decision to raise it. We all have the ability to call this presence and power of intention into action when we become conscious of our thoughts.

**Make meditation a regular practice in your life.** Even if it's only for a few moments each day while sitting at a stoplight, this practice is vital. Take some time to be silent, and repeat the sound of God as an inner mantra. Meditation allows you to make conscious contact with your Source and regain the power of intention by assisting you in cultivating a receptivity that matches up with the force of creation.

**Become conscious of the foods you eat.** There are foods that calibrate low, and there are high-energy foods as well. Foods with toxic chemicals sprayed on them will make you weak even if you have no idea that the toxins are present. Artificial foods such as sweeteners are low-energy products. In general, foods high in alkalinity such as fruits, vegetables, nuts, soy, non-yeast breads, and virgin olive oil calibrate at the high end and will strengthen you on muscle testing, while highly acidic foods such as flour-based cereals, meats, dairy, and sugars calibrate at the lower energies, which will weaken you. This is not an absolute for everyone; however, you can detect how you feel after consuming certain foods, and if you feel weak, lethargic, and fatigued, you can be pretty sure you've allowed yourself to become a low-energy system, which will attract more of the same low energy into your life.

**Retreat from low-energy substances.** I discussed in Chapter 1 how I learned that total sobriety was absolutely essential for me to achieve the level of consciousness I craved and was destined to achieve. Alcohol, and virtually all artificial drugs, legal and otherwise, lower your body's energy level and weaken you. Furthermore, they put you in a position to continue to attract more disempowering energy into your life. Simply by consuming low-energy substances, you'll find people with similar low energy showing up regularly in your life. They'll want to buy those substances for you, party with you as you get high, and urge you to do it again after your body recovers from the devastation of these low-energy substances.

**Become conscious of the energy level of the music you listen to.** Harsh, pounding, musical vibrations with repetitive, loud sounds lower your energy level and weaken you and your ability to make conscious contact with intention. Similarly, the lyrics of hate, pain, anguish, fear, and violence are low energies sending weakening messages to your subconscious and infiltrating your life with similar attractor energies. If you want to attract violence, then listen to the lyrics of violence and make violent music a part of your life. If you want to attract peace and love, then listen to the higher musical vibrations and lyrics that reflect your desires.

**Become aware of the energy levels of your home environment.** Prayers, paintings, crystals, statues, spiritual passages, books, magazines, the colors on your walls, and even the arrangement of your furniture all create energy into which you're catapulted for at least half of your waking life. While this may seem silly or absurd, I urge you to transcend your conditioned thinking and have a mind that's open to everything. The ancient Chinese art of *feng shui* has been with us for thousands of years and is a gift from our ancestors. It describes ways to increase the energy field of our home and workplace. Become aware of how being in high-energy surroundings impacts us in ways that strengthen our lives and remove barriers to our connection to intention.

**Reduce your exposure to the very low energy of commercial and cable television.** Children in America see 12,000 simulated murders in their living room before their 14th birthday! Television news programming puts a heavy emphasis on bringing the bad and the ugly into your home, and in large part, leaving out the good. It's a constant stream of negativity that invades your living space and attracts more of the same into your life. Violence is the main ingredient of television entertainment, interspersed with commercial breaks sponsored by the huge drug cartels telling us that happiness is found in their pills! The viewing public is told that it needs all sorts of low-energy medicines to overcome every mental and physical malady known to humankind.

My conclusion is that the majority of television shows provide a steady stream of low energy most of the time. This is one of the reasons I've elected to devote a significant portion of my time and efforts in support of noncommercial public television and help replace messages of negativity, hopelessness, violence, profanity, and disrespect with the higher principles that match up with the principle of intention.

**Enhance your energy field with photographs.** You may find it difficult to believe that photography is a form of energy reproduction and that every photograph contains energy. See for yourself by strategically placing photographs taken in moments of happiness, love, and receptivity to spiritual help around your living quarters, in your workplace, in your automobile, and even on your clothing or in a pocket or wallet. Arrange photographs of nature, animals, and expressions of joy and love in your environment, and let their energy radiate into your heart and provide you with their higher frequency.

**Become conscious of the energy levels of your acquaintances, friends, and extended family.** You can raise your own energy levels by being in the energy field of others who resonate closely to spiritual consciousness. Choose to be in close proximity to people who are empowering, who appeal to your sense of connection to intention, who see the greatness in you, who feel connected to God, and who live a life that gives evidence that Spirit has found celebration through them. Recall that higher energy nullifies and converts lower energy, so be conscious of being in the presence of, and interacting with, higher-energy people who are connected to Spirit and living the life they were intended to. Stay in the energy field of higher-energy people and your anger, hate, fear, and depression will melt—magically converting to the higher expressions of intention.

**Monitor your activities and where they take place.** Avoid low-energy fields where there's excessive alcohol, drug consumption, or violent behavior, and gatherings where religious or ethnic exclusion and vitriolic prejudice or judgment are the focus. All of these kinds of venues discourage you from raising your energy and encourage you to match up with lower, debilitating energy. Immerse yourself in nature, appreciating its beauty, spending time camping, hiking, swimming, taking nature walks, and reveling in the natural world. Attend lectures on spirituality, take a yoga class, give or receive a massage, visit monasteries or meditation centers, and commit to helping others in need with visits to the elderly in geriatric centers or sick children in hospitals. Every activity has an energy field. Choose to be in places where the energy fields reflect the seven faces of intention.

**Extend acts of kindness, asking for nothing in return.** Anonymously extend financial aid to those less fortunate, and do it from the kindness of your heart, expecting not even a thank you.

Activate your *magnificent obsession* by learning to be kind while keeping your ego—which expects to be told how wonderful you are—out of the picture completely. This is an essential activity for connecting to intention because the universal all-creating Spirit returns acts of kindness with the response: *How may I be kind to you?*

Pick up some litter and place it in a proper receptacle and tell no one about your actions. In fact, spend several hours doing nothing but cleaning and clearing out messes that you didn't create. Any act of kindness extended toward yourself, others, or your environment matches you up with the kindness inherent in the universal power of intention. It's an energizer for you, and causes this kind of energy to flow back into your life.

This poignant story "The Valentine," by Ruth McDonald, illustrates the kind of giving I'm suggesting here. The little boy symbolizes the magnificent obsession I just referred to.

> *He was a shy little boy, not very popular with the other children in Grade One. As Valentine's Day approached, his mother was delighted when he asked her one evening to sit down and write the names of all the children in his class so that he could make a Valentine for each. Slowly he remembered each name aloud, and his mother recorded them on a piece of paper. He worried endlessly for fear he would forget someone.*
>
> *Armed with a book of Valentines to cut out, with scissors and crayons and paste, he plodded his conscientious way down the list. When each one was finished, his mother printed the name on a piece of paper and watched him laboriously copy it. As the pile of finished Valentines grew, so did his satisfaction.*
>
> *About this time, his mother began to worry whether the other children would make Valentines for him. He hurried home so fast each afternoon to get on with his task, that it seemed likely the other children playing along the street would forget his existence altogether. How absolutely horrible if he went off to the party armed with 37 tokens of*

*love—and no one had remembered him! She wondered if there were some way she could sneak a few Valentines among those he was making so that he would be sure of receiving at least a few. But he watched his hoard so jealously, and counted them over so lovingly, that there was no chance to slip in an extra. She assumed a mother's most normal role, that of patient waiting.*

*The day of the Valentine box finally arrived, and she watched him trudge off down the snowy street, a box of heart-shaped cookies in one hand, a shopping-bag clutched in the other with 37 neat tokens of his labor. She watched him with a burning heart. "Please, God," she prayed, "let him get at least a few!"*

*All afternoon her hands were busy here and there, but her heart was at the school. At half-past three she took her knitting and sat with studied coincidence in a chair that gave a full view of the street.*

*Finally, he appeared, alone. Her heart sank. Up the street he came, turning every once in a while to back up a few steps into the wind. She strained her eyes to see his face. At that distance it was just a rosy blur.*

*It was not until he turned in at the walk that she saw it— the one lone Valentine clutched in his little red mitt. Only one. After all his work. And from the teacher probably. The knitting blurred before her eyes. If only you could stand between your child and life! She laid down her work and walked to meet him at the door.*

*"What rosy cheeks!" she said. "Here, let me untie your scarf. Were the cookies good?"*

*He turned toward her a face shining with happiness and complete fulfillment. "Do you know what?" he said. "I didn't forget a one. Not a single one!"*

**Be specific when you affirm your intentions to raise your energy level and create your desires.** Place your affirmations in strategic places where you'll notice and read them throughout the day. For example: *I intend to attract the job I desire into my life. I intend to be able to afford the specific automobile I envision myself driving by the 30th of next month. I intend to donate two hours of my time this week to the underprivileged. I intend to heal myself of this persistent fatigue.*

Written affirmations have an energy of their own and will guide you in raising your energy level. I practice this myself. A woman named Lynn Hall who lives in Toronto sent me a beautiful plaque that I look at each day. In her letter she stated: "Here is a gift for you, written solely for you in an effort to convey heartfelt gratitude for the blessing of your presence in my life. That said, I am sure that the sentiment is a universal one speaking for every other soul on the planet who has experienced the same good fortune. May the light and love that you emit forever reflect back to you in joyful abundance, Dr. Dyer." The beautiful etched-in-soul plaque reads like this:

> *Spirit*
> *Has found*
> *Great voice*
> *In you.*
> *In vibrant truths,*
> *And joyful splendor.*
>
> *Spirit*
> *Has found*
> *Revelation*
> *Through you,*
> *In resonant*
> *And reflective ways.*
>
> *Spirit*
> *Has found*
> *Celebration*
> *Through you,*
> *In infinite expanses*
> *And endless reach.*

*To*
*All those*
*Awakened*
*To the*
*Grace of*
*Your gifts—*

*Spirit*
*Has found*
*Both*
*Wings*
*And*
*Light.*

I read these words daily to remind me of my connection to Spirit, and allow the words to flow from my heart to yours, fulfilling my intentions and hopefully helping you do the same.

**As frequently as possible, hold thoughts of forgiveness in your mind.** In muscle testing, when you hold a thought of revenge, you'll go weak, while a thought of forgiveness keeps you strong. Revenge, anger, and hatred are exceedingly low energies that keep you from matching up with the attributes of the universal force. A simple thought of forgiveness toward anyone who may have angered you in the past—without any action taken on your part—will raise you to the level of Spirit and aid you in your individual intentions.

You can either serve Spirit with your mind or use that same mind to divorce yourself from Spirit. Married to the seven faces of spiritual intention, you connect to that power. Divorced, your self-importance, your ego, takes over.

Here's the final obstacle to making your connection to intention.

\* \* \*

### *Your Self-Importance*

In *The Fire from Within,* Carlos Castaneda hears these words from his sorcerer teacher: "Self-importance is man's greatest enemy. What weakens him is feeling offended by the deeds and misdeeds of his fellow man. Self-importance requires that one spend most of one's life offended by something or someone." This is a major impediment to connecting to intention; you can all too easily create a *no match* here.

Basically, your feelings of self-importance are what make you feel special, so let's deal with this concept of being special. It's essential that you have a strong self-concept and that you feel unique. The problem is when you misidentify who you truly are by identifying yourself as your body, your achievements, and your possessions. Then you identify people who have accomplished less as inferior, and your self-important superiority causes you to be constantly offended in one way or another. This misidentification is the source of most of your problems, as well as most of the problems of humankind. Feeling *special* leads us to our self-importance. Castaneda writes later in his life, many years after his initial emergence into the world of sorcery, about the futility of self-importance. "The more I thought about it, and the more I talked to and observed myself and my fellow men, the more intense the conviction that something was rendering us incapable of any activity or any interaction or any thought that didn't have the self as its focal point."

With the self as a focal point, you sustain the illusion that you are your body, which is a completely separate entity from all others. This sense of separateness leads you to compete rather than cooperate with everyone else. Ultimately, it's a no match with Spirit, and becomes a huge obstacle to your connection to the power of intention. In order to relinquish your self-importance, you'll have to become aware of how entrenched it is in your life. Ego is simply an *idea of who you are* that you carry around with you. As such, it can't be surgically removed by having an egoectomy! This *idea* of who you think you are will persistently erode any possibility you have of connecting to intention.

## Seven Steps for Overcoming Ego's Hold on You

Here are seven suggestions to help you transcend ingrained ideas of self-importance. All of these are designed to help prevent you from falsely identifying with the self-important ego.

**1. Stop being offended.** The behavior of others isn't a reason to be immobilized. That which offends you only weakens you. If you're looking for occasions to be offended, you'll find them at every turn. This is your ego at work convincing you that the world shouldn't be the way it is. But you can become an appreciator of life and match up with the universal Spirit of Creation. You can't reach the power of intention by being offended. By all means, act to eradicate the horrors of the world, which emanate from massive ego identification, but stay in peace. As *A Course in Miracles* reminds us: *Peace is of God, you who are part of God are not at home except in his peace.* Being offended creates the same destructive energy that offended you in the first place and leads to attack, counterattack, and war.

**2. Let go of your need to win.** Ego loves to divide us up into winners and losers. The pursuit of winning is a surefire means to avoid conscious contact with intention. Why? Because ultimately, winning is impossible all of the time. Someone out there will be faster, luckier, younger, stronger, and smarter—and back you'll go to feeling worthless and insignificant.

You're not your winnings or your victories. You may enjoy competing, and have fun in a world where winning is everything, but you don't have to be there in your thoughts. There are no losers in a world where we all share the same energy source. All you can say on a given day is that you performed at a certain level in comparison to the levels of others on that day. But today is another day, with other competitors and new circumstances to consider. You're still the infinite presence in a body that's another day (or decade) older. Let go of *needing* to win by not agreeing that the opposite of winning is losing. That's ego's fear. If your body isn't performing in a *winning* fashion on this day, it simply doesn't matter when you aren't identifying exclusively with your ego. Be the observer, noticing and enjoying it all without needing to win a trophy. Be at peace, and match up with the energy of intention. And ironically, although you'll hardly notice it, more of those victories will show up in your life as you pursue them less.

**3. Let go of your need to be right.** Ego is the source of a lot of conflict and dissension because it pushes you in the direction of making other people wrong. When you're hostile, you've disconnected from the power of intention. The creative Spirit is kind, loving, and receptive; and free of anger, resentment, or bitterness. Letting go of your need to be right in your discussions and relationships is like saying to ego, *I'm not a slave to you. I want to embrace kindness, and I reject your need to be right. In fact, I'm going to offer this person a chance to feel better by saying that she's right, and thank her for pointing me in the direction of truth.*

When you let go of the need to be right, you're able to strengthen your connection to the power of intention. But keep in mind that ego is a determined combatant. I've seen people willing to die rather than let go of being right. I've seen people end otherwise beautiful relationships by sticking to their need to be right. I urge you to let go of this ego-driven need to be right by stopping yourself in the middle of an argument and asking yourself, *Do I want to be right or be happy?* When you choose the happy, loving, spiritual mode, your connection to intention is strengthened. These moments ultimately expand your new connection to the power of intention. The universal Source will begin to collaborate with you in creating the life you were intended to live.

**4. Let go of your need to be superior.** True nobility isn't about being better than someone else. It's about being better than you used to be. Stay focused on your growth, with a constant awareness that no one on this planet is any better than anyone else. We all emanate from the same creative life force. We all have a mission to realize our intended essence; all that we need to fulfill our destiny is available to us. None of this is possible when you see yourself as superior to others. It's an old saw, but nonetheless true: *We are all equal in the eyes of God.* Let go of your need to feel superior by seeing the unfolding of God in everyone. Don't assess others on the basis of their appearance, achievements, possessions, and other indices of ego. When you project feelings of superiority, that's what you get back, leading to resentments and ultimately hostile feelings. These feelings become the vehicle that takes you farther away from intention. *A Course in Miracles* addresses this need to be special and superior: *Specialness always makes comparisons. It is established by a lack seen in another, and maintained by searching for, and keeping clear in sight, all lacks it can perceive.*

**5. Let go of your need to have more.** The mantra of the ego is *more.* It's never satisfied. No matter how much you achieve or acquire, your ego will insist that it isn't enough. You'll find yourself in a perpetual state of striving, and eliminate the possibility of ever arriving. Yet in reality, you've already arrived, and how you choose to use this present moment of your life is your choice. Ironically, when you stop needing more, more of what you desire seems to arrive in your life. Since you're detached from the need for it, you find it easier to pass it along to others, because you realize how little you need in order to be satisfied and at peace.

The universal Source is content with itself, constantly expanding and creating new life, never trying to hold on to its creations for its own selfish means. It creates and lets go. As you let go of ego's need to have more, you unify with that Source. You create, attract to yourself, and let it go, never demanding that more come your way. As an appreciator of all that shows up, you learn the powerful lesson St. Francis of Assisi taught: " . . . it is in giving that we receive." By allowing abundance to flow to and through you, you match up with your Source and guarantee that this energy will continue to flow.

**6. Let go of identifying yourself on the basis of your achievements.** This may be a difficult concept if you think you *are* your achievements. *God writes all the music, God sings all the songs, God builds all the buildings, God is the source of all your achievements.* I can hear your ego loudly protesting. Nevertheless, stay tuned to this idea. All emanates from Source! You and that Source are one! You're not this body and its accomplishments. You are the observer. Notice it all; and be grateful for the abilities you've been given, the motivation to achieve, and the stuff you've accumulated. But give all the credit to the power of intention, which brought you into existence and which you're a materialized part of. The less you need to take credit for your achievements and the more connected you stay to the seven faces of intention, the more you're free to achieve, and the more will show up for you. It's when you attach yourself to those achievements and believe that you alone are doing all of those things that you leave the peace and the gratitude of your Source.

**7. Let go of your reputation.** Your reputation is not located in you. It resides in the minds of others. Therefore, you have no control over it at all. If you speak to 30 people, you will have 30 reputations. Connecting to intention means listening to your heart and conducting yourself based on what your inner voice tells you is your purpose here. If you're overly concerned with how you're going to be perceived by everyone, then you've disconnected yourself from intention and allowed the opinions of others to guide you. This is your ego at work. It's an illusion that stands between you and the power of intention. There's nothing you can't do, unless you disconnect from the power source and become convinced that your purpose is to prove to others how masterful and superior you are and spend your energy attempting to win a giant reputation among other egos. Do what you do because your inner voice—always connected to and grateful to your Source—so directs you. Stay on purpose, detach from outcome, and take responsibility for what *does* reside in you: your character. Leave your reputation for others to debate; it has nothing to do with you. Or as a book title says: *What You Think of Me Is None of My Business!*

This concludes the three major obstacles to your connecting to intention: *your thoughts, your energy,* and *your self-importance.*

Here are five suggestions for overcoming the obstacles and staying permanently connected to the power of intention.

### Five Suggestions for Implementing the Ideas in This Chapter

1. *Monitor your inner dialogue.* Notice how much of your inner speech focuses on what's missing, the negative circumstances, the past, and the opinions of others. The more cognizant you become of your inner speech, the sooner you'll be able to shift right in the midst of those habitual inner proceedings, from a thought of *I resent what's missing,* to *I intend to attract what I want and stop thinking about what I dislike.* That new inner dialogue becomes the link connecting you to intention.

2. *Lighten moments of doubt and depression.* Notice the moments that aren't a part of your higher nature. Reject thoughts that support an inability on your part to match up with intention. *Remain faithful to the light* is good advice. Recently, a friend and teacher learned of a struggle I was personally going through, and wrote to me: "Remember, Wayne, the sun is shining behind the clouds." Be faithful to the light that's always there.

3. *Be aware of low energy.* Recall that everything, which includes your thoughts, has an energy frequency that can be calibrated to determine whether it will strengthen or weaken you. When you find yourself either thinking in low-energy ways, or immersed in low, weakening energy, resolve to bring a higher vibration to the presence of that debilitating situation.

4. *Talk to your ego and let it know that it has no control over you today.* In my children's bedroom here on Maui, I've framed the following observation, which they see each

morning. While they joke and laugh about it, they get the essential message and share it out loud when anyone (including me) gets upset during the day.

> *Good morning,*
> *This is God.*
> *I will be handling*
> *All of your*
> *Problems today.*
> *I will not need*
> *Your help, so have*
> *A miraculous day.*

5. *View obstacles as opportunities to circulate the power of your unbending intent.* Unbending means just what it says. *I intend to stay connected to my Source and thereby gain the power of my Source.* This means being at peace, detaching yourself from the circumstances, and seeing yourself as the observer rather than the victim . . . then turning it all over to your Source and knowing that you'll receive the guidance and assistance you require.

* * *

You've just completed a thorough examination of the three major obstacles to connecting to the power of intention, along with suggestions for eliminating them. In the next chapter, I'll explain how you impact those around you when you raise your energy level to the highest spiritual frequencies and live your days connected to intention. When you're connected to the power of intention, everywhere you go, and everyone you meet, is affected by you and the energy you radiate. As you become the power of intention, you'll see your dreams being fulfilled almost magically, and you'll see yourself creating huge ripples in the energy fields of others by your presence and nothing more.

~ * ~ * ~

# CHAPTER FIVE

## YOUR IMPACT ON OTHERS WHEN CONNECTED TO INTENTION

*"It is one of the most beautiful compensations of this life that no man can sincerely try to help another without helping himself. . . . Serve and thou shall be served."*

— Ralph Waldo Emerson

As you find yourself being more in harmony with the faces of intention, you're going to discover that you'll be impacting others in new ways. The nature of this impact is profoundly important in your quest to utilize the power of intention. You'll begin seeing in others what you're feeling within yourself. This new way of seeing will enable people in your presence to feel comforted and peaceful, and to indirectly be loving accomplices to your connection to intention.

As you'll read on the next page, the poet Hafiz states that he wants nothing, even if the person is a "drooling mess" and a potential victim. All he perceives is their divine worth, which is what you'll see in others as you connect to the power of intention.

## The Jeweler

*If a naïve and desperate man*
*Brings a precious stone*
*To the only jeweler in town,*
*Wanting to sell it,*
*The jeweler's eyes*
*Will begin to play a game,*
*Like most eyes in the world when they look at you.*

*The jeweler's face will stay calm.*
*He will not want to reveal the stone's true value,*
*But to hold the man captive to fear and greed*
*While he calculates*
*The value of the transaction.*

*But one moment with me, my dear,*
*Will show you that there is nothing, nothing Hafiz*
*   wants from you.*
*When you sit before a Master like me,*
*Even if you are a drooling mess,*
*My eyes sing with Excitement*
*They see your Divine Worth.*

— Hafiz

### *You Receive What You Desire for Others*

As you review the attributes of universal intention and simultaneously vow to be those attributes, you begin to see the significance of what you desire for all others. If you desire peace for others, you'll receive it. If you want others to feel loved, you'll be the recipient of love. If you see only beauty and worthiness in others, you'll have the same returned to you. You'll only give away what you have in your heart, and attract what you're giving away. This is a matter of great concern to you. Your impact on others—whether it be strangers, family members, co-workers, or neighbors—is evidence of the strength of your connection to the power of intention. Think of your relationships in terms of holy or unholy.

Holy relationships facilitate the power of intention at a high energy level for everyone involved. Unholy relationships keep the energy at the lower, slower levels for all concerned. You'll know your own potential for greatness when you start seeing the perfection in all relationships. When you recognize others' holiness, you'll treat them as divine expressions of the power of intention, wanting nothing from them. The irony is that they become co-creators manifesting all your desires. Want nothing from them, demand nothing from them, have no expectations for them, and they'll return this kindness. Demand from them, insist that they please you, judge them as inferior, and see them as servants, and you'll receive the same. It behooves you to be acutely aware of what you truly want for others, and to know whether you're in a holy or an unholy relationship with every person you're involved with.

**The holy relationship.** One truth that I've recognized during the years of my own growth is that it's impossible to know my perfection if I'm unable to see and honor that same perfection in others. The ability to see yourself as a temporary expression of intention and to see yourself in all of humanity is a characteristic of the holy relationship. It's the ability to celebrate and honor in all others, the place where we're all one.

In an unholy relationship, you see yourself as separate from others. It's the feeling that others are primarily useful to satisfy ego's urges, and that people are there to help you get what's missing in your life. In any kind of a relationship, this attitude of separation and potential manipulation creates a barrier between you and the power of intention. The signs of unholy relationships are quite clear: People become defensive, fearful, hostile, standoffish, and don't wish to be in your company.

As you change your thought patterns to raise your energy vibrations, and reduce the demands of your ego, you'll begin developing a reverent or holy relationship with others. Then everyone is perceived as complete. When you can celebrate differences in others as interesting or enjoyable, you're loosening your identity with ego. The holy relationship is a way of matching up with the universal Source of Creation and being peacefully joyful. Any relationship—or even an encounter—from the holy perspective, is a coming together with a beloved self-aspect and discovering a stimulating connection with the power of intention.

Recently, in a supermarket, I asked a frenzied clerk behind the seafood counter if he knew where I could find the smoked salmon. I saw myself as connected to him in spite of the frustration showing through his behavior. A man standing next to me heard my request and saw the clerk's harried demeanor. The stranger smiled at me and went to another area of the store, returning with a package of nova lox, which he handed me. He delivered to me what I was seeking! A coincidence? I think not. When I feel myself connected to others and radiate the energy of holy relationship, people react with kindness and go out of their way to assist me with my intentions.

In another example of this, I was transferred from one airline to another because of a mechanical problem that resulted in a cancellation. At my original airline, which is in my hometown, the employees know me and go out of their way to assist me. I've practiced holy relationships with everyone at the counter, at baggage check-in, on the plane, and so on. On this particular day, I was sent to the other end of the airport with seven boxes of books and tapes that had to be checked as baggage. As my assistant, Maya, and I trudged up to the counter of the other airline, pushing a cart with luggage and seven heavy boxes, the passenger agent announced that her airline did not permit more than two pieces of luggage to be checked in, and that I would have to leave three of the boxes behind. I could check in two for me and two for Maya. *Those are the rules.*

Here's where a holy relationship with a stranger has more potential for assisting you with your intentions than an unholy relationship. Rather than countering the agent with an intention that she was a clerk whose job it was to serve my needs, I chose to join her where we both are one. I let her know that I wasn't even mildly upset over this rule, and I imagined how she must feel, having to process a large number of people who weren't scheduled on this flight. I felt connected, and expressed my own feelings of frustration at having this challenge of what to do with these three extra boxes, which my originally scheduled airline had agreed to transport. I invited her to attend a lecture I was giving in town the next month, as my guest. Our entire conversation and the entire interaction was guided by my private intent that this remain a holy relationship.

The energy of this interaction shifted from weak to strong. We bonded, recognized our *self* in the other, and she checked in all of my boxes with a cheerful smile. I've never forgotten what she said to me as she handed me our boarding passes. "When you wheeled up that cart with all those boxes, I was determined that you weren't going to get them on that plane, and after a few moments of being with you, I would've carried them out and put them on the plane myself if I had to. It's a pleasure to know you. Thank you for your business, and I hope you'll consider our airline in the future."

These are two simple examples of what happens when you consciously shift from ego-dominated unholy relationships, to experiencing your connectedness through the power of intention. I urge you to establish a holy relationship with your Source, the world community, your neighbors, acquaintances, family, the animal kingdom, our planet, and yourself. Just as in my examples of the man in the store delivering me the smoked salmon I was looking for, and the airline agent assisting me in realizing my intent, you'll enjoy the power of intention through holy relationships. *It's all about relationship.*

### Alone We Can Do Nothing

When you meet anyone, treat the event as a holy encounter. It's through others that we either find or love our *self*. For you see, nothing is accomplished without others. *A Course in Miracles* says this so well:

> *Alone we can do nothing,*
> *But together our minds fuse into something*
> *Whose power is far beyond*
> *The power of its separate parts.*
> *The kingdom cannot be found alone,*
> *And you who are the kingdom*
> *Cannot find yourself alone.*

When you eliminate the concept of separation from your thoughts and your behavior, you begin to feel your connection to everything and everyone. You'll begin having a sense of belonging, which enables you to scoff at any thought of being separate. This feeling of connectedness originates with and helps you process all of your interactions from the point of view of equality. By recognizing others as co-creators, you match up with your Source and move into a state of grace. If you're seeing yourself as either inferior or superior, you've disconnected from the power of intention. Your desires will be frustrated unless you connect with and support other people.

How you interact with your universal support team is significant. How you view others is a projection of how you view yourself. Consistently seeing others as worthless means that you're erecting a roadblock for your potential allies. See others as weak, and you're simultaneously attracting weak energies. Persistently viewing others as dishonest, lazy, sinful, and so on may mean that you need to feel superior. Constantly seeing others critically can be a way of compensating for something you fear. But you don't even need to understand this psychological mechanism. All you have to do is recognize how you view others. If there's a pattern of seeing others as failures, you only need to notice the pattern as evidence of what you're attracting into your life.

It's so important to see interactions as holy encounters, because this sets in motion an attractor energy pattern. In a holy relationship, you attract the collaboration of higher energies. In an unholy relationship, the attractor pattern exists, too, attracting low energies and more unholy relationships. By bringing higher spiritual energy to everyone you encounter, you dissolve lower energies. When the energies of kindness, love, receptivity, and abundance are present in your relationships, you have brought the elixir of spiritual Creation or the love of the Creator right into the mix. Now those forces begin to work on everyone in your environment. The right people magically appear. The right materials show up. The phone rings and someone gives you the information you've been wanting for months. Strangers offer suggestions that make sense to you. As I mentioned earlier, these types of coincidences are like mathematical angles that *coincide,* or fit together perfectly. Treat others as co-creators and have divine expectations for them. Don't view anyone as ordinary, unless of course you wish to have more of the ordinary manifest into your world.

### From Ordinary to Extraordinary

Leo Tolstoy's famous story *The Death of Ivan Ilyich,* is one of my favorite pieces of literature. Tolstoy describes Ivan Ilyich as a man who's motivated almost exclusively by the expectations of others, and isn't able to live out his own dreams. The opening line of Chapter 2 in this compelling story goes like this: "The story of Ivan Ilyich's life was of the simplest, most ordinary and therefore most terrible." Tolstoy actually defines living an *ordinary* life as terrible. I couldn't agree more!

If your expectations for yourself center on being normal, just getting along, fitting in, and being an ordinary person, you'll resonate to ordinary frequencies, and you'll attract more of normal and ordinary into your life. Furthermore, your impact on others as potential allies in co-creating your intentions will also revolve around ordinary. The *power* of intention occurs when you're synchronized with the all-creating universal force, which is anything but ordinary. This is the power that's responsible for all of creation.

It's ever-expansive, and thinks and creates in terms of endless abundance. When you shift to this higher energy and resonate more in harmony with intention, you become a magnet for attracting more of this energy into your world. You also have this kind of impact on everyone and everything you're in contact with.

One of the most effective means for transcending *ordinary* and moving into the realm of *extraordinary* is saying *yes* more frequently and eliminating *no* almost completely. I call it *saying yes to life*. Say yes to yourself, to your family, your children, your co-workers, and your business. Ordinary says, *No, I don't think I can do it. No, that won't work out. No, I've tried that and it's never worked before. No, that intention is impossible for me.* With the idea of *no*, you attract *more of no*, and your impact on others whom you could help and on whom you could rely for help is also *no*. Once again, I urge you to adopt the attitude of the poet Hafiz.

> *I rarely let the word No escape*
> *From my mouth*
> *Because it is so plain to my soul*
> *That God has shouted, Yes! Yes! Yes!*
> *To every luminous movement in Existence*

Shout *yes* to everyone as often as you can. When someone seeks your permission to try something, before saying *no*, ask yourself if you want that person to stay at ordinary levels of living. When my son Sands wished to try out a new surfing area last week, my first inclination was to say, *Too dangerous, you've never been there before, you could get hurt,* and so on. But I reconsidered, and accompanied him on a new adventure. My *yes* impacted his life and mine in a positive manner.

Making *yes* your inner mantra allows you to extend *yes* outside of yourself and attract more of *yes* into your own personal intending. *Yes* is the breath of Creation. Think of a drop of rain merging with a river at the moment it becomes the river. Think of the river merging with the ocean at the moment it becomes the ocean. You can almost hear the sound of *yes* being whispered in those moments. As you merge with the universal force of Creation extending *yes* wherever feasible, you become that force of Creation itself. This will be your impact on others. No more ordinary *nos* in your life. On to the extraordinary.

Ordinary implies being stuck in a rut much like Ivan Ilyich. While in the rut, you'll attract other rut-dwellers, and your mutual impact will be to stay in your ordinary ruts—complaining, finding fault, wishing, and hoping for better days. The universal force of intention never complains; it creates and offers its options for greatness. It judges no one, and isn't stuck wishing and hoping that things will improve. It's too busy creating beauty to be so foolishly engaged. As you move your own energy level up out of a rut mentality, you'll have an uplifting effect on all of the rut-dwellers in your life. Moreover, you'll help many of them have a similar impact, and create new allies in fulfilling your own intentions. Become aware of your identification with normal or ordinary, and begin to vibrate to higher and higher energetic frequencies, which constitute a shift upward into the extraordinary dimensions of pure intent.

### How Your Energies Impact Others

When you feel connected and in harmony with intention, you sense a major difference in how other people react to you. Be cognizant of these reactions, because they'll bear directly on your abilities to fulfill your individual intentions. The more closely you automatically resonate to the frequencies of the universal all-creating Source, the more that others will be impacted and their lower energies nullified. They'll gravitate toward you, bringing peace, joy, love, beauty, and abundance into your life. What follows is my opinion on how you'll impact others when you're resonating with intention, and how different your impact is when you're dominated by your ego's separatist attitude.

Here are some of the most significant ways in which you'll impact others:

**Your presence instills calmness.** When you coincide with intention, your impact on others has a calming influence. People tend to feel more at peace, less threatened, and more at ease. The power of intention is the power of love and receptivity. It asks nothing of anyone, it judges no one, and it encourages others to be free to be themselves. As people feel calmer in your presence, they're inclined to feel safe, by virtue of the energy frequencies that you radiate. Their feelings are encouraged by your energy of love and receptivity, causing them to want to reach out and be with you. As Walt Whitman put it: "We convince by our presence."

If, instead, you bring the lower calibrations of judgment, hostility, anger, hatred, or depression to your interactions, you attract that level of energy if it's lurking in the people you're interacting with. This acts like a counterforce to those same energies if they're present in others. The impact intensifies the lower frequencies at that level and creates a field in which demands are placed as a result of feelings of inferiority or opposition.

Intention doesn't interact *against* anything. It's like gravity, which doesn't move against anything, nor does gravity itself move. Think of impacting others like gravity, with no need to move against or attack anyone. People who feel *empowered* by your presence become kindred spirits. That can only happen if they feel safe rather than attacked, secure rather than judged, calm rather than harassed.

**Your presence leaves others feeling energized.** I recall leaving a two-hour session with a spiritual master and feeling as if I could conquer the world emotionally and spiritually. The saint was Mother Meera, who'd held my head in her hands and gazed into my eyes with her egoless divinity. I felt so energized that I didn't sleep that entire night. I wanted more of what this joyous being had shown me through her presence alone.

When you bring the frequencies of intention into the presence of others, they'll feel energized just by being in your immediate circle. You don't have to say a word. You don't have to act in any prescribed fashion. Your energy of intention alone will make others in your field feel as if they've mysteriously been empowered. As you begin consciously expressing the seven faces of intention, you'll discover that others begin to comment on the impact you're making on them. They'll want to assist you in fulfilling your own dreams. They'll be energized and volunteer to help you. They'll even begin to offer to finance your dreams with their energized, new ideas. As I've grown in my consciousness of the power of intention, I've been told I've had an impact without my doing anything other than spending an evening having a meal in a restaurant. People tell me they've been energized with greater confidence and determination and inspiration after our time together. I've done nothing. They've felt impacted by the field of high energy we shared.

**Your presence allows others to feel better about themselves.** Have you ever noticed when you're in the presence of certain people that you feel better about yourself? Their compassionate energy has the noticeably pleasant impact of simply making you feel really good about yourself. You'll impact others with this energy of compassion as you develop your connection to intention. People will sense that you care about them, understand them, and are interested in them as unique individuals. With this kind of connection to intention, you're less likely to focus conversation on yourself and use others to massage your ego.

On the contrary, being in the company of someone who's disdainful or indifferent impacts you quite differently. If this is the low energy you transmit to others, they're quite likely to depart the encounter feeling less than wonderful about themselves, unless they're so strongly connected to intention that they can override the impact of this low energy. These extremely low-energy thoughts and behaviors are evident if you use every topic that's brought up as an excuse to talk about yourself. Any behavior similar to this displays ego-dominated energy that impacts others unpleasantly. Moreover, it leaves others feeling as if they're insignificant or unimportant, and obviously feeling worse about themselves when it's a repeated pattern in a significant relationship.

**Your presence allows others to feel unified.** The effect of being in the presence of people expressing high frequencies is to feel unified and connected to all of nature, all of humankind, and to intention. As you raise your frequencies, your impact on others invites them to be on the same team. You are unified and want to assist each other in the fulfillment of a common objective.

The opposite of this feeling of unity is feeling polarized and cut off. Low energy is demanding and always moves against others. Therefore, it will inevitably produce a win/lose condition. The energies of antagonism, judgment, hatred, and the like set up a counterforce in which somebody has to lose. When you have an enemy, you need to establish a defense system, and having to defend yourself becomes the nature of your relationship. One person's need to move against and polarize sets in motion the conditions for war. War is always expensive. This is all avoidable by staying connected to intention and bringing that higher energy to your relationships, allowing those you encounter to feel the oneness with you, with everyone else, with nature, and with God.

**Your presence instills a sense of purpose.** When you're in the higher spiritual energies, you bring something to others that's almost inexplicable. Your presence and behavior from a space of love, acceptance, nonjudgment, and kindness becomes a catalyst for others feeling *on purpose* in their lives.

By staying at the higher energies of optimism, forgiveness, understanding, reverence for Spirit, creativity, serenity, and bliss, you radiate this energy and convert lower energies to your higher vibrations. These people whom you so nondeliberately impact begin to feel your quiet reverence and serenity. Your own purpose, which revolves around serving others and therefore serving God, becomes fulfilled, and as a bonus, you create allies.

I've had thousands of people tell me that just by attending a lecture or a talk at a church where the primary message is hope, love, and kindness is sufficient motivation for them to make a commitment to pursuing their purpose. When I'm the speaker at such events, I always enter from the rear of the room to take some time to drink in the energy of hope, optimism, and love. I can literally feel their collective energy. It's like a peaceful wave of pleasure, as if there were a warm shower running inside of me. This is energy. It's the stuff of intention, and it's powerfully motivating in helping everyone feel purposeful and hopeful.

**Your presence allows others to trust in authentic personal connections.** By bringing the traits of intention to others, you allow trust to be present. You'll notice both an inclination and a willingness on the part of others to open up and confide in you. This is related to the quality of trust. In the atmosphere of higher energy, people trust and want to share their personal stories with you. By being so connected to intention, you are more God-like, and who would you trust more than God to share your secrets with?

Recently during an early-morning whale-watching expedition, a woman who had no idea of my identity disclosed to me her history of failed relationships and how unfulfilled she felt. In conversation with me, in an energy field that allows and encourages trust, she let herself take the risk of opening up to a stranger. (This has occurred frequently since I've been living the principles of the seven faces of intention.) As St. Francis of Assisi put it, "It is no use walking anywhere to preach unless our walking is our preaching." You'll ultimately discover that by carrying this energy of intention with you, even strangers will do what they can to serve you and help you accomplish your own intentions.

The opposite results are apparent when you emit the lower-energy frequencies. If your distrustful energy exhibits itself in anxious, judgmental, dictatorial, superior, or demanding ways, others are disinclined to help you get what you want. The truth is that your low-energy emissions often leave others with the desire to interfere with your own intentions. Why? Because your low energies help to create a counterforce, conflict erupts, winners and losers are necessary, and enemies are created—all because of your unwillingness to stay connected to the faces of intention.

**Your presence inspires others to greatness.** When you're connected to Spirit and quietly reflect this consciousness, you become a source of inspiration to others. In a sense, this is one of the most powerful effects that connecting to intention transmits to others. The word *inspiration* means "in-spirit." The fact that you're primarily in-spirit means that you inspire rather than inform with your presence. You won't inspire others by loudly insisting or demanding that others listen to your point of view.

In all the years that I've been teaching, writing, lecturing, and producing tapes and videos, I've noticed a twofold process at work. I feel on purpose, inspired, and connected to universal Spirit in all of my work, and many thousands or even millions of people become inspired as a result of my own inspiration. The second factor is the vast number of people who have helped me with my work. They've sent me materials, written me inspiring stories that I've used, and literally been my co-creators. When you inspire others by your presence, you're utilizing the originating power of intention for the benefit of all those you touch, including yourself. I wholeheartedly endorse this way of being, and I know without a doubt that you too can be a presence that's inspiring to others.

**Your presence aligns others with beauty.** When you're connected to intention, you see beauty everywhere and in everything because you're radiating the quality of beauty. Your perceptual world changes dramatically. At the higher energy of intent, you see beauty in everyone, young or old, rich or poor, dark or light, with no distinctions. Everything is perceived from a perspective of appreciation rather than judgment. As you bring this feeling of beauty appreciation to the presence of others, people are inclined to see themselves as you see them. They feel attractive and better about themselves as they circulate that high energy of beauty. When people feel beautiful, they act in beautiful ways. Your awareness of beauty impacts others to see the world around them in the same way. The benefit, once again, is twofold. First, you'll be helping others become appreciators of life and be happier by virtue of their immersion into a world of beauty. Second, your own intentions receive the assistance of those people who have acquired newly enhanced self-esteem. Beauty proliferates in others just by virtue of your presence when you're connected to intention.

**Your presence instills health rather than sickness.** Your connection to your Source keeps you focused on what you intend to manifest into your life, with no energy given to what you don't want. This internal focus doesn't permit you to complain about what ails you or to think about disease, pain, or any physical difficulties. Your energy is always on creating love, and expanding the perfection from which you originated. This includes your body and all of your beliefs about your physical self. You know in your heart that your body is a system of miracles. You have great reverence for its amazing capacity to heal itself and to function on its own without your interference. You know that your physical self is inspired by a divine force that beats its heart, digests its food, and grows its fingernails, and that this same force is receptive to endlessly abundant health.

When you bring to the presence of others a healthy appreciation for the miracle that your body represents, you defuse their efforts to dwell on disease, ill health, and deterioration. In fact, the higher your energy field resonates, the more you're able to impact others with your own healing energy. (See Chapter 13 for a more thorough treatment of healing and intention.) Become aware of your own amazing capacity to affect the healing and health of those around you simply by the silent presence of your high-energy connection to intention. This is a literal energy that emanates from you.

\* \* \*

In the hopes that you will recognize the importance of raising your energy level, I'm going to conclude this chapter with a look at how our entire civilization is impacted when energy levels are synchronized with the Source of our Creation. This will require an open mind and a bit of stretching on your part; however, it's something that I know is true, and I'd be remiss if I left it out. It may appear peculiar or even outlandish to some who fail to see the ways in which all of us on this planet are connected and therefore impact each other from distances not discernible by our senses.

### Your Impact on the Consciousness of All of Humanity

Many years ago I was with one of my daughters as she completed a lengthy program in the wilderness to help her deal more effectively with some of her teenage dilemmas. The last thing the counselor at the wilderness camp said to her was, "Remember at all times that what you think and what you do affects other people." This is true even beyond the impact we have on our friends, family, neighbors, and co-workers. I believe that we impact *all* of humanity. Thus, as you read this section, keep in mind that *what you think and do affects all other people.*

In *Power vs. Force*, Dr. David Hawkins writes: "In this interconnected universe, every improvement we make in our private world improves the world at large for everyone. We all float on the collective level of consciousness of mankind, so that any increment we add comes back to us. We all add to our common buoyancy by our efforts to benefit life. It is a scientific fact that what is good for you is good for me." Dr. Hawkins has backed up his remarks and conclusions with 29 years of hard research, which I invite you to examine if you're so inclined. I'll briefly summarize some of these conclusions and how they relate to the impact you have on others when you're connected to intention.

In essence, every single person as well as large groups of people can be calibrated for their energy levels. Generally speaking, low-energy people cannot distinguish truth from falsehood. They can be told how to think, whom to hate, whom to kill; and they can be herded into a group-think mentality based on such trivial details as what side of the river they were born on, what their parents and their grandparents believed, the shape of their eyes, and hundreds of other factors having to do with appearance and total identification with their material world. Hawkins tells us that approximately 87 percent of humanity calibrates at a collective energy level that weakens them. The higher up the ladder of frequency vibration, the fewer people there are in those high levels. The highest levels are represented by the truly great persons who originated spiritual patterns that multitudes have followed throughout the ages. They're associated with divinity, and they set in motion attractor energy fields that influence all of humankind.

Just below the energy level of pure enlightenment are the energy levels associated with the experience designated as transcendence, self-realization, or God consciousness. Here's where those who are called saintly reside. Just below this level is the place of pure joy, and the hallmark of this state is compassion. Those who attain this level have more of a desire to use their consciousness for the benefit of life itself rather than for particular individuals.

Below these supremely high levels, which few ever attain in a permanent way, are the levels of unconditional love, kindness, acceptance of everyone, beauty appreciation, and on a more limited but nonetheless profound level, all of the seven faces of intention described in the opening chapters of this book. Below the levels of energy that strengthen us are the low energy levels of anger, fear, grief, apathy, guilt, hatred, judgment, and shame—all of which weaken and impact us in such a way as to inhibit our connection to the universal energy level of intention.

What I'd like you to do here is take a leap of faith with me, while I present a few of the conclusions that Dr. Hawkins came to in his second book, called *The Eye of the I*. Through his precise kinesiological testing for truth versus falsehood, he's calibrated the approximate number of people whose energy is at or below the level that weakens. I'd like you to consider his findings and conclusions relative to your impact on civilization. Dr. Hawkins suggests that it's crucial for each of us to be aware of the significance of raising our frequency of vibration to the level where we begin to match up with the energy of the universal Source, or in other words, make our connection to the power of intention.

One of the most fascinating aspects of this line of research is the idea of counterbalancing. High-energy people counterbalance the negative effect of low-energy people. But it doesn't happen on a one-to-one basis because of that 87 percent of humanity that's in the lower weakening frequencies. One person connected to intention, as I've described it here in this book, can have an enormous impact on many people in the lower energy patterns. The higher up the scale you move toward actually being the light of enlightenment and knowing God consciousness, the more negatively vibrating energies you can counterbalance. Here are some fascinating figures from Dr. Hawkins's research for you to contemplate as you review the impact you can have on humanity simply by being on the higher rungs of the ladder to intention:

- *One individual who lives and vibrates to the energy of optimism and a willingness to be nonjudgmental of others will counterbalance the negativity of 90,000 individuals who calibrate at the lower weakening levels.*

- *One individual who lives and vibrates to the energy of pure love and reverence for all of life will counterbalance the negativity of 750,000 individuals who calibrate at the lower weakening levels.*

- *One individual who lives and vibrates to the energy of illumination, bliss, and infinite peace will counterbalance the negativity of 10 million people who calibrate at the lower weakening levels (approximately 22 such sages are alive today).*

- *One individual who lives and vibrates to the energy of grace, pure spirit beyond the body, in a world of nonduality or complete oneness, will counterbalance the negativity of 70 million people who calibrate at the lower weakening levels (approximately 10 such sages are alive today).*

Here are two compelling statistics offered by Dr. Hawkins in his 29-year study on the hidden determinants of human behavior:

1. One single avatar living at the highest level of consciousness in this period of history to whom the title *Lord* is appropriate, such as Lord Krishna, Lord Buddha, and Lord Jesus Christ, would counterbalance the collective negativity of *all of mankind* in today's world.

2. The negativity of the entire human population would self-destruct were it not for the counteracting effects of these higher energy fields.

The implications of these figures are immense for discovering ways of improving human consciousness and raising ourselves to the place where we match up with the same energy of intention from which we were intended. By raising your own frequency of vibration only slightly to a place where you regularly practice kindness, love, and receptivity, and where you see beauty and the endless potential of good in others as well as yourself, you counterbalance 90,000 people somewhere on this planet who are living in the low-energy levels of shame, anger, hatred, guilt, despair, depression, and so on.

I can't help thinking of John F. Kennedy's handling of the Cuban missile crisis in the 1960s. He was surrounded by advisors urging the use of nuclear bombs if necessary. Yet his own energy and that of a few trusted colleagues who were steeped in the potential for a peaceful resolution served to counterbalance the vast majority of those who pushed for attack and bellicosity. One person with very high spiritual energy can put the possibility of war into a last-resort category. This is true in your own life. Bring the energy of intention to the presence of conflict even in family matters, and you can nullify and convert the lower antagonistic energy with your presence.

I've done this in a hostile setting where young people influenced by alcohol and drugs were squaring off to fight while a crowd urged them on. On one occasion, I simply walked between two potential combatants humming the song, "Surely the Presence of God Is in This Place," and that energy alone softened the atmosphere, raising the level of energy to peace.

In another instance, I approached a woman who was immersed in having an angry fit with her toddler in a grocery store and screaming hateful epithets at the two-year-old. I quietly moved into the energy field, said nothing, but radiated my desire for a higher energy of love, and it nullified the low energy of hatred. Consider the importance of becoming aware of the impact you have on others, and remind yourself that by raising your own energy level to a place where you're in harmony with intention, you become an instrument, or a channel, of peace. This works everywhere, so be a part of the counterbalance to the human negativity you encounter in your life.

## Five Suggestions for Implementing the Ideas in This Chapter

1. *Become aware of the importance of making all of your relationships divine.* The holy relationship isn't based on any religion. The holy relationship emphasizes the unfolding of Spirit in everyone. Your children are spiritual beings who come *through* you, not *for* you. Your love relationship can focus on wanting for your partner what you want for yourself. If you want freedom, want it for everyone you love. If you want abundance, want it first for others. If you want happiness, want it more for others, and let them know it. The more you have holiness as the centerpiece of your relationships, the more you'll merge with intention.

2. *When a question of morality arises concerning how you should act toward others, simply ask yourself, <u>What would the Messiah do?</u>* This inner inquiry returns you to the tranquility of intention. The Messiah represents the seven faces of

intention all manifested in a spiritual being having a human experience. In this way, you're honoring the Christ in you that is also in everyone else. Practice wanting for others what you want for yourself by being Christ-like rather than a Christian, Mohammed-like rather than a Muslim, and Buddha-like rather than a Buddhist.

3. *Keep track of the judgments you direct toward yourself and others.* Make a conscious effort to shift to compassionate thoughts and feelings. Offer a silent blessing to beggars rather than judging them as lazy or a drain on the economy. Your thoughts of compassion raise your level of energy and facilitate your staying connected to intention. Be compassionate toward everyone you meet, all of humanity, the entire kingdom of animal life, and our planet and cosmos as well. In return, the universal Source of all life will bestow compassion upon you, helping you manifest your own individual intention. It's the law of attraction. Send out compassion, attract it back; send out hostility and judgment, attract it back. Watch your thoughts, and when they're anything other than compassionate, change them!

4. *Whatever others want, want it for them so strongly that you disperse this energy outward and act from this level of spiritual consciousness.* Attempt to feel what would make others most happy and fulfilled. Then send the high energy of intention to that feeling and concentrate on beaming this energy outward, particularly while in their presence. This will help to create a doubly high field for such intentions to manifest.

5. *Be continually alert to the fact that simply by thinking and feeling in harmony with the seven faces of intention, you'll be counterbalancing the collective negativity of a minimum of 90,000 people, and perhaps millions.* Nothing to do. No one to convert. No goals to accomplish. Nothing more

than raising your own energy level to the creative, kind, loving, beautiful, ever-expanding, endlessly abundant, and receptive-to-all-without-judgment frequencies. These inner attitudes will raise you to the level where your presence will impact humanity in a positive way. In *Autobiography of a Yogi,* Swami Sri Yukteswar tells Paramahansa Yogananda: "The deeper the self-realization of a man, the more he influences the whole universe by his subtle spiritual vibrations, and the less he himself is affected by the phenomenal flux."

You have a responsibility to the entire human family to stay connected to intention. Otherwise you could be depressing someone in Bulgaria right at this moment!

* * *

With these words, Mahatma Gandhi sums up this chapter on how we can impact the world by staying connected to that which intended us here in the first place: "We must be the change we wish to see in the world." By being it, we connect to the eternal part of us that originates in infinity. This whole idea of infinity and coming to grips with how it affects our ability to know and employ the power of intention is vastly mysterious. It's the subject matter for the final chapter in Part I of this book. We'll explore infinity from a body and a mind that begins and ends in time, yet somehow knows that the *I* that is in here has always been and always will be.

✳ ✳

# CHAPTER SIX

## INTENTION AND INFINITY

*"Eternity is not the hereafter . . . this is it.*
*If you don't get it here, you won't get it anywhere."*
— Joseph Campbell

Please indulge me in a little exercise right here, right now. Put this book down, and say out loud: *I'm not from here.* Let the meaning of the words be clear to you. The meaning is that you are *in* this world, but not *of* this world. You've been taught that who you are is a body with your name, made up of molecules, bones, tissue, oxygen, hydrogen, and nitrogen. You know yourself as the person with your particular name, and you identify yourself as the person with the possessions and achievements that you've accumulated. This *self* also possesses some terrifying information. It knows that *if it's lucky,* it's destined to grow old, get sick, and lose everything that it's grown to love. Then it will die. This is a shortened version of what the world has offered you, which

115

probably leaves you mystified and flabbergasted at the absurdity of this thing we call life. Into this bleak picture, which inspires fear and even terror, I'd like to introduce a concept that will eliminate the terror. I want you to know that you needn't subscribe to the idea that you are only this collection of bones and tissues, destined to be annihilated in an aging process.

You've emerged from a universal field of Creation that I've been calling *intention*. In a sense, this universal mind is totally impersonal. It is pure love, fondness, beauty, and creativity, always expanding and endlessly abundant. You emanated from this universal mind. And as I keep telling you, *universal means everywhere and at all times.* In other words, *infinite.* As long as your wishes are aligned with the forward movement of this everlasting principle, there's nothing in nature to restrict you from attaining the fulfillment of those wishes. It's only when you choose to allow ego to oppose the expanding, receptive forward movement of the infinite mind of intention that the realization of your wishes doesn't feel fulfilling. Life itself is eternal, and you spring from this infinite *no thing* called life. Your ability to connect to the eternal and live in the here-and-now will determine your staying connected to intention.

### Life Is Eternal

We all live on a stage where many infinities gather. Just take a look outside tonight and contemplate the infinity of space. There are stars so distant from you that they're measured in the distance that light travels in an Earthly year. Beyond those stars that you can see are endless galaxies that stretch out into something we call eternity. Indeed, the space that you occupy is infinite. Its vastness is too huge for us to see. We're in an infinite, never-ending, never-beginning universe.

Now pay close attention to this next sentence. *If life is infinite, then this is not life.* Read that again and consider that life truly is infinite. We can see this in everything that we scrupulously observe. Therefore, we must conclude that life, in terms of our body and all of its achievements and possessions, which without exception begins and ends in dust, isn't life itself. Grasping life's true essence could radically change *your* life for the better. This is an enormous inner shift that eliminates fear of death (how can you fear something that can't exist?) and connects you permanently to the infinite Source of Creation that *intends* everything from the world of infinite Spirit, into a finite world. Learn to be comfortable with the concept of infinity, and see yourself as an infinite being.

While we're in this finite world of beginnings and endings, the power of intention maintains its infinite nature because it's eternal. Anything you experience as other than eternal is simply not life. It's an illusion created by your ego, which strives to maintain a separate address and identity from its infinite Source. This shift toward seeing yourself as an infinite spiritual being having a human experience, rather than the reverse—that is, a human being having an occasional spiritual experience—is loaded with fear for most people. I urge you to look at those fears and face them directly right now; the result will be a permanent connection to the abundance and receptivity of the universal Source that intends all of Creation into temporary form.

### Your Fear of the Infinite

We are all in bodies that are going to die, and we know this, yet we can't imagine it for *ourselves,* so we behave as if it weren't so. It's almost as if we're saying to ourselves, *Everybody dies but me.* This is attributable to what Freud observed. Our death is unimaginable, so we simply deny it and live our lives as if we weren't going to die . . . because of the terror that our own death instills. As I sat down to write this chapter, I said to a friend that my goal was to leave the reader with a complete absence of the fear of death. Let me know if it touches you in that way, even on a minor scale.

When I was a seven-year-old, I lived with my older brother, David, in a foster home at 231 Townhall Road, in Mt. Clemens, Michigan. The people who took us in while my mother worked to reunite her family were named Mr. and Mrs. Scarf. I remember this as if it occurred yesterday. David and I were sitting on the back porch of our home, and Mrs. Scarf came outside with two bananas in her hand and tears flowing down her face. She gave us each a banana, saying, "Mr. Scarf died this morning." It was the first time I'd experienced the concept of death connected to a human being. In my seven-year-old naïveté, I asked her, attempting to soothe her obvious pain, "When will he be back?" Mrs. Scarf responded with one word that I've never forgotten. She simply said, "Never."

I went upstairs to my bunk, peeled my banana, and lay there attempting to comprehend the concept of *never*. What did being dead forever really mean? I could have handled a thousand years, or even a billion light years, but the idea of *never* was so overwhelming, with its no ending, and more no ending, that I was almost sick to my stomach. What did I do to handle this incomprehensible idea of never? Simple, I forgot about it and went on about the business of being seven years old in a foster home. This is what Castaneda meant when he said that we're all in bodies on their way to dying, but we behave as if they're not, and this is our greatest downfall.

**Your own death.** Essentially, there are two points of view regarding this dilemma of your own death. The first says that we're physical bodies that are born and we go on to live for a while; and then ultimately we deteriorate, our flesh wears out, and then we die and are dead forever. This first perspective, if you embrace it either consciously or otherwise, is terrifying from our alive viewpoint. Unless you embrace the second point of view, it's completely understandable that you fear death. Or you may welcome it if you hate or fear life. The second point of view says very simply that you're eternal, an infinite soul in a temporary expression of flesh. This second point of view says that only your physical body dies, that you were whole and perfect as you were created, and that your physicalness emanated from the universal mind of intention. That universal mind was and is formless—it's the pure energy of love, beauty, kindness, and creativity, and it can't die, since there's no form involved—no form, no death, no boundaries, no deterioration, no flesh, no possibility of it wasting away.

Now which of these two points of view gives you the most comfort? Which is associated with peace and love? Which invokes fear and anxiety? Obviously the idea of your infinite self keeps you on friendly terms with infinity. Knowing you're first and foremost an infinite being consciously connecting with your Source, which is eternal and omnipresent, is surely the more comforting prospect. Because of its infinite nature, it's everywhere, and it then follows that the whole of Spirit must be present at every point in space at the same moment.

Thus, Spirit is present in its entirety everywhere, which includes you. You can never, ever be separate from it. You'll learn to laugh at the absurd idea that you could ever be separate from the universal mind. It's your Source. You are it. God is the mind through which you think and exist. It's always connected to you, even if you don't believe in it. Even an atheist doesn't have to believe in God to experience God. The question then becomes, not whether your body is going to die, but rather, on what side of infinity you wish to live. You have two choices, either you live on the *inactive* or the *active side of infinity.* In either case, you have an appointment with infinity, and there's no way to avoid it.

**Your appointment with infinity.** Reread the Joseph Campbell quote at the beginning of this chapter. Eternity is now! Right now, right here, you're an infinite being. Once you get past the fear of death as an end, you merge with the infinite and feel the comfort and relief that this realization brings. We identify everything in this material world through a space-time continuum. Yet infinity has no preference for time and space. You aren't the elements that make up your body; you merely make use of the elements. You go beyond space and time and are merged with the infinite universal mind. If you haven't recognized it, it's because of your fear. You can keep your appointment with infinity while you're in your temporary body, with its slavish adherence to time and space. My objective in this chapter is to help you realize and do this. If you make this merger, I assure you of a life without fear of death.

Let's take a look at both of the elements in the space/time prison in which we find our material bodies and all of its treasures. The factor of space means that we're experiencing separation from everyone and everything. This is *my space* as defined by my boundaries; those are *your* spaces. Even your most cherished soul mate lives in a world apart from yours. No matter how close in space you get, the boundaries are separate. In space, we're always separate. Trying to imagine an infinite world without space and separation is extremely difficult, until we make our appointment with infinity.

Time is also a factor of separation. We're separated from all of the events and memories of our past. Everything that has happened is separate from what's happening right now. The future is also separate from the here-and-now where we're living. We can't know the future, and the past is lost to us. Therefore, we're separated from everything that ever was or ever will be by this mysterious illusion we call time.

When your infinite soul leaves the body, it's no longer subject to the constraints of time and space. Separation can no longer interfere with you. So my question to you isn't about whether you believe you have an appointment with infinity. It's about when you're going to keep that inevitable appointment. You can either do it now while you're still alive in your body in the illusion of time and space, or you can do it at death. If you decide to make your appointment with infinity while you still live and breathe, it's like learning to die while you're alive. Once you make this transition to the active side of infinity, your fear of death dissolves and you laugh at the folly of death.

Understand your true essence, look death squarely in the face, and break the shackles of slavery to that fear. *You* do not die. Announce it. Meditate on it. Look at it from this angle: *If you're not an infinite being, what would be the purpose of your life?* Surely not going through the motions of being born, working, accumulating, losing it all, getting sick, and dying. By waking up to your infinite essence and staying connected to the seven faces of intention, you begin to free yourself of the limitations your ego has placed on you. You set in motion the guidance and assistance of the infinite universal mind to work with you. And most of all, you feel the peace that overtakes you when you expel your fear of death and mortality. I'm touched by the stories of great spiritual teachers leaving this Earthly plane feeling blissful and fearless. They banished all doubt, extricated all fear, and met infinity head-on with grace. Here are the final words of a few of the people I've long admired:

*The hour I have long wished for is now come.*
— Teresa of Avila

*Let us be kinder to one another.*
— Aldous Huxley

*If this is death, it is easier than life.*
— Robert Louis Stevenson

*This is the last of earth! I am content.*
— John Quincy Adams

*I shall hear in heaven.*
— Ludwig van Beethoven

*Light, light, the world needs more light.*
— Johann Wolfgang von Goethe

*I am going to that country which I have all my life wished to see.*
— William Blake

*It is very beautiful over there.*
— Thomas Edison

*Ram, Ram, Ram* [God, God, God].
— Mahatma Gandhi

Why not write your own final words now and make your transition to being an infinite being while you still occupy your body? As you consider your appointment with infinity, look at how most of us live our lives. We know we're in a *body* that's going to die, but we behave as if it's not going to happen to us. This viewpoint is from the inactive side of infinity where we don't see our connection to intention and our ability to stay in harmony with our creative Spirit. Let's examine the essential difference between keeping your appointment with infinity now, or at your death. In one case, you'll be on the active side of infinity, and in the other, you'll avoid it by being on the inactive side.

### The Active vs. the Inactive Sides of Infinity

On the active side of infinity, you're fully cognizant that you're in a body that's going to die. Furthermore, your inner knowing is that you aren't that body, its mind, or any of its achievements and possessions. On this active side of infinity, you have a good grip on that trolley strap I described earlier, which is connected to intent, and you're an observer of all your sensory experiences. This may not sound like a big deal to you; however, I assure you that once you move your inner awareness to the active side of infinity, you'll begin to notice miraculous happenings in your daily life. On this active side of infinity, you are first and foremost an infinite spiritual being having a temporary human experience, and you do all of your living in all of your relationships from this perspective. On the inactive side of infinity, your experience of life is quite the opposite. Here, you're first and foremost a human being having an occasional spiritual experience. Your life is guided by a fear of death, a separation from others, a competitive style, and a need to dominate and be a winner. The inactive side of infinity separates you from the power of intention.

Here are some of the distinctions that I see between those who live in the active side of infinity and those who deny their eternal nature and opt for the inactive side of infinity:

**A sense of destiny.** In the active side of infinity, your connection to intention will no longer be thought of as an option, but as a calling that you must heed. The inactive side of infinity leads you to see life as chaotic, purposeless, and meaningless, while your position on the active side of infinity leads you to fulfill a destiny that you feel deep within you.

When I look back at my life, I realize that my sense of destiny was directing me at an early age. I've known since I was a child that I could manifest abundance into my life. While sitting in high school and college classrooms where I was bored to death by teachers who conveyed their lack of passion in their dreary presentations, I dreamed of talking to large audiences. I vowed in those youthful days that I'd live my passion, and somehow knew that I was here for a reason. I couldn't allow anyone or anything to deter me from my path. I've always sensed that I'm really an infinite soul, disguised at various times as a husband, father, author, lecturer, and balding six-foot-plus American male. Because I live on the active side of infinity, I have a sense of destiny that won't allow me to die with my music still in me.

You can make the same kinds of choices. Just let go of the idea that you're a body that's destined to die, and instead seek an awareness of your immortal self. On the active side of infinity, you'll find your greater self, of which a small part has materialized as your body. I guarantee you that simply recognizing yourself as an infinite and therefore indestructible being, your connection to intention and the ability to manifest all that you desire within the confines of your universal Source will become your reality. There's no other way.

Your sense of destiny lets you know that you're playing this game of life on the active side of infinity. Prior to accessing your sense of destiny, your motivation was what you wanted out of life and what you'd like to do. On the active side of infinity, you realize that it's time to do what your destiny intended you to do. Wallowing around hoping things will work out, waiting for your luck to change, and hoping others will come through for you no longer feels right. Your sense of destiny allows you to realize, *I am eternal, and that means that I showed up here from the infinitude of spiritual intention to fulfill a destiny that I must act on.* You begin stating your objectives in the language of intention, knowing they'll materialize. You enlist the power of intention to keep you on track. It can't fail because there's no failure in the infinite.

This 13th-century poem may inspire you to know you have *your* destiny:

> *You were born with potential.*
> *You were born with goodness and trust.*
> *You were born with ideals and dreams.*
> *You were born with greatness.*
> *You were born with wings.*
> *You are not meant for crawling, so don't.*
> *You have wings.*
> *Learn to use them and fly.*
>
> — Rumi

If Rumi composed his poem from the inactive side of infinity, his words might be more like the following.

> *You are an accident of nature.*
> *You are subject to the laws of luck and chance.*
> *You can be pushed around easily.*
> *Your dreams are meaningless.*
> *You were meant to live an ordinary life.*
> *You have no wings.*
> *So forget about flying and stay grounded.*

**A sense of the possible.** Creation acts upon the everlasting *possibility* that anything that is thought of, can be. Consider some of the numerous great inventions, which we take for granted today: airplanes, electric lights, telephones, television, fax machines, computers. They're all the result of creative ideas by individuals who ignored the ridicule they encountered while they stayed focused on *possible* rather than impossible. In other words, a sense of the possible grows in the fertile terrain of the active side of infinity.

I have here in my writing space a wonderful account of four children who refused to allow the word *impossible* into their hearts:

Eddie was born without hands or feet. At age five, he went to South Africa and saw a mountain he wanted to climb; he climbed it in three hours. And at age 13, he decided to play a trombone. He sees no reason why he shouldn't achieve whatever he sets out to do. He lives on the active side of infinity, consulting that world of infinite possibilities.

Abby was desperately ill and needed a heart transplant. When she saw her mother crying, she told her, "Mommy don't cry, I'm going to get better." At the 11th hour, a heart miraculously became available, and Abby *is* better. Abby's intention came from that world of infinite possibilities. It's the active side of infinity where intentions manifest.

Stephanie was five years old when she came down with meningitis and had to have both of her legs amputated. Today at age 12, she rides her own bicycle and has dreams that go way beyond those of most teenagers who possess all of their limbs. Her personal slogan is: *Push to the limit.*

After two major heart operations while just a toddler, the doctors told little Frankie's parents that they could do no more. Frankie lived only because she was on a life-support machine. When her parents were advised to have the machine turned off because Frankie couldn't survive and would only suffer, they finally agreed. But Frankie survived. She was somehow on the active side of the world of infinite possibilities. The caption beneath her photo says it all: *You didn't think you could get rid of me that easily, did you?*

The power of intention involves staying on the active side of infinite possibilities. George Bernard Shaw, who was still creating into his 90s, has been quoted as saying, "You see things as they are and you say, 'Why?' But I dream things that never were, and I say 'Why not?'" Think of Shaw's words as you practice staying on the active side of infinity and seeing the infinite possibilities that are available to all of us.

**A sense of awe.** You have to admit that just the concept of infinity is awesome. No beginning. No ending. Everywhere at once. No time. And all of it here and now. The fact that you're a part of this infinite universe and that you emerged into the finite is mind-boggling. It defies description. The active side of infinity inspires a sense of awe. When you're in a state of awe, you're in a persistent state of gratitude. Perhaps the surest way to happiness and fulfillment in life is to thank and praise your Source for *everything* that happens to you. Then, even when a calamity arises, you can be assured that you'll turn it into a blessing.

In the inactive side of infinity, you assume that you're only here temporarily, and therefore you have no obligation to the universe, the planet, or its inhabitants. By denying your infinite nature, you move through life taking everyday miracles for granted. As you become acquainted with your eternal nature, you have a very different point of view. You're in a persistent state of gratitude for all that shows up. This state is the secret to fulfilling your own individual human intentions, and without it, all of your most sincere efforts will amount to naught.

Being in a state of gratitude actually creates magnetism, and of course, a magnet draws things to itself. By giving authentic thanks for all the good you now have, as well as the challenges, through this magnetism you'll start the flow of more good into your life. Every successful person I know is grateful for *everything* he or she has. This process of giving thanks opens the door for more to come. It's how being in active infinity works. Your sense of awe at all of the miracles you see around you allows you to think, see, and live more of these miraculous occurrences. In contrast, a state of ingratitude stops the infinite flow of abundance and health. It's a door closer.

**A sense of humility.** The active side of infinity fosters a sense of humility. When humility enters your soul, you know that you're not alone in this world, because you sense the heart of the power of intention, which is in each and everyone of us. To quote the Talmud, "Even if you be otherwise perfect, you fail without humility."

When you embrace the active side of infinity, you're looking at something so enormous that your little ego is dwarfed in the process. You're looking out at *forever*, and your little life is but a tiny parenthesis in eternity.

One of the reasons for so much contemporary depression and ennui is the inability to see ourselves connected to something greater and more important than our own puny egos. Young people whose primary focus is on their possessions, their appearance, their reputations with their peers—in short, their own egos—have very little sense of humility. When the only thing you have to think about is yourself and how you appear to others, you've distanced yourself from the power of intention. If you want to feel connected to your own purpose, know this for certain: *Your purpose will only be found in service to others, and in being connected to something far greater than your body/mind/ego.*

I always told my young clients in counseling who were desperate for approval from their peers that the more they chase after approval, the more they'll be disapproved of because no one wants to be around those who beg for approval. People who receive the most approval are unconcerned about it. So, if you really want approval, stop thinking about yourself, and focus on reaching out and helping others. The active side of infinity keeps you humble. The inactive side of infinity keeps you focused on me, me, me, and ultimately is a roadblock to your connection to intention.

Wilhelm Stekel made a remarkable comment on the importance of humility (which was quoted by J. D. Salinger in *Catcher in the Rye*). Stekel wrote: "The mark of the immature man is that he wants to die nobly for a cause, while the mark of the mature man is that he wants to live humbly for one."

**A sense of generosity.** If asked, *Why do you give us light and warmth?* I believe that the sun would answer, *It's my nature to do so.* We must be like the sun, and locate and dispense our giving nature. When you're on the active side of infinity, giving is your nature.

The more you give of yourself, no matter how little, the more you open the door for life to pour in. This not only compensates you for your gift, it also increases the desire to give, and consequently the ability to receive as well. When you're on the inactive side of infinity, you view life in terms of shortages, and hoarding becomes a way of living. Generosity, as well as the inclination to reach your intentions, is lost when you think in these terms. If you can't see an infinite universe, with infinite supply, and infinite time and an infinite Source, you'll be inclined to hoard and be stingy. The power of intention is paradoxically experienced through what you're willing to give to others. Intention is a field of energy, which is emanating in infinite supply. What can you give if you don't have money to give? I love Swami Sivananda's advice, and I encourage you to consider it here. Everything that he suggests, you own in infinite amounts.

> *The best thing to give*
> *your enemy is forgiveness;*
> *to an opponent, tolerance;*
> *to a friend, your heart;*
> *to your child, a good example;*
> *to your father, deference;*
> *to your mother, conduct that will make her proud of you;*
> *to your self, respect;*
> *to all men, charity.*

Make giving a way of life. It is, after all, what Source and nature do eternally. I've heard it said about nature that trees bend low with ripened fruit; clouds hang down with gentle rain; noble men bow graciously. This is the way of generous things.

**A sense of knowing.** Your infinite Source of intention has no doubt. It knows, and consequently it acts upon that knowing. This is what will happen for you when you live on the active side of infinity. All doubt flies out of your heart forever. As an infinite being in a temporary human form, you'll identify yourself primarily on the basis of your spiritual nature.

This sense of knowing that comes from the active side of infinity means that you no longer think in terms of limits. *You* are the Source. The Source is unlimited. It knows no boundaries; it's endlessly expansive, and endlessly abundant. This is what you are, too. Discarding doubt is a decision to reconnect to your original self. This is the mark of people who live self-actualized lives. They think in no-limit, infinite ways. One of the no-limit qualities is the ability to think and act as if what they'd like to have is already present. This is another one of my ten secrets for success and inner peace in the book of the same title. The power of intention is so doubt-deficient that when you're connected to it, your sense of knowing sees what you'd like to have as already present. There are no contrary opinions whatsoever.

Here's my advice for accessing the power of intention: Stay on the active side of the infinite, where all of the energy for creation exists in everlasting supply. Night and day, dream of what you intend to do and what you intend to be, and those dreams will interpret your intentions. Let no doubt into your dreams and intentions. The dreamers are the saviors of the world. Just as the visible world is sustained by the invisible, so too do the manifestations of man find nourishment in the visions of our solitary dreamers. Be one of those dreamers.

**A sense of passion.** The Greeks have given us one of the most beautiful words of our language: *enthusiasm*. The word *enthusiasm* translates to "a God within." Within you is an infinite passionate soul that wishes to express itself. It's the God within you, urging you to fulfill a deep sense of what you were meant to be. All of our acts are measured by the inspiration from which they originate. When your acts display the faces of intention, they spring from a God residing within you. This is enthusiasm. When you emulate the power of intention, this is where you'll feel the passion you were intended to feel and live.

The beauty of feeling passionate and enthusiastic is the glorious feeling of joy and cheerfulness that comes along with it. Nothing provides me with more joy than sitting here and writing to you from my heart. I enthusiastically allow these teachings to come through me from the Source of all intention, the universal mind of all creativity. Put quite simply, I feel good, I'm in a cheerful mood, and my inspiration provides me with joy. If you want to feel great, look into the mirror, say to your image, *I am eternal; this image will fade, but I am infinite. I am here temporarily for a reason. I will be passionate about all that I do.* Then just notice how you feel as you stare at your reflection. Being cheerful is a wondrous side benefit of enthusiasm. It comes from being in the active side of infinity where there's absolutely nothing to feel bad about.

**A sense of belonging.** In a world that lasts forever, you certainly must belong! The active side of infinity inspires not only a strong sense of belonging, but a strong feeling of connectedness to everyone and everything in the cosmos. It's impossible for you not to belong, because your presence here is evidence that a divine universal Source intended you here. Yet when you live on the inactive side of infinity, you feel a sense of alienation from others. Your idea that this is all temporary and that you aren't a piece of God's infinite perfection leads you to self-doubt, anxiety, self-rejection, depression, and so many more of the low energies I've written about throughout this book. All it takes is a shift to infinite awareness to leave that feeling of misery. As Sivananda taught his devotees:

> *All life is one. The world is one home.*
> *All are members of one human family.*
> *All creation is an organic whole. No*
> *Man is independent of this whole. Man*
> *Makes himself miserable by separating*
> *Himself from others. Separation is death.*
> *Unity is eternal life.*

\* \* \*

This concludes my ideas on the active and inactive side of infinity. I urge you to remind yourself every day, as frequently as possible, of your infinite nature. It may sound like merely an intellectual shift of minor consequence, but I assure you that staying on the active side of infinity and reminding yourself of it regularly will put you in a position to manifest your desires. Of all the quotes on this subject I've read, this observation made by William Blake stands out: "If the doors of perception were cleansed, everything would appear to man as it is: infinite." Remember, we're attempting to clean up the connecting link between ourselves and the field of intention.

### Five Suggestions for Implementing the Ideas in This Chapter

1. *Since you already know that you have an appointment with infinity and that you're ultimately required to leave this corporeal world behind, make the decision to do so sooner, rather than later.* In fact today, right now, is a great time to keep that appointment, and get it over with once and for all. Simply announce to yourself: *I'm no longer identified by this body/mind, and I reject this label from this moment on. I'm infinite. I'm one with all of humanity. I'm one with my Source, and this is how I choose to view myself from this day forward.*

2. *Repeat this mantra to yourself each day as you remind yourself that God wouldn't and couldn't create something that doesn't last: I will exist for all eternity. Just as love is eternal, so is this my true nature. I'll never be afraid again, because I am forever.* This kind of inner affirmation aligns you on the active side of infinity and erases doubts about your authentic higher identity.

3. *In a meditative stance, consider the two choices of belief on this concept of infinity.* You are in the truest sense, as I've said previously, either a human being having an occasional spiritual experience, or an infinite spiritual being having a temporary human experience. Which of those gives you a feeling

of love? And which inspires fear? Now, since love is our true nature and the Source of all, anything that creates fear can't be real. As you see, the feeling of love is associated with yourself as an infinite being. Then you must rely on this feeling to tell you the truth. Your place in the active side of infinity assures you of a feeling of security, love, and permanent connection to intention.

4. *In any moment in which you find yourself thinking low-energy thoughts of fear, despair, worry, sadness, anxiety, guilt, and so on, just for a moment stop and consider whether this makes any sense from the perspective of the active side of infinity.* Knowing that you're here forever, and always connected to your Source, will give you an entirely new outlook. In the context of infinity, living any moment of your life in anything other than appreciation and love is a waste of your life energy. You can quickly dissipate those lower energies and simultaneously connect to the power of intention by cleansing those lenses of perception and seeing everything as it is—*infinite*, as William Blake suggested.

5. *Take a few moments to reflect on the people you were close to and loved who have crossed over.* Being aware of your infinite nature, and staying in infinity's active side, allows you to feel the presence of these souls, who can't die and did not die. In John O'Donohue's book of Celtic wisdom called *Anam Cara*, he offers these words with which I not only concur, but I know to be true from my own personal experience:

> I believe that our friends among the dead really mind us and look out for us . . . we might be able to link up in a very creative way with our friends in the invisible world. We do not need to grieve for the dead. Why should we grieve for them? They are now in a place where there is no more shadow, darkness, loneliness, isolation or pain. They are home. They are with God from whom they came.

You can not only communicate with and feel the presence of those who've crossed over, you yourself can die while you're alive and rid yourself now of these shadows and darkness, by living in the active side of infinity.

\* \* \*

This concludes Part I of *The Power of Intention*. Part II will be a series of chapters describing how to put this new connection to intention to work in a variety of ways in your life. As with the first part, read on with a mind that is not only open to the possibility of your achieving all that you can imagine, but to knowing that on the active side of infinity all things are possible.

Now, you tell me what that leaves out!

⌒ \* ⌒ \* ⌒

# PART II

# PUTTING
# INTENTION
# TO
# WORK

*"We are already one and we imagine we are not.
And what we have to recover is our original unity.
Whatever we have to be is what we are."*

— Thomas Merton

# CHAPTER SEVEN

## *IT IS* *MY INTENTION TO:* RESPECT MYSELF AT ALL TIMES

*"A man cannot be comfortable without his own approval."*
— Mark Twain

Here's a simple truth to begin this chapter: You did not orig-inate from a material particle as you've been led to believe. Your conception at the moment of your parents' blissful commingling was not your beginning. You had no beginning. That particle emanated from the universal energy field of intention, as do all particles. You're a piece of that universal mind of Creation, and you must see God inside of you and view yourself as a divine creation in order to access the power of intention in your life.

Give this idea a healthy dose of your attention—right now in this moment—as you read these words. Contemplate the enormity of what you're reading. You are a piece of God. You are a living, breathing creation that emanated from the universal mind of the all-creating Source. You and God are the same thing. Very simply put, when you love and trust yourself, you're loving and trusting the wisdom that created you; and when you fail to love and trust yourself, you're denying that infinite wisdom in favor of your own ego. It's important here to remember that at every single moment of your life, you have the choice to either be a host to God or a hostage to your ego.

### Host or Hostage?

Your ego is the set of beliefs that I've written about earlier in this book, which define you as what you accomplish and accumulate in a material sense. Your ego is solely responsible for the feelings of self-doubt and self-repudiation that you may carry around. When you attempt to live by the low-level standards of your ego, you're a hostage to that very same ego. Your worth as a person is measured by your acquisitions and accomplishments. If you have less stuff, you're less valuable, and therefore unworthy of respect from others. If others don't respect you, and your value depends on how others see you, then it's unimaginable for you to have self-respect. You become a hostage to this low-level ego energy, which has you constantly striving for self-respect through others.

Your ego's belief that you're separate from everyone, separate from what's missing in your life, and most egregiously, separate from God, further hampers your ability to live up to the intention of respecting yourself. Ego's idea of separation fosters your feelings of being in competition with everyone, and evaluating your worth based on how frequently you emerge as a winner. As a hostage to your ego, self-respect is unavailable because you feel judged for your failures. It's out of this bleak picture, produced by the negative ego, that self-rejection emerges. It captures you and makes a hostage of you, never allowing you to play host to that from which you originated.

Being a host to God means always seeing your authentic connection to your Source. It's knowing that it's impossible for you to ever be disconnected from the Source from which you came. Personally, I thoroughly enjoy being a host to God. As I write here each morning, I feel that I'm receiving words and ideas from the power of intention, which allows me to bring these words to this page. I trust in this Source to provide me with the words; therefore, I'm trusting in the Source that brought me into this physical world. I'm eternally connected to this Source.

This awareness simply doesn't include a lack of respect for intending this book into form. The conclusion I've come to is that I'm worthy of my intention to write this book and have it published and in your hands today. In other words, I respect the piece of God that I am. I tap in to the power of intention, and my feeling of respect for it enhances my respect for myself.

So, by loving and respecting yourself, you're hosting God *and* inviting the energy of Creation to your consciousness, to your daily life, as you connect to the power of intention.

**The energy of intention and your self-respect.** If you don't believe that you're worthy of fulfilling your intentions for health, wealth, or loving relationships, then you're creating an obstacle that will inhibit the flow of creative energy into your daily life. Recall that everything in the universe is energy, which moves at various frequencies. The higher the frequency, the closer you are to spiritual energy. In the lower frequencies, you find shortages and problems. Intention itself is a unified energy field that intends everything into existence. This field is home to the laws of nature, and is the inner domain of every human being. This is the *field of all possibilities,* and it's yours by virtue of your existence.

Having a belief system that denies your connection to intention is the only way you're unable to access the power of intention from the infinite field. If you're convinced that you're unworthy of enjoying the field of all possibilities, then you'll radiate this kind of low energy. This will, in fact, become your attracted energy pattern, and you'll send messages to the universe that you're unworthy of receiving the unlimited abundance of the originating Spirit. Soon you'll act on this inner conviction of self-disrespect. You'll regard yourself as separate from the possibility of receiving the loving support of the originating field of intention, and you'll stop the flow of that energy into your life. Why? All because you see yourself as unworthy. This disrespect alone is sufficient to impede the arrival of your intentions into your life.

The law of attraction attracts disrespect when you're affirming that you're unworthy of being respected. Send out the message to the provider of all that you're unworthy, and you literally say to the universal Source of all, *Stop the flow of anything I desire, which is coming in my direction, because I don't believe I'm worthy of receiving it.* The universal Source will respond by halting this flow, causing you to reaffirm your inner conviction of unworthiness and attract even more disrespect in a multitude of ways. You'll disrespect your body by overfeeding it and poisoning it with toxic substances. You'll display your lack of self-respect in how you carry yourself, how you dress, how you fail to exercise, how you treat others . . . on and on goes the list.

The antidote to this dreary picture is to make an internal commitment to respect yourself and to feel worthy of all that the universe has to offer. If *anyone* is entitled to success and happiness, *everyone* is, because everyone is always connected to intention. Simply put, disrespecting yourself is not only disrespecting one of God's greatest creations, it's disrespecting God. When you disrespect your Source, you say no to it, and you turn away from the power of intention. This stops the flow of energy that allows you to put your individual unbending intent into practice. All of the positive thinking in the world will do you absolutely no good if those thoughts don't emanate from respect for your connection to intention. The *source* of your thoughts must be celebrated and loved, and this means having the self-respect that's in harmony with the omniscient Source of intelligence. What's the source of your thoughts? Your *beingness.* Your beingness is the place from which your thoughts and actions come. When you disrespect your being, you set into motion a chain reaction culminating in unfulfilled intentions.

Self-respect should be a natural state for you, just as it is for all of the animal kingdom. There's no raccoon out there who believes himself unworthy of what he intends to have. Were that so, the raccoon would simply die by acting on the basis of his inner conviction that he was unworthy of food or shelter, and whatever else raccoons desire. He knows he's respectable, never finds any reason for self-repudiation, and lives out his raccoon-ness in perfect order. The universe provides, and he attracts those provisions into his world.

### What You Think of Yourself Is
### What You Think of the World

How do you see the world you live in? What do you think people in general are really like? Do you believe that evil is triumphing over good? Is the world filled with egocentric, selfish people? Can the little guy ever get ahead? Are government entities and all their representatives corrupt and untrustworthy? Is life unfair? Is it impossible to get ahead if you don't have connections?

All of these attitudes emerge from your own assessment of your personal interaction with life. If your thoughts reflect a pessimistic view of the world, then that's actually how you feel about yourself. If your thoughts reflect an optimistic view of the world, then *that's* how you feel about your life. Whatever attitude you have about the world in general is a good indicator of the respect you have for your abilities to intend into this world what you desire. Pessimism strongly suggests that you don't subscribe to the idea that you can access the power of intention to help you create your own blissful reality.

I recall hearing the following conversation after the events of 9/11 in New York City. A grandfather was talking to his grandson, telling him, "I have two wolves barking inside of me. The first wolf is filled with anger, hatred, bitterness, and mostly revenge. The second wolf inside of me is filled with love, kindness, compassion, and mostly forgiveness."

"Which wolf do you think will win?" the young boy inquired.

The grandfather responded, "Whichever one I feed."

There are always two ways to look at the conditions of our world. We can see the hate, prejudice, mistreatment, starvation, poverty, and crime and conclude that this is a horrible world. We can feed this barking wolf and see more and more of what we despise. But this will only fill us with the same things that we find so malignant. Or we can look at the world from a position of self-love and self-respect, and see the improvements that have been made in race relations in our lifetime; the fall of so many dictatorships, lower crime rates, the dismantling of the atrocious apartheid systems, the elevated consciousness of the environmental movement, and the desire on the part of so many to rid our world of nuclear weapons and instruments of mass destruction. We can remind ourselves that for every act of evil in the world, there are a million acts of kindness, and we can then feed the second wolf that barks from a position of hope for humanity. If you see yourself as a divine creation, you'll look for this in your worldview, and the gloom-and-doom naysayers will have no impact on you and your self-respect.

When you have a gloomy picture of what the world looks like, you're unreceptive to the potential assistance that's there to help you with your own individual intentions. Why would others want to come to your aid when you view them as contemptible? Why would the universal force be attracted to that which repels it? How could a world that's so corrupt ever be of assistance to someone who has noble intentions? The answers to these questions are obvious. You attract into your life what you feel inside. If you feel that you're not worthy of being respected, you attract disrespect. This weak self-respect is the result of an exceptionally rusty link to the field of intention. This link must be cleansed and purified, and that takes place within your own mind.

I've specifically chosen *self-respect* as the first chapter in Part II on applying intention, because without high esteem for yourself, you shut down the entire process of intention. Without unflagging self-respect, the process of intention is operating at the lowest levels. The universal field of intention is love, kindness, and beauty, which it has for all that it brings into the material world. Those who wish to replicate the works of the universal all-creating mind must be in harmony with the attributes of love, kindness, and beauty. If you disrespect anyone or anything that God creates, you disrespect that creative force. You are one of those creations. If you view yourself disrespectfully, you've forsaken, cast aside, or at the very least, sullied your connection to the power of intention.

It's important that you recognize that your entire worldview is based on how much respect you have for yourself. Believe in infinite possibilities and you cast a vote for your own possibilities. Stand firm on the potential for humans to live in peace and be receptive to all, and you're someone who's at peace and receptive to life's possibilities. Know that the universe is filled with abundance and prosperity and is available to everyone, and you come down on the side of having that abundance show up for you as well. Your level of self-regard must come from your knowing within yourself that you have a sacred connection. Let nothing shake that divine foundation. In this way, your link to intention is cleansed, and you always know that self-respect is your personal choice. It has nothing to do with what others may think of you. Your self-respect comes from the self and the self alone.

**The *self* in self-respect.** Perhaps the greatest mistake we make, which causes a loss of self-respect, is making the opinions of others more important than our own opinion of ourselves. Self-respect means just what it says—it originates from the self. This *self* originated in a universal field of intention that intended you here—from the infinite formless state to a being of molecules and physical substance. If you fail to respect yourself, you're showing contempt for the process of Creation.

You'll find no shortage of opinions directed at you. If you allow them to undermine your self-respect, you're seeking the respect of others over your own, and you're abdicating yourself. Then you're attempting to reconnect to the field of intention with low-energy attitudes of judgment, hostility, and anxiety. You'll cycle into low-energy vibrations that will simply force you to attract more and more of these lower energies into your life. Remember, it's high energy that nullifies and converts lower energy. Light eradicates darkness; love dissolves hate. If you've allowed any of those lower negative thoughts and opinions directed your way to become the basis of your self-portrait, you're asking the universal mind do the same. Why? Because at the high frequencies, the universal Source of intention is pure creativeness, love, kindness, beauty, and abundance. *Self-respect attracts the higher energy.* Lack of self-respect attracts the lower. It knows no other way.

The negative viewpoints of others represent *their low-energy ego* working on you. Very simply, if you're judging anyone, you aren't loving them at that moment. The judgments coming your way, likewise, are unloving but have nothing to do with your self-respect. Their judgments (and yours as well) distance you from your Source, and therefore away from the *power* of intention. As my friend and colleague Gerald Jampolsky observed, "When I am able to resist the temptation to judge others, I can see them as teachers of forgiveness in my life, reminding me that I can only have peace of mind when I forgive rather than judge."

This is how you return to the *self* in self-respect. Rather than judging those who judge you, thereby lowering your self-respect, you send them a silent blessing of forgiveness and imagine them doing the same toward you. You're connecting to intention and guaranteeing that you'll always respect the divinity that you are. You've cleared the path to be able to enjoy the great power that is yours in the field of intention.

### Making Your Intention Your Reality

In this concluding section, you'll find ten ways to practice nurturing your intention to respect yourself at all times.

**Step 1: Look into a mirror, make eye connection with yourself, and say *"I love me"* as many times as possible during your day.** *I love me:* These three magic words help you maintain your self-respect. Now, be aware that saying these words may be difficult at first because of the conditions you've been exposed to over a lifetime, and because the words may bring to the surface remnants of disrespect that your ego wants you to hold on to.

Your immediate impulse might be to see this as an expression of your ego's desire to be superior to everyone else. But this is not an ego statement at all—it's an affirmation of self-respect. Transcend that ego mind and affirm your love for yourself and your connection to the Spirit of God. This doesn't make you superior to anyone; it makes you equal to all and celebrates that you're a piece of God. Affirm it for your own self-respect. Affirm it in order to be respectful of that which intended you here. Affirm it because it's the way you'll stay connected to your Source and regain the power of intention. *I love me.* Say it without embarrassment. Say it proudly, and be that image of love and self-respect.

**Step 2: Write the following affirmation and repeat it over and over again to yourself:** *I am whole and perfect as I was created!* Carry this thought with you wherever you go. Have it laminated, and place it in your pocket, on your dashboard, on your refrigerator, or next to your bed—allow the words to become a source of high energy and self-respect. By simply carrying these words with you and being in the same space with them, their energy will flow directly to you.

Self-respect emerges from the fact that you respect the Source from which you came and you've made a decision to reconnect to that Source, regardless of what anyone else might think. It's very important to keep reminding yourself at the beginning that you're worthy of infinite respect from the one Source you can always count on, the piece of God energy that defines you. This reminder will do wonders for your self-respect, and consequently your ability to use the power of intention in your life. Over and over, remind yourself: *I'm not my body. I'm not my accumulations. I'm not my achievements. I'm not my reputation. I am whole and perfect as I was created!*

**Step 3: Extend more respect to others and to all of life.** Perhaps the greatest secret of self-esteem is to appreciate other people more. The easiest way to do this is to see the unfolding of God in them. Look past the judgments of others' appearance, failures, and successes, their status in society, their wealth or lack of it . . . and extend appreciation and love to the Source from which they came. Everyone is a child of God—everyone! Try to see this even in those who behave in what appears to be a godless fashion. Know that by extending love and respect, you can turn that energy around so that it's heading back to its Source rather than away from it. In short, send out respect because that is what you have to give away. Send out judgment and low energy and that is what you'll attract back. Remember, when you judge others, you do not define them, you define yourself as someone who needs to judge. The same applies to judgments directed at you.

**Step 4: Affirm to yourself and all others that you meet, *I belong!*** A sense of belonging is one of the highest attributes on Abraham Maslow's pyramid of self-actualization (which I discuss at the beginning of the next chapter). Feeling that you don't belong or you're in the wrong place can be due to a lack of self-respect. Respect yourself and your divinity by knowing that everyone belongs. This should never come into question. Your presence here in the universe is proof alone that you belong here. No person decides if you belong here. No government determines if some belong and some don't. This is an intelligent system that you're a part of. The wisdom of Creation intended you to be here, in this place, in this family with these siblings and parents, occupying this precious space. Say it to yourself and affirm it whenever necessary: *I belong!* And so does everyone else. No one is here by accident!

**Step 5: Remind yourself that you're never alone.** My self-respect stays intact as long as I know that it's impossible for me to be alone. I have a *"senior partner"* who's never abandoned me and who's stuck with me even in moments when I had seemingly deserted my Source. I feel that if the universal mind has enough respect to allow me to come here and to work through me—and to protect me in times when I strayed onto dangerous nonspiritual turf—then this partnership deserves my reciprocal respect. I recall my friend Pat McMahon, a talk-show host on KTAR radio in Phoenix, Arizona, telling me about his encounter with Mother Teresa in his studio before interviewing her for his program. He pleaded with her to allow him to do something for her. "Anything at all," he begged. "I'd just like to help you in some way." She looked at him and said, "Tomorrow morning get up at 4:00 A.M. and go out onto the streets of Phoenix. Find someone who lives there and believes that he's alone, and convince him that he's not." Great advice, because everyone who wallows in self-doubt or appears to be lost . . . has lost their self-respect because they've forgotten that they're not alone.

**Step 6: Respect your body!** You've been provided with a perfect body to house your inner invisible being for a few brief moments in eternity. Regardless of its size, shape, color, or any imagined infirmities, it's a perfect creation for the purpose that you were intended here for. You don't need to work at getting healthy; health is something you already have if you don't disturb it. You may have disturbed your healthy body by overfeeding it, underexercising it, and overstimulating it with toxins or drugs that make it sick, fatigued, jumpy, anxious, depressed, bloated, ornery, or an endless list of maladies. You can begin the fulfillment of this intention to live a life of self-respect by honoring the temple that houses you. You know what to do. You don't need another diet, workout manual, or personal trainer. Go within, listen to your body, and treat it with all of the dignity and love that your self-respect demands.

**Step 7: Meditate to stay in conscious contact with your Source, which always respects you.** I can't say this enough: Meditation is a way to experience what the five senses can't detect. When you're connected to the field of intention, you're connected to the wisdom that's within you. That divine wisdom has great respect for you, and it cherishes you while you're here. Meditation is a way to ensure that you stay in a state of self-respect. Regardless of all that goes on around you, when you enter into that sacred space of meditation, all doubts about your value as an esteemed creation dissolve. You'll emerge from the solemnity of meditation feeling connected to your Source and enjoying respect for all beings, particularly yourself.

**Step 8: Make amends with adversaries.** The act of making amends sends out a signal of respect for your adversaries. By radiating this forgiving energy outward, you'll find this same kind of respectful positive energy flowing back toward you. By being big enough to make amends and replace the energy of anger, bitterness, and tension with kindness—even if you still insist that you're right—you'll respect yourself much more than prior to your act of forgiveness. If you're filled with rage toward anyone, there's a huge part of you that resents the presence of this debilitating energy. Take a moment right here and now to simply face that person who stands out in your mind as someone you hurt, or directed hurt to you, and tell him or her that you'd like to make amends. You'll notice how much better you feel. That good feeling of having cleared the air is self-respect. It takes much more courage, strength of character, and inner conviction to make amends than it does to hang on to the low-energy feelings.

**Step 9: Always remember the *self* in self-respect.** In order to do this, you must recognize that the opinions of others toward you aren't facts, they're opinions. When I speak to an audience of 500 people, there are 500 opinions of me in the room at the end of the evening. I'm none of those opinions. I can't be responsible for how they view me. The only thing I can be responsible for is my own character, and this is true for every one of us. If I respect myself, then I'm relying on the *self* in self-respect. If I doubt myself, or punish myself, I've not only lost my self-respect, I'll continue to attract more and more doubt and lower-energy opinions with which to further punish myself. You can't stay linked to the universal mind, which intends all of us here, if you fail to rely on your self for your self-respect.

**Step 10: Be in a state of gratitude.** You'll discover that gratitude is the final step in each succeeding chapter. Be an appreciator rather than a depreciator of everything that shows up in your life. When you're saying *Thank you, God, for everything,* and when you're expressing gratitude for your life and all that you see and experience, you're respecting Creation. This respect is within you, and you can only give away what you have inside. Being in a state of gratitude is the exact same thing as being in a state of respect—respect for yourself, which you give away freely, and which will return to you tenfold.

I close this chapter with the words of Jesus of Nazareth, speaking through his apostle Saint Matthew (Matthew 5:48): "Be perfect, therefore, as your heavenly Father is perfect." Reconnect to the perfection from which you originated.

You can't have any more self-respect than that!

✻ ✻

# CHAPTER EIGHT

# IT IS
# MY INTENTION TO:
# LIVE MY LIFE
# ON PURPOSE

*"Those who have failed to work toward the truth
have missed the purpose of living."*

— Buddha

*"Your sole business in life is to attain God-realization.
All else is useless and worthless."*

— Sivananda

A sense of purpose is at the very top of the pyramid of self-actualization created by Abraham Maslow more than 50 years ago. Through his research, Dr. Maslow discovered that those who feel purposeful are living the highest qualities that humanity has to offer. During the many years I've been in the fields of human development, motivation, and spiritual awareness, this is the topic that more people inquire about than anything else. I'm repeatedly asked questions such as: *How do I find my purpose? Does such a thing really exist? Why don't I know my purpose in life?* Being on purpose is what the most self-actualized people accomplish on their life journeys. But many individuals feel little sense of purpose, and may even *doubt* that they have a purpose in life.

## *Purpose and Intention*

The theme of this book is that intention is a force in the universe, and that everything and everyone is connected to this invisible force. Since this is an intelligent system we're all a part of, and everything that arrives here came from that intelligence, it follows that if it wasn't supposed to be here, then it wouldn't be here. And if it's here, then it's supposed to be, and that's enough for me. The very fact of your existence indicates that you have a purpose. As I mentioned, the key question for most of us is: "What is my purpose?" And I hear that question in as many forms as there are people wondering about it: *What am I supposed to be doing? Should I be an architect, a florist, or a veterinarian? Should I help people or fix automobiles? Am I supposed to have a family or be in the jungle saving the chimpanzees?* We're befuddled by the endless number of options available to us, and wonder whether we're doing the right thing.

In this chapter, I urge you to forget these questions. Move instead to a place of faith and trust in the universal mind of intention, remembering that you emanated from this mind and that you're a piece of it at all times.

Intention and purpose are as beautifully and naturally intertwined as the double helix of your DNA. There are no accidents. You're here for the purpose that you signed up for before you entered the world of particles and form. Many of the things that you refer to as problems result from the fact that you're disconnected from intention and therefore unaware of your true spiritual identity. The process of polishing that connecting link and reconnecting is basic to your intention to live your life on purpose. As you cleanse this link, you'll make two very important discoveries. First, you'll discover that your purpose is not as much about what you do as it is about how you feel. Your second discovery will be that feeling purposeful activates your power of intention to create anything that's consistent with the seven faces of intention.

**Feeling purposeful.** In response to the question *What should I do with my life?*, I suggest that there's only one thing you *can* do with it, since you came into this life with nothing and you'll leave with nothing: *You can give it away.* You'll feel most on purpose when you're giving your life away by serving others. When you're giving to others, to your planet, and to your Source, you're being purposeful. Whatever it is that you choose to do, if you're motivated to be of service to others while being authentically detached from the outcome, you'll feel on purpose, regardless of how much abundance flows back to you.

So, your intention is to live your life on purpose. But what is the spiritual Source like in this regard? It's perpetually in the process of giving its life force away to create something from nothing. When you do the same, regardless of what you're giving or creating, you're in harmony with intention. You're then on purpose, just as the universal mind is always acting purposefully.

Take this one step further. Does the universal Source of all life have to think about what it's doing with its powers? Is it concerned with bringing in gazelles or centipedes? Does it concern itself with where it lives or what it ultimately creates? No. Your Source is simply in the business of expressing itself through the seven faces of intention. The details are taken care of automatically. Likewise, your feelings of being on purpose in your life flow through expression of the seven faces of intention.

Allow yourself to be in the feeling place within you that's unconcerned with such things as vocational choices or doing the things you were destined to do. When you're in the service of others, or extend kindness beyond your own boundaries, you'll feel connected to your Source. You'll feel happy and content, knowing that you're doing the right thing.

I get that feeling of inner completion and contentment that lets me know that I'm on purpose by reading my mail or hearing the comments I so frequently hear when I'm walking through airports or eating at restaurants: *You changed my life, Wayne Dyer. You were there for me when I felt lost.* This is different from receiving a royalty payment or a great review, which I also enjoy. The personal expressions of gratitude are what sustain me in knowing that I'm on purpose.

153

Outside of my chosen occupation, I feel purposeful in a myriad of ways virtually every single day. When I extend assistance to someone in need, when I take a moment to cheer up a disgruntled employee in a restaurant or a store, when I make a child laugh who sits otherwise ignored in a stroller, or even when I pick up a piece of litter and place it in a trash can, I feel that I'm giving myself away and, as such, feel purposeful.

Essentially what I'm saying is: Stay on purpose by expressing the seven faces of intention, and the details will find you. You'll never have to ask what your purpose is or how to find it.

**Your purpose will find you.** In a previous chapter, I reviewed the obstacles to connecting to intention and pointed out that our thoughts are one of the major roadblocks. I stressed that we become what we think about all day long. What thoughts do *you* have that inhibit you from feeling as if you're on purpose in your life? For instance, if you think that you're separate from your purpose and that you're drifting without direction through your life, then that's precisely what you'll attract.

Suppose, instead, that you know this is a purposeful universe where your thoughts, emotions, and actions are a part of your free will and are also connected to the power of intention. Suppose that your thoughts of being purposeless and aimless are really a *part* of your purpose. Just as the thought of losing someone you love makes you love them even more, or an illness makes you treasure your health, suppose that it takes the thought of your unimportance to make you realize your value.

When you're awake enough to question your purpose and ask how to connect to it, you're being prodded by the power of intention. The very act of questioning why you're here is an indication that your thoughts are nudging you to reconnect to the field of intention. What's the source of your thoughts about your purpose? Why do you want to feel purposeful? Why is a sense of purpose considered the highest attribute of a fully functioning person? The source of thought is an infinite reservoir of energy and intelligence. In a sense, *thoughts about your purpose are really your purpose trying to reconnect to you.* This infinite reservoir of loving, kind, creative, abundant energy grew out of the originating intelligence, and is stimulating you to express this universal mind in your own unique way.

Reread the two display quotes at the beginning of this chapter. Buddha refers to *the truth,* and Sivananda suggests that *God realization* is our true purpose. This entire book is dedicated to connecting to the power of intention and letting go of ego, which tries to make us believe that we're separate from our divine originating Source and tries to separate us from realizing ultimate truth. This ultimate truth is the source of your thoughts.

That inner beingness knows why you're here, but your ego prods you to chase after money, prestige, popularity, and sensory pleasures and *miss the purpose of living.* You may feel sated and gain a reputation, but inside there's that gnawing feeling typified by the old Peggy Lee song "Is That All There Is?" Focusing on the demands of the ego leaves you feeling unfulfilled. Deep within you, at the level of your being, is what you were intended to become, to accomplish, and to be. In that inner placeless place, you're connected to the power of intention. It will find you. Make a conscious effort to contact it and listen. Practice being what you are at the source of your soul. Go to your soul level, where intention and purpose fit together so perfectly that you achieve the epiphany of simply *knowing this is it.*

**Your silent inner knowing.** Esteemed psychologist and philosopher William James once wrote: "In the dim background of our mind we know meanwhile what we ought to be doing. . . . But somehow we cannot start. . . . Every moment we expect the spell to break . . . but it does continue, pulse after pulse, and we float with it. . . ."

In my experience as a therapist, and as a speaker talking with thousands of people about their lives, I've come to the same conclusion. Somewhere, buried deep within each of us, is a call to purpose. It's not always rational, not always clearly delineated, and sometimes even seemingly absurd, but the knowing is there.

There's a silent something within that *intends* you to express yourself. That something is your soul telling you to listen and connect through love, kindness, and receptivity to the power of intention. That silent inner knowing will never leave you alone. You may try to ignore it and pretend it doesn't exist, but in honest, alone moments of contemplative communion with yourself, you sense the emptiness waiting for you to fill it with your music. It wants you to take the risks involved, and to ignore your ego and the egos of others who tell you that an easier, safer, or more secure path is best for you.

Ironically, it's not necessarily about performing a specific task or being in a certain occupation or living in a specific location. It's about sharing yourself in a creative, loving way using the skills and interests that are inherently part of you. It can involve any activity: dancing, writing, healing, gardening, cooking, parenting, teaching, composing, singing, surfing—whatever. There's no limit to this list. But everything on the list can be done to *pump up your ego* or *to serve others*. Satisfying your ego ultimately means being unfulfilled and questioning your purpose. This is because your Source is egoless, and you're attempting to connect to your Source, where your purpose originates. If the activities on the list are in service to others, you feel the bliss of purposeful living, while paradoxically attracting more of what you'd like to have in your life.

My daughter Skye is an example of what I'm presenting here. Skye has known since she could first speak that she wanted to sing. It was almost as if she showed up here in the world with a destiny to sing for others. Over the years, she's sung at my public appearances, first as a 4-year-old, and then at every age up until now, her 21st year. She has also sung on my public television specials, and the reaction to her singing has always been gratifying.

As a student immersed in a music program at a major university, Skye studied from academic and theoretical perspectives. One day in her junior year, we had a discussion that centered on her purpose and the silent inner knowing she's always had. "Would you be upset," she inquired, "if I left college? I just don't feel like I can do what I know I have to do by sitting in a classroom and studying music theory any longer. I just want to write my own music and sing. It's the only thing I think about, but I don't want to disappoint you and Mom."

How could I, who tells his readers not to die with their music still in them, tell my 21-year-old daughter to stay in college because that's the right way, and it's what I did? I encouraged her to listen to the silent knowing that I've seen evidence of since she was a toddler, and to follow her heart. As Gandhi once said: "To give one's heart is to give all." This is where God exists in Skye . . . and in you.

I did ask Skye to make a supreme effort to live her purpose by serving those who will listen to her music rather than focusing her attention on being famous or making money. "Let the universe handle those details," I reminded her. "You write and sing because you have to express what is in that beautiful heart of yours." I then asked her to think from the end, and act as if all that she wanted to create for herself was already here, waiting for her to connect to it.

Recently she voiced dismay at not having her own CD out in the world, and she was acting with thoughts of *not having a CD out in the world*. Consequently, no CD and lots of frustration. I strongly encouraged her to start thinking from the end by seeing the studio being available, the musicians ready to collaborate with her, the CD as a finished product, and her intention as a reality. I gave her a deadline to have a CD completed that I could make available at my lectures. I told her that she could sing to these audiences, as she has done sporadically in her life as well as on my public-television pledge shows.

Her thinking from the end materialized everything she needed, and the universal Spirit began to work with her unbending intent. She found the studio, the musicians she needed magically appeared, and she was able to have the CD produced.

Skye worked tirelessly day after day singing her own favorites, as well as several that I wanted her to sing at my appearances, including "Amazing Grace," "The Prayer of St. Francis," and her own composition, "Lavender Fields," which she sings from deep pride and passion. And lo and behold, today her CD, *This Skye Has*

*No Limits,* is now out and is being offered to the public whenever she sings at my lectures.

Skye's presence on the stage with me brings so much joy and love to the presentation because she's as closely aligned with those seven faces of intention as any human being I've ever known. So it's no secret why this book is also dedicated to her—one of my angels of spiritual intention.

### Inspiration and Purpose

When you're inspired by a great purpose, everything will begin to work for you. Inspiration comes from moving back in-spirit and connecting to the seven faces of intention. When you feel inspired, what appeared to be risky becomes a path you feel compelled to follow. The risks are gone because you're following your bliss, which is the truth within you. This is really love working in harmony with your intention. Essentially, if you don't feel love, you don't feel the truth, and your truth is all wrapped up in your connection to Spirit. This is why inspiration is such an important part of the fulfillment of your intention to live a life on purpose.

When I left the work that no longer inspired me, every single detail that I'd worried about was almost magically taken care of for me. I'd spent several months working for a large corporation where I was offered a salary three times higher than I'd been paid as a teacher, but I wasn't in-spirit. That prodding inner knowing said, *Do what you're here to do,* and teaching/counseling became my manifested daily purpose.

When I left a professorship at a major university for writing and public speaking, it wasn't a risk; it was something I had to do because I knew that I couldn't feel happy with myself if I didn't follow my heart. The universe handled the details, because I was feeling love for what I was doing, and consequently, I was living my truth. By teaching love, that very same love guided me to my purpose, and the financial remuneration flowed to me with that same energy of love. I couldn't see how it would work out, but I followed an inner knowing and never regretted it!

You may think it's too risky to give up a salary, a pension, job security, or familiar surroundings because of a dim night-light in your mind that draws you to see why it's turned on. I suggest that there are no risks at all if you pay attention to that light, which is your knowing. Combine your strong knowing with the faith that Spirit will provide, and you acknowledge the power of intention at work. Your trust in this inner knowing is all you need. I call it *faith*— not faith in an external god to provide you with a purpose, but faith in the call you're hearing from the center of your being. You are a divine, infinite creation making the choice to be on purpose and to be connected to the power of intention. It all revolves around your being harmoniously connected to your Source. Faith eliminates the risk when you choose to trust that inner knowing about your purpose and become a channel for the power of intention.

### Making Intention Your Reality

Below are ten ways to practice fulfilling your intention to live your life on purpose from this day forward:

**Step 1: Affirm that in an intelligent system, no one shows up by accident, including you.** The universal mind of intention is responsible for all of creation. It knows what it's doing. You came from that mind, and you're infinitely connected to it. There's meaning in your existence, and you have the capacity to live from a perspective of purpose. The first step is to know that you're here on purpose. This is not the same as knowing what you're supposed to do. Throughout your life, what you do will change and shift. In fact, the changes can occur from hour to hour in each day of your life. Your purpose is not about what you do, it's about your beingness, that place within you from which your thoughts emerge. This is why you're called a *human being* rather than a *human doing!* Affirm in your own words, both in writing and in your thoughts, that you are here on purpose, and intend to live from this awareness at all times.

**Step 2: Seize every opportunity, no matter how small, to give your life away in service.** Get your ego out of your intention to live a life of purpose. Whatever it is that you want to do in life, make the primary motivation for your effort something or somebody other than your desire for gratification or reward.

The irony here is that your personal rewards will multiply when you're focused on giving rather than receiving. Fall in love with what you're doing, and let that love come from the deep, inner-dwelling place of Spirit. Then sell the feeling of love, enthusiasm, and joy generated by your efforts. If your purpose is felt by being Supermom, then put your energy and inner drive into those children. If it's felt writing poetry or straightening teeth, then get your ego out of the way and do what you love doing. Do it from the perspective of making a difference for someone or for some cause, and let the universe handle the details of your personal rewards. Live your purpose doing what you do with pure love—then you'll co-create with the power of the universal mind of intention, which is ultimately responsible for all of creation.

**Step 3: Align your purpose with the field of intention.** This is the most important thing you can do to fulfill your intentions. Being aligned with the universal field means having faith that your Creator knows why you're here, even if you don't. It means surrendering the little mind to the big mind, and remembering that your purpose will be revealed in the same way that *you* were revealed. Purpose, too, is birthed from creativeness, kindness, love, and receptivity to an endlessly abundant world. Keep this connection pure, and you'll be guided in all of your actions.

It's not fatalism to say that *if it's meant to be, then it can't be stopped.* This is having faith in the power of intention, which originated with you and is within you. When you're aligned with your originating Source, then this same Source will aid you in creating the life of your choice. Then, what happens feels exactly as if it was meant to be. And that's because it is! You always have a choice in how to align yourself. If you stay focused on making demands on the universe, you'll feel as if demands are being placed on you in your life. Stay focused on lovingly asking, *How may I use my innate talents and desire to serve?* and the universe will respond with the identical energy by asking you, *How may I serve you?*

**Step 4: Ignore what anyone else tells you about your purpose.** Regardless of what anyone might say to you, the truth about your feeling purposeful is that only *you* can know it, and if you don't feel it in that inner place where a burning desire resides, it isn't your purpose. Your relatives and friends may attempt to convince you that what *they* feel is *your* destiny. They may see talents that they think will help you make a great living, or they may want you to follow in their footsteps because they think you'll be happy doing what they've done for a lifetime. Your skill at mathematics or decorating or fixing electronic equipment might indicate a high aptitude for a given pursuit—but in the end, if you don't feel it, nothing can make it resonate with you.

Your purpose is between you and your Source, and the closer you get to what that field of intention looks and acts like, the more you'll know that you're being purposefully guided. You might have zero measurable aptitudes and skills in a given area, yet feel inwardly drawn to doing it. Forget the aptitude-test results, forget the absence of skills or know-how, and most important, ignore the opinions of others and *listen to your heart.*

**Step 5: Remember that the all-creating field of intention will work on your behalf.** Albert Einstein is credited with saying that the most important decision we ever make is whether we believe we live in a friendly universe or a hostile universe. It's imperative that you know that the all-creating field of intention is friendly and will work with you as long as you see it that way. The universe supports life; it flows freely to all and is endlessly abundant. Why choose to look at it in any other way? All of the problems we face are created by our belief that we're separate from God and each other, leading us to be in a state of conflict. This state of conflict creates a counterforce causing millions of humans to be confused about their purpose. Know that the universe is always willing to work with you on your behalf, and that you're always in a friendly, rather than hostile, world.

**Step 6: Study and replicate the lives of people who've known their purpose.** Whom do you admire the most? I urge you to read biographies of these people and explore how they lived and what motivated them to stay on purpose when obstacles surfaced. I've always been fascinated by Saul of Tarsus (later called St. Paul), whose letters and teachings became the source of a major portion of the New Testament. Taylor Caldwell wrote a definitive fictional account of St. Paul's life called *Great Lion of God,* which inspired me enormously. I was also deeply touched by the purposeful manner in which St. Francis of Assisi lived his life as exemplified in the novel *St. Francis,* by Nikos Kazantzakis. I make it a point to use my free time to read about people who are models for purposeful living, and I encourage you to do the same.

**Step 7: Act as if you're living the life you were intended to live, even if you feel confused about this thing called purpose.** Invite into your life every day whatever it might be that makes you feel closer to God and brings you a sense of joy. View the events you consider obstacles as perfect opportunities to test your resolve and find your purpose. Treat everything from a broken fingernail to an illness to the loss of a job to a geographical move as an opportunity to get away from your familiar routine and move to purpose. By acting as if you're on purpose and treating the hurdles as friendly reminders to trust in what you feel deeply within you, you'll be fulfilling your own intention to be a purposeful person.

**Step 8: Meditate to stay on purpose.** Use the technique of Japa, which I mentioned earlier, and focus your inner attention on asking your Source to guide you in fulfilling your destiny. This letter from Matthew McQuaid describes the exciting results of meditating to stay on purpose:

*Dear Dr. Dyer,*

*My wife, Michelle, is pregnant by a miracle—a miracle manifest from Spirit using all of your suggestions. For five years, Michelle and I were challenged by infertility. You name it, we tried it. None of the expensive and sophisticated treatments worked. The doctors had given up. Our own faith was tested over and over with each failed treatment cycle. Our doctor managed to freeze embryos from earlier cycles of treatment. Throughout the years, over 50 embryos had been transferred to Michelle's uterus. The odds of a frozen embryo successfully initiating pregnancy in our case were close to zero. As you know, zero is a word not found in the spiritual vocabulary. One precious frozen embryo, surviving minus 250 degrees for six months, has taken up a new home in Michelle's womb. She is now in her second trimester.*

*Okay, "So what," you might say. "I get letters like this every day." However, this letter contains proof of God. A tiny drop of protoplasm, as you have so eloquently written on many occasions, a physical mass of cells alive with the future pull of a human being, turned on in a laboratory, then turned off in a freezer. All molecular motion and biochemical processes halted, suspended. Yet, the essence of being was there prior to freezing. Where did the spiritual essence go while frozen? The cells were turned on, then turned off, but the spiritual essence had to prevail despite the physical state of the cells. The frequency of vibration of the frozen cells was low, but the vibrational frequency of its spirit must be beyond measure. The essence of the being had to reside outside of the physical plane or mass of cells. It couldn't go anywhere except to the realm of spirit, where it waited. It waited to thaw and manifest into a being it always has been. I hope you find this story as compelling as I do, as nothing less than a miracle. An example of spirit in body, rather then a body with a spirit.*

*And now for the million-dollar question. Could this one embryo survive such hostile frozen conditions and still manifest because I practiced the Japa mediation? Just because I opened my mouth and said, "Aaaahhh"? I had a knowing, no question about it. Japa meditation and surrendering to infinite patience are daily practices. During my quiet moments, I can smell this baby. Michelle will thank me for my conviction and faith during the dark times. I praise your work for guiding me. Thank you. Now, nothing is impossible for me. When I compare what I have manifested now in Michelle's womb to anything else I might desire, the process is without effort. After you truly surrender, everything you could ever want just seems to show up, right on schedule. The next amazing manifestation will be to help other infertile couples realize their dreams. Somehow, I will help those who feel there is no hope.*

*Sincerely,*
*Matthew McQuaid*

Many people have written to me about their success with staying on purpose through the practice of Japa meditation. I'm deeply touched by the power of intention when I read about people who use Japa to help achieve a pregnancy, which they felt was their divine mission. I particularly like Matthew's decision to use this experience to help other infertile couples.

**Step 9: Keep your thoughts and feelings in harmony with your actions.** The surest way to realize your purpose is to eliminate any conflict or dissonance that exists between what you're thinking and feeling and how you're living your days. If you're in disharmony, you activate ego-dominated attitudes of fear of failure, or disappointing others, which distance you from your purpose. Your actions need to be in harmony with your thoughts. Trust in those thoughts that harmonize, and be willing to act upon them. Refuse to see yourself as inauthentic or cowardly, because those thoughts will keep you from acting on what you know you were meant to be. Take daily steps to bring your thoughts and feeling of your grand heroic mission into harmony with both your daily activities and of course, with that ever-present field of intention. Being in harmony with God's will is the highest state of purpose you can attain.

**Step 10: Stay in a state of gratitude.** Be thankful for even being able to contemplate your purpose. Be thankful for the wonderful gift of being able to serve humanity, your planet, and your God. Be thankful for the seeming roadblocks to your purpose. Remember, as Gandhi reminded us: "Divine guidance often comes when the horizon is the blackest." Look at the entire kaleidoscope of your life, including all of the people who have crossed your path. See all of the jobs, successes, apparent failures, possessions, losses, wins—everything—from a perspective of gratitude. You're here for a reason; this is the key to feeling purposeful. Be grateful for the opportunity to live your life purposefully in tune with the will of the Source of all. That's a lot to be grateful for.

\* \* \*

It seems to me that searching for our purpose is like searching for happiness. There's no way to happiness; happiness *is* the way. And so it is with living your life on purpose. It's not something you find; it's how you live your life serving others, and bringing purpose to everything you do. That's precisely how you fulfill the intention that is the title of this chapter. When you're living your life from purpose, you're dwelling in love. When you're not dwelling in love, you're off purpose. This is true for individuals, institutions, business, and our governments as well. When a government gouges its citizens with excessive fees for any service, they're off purpose. When a government pursues violence as a means for resolving disputes, it's off purpose regardless of how it justifies its actions. When businesses overcharge, cheat, or manipulate in the name of profit-making, they're off purpose. When religions permit prejudice and hatred or mistreat their parishioners, they're off purpose. And it's true for you as well.

165

Your goal in accessing the power of intention is to return to your Source and live from that awareness, replicating the very actions of intention itself. That Source is love. Therefore, the quickest method for understanding and living your purpose is to ask yourself if you're thinking in loving ways. Do your thoughts flow from a Source of love within you? Are you acting on those loving thoughts? If the answers are yes and yes, then you're on purpose. I can say no more!

~ * ~ * ~

# CHAPTER NINE

# IT IS MY INTENTION TO: BE AUTHENTIC AND PEACEFUL WITH ALL OF MY RELATIVES

*"Your friends are God's way of apologizing for your relatives!"*
— Dr. Wayne W. Dyer

Somehow we allow the expectations and demands of our family members to be the source of so much unhappiness and stress, when what we want is to be authentically ourselves and at peace with our relatives. The conflict seems too often to be a choice between being authentic, which means no peace with certain relatives, or having peace at the price of being inauthentic. Making the connection to the power of intention in regard to being around your relatives may sound like an oxymoron to you, but it isn't. Being peaceful and authentic can define your relationship with your relatives. First, though, you may have to assess your relationship with the closest relative of all—you. How others treat you, you'll discover, has a lot to do with how you treat yourself and thereby teach others to treat you.

### You Get Treated the Way You Teach Others to Treat You

In an earlier chapter, I urged you to notice your inner dialogue. One of the greatest obstacles to connecting to intention are your thoughts of what others want or expect from you. The more you focus on how upsetting it is that your family doesn't understand or appreciate you, the more you'll attract their misunderstanding or lack of appreciation. Why? Because what you think about expands, even when you think about what you find unnerving, and even when you think about what you don't want in your life.

If you're attracted to this intention, then you most likely already know which family members push your buttons. If you feel as though you're unduly influenced by their expectations, or you're a victim of their way of being, you'll need to begin by shifting from thoughts of what *they're doing* to what *you're thinking*. Say to yourself, *I've taught all these people how to treat me as a result of my willingness to make their opinions of me more important than my own.* You might want to follow this up by emphatically stating, *And it's my intention to teach them how I desire to be treated from now on!* Taking responsibility for how your family members treat you helps you create the kind of relationship with all of your relatives that matches up with the universal mind of intention.

You may be asking yourself how you can possibly be responsible for teaching people how to treat you. The answer is, in large part, your willingness to not only put up with listening to those familial pressures—some of which are long-term traditions running back countless generations—but also with allowing yourself to disconnect from your divine Source and indulge in low-energy emotions as humiliation, blame, despair, regret, anxiety, and even hatred. You and only you taught your kin how to treat you through your willingness to accept critical comments from that well-meaning, but often interfering and bothersome, tribe.

**Your family relationships are in your mind.** When you close your eyes, your family disappears. Where did they go? Nowhere, but doing this exercise helps you recognize that your relatives exist as thoughts in your mind. And recall that God is the mind with which you're thinking. Are you using your mind to process your relatives in harmony with intention? Or have you abandoned or separated yourself in your mind by viewing your family in ways contrary to the universal Source of intention? These people who are related to you are all ideas in your mind. Whatever power they have, you've given to them. What you feel is wrong or missing in these relationships is an indication that something is amiss within you, because broadly speaking, anything you see in anyone else is a reflection of some aspect of you—otherwise you wouldn't be bothered by it, because you wouldn't notice it in the first place.

In order to change the nature of family relationships, you'll have to change your mind about them and do a somersault into the inconceivable. And what is the inconceivable? It's the idea that *you are the source of the anguish* in your relationships, rather than the individual whom you've pegged as the most outrageous, the most despicable, or the most infuriating. Over the years, all of these individuals have been treating you exactly as you've allowed them to with your reactions and behaviors. All of them exist as ideas in your mind that have separated you from your source of intention. This can miraculously change when you choose to be at peace with everyone in your life—most particularly, your relatives.

If the focus of your inner dialogue about your family members is on what they're doing that's wrong, then that's precisely how your relationship with them will be experienced. If your inner speech centers on what's annoying about them, that's what you'll notice. As much as you're inclined to blame them for your annoyance, it's yours, and it's coming from your thoughts. If you make a decision to put your inner attention, your life energy, on something quite different, your relationship will change. In your thoughts, where your family relationships exist, you'll no longer be annoyed, angry, hurt, or depressed. If in your mind you're thinking, *My intention is to be authentic and peaceful with this relative,* then that's what you'll experience—even if that relative continues to be exactly the way he or she has always been.

**Changing your mind is changing your relationships.** Being authentic and peaceful with your relatives is only a thought away. You can learn to change your thoughts by intending to create authentic and peaceful feelings within yourself. No one is capable of making you upset without your consent, and you've given your consent too frequently in the past. When you begin practicing the intention to be authentic and peaceful, you withdraw your consent to be in the lower energy. You connect to peace itself, and decide to bring peace to your relatives, thereby immediately gaining the power to change the energy of family gatherings.

Think of the relatives whom you've blamed for your feelings of anxiety, annoyance, or depression. You've focused on what you disliked about them or how they treated you, and your relationship has always had an uncomfortable edge to it. Now imagine yourself doing this from a new point of view: Rather than reacting to their low energy of hostility or bragging with a hostile or bragging reaction of your own—lowering the energy field for everyone involved— you instead bring your intention of peace to the interaction. Remember, it's the higher energy of love that can dissolve all the lower energies. When you react to low energy with more of the same, you're not being peacefully authentic or connected to the power of intention. In the low energy, you say or think sentences like, *I disrespect you for being so disrespectful. I'm angry at you for being so angry at the world. I dislike you because you're such a braggart.*

By putting your attention on what you intend to manifest rather than on the same low energy that you encounter, you make a decision to connect to intention and bring the attributes of your universal Source to the presence of that low energy. Try to imagine Jesus of Nazareth saying to his followers, "I despise those people who despise me, and I want nothing to do with them." Or, "It makes me so angry when people judge me. How can I have peace when there are so many hostile people around me?" This is absurd, because Jesus represents the highest loving energy in the universe.

That's precisely what he brought to the presence of doubting, hostile people, and his presence alone would raise the energy of those around him. Now I know you're not the Christ, but you do have some great spiritual lessons to learn from our greatest teachers. If you have the intention to bring peace to a situation and you're living at the level of intention, you'll leave that situation feeling peaceful. I learned this lesson years ago with my in-laws.

Prior to my waking up to the power of intention, family visits were events that caused me consternation because of the attitudes and behavior of some of my wife's relatives. I'd prepare for a Sunday-afternoon family visit by getting anxious and upset over what I anticipated to be a fretful, lousy experience. And I seldom disappointed myself! I'd focus my thoughts on what I didn't like, and I defined my relationship with my in-laws in this manner. Gradually, as I began to understand the power of intention and left my ego behind, I substituted kindness, receptivity, love, and even beauty for my former annoyed and angry assessments.

Before family get-togethers, I'd remind myself that I am what I choose to be in any and all circumstances, and I chose to be authentically peaceful and have a good time. In response to something that used to annoy me, I'd now say to my mother-in-law in a loving way, "I never thought of it that way; tell me more." In response to what I previously considered to be an ignorant comment, I'd respond, "That's an interesting point of view; when did you first learn about this?" In other words, I was bringing my own intention to be in a state of peace to this encounter, and was refusing to judge them.

The most amazing thing began to happen: I started looking forward to having these family members at our home. I began to see them as much more enlightened than I'd previously thought. I actually enjoyed our times together, and every time something came up that I'd found annoying in the past, I'd overlook it and respond with love and kindness instead. At an earlier stage of my life, expressions of racial or religious prejudice were a stimulus for my anger and resentment. Now I'd quietly respond with a kind and gentle reminder of my own opinions, and simply let the matter drop.

Over the years, I found that not only did the racial and religious slurs diminish to zero, but I noticed that my in-laws were expressing tolerance—and even love—toward minorities, as well as those who practiced religions different from their own.

Although my primary intention was to stay in a state of peace, I discovered that by not joining in the low energies of my in-laws, not only was the entire family more peaceful, but many enjoyable and even enlightening conversations developed. I had as much to learn from my in-laws as I had to teach. Even when I disagreed vehemently with a judgment directed at me, if I remembered my intention to have a peaceful relationship with them, I was able to do just that. No longer did I think about what I disliked, what was missing, or what always had been. I stayed focused on making these gatherings fun, loving, and most important to me, peaceful.

\* \* \*

Let's take a look at the steps you need to take in order to make the stated intention of this chapter and all succeeding ones a reality.

**Step 1: Identify your intention verbally and in writing, and develop a deep yearning for it.** When you create a great longing for the experience of a peaceful family, everything will begin to happen to fulfill this yearning spontaneously and naturally. Rather than praying to a saint or God for a miracle, pray for the miracle of the inner awakening, which will never leave you. The awakening of this inner light, once experienced, will become your constant companion, regardless of who you are with or where you are. The dynamic force is within you. This force is felt as great joy running through your body. Ultimately, your thinking will become sublime, and your inner and outer world will become one. Yearn for this awakening to the inner light, and long for your intention to manifest.

**Step 2: Intend for all of your relatives what you intend for yourself.** When anyone criticizes, judges, acts angry, expresses hatred, or finds fault with you, they're not at peace with themselves. Want this peace for them even more than you desire it for yourself. By having this kind of intention for them, you take the focus off of you. This doesn't require words or actions on your part. Simply picture the people in your family with whom you're not at peace, and feel the peace you crave for them. Your inner speech will change, and you'll begin to experience the peaceful authenticity of both your beings.

**Step 3: Be the peace you're seeking from others.** If peace is missing in your relationships with your family, it means that you have a place within you that's occupied by non-peace. It may be filled with anxiety, fear, anger, depression, guilt, or any low-energy emotions. Rather than attempting to rid yourself of these feelings all at once, treat them the same as you do your relatives. Say a friendly *Hello* to the non-peace, and let it be. You're sending a peaceful feeling to the non-peace feeling. The lower energies you're experiencing will be strengthened by your peaceful *Hi* or *Hello,* and eventually vanish as the divine grows within you. The way to this peace is through any form of quiet and meditation that works for you. Even if it's only a two-minute respite during which time you're silent, concentrate on the name of the divine, or repeat that sound of "Aaahh" as an inner mantra.

**Step 4: Match up with the seven faces of intention.** If you've forgotten what the universal mind of intention looks like, it's creative, kind, loving, beautiful, always expanding, endlessly abundant, and receptive to all of life. Play the match game that I introduced earlier in this book, and very quietly and with unbending intent bring the face of the universal Source of all to the presence of everyone whom you feel brings you down or interferes with your peace. This kind of spiritual energy will be transformative—not only for you, but also for your relatives. Your intention to be in peaceful relationships is now taking form—first in your mind, then in your heart—and ultimately, it will materialize.

**Step 5: Review all the obstacles that have been erected on your path to familial peace.** Listen to any inner dialogue that focuses on your resentment of others' expectations for you. Remind yourself that when you think about what you resent, you act upon what you think about, while simultaneously attracting more of it to you. Examine your energy level for your tendency to react to lower energies with more of the same, and give your ego a reminder that you'll no longer opt to be offended, or need to be right in these relationships.

**Step 6: Act *as if*.** Begin the process of acting *as if what you intend to manifest is already true*. See everyone in your family in the love and light that is their true identity. When someone asked Baba Muktananda, a great saint in India, "Baba, what do you see when you look at me?" Baba said, "I see the light in you." The person replied, "How can that be, Baba? I am an angry person. I am terrible. You must see all that." Baba said, "No, I see light." (This story is told by Swami Chidvilasananda Gurumayi in *Kindle My Heart*.)

So, see the light in those *others,* and treat them *as if* that is all you see.

**Step 7: Detach from the outcome.** Don't let your authentic and peaceful attitude depend on your relatives' behavior. As long as you remain connected to intention and radiate outward the high energy, you've achieved your peace. It's not your place or your purpose to make everyone else in your family think, feel, and believe as you do. The likelihood is great that you'll see dramatic changes in your relatives as you teach them with your own persona how you intend to be treated. But if they don't change, and if they continue their nonpeaceful ways, let go of your need to see them transformed. It all works in divine order, and the saying *Letting go and letting God* is a helpful reminder for you. By letting go, you guarantee your own peace, and you dramatically increase the odds of helping others to do the same.

**Step 8: Affirm:** *I attract only peace into my life.* I remind myself of this affirmation many times on a given day, particularly with my children and other more distant relatives. I also practice this in grocery stores, when greeting flight attendants, when visiting the post office, and while driving my automobile. I say this silently to myself as an absolute truth with unbending intent on my part, and it works for me all the time. People respond to me with smiles, acknowledgments, friendly gestures, and kind greetings all day long. I also remind myself of the cogent observation from *A Course in Miracles* when I feel other than peaceful in any given moment with my family: *I can choose peace, rather than this.*

**Step 9: Hold no grudges, and practice forgiveness.** The key to having peace in all your family relationships is forgiveness. Your relatives are simply doing what they've been taught to do over a lifetime, and the lifetimes of many of their ancestors. Shower them with understanding and forgiveness from your heart.

This passage from *A Course in Miracles* offers so much in the fulfillment of this intention:

> *Do you want peace? Forgiveness offers it.*
> *Do you want happiness, a quiet mind,*
> *a certainty of purpose,*
> *and a sense of worth and beauty*
> *that transcends the world?*
> *Do you want a quietness that cannot be disturbed,*
> *a gentleness that can never be hurt,*
> *a deep abiding comfort,*
> *and a rest so perfect it can never be upset?*
> *All this forgiveness offers you.*

**Step 10: Be in a state of gratitude.** Rather than being in a state of non-peace concerning any family members, say a prayer of gratitude for their presence in your life and all that they have come to teach you.

\* \* \*

These are the ten steps that you can practice each day. As you work toward the absolute knowing that this intention will manifest for you, remind yourself on a daily basis that you can never remedy a bad relationship by condemning it.

$\backsim$ * $\backsim$ * $\backsim$

# CHAPTER TEN

# *IT IS MY INTENTION TO:*
# FEEL SUCCESSFUL AND
# ATTRACT ABUNDANCE
# INTO MY LIFE

*"God is able to provide you with every blessing in abundance."*

— St. Paul

*"When you realize there is nothing lacking, the whole world belongs to you."*

— Lao Tzu

One of my secrets for feeling successful and attracting bountiful abundance into my life has been an internal axiom that I use virtually every day of my life. It goes like this: *Change the way you look at things, and the things you look at change.* This has always worked for me.

The truth of this little maxim is actually found in the field of quantum physics, which, according to some, is a subject that's not only stranger than you think it is, it's stranger than you can *think*. It turns out that at the tiniest subatomic level, the actual act of observing a particle changes the particle. The way we observe these infinitely small building blocks of life is a determining factor in what they ultimately become. If we extend this metaphor to larger and larger particles and begin to see ourselves as particles in a larger body called humanity or even larger—life itself—then it's not such a huge stretch to imagine that the *way* we observe the world we live in affects that world. It's been said repeatedly in a number of different ways: *As is the microcosm, so is the macrocosm.* As you read this chapter, remember this little journey into quantum physics as a metaphor for your life.

This being the case, your intention to feel successful and experience prosperity and abundance depends on what view you have of yourself, the universe, and most important, the field of intention from which success and abundance will come. My little maxim about changing the way you look at things is an extremely powerful tool that will allow you to bring the intention of this chapter into your life. First examine how *you* look at things, and then how the spirit of intention does the same.

### How Do You Look at Life?

The way you look at life is essentially a barometer of your expectations, based on what you've been taught you're worthy of and capable of achieving. These expectations are largely imposed by external influences such as family, community, and institutions, but they're also influenced by that ever-present inner companion: your ego. These sources of your expectations are largely based on the beliefs of limitation, scarcity, and pessimism about what's possible for you. If these beliefs are the basis for how you look at life, then this perception of the world is what you expect for yourself. Attracting abundance, prosperity, and success from these limiting viewpoints is an impossibility.

In my heart, I know that attracting abundance and feeling successful is possible, because, as I touched on earlier, *I* had an early life of enormous scarcity. I lived in foster homes, away from my mother and my absentee, alcoholic, often-imprisoned father. I know that these truths can work for you, because if they've worked for any one of us, they can work for *all* of us, since we all share the same abundant divine force and emanated from the same field of intention.

Take an inventory of how you look at the world, asking yourself how much of your life energy is focused on explaining away potentially optimistic viewpoints by preferring to see the inequities and inconsistencies in the abundance-for-all philosophy. Can you change the way you look at things? Can you see potential for prosperity where you've always seen scarcity? Can you change *what is* by simply changing the way you see it? I say a resounding *yes* to these questions. And the way to work at changing the way you see things is to take a hard look at something you may not have previously considered.

### How Does the Universal All-Creating Field of Intention Look at Life?

The field of intention, which is responsible for all creation, is constantly giving—in fact, it knows no bounds to its giving. It just keeps on converting pure formless spirit into a myriad of material forms. Furthermore, this field of intention *gives* in unlimited supplies. There is no such concept as shortage or scarcity when it comes to the originating Source. So we're looking at two major conceptualizations when we think of the universal mind's natural abundance. The first is that it's perpetually giving, and the second is that it offers an infinite supply.

The power of intention is perpetually giving and infinite, so it seems obvious that you'll need to adopt these same two attributes if you're to fulfill your own personal intention to live successfully and attract abundance into your life. What should your message back to the universe be if you want to *be* abundance and success rather than strive for it? Your Source is abundant and you are your Source; therefore, you must communicate this back. Since your Source is always serving and giving, and you are your Source, then you must be always in a state of serving and giving. *This Source can only work with you when you are in harmony with it!*

179

A message to the field of intention that says *Please send me more money* is interpreted as your seeing yourself in a state of scarcity, but this Source has no concept of scarcity. It doesn't even know what not having enough money means. Thus, its response back to you will be: *Here's a state of needing more money because that's how you think, and I'm the mind with which you think, so here's more of what you don't want and don't have.* Your ego-dominated response will be: *My desires are being denied!* But the real truth is, the universal Source knows only abundance and giving, and will respond with money flowing to you if your intention is: *I have enough money, and I allow what I already have enough of to flow to me.*

Now this may appear to be mumbo jumbo and nothing more than twisting words around, but I assure you that it's exactly how the universal mind of intention operates. The more you get back into gear with that which intended you here, the more you'll see that unlimited abundance showing up. Get rid of the concept of shortages, because God hasn't got a clue about such things. The creative Source reacts to your belief in shortages with a fulfillment of your belief.

Now, think back to my opening observation in this chapter: *Change the way you look at things, and the things you look at change.* I can guarantee you that the universal mind only flows in harmony with its own nature, which is providing endless abundance. Stay in harmony with this nature, and all of your desires *have* to manifest for you—the universe knows no other way to be. If you tell the universal mind what you want, it will respond by leaving you in a state of wanting, never arriving and always needing more. If, however, you feel that what you intend to manifest has already manifested, you're unified with your intention. Never allowing a moment of doubt or listening to naysayers, you'll be in the presence of that all-creating field of intention.

You can't come from shortage, you can't come from scarcity, and you can't come from wanting. You must come from the same attributes as that which allows everything. This is a key word, *allowing*. Let's take a look at how *allowing* is so often ignored in attempts to manifest feeling successful and attracting abundance.

## The Art of Allowing

The universal mind of Creation is in a constant state of supplying. It never shuts down, it takes no vacations, there are no days off, and it's perpetually giving forth. Everything and everyone, without exception, emanates from this universal mind we're calling intention. So if everything comes from this infinite field of invisible energy, why is it that some are able to partake of it, while others seem so separated from it? If it's always giving forth in an endless stream of abundance, somehow there must be resistance to allowing it to come into your life if you're experiencing shortages or scarcity in any way.

Allowing this all-giving Source into your life means becoming aware of the resistance that you may be placing in the way of the abundance that's always being supplied. If the universe is based on energy and attraction, this means that everything is vibrating to particular frequencies. When the frequency with which you're vibrating is in contradiction with the frequency of the universal supply, you create a resistance, thereby inhibiting that flow of abundance into your life space. Your individual vibrations are the key to understanding the art of allowing. The nonharmonious vibrations are largely in the form of your thoughts and feelings. Thoughts that emphasize what you don't believe you deserve set up a contradiction in energy. That contradiction puts a stop to a hooking up of identical energies, and you've created a field of disallowing. Remember, it's always about being in harmony with your Source. Your thoughts can either emerge from a beingness that's in rapport with intention or in contradiction with it.

Keep in mind that you're a part of the universal mind, so if you see yourself in a harmonious way with the seven faces of intention, the universal mind can only work harmoniously with you. For example, suppose that you want a better job with a higher salary. Imagine yourself as already having it, knowing in your thoughts that you're entitled to it, with no doubts about the job showing up because you can see it within. The universal mind now has no choice in the matter, since you're a part of that all-creating mind and there's no vibrational contradiction. So what can go wrong here? The art of allowing gets hampered by your habit of disallowing.

There's a long history of countless thoughts that have formed a field of resistance to allowing the free flow of abundance. This habit of disallowing grew from the belief system that you've cultivated over the years and that you rely on. Furthermore, you've allowed the resistance of others to enter this picture, and you surround yourself with the need for their approval in these matters. You solicit their resistant opinions, read newspaper accounts of all those who've failed to manifest the jobs of their choice, examine government reports about the poor job prospects and the declining economy, watch the television reports belaboring the sorry state of affairs in the world, and your resistance becomes even more convincingly entrenched. You've aligned yourself with the proponents of disallowing.

What you need to do is look at this belief system and all of the factors that continue to support it and say, *It's too big of a job to change the entire thing. Instead, I'm going to start changing the thoughts that activate disallowing right here, right now.* It doesn't matter what you thought before, or for how long, or how many pressures you're under to maintain your resistance. Instead, stop activating disallowing thoughts today, one thought at a time. You can do so by stating, *I feel successful, I intend to feel the abundance that is here, now.* Repeat these words, or create your arrangement of words, which continually inundate your thoughts during your waking hours, with a new belief of being successful and abundant. When you've activated these thoughts enough times, they'll become your habitual way of thinking, and you will have taken the steps to eliminating your resistance to allowing.

Those thoughts will then become what you say in silent, prayer-like messages to yourself: *I am success; I am abundance.* When you're success itself, when you're abundance itself, you're in harmony with the all-creating Source, and it will do the only thing it knows how to do. It will be endlessly giving and forthcoming with that which has no resistance to it—namely, you. You're no longer vibrating to scarcity; your every individual vibrational utterance is in concert with what you summon from your Source. You and your Source are one in your thoughts. You've chosen to identify thoughts of resistance and have simultaneously decided to stay out of your own way.

As you practice allowing and living the faith of least resistance, success is no longer something you choose; it's something that you are. Abundance no longer eludes you. You are it, and it is you. It flows unimpeded beyond your resistance. Herein lies another clue to the free flow of abundance: *You must avoid becoming attached to and hoarding what shows up in your life.*

### Abundance, Detachment, and Your Feelings

While it's crucial for you to have a firm vibrational match-up with the all-creating abundance of intention, it's just as crucial for you to know that you can't hang on to and own any of the abundance that will be coming your way. This is because the you that would like to hang on to and become attached to your success and your wealth is not really you, it's that troublesome ego of yours. You're not what you have and what you do; you're an infinite, divine being disguised as a successful person who has accumulated a certain amount of stuff. *The stuff is not you.* This is why you must avoid being attached to it in any way.

Detachment comes from knowing that your true essence is a piece of the infinitely divine field of intention. It's then that you become aware of the importance of your feelings. Feeling good becomes much more valuable than polishing your jewelry. Feeling abundant surpasses the money in your bank account and transcends what others may think of you. Genuinely feeling abundant and successful is possible when you detach yourself from the things you desire and allow them to flow to you, and just as important, *through* you. Anything that inhibits the flow of energy stops the creating process of intention right where the obstacle is erected.

Attachment is one such roadblock. When you hang on to that which arrives, rather than allowing it to move through you, you stop

183

the flow. You hoard it or decide to own it, and the flow is disrupted. You must keep it circulating, always knowing that nothing can stop it from coming into your life except any resistance you place in its way. Your feelings and emotions are sensational barometers for detecting resistance and evaluating your ability to experience success and abundance.

**Paying attention to your feelings.** Your emotions are the inner experiences that tell you how much of the divine energy you're summoning for the manifestation of your desires. Feelings can be measuring tools that gauge how you're doing in the manifestation process. An exceptionally positive emotional response indicates that you're summoning the divine energy of intention and allowing that energy to flow to you in a nonresistant manner. Feelings of passion, pure bliss, reverence, unmitigated optimism, unquestioned trust, and even illumination indicate that your desire to manifest success and abundance, for example, have an extremely strong pulling power from the universal Source to you. You must learn to pay close attention to the presence of these feelings. These emotions aren't just facets of your life that are empty of energy— they're agents that are in charge of how you clean and purify the connecting link to intention. These emotions tell you precisely how much of the life force you're summoning, and how much *pulling power* you have going for you at that moment.

Abundance is the natural state of the nature of intention. Your desire for abundance must flow free of resistance. Any discrepancy between your individual intention or desire, and your belief concerning the possibility of summoning it into your life, creates resistance. If you want it but believe it's impossible or that you're unworthy, or that you don't have the skills or perseverance, then you've created resistance and you're disallowing. Your feelings indicate how well you're attracting the energy necessary for the fulfillment of your desire. Strong feelings of despair, anxiety, blame, hate, fear, shame, and anger are sending you the message that you want success and abundance but you don't believe it's possible for you. These negative feelings are your clues to get busy and balance your desires with those of the universal mind of intention, which is the only source of that which you desire. Negative emotions tell you that your pulling power from intention is weak or even non-existent. Positive emotions tell you that you're connecting to and accessing the power of intention.

Concerning abundance, one of the most effective ways to increase that pulling power from intention to you is to take the focus off of dollars and place it on creating abundant friendship, security, happiness, health, and high energy. It's here that you'll begin to feel those higher emotions, which let you know that you're back in the match game with the all-creating Source. As you focus on having abundant happiness, health, security, and friendship, the means for acquiring all of this will be flowing toward you. Money is only one of those means, and the faster your vibrational energy around abundance radiates, the more money will show up in significant amounts. These positive feelings as indicators of your pulling power for success and abundance will put you into an active mode for co-creating your intentions.

I'm not suggesting that you just wait for everything to fall into place. I'm suggesting that by declaring, *I intend to feel successful and attract prosperity*, your emotional energy will shift and you'll act as if what you desire were already true. Your actions will be in harmony with the faces of intention, and you'll be provided with what you *are*, rather than attempting to be provided with what's missing.

At this point in my life, I refuse to participate in any desire unless I have total, nonresistant knowing that it can and will manifest into my life from the all-creating Source of intention. My desires for personal indicators of abundance have all manifested by practicing what I write here, and in the ten-step program that follows. I've been able to *allow* by removing resistance and connecting to my originating, all-creating Source. I trust in it completely. Over the years, I've learned that when I've desired something seemingly impossible, I felt poorly as a result. I then figured that I should desire less, but all that did was make me even further removed from the unlimited power of intention. I was still in vibratory *disharmony* with the abundance of the universe.

I began to understand that my being in harmony with abundance didn't cause others to be poor or hungry. On the contrary, the abundance I created gave me the chance to help eradicate poverty and hunger. But the significant awareness was realizing that I had less of a chance to help others when I was in the lower frequencies. I learned that I had to get myself into vibratory harmony with my Source. One of my reasons for writing this chapter in this fashion is to convince you that you don't have to ask for less, or feel guilty about wanting abundance—it's there for you and everyone in an unlimited supply.

\* \* \*

I live and breathe what I'm writing here about success and abundance. I know beyond any doubt (resistance) that you can attract abundance and feel successful by absorbing the messages of this chapter, which, like the abundance you seek, have flowed from that universal Source through me and onto these pages. There's no discrepancy between my desire to write it all out here and my willingness to allow it to flow unimpeded to you. How do I know this? My emotion in this moment is ineffable bliss, serenity, and reverence. I trust this emotional state, which indicates to me that I've been utilizing a very strong pulling power to create these messages from the all-creating Spirit of intention. I'm in vibratory harmony and abundance, and feelings of success are my intentions herewith manifested. Try it on anything you'd like to see flowing abundantly into your life.

### Making Your Intention Your Reality

Below is a ten-step program for implementing the intention of this chapter—that is, to feel successful and attract abundance into your life:

**Step 1: See the world as an abundant, providing, friendly place.** Again, when you change the way you look at things, the things you look at change. When you see the world as abundant and friendly, your intentions are genuine possibilities. They will, in fact, become a certainty, because your world will be experienced from the higher frequencies. In this first step, you're receptive to a world that provides rather than restricts. You'll see a world that wants you to be successful and abundant, rather than one that conspires against you.

**Step 2: Affirm:** *I attract success and abundance into my life because that is who I am.* This puts you into vibratory harmony with your Source. You goal is to eliminate any distance between what you desire and that from which you pull it into your life. Abundance and success aren't out there waiting to show up for you. You are already it, and the Source can only provide you with what it is, and, consequently, what you are already.

**Step 3: Stay in an attitude of allowing.** *Resistance* is disharmony between your desire for abundance and your beliefs about your ability or unworthiness. *Allowing* means a perfect alignment. An attitude of allowing means that you ignore efforts by others to dissuade you. It also means that you don't rely on your previous ego-oriented beliefs about abundance being a part of or not a part of your life. In an attitude of *allowing*, all resistance in the form of thoughts of negativity or doubt are replaced with simply knowing that you and your Source are one and the same. Picture the abundance you desire freely flowing directly to you. Refuse to do anything or have any thought that compromises your alignment with Source.

**Step 4: Use your present moments to activate thoughts that are in harmony with the seven faces of intention.** The key phrase here is *present moments.* Notice right now, in this moment, if you're thinking that it's hopeless at this stage of your life to change the thoughts that comprise your belief system. Do you defeat

187

yourself with thoughts of having had such a long life practicing affirmations of scarcity and creating resistance to your success and abundance that you don't have enough time left to counterbalance the thoughts that comprise your past belief system?

Make the choice to let go of that lifetime of beliefs, and begin activating thoughts right now that allow you to feel good. Say *I want to feel good* whenever anyone tries to convince you that your desires are futile. Say *I want to feel good* when you're tempted to return to low-energy thoughts of disharmony with intention. Eventually your present moments will activate thoughts that make you feel good, and this is an indicator that you're reconnecting to intention. Wanting to feel good is synonymous with wanting to feel *God*. Remember, "God is good, and all that God created was good."

**Step 5: Initiate actions that support your feelings of abundance and success.** Here, the key word is *actions*. I've been calling this *acting as if* or *thinking from the end* and acting that way. Put your body into a gear that pushes you toward abundance and feeling successful. Act on those passionate emotions as if the abundance and success you seek is already here. Speak to strangers with passion in your voice. Answer the telephone in an inspired way. Do a job interview from the place of confidence and joy. Read the books that mysteriously show up, and pay close attention to conversations that seem to indicate you're being called to something new.

**Step 6: Remember that your prosperity and success will benefit others, and that no one lacks abundance because you've opted for it.** Once again, the supply is unlimited. The more you partake of the universal generosity, the more you'll have to share with others. In writing this book, wonderful abundance has flowed into my life in many ways. But even more significantly, book editors and graphic designers, the truck drivers who deliver the book, the auto workers who build the trucks, the farmers who feed the auto workers, the bookstore clerks . . . all receive abundance because I've followed my bliss and have written this book.

**Step 7: Monitor your emotions as a guidance system for your connection to the universal mind of intention.** Strong emotions such as passion and bliss are indications that you're connected to Spirit, or *inspired,* if you will. When you're inspired, you activate dormant forces, and the abundance you seek in any form comes streaming into your life. When you're experiencing low-energy emotions of rage, anger, hatred, anxiety, despair, and the like, that's a clue that while your desires may be strong, they're completely out of sync with the field of intention. Remind yourself in these moments that you want to feel good, and see if you can activate a thought that *supports* your feeling good.

**Step 8: Become as generous to the world with your abundance as the field of intention is to you.** Don't stop the flow of abundant energy by hoarding or owning what you receive. Keep it moving. Use your prosperity in the service of others, and for causes greater than your ego. The more you practice detachment, the more you'll stay in vibratory harmony with the all-giving Source of everything.

**Step 9: Devote the necessary time to meditate on the Spirit within as the source of your success and abundance.** There's no substitute for the practice of meditation. This is particularly relevant with abundance. You must have an understanding that your *consciousness of the presence* is your supply. By repeating the sound that is in the name of God as a mantra, you're using a technique for manifesting as ancient as recorded history. I am particularly drawn to the form of meditation I've mentioned previously, called Japa. I know it works.

**Step 10: Develop an attitude of gratitude for all that manifests into your life.** Be thankful and filled with awe and appreciation, even if what you desire hasn't arrived yet. Even the darkest days of your life are to be looked on with gratitude. Everything coming from Source is on purpose. Be thankful while empowering your reconnection to that from which you and everything else originated.

* * *

The energy that creates worlds and universes is within you. It works through attraction and energy. Everything vibrates; everything has a vibratory frequency. As St. Paul said, "God is able to provide you with every blessing in abundance." Tune in to God's frequency, and you will know it beyond any and all doubt!

〜 ✱ 〜 ✱ 〜

# CHAPTER ELEVEN

# *IT IS MY INTENTION TO:*
# LIVE A STRESS-FREE,
# TRANQUIL LIFE

*"Anxiety is the mark of spiritual insecurity."*
— Thomas Merton

*"So long as we believe in our heart of hearts that our
capacity is limited and we grow anxious and unhappy, we
are lacking in faith. One who truly trusts in God has no
right to be anxious about anything."*
— Paramahansa Yogananda

Fulfilling this intention to live a stress-free and tranquil life
is a way of manifesting your grandest destiny. It seems to me
that what our Source had in mind when we were intended
here is for us to have happy and joyous experiences of life on Earth.
When you're in a state of joy and happiness, you've returned to the
pure, creative, blissful, nonjudgmental joy that intention truly is.
Your natural state—the state from which you were created—is that
feeling of well-being. This chapter is concerned with having you
return to, and access, this natural state.

You were created from a Source that is peaceful and joyful.
When you're in that state of exuberant joy, you're at peace with
everything. This is what intended you here and what you're determined

to match up with in your thoughts, feelings, and actions. In a state of joy, you feel fulfilled and inspired in all facets of your life. In short, gaining freedom from anxiety and stress is a pathway to rejoicing with the field of intention. The moments of your life, which you spend being happy and joyful and allowing yourself to be fully alive and on purpose, are the times when you're aligned with the all-creating universal mind of intention.

There's nothing natural about living a life filled with stress and anxiety, having feelings of despair and depression, and needing pills to tranquilize yourself. Agitated thoughts that produce high blood pressure, a nervous stomach, persistent feelings of discomfort, an inability to relax or sleep, and frequent displays of displeasure and outrage are violating your natural state. Believe it or not, you have the power to create the naturally stress-free and tranquil life you desire. You can utilize this power to attract frustration or joy, anxiety or peace. When you're in harmony with the seven faces of intention, you can access and pull from the Source of all in order to fulfill your intention of being stress free and tranquil.

So if it's natural to have feelings of well-being, why is it that we seem to experience so much "unwellness" and tension? The answer to this question provides you with the key that leads to the peaceful life you desire.

### Stress Is a Desire of the Ego

That pesky ego is at work when you're experiencing stress or anxiety. Perhaps your ego-self feels more effective dealing and coping with stress because you feel you're actually doing something in the world. Perhaps it's habit, custom, or believing that this is the right way to be. Only you can analyze the *why.* But the fact is that stress is familiar, and tranquility is unfamiliar, so ego desires stress.

But there's no actual stress or anxiety in the world; it's your thoughts that create these false beliefs. You can't package stress, touch it, or see it. There are only people engaged in stressful thinking. When we think stressfully, we create reactions in the body, valuable messages or signals requesting our attention. These messages might reveal themselves as nausea, elevated blood pressure, stomach tension, indigestion, ulcers, headaches, increased heart rate, difficulty breathing, and a zillion other feelings—from minor discomfort to serious, life-threatening illness.

We speak of stress as if it were present in the world as something that attacks us. We say things like *I'm having an anxiety attack* as if anxiety is a combatant. But the stress in your body is rarely the result of external forces or entities attacking you; it's the result of the weakened connecting link to intention caused by your belief that ego is who you are. You are peace and joy, but you've allowed your ego to dominate your life. Here's a short list of stress-inducing thoughts that originate in your ego self:

- *It's more important to be right than to be happy.*

- *Winning is the only thing. When you lose, you should be stressed.*

- *Your reputation is more important than your relationship with your Source.*

- *Success is measured in dollars and accumulations rather than in feeling happy and content.*

- *Being superior to others is more important than being kind to others.*

The following lighthearted way to stop taking yourself so seriously is from a book by Rosamund and Benjamin Zander (he's the conductor of the Boston Philharmonic) titled *The Art of Possibility*. It illustrates in a delightful way how we allow ego to create many of the problems we encounter that we label stress and anxiety.

> Two prime ministers are sitting in a room discussing affairs of state. Suddenly a man bursts in, apoplectic with fury, shouting and stamping and banging his fist on the desk. The resident

prime minister admonishes him: "Peter," he says, "kindly remember Rule Number 6," whereupon Peter is instantly restored to complete calm, apologizes, and withdraws. The politicians return to their conversation, only to be interrupted yet again twenty minutes later by an hysterical woman gesticulating wildly, her hair flying. Again the intruder is greeted with the words: "Marie, please remember Rule Number 6." Complete calm descends once more, and she too withdraws with a bow and an apology. When the scene is repeated for a third time, the visiting prime minister addresses his colleague: "My dear friend, I've seen many things in my life, but never anything as remarkable as this. Would you be willing to share with me the secret of Rule Number 6?" "Very simple," replies the resident prime minister. "Rule Number 6 is 'Don't take yourself so goddamn seriously.'" "Ah," says his visitor, "that is a fine rule." After a moment of pondering, he inquires, "And what, may I ask, are the other rules?"

"There aren't any."

As you encounter stress, pressure, or anxiety in your life, remember "Rule Number 6" at the moment you realize you're thinking stressful thoughts. By noticing and discontinuing the inner dialogue that's causing stress, you may be able to prevent its physical symptoms. What are the inner thoughts that produce stress? *I'm more important than those around me. My expectations aren't being met. I shouldn't have to wait, I'm too important. I'm the customer here, and I demand attention. No one else has these pressures.* All of the above, along with a potentially endless inventory of "Rule Number 6" thoughts are from the ego's bag of tricks.

You aren't your work, your accomplishments, your possessions, your home, your family . . . your anything. You're an aspect of the power of intention, dressed in a physical human body intended to experience and enjoy life on Earth. This is the intention that you want to bring to the presence of stress.

**Bringing intention to the presence of stress.** In any given day, you have hundreds of opportunities to implement "Rule Number 6" by bringing the power of intention into the moment and eliminating the potential for stress. Here are a few examples of how I've employed this strategy. In each of these examples, I activated an inner thought that was in vibrational harmony with the universal field of intention, and I fulfilled my personal intention to be tranquil. These examples occurred in a three-hour period of a normal day. I offer them to you to remind you that stress and anxiety are choices that we make to process events, rather than entities that are out there waiting to invade our lives.

— I'm dropping off a prescription at the drugstore and the person ahead of me is talking to the pharmacist, asking a series of seemingly inane questions—all of which, my stress-producing ego tells me, are intended to deliberately delay and annoy me. My inner dialogue might go like this: *I'm being victimized! There's always someone just ahead of me in line who fumbles with money, can't find what's needed to prove participation in some kind of an insurance plan, and has to ask silly questions designed to keep me from dropping off a prescription.*

I use those thoughts as a signal to change my inner dialogue to: *Wayne, stop taking yourself so goddamn seriously!* I immediately make the shift from pissed to blissed. I take the focus off of myself, and at the same time, I remove resistance to my intention to live a stress-free and tranquil life. I now see this person as an angel who's ahead of me in line to assist me in reconnecting to intention. I stop judging, and actually see beauty in the slow, deliberate gestures. I'm kind in my mind toward this *angel*. I've moved from hostility to love in my thoughts, and my emotions have shifted from discomfort to ease. Stress is absolutely impossible in the moment.

— My 17-year-old daughter tells me about her disagreement with a school official who's taken action against some of her friends, an act she considers totally unfair. It's Saturday morning and nothing can be done until Monday. The choice? Spend two days in misery replaying the details of her story, and have a weekend of inner stress, or remind her how to activate thoughts that will make her feel good. I ask her to describe her feelings. She responds that she's "angry, upset, and hurt." I ask her to think about "Rule Number 6" and see if there's any other thought she could activate.

195

She laughs at me, telling me how crazy I am. "But," she admits, "it really doesn't make any sense to be upset for the entire weekend, and I'm going to stop thinking thoughts that make me feel bad."

"On Monday we'll do what we can to rectify the situation," I tell her. "But for now—and now is all you have—put 'Rule Number 6' into play and rejoin the field of intention where stress, anxiety, and pressure don't exist."

To fulfill the intention of this chapter, *to live a stress-free and tranquil life,* you must become conscious of the need to activate thought responses that match your intention. These new responses will become habitual, and replace your old habit of responding in stress-producing ways. When you examine segments of stress-producing incidents, you always have a choice: *Do I stay with thoughts that produce stress within me, or do I work to activate thoughts that make stress impossible?* Here's another easy tool that will help you replace the habit of choosing anxiety and stress.

**Five magic words: I want to feel good!** In an earlier chapter, I described how your emotions are a guidance system informing you of whether or not you're creating resistance to your intentions. Feeling bad lets you know that you're not connected to the power of intention. Your intention here is to be tranquil and stress free. When you feel good, you're connected to your intentions, regardless of what goes on around you or what others expect you to feel. If there's a war going on, you still have the option to feel good. If the economy goes further into the toilet, you have the option to feel good. In the event of any catastrophe, you can still feel good. Feeling good isn't an indication that you're callous, indifferent, or cruel—it's a choice you make. Say it out loud: *I want to feel good!* Then convert it to: *I intend to feel good.* Feel the stress, and then send it the love and respect of the seven faces of intention. The seven faces smile and say hello to what you label as feeling bad. It's that feeling that wants to feel good. You must be to your feelings as your Source is to you, in order to counteract the desires of your ego.

Many events will transpire in which your conditioned response is to feel bad. Be aware of these outer incidents, and say the five magic words: *I want to feel good.* In that precise moment, ask yourself if feeling bad is going to make the situation any better. You'll discover that the only thing that feeling bad accomplishes in response to outer situations is to plummet you into anxiety, despair, depression, and of course, stress. Instead, ask yourself in that moment what thought you can have that will make you feel good. When you discover that it's responding with kindness and love to the bad feeling (which is quite different from wallowing in it), you'll begin experiencing a shift in your emotional state. Now you're in vibrational harmony with your Source, since the power of intention knows only peace, kindness, and love.

This newly activated thought, which allows you to feel good, may only last a few moments, and you might go back to your previous way of processing unpleasant events. Also treat that old way of processing with respect, love, and understanding, but remember that it's your ego-self trying to protect you from its perception of danger. Any stress signal is a way of alerting you to say the five magic words *I want to feel good.* Stress wants your attention! By saying the five magic words and extending love to your bad feelings, you'll have begun the process of fulfilling your stated intention of being tranquil and stress free. Now you can practice activating these thoughts in the toughest of moments, and before long, you'll be living the message offered to all of us in the book of Job: "You will decide on a matter and it will be established for you, and light will shine on your ways"[Job 22:28]. The word *light* in this biblical reference means that you'll have the assistance of the divine mind of intention once you decide on a matter that is consistent with that light.

I assure you that your decision to feel good is a way of connecting to Spirit. It isn't an indifferent response to events. By feeling good, you become an instrument of peace, and it's through this channel that you eradicate problems. By feeling bad, you stay in the energy field that creates resistance to positive change; and experience a stressful, anxious state as a by-product. The things you call problems will perpetually present themselves to you. They'll never go away. Resolve one . . . and another will surface!

**You'll never get it done.** In Chapter 6, I reminded you of your infinite nature. Since you're an infinite spiritual being disguised as a temporary human being, it's essential to understand that in infinity there's no beginning and no ending. Therefore, your desires, goals, hopes, and dreams will never be finished—ever! As soon as you manifest one of your dreams, another will most assuredly pop up. The nature of the universal force of intention from which you emigrated into a temporary material being is always creating and giving forth. Furthermore, it's in a continuous state of expansion. Your desires to manifest into your life are a part of this infinite nature. Even if you desire to have no desires, that's a desire!

I urge you to simply accept the fact that you'll never get it all done, and begin to live more fully in the only moment that you have—now! The secret to removing the harmful effects of feeling stressed and under pressure is to be in the now. Announce out loud to yourself and all who are willing to listen to you: *I'm an incomplete being. I'll always be incomplete because I can never get it done. Therefore, I choose to feel good while I'm in the moment, attracting into my life the manifestations of my desires. I am complete in my incompleteness!* I can assure you that a follow-up on this statement will eradicate all anxiety and stress, which is precisely the intention of this chapter. All resistance melts away when you can feel complete in your incompleteness.

### The Path of Least Resistance

You live in a universe that has limitless potential for joy built into the creation process. Your Source, which we call the universal mind of intention, adores you beyond anything you can possibly imagine. When you adore yourself in the same proportion, you're matched up with the field of intention, and you've opted for the path of no resistance. As long as you have even a pinch of an ego, you'll retain some resistance, so I urge you to take the path in which resistance is minimized.

The shape and quantity of your thoughts determine the amount of resistance. Thoughts that generate bad feelings are resistant thoughts. Any thought that puts a barrier between what you would like to have and your ability to attract it into your life is resistance. Your intention is to live a tranquil life, free of stress and anxiety. You know that stress doesn't exist in the world, and that there are only people thinking stressful thoughts. Stressful thoughts all by themselves are a form of resistance. You don't want stressful, resistant thoughts to be your habitual way of reacting to your world. By practicing thoughts of minimal resistance, you'll train yourself to make this your natural way of reacting, and eventually you'll become the tranquil person you desire to be, a stress-free person free of the "dis-ease" that stress brings to the body. Stressful thoughts *all by themselves* are the resistance that you construct that impedes your connection to the power of intention.

We're in a world that advertises and promotes reasons to be anxious. You've been taught that feeling good in a world where so much suffering exists is an immoral stance to take. You've been convinced that choosing to feel good in bad economic times, in times of war, in times of uncertainty or death, or in the face of any catastrophe anywhere in the world is crass and inappropriate. Since these conditions will always be in the world someplace, you believe you can't have joy and still be a good person. But it may not have occurred to you that in a universe based on energy and attraction, thoughts that evoke feeling bad originate in the same energy Source that attracts more of the same into your life. These are resistant thoughts.

Here are some examples of sentences on the **path of resistance,** which are then changed to sentences on the *path of least resistance.*

**I feel uneasy about the state of the economy; I've already lost so much money.**
*I live in an abundant universe; I choose to think about what I have and I will be fine. The universe will provide.*

**I have so many things to do that I can never get caught up.**
*I'm at peace in this moment. I'll only think about the one thing I'm doing. I will have peaceful thoughts.*

**I can never get ahead in this job.**
*I choose to appreciate what I'm doing right now, and I'll attract an even greater opportunity.*

**My health is a huge concern. I worry about getting old and becoming dependent and sick.**
*I'm healthy, and I think healthy. I live in a universe that attracts healing, and I refuse to anticipate sickness.*

**My family members are causing me to feel anxious and fearful.**
*I choose thoughts that make me feel good, and this will help me uplift those family members in need.*

**I don't deserve to feel good when so many people are suffering.**
*I didn't come into a world where everyone is going to have the same identical experiences. I'll feel good, and by being uplifted, I'll help eradicate some of the suffering.*

**I can't be happy when the person I really care about loves another and has abandoned me.**
*Feeling bad won't change this scenario. I trust that love will return to my life if I'm in harmony with the loving Source. I choose to feel good right now and focus on what I have, rather than what's missing.*

All stressful thoughts represent a form of resistance you wish to eradicate. Change those thoughts by monitoring your feelings and opting for joy rather than anxiety, and you'll access the power of intention.

### Making Your Intention Your Reality

Below is my ten-step program for creating a stress-free, tranquil life:

**Step 1: Remember that your natural state is joy.** You are a product of joy and love; it's natural for you to experience these feelings. You've come to believe that feeling bad, anxious, or even depressed is natural, particularly when people and events around you are in low-energy modes. Remind yourself as frequently as necessary: *I come from peace and joy. I must stay in harmony with that from which I came in order to fulfill my dreams and desires. I choose to stay in my natural state. Anytime I'm anxious, stressed out, depressed, or fearful, I've abandoned my natural state.*

**Step 2: Your thoughts, not the world, cause your stress.** Your thoughts activate stressful reactions in your body. Stressful thoughts create resistance to the joy, happiness, and abundance that you desire to create in your life. These thoughts include: *I can't, I'm too overworked, I worry, I'm afraid, I'm unworthy, It will never happen, I'm not smart enough, I'm too old (young),* and so on. These thoughts are like a program to resist being tranquil and stress free, and they keep you from manifesting your desires.

**Step 3: You can change your thoughts of stress in any given moment, and eliminate the anxiety for the next few moments, or even hours and days.** By making a conscious decision to distract yourself from worry, you've inaugurated the process of stress reduction, while simultaneously reconnecting to the field of all-creating intention. It's from this place of peace and tranquility that you become a co-creator with God. You can't be connected to your Source and be stressed at the same time—this is mutually exclusive. Your Source doesn't create from a position of anxiety, nor does it need to swallow antidepressants. You've left behind your capacity to manifest your desires when you don't choose in the moment to eliminate a stressful thought.

**Step 4: Monitor your stressful thoughts by checking on your emotional state right in the moment.** Ask yourself the key question: *Do I feel good right now?* If the answer is no, then repeat those five magic words: *I want to feel good,* then shift to: *I intend to feel good.* Monitor your emotions, and detect how much stress- and anxiety-producing thinking you're engaging in. This monitoring process keeps you apprised of whether you're on the path of least resistance or going in the other direction.

**Step 5: Make a conscious choice to select a thought that will activate good feelings.** I urge you to choose your thought based exclusively on how it makes you feel, rather than on how popular it is or how well advertised. Ask yourself: *Does this new thought make me feel good? No? Well, how about this thought? Not really? Here's another.* Ultimately you'll come up with one that you agree makes you feel good, if only temporarily. Your choice might be the thought of a beautiful sunset, the expression on the face of someone you love, or a thrilling experience. It's only important that it resonate within you emotionally and physically as a good feeling.

In the moment of experiencing an anxious or stressful thought, change to the thought you chose, which makes you feel good. Plug it in. Think it and feel it in your body if you can. This new thought that makes you feel good will be of appreciation rather than depreciation. It will be of love, beauty, receptivity to happiness, or in other words, it will align perfectly with those seven faces of intention I've been harping about since the opening pages of this book.

**Step 6: Spend some time observing babies, and vow to emulate their joy.** You didn't come forth into this world to suffer, to be anxious, fearful, stressful, or depressed. You came from the God-consciousness of joy. Just watch little babies. They've done nothing to be so happy about. They don't work; they poop in their pants; and they have no goals other than to expand, grow, and explore this amazing world. They love everyone, they're completely entertained by a plastic bottle or goofy faces, and they're in a constant state of love—yet they have no teeth, no hair, and they're pudgy and flatulent. How could they possibly be so joyful and easily pleased? Because they're still in harmony with the Source that intended them here; they have no resistance to being joyful. Be like that baby you once were in terms of being joyful. You don't need a reason to be happy . . . your desire to be so is sufficient.

**Step 7: Keep "Rule Number 6" in mind.** This means to suspend the demands of your ego, which keep you separated from intention. When you have a choice to be right or to be kind, pick kind, and push the ego's demand out of the way. Kindness is what you emanated from, and by practicing it, rather than being right, you eliminate the possibility of stress in your moment of kindness. When you find yourself being impatient with anyone, simply say to yourself: "Rule Number 6," and you'll immediately laugh at the piddly little ego that wants you to be first, faster, number one, and to be treated better than the other guy.

**Step 8: Accept the guidance of your Source of intention.** You will only come to know the Father by being as He is. You'll only be able to access the guidance of this field of intention by being as *it* is. Stress, anxiety, and depression will be lifted from you with the assistance of that same force that created you. If it can create worlds out of nothing, and you out of nothing, surely the removal of some stress isn't such a big task. I believe that God's desire for you is that you not only know joy, but that you become it.

**Step 9: Practice being in silence and meditation.** Nothing relieves stress, depression, anxiety, and all forms of low-energy emotions like silence and meditation. Here, you make conscious contact with your Source and cleanse your connecting link to intention. Take time every day for moments of quiet contemplation, and make meditation a part of your stress-reducing ritual.

**Step 10: Stay in a state of gratitude and awe.** Go on a rampage of appreciation for all that you have, all that you are, and all that you observe. Gratitude is the tenth step in every ten-step program for manifesting your intentions, because it's the surest way to stop the incessant inner dialogue that leads you away from the joy and perfection of the Source. You can't feel stressed and appreciative at the same time.

\* \* \*

I conclude this chapter on your intention to lead a tranquil life with a poem by the famous Bengali poet of Calcutta, Rabindranath Tagore, one of my favorite spiritual teachers:

*I slept and dreamt that life was joy*
*I awoke and saw that life was service*
*I acted and behold service was joy*

It can all be joy in your inner world. Sleep and dream of joy, and remember above all else: *You feel good not because the world is right, but your world is right because you feel good.*

∽ \* ∽ \* ∽

# CHAPTER TWELVE

## *It Is My Intention to:* Attract Ideal People and Divine Relationships

*"The moment one definitely commits oneself, then Providence moves too. All sorts of things occur to help one that would never otherwise have occurred . . . unforeseen incidents, meetings, and material assistance, which no man could have dreamed would have come his way."*

— Johann Wolfgang von Goethe

I f you saw the 1989 movie *Field of Dreams,* you probably came away remembering the concept that if you pursue a dream, you will succeed (or, "If you build it, they will come"). I thought of this as I began writing this chapter because I'm suggesting that if you commit yourself to matching up with the field of intention, everyone you desire or need to fulfill your personal intention will appear. How can that be? In the quote above, Goethe, one of the most brilliantly gifted scholars and achievers in the history of humanity, gives you the answer. The moment you definitely commit yourself to being a part of the power of intention, "then Providence moves too," and unforeseen assistance comes your way.

The right people will arrive to assist you in every aspect of your life: The people who will support you in your career are there; the people who will help you create your perfect home show up; the people who will arrange the finances for whatever you desire are available; the driver you need to get you to the airport is waiting for you; the designer you've admired wants to work with you; the dentist you need in an emergency when you're on vacation just happens to be there; and your spiritual soul mate finds you.

The list is endless, because we're all in relationship to each other, we all emanate from the same Source, and we all share the same divine energy of intention. There's no place that this universal mind is not; therefore, you share it with everyone you attract into your life.

You'll have to let go of any resistance to your ability to attract the right people, or you won't recognize them when they show up in your everyday life. Resistance may be difficult to recognize at first, because it's such a familiar form of your thoughts, your emotions, and your energy levels. If you believe that you're powerless to attract the right people, then you've attracted powerlessness to your experience. If you're attached to the idea of being stuck with the wrong people or no people at all, then your energy isn't aligned with the power of intention, and resistance reigns. The field of intention has no choice but to send you more of what you're desiring. Once again, make a somersault into the inconceivable, where you have faith and trust in the universal mind of intention, and allow the right people to arrive in your life space right on schedule.

### Removing Resistance by Allowing

Your intention is absolutely clear here. You want to attract the people who are intended to be part of your life, and you want to have a happy, fulfilling, spiritual relationship. The universal all-creating field is already cooperating with your intention. These very people are obviously already here, otherwise you'd want something that hasn't been created. Not only are the right people here, but you also share the same divine Source of all life with them, since everyone emanates from that Source. In some invisible way, you're already connected spiritually to those *perfect-for-you* people. So why can't you see them, touch them, or hold them, and why aren't they there when you need them?

What you need in the way of the *right people* showing up will appear for you only when you're ready and willing to receive them. They've always been there. They're there right now. They'll always be there. The questions you need to ask yourself are: *Am I ready? Am I willing?* and *How much am I willing to have it?* If your responses to these questions are a readiness and willingness to experience your desires, then you'll begin seeing people not only as a body with a soul, but as a spiritual being clothed in a unique body. You'll see the infinite souls that we all are: *infinite*, meaning always and everywhere; and *everywhere*, meaning with you right now if that's your spiritual desire.

**Giving forth what you want to attract.** Once you've formed a picture in your mind of the person or people that you intend to show up in your immediate life space, and you know how you want them to treat you and what they'll be like, you must be what it is that you're seeking. This is a universe of attraction and energy. You can't have a desire to attract a mate who's confident, generous, nonjudgmental, and gentle, and expect that desire to be manifested if you're thinking and acting in nonconfident, selfish, judgmental, or arrogant ways—which is why most people don't attract the right people at the right time.

Almost 30 years ago, I wanted to attract a publisher into my life for my book, *Your Erroneous Zones.* This publisher would have to be understanding, since I was an unknown writer at the time, and would have to be a risk taker, willing to let go of any doubts about me.

My literary agent arranged a meeting with an executive editor, whom I'll refer to as George, at a large New York publishing house. As I sat down to talk with him, it was obvious to me that he was personally distraught. I asked him what was troubling him, and we proceeded to spend the next three to four hours talking about a devastating personal matter that had just transpired the night before. George's wife had told him that she was going to seek a divorce, and he felt as though he'd been blindsided by this news. I let go of my own desires to talk about getting my book published and became what it was that I was seeking: an understanding, confident, risk-taking person. By being that very thing and detaching from my ego-dominated desires, I was able to help George out that afternoon, which I've never forgotten.

I left George's office that day without even discussing my book proposal. When I told my literary agent this story, he was convinced that I'd blown my one opportunity with a major publishing house by not making a strong pitch for my book. The following day, George called my agent, telling him, "I really don't even know what Dyer's book proposal entails, but I want that man as one of our authors."

At the time, I didn't realize what was happening. Now, with a quarter century of living in this world of spiritual inquiry, I see it quite clearly. The right people will show up precisely when you need them and when you're able to match up. You must be that which you desire. When you *are* what you desire, you attract it by radiating it outward. You have this ability to match up with the power of intention and fulfill your intention to attract ideal people and divine relationships.

### Attracting Spiritual Partnerships

There's no point whatsoever in an unloving man or woman bemoaning their inability to find a partner. They're doomed to endless frustration because they don't recognize the perfect match when it appears. That loving person could be right there, right now, and their resistance doesn't allow them to see it. The unloving person continues to blame bad luck or a series of external factors for their not having a loving relationship.

Love can only be attracted by and returned by love. The best advice I can give for attracting and maintaining spiritual partnerships, as I've been emphasizing in this chapter, is to *be what it is that you're seeking.* Most relationships that fail to sustain themselves are based on one or both of the partners feeling as if their freedom has been compromised in some way. Spiritual partnerships, on the other hand, are never about making another person feel inferior or ignored in any way. The term *spiritual partnership* simply means that the energy that holds the two of you together is in close harmony with the Source energy of intention.

This means that an *allowing* philosophy flows through the partnership, and you need never fear that your freedom to fulfill your own inner knowing about your purpose is questioned. It's as if each person has whispered silently to the other, *You are Source energy in a physical body, and the better you feel, the more of this loving, kind, beautiful, receptive, abundant, expanding, and creative energy is flowing through you. I respect this Source energy, and I share it with you as well. When either of us feels downhearted, there's less of this energy of intention flowing. We must always remember that nothing is disallowed by the universal mind. Whatever is not allowing us to be happy is being disallowed by us. I'm committed to staying in this energy field of intention and watching myself whenever I slip. It's that very Source that brought us together, and I'll work to stay in harmony with it.* This kind of inner commitment is what Goethe was speaking about in that opening quotation. It allows providence to move and helps things to occur, "which no man could have dreamed would come his way."

**You're already connected to those you want in your life— so act like it.** Mystically speaking, there's no difference between you and another person. A weird concept, perhaps, but nevertheless valid. This explains why you can't hurt another person without hurting yourself, nor can you help another person without helping yourself. You share the same Source energy with everyone, and consequently, you must begin to think and act in a way that reflects your awareness of this principle. When you feel the need to have the right person show up, begin to change your inner dialogue to reflect this awareness. Rather than saying, *I wish this person would show up because I need to get out of this rut,* activate a thought that reflects your connection, such as: *I know the right person will be arriving in divine order at precisely the perfect time.*

Now you'll act on this inner thought. You'll be *thinking from the end,* and anticipating this arrival. Your anticipation will make you alert. You've revised your energy level to the same receptivity as the power of intention that intends everything and everyone here. When you reach these higher energy levels, you access higher information. Your intuition clicks in, and you can feel the presence of the person or people you want in your life. Now you act on that intuition with a deep sense of knowing that you're on track. You're acting in accordance with this new awareness. You become a co-creator. New insight becomes activated within you as well. You're looking at the face of the Creator, and you see yourself co-creating. You know whom to call, where to look, when to trust, and what to do. You're being guided to connect to that which you're bringing forth.

If a friendship or partnership requires the submission of your higher original nature and dignity, it's simply wrong. When you truly know what it is to love, as you're loved by your Source, you won't experience the kind of pain you did in the past when your love was unnoticed or rejected. It will, instead, be similar to how a friend described her experience of choosing to leave a relationship: "My heart was broken, but it felt like it was stuck in the open position. I felt love flowing toward this person who couldn't love me the way I wanted to be loved, even as I left that relationship to seek the love I felt inside of me. It was strange to feel the pain of my broken heart, and at the same time feel its openness. I kept thinking, *My heart's broken, but it's broken open.* I shifted to an entirely new level of loving and being loved. The relationship I'd dreamed of having manifested 18 months later!"

You are love. You emanated from pure love. You're connected to this Source of love at all times. Think this way, feel this way, and you'll soon act this way. And all that you think, feel, and do will be reciprocated in exactly the same fashion. Believe it or not, this principle of the right person showing up has been in place forever. It's only your ego that's kept you from seeing it clearly.

**It's all unfolding in divine order.** By now you should be affirming that everyone you need for this journey of yours will show up, and that they'll be perfect in every way for whatever needs you have at this time. Furthermore, they'll arrive at precisely the right moment. In this intelligent system that you're a part of, everything arrives from the field of intention where the infinite, invisible life force flows through everyone and everything. This includes you, and everyone else as well. Trust in this invisible life force and the all-creating mind that intends everything into existence.

I suggest that you do a quick review, and note all of the people who've shown up as characters in this play called your life. It has all been perfect. Your ex-spouse showed up at just the right time—when you needed to create those children you love so much. The father who walked out on you so that you could learn self-reliance left right on time. The lover who abandoned you was a part of this perfection. The lover who stayed with you was also taking his or her cues from Source. The good times, the struggles, the tears, the abuse—all of it involved people coming into your life and then leaving. And all of your tears will not and cannot wash out one word of it.

This is your past, and whatever your energy level at the time, whatever your needs, whatever your station in life, you attracted the right people and events to you. You may feel that they didn't show up when you needed them, that in fact, you were alone and no one showed up at all, but I urge you to see it from the perspective of all of life being in divine order. If no one showed up, it was because you needed to handle something on your own and therefore attracted no one to fulfill your energy level at that time. Viewing the past as a play in which all characters and all entrances and exits were scripted by your Source and was what you attracted at the time, frees you from the very low energies of guilt, regret, and even revenge.

As a result, you'll go from being an actor who's influenced by others playing the roles of producer and director, to being the writer, producer, director, and star of your glorious life. You'll also be the casting director who possesses the ability to audition anyone you choose. Base your choices on taking the path of no resistance and staying harmonized with the ultimate producer of this entire drama: the universal all-creating mind of intention.

**A few words about patience.** There's a wonderfully paradoxical line in *A Course in Miracles:* "Infinite patience produces immediate results." To be infinitely patient means to have an absolute knowing within you that you're in vibrational harmony with the all-creating force that intended you here. You are, in fact, a co-creator of your life. You know that the right people will show up on divinely ordained schedule. Attempting to rush the schedule based on your own timetable is akin to getting down on your knees and tugging at an emerging tulip shoot, insisting that you need the flower now. Creation reveals its secrets by and by, not according to your agenda. The immediate result that you'll receive from your infinite patience is a deep sense of peace. You'll feel the love of the creation process, you'll stop making incessant demands, and you'll start being on the lookout for exactly the right person.

I write this with the idea of infinite patience producing immediate results. I know that I'm not alone as I sit here writing. I know that the right people will magically appear to provide me with whatever incentive or material I might need. I have total faith in this process, and I stay harmoniously in tune with my Source. The phone will ring, and someone has a tape they think I'll like. Two weeks ago, it wouldn't have clicked with me, but on this day, I listen to that tape while exercising, and it provides me with exactly what I need. I pass someone on a walk, and they stop to talk. They tell me about a book they're sure I'd love. I jot down the title, look it up, and sure enough, I have what I need.

This goes on every day in some way or another as I surrender my ego-mind to the universal mind of intention, and allow precisely the right people to help me with my individual intention. The immediate result of infinite patience is the inner peace that comes from knowing that I have a "senior partner" who will either send me someone, or leave me alone to work it out myself. This is called practical faith, and I urge you to trust in it, be infinitely patient with it, and have an attitude of radical appreciation and awe each time the right person mysteriously appears in your immediate life space.

### Making Your Intention Your Reality

Below is my ten-step program for implementing the intention of this chapter:

**Step 1: Move away from hoping, wishing, praying, and begging for the right person or people to show up in your life.** Know that this is a universe that works on energy and attraction. Remind yourself that you have the power to attract the right people to assist you with any desire as long as you're able to shift from ego-driven energy to match up with the all-providing Source of intention. This first step is crucial, because if you can't banish all doubt about your ability to attract helpful, creative, loving people, then the remaining nine steps will be of little use to you. Intending ideal people and divine partners begins with knowing in your heart that it's not only a possibility, but a certainty.

**Step 2: Conceptualize your invisible connection to the people you'd like to attract to your life.** Let go of your exclusive identification with the appearance of your body and its possessions. Identify with the invisible energy within you that sustains your life by directing the functions of your body. Now recognize that same energy Source flowing through the people you perceive to be missing from your life, and then realign yourself in thought with that person or persons. Know within you that this power of intention connects the two of you. Your thoughts of creating this merger also emanate from that same field of universal intention.

**Step 3: Form a picture in your mind of meeting the person(s) you'd like to have assist you or be in partnership with you.** Manifesting is a function of spiritual intention matching up in vibrational harmony with your desires. Be as specific as you'd like, but don't share this visualizing technique with anyone because you'll be asked to explain yourself, defend yourself, and have to deal with the low energy of doubt that will inevitably occur. This is a private exercise between you and God. Never, *never* allow your picture to be blurred or corroded by negativity or doubt. Regardless of any obstacles that may surface, hang on to this picture, and stay in loving, kind, creative, peaceful harmony with your always-expanding and endlessly receptive Source of intention.

**Step 4: Act upon the inner picture.** Begin to act as if everyone you meet is a part of your intention to attract ideal people into your life. Share with others your needs and desires without going into detail about your spiritual methodology. Make calls to experts who might be of assistance, and state your desires. They'll want to help you. Don't expect anyone else to do the work of attracting the right people for whatever you seek—be it a job, admission to a college, a financial boost, or a person to repair your automobile. Be proactive, and stay alert for signs of synchronicity, never ignoring them. If a truck drives by with a phone number advertising what you need, jot the number down and call. See all so-called bizarre coincidences surrounding your desires as messages from Source, and act upon them immediately. I assure you that they'll occur repeatedly.

**Step 5: Take the path of least resistance.** I use the word *resistance* here, as I have several times in Part II of this book. Thoughts such as the following are actually a form of resistance to having your intentions manifest: *This stuff isn't practical. I can't just materialize my ideal person by my thoughts. Why should I be treated any better than all of those others who are still waiting for Mr. Right? I tried this before, and a real idiot came into my life.* These are thoughts of resistance that you're placing right in the way of

Source sending you someone. Resistance is lowered energy. Source is high, creative, expansive energy. When your thoughts are low-energy vibrations, you simply can't attract the high-energy people you need or desire. Even if they came rushing up to you announcing: *Here I am, how can I serve you, I'm willing and able,* and carrying a sign saying *I'M YOURS,* you wouldn't recognize or believe them while you're so busy trying to attract more of what you *can't have and don't deserve.*

**Step 6: Practice being the kind of person you wish to attract.** As I've touched on before, if you want to be loved unconditionally, *practice* loving unconditionally. If you want assistance from others, *extend* assistance whenever and wherever you have the opportunity. If you'd like to be the recipient of generosity, then *be* as generous as you can, as frequently as you can. This is one of the simplest and most effective ways of attracting the power of intention. Match up with the *forthcomingness* of the universal mind from which everyone and everything originates while extending it outward, and you'll attract back to yourself all that you intend to manifest.

**Step 7: Detach from the outcome, and practice infinite patience.** This is the crucial step of faith. Don't make the mistake of evaluating your intentions as successes or failures on the basis of your little ego and its time schedule. Put out your intention, and practice everything that's written in this chapter and in this book . . . and then let go. Create a knowing within, and let the universal mind of intention handle the details.

**Step 8: Practice meditation, particularly the Japa meditation, to attract ideal people and divine relationships.** Practice the repetition of the sound that is in the name of God as a mantra, literally seeing in your mind's eye the energy you're radiating, bringing the people you desire into your life. You will be astounded at the results. I've provided examples throughout this book of how the practice of Japa meditation has helped people manifest their dreams, almost like magic.

**Step 9: Look upon everyone who has ever played any role in your life as having been sent to you for your benefit.** In a universe peopled by a creative, divine, organizing intelligence, which I'm calling *the power of intention,* there are simply no accidents. The wake of your life is like the wake of a boat. It's nothing more than the trail that's left behind. The wake doesn't drive the boat. The wake is not driving your life. Everything and everyone in your personal history had to be there when they were. And what's the evidence for this? *They were there!* That's all you need to know. Don't use what transpired in the wake, or the wrong people who showed up in your wake, as a reason why you can't attract the right people today. It's your past . . . nothing more than a trail you've left behind.

**Step 10: As always, remain in a state of eternal gratitude.** Even be grateful for those whose presence may have caused you pain and suffering. Be thankful to your Source for sending them, and to yourself for attracting them to you. They all had something to teach you. Now be grateful for everyone God sends to your path, and know as a co-creator that it's up to you to either resonate with the high, loving energy of intention and keep those like-energized people in your life, or to give them a silent blessing and a pleasant *no thank you.* And the emphasis is on the *thank you,* for that is true gratitude in action.

\* \* \*

In Lynne McTaggart's fabulous book *The Field: The Quest for the Secret Force of the Universe,* she offers us this scientific perspective on what I've written in this chapter: "Our natural state of being is a relationship, a tango, a constant state of one influencing the other. Just as the subatomic particles that compose us cannot be separated from the space and particles surrounding them, so living beings cannot be isolated from each other. . . . By the act of observation and *intention,* we have the ability to extend a kind of super-radiance to the world." [Emphasis mine]

Through relationships with others and by using the power of intention, we can radiate outward all of the energy necessary to attract what we desire. I urge you to move into this awareness now and know in your heart, just as the farmer in *Field of Dreams* knew, that *if you build this inner dream, surely, it will come!*

✽ ✽

# CHAPTER THIRTEEN

## IT IS MY INTENTION TO: OPTIMIZE MY CAPACITY TO HEAL AND BE HEALED

*"No one can ask another to be healed. But he can let himself be healed, and thus offer the other what he has received. Who can bestow upon another what he does not have? And who can share what he denies himself?"*

—A Course in Miracles

Every single person on the planet has within them the potential to be a healer. In order to make conscious contact with your inherent healing powers, you must first make the decision to be healed yourself. As *A Course in Miracles* reminds us: "Those who are healed become the instruments of healing," and "The only way to heal is to be healed." Thus, there's a twofold advantage in this intention to be healed. Once you've accepted your power to heal yourself and optimize your health, you become someone who's capable of healing others as well.

One of the many fascinating observations that David Hawkins made in his book *Power vs. Force* is the relationship between a person's calibrated level of energy and their capacity to heal. People who calibrated above 600 on his map of consciousness scale (which is an exceptionally high-energy score indicating illumination and supreme enlightenment) radiated healing energy. Disease, as we know it, can't exist in the presence of such high spiritual energy. This explains the miraculous healing powers of Jesus of Nazareth, St. Francis of Assisi, and Ramana Maharshi. Their exceptionally high energy is sufficient to counterbalance disease.

As you read this, keep in mind that you too emanated from the highest spiritual loving energy field of intention, and you have within you this capacity. In order to fulfill the intention of this chapter, you must, as Gandhi states in the quotation above, "be the change that you wish to see in others." You must focus on healing yourself so you'll have this healing ability to offer others. If you reach a level of blissful illumination where you're reconnected to Source and are harmonized vibrationally, you'll begin to radiate the energy that converts disease to health.

In St. Francis's powerful prayer, he asks of his Source, "Where there is injury, let me sow pardon," meaning, *allow me to be a person who gives others healing energy.* This principle has been repeated throughout the pages of this book: Bring higher/spiritual energy to the presence of lower/diseased energy, and it not only nullifies the lower energy, but converts it to healthy spiritual energy. In the field of energy medicine where these principles are being applied, tumors are bombarded with exceptionally high-laser energy that dissolves and converts them to healthy tissue. Energy medicine is the discipline of the future, and relies on the ancient spiritual practice of *being the change,* or healing others by first healing ourselves.

### Becoming the Healing

*Reconnect to the disease-free loving perfection from which you came* is a succinct statement of what the self-healing process requires. The universal mind of intention knows precisely what you need in order to optimize your health. What *you* must do is notice your thoughts and behaviors, which are creating *resistance,* and interfering with healing, which is the flow of intentional energy. Recognizing your resistance is something that's entirely up to you. You must dedicate yourself to this awareness so that you can make a shift to pure healing intention.

While I was on the treadmill at the gym yesterday, I talked to a gentleman for five minutes, and in that brief span of time, he regaled me with a laundry list of ailments, surgeries, heart procedures, diseases, and projected joint replacements—all in five minutes! This was his calling card. Those thoughts and recapitulations of bodily afflictions are resistance to the healing energy that's available.

As I talked to the complaining man on the treadmill, I attempted to get him to shift even momentarily away from his resistance to receiving healing energy. But he was absolutely determined to wallow in his disabilities, wearing them as a badge of honor, arguing vehemently for his limitations. He seemed to cherish and cling to his self-loathing for his deteriorating body. I attempted to surround him with light and sent him a silent blessing, congratulating him for doing a treadmill exercise as I moved on to my own workout. But I was struck by how much of this man's inner focus was on dis-order, dis-harmony, and dis-ease as he related to his own body.

Reading about the role of thoughts in reports of spontaneous recovery from irreversible and incurable disease is fascinating. Dr. Hawkins, writing in *Power vs. Force,* offers us this wisdom: "In every studied case of recovery from hopeless and untreatable disease, there has been a major shift in consciousness, so that the attractor patterns that resulted in the pathologic process no longer dominated." Every case! Imagine that. And look at that term *attractor patterns:* We attract into our lives through our level of consciousness, and we can change what we attract. This is a very powerful idea and the basis for accessing the power of intention not only in healing, but in every area where we have desires, aspirations, and individual intentions. Hawkins goes on to say that "in spontaneous recovery, there is frequently a marked increase in the capacity

221

to love and the awareness of the importance of love as a healing factor."

Your intention in this chapter is facilitated by looking at the larger objective of returning to your Source, and vibrating more in harmony with the energy of the power of intention. That Source is never focused on what's wrong, what's missing, or what's sickly. True healing takes you back to the Source. Anything short of this connection is a temporary fix. When you clean up the connecting link to your Source, *attractor patterns* of energy are drawn to you. If you don't believe that this is possible, then you've created resistance to your intention to heal and be healed. If you believe that it *is* possible, but not for you, then you have more resistance. If you believe you're being punished by the absence of health, that's also resistance. These inner thoughts about your ability to be healed play a dominant role in your physical experience.

Becoming a healer by healing oneself involves another one of those imaginary somersaults into the inconceivable, wherein you land upright and balanced in your thoughts, face-to-face with your Source. You realize, perhaps for the first time, that you and your Source are one when you let go of the ego-mind, which has convinced you that you're separate from the power of intention.

**Healing others by healing yourself.** In Lynne McTaggart's book *The Field,* which I've mentioned previously, the author has taken the time and trouble to report the hard scientific research conducted around the world in the past 20 years regarding this field I'm calling intention. In a chapter that is relevant here, called "The Healing Field," McTaggart describes a number of research studies. Here are just five of the intriguing conclusions that researchers have come to concerning intention and healing. I present these to you to stimulate an awareness of your potential for healing the physical body you've opted for in this lifetime, as well as the corollary capacity to offer healing to others. (I haven't reiterated the obvious need for a healthy diet and a sensible exercise routine, which I'm assuming you're aware of and practicing. Bookstores now have entire sections on healthy alternatives for this purpose.)

## Five Conclusions about Healing from the World of Hard Research

1. **Healing through intention is available to ordinary people, and healers may be more experienced or naturally talented in tapping in to the field.** There's physical evidence that those who are capable of healing through intention have a greater coherence and a greater ability to marshal quantum energy and transfer it to those in need of healing. I interpret this scientific evidence to mean that deciding to focus life energy on being in coherence with the power of intention gives you the capacity to heal yourself and others. This means essentially abandoning the fear that permeates your consciousness. And it also means recognizing the fear-based energy promoted by much of the health-care industry. The field of intention has no fear in it. Any disease process is evidence that something is amiss. Any fear associated with the disease process is further evidence that something is amiss in the working of the mind. Health and peace are the natural state when that which prevents them is removed. Research shows that healing through intention, which is actually healing through connecting to the field of intention, is possible for everyone.

2. **Most authentic healers claim to have put out their intention and then stepped back and surrendered to some other kind of healing force, as though they were opening a door and allowing something greater in.** The most effective healers ask for assistance from the universal Source, knowing that their job is to be uplifting and allow the Source of healing to flow. Healers know that the body is the hero, and the life force itself is what does the healing. By removing ego and allowing that force to flow freely, healing is facilitated. Medically trained professionals often do the opposite of allowing and uplifting. They frequently convey the message that the medicine does the healing, and

communicate disbelief in anything other than their pre-scribed procedures. Patients often feel anything but uplifted and hopeful, and diagnosis and prognosis are usually fear based and excessively pessimistic to avoid legal proceedings. *Tell them the worst and hope for the best* is often the medical operating philosophy.

The ability to heal yourself seems to be available to those who have an intuitive knowing about the power of the Spirit. The healing inner speech has to do with relaxing, removing thoughts of resistance, and allowing the spirit of light and love to flow. A powerful healer from the island of Fiji once told me about the efficacy of the native healers. He said, "When a knowing confronts a belief in a disease process, the knowing will always triumph." *A knowing is faith in the power of intention.* A knowing also involves an awareness of always being connected to this Source. And finally, a knowing means getting one's ego out of the way and surrendering to the omnipotent, omnipresent, and omniscient Source, the power of intention, which is the source of all, including all healing.

3. **It didn't seem to matter what method was used, so long as the healer held an intention for a patient to heal.** Healers relied upon profoundly different techniques, including a Christian image, a kabbalist energy pattern, a Native American spirit, a totem, a statue of a saint, and incantations and chants to a healing spirit. As long as the healer held firm to an intention and had a knowing beyond any and all doubts that he could touch the patient with the spirit of intention, the healing was effective as measured by scientific validation.

It's crucial for you to hold an absolute intention for yourself to heal, regardless of what goes on around you, or what others might offer you in the way of discouragement or "getting real." Your intention is strong because it isn't ego's intention, but a match-up with the universal Source. It's

God-realization at work in your approach to healing and being healed.

As an *infinite being,* you know that your own death, and the death of everyone else, is programmed in the energy field from which you emanated. Just as all of your physical characteristics were determined by that future pull, so, too, is your death. So let go of fear of your death, and decide to hold the same intention that intended you here from the world of formlessness. You came from a natural state of well-being, and you intend to be there in your mind, regardless of what transpires in and around your body. Hold that intention for yourself until you leave this body, and hold that same invisible intention for others. This is the one quality that all healers shared. I encourage you to emphasize it, too, right here, right now, and don't let anyone or any prognosis deter you from it.

4. **Research suggests that intention on its own heals, but that healing is a collective memory of a healing spirit, which can be gathered as a medicinal force.** Healing itself may in fact be a force that's available to all of humankind. It's the universal mind of intention. Further, research suggests that individuals and groups of individuals can gather this collective memory and apply it to themselves and to those who suffer with epidemic diseases as well. Since we're all connected to intention, we all share the same life force, and we all emanated from the same universal mind of God, it's not so far-fetched to assume that by tapping in to this energy field, we can gather healing energy and spread it to all who enter our enlightened spheres. This would explain the enormous collective healing power of saints, and make the case for each of us holding the intention to eradicate such things as AIDS, smallpox, worldwide influenzas, and even the cancer epidemic we live with today.

When illness is viewed in isolation, it's disconnected from the collective health of the universal field. Several studies report that the AIDS virus seems to feed on fear, the kind of fear that's experienced when a person is shunned or isolated from the community. Studies on heart patients reveal that those who felt isolated from their family, their community, and especially their spirituality, were more susceptible to disease. Studies on longevity show that those who live longer have a strong spiritual belief and a sense of belonging to a community. The capacity to heal collectively is one of the powerful benefits that's available when you raise your energy level and connect to the faces of intention.

5. **The most important treatment any healer can offer is hope for the health and well-being of those who suffer disease or trauma.** Healers do a self-analysis of what's present in their consciousness before they focus on someone in need of healing. The key word here is *hope*. The presence of hope conveyed boils down to faith. I would also call it *knowing*, a knowing that connection to one's Source is a connection to the source of all healing. When we live this way, we always see hope. We know that miracles are always a possibility. Staying in that mind-set, fear and doubt are banished from the landscape. If you give up hope, you change the energy level of your life to vibrate at fear and doubt levels. Yet we know that the all-creating Source of intention knows no fear or doubt.

My favorite quote from Michelangelo is on the value of hope: "The greater danger for most of us is not that our aim is too high and we miss it, but that it is too low and we reach it." Just imagine—the intention of healers and the hopes they have for themselves and others may be even more important than the medicine being offered. The simple thought of dislike toward another impedes the potential for healing. Lack of faith in the power of Spirit to heal plays a deleterious role in the healing process. Any low-energy thoughts you have undermine your ability to heal yourself. All five of these research-backed conclusions lead us to an awareness of the importance of shifting our focus and connecting to the all-healing field of intention and harmonizing with it.

### From Thoughts of Sickness to Intentions of Wellness

You're probably familiar with the phrase "And God intended, 'Let there be light!' and there was light," from the Old Testament. If you look in an English-Hebrew dictionary, you'll find that the English translation of the Hebrew can be read as: "And god *intended* . . ." The decision to *create* is the decision to *intend*. To create healing, you can't have thoughts of illness and anticipate your body falling victim to disease. Become aware of the thoughts you have that support the idea of sickness as something to be expected. Begin noticing the frequency of those thoughts. The more they occupy your mental landscape, the more resistance you're creating to realizing your intention.

You know what those thoughts of resistance sound like: *I can't do anything about this arthritis. It's the flu season. I feel okay now, but by the weekend, it will be in my chest and I'll have a fever. We live in a carcinogenic world. Everything is either fattening or filled with chemicals. I feel so tired all the time.* On and on they go. They're like huge barricades blocking the realization of your intention. Notice the thoughts that represent a decision on your part to buy into the illness mentality of the huge profit-making drug companies and a health-care industry that thrives on your fears.

But you're the divine, remember? You're a piece of the universal mind of intention, and you don't have to think in these ways. You can opt to think that you have the ability to raise your energy level, even if all of the advertising around you points to a different conclusion. You can go within and hold an intention that says: *I want to feel good, I intend to feel good, I intend to return to my Source, and I refuse to allow any other thoughts of dis-order or dis-ease in.* This is the beginning. You'll feel empowered by this unique experience. Then in any given moment of not feeling well, choose thoughts of healing and feeling good. In that instant, feeling good takes over, if only for a few seconds.

When you refuse to live in low energy, and you work moment by moment to introduce thoughts that support your intention, you've effectively decided that wellness is your choice and that being a healer is a part of that decision. At this time, wheels of creation are set in motion, and what you've imagined and created in your mind begins to take form in your everyday life.

Give it a shot the next time you're low-energy thinking of any kind. Just note how quickly you can change how you feel by refusing to think thoughts that are out of harmony with your Source of intention. It works for me, and I encourage you to do so as well. I simply will not think any longer that I must be a victim of illness or disability, and I will not spend the precious moments of my life discussing illness. I am a healer. I heal myself by co-creating health with God, and I give this gift to others as well. This is my intention.

### Illness Is Not a Punishment

Illness became a component of the human condition when we separated ourselves from the perfect health from which we were intended. Rather than attempting to intellectualize reasons why people get sick and come up with a rationale for understanding illness, I encourage you to think of yourself as having the potential to become a master healer. Try visualizing all of human illness from the perspective of something that the human race has collectively brought upon itself by identifying with the ego rather than staying with the divinity from which we emanated. Out of this collective ego identification, we brought about all that goes with the ego problems—fear, hate, despair, anxiety, depression—all of it. The ego feeds on these emotions because it's insistent on its own identity as a separate entity apart from this God-force that intended us here. In one way or another, virtually every single member of the human race bought into this idea of separation and ego identification. Consequently, illness, disease, sickness, and the need for healing simply come with the territory of being human.

However, you needn't feel stuck there. The power of intention is about returning to the Source of perfection. It's about knowing that the power to heal is all wrapped up in making that divine connection, and that the Source of all life does not punish, offering karmic paybacks through suffering and hardship. You don't have a need for healing because you were bad or ignorant, or as retribution for past-life offenses. You've taken on whatever you're experiencing for whatever lessons you need to learn on this journey, which is being orchestrated by the all-providing intelligence that we're calling intention.

In an eternal universe, you must view yourself and all others in infinite terms. Infinite terms mean that you have an infinite number of opportunities to show up in a material body to co-create anything. As you view the sickness of the mind and body that permeates your own life as well as the rest of humanity, try viewing it as part of the infinite nature of our world. If starvation, pestilence, or disease are a part of the perfection of the universe, then so is your intention to end these things a part of that same perfection. Now decide to stay with that intention—first in your own life, then in the lives of others. Your intention will match up with the intention of the universe, which knows nothing of egos and separation, and all thoughts of illness as punishment and karmic paybacks will cease to exist.

### Making Your Intention Your Reality

Below is my ten-step plan for implementing the intention of this chapter to optimize your capacity to heal and be healed:

**Step 1: You can't heal anyone until you allow yourself to be healed.** Work in a collaborative effort with your Source to create a sense of your own healing. Put all of your focused energy on knowing that you can be healed of physical or emotional disruptions to your perfect health. Connect to a loving, kind, receptive-to-healing energy, which is the field that intended you here. Be willing to accept the fact that you're a part of the healing energy of all of life. The same force that heals a cut on your hand and grows the new skin to repair it permanently is both in your hand and in the universe as well. You are it, it is you; there's no separation. Be conscious of staying in contact with this healing energy, because it's impossible to separate from it except in your ego-diminished thoughts.

**Step 2: The healing energy that you're connected to at all times is what you have to give away to others.** Offer this energy freely, and keep your ego entirely out of the healing process. Remember how St. Francis responded when asked why he didn't heal himself of his diseases, which would cause his death at the age of 45: "I want everyone to know that it is God who does this healing." St. Francis was healed of ego domination, and he deliberately held on to his infirmities to teach others that it was God's energy working through him that provided the energy for all of his miraculous healings.

**Step 3: By raising your energy to a vibrational match with the field of intention, you're strengthening your immune system and increasing the production of well-being enzymes in the brain.** A change in personality from being spiteful, pessimistic, angry, sullen, and disagreeable to one of passion, optimism, kindness, joy, and understanding is often the key when witnessing miraculous acts of spontaneous recovery from fatalistic prognostications.

**Step 4: Practice surrender!** *Let go and let God* is a great theme in the recovery movement. It's also a wonderful reminder in the world of healing. By surrendering, you're able to have reverence for, and commune with, the Source of all healing. Remember that the field of intention doesn't know anything about healing *per se*, because it's spiritual perfection already, and it creates from that perspective. It's ego consciousness that creates the dis-order, dis-harmony, and dis-eases of our world, and it is in returning to that spiritual perfection that harmony of body, mind, and spirit are realized. When this balance or symmetry is restored, we call it healing, but the Source knows nothing of healing because it creates only perfect health. It's to this perfect health that you must surrender.

**Step 5: Don't ask to be healed, ask to be restored to that perfection from which you emanated.** Here's where you want to hold an intention for yourself and for others in an unbending, non-negotiable way. Let nothing interfere with the intention you have to heal and be healed. Discard all negativity that you encounter. Refuse to let in any energy that will weaken your body or your resolve. Convey this to others as well. Remember, you're not asking your Source to heal you, because this assumes health is missing from your life. It assumes scarcity, but the Source can only recognize and respond to what it is already, and you too are a component of that Source. Come to the Source as whole and complete, banish all thoughts of illness, and know that by connecting back to this Source—filling yourself with it and offering it to others—you become healing itself.

**Step 6: Know that you are adored.** Look for reasons to praise and feel good. In the moment in which you're experiencing thoughts that make you feel sick or bad, do your best to change them to thoughts that support your feeling good, and if that seems impossible, then do your very best to say nothing at all. Refuse to talk about disease, and work to activate thoughts that predict recovery, feeling good, and perfect health. Picture yourself as healthy and free of disability. Be on the lookout for the opportunity to literally say to yourself, *I feel good. I intend to attract more of this good feeling, and I intend to give it away to any and all in need of it.*

**Step 7: Seek out and cherish the silence.** Many people who have suffered with long-term illnesses have been able to return to their Source through the channel of nature and contemplative silence. Spend time in quiet meditation visualizing yourself coupled with the perfectly healthy field of intention. Commune with this Source of all that is good, all that is well, and practice accessing this high spiritual energy, bathing your entire being in this light.

Meditation is always healing for me. When I'm fatigued, a few moments in silence accessing higher, loving, kind vibrations energizes me. When I feel out of sorts, a few moments in quietude making conscious contact with God provides me with all that I need to not only feel good, but to help others do the same. I always remember Herman Melville's timely words: "Silence is the only Voice of our God."

Here's an excerpt from a letter written to me by Darby Hebert, who now lives in Jackson Hole, Wyoming. For more than two decades, she struggled with feeling used as well as watching her own physical condition deteriorate. She opted for nature, silence, and meditation. I repeat her words (with her permission) below:

> For a year I lived out of boxes in an empty house. Then, to remove myself from this negative energy field and the scorn of people who were sitting in judgment, I moved 2,000 miles away to Jackson Hole. The magnificence, grandeur, and peace of this sacred, enchanted place began to work its magic immediately. I have lived in silence for almost two years. Meditation and appreciation have become my way of life. Leaving low energy, and moving into high energy, with your help, has worked miracles. I have moved from hemorrhaging eyes, internal lesions, aseptic meningitis, and severe muscle pain to a health that includes all-day mountain hiking and cross-country skiing. I am slowly getting off of the dangerous drugs used to control the diseases, and I _know_ I can do it. You have shown me the way to being well, and I will forever be grateful. God bless you a thousandfold, Wayne, for following your bliss and helping others to find theirs. I hope there will come a time when I can express my gratitude in person. Until then, I'll see you in the Gap.

**Step 8: To *be* health, you must totally identify with the wholeness that you are.** You can stop seeing yourself as a physical body and immerse yourself in the idea of absolute well-being. This can become your new identification card. Here, you breathe only wellness, you think only perfect health, and you detach from appearances of illness in the world. Soon you recognize only perfection in others. You stand firm in your truth, reflecting only thoughts of well-being, and speaking only words of the infinite possibility for healing any and all disease processes. This is your rightful identity of wholeness, and you live it as if you and the Source that creates all are one and the same. This is your ultimate truth, and you can allow this dynamic aura of wholeness to saturate and animate your every thought until it is all that you have to give away. This is how you heal, from that inner knowing and trust of your wholeness.

**Step 9: Allow health to stream into your life.** Become conscious of resistance, which interferes with the natural flow of healthy energy to you. This resistance is in the form of your thoughts. Any thought that's out of sync with the seven faces of intention is a resistant thought. Any thought that says that *it's impossible to heal* is a resistant thought. Any thought of doubt or fear is a resistant thought. When you observe these thoughts, note them carefully, and then deliberately activate thoughts that are in energetic, vibrational balance with the all-providing Source of intention.

**Step 10: Stay immersed in a state of gratitude.** Be grateful for every breath you take . . . for all of your internal organs that work together in harmony . . . for the wholeness that is your body . . . for the blood streaming through your veins . . . for your brain that allows you to process these words and the eyes that allow you to read them. Look in the mirror at least once every day and give thanks for that heart that continues to beat and the invisible force on which those heartbeats depend. Stay in gratitude. This is the surest way to keep the connecting link to perfect health clean and pure.

* * *

One of the messages of Jesus of Nazareth is apropos of all that I've presented in this chapter on having a healing intention:

*If you bring forth what is inside you,*
*what you bring forth will save you.*
*If you don't bring forth what is inside you,*
*what you don't bring forth will destroy you.*

What is inside you is the power of intention. No microscope will reveal it. You can find the command center with x-ray technology, but the *commander* in the command center remains impervious to our sophisticated probing instruments. *You are that commander.* You must allow yourself to be in vibrational harmony with the greatest commander of all and bring it forth to serve you, rather than allowing yourself to be in a state of disrepair.

~ * ~ * ~

# — CHAPTER FOURTEEN

## *It Is My Intention to:* Appreciate and Express the Genius That I Am

*"Everyone is born a genius, but the process of living de-geniuses them."*

— Buckminster Fuller

onsider that all human beings have within themselves the same essence of consciousness, and that the process of creativity and genius are attributes of human consciousness. Therefore, genius is a potential that lives within you and every other human being. You have many moments of genius in your lifetime. These are the times when you have a uniquely brilliant idea and implement it even if only you are aware of how fantastic it is. Perhaps you created something absolutely astonishing and you even amazed yourself. Then there are the moments when you make exactly the right shot in a round of golf or a tennis match and you realize with immense pleasure what you've just accomplished. You are a genius.

You may never have thought of yourself as a person who has genius residing within. You may have thought that *genius* is a word reserved for the Mozarts, Michelangelos, Einsteins, Madame Curies, Virginia Woolfs, Stephen Hawkings, and others whose lives and accomplishments have been publicized. But keep in mind that they share the same essence of consciousness that you do. They emanated from the same power of intention as you did. They have all shared the same life force animating them as you do. Your genius is in your very existence, awaiting the right circumstances to express itself.

There is no such thing as *luck* or *accidents* in this purposeful universe. Not only is everything connected to everything else, but no one is excluded from the universal Source called intention. And genius, since it's a characteristic of the universal Source, must be universal, which means that it's in no way restricted. It's available to every single human being. It certainly can and does show up differently in every single one of us. The qualities of creativity and genius are within you, awaiting your decision to match up with the power of intention.

### Changing Your Energy Level to Access the Genius Within You

In his illuminating book, *Power vs. Force,* David Hawkins wrote: "Genius is by definition a style of consciousness characterized by the ability to access high energy attractor patterns. It is not a personality characteristic. It is not something that a person *has,* nor even something that someone *is.* Those in whom we recognize genius commonly disclaim it. A universal characteristic of genius is humility. The genius has always attributed his insights to some higher influence." Genius is a characteristic of the creative force (the first of the seven faces of intention) that allows all of material creation to come into form. It is an expression of the divine.

No one who's considered a genius—be it Sir Laurence Olivier onstage as Hamlet; Michael Jordan gracefully gliding toward a dunk on the basketball court; Clarence Darrow speaking to a jury; Joan of Arc inspiring a nation; or Mrs. Fuehrer, my eighth-grade teacher making a story come alive in the classroom—can explain where the energy to perform at those levels came from. Sir Laurence Olivier is said to have been distraught after giving one of the greatest stage performances of *Hamlet* ever seen in London. When asked why he was so upset after the thundering ovation from the audience, he replied (I paraphrase), "I know it was my best performance, but I don't know how I did it, where it came from, and if I can ever do it again." Ego and genius are mutually exclusive. Genius is a function of surrendering to the Source or reconnecting to it so dramatically that one's ego is substantially minimized. This is what Dr. Hawkins means by *accessing higher energy patterns*.

Higher energy is the energy of light, which is a way of describing spiritual energy. The seven faces of intention are the ingredients of this spiritual energy. When you shift your thoughts, emotions, and life activities into these realms and deactivate the lower energies of the ego, the God force within you begins to take over. It's so automatic that it travels faster than your thoughts. This is why your thoughts about how you did something are so bewildering. The higher energy level actually transcends thought, moving into vibrational harmony with the Source energy of intention. As you release ego-dominated thoughts (which convince you that you're doing these amazing things and are responsible for these unbelievable accomplishments), you tap in to the power of intention. This is where the genius that you truly are resides.

Many people never get acquainted with this inner world of their personal genius, and think that genius is only measured in intellectual or artistic endeavors. Genius remains in the shadows of their thoughts, unnoticed during their occasional forays inward, and may even be padlocked and chained! If you've been taught to avoid thinking too highly of yourself, and that genius is reserved for a handful of select individuals, you probably resist this idea. You won't recognize your genius aspect if you've been conditioned to believe that you should accept your lot in life, think small, try to fit in with *normal* groups of people, and not aim too high in order to avoid disappointment.

I'd like you to consider what may seem like a radical idea: *Genius can show up in as many ways as there are human beings.* Anything in any field that anyone has ever accomplished is shared by you. You're connected to every being that has ever lived or ever will live, and you share the exact same energy of intention that flowed through Archimedes, Leonardo da Vinci, the Virgin Mother, and Jonas Salk. You can access this energy. At the deepest level, all things and all people are composed of vibrations organized into fields that permeate the entire structure of the universe. You share these vibrations, and you are in this field.

The starting point is knowing and understanding that this level of creativity and functioning called *genius* resides within you. Then begin to deconstruct doubts about your role here. Make a commitment to raise your energy levels to vibrate harmoniously with the field of intention despite attempts by your ego and others' egos to dissuade you.

Dr. Valerie Hunt in *Infinite Mind: Science of Human Vibrations of Consciousness,* reminds us: "Lower vibrations exist with material reality, higher ones with mystical reality, and a full vibrational spectrum with expanded reality." To fulfill this intention of appreciating and expressing the genius that you are, you're going to have to strive for that *full vibrational spectrum.* This is the idea of expansion, which is crucial to knowing your true potential. It's what you signed up for when you left the formless world of spiritual intention. You co-created a body and a life to express that inner genius, which you may have locked away in an almost inaccessible chamber.

### Expanding Your Reality

The universal force that created you is always expanding, and your objective is to achieve harmony with that Source and thereby regain the power of intention. So what is it that keeps you from expanding to the mystical reality and full vibrational spectrum that Dr. Hunt refers to? I like this answer from William James, who is often referred to as the father of modern psychology: "Genius means little more than the faculty of perceiving in an unhabitual way." To expand your reality to match the expansiveness of the all-creating field of intention, you have to peel away your old habits of thought. These habits have pigeonholed you to a point where you allow labels to be attached to you. These labels define you in many ways.

Most of the labels are from other people who need to describe what you are not, because they feel safer predicting what can't be than what can be: *She's never been very artistic. He's a tad clumsy, so he won't be an athlete. Mathematics was never her strong suit. He's a bit shy, so he won't be good dealing with the public.* You've heard these pronouncements for so long that you believe them. They've become a habitual way of thinking about your abilities and poten-tialities. As William James suggested, *genius means making a shift in your thinking* so that you let go of those habits and open your-self to possibilities of greatness.

I've heard the stereotype about writers and speakers since I was a young man. If you're a writer, you're introverted, and writers don't make dynamic speakers. I chose to shift from that programmed and stereotypical way of thinking and decided that I could excel at any-thing I affirmed and intended for myself. I chose to believe that when I came into this world of boundaries and form, there were no restrictions on me. I was intended here from an expansive energy field that knows nothing of limits or labels. I decided that I'd be both an introverted writer *and* a dynamic extroverted speaker. Similarly, I've broken through many socially imposed habitual ways of labeling people. I can be a genius in any area if, accord-ing to the father of modern psychology, I learn to *perceive in unhabitual ways.* I can sing tender songs, write sentimental poetry, create exquisite paintings, and at the same time in the same body, excel as an athlete in any sport, build a fine piece of furniture, repair my automobile, wrestle with my children, and surf in the ocean.

Pay attention to yourself in ways that allow the expansion of the infinite possibilities that you're potentially capable of. You may decide, as I have, that repairing an automobile and surfing in the ocean aren't what you enjoy doing. So leave those activities to others, and use your genius to engage in pursuits that please and attract you. Expand your reality to the point where you pursue what you love doing and excel at it. Involve yourself in the high-energy levels of trust, optimism, appreciation, reverence, joy, and love. That means love for what you're doing, love for yourself, and love for your genius, which allows you to immerse yourself in any activity and enjoy the process of experiencing it fully.

**Trusting your insights.** The process of appreciating your genius involves trusting those inner flashes of creative insight that are worthy of expression. The song you're composing in your head. The weird storyline that you keep dreaming about that would make a fabulous movie. The crazy idea about combining peas and carrots in a seed and growing *parrot* vegetables. The new car design you've always contemplated. The fashion idea that would become the next fad. The toy that every child will yearn to have. The musical extravaganza you've seen in your mind. These ideas and thousands like them are the creative genius within you at work. These ideas in your imagination are *distributions of God* taking place. They're not from your ego, which squashes them with fear and doubt. Your insights are divinely inspired. Your creative mind is how your higher self vibrates harmoniously with the field of intention, which is always creating.

Banishing doubt regarding those brilliant flashes of insight will allow you to express these ideas and begin the process of acting on them. Having the thoughts and squelching them because you think they aren't good enough or they don't merit any action is denying the connection that you have to the power of intention. You have a connecting link to intention, but you're allowing it to be weakened by living at ordinary levels of ego consciousness. Remember that you're a piece of God, and the inner spark of genius in your imagination—that intuitive inner voice—is really God reminding you of your uniqueness. You're having these inner insights because this is precisely how you stay connected to the all-creating genius that intended you here. As I've said earlier, trusting in yourself is trusting in the wisdom that created you.

Never, ever regard any creative thought that you're having as anything other than a worthy potential expression of your inner genius. The only caveat here is that these thoughts must be in vibrational harmony with the seven faces of intention. Inner thoughts of hatred, anger, fear, despair, and destruction simply don't foster creative insights. The low-energy, ego-dominated thoughts must be replaced and converted to the power of intention. Your creative impulses are real, they're vital, they're worthy, and they crave expression. The fact that you can conceive of them is proof of this. Your thoughts are real. They're pure energy, and they're telling you to pay attention and get that connecting link to the power of intention polished through living at different levels than you've accepted as normal or ordinary. At these levels, everyone is a genius.

**Appreciating the genius in others.** Every person you interact with should feel the inner glow that comes from being appreciated, particularly for the ways in which they express their creativity. A core theme, which strengthens the flow of the power of intention, is wanting for others as much as you intend for yourself. Appreciating the genius in others attracts high levels of competent energy to you. By seeing and celebrating the creative genius, you open a channel within yourself for receiving the creative energy from the field of intention.

My 15-year-old son, Sands, has a unique way of riding a surfboard unlike everyone around him in the ocean. I encourage him to do what comes naturally and express it with pride. He also created a unique language of communication, similar to my brother David, which others in the family and close personal acquaintances emulate. Creating a language that others use is the work of a genius! I tell Sands this, and my brother, too, whose unique language I've spoken for over half a century. My daughter Skye has a distinctive one-of-a-kind singing voice that I love. I tell her so, and point out that it's an expression of her genius.

All of my children, and yours as well (including the child within you) have unparalleled characteristics in many of the ways they express themselves. From the way that they dress, to the little tattoo, to their signature, to their mannerisms, to their unmatched personality quirks, you can appreciate their genius. Notice and appreciate *your* genius, too. When you're just like everybody else, you've nothing to offer other than your conformity.

Take the road of *seeing the face of God in everyone* you encounter. Look for something to appreciate in others, and be willing to communicate it to them and anyone who's willing to listen. When you see this quality in others, you'll soon begin to realize that this potential is available to all of humanity. This obviously includes you. Recognizing genius in yourself is an integral part of the dynamic. As Dr. Hawkins tells us in *Power vs. Force:* "Until one acknowledges the genius within oneself, one will have great difficulty recognizing it in others."

**Genius and simplicity.** Begin to realize the intention of this chapter by uncomplicating your life as much as possible. Genius thrives in a contemplative environment, where every minute isn't filled with obligations or hoards of people offering advice and insisting on your constant participation in ordinary, mundane endeavors. The genius in you isn't seeking confirmation from others, but quiet space for its ideas to blossom. Genius isn't as much about achieving a high IQ on a standardized test, as it is the exceptionally high level of plain old savvy in any given field of human endeavor. Genius-at-work may be the person who finds tinkering with an electronic gadget for hours on end exhilarating, and also can be entranced by puttering in the garden or observing the communication patterns between bats on a starry night. An uncomplicated life with fewer intrusions tolerated, in a simple setting, allows your creative genius to surface and express itself. The simplicity establishes a link to the power of intention, and your genius will flourish.

*Making Your Intention Your Reality*

Below is my ten-step program for putting this intention to appreciate and express the *genius* within you to work.

**Step 1: Declare yourself to be a genius!** This shouldn't be a public pronouncement, but a statement of intention between you and your Creator. Remind yourself that you're one of the masterpieces that emanated from the universal field of intention. You don't have to prove that you're a genius, nor do you need to compare any of your accomplishments to those of others. You have a unique gift to offer this world, and you are unique in the entire history of creation.

**Step 2: Make a decision to listen more carefully to your inner insights, no matter how small or insignificant you may have previously judged them to be.** These thoughts, which you may have viewed as silly or unworthy of attention, are your private connection to the field of intention. Thoughts that seem to persist, particularly if they relate to new activities and adventures, aren't in your mind accidentally. Those tenacious thoughts that don't go away should be viewed by you as intention talking to you, saying, *You signed up to express your unique brilliance, so why do you keep ignoring the genius in favor of settling for less?*

**Step 3: Take constructive action toward implementing your inner intuitive inclinations.** Any step in the direction of expressing your creative impulses is a step in the direction of actualizing the genius that resides within you—for example, writing and submitting a book outline, regardless of how you may have doubted yourself up until now; recording a CD of yourself reading poetry or singing the songs you've written; purchasing an easel and art paraphernalia and spending an afternoon painting; or visiting an expert in the field that interests you.

During a recent photo shoot, a photographer told me that years earlier he'd arranged a meeting with a world-renowned photographer, and that visit sent him on the road to doing the work that he loved. To me, this man was a genius. Photography had always intrigued him. The early prodding in his life that he acted on allowed him to *appreciate the genius* within him, then one meeting with one man taught him to trust in that *intrigue* and to use it as a means for communicating his genius to the entire world.

**Step 4: Know that any and all thoughts that you have regarding your own skills, interests, and inclinations are valid.** To reinforce the validity of your thoughts, *keep them private.* Tell yourself that they're between you and God. If you keep them in the spiritual domain, you don't have to introduce them to your ego or expose them to the egos of those around you. This means that you'll never have to compromise them by explaining and defending them to others.

**Step 5: Remind yourself that aligning with spiritual energy is how you will find and convey the genius within you.** In *Power vs. Force,* David Hawkins concluded: "From our studies it appears that the alignment of one's goals and values with high energy attractors is more closely associated with genius than anything else." This is completely in line with understanding and implementing the power of intention. Shift your energy to harmonize vibrationally with the energy of Source. Be an appreciator of life, and refuse to have thoughts of hatred, anxiety, anger, and judgment. Trust yourself as a piece of God and your genius will flourish.

**Step 6: Practice radical humility.** Take no credit for your talents, intellectual abilities, aptitudes, or proficiencies. Be in a state of awe and bewilderment. Even as I sit here with my pen in my hand, observing how words appear before me, I'm in a state of bewilderment. Where do these words come from? How does my hand know how to translate my invisible thoughts into decipherable words, sentences, and paragraphs? Where do the thoughts come from that precede the words? Is this really Wayne Dyer writing, or am I watching Wayne Dyer put these words on the paper? Is God writing this book through me? Was I intended to be this messenger before I showed up here as a baby on the 10th of May, 1940? Will these words live beyond my lifetime? I'm bewildered by it all. I'm humble in my inability to know where any of my accomplishments come from. Practice radical humility, and give credit everywhere except to your ego.

**Step 7: Remove resistance to actualizing your genius.** Resistance always shows up in the form of your thoughts. Watch for thoughts that convey your inability to think of yourself in genius terms . . . thoughts of doubt about your abilities . . . or thoughts that reinforce what you've been taught about a lack of talent or lack of aptitude. All of these kinds of thoughts are a misalignment and don't allow you to be in vibrational harmony with the universal all-creating field of intention. Your Source knows that you're a genius. Any thought you have that challenges this notion is resistance, which will inhibit you from realizing your intention.

**Step 8: Look for the genius in others.** Pay attention to the greatness you observe in as many people as possible, and if you don't see it at first, then spend some mental energy looking for it. The more you're inclined to think in genius terms, the more natural it becomes for you to apply the same standards to yourself. Tell others about their genius. Be as complimentary and authentic as you can. In doing so, you'll radiate loving, kind, abundant, creative energy. In a universe that operates on energy and attraction, you'll find these same qualities returning to you.

**Step 9: Simplify your life.** Take the complications, rules, *shoulds, musts, have tos*, and so on out of your life. By uncomplicating your life and removing the trivial pursuits that occupy so much of it, you open a channel for the genius within you to emerge. One of the most effective techniques for simplifying life is to take time each day to spend 20 or so minutes in silence and meditation. The more conscious contact you make with your Source, the more you come to appreciate your own highest self.

And it's from this highest self that your own genius will be manifested.

**Step 10: Remain humble while staying in a state of gratitude.** This genius that you are has nothing at all to do with your ego-mind. Be ever so grateful to the Source of intention for providing you with the life force to express the genius that resides within you. Those who attribute their inspiration and success to their ego soon lose this capacity, or they allow the approval and attention of others to destroy them. Remain humble and grateful, and more of your genius will surface as you remain in a constant state of expansion. Gratitude is a sacred space where you *allow* and *know* that a force greater than your ego is always at work and always available.

\* \* \*

The man who inspires me every day, Ralph Waldo Emerson, whose photograph looks back at me as I write, put it this way: "To believe your own thoughts, to believe that what is true for you in your private heart is true for all men—that is genius."

Take this awareness and apply it in your life. Another genius tells us just how to do this. Thomas Edison said, "Genius is one percent inspiration, and ninety-nine percent perspiration." Are you sweating yet?

∾ \* ∾ \* ∾

# PART III

# THE
# CONNECTION

"Man is in the process of changing, to forms that are not of this world; grows he in time to the formless, a plane on the cycle above. Know ye, ye must become formless before ye are one with the light."

— adapted from *The Emerald Tablets of Thoth*

# CHAPTER FIFTEEN

# A Portrait of a Person Connected to the Field of Intention

*"Self-actualizing people must be what they can be."*

— Abraham Maslow

A person who lives in a state of unity with the Source of all life doesn't look any different from ordinary folks. These people don't wear a halo or dress in special garments that announce their godlike qualities. But when you notice that they go through life as the *lucky ones* who seem to get all the breaks, and when you begin to talk to them, you realize how distinctive they are compared to people living at ordinary levels of awareness. Spend a few moments in conversation with these people who are connected to the power of intention and you see how unique they are.

These people, whom I call *connectors* to signify their harmonious connection with the field of intention, are individuals who have made themselves available for success. It's impossible to get them to be pessimistic about achieving what they desire in their lives. Rather than using language that indicates that their desires may not materialize, they speak from an inner conviction that communicates their profound and simple knowing that the universal Source supplies everything.

They don't say, *With my luck things won't work out.* Instead, you're much more likely to hear something like, *I intend to create this and I know it will work out.* No matter how you might attempt to dissuade them by pointing out all the reasons why their optimism ought to be curtailed, they seem blissfully blind to reality-check repercussions. It's almost as if they're in a different world, a world in which they can't hear the reasons why things won't work out.

If you engage them in conversation about this idea, they simply say something like, *I refuse to think about what can't happen, because I'll attract exactly what I think about, so I only think about what I know will happen.* It doesn't matter to them what's happened before. They don't relate to the concepts of *failure* or *it's impossible.* They simply, without fanfare, are unaffected by reasons for being pessimistic. They've made themselves available for success, and they know and trust in an invisible force that's all-providing. They're so well connected to the all-providing Source that it's as if they have a natural aura preventing anything from getting through that might weaken their connection to the creative energy of the power of intention.

Connectors don't place their thoughts on what they don't want, because, as they'll tell you: *The Source of all can only respond with what it is, and what it is, is infinite supply. It can't relate to scarcity, or things not working out, because it's none of these things. If I say to the Source of all things, "It probably won't work out," I'll receive back from it precisely what I sent to it, so I know better than to think anything other than what my Source is.*

To the average person who has fears about the future, this all sounds like mumbo jumbo. They'll tell their connector friend to do a reality check and look realistically at the world they live in. But connectors aren't distracted from their inner knowing. They'll tell you, if you choose to listen, that this is a universe of energy and attraction, and that the reason so many people live lives of fear and scarcity is because they rely on their ego to fulfill their desires. *It's simple,* they'll tell you. *Just reconnect to your Source, and be like your Source, and your intentions will match up perfectly with the all-providing Source.*

To connectors, it all seems so simple. Keep your thoughts on what you intend to create. Stay consistently matched up with the field of intention, and then watch for the clues that what you're summoning from the all-creative Source is arriving in your life. To a connector, there are simply no accidents. They perceive seemingly insignificant events as being orchestrated in perfect harmony. They believe in synchronicity and aren't surprised when the perfect person for a situation appears, or when someone they've been thinking about calls out of the blue, or when a book arrives unexpectedly in the mail giving them the information they needed, or when the money to finance a project they've been intending mysteriously shows up.

Connectors won't attempt to win you over to their point of view with debates. They know better than to place a lot of energy on arguing or being frustrated, because that attracts argumentation and frustration into their lives. They know what they know, and they aren't seduced into constructing a counterforce of resistance to people who live otherwise. They accept the idea that there are no accidents in a universe that has an invisible force of energy as its Source that continuously creates and provides an infinite supply to all who wish to partake of it. They'll tell you plain and simple if you inquire: *All you have to do to tap in to the power of intention is to be in a perfect match with the Source of everything, and I'm choosing to be as closely aligned to that Source as I can.*

To connectors, everything that shows up in their life is there because the power of intention intended it there. So they're always in a state of gratitude. They feel thankful for everything, even things that might seem to be obstacles. They have the ability and desire to see a temporary illness as a blessing, and they know in their heart that somewhere an opportunity exists in the setback, and that is what they look for in everything that shows up in their life. Through their thanks, they honor all possibilities, rather than asking their Source for something, because that seems to give power to what's missing. They commune with the Source in a state of reverent gratitude for all that's present in their lives, *knowing* that this empowers their intention to manifest precisely what they need.

Connectors describe themselves as living in a state of appreciation and bewilderment. You're unlikely to hear them complain about anything. They aren't faultfinders. If it rains, they enjoy it, knowing that they won't get where they want to go if they only travel on sunny days. This is how they react to all of nature, with appreciative harmony. The snow, the wind, the sun, and the sounds of nature are all reminders to connectors that they're a part of the natural world. The air—regardless of its temperature or wind velocity—is the revered air that is the breath of life.

Connectors appreciate the world and everything in it. The same connection that they experience with nature they feel toward all beings, including those who lived before and those who have yet to arrive. They have a consciousness of the oneness, and therefore they make no distinctions such as *them* or *those other people*. To a connector, it is all *we*. If you could observe their inner world, you'd discover that they're hurt by pain inflicted on others. They don't have the concept of enemies, since they know that all of us emanate from the same divine Source. They enjoy the differences in the appearance and customs of others rather than disliking, criticizing, or feeling threatened by them. Their connection to others is of a spiritual nature, but they don't separate themselves spiritually from anyone regardless of where they might live or how different their appearances or customs may be from their own. In their heart, connectors feel an affinity to all of life, as well as to the Source of all of life.

It's because of this connecting link that connectors are so adept at attracting into their lives the cooperation and assistance of others in fulfilling their own intentions. The very fact of feeling connected means that in the connectors' minds, there's no one on this planet who they're not joined up with in a spiritual sense. Consequently, living in the field of intention, the entire system of life in the universe is available to access anything their attention is on, because they're already connected to this life-giving energy system and all of its creations. They appreciate this spiritual connection, and expend no energy on depreciating or criticizing it. They never feel separated from the assistance that this entire life-giving system offers.

Therefore, connectors aren't surprised when synchronicity or coincidence brings them the fruits of their intentions. They know in their hearts that those seemingly miraculous happenings were brought into their immediate life space because they were already connected to them. Ask connectors about it and they'll tell you, *Of course, it's the law of attraction at work. Stay tuned vibrationally to the Source of all life that intended you, and everyone else here and all of the powers of that field of intention will cooperate with you to bring into your life what you desire.* They know that this is how the universe works. Others may insist that connectors are just plain lucky, but the people who enjoy the power of intention know otherwise. They know that they can negotiate the presence of anything they place their attention on as long as they stay consistent with the seven faces of intention.

Connectors don't brag about their good fortune, but are in a perpetual state of gratitude and radical humility. They understand how the universe works, and they stay blissfully in tune with it, rather than challenging or finding fault with it. Ask them about this and they'll tell you that we're part of a dynamic energy system. *Energy that moves faster,* they explain, *dissolves and nullifies slower-moving energy.* These people choose to be in harmony with the invisible spiritual energy. They've trained their thoughts to move at the levels of the higher vibrations, and consequently they're able to deflect lower/slower vibrations.

Connectors have an uplifting effect when they come into contact with people who are living in lower energy levels. Their peacefulness causes others to feel calm and assured, and they radiate an energy of serenity and peace. They're not interested in winning arguments or accumulating allies. Rather than trying to persuade you to think like they do, they're convincing through the energy they exude. People feel loved by connectors, because they're merged with the Source of all life, which is love.

Connectors tell you without hesitation that they choose to feel good regardless of what's going on around them or how others might judge them. They know that feeling bad is a choice, and that it isn't useful for correcting unpleasant situations in the world. So they use their emotions as a guidance system to determine how attuned they are to the power of intention. If they feel bad in any way, they use this as an indicator that it's time to change their energy level so that it matches up with the peaceful, loving energy of the Source. They'll repeat to themselves: *I want to feel good,* and they'll bring their thoughts into harmony with this desire.

If the world is at war, they still opt to feel good. If the economy takes a nosedive, they still want to feel good. If crime rates go up or hurricanes rage somewhere on the planet, they still choose to feel good. If you ask them why they don't feel bad when so many bad things are happening in the world, they'll smile and remind you that *the world of spirit from which all is intended works in peace, love, harmony, kindness, and abundance, and that is where I choose to reside within myself. My feeling bad will only ensure that I attract more of feeling bad into my life.*

Connectors simply don't allow their well-being to be contingent on anything external to themselves—not the weather, not the wars someplace on the globe, not the political landscape, not the economy, and certainly not anyone else's decision to be low energy. They work with the field of intention, emulating what they know is the creative Source of all.

Connectors are always in touch with their infinite nature. Death is not something that they fear, and they'll tell you, if you ask, that they were never truly born nor will they ever die. They see death as taking off a garment or moving from one room into another—merely a transition. They point to the invisible energy that intends everything into existence and see this as their true self. Because connectors always feel aligned to everyone and everything in the universe, they don't experience the feeling of being separate from anyone else or from what they'd like to attract into their lives. Their connection is invisible and nonmaterial, but it's never doubted. Consequently, they rely on this inner, invisible spiritual energy that permeates all things. They live in harmony with Spirit, never seeing themselves as separate. This awareness is key to their seeing the power of intention at work on a daily basis.

You simply can't convince connectors that what they're intending won't materialize, because they trust in their connection to Source energy so strongly. They'll invite you to choose which possibility you're going to identify with, and then encourage you to live as if it had already occurred. If you can't do it, and are stuck in worry, doubt, and fear, they'll wish you well, but they'll continue what they call *thinking from the end*. They can see what it is they intend to manifest into their lives as if it already had materialized, and for them, because it's so real in their thoughts, it's their reality. They'll tell you forthrightly: *My thoughts, when harmonized with the field of intention, are God's thoughts, and this is how I choose to think.* You'll see if you follow them closely enough that they're exceptional at realizing the fruits of their intentions.

Connector people are exceptionally generous. It's as if what they want for themselves is dwarfed only by wanting it even more for other people. They take great pleasure in giving. Others may wonder how they ever accumulate anything for themselves, yet their lives are filled with abundance, and they seem to lack nothing that they desire. *The secret to the power of intention,* they'll tell you, *is in thinking and acting the same as the all-providing Source from which all originates. It's always providing, and I choose to be a provider, too. The more I give of myself and all that flows to me, the more I see flowing back to me.*

Connectors are highly inspired people. They live more in spirit than in form. Consequently, they're inspired and inspiring, as opposed to informed and filled with information. These are people who have a strong sense of their own destiny. They know why they're here, and they know that they're more than an encapsulated collection of bones, blood, and organs in a skin- and hair-covered body. They're all about living this purpose and choosing to avoid being distracted by the demands of the ego. They have great reverence for the world of Spirit, and by communing with this Source, they stay inspired.

Their level of energy is exceptionally high. It's an energy that defines them as connectors. It's the energy of the Source, a fast vibrational frequency that brings love to the presence of hatred and converts that hatred to love. They bring a peaceful countenance to the presence of chaos and disharmony, and convert the lower energies to the higher energy of peace. When you're around those who dwell in the field of intention, you'll feel energized, cleansed, healthier, and inspired. They have a noticeable absence of judgment toward others, and they aren't immobilized by the thoughts or actions of others. They often get labeled as aloof and distant because they don't gravitate toward small talk and gossip. They'll tell you that it is the Spirit that gives life, and that everyone on this planet has this Spirit within them as an all-powerful force for good. They believe it, they live it, and they inspire others.

They'll even go so far as to tell you that imbalances in the earth such as earthquakes, volcanic eruptions, and extreme weather patterns are the result of a collective imbalance in human consciousness. They'll remind you that our bodies are made up of the same materials as the earth, that the fluid that comprises 98 percent of our blood was once ocean water, and that the minerals in our bones were components of the finite supply of minerals in the earth. They view themselves as one with the planet, and feel a responsibility to stay in balanced harmony with the field of intention to help to stabilize and harmonize the forces of the universe that can get out of balance when we live from excessive ego. They'll tell you that all thoughts, feelings, and emotions are vibrations, and that the frequency of these vibrations can create disturbances—not only in ourselves, but in everything that's made of the same materials.

Connectors will encourage you to stay in vibrational harmony with Source out of a sense of responsibility to the entire planet, and they regard this as a vital function to emulate. This isn't something they think about and discuss from a purely intellectual perspective; it's what they feel deeply within themselves and live passionately every day.

As you observe these connectors, you'll note that they don't dwell on illness and disease. They move through their life as if their body is in perfect health. They actually think and feel that any current disease pattern has never been present, and they believe that they're already healed. They believe that they attract the new outcome, because they know that there are many possible outcomes for any given condition, even for a condition that may seem to others to be impossible to overcome. They'll tell you that the possibilities for healing outcomes are here and now, and the course that an illness will take is a matter of their own perspective. Just as they believe that external turbulent systems become peaceful in the presence of our peace, they see this as a possibility for internal turbulence. Ask them about their healing capabilities and they'll say, *I'm already healed, and I think and feel from only this perspective.*

You'll often see your illnesses and physical complaints disappear when you're in the presence of exceptionally high-energy connectors. Why? Because their high spiritual energy nullifies and eradicates the lower energies of illness. Just as being in the presence of connectors makes you feel better because they exude and radiate joyful appreciative energy, so too will your body heal by being in this kind of energy field.

Connectors are aware of the need to avoid low energy. They'll quietly retreat from loud, bellicose, opinionated people, sending them a silent blessing and unobtrusively moving along. They don't spend time watching violent TV shows or reading accounts of atrocities and war statistics. They might appear docile or uninteresting to people who wallow in the horrors being discussed and broadcast. Since connectors have no need to win, to be right, or to dominate others, their power is the fact that they uplift others with their presence. They communicate their views by being in harmony with the creative energy of the Source. They're never offended, because their ego isn't involved in their opinions.

Connectors live their lives matched up vibrationally to the field of intention. To them, everything is energy. They know that being hostile, hateful, or even angry toward people who believe in and support low-energy activities, which involve violence in any form, will only contribute to that kind of debilitating activity in the world.

The connectors live through higher/faster energy that allows them to access their intuitive powers readily. They have an inner knowing about what's coming. If you ask them about it, they'll tell you, *I can't explain it, but I just know it because I feel it inside.* Consequently, they're seldom confounded when the events they anticipate and intend to create . . . manifest. Rather than being surprised, they actually expect things to work out. By staying so connected to Source energy, they're able to activate their intuition and have insight into what is possible and how to go about achieving it. Their inner knowing allows them to be infinitely patient, and they're never dissatisfied with the speed or the manner in which their intentions are manifesting.

Connectors frequently mirror the seven faces of intention written about throughout the pages of this book. You'll see people who are extraordinarily creative, who have no need to fit in or to do things the way others expect them to. They apply their unique individuality to tasks, and they'll tell you that they can create anything that they place their attention and imagination on.

Connectors are exceptionally kind and loving people. They know that harmonizing with Source energy is replicating the kindness from which they originated. Yet it's not an effort for connectors to be kind. They're always grateful for what comes to them, and they know that kindness toward all of life and our planet is how to display gratitude. By being kind, others want to return the favor and become allies in helping them achieve their intentions. They associate with an unlimited number of people, all of whom are full of love, kindness, and generosity—assisting each other in fulfilling their desires.

You'll also notice how connectors see the beauty in our world. They always find something to appreciate. They can get lost in the beauty of a starry night or a frog on a lily pad. They see beauty in children, and they find a natural radiance and splendor in the aged. They have no desire to judge anyone in low-energy negative terms, and they know that the all-creating Source brings only beauty into material form and so it is always available.

Connectors never know enough! They're inquisitive about life, and they're attracted to every manner of activity. They find something to enjoy in all fields of human and creative endeavors, and are always expanding their own horizons. This openness to everything and all possibilities, and this quality of always expanding, characterizes their proficiency at manifesting their desires. They never say *no* to the universe. Whatever life sends them, they say, *Thank you. What can I learn, and how can I grow from what I'm receiving?* They refuse to judge anyone or anything that the Source offers them, and this always-expanding attitude is what ultimately matches them up with Source energy and opens up their life to receiving all that the Source is willing to provide. They're an open door that's never closed to possibilities. This makes them totally receptive to the abundance that's always ceaselessly flowing.

These attitudes that you see in connector people are precisely the reason that these folks seem so lucky in life. When you're around them, you feel energized, purposeful, inspired, and unified. You're seeing people whom you want to hang around with because they energize you, and this brings you a feeling of empowerment. When you feel empowered and energized, you step into the flow of abundant Source energy yourself, and you inadvertently invite others to do the same. The connection isn't just to Source energy, it's to everyone else and everything in the universe. Connectors are aligned with the entire cosmos and every particle within the cosmos. This connection makes the infinite power of intention possible and available.

These highly realized people think *from the end*, experiencing what they wish to intend before it shows up in material form. They use their feelings as a gauge to determine if they're synchronized with the power of intention. If they feel good, they know that they're in vibrational harmony with Source. If they feel bad, they use this indicator to adjust to higher energy levels. And finally, they act on these thoughts of intention and good feelings as if all that they desired were already here. If you ask them what you can do to make your desires come true, they'll unhesitatingly advise you to *change the way you look at things, and the things you look at will change.*

I urge you to replicate their inner world, and rejoice in the infinitely magnificent power of intention.

It works—I guarantee it!

～ ✳ ～ ✳ ～

# ACKNOWLEDGMENTS

I would like to acknowledge Joanna Pyle, who has been my personal editor for two decades. You, Joanna, make my ideas and my disjointed stream-of-consciousness writing into a cogent format called a book. I couldn't do it without you, and I'm deeply grateful for your loving presence in my life.

To my personal manager, Maya Labos, for almost a quarter of a century you've been there for me, and you've never once said, "That's not my job." Other writers and speakers have 25 assistants every year; I've had only *one* for 25 years. Thank you, thank you, thank you!

For my publisher and my close personal friend, Reid Tracy, at Hay House, you've believed in this project from the very beginning, and you were willing to do what it took to make it all happen. Thanks, friend. I love and respect you and your courage.

I'd also like to recognize the teachings of Abraham, as brought to us through Esther and Jerry Hicks.

And finally, to Ellen Beth Goldhar, your loving inspiration guided me throughout the writing of this book. Thank you for your spirited suggestions and critical analysis of these ideas on intention as a synonym for the loving Source from which we all emanate and to which we all aspire to reconnect.

⌁ ✳ ⌁ ✳ ⌁

# INSPIRATION

*For my mother, Hazel Irene Dyer.*
*You inspire me—*
*thank you, thank you, thank you!*

*For Immaculée Ilibagiza.*
*You could never even imagine*
*how much better off this world is*
*because you were "left to tell."*
*I love you.*

# INTRODUCTION

**I LOVE BEING INSPIRED,** and I trust that the idea of living an inspired life appeals to you as well. I've written this book with the paramount idea of showing you what I've learned about this magical concept.

Writing this book has been a transcendent experience for me. For many months I awoke every morning at approximately 3:30, and after spending my own personal, private moments with God, I sat down to write. Every word of this book was written out longhand. I'd place my hand on the table and allow the ideas to flow from the invisible world of Spirit through my heart and onto the pages. I know deep within me that I do not own these words—I'm merely an instrument through which these ideas are expressed. I trust in this process, and it works as long as I remain "in-Spirit" while I write. I also trust that these ideas will work for you.

This is the most personal book I've written in my 35 years as an author. I've chosen to use examples from my own life—that is, those I've experienced firsthand. The personal nature of this book is a deliberate choice. I discovered as I went along that, in order to write about such a deeply felt subject as inspiration, I needed to convey what I felt as authentically as possible. Just as one can never actually know what a mango tastes like from another person's description, I wouldn't have been able to adequately convey my familiarity with the experience of inspiration by citing case studies of others. By writing from my heart, I've been able to keep the flavor of inspiration alive here in these pages.

(By the way, if you're interested in why I appear on the cover of this book looking blissfully at a butterfly, read the final chapter, "How Life Looks When I Am Inspired." As I was finishing this work, I had an incredible mystical encounter with one of God's most fragile creations. In the last chapter I've described that astonishing experience, along with what *your* life might begin to look like if you apply the insights offered throughout *Inspiration*.)

I'm also well aware that I've repeated one theme over and over throughout these pages. I decided not to edit out this repetition because I see this book as an instrument for moving you to a place where you truly understand what it means to be in-Spirit. This oft-repeated theme is: *Live in-Spirit. You came from Spirit, and to be inspired you must become more like where you came from. You must live so as to become more like God.*

One of my favorite mentors and storytellers, Anthony de Mello, was a Catholic priest who lived in India and could convert complex philosophical issues into understandable and simple teachings using the art of storytelling. Here's a short tale from *The Heart of the Enlightened*, in which Father de Mello does such a good job of summing up much of what I want to convey to you about living in-Spirit:

> The devotee knelt to be initiated into discipleship. The guru whispered the sacred mantra into his ear, warning him not to reveal it to anyone.
> "What will happen if I do?" asked the devotee.
> Said the guru, "Anyone you reveal the mantra to will be

liberated from the bondage of ignorance and suffering, but you yourself will be excluded from discipleship and suffer damnation."

No sooner had he heard those words than the devotee rushed to the marketplace, collected a large crowd around him, and repeated the sacred mantra for all to hear.

The disciples later reported this to the guru and demanded that the man be expelled from the monastery for his disobedience.

The guru smiled and said, "He has no need of anything I can teach. His action has shown him to be a guru in his own right."

I trust that the meaning of this story will become clearer and clearer as you immerse yourself in this book. You have a profound calling back to Spirit. It is working right now in your life, otherwise you wouldn't be reading these very words in this very instant. I urge you to heed that calling and come to know the pure bliss that awaits you as you make an inspired life your reality.

In-Spirit,
Wayne W. Dyer

"The highest knowledge man can attain
is the yearning for peace, for the union
of his will with an infinite will,
his human will with God's will."

— ALBERT SCHWEITZER

"Every tree and plant in the meadow
seemed to be dancing,
those which average eyes would see
as fixed and still."

— RUMI

"Let me have the glory with Thee
that I had with Thee even before the beginning."

— JESUS OF NAZARETH

# PART I

# INSPIRATION—
# LIVING IN-SPIRIT

*"A physical body was given him [man]
by Nature at birth. Somewhere exists
the original Divine spark launched
from God and which, refound,
will be his conscious spirit."*

— RODNEY COLLIN
from *The Theory of Conscious Harmony*

# CHAPTER 1

# LIVING YOUR LIFE IN-SPIRIT

*"When you are inspired . . .*
*dormant forces, faculties, and talents become alive,*
*and you discover yourself to be a greater person*
*by far than you ever dreamed yoursef to be."*

— PATANJALI

**IN THE TITLE OF THIS BOOK,** I've deliberately used the word *calling* to indicate the importance of inspiration as it applies to our lives. There's a voice in the Universe entreating us to remember our purpose, our reason for being here now in this world of impermanence. The voice whispers, shouts, and sings to us that this experience—of being in form in space and time—has meaning. That voice belongs to inspiration, which is within each and every one of us.

Inspiration responds to our attentiveness in various and sometimes unexpected ways. For example, when I began writing this book, I debated between the two titles *Inspiration: Your Ultimate Destiny* or *Inspiration: Your Ultimate Calling.* One day while swimming in the ocean, I was going back and forth in my mind, trying out both titles. Still uncertain when I'd finished my swim, I called Reid Tracy, president and CEO of Hay House, the company that publishes my books, from a pay phone to get his opinion about the title. While I waited for him to answer, the word *calling* appeared on the miniature screen of the phone. Nothing else, just *calling*. And then the word began to flash on and off as if it were trying to get my attention.

When Reid answered, I told him what had just occurred, and we both agreed on *Inspiration: Your Ultimate Calling* for the title of my new book. All of this may appear to be nothing more than a silly coincidence, but I know better.

Consider that the word *coincidence* itself relates to the mathematical idea of angles that coincide. When two angles join in this way, they're said to fit together perfectly. Not accidentally— *perfectly*. Any so-called coincidence might then just be an alignment of forces fitting together in flawless harmony. The word *calling* flashing before my eyes, for instance, at the exact moment that I was trying to choose between *calling* or *destiny* exemplifies an opportunity to notice something important. You see, what catches our attention might be more than a coincidence—it might also be a potential incident of inspiration.

We know that there's something deep within us waiting to be known, which we sometimes call a "gut reaction" to life's events. We have a built-in yearning to seek our inspired self and feel wholeness, a kind of inexplicable sense that patiently demands recognition and action. We might describe it as a mechanism persistently projecting the words *destiny, mission,* or *purpose* on our inner screen. It's possible to have our daily behavior so aligned with these inner feelings that we unequivocally know what our calling is. In fact, if you put this book aside and check in with what you're feeling at this moment, my guess is that you'll hear a part of yourself crying out, "Yes, I want to have more inspiration in my life! I want to know my calling!"

I promise you that after your first reading of this book, you'll begin to be intimately connected to your inspired self. I say this with such certainty because it's *my* calling to write and publish these words. You see, *you're* a component of *my* ultimate calling.

I think of the word *inspiration* as meaning "being in-Spirit." When we're in-Spirit, we're inspired . . . and when we're inspired, it's because we're back in-Spirit, fully awake to Spirit within us. Being inspired is an experience of joy: We feel completely connected to our Source and totally on purpose; our creative juices flow, and we bring exceptionally high energy to our daily life. We're not judging others or ourselves—we're uncritical and unbothered by behaviors or attitudes that in uninspired moments are frustrating. Our heart sings in appreciation for every breath; and we're tolerant, joyful, and loving.

Being in-Spirit isn't necessarily restricted to the work we do or the activities of our daily life. We can be inspired and at the same time be unsure of what vocation to pursue or what activities we want to schedule. Inspiration is a simple recognition of Spirit within ourselves. It's a return to that invisible, formless field from which all things emanate, a field of energy that I called "intention" in my previous book *The Power of Intention*.

In *this* book I'm going beyond an understanding of the inherent power of intention, however, by describing how to live in-Spirit and hear the voice of inspiration even when we're doing absolutely nothing that we'd call purposeful. This is quite different from being highly motivated; in fact, it's almost the opposite of motivation.

### Motivation vs. Inspiration

It's important to note that whatever is needed to fulfill our calling is part of the present process. Arthur Miller, who was perhaps the most accomplished dramatist in the U.S., is an example of a man who knew this. In an interview late in his life, he was asked, "Are you working on a new play?" Mr. Miller's answer went something like this: "I don't know if I am or not, but I probably am." This delightful response suggests that Miller's writing came from inspiration—that is, something other than ego spurred him on.

By contrast, highly motivated people have a kind of ego determination driving them over obstacles and toward goals—*nothing* gets in their way. Now, most of us have been taught that this is an admirable trait; in fact, when we're not accomplishing and demonstrating drive and ambition, we've been told to "get motivated!" Lectures, books, videos, and audio recordings abound that preach that all we have to do is dedicate ourselves to an idea with actions designed to make it a reality. This is a beneficial approach for a different level of accomplishment—but what we're exploring in these pages is what leads us to precisely what we're meant to be and do . . . our ultimate calling.

If motivation is grabbing an idea and carrying it through to an acceptable conclusion, then inspiration is the reverse. When we're in the grip of inspiration, an idea has taken hold of us from the invisible reality of Spirit. Something that seems to come from afar, where we allow ourselves to be moved by a force that's more powerful than our ego and all of its illusions, is inspiration. And being in-Spirit is the place where we connect to the invisible reality that ultimately directs us toward our calling. Often we can identify these inspired times by their insistence, and because they seem not to make sense while at the same time they keep appearing in our consciousness.

If we ignore inspiration's powerful attraction, the result is personal discomfort or a sense of disconnection from ourselves. For any number of reasons, we might be resistant when we feel called to create, perform, visit a foreign place, meet someone, express ourselves, help another, or be a part of a cause. Inspiration is a calling to proceed even though we're unsure of goals or achievements—it may even insist that we go in the direction of uncharted territory.

Throughout various stages of life, inspiration is the thought or idea reconnecting us to the energy we were part of prior to becoming a microscopic particle. I call this "surrendering to our destiny and allowing ourselves to hear the call." At this point we can differentiate between the demands of our ego and those of the ego-dominated people and institutions that deflect us from the call of inspiration. As we move more deeply into Spirit, we cease to be guided by the ego demands of others or ourselves. We surrender to the always-present force that urges us to be in this blissful state of inspiration. We're guided by our ultimate calling, which is truly our life purpose.

### A Force Beyond Even Our Own Life

The invisible reality, where all physical life originates, is more powerful and significant than the tiny parenthesis in eternity that we call "life," or what comes between birth and death. The spiritual dimension of the invisible reality calls to us in this material world of beginnings and endings. This spiritual essence is our Source, which is magnificent and stupendous compared to our earthly self. When we're inspired (as I refer to it in this book), we're connected to this force that's greater in every respect than our physical being. It was in-Spirit that our purpose was laid out, and it's in-Spirit where our magnificence is absolute and irrefutable. Before merging into form, we were a part of God, with all the inherent qualities of a Creator who sends forth abundance, creativity, love, peace, joy, and well-being.

When we feel what Arthur Miller apparently did, we acknowledge and rejoin that more expansive energy field running through us, and we invite this Source to participate in our daily life. We suspend our ego identification and warm to the idea of trusting the energy that created us. We choose to live in-Spirit, entrusting ourselves to something greater than our life as a physical being. When we listen and allow it to, Spirit guides us; when we fail to listen—or allow our ego to get in the way and run the show—we're going to be uninspired. It's that simple.

Later in this book there are specific suggestions for communing with and connecting to this part of ourselves. First, I'd like to share some of the personal experiences I've had when I've been in-Spirit.

### My Experience with Being in-Spirit

When I'm in-Spirit, I have a feeling of contentment, but more than this, I experience joy. I'm able to receive the vibrational energies of my Source—call them voices, messages, silent reminders, invisible suggestions, or what have you, but they're vibrations of energy that I'm able to align with as I get myself out of the way. Wolfgang Amadeus Mozart, one of the world's great geniuses, once remarked: "When I am, as it were, completely myself, entirely alone, and of good cheer—say, traveling in a carriage, or walking after a good meal, or during the night when I cannot sleep—it is on such occasions that my ideas flow best and most abundantly. Whence and how they come, I know not, nor can I force them."

We don't have to be a genius to know what Mozart speaks of—the same force in a different way is flowing through you and me right now. I've learned to remove resistance to the free flow of this spiritual energy by reminding myself to align with it, or to be in-Spirit in my thoughts and expectations.

Spirit doesn't dwell on the impossibility of anything—that is, it doesn't focus on not being able to create, on things not working out, on expecting the worst, or on being stuck in place. When I'm in-Spirit, I want my present moment and thoughts to align perfectly with what I desire. I want to offer an experience of inspiration to my audience, so I don't give a speech thinking, *I'll probably disappoint them.* I choose to know that if I stumble or forget something in the middle of my talk, the inspiration to get me through it will be there. The results are exhilarating feelings of inspiration.

When I sit down to write, my desire is to invite Spirit to express through me, and I encourage ideas to flow freely. Like Mozart, I'm connected, as it were, to my Source in-Spirit, thinking and expecting to be the instrument of my spiritual Source. Ideas flow, and whatever assistance I need just shows up. And like Mozart, I can't describe how the ideas come, and I can't force them. Staying in-Spirit seems to be the secret to this feeling of being inspired.

I also find that inspiration flows in other areas of my life when my primary mission is like what Michael Berg so beautifully describes in *Becoming Like God: Kabbalah and Our Ultimate Destiny:* ". . . just as every being is God's business, every being becomes our business as well." That is, being inspired necessitates the willingness to suspend ego and enter a space where I want to share who I am and what I have in a completely unlimited fashion.

At a recent lecture, for instance, a woman named Rolina De Silva approached me at the break to ask if I'd visit her teenage daughter, Alison, in The Hospital for Sick Children in Toronto. Alison had been hospitalized for many, many months due to a rare disease that's characterized by a breakdown of the lymphatic system. Her intestines had been perforated, so she was unable to process proteins and fats . . . and her prognosis was dismal at best.

As I sat with Alison on my third visit with her, I held her hand and noticed that a scab was forming on the top of her hand from a minor injury brought about by an intravenous injection. Something came over me in that moment, and I looked into the girl's eyes and reminded her that the scab was a gift to her. It indicated that the essence of well-being (our Source) was working within her. I reminded her that all she had to do was to summon that same well-being to her abdomen. "You're already connected to Spirit," I almost shouted, "otherwise you wouldn't be growing a scab over that cut on your hand!"

When I spoke with Rolina 14 months later, I asked if she remembered that day in the hospital when I held Alison's hand and felt inspired by the scab. Rolina replied that that day was a new beginning for her daughter, as something inside of her opened. Always before she'd had a blank look on her face, yet she gave off an air of intolerance about the entire process. When the girl realized that she was indeed connected to Spirit, evinced by the presence of the scab forming on her hand, she changed her attitude completely.

Today Alison is back home and actually doing work to raise money for that same hospital where she spent so many months as a critical-care patient. (If you ever see me speaking on television or in person, you'll notice a little angel pin that I wear, which was given to me by Alison as a thank-you gift. To me, this pin is a symbol of the angel that guided me that day to speak to Alison as I did.)

I know in my heart that when we remember we're always connected to this Source and that we can summon the well-being of

God, it is then that we're said to be inspired. Whether the outcome is miraculous, as was Alison's, or our physical reconnection to our Source is completed through the death of our body, we live out our moment in-Spirit. It's important to understand that *each and every one of us represents God or Spirit revealing Itself here on our planet.*

Also, keep in mind that our creative force is a forthcoming energy. I find that when I emulate it, the result is inspiration flowing through my life, and I'm living a life that is my ultimate calling. If I feel called to something higher and then do nothing about it, I'll generally find myself experiencing discontentment and disappointment. But when I act upon that calling by being in vibrational harmony with it, and by being willing to share it with as many people as possible, I feel inspired.

When I donate books to a prison or a library, for example, I feel my ultimate calling being fulfilled by my actions. And just this morning I received a thank-you call from a woman who'd asked me for an endorsement for her work. I'd taken the time to respond with an appraisal of how her spiritual practice of healing hypnosis had benefited me and what I thought it could do for others. She said, "Your words were the greatest Christmas gift I ever received." So why am *I* still inspired by this? Because I left the world of ego and entered the world of expressing Spirit to benefit another person.

These experiences of being in-Spirit are available to all of us— I've simply used some personal vignettes here to illustrate ways to discover the calling for each of us. I've felt called to help others, and my life has taken me in that direction.

### In What Direction Are <u>You</u> Moving?

Being in-Spirit is a direction we take, rather than a destination to be reached. Living our life in-Spirit requires us to determine that direction, and we do so by noticing our thoughts and behaviors. Thoughts that are in-Spirit reflect a vibrational alignment moving us toward our ultimate calling—and, obviously, this is the direction we want to take. Once we begin to observe our thoughts, we realize that there are many times we're going in the opposite direction. When we catch ourselves, with conscious effort we can make a U-turn with new thoughts. For example, blaming something we call "evil" is thinking in the wrong direction. When we see things in our world that we label evil, what we're really seeing are people moving away from their Source, not individuals in the grip of an evil power.

In our world there are many activities that seem to be motivated by evil, but we must be careful not to assign power to a force that doesn't exist. There are only people moving away from Source with behavior that contradicts the creative energy that's within them. When we have thoughts that reflect hatred, judgment, and exclusion, we're moving away from our Source. When those non-spiritual thoughts explode in the painful form of terrorist activities, for instance, we call them evil. While the pejorative labels that we use may alleviate our feelings of anger and helplessness, they don't help us be in-Spirit. It's imperative for all who seek an inspired life to assess the direction of their thoughts and behaviors in terms of going toward, or away from, Spirit. Condemning behavior as an evil force is thinking that takes us away from living in-Spirit.

To become inspired on a daily basis, we must be able to quickly identify any thoughts that are moving us away from our Source, and then shift the direction. We need to bring love to the presence of hatred, as Saint Francis advised. When we're consumed with thoughts we've labeled as evil, we need to notice that we're headed in the wrong direction. It's difficult to comprehend because we're accustomed to blaming our problems on external forces such as evil or hate, but we know better. We can make that U-turn by using the same energy within us that has us traveling away from God.

Evil, hatred, fear, and even illness soften with love and kindness when we're in-Spirit. When we make that U-turn, we make an alignment correction and move back into the space of Spirit in our thoughts and actions.

# Some Suggestions for Putting
# the Ideas in This Chapter
# to Work for You

— Commit to at least one daily experience where you share something of yourself with no expectation of being acknowledged or thanked. For example, before I begin my daily routine of exercise, meditation, or writing, I go to my desk and choose my gift for that day. Sometimes it's just a phone call to a stranger who's written to me, or perhaps I order flowers or send a book or present to someone who has helped me in a local store. On one occasion I wrote to the president of the university I graduated from to start a scholarship fund, on another day I took a calender to the yard man, on another I sent a check to Habitat for Humanity, and on another I sent three rolls of postage stamps to my son who'd just started his own business. It doesn't matter if this activity is big or small—it's a way to begin the day in-Spirit.

— Become conscious of all thoughts that aren't aligned with your Source. The moment you catch yourself excluding someone or having a judgmental thought, say the words "in-Spirit" to yourself. Then make a silent effort to shift that thought to match up with Source energy.

— In the morning before you're fully awake, and again as you're going to sleep, take one or two minutes of what I call "quiet time with God." Be in a state of appreciation and say aloud, "I want to feel good."

— *My life is bigger than I am.* Remind yourself of this statement. Print it out and post it strategically in your home, car, or workplace. The "I" is your ego identification. Your life is Spirit flowing through you unhindered by ego—it's what you showed up here to actualize—and is infinite. The "I" that identifies you is a fleeting snippet.

— Dedicate your life to something that reflects an awareness of your Divinity. You are greatness personified, a resident genius, and a creative master—regardless of anyone's opinion. Make a silent dedication to encourage and express your Divine nature.

\* \* \*

*A Course in Miracles* quotes Jesus as saying: "If you want to be like me I will help you, knowing that we are alike. If you want to be different, I will wait until you change your mind." Being inspired is truly being like your Source. If you're not, then your Source is politely waiting for you to do something as simple as *change your mind.*

CHAPTER 2

# YOUR LIFE BEFORE YOUR BIRTH INTO A BODY

*"All bodies emerge from the Soul and return to it.*
*The visible emerges from the invisible,*
*is controlled by it, and returns to it."*

— LAO RUSSELL

**QUANTUM PHYSICISTS TELL US** that particles don't create more particles; rather, they're said to proceed from what are described as "waves of energy." And physicists and metaphysicists agree that, in a physical sense, life as we know it springs from an invisibleness that we often call Spirit. I'm sure that it comes as no surprise to you that the invisible world of Spirit from which all physical particles originate isn't explainable or verifiable. Words can't define with precision what's inherently clear to us at moments of *knowing*.

This is clearly a purposeful Universe, with an intelligence supporting its creation and continuing evolution—and we're pieces of that intelligence by virtue of having emerged from it. Consider, for example, that scientific analysis of even a droplet of blood reveals all of the characteristics in our entire body's supply. The percentage of iron in that droplet is proportionately the same as in that which flows through our entire body—so it's easy to agree that the drop of blood is identical to the source from which it was removed.

Now think about what happens to that droplet of blood when it remains in the state of separation: It can't fortify or heal us, and it can't circulate freely. Disconnected from its source long enough, it will simply dry up, decay, and disintegrate, even though it contains all of the physical properties necessary to survive that its original source does.

I believe that our transition from spiritual Source to physical beings made up of particles is similar to that bit of blood in that we contain all of the same properties as our Source—but unlike that droplet, we're never completely separated from our Source. I know that there are no accidents in a Universe directed by a Source energy that creates endless real magic in the form of Its creations. I know that we agreed to move from the world of Spirit into the world of particles and form, to come forth at the exact time that we did, and to leave when we've agreed to do so. I also know that we decided to bring joyful perfection to this world, and to share that God-like energy with everyone we encounter here on Earth. It's our nature to do so!

Ancient mystical traditions teach that our planet exists as a vehicle to share the Creator's universal love, beauty, and abundance. When we leave Spirit, we don't necessarily have to separate from our original nature, but that's what seems to happen. Becoming inspired requires our being curious about, and attentive to, feelings that emerge to help us reconnect with our original self.

Inspiration flowing through us is a messenger from the realm of our nonphysical self, from where we were before we entered this visible world of form. We have the ability to return to that formlessness right now, in our body, without experiencing physical death.

This is largely a mental excursion, which requires us to think in ways that we imagine the All-Creating Energy, or God, thinks. What must it have been like just before we made the transition from Spirit to form? In the infinite oneness that we were (and still are), something took place to allow that aforementioned wave of energy to manifest into a tiny subatomic particle, and then to a quark, an electron, an atom, a molecule, and ultimately a cell that comprised all that we needed for the physical manifestation of our body and all of its pursuits, accomplishments, acquisitions, and physical properties.

Our life before becoming an embodiment of Spirit was exactly like our Source. Then we began the transition process and became a tiny fetus intended to spend nine months developing in our mother's womb. I contend that we've *chosen* to enter this world of particles and form. In ways that we don't readily comprehend now, when we were in our place of origin we knew what we were coming here to accomplish, and we participated in setting this life process in motion.

Why place the responsibility or blame on any *one* or any *thing* that's not a part of us? On Earth we have been given the gift of volition (that is, we can choose), so let's assume that we had the same capacity when we resided exclusively in the spiritual realm. We chose our physical body, just as we chose the parents we needed for the trip. And it doesn't seem too great a stretch to believe that we chose this life in concert with our Source.

The very first particle of human protoplasm intended to be our self wasn't the architect of our physical being—instead, it was an aspect of an invisible, formless energy field that was our self *manifesting.* In the particle, and the energy field from which it emanated, were the size and shape of our eyes, our legs, our mouth, and so on. So it feels intuitively natural to me to assume that in that field of energy, the very shape of our life was also encapsulated.

You see, deep within us lies an awareness of what shape our life is to take. We can hear that voice, the one that wants us to know our calling, if we choose . . . but first we need to surrender to that Divine plan we signed up for before our conception.

### Our First Nine Months in Form

Let's take a second to go back to what took place from the first moment of our manifestation into a particle, right up until the instant that we emerged from our mother's womb.

Our embryo became a fetus in a space of total faith and harmony—it had no demands, since it was simply carried along by the Divine forces of nature. The basics of our development occurred without our interference: Our brain developed independent of our ideas about how it should be done; our heart, liver, kidneys, toes, fingers, eyebrows, and every other feature appeared on a schedule that seems miraculous from this side of the womb! For most of us, it was nine months in the hands of the Source of life inside a woman's womb (who may or may not have been welcoming our existence). Whatever energy we needed to grow into the being that we signed up to be flowed directly to and through us.

How could we have gotten along so well in those first nine months with only the cooperation of our mother allowing us to develop inside of her? How could everything we required for the beginning of our human journey be so perfectly aligned with the Creative Spirit? The seed that we came from was so tiny that millions of them could fit on the head of a pin, and it looked identical to the seed that begins a giraffe, a palm tree, or any other living organism. So how did it eventually become you or me?

The seed materialized into what we intended to become under the auspices of the Creative Intelligence, and it flourished with the assistance of that remarkable Spirit that's responsible for all of life. The entire process of creation simply unfolded. . . . During those months that we lived in the womb, it's safe to say that we were in-Spirit—we were allowing Spirit to perfectly align without any effort on our part. We were provided for entirely by a life force that none of us can completely describe or explain. We were a little larvae-shaped ooze ball that, in a relatively short period of time, became a human being with the apparatus necessary to support life outside of the womb.

We can see that there's a force in the Universe that's 100 percent trustworthy, one that we relied upon to get us here. It creates and manifests from a spirit of love, cooperation, beauty, and expansiveness, and it's to this flawless work of Spirit that we can return in order to know inspiration. Throughout our life, we continue our development outside of the womb, wherein we rely on the energy of creation to fuel the light of inspiration within us.

Now I'd like to share a conversation I was privileged to have with my originating Spirit. (As I mentioned previously, this is an exercise that we can all do in our imagination.) It was an amazing experience, which I encourage everyone to seek the opportunity to have, or at least be on the lookout for circumstances that will make it happen.

## My Conversation with My Spirit
## Before Manifesting into
## a Physical Particle

Being in a Universe that's created and guided by an organizing intelligence that precludes accidents and coincidences, I've always felt that my presence here at this time is a component of that intelligent system. In a powerful experience of hypnosis, I re-created a conversation between my highest spiritual self and my originating Source to which I'm still connected. This one imaginary exchange has been exceedingly helpful to me for the major portion of my adult life.

I was conceived on the first day of September in 1939 and born on the tenth day of May in 1940. The day of my conception was the same day that Adolf Hitler invaded Poland; two days later, World War II was initiated. I was born on the same day that the Nazis invaded and occupied Belgium, the Netherlands, and Luxembourg, and I saw the Holocaust coming. I knew that I was to play a dominant role in reversing the kind of hatred that precipitated the horrendous actions that resulted in the slaughter of millions.

I came here to teach self-reliance and compassion, just as in an earlier incarnation in the 13th century when I wandered through Europe and Asia with or as Francesco Bernadone (who later became Saint Francis of Assisi), attempting to stop the vicious activities known as the Crusades. My infinite soul was, and still is, tormented by human beings' inhumanity to their fellow humans and wants to eradicate suffering caused by separating ourselves collectively and individually and using violence to settle disputes. The answer, it seems to me, is to teach others how to connect to their Source and stay in this consciousness of love, peace, kindness, and one-ness. When enough of us make this journey back to being in-Spirit, our groups and collectives will reflect the inspiration I'm called to promote in one way or another.

As I readied myself to make the shift from an exclusively spiritual being into the world of particles in 1939, I had the following conversation with the Creative Intelligence I'll call God.

**God:** What would you like to accomplish on this journey you're about to undertake?

**Me:** I'd like to teach self-reliance, compassion, and forgiveness.

**God:** Are you certain this is what you wish to dedicate this lifetime to?

**Me:** Yes. I can see the need even more clearly now.

**God:** Well, then, I think we'd better put your little ass into a series of foster homes and have you stay there for a decade or so, where you'll learn to experience relying upon yourself. And we'll remove your parents so that you won't be dissuaded from your mission.

**Me:** I accept that. But what about my parents? Who will best facilitate my life's purpose?

**God:** You can select Melvin Lyle Dyer as your father. A prisoner, an alcoholic, and a thief, he'll abandon you as a baby and never show up in your life. You'll first practice hating him and seeking revenge, but you'll ultimately forgive him, long after he's left his body. This act of forgiveness will be the single-most important event of your life. It will put you on the path that you're signing up for.

**Me:** And my mother?

**God:** Take Hazel Dyer, Lyle's wife. Her compassion for all of her children will give you an example to follow. She'll steadfastly work herself to the bone to reunite you and your brothers after ten years or so of her own suffering.

**Me:** Isn't it an awfully cruel fate for my father?

**God:** Not at all. He signed up for this 25 years ago. He dedicated this entire lifetime to teach one of his children the lesson of forgiveness—a noble gesture, wouldn't you say? And your mother is here to show you how true compassion shows up every day. Now get down there and participate in becoming a particle.

In the Introduction of my book *You'll See It When You Believe It,* I wrote about finding my father and visiting his grave in the early 1970s. The facts that led me there defy the laws of logic—and visiting it was the final hurdle I needed to overcome before initiating my writing and speaking career, or the mission I'd signed up for back in 1939.

I've also visited the Holocaust sites of Europe and read and reread the history of events that contributed to the hatred that created war. In the 1960s I worked to bring peace to the events surrounding the horrible Vietnam War, and today my attention is often focused on finding an alternative to the violence and hatred in Africa, the Middle East, and particularly Iraq. My calling is deep within me and has a hold on me. Like Arthur Miller, I don't know what I'm going to do next, but I'm probably being guided by what Spirit and I decided at the inception of this journey. One thing I know for certain is that I'm inspired!

I've described my personal insight about my calling to encourage all of you to examine your own life—including all of its travails and success—as a necessary experience in order to fulfill your mission. Looking at life from this perspective nurtures the deep yearning within that will beckon you back to Spirit.

### *Looking at Life from an Inspired Perspective*

As you can see from my own example, it can be a great help to look at your entire life as the unfolding of a plan that you participated in before you even arrived here. By doing so, you shift from blaming others and circumstances to being responsible and feeling your purpose. Whatever shows up in your life then becomes a part of the perfection of this plan. When everything you experience seems unwelcome, for instance, you can search for what you gain from the apparent obstacles.

If we can remember that we're responsible for what we're attracting, we can then eliminate the negative energy we wallow in. If what we desire is to be inspired and feel joy, but the opposite keeps showing up, rather than cursing fate, we can view ourselves as simply being out of creative vibrational alignment. We can shift our vibrations, in the form of thoughts, to those that are more harmonious with our desires, and we can then begin to take the small steps necessary for our inspiration to be sensed. Source energy will cooperate with us when we seek it energetically—moreover, we can begin to reassess our lives for misaligned attractions and imagined bad luck.

With a mental shift of this nature, someone could question why he'd elect to come here as a homosexual, when all it's done is bring him trouble: Parents rejected him, he was the recipient of ridicule throughout childhood, employment opportunities eluded him, and he faced discrimination in every area of his life. Well, maybe if he looks deeper into his spiritual origins, he'd discover that he signed up to teach others to love and accept those who aren't in the mainstream of life. What better way to do so than to have a life in a body that's so easily stereotyped? If this felt true, that person would recognize his calling to be involved in changing prejudicial reactions. Regardless of what goes on in the world of form, inside himself he'd be living in-Spirit.

When we feel peaceful within, we begin to attract more of the peace we desire because we're functioning from a spiritual place of peace. When we engage Spirit, we regain the power of our ultimate Source. Likewise, a beggar on a street corner may have agreed to come into this world of boundaries to teach and generate the awareness that leads to more compassion in this world—or even to teach a single person (perhaps you) to be more compassionate. After all, Source shows up in an endless array of costumes. . . .

In an infinite Universe, there's no time restriction on how many lifetimes we get. With an infinity before us, spending one lifetime teaching compassion doesn't seem outrageous. Similarly, the autistic child, the blind person, the victim of violence, the aborted fetus, the quadriplegic, the starving child, and you—with whatever infirmities and difficulties you've attracted—are part of the perfection of this Universe. The desire to change and improve our world is also a part of that perfection. Therefore, an inspirational attitude is less judgmental and more appreciative, with a keen eye for how God, or Source energy, manifests. And remember: *Source can't be removed from what It creates.*

I love this story that Sri Swami Satchidananda tells in his wonderful book *Beyond Words*. I had the great pleasure of meeting with Swami on several occasions, and he was a supremely inspired being right up until his transition back to nonphysical spirit a few years ago.

> There was a man a long time ago who prayed every day, "God, I really want You to come in person, to have a nice sumptuous lunch with me."
>
> Because he was constantly nagging, God appeared one day and said, "Okay, I'll come."
>
> "God, I'm so happy. When can You come? You must give me some time to prepare everything."
>
> "Okay, I'll come on Friday."
>
> Before He left, the man asked, "Can I invite my friends?"
>
> "Sure," God said. And then He disappeared.

The man invited everybody and started preparing all kinds of delicious food. Friday at noon a huge dining table was set up. Everybody was there, with a big garland and water to wash God's feet. The man knew that God is punctual. When he heard the clock chiming twelve, he said, "What happened? God wouldn't disappoint me. He can't be late. Human beings can be late, but not God."

He was a little puzzled but decided to wait another half hour as a courtesy. Still no God. Then the guests began speaking, "You fool, you said God was coming. We had doubts. Why on Earth would God come and eat with you? Come, let's go."

The man said, "No, wait," and walked inside to see what was happening.

To his great anxiety, he saw a big black dog on the dining table, eating everything there. "Oh, no! God sensed that the lunch was already eaten by a dog. That's why he didn't want to come." He took a big club and started beating the dog. The dog cried and ran away.

Then the man came out to his guests and said, "What can I do? Now, neither God nor you can eat because the food was polluted by a dog. I know that's why God didn't come." He felt so bad that he went back and started praying. Finally God appeared to him again, but there were wounds and bandages all over his body.

"What happened?" asked the man. "You must have gotten into a terrible accident."

"It was no accident," said God. "It was you!"

"Why do You blame me?"

"Because I came punctually at noon and started eating. Then you came and beat Me. You clubbed Me and broke My bones."

"But You didn't come!"

"Are you sure nobody was eating your food?"

"Well, yes, there was a black dog."

"Who is that, then, if not Me? I really wanted to enjoy your food, so I came as a dog."

Everyone and everything contains God or the Source, so be on the lookout for the God-force in every living thing. Explore how this force has delivered to us many blessings in disguise.

We came from a world of pure Spirit and allowed that Source

to take over without any interference or questioning on our part. As long as we were in-Spirit, our Source materialized in a multitude of ways to handle everything. Then, almost immediately after our birth into form, we initiated a program to deny Spirit and emphasize the ego.

But now, as you read these words, you're on the threshold of dropping ego identity and returning to a life where inspiration awaits you. Here are some suggestions to assist you in crossing that threshold.

## Some Suggestions for Putting the Ideas in This Chapter to Work for You

— See yourself as a single cell in a body called humanity, and vow to be a cell that cooperates with all adjacent cells with a sense of belonging to the whole. View uninspired thoughts and actions as impinging on your well-being *and* that of all humanity.

— Make a concerted effort to allow the natural-healing and well-being capacity of your body to play itself out. Refuse to focus on what's wrong in your body and in your life; rather, shift your thoughts to those that allow you to stay in harmony with your Source energy. For example, rather than saying, "I feel sick [or tired]," say, "I want to feel good, so I'll allow my natural connection to well-being to take over right now." Your reformed self-talk invites the flow of inspiration.

— Inventory all the people who were negative and/or destructive elements in your past, and search for ways that their actions might have been helpful events and attitudes that were just disguised as impediments to happiness. For example, my stepfather's alcoholism and drunken ways, which I despised at the time, were powerfully instrumental in helping me deal with my own addictions later on in life. Abandonment, abuse, and disloyalty can be painfully difficult and valuable teachers when you see yourself as having experienced them for a greater good.

— Imagine a conversation, just before your conception, with the Creative Spirit that you materialized from. Review the parents and siblings you selected, as well as the timing of your birth. Find ways that those participants in your life were aligned with the deep inner urge you had as an exclusively spiritual entity to accomplish a calling. Try to make sense of what may at first appear to be a jumble of unrelated items in your life. If this exercise satisfies and inspires you, there's no need to convince anyone else.

— Be mindful of the perfection of the Universe and the Creative Source behind it by noticing whenever you bang your elbow, stub your toe, get hit by a falling tree branch, and so forth. When such events happen, stop and ask yourself, "What was I thinking in that precise moment, and how is it related to what appeared to be an accident?" You'll discover a pattern: What you're thinking is usually mysteriously tied in with what's taking place from moment to moment. Do this to create a constant awareness of your Source and the direction of your life.

\* \* \*

In the next chapter, we'll explore why we left the world where we were in-Spirit. Keep in mind the ancient simple truth that *the mighty oak was once a little nut that held its ground.* We're all a mighty oak in the making, and it's all right to be a little nutty as long as we also hold our ground!

# CHAPTER 3

# WHY WE LEFT OUR FULL-TIME SPIRITUAL IDENTITY BEHIND

*"A sense of separation from God
is the only lack you really need correct."*

— FROM *A COURSE IN MIRACLES*

**WE NOW UNDERSTAND** that we were created out of Spirit, so It must be a part of us. We also realize that for nine months, we totally trusted in this originating Spirit, and all we needed was ·provided for—and then we arrived as a pure representation of Spirit. So why did most of us trade in the "spiritual identity card" for one that wants us to believe in things that are nonexistent where we came from, such as suffering, fear, anxiety, limits, and worries? The answer lies in understanding why we left behind our full-time participation in the world of Spirit.

I've used the term *full-time* to signify that we're always connected to Spirit, even when we think and behave in ways that don't reflect spiritual consciousness. What I'm offering in this book is the awareness that we can return to a full-time position of inspiration, which is the true meaning of our life.

Inspiration can be cultivated and be a driving enthusiasm

*throughout* life, rather than showing up every now and then and just as mysteriously disappearing, seemingly independent of our desire. And it's *everyone's* Divine birthright—that is, it isn't reserved for high-profile creative geniuses in the arts and sciences. The problem is that from birth we're gradually taught to believe exclusively in the world ruled by Club Ego . . . and we put our full-time membership in Club Spirit on hold.

### Our Initiation into Club Ego

When we arrive in this physical world, we're immediately cared for by well-meaning folks who've been taught to believe in the illusion of what Patanjali called "the false self." They think that they're not defined by the spiritual essence from which they came, but by their uniquely special individuality, their possessions, and their accomplishments. They see themselves as separate from each other, from what's materially missing in their lives, and from God.

You can see why the word *ego* is often referred to as an acronym for **e**dging **G**od **o**ut. Ego, you see, is an idea that we acquire from our clogged environment, which is stuffed full of ego-dominated folks. I'm not using the word *ego* to describe overly self-important people who thrive on nauseating delusions of grandeur; rather, I mean it as a catch-all term for defining identification with the false self.

Very early on, ego tells us that we're separate from everyone else—directly contradicting Spirit, which reminds us that we share the same life force with everyone. Ego nags us to compete and insists that we've failed when others defeat us or have more than we do. And more than anything else, ego fears our living an inspired life because then we'll have no need for it.

As we progressed through our developmental years, we weren't trained to stay in-Spirit—quite the opposite! We were constantly reminded that we were what we did in life, and failure to accomplish the kind of life that others saw for us meant that we should feel dejected. Our culture wanted us to learn early that we are what we acquire, and if we have or want very little, then *we* are of very little value. Furthermore, we are what others think of us, so if our reputation is sullied, we're of even less value!

We were indoctrinated in these lessons by family, church, community, school, the media, and even strangers. These ego-dominated edicts were force-fed to us and allowed to mute the deep inner voice that beckoned us to remember why we're here. Eventually, we learned to ignore those in-Spirit murmurs and replace joy, contentment, and bliss with an emptiness that wonders, *What's it all about?* We opted to fit in, chasing someone else's dream and counting up our earnings and possessions to measure our level of success. The nagging feeling that resulted is the result of relinquishing our true spiritual self as an active participant in this life. But take heart: It never left us, and is alive within us today.

### *Ego's Dominating Messages*

We can start returning to being in-Spirit by examining what ego has accomplished in our life, as well as making a determined effort to resist the powerful pressures of *our culture's* ego in favor of an inspired life. Ego is just an illusion . . . so ask yourself if you wish to continue to be controlled by something that isn't true, or would you rather look into what's real and never changes? Keep in mind that Spirit is fixed, permanent, and infinite, while ego comes and goes with the wind.

To continue on with this discussion, I've adapted the following list from a fascinating book called *The Disappearance of the Universe* (Hay House, 2004) by Gary Renard, which gives an account of two spiritual visitors teaching Gary the significance of *A Course in Miracles*. Whether you accept the premise or not is your option—*I* find these teachings to be profound, and they merit consideration.

**1. The ego says, "You're a body." The Holy Spirit says, "You're not even a person—you're just like Me, your Source of being."** This teaching shows that our ego insists we're impermanent, which is opposed to our being what Lao-tzu (the mystical spiritual teacher of the 6th century B.C.) taught: that which never changes. When we think about our life here on Earth, we can't avoid the awareness that everything we experience, including our body, returns to dust to be recycled by Spirit. Our ego finds this concept impossible to accept.

**2. The ego says, "Your thoughts are very important." The Holy Spirit insists, "Only thoughts you think with God are real—nothing else matters."** This teaching explains that thoughts centering on ourselves, appearance, possessions, fears, or relationship problems are not only unimportant, they're not real. *Ouch!* The ego flinches at such commentary. But if we examine these thoughts from Spirit's infinite perspective, we see that they're indeed unreal. When we were totally immersed in-Spirit, we only had thoughts of Spirit because that's all we were; when we left It behind, we opted for thoughts that our ego told us were important. *A Course in Miracles* tells us that we didn't even have to think in heaven because we were thought by God. So we can access permanent inspiration by letting ourselves once again be thought by God and achieve a state of heaven on Earth.

**3. Your ego says, "The Lord giveth and the Lord taketh away." The Holy Spirit asserts, "God only gives and never takes away."** When living an inspired life, we're focused on giving our life away and simultaneously observing how it's returned, thus fortifying the idea of what goes around comes around. Ego is constantly telling us to be fearful about losing what we have and warning us of greedy others who'll take what's ours—but God doesn't take away from us. As we learn to think this way, we attract more of what's missing in our life. The reason for this is simple: We become what we think about. If we think about giving, like God does, the

Universe will provide. If we think about things being taken away, then that's what we'll attract.

**4. The ego says, "There's good and bad." The Holy Spirit maintains, "There's nothing to judge because it isn't real in the first place."** When we accept the ego identification card, we agree to judge almost everyone and everything in terms of good or bad. The problem with this is that we *all* contain the same Spirit from which we originated. If I make you bad and myself good, for instance, I deny the presence of Spirit in you whom I elected to judge. God sees it quite differently: Our spiritual Source knows that *only It is real*—all of the ephemeral world of form and boundaries is not of Its infinite nature. At our core, the place where we all originate from and return to, there's no one and nothing to judge. This takes some time to get used to, but once we grasp the truth of this observation, we're free to tap in to authentic inspiration.

**5. The ego directs love and hate toward individuals. The Holy Spirit's love is nonspecific and all-encompassing.** Ego directs us to love some, be indifferent toward many, and hate all others. When we learn to be back in-Spirit on a full-time basis, we discover what we knew in our pre-ego time: There's no "they," there's only "one." The one Source of all-encompassing love knows nothing of boundaries; differing customs; geographic divisions; family splits; or differences in race, creed, sex, and so on—It only knows *love for all.*

Ego is probably working on you right now as you read, attempting to convince you of the folly of such thinking. It may retort, "How can you love those who would harm you and are your declared enemies?" When your ego speaks in this way, recall the words of Jesus: "You have heard that it was said 'love your neighbor and hate your enemy'" (Matt. 5:43). This is how ego works—it tells you to divide your love for some and offer your hate to others. Yet Jesus, who lived totally in-Spirit, goes on to say, "But I tell you: love your enemies and pray for those who persecute you, that you may be sons of your Father in heaven" (Matt. 5:44–45).

Jesus points so perfectly to the differences between ego and Spirit. When we were in-Spirit, we were a child of our Father in heaven and "He causes his sun to rise on the evil and the good" (Matt. 5:45). This, of course, means that it's all one: Evil, good, righteous, and unrighteous are all the same—some move away from the Father, some move toward Him. This is such an important and powerful lesson to get as we move toward becoming inspired by living in-Spirit.

**6. The ego devises clever reasons why we should continue to listen to its selfish counsel. The Holy Spirit is certain that at some point we'll turn toward It and ultimately return.** Ego will tout its irresistible logic to assure us that our body, our possessions, and our achievements are all very real and important. It convinces us by insisting that what's real is what we can see, touch, hear, taste, and smell; therefore, invisible Spirit isn't real. So ego continues to be attached to stuff and to make the acquisition of money and power a lifelong objective. To that end, it wants us to disdain forgiveness in favor of seeking revenge—very persuasive logic when we look around and see almost everyone doing just that.

Through the lens of inspiration, however, we're able to see how ego has distorted the message of the Holy Spirit—instead of seeking revenge, we're more likely to see a very sad nation of strivers and virtually no arrivers; a gaggle of pill poppers, searching outside of themselves for a resolution to their depressing, anxiety-filled, joyless, and often lonely lives. As we return to the Holy Spirit, we'll no longer be under the influence of ego's absurd counsel.

**7. The ego wants us to regret our past. The Holy Spirit wants us to practice unconditional forgiveness.** The Holy Spirit isn't limited by a past or a future—there's only the eternal now. Any energy we place on what transpired in the past is groundwork for guilt, and ego *loves* guilt. Such negative energy fabricates an excuse for why our present moments are troubled and gives us a cop-out, a reason to stay out of Spirit. And thinking about where we've been or what we did wrong in the past are great impediments to an inspired life.

On the other hand, when we're inspired, we're totally engaged in the now. In an infinite never-beginning and never-ending Universe, there can be no past. All guilt and regret simply serve as ways to avoid being here in the only moment we have, which is now. This is where we reconnect to Spirit—*now*. If we choose to use up this holy instant with regrets about a past that's only an illusory thought, then we're unable to be in the joyful, loving, peaceful, present moment. Cramming this holy moment with thoughts of guilt, remorse, and regret is great for ego . . . and keeps us totally resistant to being in-Spirit.

These seven messages are the dominant ones the ego drones on about. If we don't listen, it will try to drown out inspiration by intensifying worrisome and fearful thoughts. I've managed to tame this annoying voice of the ego so that its influence is almost negligible in my life, and I know you can, too.

### How I Learned to Slay the Ego Intruder

I realize that the ego's voice has most of us convinced that we're powerless to manage our own destiny. There was a time when I felt much more kindly toward the ego, since it plays such a dominant role in the lives of so many people—but today I see it as something that needs to be destroyed. I no longer agree that since it's in our lives, we might just as well learn to love and accept it, troublesome as it might be; nor do I believe that it serves some useful purpose. Knowing that we've been created in the image of our Creator, and therefore have the same essence *and* the same ultimate potential, means that ego is out of the picture! Ego denies our original invisible reality, so it must be removed and completely banished from our awareness.

Realizing that ego is a traitor to our greatness is what ultimately set me free of its pull. I keep remembering that ego isn't real, even as it still protests and attempts to delete my feelings of inspiration. My highest self responds with, "But remember, Wayne, what's trying to drag you down isn't real."

What also helps to keep me on track is parenting. I'm the father of eight children, so I can recall thousands of instances of being sucked into a black hole of confusion and uncertainty with my kids. Arguments with them concerning schoolwork, questionable friendships, curfews, staying at a pal's house, dress codes, dating, cigarettes or drugs, what was right from my perspective and wrong from theirs (and vice versa) . . . on and on this list could go. There were anger and hurt feelings, sleepless nights, and of course, much happiness, joy, and contentment, too.

As I look back on those years of parent/child conflicts, I realize today, in this now moment, that none of it exists. It isn't real because it's in the changing world of time and space. Similarly, I now realize that every conflict or struggle that exists, as well as those experiences I'd call good and joyful, are not real from the inspirational point of view. So if anything I experience is immediately going to fall into illusion, why not simply stay connected to Spirit through it all?

While I still have occasions when I slip, today I'm able to say that every conflict I have with my mostly now-adult children (or anyone else for that matter) isn't really between me and them—it's between me and God. I look for a way to be like God and stay loving, caring, forgiving, and peaceful within myself, suspending my need to be right and knowing that in the next moment it will all be gone . . . which is true of everything that's being played out in this illusory world.

I want to emphasize that I'm not suggesting that peace means being in a place where there's no noise or trouble; rather, it means that in the *midst* of turmoil, I can still feel calm. Not one of the things that I was so upset and out of control over matters today— not one. It's all illusion fed by my ego's need to make me important by "winning," "being right," or "coming out on top."

❋ ❋ ❋

I'll conclude this chapter a little differently by presenting a few passages from the Bhagavad Gita, the holy book of the Hindus, on which Mahatma Gandhi based his life. These passages speak to our leaving that world of pure Spirit and inspiration and incarnating into a body and reflect, in ancient spiritual verse, what I've attempted to convey. (Notice in this highly respected spiritual text that the word *Self* is capitalized—this is to signify the spiritual, eternal Self.)

*The Self dwells in the house of the body,*
*Which passes through childhood, youth, and old age.*
*So passes the Self at the time of death*
*Into another body. The wise know this truth*
*And are not deceived by it.*

*When the senses come in contact with sense-objects*
*They give rise to feelings of heat and cold,*
*Pleasure and pain, which come and go.*
*Accept them calmly, as do the wise.*

*The wise, who live free from pleasure and pain,*
*Are worthy of immortality.*

As I've tried to express in this chapter, pleasure and pain and troubles and good times aren't eternal—Krishna advises us to accept them calmly, but stay detached. If we do, we'll live in-Spirit in what I call immortality.

*Not pierced by arrows nor burnt by fire,*
*Affected by neither water nor wind,*
*The Self is not a physical creature.*

*Not wounded, not burnt, not wetted, not dried,*
*The Self is ever and everywhere,*
*Immovable and everlasting.*

This spiritual classic reminds us that we're not only physical creatures with egos—we're a Self to which we wish to be wedded in-Spirit, which is everywhere and everlasting. This is our true essence. When we move into this space within ourselves and see all of our life experiences from this point of view, we'll be permanently inspired.

*Some there are who have realized the Self*
*In all its wonder. Others can speak of it*
*As wonderful. But there are many*
*Who don't understand even when they hear.*

*Deathless is the Self in every creature.*
*Know this truth, and leave all sorrow behind.*

When we do as Krishna advises and realize the Self, we live knowing that our true being is deathless. This is a great comfort, as we can leave sorrow behind and be inspired.

## Some Suggestions for Putting the Ideas in This Chapter to Work for You

— Seeing this physical world as an illusion ironically allows you to enjoy it more and stay inspired. Practice laughing at the importance that you and so many people place on everyday circumstances. View it from an eternal perspective, and you'll find yourself lightening that heavy load. (I've personally often cited the words *this too shall pass* to keep me unburdened when my imagined problems feel troublesome.)

Your ego wants you to live in a state of self-importance, but your Holy Spirit knows that the only thing that's truly important is being in alignment with Spirit. Therefore, anything that's not of Spirit—such as fear, illness, worry, shame, anger, and the like—is worthy of your laughter.

— When others attempt to seduce you into feeling bad, guilty, worried, fearful, or anything that isn't of Spirit, practice stepping outside of yourself and becoming the observer to all things transitory, which is your entire physical world. Repeat sentiments such as "This isn't mine," "I refuse to own it," and "I'll not be misaligned with Spirit." At any moment of your life, you can practice this observer technique: Just mentally step outside of your body and observe what's trying to keep you from being inspired. Then vow to return to Spirit by repeating the above statements.

— Continually remind yourself of the physical and metaphysical truth that there's no place anywhere in this Universe that's devoid of Spirit. Everything and everyone is of Spirit before, during, and after manifestation into physical form. I urge you to seek this Spirit when your ego has convinced you that It's absent. In all of your noninspired moments, practice stopping the chatter of the ego and look for the good, or a reason for what's happening. Even in devastating natural disasters such as hurricanes, tsunamis, floods, fires, and the like, look for the good. There's no death from the perspective of infinity, so once you've removed the horror of dying from the equation, you'll have a different perspective.

— The lost lives of others teach us all to be more in-Spirit: to be kinder, to grow in caring and compassion, creating an increased sensitivity to the oneness in the Universe. We can translate these heightened sensitivities into behavior that's more giving and forgiving, extending assistance and cooperating with each other. You'll discover a way of following your own instincts to be more in-Spirit and less in fear and anger.

— Die while you're alive. Live the words of the New Testament that tell you that you're *in* this world but not *of* it. You can be here without being attached to here by simply discarding your body identification: Imagine yourself as a decomposed energy field that's impervious to anything not of Spirit. Envision, for example, that criticism and feelings of inadequacy are *in* this world and thus unable to enter your body because you've left it and are a translucent glob of nonparticles that's no longer *of* this world.

This exercise will liberate you from so many of the problems you've connected to in your mind. You only have now, and even it will disappear in a flash. Welcome to the infinite world of Spirit! As H. L. Mencken, a famous journalist/satirist of a generation ago, wrote: "We are here and it is now: further than that, all human knowledge is moonshine."

— Work every day to tame ego's demands. Ultimately, make it your goal to unashamedly slay your ego while you're still in your body—it's doomed to destruction at the moment you die and re-enter the realm of reality from which you came anyway. Keep in mind that you're not being cruel by destroying your ego, since it's a false self to begin with.

✳ ✳ ✳

The best way I can think of to summarize and conclude this chapter is to take you back to the opening quotation from *A Course in Miracles*. To me, this observation helps us understand why we've left our spiritual identification: "A sense of separation from God is the only lack you really need correct."

Now let's work on correcting that separation.

CHAPTER 4

# HOW IT FEELS TO RETURN TO SPIRIT

*"The aim and purpose of human life*
*is the unitive knowledge of God."*

— ALDOUS HUXLEY

**THIS MUCH SHOULD BE CLEAR BY NOW:** We originated in a field of energy that has no boundaries. Before entering the world of form, we were in-Spirit—a piece of God, if you will. We began entering this physical world first as a particle, then as a cell, then as a fetus, then as an infant, and ultimately as a fully developed human being. But our ultimate purpose all along was to experience "the unitive knowledge of God," as Huxley so beautifully puts it.

Sadly, when we began our human training, we were taught to abandon most of our spiritual identity and adopt a new one based on ego consciousness, or a sense of being separate from Spirit. In other words, we came here from a place of inspiration and intended to stay that way—unfortunately, we forgot to do so, and we ended up abandoning most of our inspiring notions in favor of a consensus of "reality" that didn't include Spirit. We chose the false self, which is why we so inexplicably feel off-purpose.

In the West, traditional psychology hasn't wholeheartedly embraced the existence of Atman, the godhead within humans, and our psychological and spiritual teachings don't show us how to achieve the union of perfect yoga. (For this kind of learning, we'd have to study with a teacher of yoga or organized religion.) Now we'd like to reconnect to the world of Spirit, while at the same time not shed the familiar body we've worn for a lifetime. That's where Patanjali's teachings come in.

Patanjali was considered a saint in his lifetime, teaching *sutras* (the essential threads of a philosophy) that elevated human beings to their highest potential. He taught about knowing God through the practice of meditation and yoga in order to attain a point of union with the Source. He also described our ability to perform miracles—these feats involved specific spiritual aphorisms and the daily practice of yoga. The remainder of this chapter is devoted to my impression of Patanjali's 2,300-year-old observations on inspiration.

### When You Are Inspired . . .

My personal view of the six ideas presented here includes my belief in the existence of a God-consciousness within every one of us. And my purpose in the next few pages is to help you achieve this perfect union of yoga and live from this inspired perspective every day.

Here's what Patanjali offered us more than 2,000 years ago, which is the most profound statement I've ever found on the significance of the role of our ultimate calling:

> When you are inspired by some great purpose, some extraordinary project, all your thoughts break their bonds, your mind transcends limitations, your consciousness expands in every direction, and you find yourself in a new, great, and wonderful world. Dormant forces, faculties, and talents become alive, and you discover yourself to be a greater person by far than you ever dreamed yourself to be.

Patanjali opens his aphorism with an observation on inspiration and follows it up with six conclusions. These six key points are the basis for this chapter, as they describe what it feels like when we return to the world of Spirit.

## 1. When You Are Inspired . . .
## All Your Thoughts Break Their Bonds

As I explained earlier, being inspired is equivalent to being back in-Spirit. Before we showed up in form, our mind and the mind of God were synonymous, which means that we were free from the bonds of the ego mind. This is simply how the world of Spirit works: It's impossible to have limiting boundaries or self-imposed shackles placed on us. When we're in harmony with the mind of God, we simply don't have thoughts that tell us we can't accomplish some-thing—after all, our thoughts are of a higher energy.

Every desire we have has an energy-vibration component to it. When we launch that desire in the form of a thought, it generally matches up with the same energy vibration of our spiritual Source: *I want to attract prosperity, I want to experience physical well-being, I want to have a peaceful relationship, I want to feel good about my life,* and so on. The energy of our thoughts determines whether or not we're living at an inspired level, so any doubt in our ability to manifest our desire or to receive spiritual guidance is vibrationally out of tune with that desire. And when this occurs, we automati-cally impose bonds on our mind—which most frequently assume the form of thoughts that imperil our ability to be inspired.

Returning to Spirit results in a grand sense of being in tune with our uniquely Divine purpose. Just imagine being able to go on and on for hours at a time without experiencing fatigue, hunger, thirst, or mental exhaustion, all thanks to one factor: the willingness to be back in-Spirit. I've personally found that when I have thoughts of being "inspired by some great purpose [or] extraordinary project," I let go of fatigue; that is, being in-Spirit somehow eliminates thoughts that send the "I'm exhausted" signals to my body. In the middle of writing, speaking, touring with my family, playing a tennis match, or anything that inspires me, all bonds are shattered by my mind, and fatigue is impossible.

Furthermore, matching up my desires with plans and behavior in the form of my thoughts and actions breaks down the bonds of hunger and discomfort. I've literally written for up to 14 hours without eating or experiencing any hunger pangs. Somehow being inspired allows my thoughts to remove any of the bonds that can serve as excuses not to do what I know I'm here to accomplish.

This observation that Patanjali made so long ago is awesome. Why not practice returning to Spirit and allowing all thoughts to be in agreement with that originating Spirit? Your thoughts will work on your body and surroundings, transforming obstacles into the fulfillment of desires.

## 2. When You Are Inspired . . .
## Your Mind Transcends Limitations

Next, imagine what it must feel like to have absolute faith—an inner knowing that it's impossible to fail, a complete absence of doubt concerning your ability to create anything you place your attention on. I imagine that must be how God feels when preparing to create—He must have this kind of confidence about the outcome.

Well, when we're inspired, we remember that God is always in us and we're always in God, so we're incapable of thinking limited thoughts. We're transcendent; we've gone beyond the world of boundaries and entered a space of creative knowing. In other words, we surrender . . . we put ourselves under the guidance and control of our Purposeful Force.

I can personally vouch for this surrendering process. During my life I've had an unshakable faith in my ability to attract money and prosperity—even as a youngster living in foster homes, I always felt I was entitled to have wealth. I just *knew* there was an inexhaustible supply and that it was totally neutral, simply an energy that goes wherever it's called to go. I don't know why I've known this my entire life, but I know it even more today.

A television interviewer once asked me if I ever felt guilty about making so much from my writings and recordings. I responded, much to her surprise, "I would feel guilty, except that it's not my fault." When she asked what I meant, I explained that money has always come to me because I've always felt within me that I *am* money. I attract prosperity because I feel entitled to it; in fact, I feel that it's actually a definition of me. Money has always come to me, and because it has, I direct *it* wherever I perceive it to be needed. It's simply an energy system that my mind has created—it flows to me because it's who I am. I've never doubted that I came from an energy field of pure unlimited abundance, and because of my unshakable faith, I've always acted on this prosperity consciousness. I've never known a moment of unemployment, through good or bad economic times.

When I was a little kid, I saw that collecting soda-pop bottles would bring in pennies and that pennies became dollars. I saw that helping ladies with their groceries, shoveling their snow, or emptying their ashes from the coal furnaces were acts of prosperity. And today, I'm still collecting pop bottles, shoveling snow, and carrying out ashes on a much larger scale. Prosperity continues to chase after me because I'm still in total harmony with my originating Spirit, which is abundance and prosperity.

A few months back, the NFL's rushing champion of 2004, Curtis Martin of the New York Jets, was in the front row of a lecture I presented at Westbury Music Fair on Long Island. At the conclusion of the evening, this gentleman—who's reached the pinnacle in his own profession—came up to me and pressed a piece of paper into my hand as he thanked me for the lecture.

Back in my hotel room, I realized that Mr. Martin had given me a personal check for $5,000, with no restrictions or instructions. You see, as I told the interviewer, it's not my fault! (I matched the gift that Curtis gave to me and contributed it toward a van for a woman on Maui who's been in a wheelchair for more than 22 years.) Indeed, when we're inspired, we attract the abundance from that which we originated. And the mind then truly transcends every limitation.

## 3. When You Are Inspired . . .
## Your Consciousness Expands in Every Direction

Now try to imagine yourself living in a world that has no direction: There's no north, south, east, or west; there's no up or down; and there's no past or future. In this world, *any* direction is *every* direction. As difficult as it is to imagine a direction-less Universe, that's exactly what the world of Spirit looks and feels like.

When we're in-Spirit, every direction is possible for us at every moment because our consciousness happens within our mind. Now this inner world of ours, reunited with its originating essence, doesn't think in only one direction; rather, it allows all possibilities. Our consciousness is in the absolute state of allowing—all resistance, in the form of thoughts, is nonexistent.

I'm speaking of a feeling that comes over us when we're inspired by a "great purpose, [an] extraordinary project," where we experience the bliss of an expanded consciousness with the unsurpassed allowing of any and all possibilities to enter into our daily life. We cease looking for answers in a directional way—they don't come from someplace north or west of us, nor are they arriving from up above or impeded by something down below. We begin to feel the larger sense of life, what being a part of *all* is like once again.

Is there any place that God isn't? And if we came from God, then mustn't we be like God? You see, we're already connected to everything we need when we're inspired—what takes place is a realignment within us that allows for every thing, every event, and every person to merge in our inspirited consciousness. When we reemerge into the perfect oneness of Spirit, we view everyone we meet as an ally through our inspired way of life. We feel extraordinarily guided and attract people, events, and circumstances to join us in our inspired state because our world has transcended from the elementary cause-and-effect, birth-to-death path to all directions simultaneously. We're living at maximum *allowing,* with nonexistent resistance. We're back in-Spirit.

## 4. When You Are Inspired . . .
## You Find Yourself in a New, Great, and Wonderful World

Patanjali was so right with this conclusion—we absolutely enter into a new world when we become inspired. We feel different because we're no longer edging God out. We're back in vibrational alignment where limitations don't exist and there are no bonds, and we've left our body and all of its boundaries to live in an expanded consciousness in our mind. We now begin to think in terms of miracles being not only possible, but actively en route. Soon we stop being surprised by all the things that are going our way and instead affirm: *What is needed is on its way.* The phrase *We expect miracles* is more than a New Age slogan, it's how we feel when we live each day in-Spirit. We leave the world of anxiety, fear, doubt, and impossibility and enter a new, wonderful world of Spirit, where all things are possible.

In 1976, I made the choice to live in-Spirit on a full-time basis. I resigned from my professorship at St. John's University to teach and write on a much larger stage. I knew within myself that I was finally listening in earnest to the inner voice that chose my destiny before I was conceived. I incarnated to teach self-reliance and to help our planet move to a more unified means of living in heaven on Earth, but I was here for 35 years before devoting myself exclusively to my mission.

At the age of 36, I was consumed by my writing and by telling the world about my book *Your Erroneous Zones*—I was filled with excitement and passion about what I was involved in. I had never felt as complete in my previous 35 years, even though I had an exciting and thoroughly satisfying career teaching and counseling. The moment I resigned from being an employee to living my dream—when I mustered up the courage to be in-Spirit—lives in my mind even today, some 30 years later. What happened from that moment on is precisely what Patanjali suggests. I found myself in a "new, great, and wonderful world." It was as if a huge blanket had been removed from me, and breezes were allowed to refresh me at every turn I made. The world became my oyster when I shifted into the world of inspiration.

Suddenly I began receiving requests to appear on radio and TV shows to discuss what I believed in so passionately. The more I spoke (from what I now recognize as inspiration), the more invitations I received. Radio hosts began asking me to fill in—sometimes for six or seven hours on all-night shows, and then for a week at a time—in cities across the country. I stayed with my inspiration, loving every moment, working 18-hour days, and being willing to do whatever it took to stay in-Spirit.

Soon national shows took an interest in me, and all the while, precisely the right people showed up to teach and guide me through this process. Publicists, editors, book distributors, talent coordinators, travel agents, bankers . . . everyone who was needed kept surfacing. All I had to do was stay inspired, and "follow [my] bliss," in the words of Joseph Campbell—it was as if a gigantic hand was pulling the right strings. Moment by moment, day by day, I was in awe of it all at the time, and I'm still in awe as I write these words many years later. Today, more than ever, I trust in Patanjali's advice to stay in-Spirit.

This is not to say that many obstacles didn't surface, as they continue to today. There are times when I still can't fathom why I have to go through so many difficulties. At the age of 65 I thought I was through with heartbreak, yet I still have it coming at me. A debilitating heart attack, a personal tragedy in my private life, and serious addiction challenges within my family have all been recent occurrences. Despite all the hardships that have surfaced, I've found that all these experiences are valuable because of the compassion, forgiveness, and kindness that I've developed.

These so-called negative situations have impacted my writing and speaking and have caused me to reach out to a much larger audience through public television, where I offer a positive, inspired message. My lesson has been to stay in-Spirit and step outside my body and my life circumstances to observe all that has and continues to flow to me from a perspective of detachment. It's not about me; it's about staying in-Spirit, knowing that all that comes my way is a Divine blessing—even the struggles.

Here's a tale about ways of dealing with adversity that I find particularly thought provoking and inspiring:

## Carrots, Eggs, and Coffee

A young woman complained to her mother about the hardships and difficulties in her life. She didn't know how she was going to continue and wanted to give up. The young woman said, "I'm tired of fighting and struggling. It seems that as soon as one problem is solved, a new one appears." In response, her mother took her to the kitchen and filled three pots with water, placing each on the stove over a high flame.

Soon the water came to boil. In the first pot she placed carrots, in the second she placed eggs, and in the last she placed ground coffee beans. She let them sit and boil, without saying a word. In about 20 minutes, she turned off the burners. The mother then fished the carrots out and placed them in a bowl. She removed the eggs and placed them in a bowl. Then she ladled the coffee out and placed it in a bowl. Turning to her daughter, she said, "Tell me what you see."

"Carrots, eggs, and coffee," the daughter replied. Her mother brought her closer and asked her to feel the carrots. She did and noted that they were soft. The mother then asked the daughter to take an egg and break it. After peeling off the shell, she observed the hard-boiled egg. Finally, the mother asked the daughter to sip the coffee. The daughter smiled as she tasted its rich flavor.

The daughter then asked, "What does it mean, Mother?"

Her mother explained that each of these objects had faced the same adversity, boiling water, and each reacted differently. The carrot went in strong, hard, and unrelenting. However, after being subjected to the boiling water, it softened and became weak. The egg had been fragile, its thin outer shell protecting its liquid interior, but after the boiling water, its inside became hardened. But the ground coffee beans were unique—after they were in the boiling water, they'd changed the water itself.

The message? Stay in-Spirit and change adversity into a component of a new, great, and wonderful world, just as the coffee did.

## 5. When You Are Inspired . . .
## Dormant Forces, Faculties, and Talents Become Alive

I love Patanjali for teaching me this powerful truth. Essentially, he's telling us that when we move into an awareness of inspiration, forces that we thought were either dead or unavailable come alive and are available for us to use to manifest our inspired desires. Could this be true? Does the Universe collaborate with us in awakening long-slumbering forces, faculties, and talents? I know it to be true, so my answer is an unqualified *yes!* I use this particular insight every day of my life—in fact, I'm using it in this very moment.

I'm confident that what I'm supposed to say in these pages will come to me in one form or another, especially since I live and breathe this idea of inspiration—I'm so passionate about helping others learn how important it is to hear *their* ultimate calling. I sleep with a pad of paper and a pen next to my bed because much of what I wish to convey comes via my dream state. As I walk along the beach here on Maui, watching the humpback whales and dolphins dancing offshore, I ask them for guidance. I receive it, note it, and share it with you.

I know that forces exist to guide me through every stage of this writing. When I pick up a book, I often open it to precisely the right page, and exactly what I need appears before me. I smile inwardly and say aloud, "Thank you, God. You're always there for me when I write, seemingly alone here in my dining room and looking out at the magnificent ocean."

I love watching those dormant forces come alive and guide me in my own inspired offerings. I so appreciate the talent that's rested within me for so long awakening when I do what I know I'm here to do. I certainly couldn't access the forces if I were living at the ordinary level of consciousness that had been laid out for me by external well-meaning forces. I can only access the dormant forces when I'm inspired—that is, when I let go of my ego demands and reenter that magical realm of Spirit.

These dormant forces will come to all of us—they're actually alive and well and have been working on our behalf for as long as we've been here. Yet they appear to be dead to us because we've left behind our Divine purpose, which we decided on long before we took on the insane ego.

I've always loved great stories of synchronicity. Here's one (considered to be an urban legend by some) that illustrates how the Universe conspires to guide those who opt for a life of inspiration:

A poor Scottish farmer named Fleming heard a cry for help coming from a nearby bog. He dropped his tools and ran to it. There, mired up to his waist in black muck, was a terrified boy, screaming and trying to free himself. Farmer Fleming saved the child from what could have been a slow and horrible death. On the following day, a fancy carriage pulled up to the Scotsman's sparse surroundings. An elegantly dressed nobleman stepped out and introduced himself as the father of the boy Farmer Fleming had saved. "I want to repay you," said the nobleman. "You saved my son's life."

"No, I can't accept payment for what I did," the Scottish farmer replied, waving off the offer. At that moment, the farmer's son came to the door of the family hovel.

"Is that your son?" the nobleman asked.

"Yes," the farmer replied proudly.

"I'll make you a deal. Let me provide him with the level of education that my son will enjoy. If the lad is anything like his father, he'll no doubt grow to be a man we both will be proud of." And that he did.

Farmer Fleming's son attended the very best schools and in time, he graduated from St. Mary's Hospital Medical School, London University, and went on to become known throughout the world as the noted Sir Alexander Fleming, the man who discovered penicillin.

Years afterward, the same nobleman's son who was saved from the bog was stricken with pneumonia. What saved his life this time? Penicillin. The name of the nobleman? Lord Randolph Churchill. His son's name? Sir Winston Churchill.

What force is operating here? It's the same one that seeks to work with us when we choose to live the inspired life we signed up for.

### 6. When You Are Inspired . . .
### You Discover Yourself to Be a Greater Person by Far
### Than You Ever Dreamed Yourself to Be

The act of being inspired by some great purpose allows us to feel the essence of a spiritual being having a human experience, rather than the other way around. Patanjali suggests that we could never even dream of our greatness because we've been imprisoned by our beliefs about who we are. We've bought into the idea that we were limited in our ability to create an all-encompassing life, and we were certain that we had no choice in our own destiny. We defended our need to acquire more and to live a scarcity consciousness in which we competed with everyone else for a meager slice of the whole pie. All of these imprisoning thoughts result when we're not guided by Spirit.

Moving into a state of inspiration removes all of those restraining ideas. As Patanjali notes, we'll discover someone we couldn't imagine because we were incarcerated in ego's jail, imprisoned by what we now recognize from our inspired viewpoint is an illusion. The poet Rabindranath Tagore (winner of the Nobel Prize for Literature in 1913) writes of those who live exclusively in the false identity of the ego: "He who, in the world of men, goes about singing for alms from door to door, with his one-stringed instrument and long robe of patched-up rags on his back." Tagore is describing how limited our thoughts and our lives are when we're not in-Spirit.

As we move toward heeding the ultimate calling, we no longer live exclusively "in the world of men," so we know that we all have greatness awaiting us. We need to awaken from the bad dream that has stupefied us in the fog of ego, and live from the blissful perspective offered by being in-Spirit.

# Some Suggestions for Putting the Ideas in This Chapter to Work for You

— Monitor your thoughts for any that put bonds on your ability to manifest. Even a seemingly insignificant one that questions your resolve to live in-Spirit represents an energy vibration that inhibits you from creating your desires. Change a thought from *This is unlikely to happen because I've never been lucky before* to *What I need is on its way; I'm going to look everywhere for evidence that I'm aligned with the same energy vibrations as my desire.* Be alert for thoughts that creep in by force of habit and reflect the idea that you can't manifest your desires.

— Repeat this mantra to yourself as often as you can, making it a ritual that only you are privy to: *I have absolutely no limits on what I intend to create.* By repeating these words, you'll find that you slip into the world of Spirit where limitlessness defines all reality.

— Make an attempt to spend some time each day in a state of meditation, wherein you let go of all ideas about time, space, and linear directionality. Just allow yourself to be. . . . Imagine yourself without a body or any possessions and attachments—in this way, you'll begin to emulate the world of Spirit. It's out of this nondirectionality, with no backward or forward, up or down, or north and south, that you'll brush right up against inspiration. Such a feeling may come out of nowhere, but it will appear when you do everything you can to emulate connectedness with Spirit.

— Develop a private trust in your ability to activate and attract dormant forces. Visualize yourself as a being who can command these seemingly inert forces to work with you. Remind yourself of this truth: *If I stay in harmony with my originating Spirit, that invisible All-Creating Force will go to work on my behalf.* Just know this within. Then begin to look for even the slightest hint that those

319

hibernating forces are awakening from their apparent slumber to work with you. In reality, these forces never sleep; rather, they only work with you when you're a vibrational match to them. So change your expectations for yourself—expect the best, expect guidance, expect your fortunes to change, expect a miracle!

\* \* \*

Remember the words of Michelangelo: "The greater danger for most of us lies not in setting our aim too high and falling short; but in setting our aim too low, and achieving our mark." When you were in-Spirit prior to materializing, your aim was high and your expectations were God-like. Reacquaint yourself with that vision and begin living an inspired life . . . just turn the page to begin.

CHAPTER 5

# FINDING YOUR WAY TO AN INSPIRED LIFE

*"If we examine every stage of our lives, we find that
from our first breath to our last we are under the constraint
of circumstances. And yet we still possess the greatest of all
freedoms, the power of developing our innermost selves in
harmony with the moral order of the Universe, and so
winning peace at heart whatever obstacles we meet.*

*"It is easy to say this and to write this. But it always remains
a task to which every day must be devoted. Every morning
cries to us: 'Do what you ought and trust what may be.'"*

— JOHANN WOLFGANG VON GOETHE

**WHEN I SPEAK ABOUT INSPIRATION AND PURPOSE,**
I frequently hear people ask, "But what if I don't really know what
would inspire me?" or "How do I find my purpose when nothing
seems to resonate with me at the level of bliss you speak about?"
That's why this chapter and the following one are dedicated to
my heartfelt answers to these questions, which seem most bothersome to those who'd really love to heed their ultimate calling.

Just the mere act of questioning our ability to live an inspired
life represents resistance that we need to examine because it implies
that we're deficient in our spiritual quest. Of course, nothing could
be further from the truth: In the world of Spirit from whence we
came, there are no deficits, lacks, or shortages; and there's definitely
no such thing as purposelessness. This is an intelligent system that
we're a part of—we're Divine beings who are a piece of the entire
pie of creation. By questioning our ability to activate a connection

to inspiration, we give evidence of our lack of belief in our divinity. With this minor reproach in mind, I'll now explain ways to believe in, and connect with, our ultimate calling.

First, in order to put to rest any question regarding our personal right to live an inspired life, we must claim our divinity. The fundamental truth each of us needs to affirm is: *I am a Divine creation. All creation has purpose. I am here to be like God.* We should tattoo this statement on our consciousness and wear it proudly!

We must begin the process of getting in-Spirit with a firm declaration from which we never waver. Here's a poetic reminder of this truth from Walt Whitman: ". . . perhaps the deepest, most eternal thought latent in the human soul [is] the thought of God, merged in the thoughts of moral right and the immortality of identity. Great, great is this thought—aye, greater than all else."

Yes, as Whitman says, this thought of being merged with God is greater than any we could ever have. Once we've accepted this, we can move on to knowing why we're here and what inspires us. We can begin to trust in the intelligence that beats our heart 50 or 60 times every minute and at the same time turns the earth once every 24 hours, keeps the planets aligned, and creates every millisecond. Our job is to be as much like the Source of All Being as we can, and the nagging questions about what inspires us and why we're here dissolve in this grand desire. Once we declare our holy, Divine nature to be our essence, rather than something to be verified, it all seems so obvious: The journey to feeling purposeful and inspired begins by seeking to be like God in all of our thoughts and actions.

I quoted Goethe at the beginning of the chapter because I consider him to be among the most intellectually and spiritually gifted Renaissance men who ever lived. Study his words thoughtfully as you read this chapter, and keep in mind that every one of us is capable of being inspired every day of our life; after all, this is our entitlement offered by God, with Whom we collaborated before ever arriving here.

### *Sharing Is Inspiration*

Oneness with our Source is achieved by becoming like It, and Its essence is giving and sharing. Therefore, in order to know our purpose and heed our ultimate call to inspiration, we must also become a being who's more focused on sharing than on receiving.

This Universe works on the Law of Attraction—so the more we shift the focus from our desires to wanting more for others, the richer we become. When we tell the Universe to "Gimme, gimme, gimme," it responds in like fashion, and we find ourselves feeling put upon and out of balance. But when we ask the Universe, "How may I share?" it will ask, "How may *I* share with *you?* You are a being of sharing, and I return the same energy back to you."

Now this may at first seem absurd, particularly if we've been raised on an ego consciousness that's stressed the need to "look out for number one," and "get what I can before someone else does." But I assure you that when we make the transformation to a being of sharing, the question of how to become inspired will disappear. So whenever we find ourselves "wanting more," the solution is to do more for society, for humanity, or for the environment. Any act of sharing as a response to our wants leads to feeling inspired. The fact is, it just plain feels good to do something for others.

When I completed writing *The Power of Intention* a couple of years ago, for instance, I had such a glorious feeling of having been guided through the writing that I wanted to express my gratitude in some way other than taking credit for it or thinking about myself. That's when I thought of my personal editor, Joanna Pyle, who has taken my disjointed thoughts and ramblings and turned them into cohesive books for almost three decades. I knew that in all of her 65 years, my friend had never known the joy of owning a new car—it simply hadn't been a priority in her life. So I arranged for Joanna to receive a brand-new camper van as an expression of my gratitude for all of her brilliant editing, going back to the 1970s. In that single act of sharing, I received as much joy and fulfillment as I did from writing the contents of a book that consumed me for almost a year.

Understand that this isn't necessarily about giving our possessions or money away; rather, it's about living in the same vibrational energy as our Source and attracting that energy in each other. It's about thinking of others before ourselves and offering the love we feel for all of life, first in our thoughts and then in our actions . . . and that's how we make a connection to inspiration. This is because we've become one with our Source in thought and then action, or as Goethe puts it so perfectly, "[W]e still possess the greatest of all freedoms, the power of developing our innermost selves in harmony with the moral order of the Universe, and so winning peace at heart." A being of sharing frequently thinks in those terms.

When we contemplate our Creator, we realize that God simply gives and imparts without demanding anything in return. We aren't required to give to, pay homage to, or do anything for God. It's *our* demands that distance us from feeling inspired—so we need to let go of them and extend ourselves in an attitude of sharing. I speak here of an inner transformation in which extending love outward is our predominant disposition. This can take the form of a silent blessing toward someone we might have previously judged, a loving greeting, a kind remark, or a thought wishing the highest good for all concerned. As simple as it sounds, this is the ultimate impetus for feeling inspired.

### Blocking the Bliss of Inspiration

The most frequent lament I hear from people who want to feel inspired is, "I don't have any idea what I should be doing, so how can I find my inspiration?" My answer is always the same: "Inspiration isn't what we receive from what we do—it's what we bring to our actions." In other words, when we're living in-Spirit, we can feel inspired doing anything. Our job is to stay connected to our spiritual essence, rather than looking for a position that we think will provide us with that connection.

When we feel confused about what we should do to feel inspired, it's time to go to a quiet place. It could be in our home, down by the sea, in a meadow, or deep in the woods—it just needs to be a place where we can be alone with God. Once there, we can imagine talking to our beloved Creator, Who's trusted more than anyone else. Conversing with God will just affirm the answers we already have within us, and we can then awaken to a realization of what we're to do. It isn't about getting the right job—whatever we're doing at the moment provides us with a unique opportunity to bring inspiration to our workplace. We can do this by becoming a being of sharing and extending the love we came from to everyone we encounter, particularly those who seem to be the most annoying or those we tend to blame for our absence of inspiration.

Basically, we have two choices for meeting any problem that seems to be blocking us from the bliss of inspiration. The first choice is *the way of frailty*, in which we assure ourselves that we're weak and incapable. Frustration, grief, fears, and tears are the hallmarks of this choice, wherein we attempt to cure a wrong with another wrong. The frailty method multiplies tensions by focusing on what's missing, and often invites the advice of others in an attempt to resolve our inner tension and lack of inspiration.

The second choice is *to go within* and know that at our core, beyond all physical and mental factors, there resides the Spirit that's always connected to God. Any problem, and I emphasize *any* problem, represents our inability to consciously connect to our Source in the moment. With a conscious connection, we don't seek the advice of others, we seek *information*—so our decisions are made between ourselves and our Creator. We frequently have quiet interchanges with God, and we know and trust that spiritual guidance is available as an alignment of energy.

When we feel uninspired, we recognize that we need to make a vibrational adjustment that puts our thoughts and behaviors back in alignment with the *desire* to be inspired. Then when this realignment takes place, we can laugh at the folly of seeking something outside of ourselves (such as an activity or a job) to inspire us. By simply realigning and harmonizing with Spirit, we let inspiration blossom in the field of harmony.

### *Listening to the Voice of God*

When we make the decision to become a being of sharing, and practice keeping our thoughts harmonized with Spirit energy on a daily basis, our purpose will not only find us, it will *chase after* us wherever we go. Since we've become aligned with our Creator, we won't be able to escape it. You see, when we live as much of life as possible in God-realization, nothing can go wrong. What and who we need will surface, and we'll notice that we can't escape feeling that something much greater than our individual life is at work within and around us.

Our number one relationship must be to this creative energy of God. When we go to our Source, we activate the energy that reconnects us to our purpose—inspiration then shows up right before our eyes, even when we may have stopped thinking about it. Our purpose manifests in many ways and won't be limited to a career slot; in fact, it's often something that requires us to leave a particular kind of employment to pursue something we'd never considered.

We must trust that inspiration is already here—it only eludes us because we've disconnected in some way from the Spirit that was and always will be our essence. I recently received a letter from a woman in Kansas that illustrates this message perfectly. Just out of the blue, she felt compelled to do something that she'd never contemplated before, and *voilà!*—she was inspired and remains so today. With Gail's permission, here is her letter, which has been edited for clarity. (For more on Japa, which is a form of meditation, please see my book *Getting in the Gap*.)

> *Dear Wayne,*
> *Thank you so much for your presentations and tapes. You are frequently my traveling companion as I drive in my job. I just wanted to add my testimony to the power of Japa.*
> *I was an on-and-off meditator but realized how much more smoothly my days went when I was "on" it. I visited Kenya, Africa, in June of 2002 and met an eight-year-old orphan girl there. As I sat on the ground, she crawled into my lap, and a*

*voice said, "Take her home." I physically turned around, but no one was there. Again the voice said, "Take her home." I asked my 18-year-old daughter (who was with me on the trip) what she thought about my adopting this beautiful child. With the quickness of a sprinter, she replied, "Go for it."*

*When we returned to the States a week later, I realized that if I didn't follow through with this adoption, I'd always regret it. Regret seemed much larger than the task of adopting! I began doing Japa each morning, and through a series of miracles, that special little girl was able to come to this country. I named her Nellie, and she has been a blessing to me and my other children.*

*Nellie's adoption was part two of God's plan. Part one had unfolded a couple of years before, when I felt guided to sponsor a series of workshops for which I profited $10,000 with very little time or work. And guess what the final cost of adopting Nellie was? The first time I heard the voice, I chose to disregard it and/or think it through, making lists of pros and cons. But I could not rest until I proceeded with the workshops. That's how I explained to my family that I needed to proceed with adopting Nellie—obedience had brought abundance into our lives, and now it was time to share that abundance. Nellie has brought the abundance of love and forgiveness into our home. She is truly a treasure.*

*Thank you for sharing your gift of this wonderful meditation. It changed my life and the life of a little girl.*

*Sincerely,*
*Gail Beale*
*Topeka, Kansas*

Gail used her meditation practice to stay connected to her Creator and to be open to having her purpose in life find her—and when a small orphaned child in Kenya crawled into her lap, purpose did indeed find her. Gail calls this "God's plan," but she's actually a piece of God. She came from God, so she must be like what she came from. Hence, God's plan is her plan, and vice versa. In her meditation practice, Gail heard a voice—that voice belonged to her highest self, the part that never left Spirit, is always inspired, and can be heard when allowed to come through. It's a voice that lives in each and every one of us, too.

### *Ask, and It Will Be Given*

It may sound too simplistic, but the ancient biblical advice to "ask, and it will be given" carries a great message for us as we attempt to find our way to an inspired life. I interpret *to ask* as being identical to allowing the guidance of our Source to flow back to us. Recall that allowing is an absence of resistance, which means that we're in the process of reconnecting to the vibrational energy of Spirit, not making a plea to a disconnected being residing outside of us. When we're in harmony with Spirit, we're just like God, so our desires are the same. In this state, we're asking our highest self to get back into balance and allow our desires to be in this spiritual proportion.

The greater our desire, the more horsepower we'll apply to its fulfillment. This is what true asking is: a plea for the assistance to put into practice that which matches up with our desires. The more intense our desires, the greater the measure of love going into our asking and our labor will be—and coming in contact with love is the very essence of Spirit and inspiration. Weak desire will attract doubt and weakness, which will cause us to experience monotony and drudgery in our efforts. With monotony, we'll give up, but with love, we'll be available to abundant hope.

For example, I find it impossible to think in boring terms when it comes to my writing. My desire is so intense that I feel love for what I'm doing and joyful when I even pass by my writing space. I get a warm feeling throughout my body because my desire to convey these ideas and express what I'm learning each day is so intense that it matches up with the spiritual energy of the Source of All Creation. When I ask, it's for the intensity of my desire to be matched up with my spiritual Source so that I can accomplish that desire. Obviously when I'm asking for guidance, my thoughts or queries go out to my spirit, which then matches up with the Divine Source.

The quality that stands out among those who feel inspired is one of an intense, burning desire—it goes beyond talent and ability as a measure of success. We need to ask this highest part of ourselves to align with Source, and for the intensity of our desire to be so great that our love for who we are and what we do precludes the possibility of any boredom, tedium, or weariness. In this manner, our inspired vision will be forthcoming.

### Creating and Holding on to Our Vision

The desire to find our way to inspiration involves creating a vision of living in-Spirit 100 percent of the time. Even if we don't have a clue what we should be doing or what our mission is, we need to practice creating this vision anyway. Our inner picture has to be based on our intention to feel good, which is of course synonymous with feeling *God.*

If we make this an inner mantra: *I intend to feel good,* we can picture ourselves experiencing joy regardless of what's going on around us. We can remind ourselves that whatever we desire is on its way, in amounts greater than ever imagined. If we keep this vision uppermost in mind, then before long, the All-Creating Source will conspire to bring our vision into our physical life. Most important, we'll begin to act on our vision and receive Divine guidance.

Here's a Lao Russell quote that I hold close to my heart:

> Whatever work you perform with deep desire, God will work with you by doing exactly as much for you as you do to manifest Him. The farmers, or gardeners, or foresters know this. They

know that a little work given by them brings but little work done by Nature. The giving and regiving are always equal. The more service you give to Nature, the more Nature will work with you in her regivings.

It all begins and ends with our willingness to hold a desire in our inner vision despite what we see around us now. The inner picture is what we'll ultimately have to act upon, so we want to be very careful about what we create and hold for ourselves. If we see ourselves as limited, unworthy, weak, timid, or sickly, then we'll act on these inner portraits. For example, I was touched by Ram Dass's description of wondering what it would feel like to be old and infirm in his book *Still Here*. He held that thought and almost immediately experienced a stroke, requiring his need for continuous care by others. "Thinking old" attracted the element of old that he so feared.

The truth is that we react to the vision we create and hold— and so do all of the cells in our body. So it's vitally important to hold a clear vision of ourselves as deserving of feeling inspired, knowing that it's our ultimate calling, and choosing to be in-Spirit even when everything around us suggests otherwise. We need to opt to be a being of sharing, living as close to God-realization as is possible. The ancient Persian poet Rumi states this so perfectly with the following lines:

*The garden of the world has no limits*
*except in your mind.*

*Its presence is more beautiful than the stars,*
*with more clarity*
*than the polished mirror of your heart.*

Clear your mind of limits, and move into Spirit, Whose presence, as Rumi tells us, is "more beautiful than the stars."

# Some Suggestions for Putting
# the Ideas in This Chapter
# to Work for You

— Practice sharing anonymously. The goal is to be at one with the Creator, and It isn't looking for credit, a reward, or even a thank-you. The more you practice being a sharing person rather than one who continually wonders, *What's in it for me?* the more flows back to you when you least expect it. You don't have to make deals with God in which you perform acts of sharing in exchange for special favors—just work at becoming a being of sharing *with no expectation of receiving anything in return*. You'll be pleasantly surprised at how inspired you'll feel.

— Give yourself the time and quiet space to enter into dialogue with your Source. Be willing to ask the questions that you need to feel guided by Spirit—the answers you seek will come rushing toward you when you're in authentic communication. I've found that very early in the morning is such a powerful time for me that I call it my "being-with-God time." Every morning when I awake, I lie in bed and say, "I'm going to spend a few quiet moments with God and ask for guidance for this day," and I always hear instructions to begin by sharing something with someone. I treasure those 10 or 15 minutes of being with my Source as I start the day in gratitude for being alive, healthy, and able to help others.

— Keep an open mind about what it takes to feel inspired. It may not necessarily mean a change of career; it might simply involve writing your equivalent of *Mr. Holland's Opus,* helping orphaned children, purchasing a horse for riding and competing, or buying a piece of vacant property and planning a vacation getaway spot. However, it is entirely possible that a change in job and location *is* beckoning you, so stay open and allow it to find you. Regardless, you should always stay connected to Spirit and trust the messages you receive.

— Remember this simple truth: *The answer to how is yes.* You may never know exactly how you're going to accomplish the feeling of inspiration, but by saying *yes!* to life and all that calls you, the how will take care of itself.

— Remove inner references and visions of what you don't want. Instead of thinking, *I will not attract sickness into my world,* affirm, *I attract health into my world* and *I will never allow my brain to atrophy; I will stay active throughout all of my life.* Know that you are connected to a continual stream of well-being, and let this knowing guide you in all of your visions for inspiration.

✳ ✳ ✳

Here's a question that Ralph Waldo Emerson posed, which I'd like you to ponder before turning to the next section: "We are very near to greatness: one step and we are safe; can we not take the leap?"

One step. Surely you can take one step for your own inspired greatness. . . .

# PART II

# THE FUNDAMENTALS OF INSPIRATION

*"The philosophy of six thousand years has not searched the chambers and magazines of the soul.*

*"In its experiments there has always remained, in the last analysis, a residuum it could not resolve. Man is a stream whose source is hidden. Our being is descending into us from we know not whence. . . .*

*"I am constrained every moment to acknowledge a higher origin for events than the will I call mine."*

— RALPH WALDO EMERSON
from *"Essay IX: The Over-Soul"*

CHAPTER 6

# ESSENTIAL PRINCIPLES FOR FINDING YOUR WAY TO AN INSPIRED LIFE

*"Well, every man has a religion;*
*has something in heaven or earth which he will give up*
*everything else for—something which absorbs him—which may*
*be regarded by others as being useless—yet it is his dream,*
*it is his lodestar, it is his master. That, whatever it is,*
*seized upon me, made me its servant, slave—induced me to set*
*aside the other ambitions—a trail of glory in the heavens,*
*which I followed, followed with a full heart. . . .*
*When once I am convinced, I never let go . . ."*

— WALT WHITMAN

**THIS CHAPTER PRESENTS SIX PRINCIPLES** that are important to observe as we seek an inspired life—they're a blueprint to refer to as we reconstruct a life in-Spirit. I'm listing them in no particular order of importance because I believe that they're equally essential.

***Principle #1:*** *Be Independent of the Good Opinion of Others*

In order to live in-Spirit, we must adopt Arthur Miller's trust that the Source is always working within us, or Walt Whitman's belief that our ultimate calling "may be regarded by others as being useless—yet it is [our] dream, it is [our] lodestar." In other words, inspiration must be our master, even though following it might disappoint others.

When inspiration makes its presence known, we must pay attention if our priority is to be who or what we were meant to be. William Shakespeare's famous query, "To be or not to be: that is the question," symbolizes the urgent choices that we have to make—that is, do we become what we came here to be, or do we ignore that calling? In this oft-quoted soliloquy, Hamlet delves deeper by wondering, "Whether 'tis nobler in the mind to suffer / The slings and arrows of outrageous fortune, / Or to take arms against a sea of troubles, / And by opposing end them? . . ." Suffering the consequences of living according to someone else's wishes doesn't make any sense; rather, we need to oppose the external opinions that try to force us to be what we're not intended to be.

There are many well-meaning people in our lives who have ideas about what we should or shouldn't be doing . . . relatives tend to be specialists in this area! If we let them guide us with advice that isn't congruent with our inner calling, we'll suffer the anguish—the "slings and arrows"—of an uninspired life. Each of us can feel what we're being called to be; when we listen, we can hear our own impatient voices coaxing us to listen and complete the assignments we brought with us from the world of Spirit. But when we allow the opinions and dictates of others to determine what we're going to be, we lose sight of our objective to live an inspired life.

We need to determine for ourselves how much we've allowed others to decide issues such as what we do, where we live, with whom we live, and even how we're treated. We must know that absolutely no one else truly knows and feels what we're here to accomplish, so we must give ourselves permission to hear our inner guidance and ignore the pressure from others. Regardless of how absurd our inner calling might seem, it's authentically *ours* and doesn't have to make sense to anyone else. The willingness to listen and act on our inspiration, independent of the opinions of others, is imperative.

***Principle #2:*** *Be Willing to Accept the Disapproval of Others*

Logically following the last principle, this one notes that we're going to incur the disfavor of many people when we follow our inclinations to be in-Spirit and live the life we came here to live. This isn't a selfish or cynical attitude: When we begin to follow our ultimate calling, there *will* be a lot of resistance. In fact, the purpose of the "slings and arrows" sent our way is to get us to change our mind and be "reasonable," which translates to "Do it *my* way!"

However, as we gain the strength to ignore the pressure to conform, resistance will diminish and ultimately change to respect. When we steadfastly refuse to think, act, and conform to the mandates of others, the pressure to do so loses its momentum. All we have to do is endure some initial disapproval such as dogmatic persuasion, anger, pouting, silence, and long-winded lectures . . . and then we're on our way to inspiration rather than frustration.

Here's a recent example of this from my own life. I elected to have most of the royalties and all of the advance payments for this book go to a scholarship fund, and there were people who tried to get me to "come to my senses" and not "throw my money away," which was how they viewed my decision. I have an inner voice that is overwhelmingly powerful, and I trust in what truly inspires me. I'd known for many years that one day I'd endow a scholarship fund at my alma mater, for instance—the thought of young, financially challenged students having the opportunity that I'd received as a young military veteran inspires me more than I can relate to you here in these pages. So I was comfortable with, and able to ignore, the disapproval I encountered, giving responses such as, "I know what I'm doing and why I'm doing it," and "Don't waste your time and mine attempting to convince me otherwise." And sure enough, the resistance I met was converted to acceptance.

The people who receive the most approval in life are the ones who care the least about it—so technically, if we want the approval of others, we need to stop caring about it and turn our attention to becoming an inspired being of sharing. One little note of caution here: When we raise our children according to these principles, and they observe us living them on a daily basis, we'll have to deal with their determination to respect their inner calling. For example, when my daughter Sommer was about 11 years old and I asked to see her report card, I was a bit taken aback by her response. "Why do you want to see it?" she asked.

When I said, "Well, I'm your father, and I think I should know how you're doing in school," she matter-of-factly replied, "But these are my grades, not yours, and if I thought you needed to see them, I would've shown them to you already."

I assure you that she wasn't being disrespectful; she simply had no need to share her grades with me. Since I knew that she was doing very well in school, I let it go—and let her be who she wanted to be.

**Principle #3:** *Stay Detached from Outcomes*

Inspiration doesn't come from completing tasks or meeting goals; in fact, that's the sure way to have it elude us. Returning to Spirit, you see, is an experience of living fully in the present moment. Our purpose in life isn't to arrive at a destination where we find inspiration, just as the purpose of dancing isn't to end up at a particular spot on the floor. The purpose of dancing—and of life—is to enjoy every moment and every step, regardless of where we are when the music ends.

Many of us are seduced into believing that having goals is necessary for a successful life, especially since we've been brainwashed by slogans such as "If you don't know where you're going, how will you know when you're there?" and "Not having a goal is more to be feared than not reaching a goal." This kind of logic keeps us from feeling inspired because we live a life of *striving* while foregoing *arriving*.

A more rewarding spiritual truth is that there's only now—and when this moment passes, it will be replaced by another one, ad infinitum. To use up our "present now" being consumed with a "future now" that will only turn into a "then" is the prescription for the absence of inspiration. Since there's only now, learning to live in it and enjoy every present moment is the same as being in-Spirit, while being focused on an outcome to determine our level of happiness and success keeps us out of Spirit.

Yoga master Sri Swami Sivananda offered the only worthwhile goal I know of when he said that the goal of life is God-realization. Now *here's* a goal I can live with! After all, this allows me to live in-Spirit every moment of my life, while simultaneously thinking ahead to the next God-realized moment (and the next). As the great Indian sage Ramana Maharshi once remarked, "There is no goal to be reached. There is nothing to be attained. You are the Self. You exist always." Now this is real inspiration.

As I sit here writing, I don't have a goal in mind, yet I trust that the book will be completed. I've seen it, even though I'm months away from the final product. I live in the bliss of creating right here, right now, and I relish these moments. I trust that the outcome will be handled by the same Source that inspires these words to appear seemingly out of nowhere. I'm here now—in peace, in love, and in awe—and my only goal is to stay in this consciousness and enjoy every moment, putting into practice what I agreed to when I was in-Spirit before becoming the particle that began this glorious journey.

***Principle #4:*** *Know That We Need Nothing/No Things to Be Inspired*

We came into this world of boundaries from a formless energy field of Spirit. We arrived here with nothing/no things, we'll make our exit with nothing/no things, and our purpose (God-realization) requires nothing/no things. We are all that we need to be inspired and living on purpose, and the things that continue to flow into our life are just symbols of the unlimited abundance of our Source. In other words, these things have no value in and of themselves because everything in the physical world is changing and will dissolve back to nothingness anyway.

The objective Universe is *not* made up of things—it's made up of waves of motion that *simulate* the things we're taught to believe are real. Once we accept that, from an infinite perspective, everything we see in nature isn't really what it seems to be, we're able to convert what we view with our eyes into a knowing about all things. Then we can recognize that the objects we believed we needed to feel inspired are nothing from Spirit's perspective. This is what distinguishes the physical person from the spiritual person, the inspired person from the uninspired person.

We're beings of Spirit, living from mind (rather than the body with all of its inherent restrictions), so if we communicate with God in the language of light and energy, we'll see His tolerant amusement at our preoccupation with the illusion of possessions. We don't need more of anything to become inspired; rather, we need to take our attention away from what we see and move into the miraculous world of Spirit, where joy and bliss await us.

Remember: *We're already connected to everything that we think is missing from our life.* Below and above the ranges that our eyes and ears perceive, the entire activity of creation remains invisible and inaccessible—but when we shift from sensory searching to trusting what we know, we discover the folly of chasing after anything in order to feel inspired. All we need is a conscious realignment so that our thoughts begin to match up vibrationally with Spirit, which we know is a part of us already. And our state of inspiration is what allows for this realignment.

When we tune in to what we know rather than what we see, we immediately find that every thought of God is repeated throughout the Universe. We can watch as some things enter our life and others leave, all the while remaining in-Spirit, knowing that all of those things have nothing to do with our state of inspiration. We need nothing more to be inspired, since we're connected to Spirit already. The ancient Persian poet Omar Khayyam offered us these words, which summarize this principle that we don't need another thing to be inspired—it's all right here, right now:

*Forget the day that has been cut off*
*from thy existence;*
*disturb not thyself about tomorrow,*
*which has not yet come,*
*rest not upon that which is no more;*
*live happily one instant,*
*and throw not thy life to the winds.*


***Principle #5:*** *"Don't Die Wondering"*

This principle is extremely important in working toward an in-spired life because it motivates us to act—after all, we don't want to be full of regrets because we failed to heed our ultimate calling. Attempting to do something, even if it doesn't succeed, is inspiring because we don't tend to regret what we do, we regret what we *didn't* do. Even following a futile attempt, we're inspired because we know that we gave it a shot. It's wondering whether we should or shouldn't try something that leaves us feeling stressed and incomplete.

When I'm playing a tennis match and being tentative in anticipation of losing a point, for example, I've created a situation in which I'll wonder what kind of a game it would have been had I re-ally gone for it. It's in these moments that I remind myself, "Don't die wondering."

Inspiration has nothing to do with whether we win or lose; in fact, if we just play the game of life, we'll have plenty of wins and losses, regardless of our talent level. If we fail to even try because of fear of rejection or doubt about our talent, we're going to go through life won-dering, and that's what keeps us from finding and feeling inspiration.

Most of us, myself included, can remember the intensity of our first romantic attraction—just as we can recall what happened when we didn't follow our inspiration. I've always wondered what would have happened if I'd been able to act on that strong inner call in high school, when I had an enormous crush on a beautiful girl named Janice Nelson. I wanted to ask her out, but I let my fear of being re-jected keep me from taking the steps to act upon my inner desires.

On several occasions I even dialed her phone number and hung up when she answered. I never overcame my foreboding thoughts and, in effect, was left to die wondering.

Many years later, I danced with Janice at our 30-year high school reunion and told her how I felt back then. I even confessed the way I'd hang up the phone because of my trepidation. Janice, to my everlasting delight—and chagrin—said, "*I always had a crush on you.* I would've loved to have gone out with you, and in fact I tried to leave you clues to call me. But you never did." *Ouch!* That's a perfect example of regretting what I didn't do.

Goethe, writing in *Faust,* provides a poetic description of the two souls living within us: one, a spirit that allows us to make the phone call and ask for the date regardless of the outcome, and the other that clings to the world of fear, and lives to die wondering:

> *Alas, two souls are living in my breast,*
> *And one wants to separate itself from the other.*
> *One holds fast to the world with earthy passion*
> *And clings with twining tendrils:*
> *The other lifts itself with forceful craving*
> *To the very roof of heaven.*

If we lift ourselves "with forceful craving to the very roof of heaven," we'll never die wondering.

**Principle #6:** *Remember That Our Desires Won't Arrive by Our Schedule*

There's an ancient aphorism that goes: "If you really want to make God laugh, tell Him your plans." In essence this means that all we desire will arrive in our life when and only when we're aligned vibrationally with the energy of our Source. Our ego won't be consulted or get to determine the schedule—the Creator reveals Its secrets when It's good and ready. Our job is to take the focus off of the *when* and put it on being connected to our originating

Spirit. Our job is to stop challenging and demanding responses from God, and instead be more like Him. Our job is to understand and accept that all of the things that show up in our life, which we often find contradictory or troublesome, are there because we've attracted them . . . and we need to have these obstacles in order to clear an opening for our true Spirit purpose to emerge. This may require a change in thinking patterns, which is something Tom Barber knows all too well.

Tom is the head golf pro at Griffith Park in Los Angeles and owns and operates the Tom Barber Golf Center in Southern California; his father, Jerry, was the PGA champion in 1961. Tom is a close friend whom I can talk to straight about virtually anything. For example, he once admitted to me that business had fallen off, and he was concerned about a deterioration in income due to fewer customers golfing in an economy on the downturn.

He'd gone on for about as long as I was willing to absorb this kind of energy when I finally said, "Tom, you're approaching the whole issue from a perspective that almost guarantees that this financial headache will continue to grow. Try affirming: *What I desire is on its way. It will arrive precisely on God's time-table, not on mine. Everything that I'm experiencing now is disguised as a problem, but I know that it's a blessing. What I desire is on its way, and it's coming to me in amounts even greater that I can imagine. This is my vision, and I'll hold on to it in a state of gratitude, no matter what.*"

I received a letter from my friend about two months after our conversation, in which he wrote: "Thanks for the pep talk. Once I started to say that the business I'm seeking and the finances I need are on their way, everything started to turn around." What happened is that Tom decided to align with the unrestricted abundance of Spirit energy.

As you can see from Tom's example, rather than making demands of God to follow our schedule in order to feel inspired, we can let go, surrender, and remind ourselves that all is in Divine order. We're much more successful when we allow inspiration to flow in on God's terms than when we're impatient and demanding. As always, our job in God-realization is to become more like God—that means surrendering to the timetable that's always perfect, even when it seems to be full of errors.

Keep these six principles handy and access them anytime you find yourself lacking inspiration. Remember, too, that we're called to this world of inspiration, which beckons us to "let go and let God," as they say in the recovery movement. I also love this advice, which was tendered by one of my favorite teachers, Napoleon Hill: "If you can't do great things, do small things in a great way. Don't wait for great opportunities. Seize common, everyday ones and make them great."

## Some Suggestions for Putting the Ideas in This Chapter to Work for You

— Make a written commitment to be free of the pressures of people who try to dictate the course of your life, such as: *I intend to listen to my own thoughts concerning my life. I'll be receptive to advice, but I'll do what my conscience dictates, even if I incur disapproval.* By writing your intentions and having them readily available to refer to, you nurture the inspirational energy to follow through on your interests. The intention behind the words guides and reminds you to be steadfast about seeking your own inspiration. Don't employ anger or aggression as ways of being independent of others' opinions—you're Spirit energy from a field of love, and you must *be* love in order to be in-Spirit.

— Small steps will activate matching vibrations to what you desire. So if you want to live close to nature, plan a visit to the place of your dreams and take the small steps to experience what it feels like. If you can't or won't do that, or if you aren't ready to go yet, you can read books or rent movies in order to have the experience vicariously. But be alert to the vibrational energy of thought and action that you offer Spirit.

When my daughter Skye wanted to produce a CD of her own compositions, it seemed like a daunting task to write, perform, record, and arrange for all of the studio time and musicians. She continued to shy away from what inspired her, so I encouraged her to take a small step and write just one song. I gave her a suggestion for a title and gave her a deadline—and then I watched with joy and pride as she sat at her piano, engrossed in her inspiration, creating. One small step put her on the path of inspiration, as Napoleon Hill suggested.

— Instead of goals, make the commitment to live joyfully in the moment. Stop dreaming about the future and get back to the only thing any of us have: now. Decide to live fully in the present, withdrawing attention from past and future. Your desire for inspiration activates the world of Spirit from which you came. Your imagined future, the stuff of goals, is an unnecessary way of squandering the present moment. *Be Here Now* is more than a great book title by Ram Dass, it's the essence of inspiration. Being in the now is the way to remove anxiety, stress, and even some illnesses.

As I sit here writing, I can daydream all I want about completing this book, but in reality, all I can really do (which is precisely what I *am* doing) is listen to my inner voice, offer a matching vibration to those inner pleadings, and feel the joy of allowing the thoughts to come through me onto the pages. The "goal" has been suspended in favor of being here now, living out what I'm being directed by my "Senior Partner" to do. The end result takes care of itself, particularly since I see the end result in my mind, and I use my present moments in harmony with that vision.

— Respect the silent and burning desire that's within you— don't scoff at it, and refuse to be critical or judgmental. Create a sacred space within your home, some private corner where you can have an altar for the symbolic residence of your inner vision. When you walk by this altar, offer a silent blessing and express gratitude for the presence of inspiration in your life. The altar can have photographs, magazine articles, artifacts, totems, crystals, jewelry, plaques . . . anything that reminds you of your own passions. As "silly" or "far-fetched" as this might appear, it's nevertheless true that when you talk and live with daily reminders of Spirit, you become a vibrational match to your ultimate calling.

When I was much younger, many people ridiculed and disregarded my vision of being a writer and a performer, but I treated my inner vision with the veneration that the sacred deserves. Holding my inner knowing in high esteem during my teen years allowed me to undertake writing a novel, irrespective of what anyone around me expressed. When you trust in *your* inner vision, you're trusting the same wisdom that created you.

— Make an affirmation that whatever brings passion, enthusiasm, and inspiration to you is on its way. Say it often: *It is on its way, it will arrive on time, and it will arrive in greater amounts than I imagined.* Then look for even the tiniest clue that will help you be a vibrational match with your affirmation. You'll get what you think about, whether you want it or not!

✻✻✻

The words of a man who was both a philosopher and a Roman emperor will close this chapter. Marcus Aurelius disdained thoughts of violence and refused to go to war; in fact, he presided over his empire with a philosophy of peace and respect for all of his fellow men. Here, he speaks of the things we've forgotten when we're uninspired or not focused in-Spirit.

> When thou art troubled about anything, thou hast forgotten this, that all things happen according to the universal nature; and forgotten this, that a man's wrongful act is nothing to thee; and further thou hast forgotten this, that everything which happens, always happened so and will happen so, and now happens so everywhere; forgotten this too, how close is the kinship between

a man and the whole human race, for it is a community, not of a little blood or seed, but of intelligence. And thou hast forgotten this too, that every man's intelligence is a god, and is an efflux of the deity; and forgotten this, that nothing is a man's own, but that his child and his body and his very soul came from the deity; forgotten this, that everything is opinion; and lastly thou hast forgotten that every man lives the present time only, and loses only this.

Use his words as an inventory of things to remember as you seek to find your way back to inspiration.

CHAPTER 7

# INSPIRATION AND YOUR OWN MAGNIFICENCE

*"What is necessary to change a person
is to change his awareness of himself."*

— ABRAHAM MASLOW

*"You are a primary existence. You are a distinct portion
of the essence of God, and contain a certain part of Him
in yourself. Why then are you ignorant of your noble birth?
You carry a God about within you, poor wretch,
and know nothing of it."*

— EPICTETUS

**IN THIS CHAPTER,** we'll look at our Divine magnificence and examine the ways in which we can view ourselves in these terms for the rest of our life.

It's imperative to eliminate self-perceptions that might cloud our vision or make us question our Divine magnificence. The quote from Abraham Maslow above sets the tone for what we can do: If we want to move from disenchantment to inspiration, or from apathy and indifference to passion and enthusiasm, then it's necessary to alter our awareness of ourselves.

I'm a people watcher, and every day of my life I observe how others carry themselves and treat their body, what they eat, and how they move; I also listen carefully to the seemingly nonchalant verbal utterances that reflect their opinion of themselves. I'm fascinated by what people think of themselves—it's the rare individual who reflects the image that Epictetus describes in the opening quotation.

So what prevents us from seeing ourselves as containing "the essence of God" and knowing that we're of "noble birth"? Only ego, and only when we allow it. A non-ego-based point of view must be firmly in place on the journey to an inspired, passionate life. We must make a decision to see ourselves in the same manner that we knew to be true when we were in the formless dimension contemplating our transformation into a physical being with a purpose.

*Who am I?* is *the* "big question." We're so accustomed to identifying ourselves by what we have, what we accomplish, what we earn, and what others think of us that we've lost touch with our original self. The answer to this question is: *I'm a unique portion of the essence of God. I originated in-Spirit, yet I've forgotten this fundamental truth.* With this kind of awareness, we'd all be determined to seek our ultimate calling and live an inspired life. Our perception of ourselves would be of a spiritual being who's free of limitations and who trusts that Divine guidance is available at every moment. If we don't currently feel this way, then it's vital that we do what Dr. Maslow suggests and change it.

### *Changing Our Awareness of Ourselves*

How would we think and act in daily life if we were truly aware of our Divine essence? Obviously there wouldn't be room to reproach ourselves because we wouldn't doubt our abilities. In fact, we'd never look in the mirror and feel anything but love and appreciation: We'd see ourselves as fully capable of attracting all we desire; we'd treat our body with reverence and care, giving thanks for its Divine design; we'd celebrate every thought we have, knowing its Divine origin; and we'd become aware of our enormous talents and be awed by all that we are.

We need to encourage the awareness of our magnificence in every regard. When that awareness has been reawakened, the seedlings of inspiration will begin blossoming. Here's a way of expressing these fundamental truths, offered to us by the writings of Bahaullah, of the Baha'i faith: "This most great, this fathomless and surging Ocean is near, astonishingly near, unto you. Behold it is closer to you than your life-vein! Swift as the twinkling of an eye ye can, if ye but wish it, reach and partake of this imperishable favor, this God-given grace, this incorruptible gift, this most potent and unspeakably glorious bounty."

There's no way to be in-Spirit without a changed awareness—so when we accomplish this, we give ourselves the gift of moving from being flawed, limited, lacking, and imperfect to being completely comfortable with our magnificence.

This unspeakably glorious bounty is so close to us . . . all we have to do is to make a few "twinkling-of-an-eye" adjustments, so why not begin now?

Following are three of the most obvious and important changes in awareness that we can make.

### 1. Changing the Awareness of Our Magnificent Talents and Abilities

I want to emphasize an extremely important point: I'm not writing about self-esteem here, nor am I referring to levels of confidence. Rather, I'm saying that we need to keep the important question *Who am I?* in the forefront of our mind. This question doesn't revolve around previous life experiences, has nothing to do with what we've been told our special qualities or unique abilities are, and isn't related to how worthy or worthless we feel about ourselves—it has to do with a simple truth.

As Epictetus, a philosopher in the 1st century A.D. said, "You carry a God about within you, poor wretch, and know nothing of it." Just like Epictetus, who was born into slavery yet became one of our most profound teachers, we came into this world with an inexhaustible supply of talent. Our abilities are as limitless as God's are because we're a distinct portion of the essence of Him—and there's an infallible way

351

to begin entertaining those abilities and creating as He does.

That way is to become aware that anything that excites us is a clue that we have the ability to pursue it. Anything that truly intrigues us is evidence of a Divine (albeit latent) talent that's signaling our awareness. Having an interest in something is the clue to a thought that's connected to our calling—that thought is a vibration of energy in this vast Universe. If something *really* appeals to us and we feel excited, but perceive ourselves as devoid of the talent we think is necessary, it's probably an even higher vibration.

Anything that's causing excitement within us is evidence of a Spirit message that's saying, "You can do this—yes, you can!" If we react to this message with anything other than "You're correct—I *can* do this! I have the ability to do it," then we've selected the vibration of resistance and ignored the vibration of excitement and interest that spoke to us.

How could it be any other way? We wouldn't think of things that are interesting and exciting to us if we didn't have the inherent ability to act on these thoughts, especially since we're a portion of the All-Creating, All-Capable, All-Wise Force. Just the fact that we're interested and excited about doing something is all the evidence we need—this is inspiration right in front of us, begging us to pay attention to the feeling. Therefore, we need to change our awareness in order to take note of our stimulation, rather than of the opinions of others. We need to ignore the scores on some standardized test, or worse yet, our own inventory of past experiences that led us to conclude that we're untalented and incapable.

Our thoughts about who we are, what excites us, and what we feel called to be and do are all Divinely inspired and come with whatever guidance and assistance we'll need to actualize these goals. The decision at this point is: Are we willing to listen to these Divine thoughts that pique our interest, or do we go on listening to the false self that's made us what Epictetus called a "poor wretch"?

\* \* \*

Rather than case studies of which I have only secondhand knowledge, I'm going to use some examples from my own life that illustrate listening to the false self.

My background would appear to be an unlikely one for what I'm calling *magnificence*. Here's what it would look like on paper: *Fathered by an alcoholic who abandoned his three children; childhood years spent in foster homes; a classic underachiever educated in public schools; grew up at the low end of the socioeconomic scale; no financial advantages; no examples of, or ambitions for, higher education; four years as an enlisted man in the United States Navy; admitted to a university on a provisional acceptance at the age of 22 due to lower-than-average grades in high school; worked his way through three advanced degrees by being a cashier and stock boy in a grocery store in Detroit.* This isn't exactly what you'd call a prescription for becoming the best-selling author of 25 books and a successful public speaker.

I couldn't begin to tell you how many teachers of creative writing and speech gave me low grades for my efforts in these fields. All I can say for certain is that I've always had a knowing about my interest in writing, and have been excited by the prospect of entertaining and informing an audience—any audience! By all of the "accepted" standards, I didn't have any writing ability. What I did have (and still do) was an interest and a passion for writing: It inspired and thrilled me, and I simply loved it. From the perspective of inspiration, I had the ability to do it, and that's all I needed to know.

Then, as now, I trusted that the Universe would handle all of the details, including: *Will I be published? Will the critics approve? Will my book be a bestseller? Will my mother approve? Will I get an apology from any of my old English teachers?* But really, who cares about all this? The fact that writing excites me is all I've ever needed to know. When I follow that thought and stay with it, I conclude that I have the ability and the talent . . . and so do you.

Like me, it's easy to find what excites you. What do you find intriguing? Does learning yoga and becoming an instructor interest you? Then you have your answer. The issue isn't about ability, it's about being matched up in-Spirit with your current thoughts and behaviors. I still remember the excitement I felt at being admitted to a doctoral program. Despite the fact that no one in my family had ever entertained such a possibility and I didn't know one single person who had entered, let alone completed, an advanced-degree program, I was excited beyond what I can convey to you here. I knew that whatever I needed in the way of ability and talent would be there.

So how about you—do you live with resistance, or do you allow your enthusiasm and excitement to be a vibrational match to what intrigues you? Keep in mind that as one of God's glorious thoughts, you've originated out of an energy field that knows only possibility. So stay in vibrational harmony with this idea and know that your thoughts—which emerge as interests, excitement, inner thrills, and illuminating sensations—are indications that you have the necessary ability to merge with your magnificent creativity. You came from magnificence, and you are magnificent still.

## 2. Changing the Awareness of Our Magnificent Physical Presence

During the writing of this book, I was engaged in a passionate tennis match when I overheard a woman on her cell phone saying, "I can't believe she would even say something like that—she's such an unattractive person herself." I was getting ready to serve the ball to my opponent and actually had to stop to make a note to write about this incident and the question it raises. *How is it possible for a creation of God to be unattractive in any way?* I wondered.

I thought about an apple pie: One slice must be the same as the entire pie—it can't suddenly be pineapple or banana. The same logic applies to all of us: If we came from Source, how is it possible for us to be different from It? I doubt that the woman on the cell phone would ever deign to call God unattractive, yet that's exactly what she was inadvertently doing. And we do the very same thing when we place pejorative labels on our body, the magnificent temple we occupy.

In the previous section, we answered the question *Who am I?* in spiritual rather than physical terms. Now let's ask a similar question regarding our physical body. Even though we've been living in it ever since we began as an embryo, it's still relevant to ask, *What is this body that emerged from Spirit?*

Our body is made up of chemicals, far too many for me to elaborate here, but some of them are iron, magnesium, calcium, nitrogen, hydrogen . . . and on and on goes the list. These chemicals are part of a finite supply here on Earth, so what flows through our veins is part of that finite supply. To that end, the iron that's in our blood was once somewhere else—perhaps in a dinosaur, in the body of Jesus, or in a mountain in Afghanistan—and now it's in our body. And when we leave our body, our iron supply will reside someplace else on Earth as a part of that finite supply.

In other words, our entire planet is made up of the exact same chemicals that constitute our physical makeup. Chemically speaking, there's no difference between humans and rocks, trees, orangutans, or distant stars—grind them all up and their chemical composition isn't what distinguishes one from the other. Our physical presence is a spiritually directed conglomeration of a hodgepodge of chemicals, and the end result is that we're beings made up of the same stuff that makes up the stars. We're made up of stardust. That's right, the stuff of dreams—twinkling, magical, beautiful, light-filled stardust!

Remember that the Spirit from which we originated can create anything, including worlds, so why would it choose ugly or unattractive creations? We're here in the perfect body for our time in this incarnation, and it's a living, breathing miracle in every way. It's guided and being directed by an invisible Force that directs everything and everyone in the Universe: It beats our heart, digests our food, circulates our blood, grows our hair, and repairs our cuts and bruises, all independent of our opinions.

I wrote earlier about being independent of the opinions of others. Well, we aren't beautiful or attractive because of how we stack up against a runway model—we're beautiful because we came from beauty, so we must be the same as what we came from. All labels such as *unattractive, ugly, homely,* and *unbecoming* (as well as *pretty, attractive, handsome,* and *beautiful*) are judgments designed to compare one person to another using artificial standards set up by ego-dominated people and organizations.

Living in-Spirit means that we see our body with all of its unique characteristics and feel thankful for the perfect temple that's temporarily housing our true "primary existence." If it's short or tall, bald or hairy, stumpy or slender, extend loving appreciation to it every day. If it can't see or hear, resides in a wheelchair or a hospital bed, has crooked teeth or only three toes—whatever—love this collection of stardust! A prayerful thought might go like this: *I think of my body as a piece of the eternal, an individualized expression of God. I live in-Spirit, inspired because I'm the same as the loving energy that created me, which is perfect.*

Think about the logic of what I'm saying here. Obviously we can't live a life of inspiration if the physical shell we take with us everywhere is perceived as anything other than a Divine, perfect creation. Our attitude toward our body, along with how we feed and exercise it, must match up with Spirit. We came from love, so we must extend that love and appreciation to our body at all times in order to be genuinely inspired.

### 3. Changing the Awareness of Our Magnificent Personal History

This third and final element of our inspirational magnificence is perhaps our greatest challenge. How can we look upon all that we've done (or failed to do) and view it through the lens of our magnificence, especially when we've been trained to feel shame and self-reproach as a result of our perceived failures or flaws. Early on we're taught to evaluate our worth as a human being based on how well we fit in, what grades we get, and what merit badges we acquire. Then, as adults, we're measured by the amount of money we make, the promotions we receive, whom we've pleased or disappointed, and what sins we've committed. On and on goes this ego-dominated list of judgments that we've had imposed on us and have imposed on ourselves.

At this stage, we need to view our past from the perspective of everything that we've ever done or not done being over. We can't *un*do or *re*do it—we have the choice to look back at the past either through eyes clouded by ego judgments or through an inspired point of view. We can forgive ourselves or we can shame ourselves. Since our goal is to be more like our Creative Source, which is loving and giving, we should adopt forgiveness—but this isn't in ego's script.

We've all reacted to situations in the past in ways that we wouldn't want to today. I personally have done many things that I wouldn't choose to repeat—yet every recovering or recovered addict looks back with gratitude for the experience that brought him or her to a higher, more loving, sober place. As I've said in other places, true nobility is not about being better than someone else, it's about being better than we used to be. Every single experience in my life, right up to this day, was something I needed to go through in order to get to be here now, writing these words. What proof can I offer for this assertion? It happened—that's all the proof I need.

As we look back on our life, we've failed at nothing . . . all we've done is produce some results. It's imperative that we send love to those who were hurt by us and forgiveness to ourselves to heal our inner agony. We can then view it all as what we needed to experience in order to get to a higher place. One thing I've learned in my 65 years is that virtually every spiritual advance I've made toward a closer alignment with God energy has been preceded by some kind of fall from grace. Such "mistakes" allow me to write and speak from a more compassionate stance—that is, they always seem to provide me with the energy to propel myself to a higher place. Truly, I bless all of these "failures" because I know I needed to go *there* in order to get *here*.

Be gentle and forgiving with yourself, abandon any and all shame, and refuse to engage in any self-repudiation. Instead, learn from Leo Tolstoy, who said that "the most difficult thing—but an essential one—is to love Life, to love it even while one suffers, because Life is all. Life is God, and to love Life means to love God."

So love every moment of life, especially your blunder-filled past.

# Some Suggestions for Putting the Ideas in This Chapter to Work for You

— When you see people you're used to judging as less than perfect, stop in midthought and remember that they share the same God-force as you. Replace judgments of *grossly overweight, dirty, slovenly, disfigured,* or whatever terminology you normally use, with a nonjudgmental thought of pure love, remembering that no one is unappealing to God. Look for opportunities to replace scornful thoughts with loving ones. Trust me—every time you extend love to those who usually receive anything but is a seed of inspiration.

— Forgiving yourself for everything you've felt shame about is highly important. Whatever happened was necessary, so let go of regret and replace your negative feelings with gratitude for what you've learned. If your objective is to be inspired, then you must eradicate your resistance to that magnificent state of being.

After you've forgiven yourself, extend the same courtesy to everyone who you feel mistreated you. There are three people in my life whom I once felt so much anger and hatred toward that I'd get sick to my stomach whenever I thought of them. However, since I've extended love to these individuals, all manner of great things have flowed to me from the world of Spirit.

Practice forgiveness every day. The most difficult or impossible situations are the most essential!

— Keep a list of everything that interests and excites you, no matter how insignificant. Remind yourself that these are indicators or clues that within and around you lie both the talent and the necessary Spirit assistance to bring them into your reality.

— How about taking the time to give the temple in which you reside the ultimate love and respect? Your physical body is sacred space—it's Divine, beautiful, and perfect—yet you can certainly choose to bestow upon it whatever improvements you wish. There are lots of beneficial housekeeping choices you can make: Firm it up, eliminate toxins, even redecorate it, but keep the awareness of your blessed, Divine, perfect body that's capable of anything you desire from the place of being in-Spirit.

— Here's an inspiring thought to keep close to your heart: *Just as you'll never find light by analyzing the darkness, you'll never find your magnificence by analyzing what you believe to be undistinguished about yourself.* Look for opportunities to verify your greatness, and expand your view of yourself as a splendid creation. Whenever a thought of ordinariness pops into your mind, put the brakes on immediately and affirm something like: *I'm a Divine being, a distinct portion of the essence of God.* This silent reminder will do more for your inspiration than a thousand books and a hundred seminars.

* * *

Dr. Abraham Maslow, perhaps the most influential person in my life many years ago, is quoted at the beginning of this chapter as saying: "What is necessary to change a person is to change his awareness of himself." Consider how you might want to follow his advice. You can never be mediocre because you are magnificent in every way. So seek ways to change your awareness of yourself so that you're fully aware of your magnificence and can become receptive to inspiration, your ultimate calling.

CHAPTER 8

# INSPIRATION IS SIMPLE

*"I have lived long enough to learn how much there is I can really do without. . . . He is nearest to God who needs the fewest things."*

— SOCRATES

**FOR A MOMENT, LET'S IMAGINE** what it would be like to be fully alive without a physical shell or any of the stuff we need and desire for maintaining life on Earth. We'd have a mental energy that allowed us to move forward or backward, up or down, instantly creating whatever we desired. We'd be free to wallow in an exquisite existence without time or space as we know it. We'd be in a state of pure bliss, in love with everything and everyone. We'd have no duties or bills to tend to, no fear of losing anything, no one judging us, no possessions to insure, no demands on our time, and no goals to achieve.

What we're envisioning is actually the world of Spirit, which we experienced before we came here and will return to when we shed our body (or as William Butler Yeats poetically called it, our "tattered coat upon a stick").

Remember that a central premise of this book is that inspiration is a state of being here now in this material world, while at the same time reconnecting to our spiritual origins. In order to be receptive to inspiration, we need to eliminate the ego clutter that accumulates all too easily for most of us—after all, if we're preoccupied with events and activities that have nothing to do with inspiration, we're unlikely to notice its summons. So in order to achieve a reunion with our ultimate calling, we need to emulate the clear, uncomplicated world of Spirit.

### Three Keys to Keeping Life Simple

While the theme of this chapter is that inspiration is simple, this doesn't mean that we should sit around doing nothing, awaiting Spirit's arrival; instead, it means having faith that our spiritual connection flourishes in a life dedicated to joy, love, and peace. If our daily activities are so overwhelming that we don't make these three things our priority, then we're disregarding the value of living a simple life.

Let's now look at each "simple key" in more detail.

## Joy

A hectic schedule crammed with nonpurposeful activities precludes an experience of inspiration. For example, when we accept obligatory committee assignments or board appointments, requests to write on subjects that don't inspire us, or invitations to gatherings we don't want to attend, we feel joy draining from our body and spirit.

Our life must be open to Spirit's guidance in order for us to feel inspired. When the calendar becomes frenzied, full of unnecessary turbulence because we've failed to simplify, we won't be able to hear those long-distance calls from our Source . . . and we'll slip into stress, anguish, and even depression. So whatever it takes to feel joy, we simply must act upon it.

Regardless of our current station in life, we have a spiritual contract to make joy our constant companion—so we must learn to make a conscious choice to say no to anything that takes us away from an inspired life. This can be done gently, while clearly showing others that this is how we choose to live. We can start by turning down requests that involve actions that don't correspond with our inner knowing about why we're here.

Even at work, we can find ways to keep ourselves on an inspirational agenda. For example, during my years as a college professor, I recall being asked over and over to partake in activities that didn't correspond with my own inspiration. So I devised a simple solution: I took on more teaching assignments, and in exchange, my colleagues attended curriculum meetings, served on research committees, and wrote building-improvement reports. I consistently listened to my heart, which always demanded joy.

Keep in mind that it's only difficult or impossible to accomplish joy when we engage in resistant vibrational thinking. If we know that we don't have to live a life stuffed with nonjoyful activities, then we can choose the way of inspiration. Opting for joy involves giving ourselves time for play instead of scheduling a workaholic nightmare. *We deserve to feel joy—it's our spiritual calling.* By giving ourselves free time to read, meditate, exercise, and walk in nature, we're inviting the guidance that's waiting patiently to come calling with inspirational messages.

There's also no law requiring us to be at the continual beck and call of our family members. I see no reason to feel anything but joy when we know it's right to choose to do what we're called to do, even when it interferes with another family member's calling. In fact, children benefit by knowing that the business of parenting is to teach them how *not* to lean on their parents. Raising independent kids to find their own inspiration and look for their own joy is important for everyone—we want them to be doing what they're called to do, ultimately for themselves, not for us. We can take great joy in attending their soccer games and recitals and in being with them and their friends—and when we're inspired, we actually *enjoy* their activities. But let's help them to live their joy, and be able to do it with *or without* us there to cheer them on.

The bottom line is that we can simplify life by cutting down on the busywork that keeps us off purpose. We must curtail such activities and listen to Spirit, staying aware of joy and how simple it is to access.

## Love

Thoughts or actions that aren't tuned to love will prevent inspiration from getting through to us—we need to remember that we come from a Source of pure love, so a simple life means incorporating that love as one of the three mainstays of our material existence.

This little four-line poem from the *Rubaiyat of Omar Khayyam,* written approximately 1,000 years ago, says so much about staying focused on love:

> *Ah, love! could thou and I with fate conspire*
> *To grasp this sorry scheme of things entire,*
> *Would not we shatter it to bits—and then*
> *Re-mould it nearer to the heart's desire!*

On the fateful day of September 11, 2001, what stuck in my mind were the cell-phone calls made by the people on the ill-fated planes. Every single call was made to a loved one, to connect back in love or to express final words of love. No one called the office or asked their stockbroker for a final appraisal of their financial status, as relationships that weren't love based didn't enter the thoughts of those who knew they were leaving this physical world. Their top priority was to be certain to close out their lives in love: "Tell the kids that I love them." "I love you!" "Give Mom and Dad my love."

Just as love is the priority in the final moments of life, so it must be as we simplify life *now.* We can go toward a clearer life by examining and purifying our relationships with those we love, with ourselves, and with God. What we're looking for are connections that keep us in an energy of love, which is the highest and fastest energy in the Universe.

Love is also incredibly healing, which reminds me of an article I recently read. Called "The Rescuing Hug," it detailed the first week in the life of a set of twins, one of whom wasn't expected to live. The babies were in two separate incubators, but nurse Gayle Kasparian fought hospital rules to place them together in one. When Gayle did so, the healthier of the twins threw an arm over her sister in an endearing embrace—at which point, the weaker baby's heart rate stabilized and her temperature rose to normal.

Even as tiny infants, our spiritually based instincts tell us to love one another. It's such a simple message, yet it's so powerful. If we organize our life around love—for God, for ourselves, for family and friends, for all humankind, and for the environment—we'll remove a lot of the chaos and disorder that defines our life. This is a way to simplify our life, but more than that, it's a way to attract inspiration.

## Peace

Isn't our all-time highest priority to live in peace? We come from a place of peace, yet we've somehow gotten farther and farther away from these origins. When we hooked up with ego, we opted for chaos, even though peace was right there for us. And inspiration and being peaceful go hand in hand.

I know that having inner and outer peace is simply crucial for me. I eschew turmoil, conflict, and agitation and remove myself from these noninspiring elements at every opportunity. After all, I can't be the spiritual being I desire to be or live in God-realization when I'm engaged in any form of bedlam.

Somehow I've been directed to maintain the peacefulness I crave by having those "dormant forces" Patanjali spoke about earlier in the book work for me throughout my career. Many people who have a similar semi-celebrity status as myself are surrounded by a long list of people who orchestrate virtually every aspect of their lives. I, however, have chosen a simpler route, and the Universe has responded by sending me a very few individuals who've supported my desire for peace. I'd like to spend the rest of this section discussing each one of them so that you'll have some clear illustrations of how these wonderful people have helped me stay in-Spirit.

— Years ago I realized that I needed help in managing the affairs of my growing enterprise, yet the idea of agents, business managers, advisors, attorneys, accountants, mediators, personal trainers, bodyguards, and any number of people to represent me seemed beyond my tolerance level. Many of those who do what I do even on a smaller scale have a large entourage of attendants for all manner of duties and activities. And I've had these contemporaries complain to me about being burdened with all of their representatives and spending more than they take in to support the services of all these individuals.

This is not my way—in fact, I have *one person* who handles almost all of my requirements. One day while running a training session for a marathon, God sent me the perfect person to handle so many of my upcoming unforeseen pressures and requirements, in the form of a woman who'd left high school in a foreign country to come to America with her two daughters. She doesn't have any fancy degrees or specialized skills, but what she does have is a heart as big as the sky, fierce loyalty, and a willingness to do whatever it takes to learn with on-the-job training.

Originally from Finland (but now a U.S. citizen), Maya Labos is the ultimate definition of a multitasker. In three decades, she's never said, "I can't do that; it's not my job." She manages every request, answers my mail, books all of my talks and my appearances with the media, takes me to and from airports, maintains my personal privacy by deflecting low-energy requests, and deals with the hundreds of appeals I get for endorsements and writing requests. Yet she also handles innumerable tasks, including grocery shopping, vitamin purchasing, office tidying, or bringing clothes to the cleaners—I can count on her to take care of everything and anything I need.

When I met Maya almost 30 years ago, she was completely broke; today she owns her own home by the ocean and is my best friend, confidante, and associate. You see, when we're open to matching up our desire for peace and simplicity with the peace and simplicity from which we originated, God sends what we need. In my case, I got an "entourage of one" to handle what myriad "specialists" can't do for so many of my contemporaries.

— Every writer needs an editor. Almost 30 years ago, God saw this and sent one to me in the form of the enormously well-read and competent Joanna Pyle. She's been my one and only editorial person for the 25 books I've written; I don't submit to editorial boards. Joanna does for me what many writers ask for from their team of editors, editorial assistants, line editors, rewriters, revisers, amenders, annotators, and so on. I want to keep it simple, and Joanna knows how I write. She's also the only person who can read my scribbles, since I write in longhand.

As the computer age dawned on the publishing world, Joanna trained herself to meet these newly emerging technological requirements—she didn't ask me to write on a computer or to change anything. She knows my desire for simplicity and peace, and she accommodates me perfectly. When I finish a chapter, I send it to Joanna with complete trust that she'll edit it in such a manner that it will be consistent with my original intent. She transcribes it, types it, reorganizes it, and computerizes it—all with a smile and genuine gratitude for being able to fulfill her purpose. Joanna is me; I am Joanna. Once I was able to convince her to leave her nonfulfilling employment as a flight attendant and pursue her bliss as an editor full-time, she was finally able to feel the joy and peace that comes from matching up her energy with her desires. She lives inspiration, and she allows me to do the same.

— I only employ one individual who handles any and all matters related to the complexities of taxes, particularly where foreign royalties are concerned. I don't use a team of legal experts who charge by the hour, or tax consultants who receive as much as what I owe the government. One man, Bob Adelson, knows my desire for peace by keeping it simple, so he organizes everything for me. He works diligently and thoroughly, doing what he loves, and I treasure his presence in my life.

— In 1976, after *Your Erroneous Zones* was published, I decided to move from New York to Florida. I knew absolutely no one in my new hometown, yet I needed an investment person whom I could trust to help me with the bonuses I'd received from the success of my first book. Having been a teacher and university professor before this point, with no experience in (or money for) investing, I knew practically nothing about this world. While contemplating how to start an investment portfolio, I pulled into a gas station, filled my tank, and drove away without realizing that my wallet, which contained $800 in cash, had fallen out of the car and was lying next to the pump.

Just a few hours later, a man called to tell me that he'd found my wallet—including the cash. I went to meet John Darling, who was my angel sent from God to take care of all of my investments for the next 29 years (and he continues to be one of my very best friends and confidants). When I needed someone I could trust, the Universe sent me a stranger who returned my $800 . . . and I've never had a moment of nonpeace regarding investments in the past three decades. John has managed it all for me—always keeping in mind how I like things to be simple, risk free, and uncomplicated—knowing what my ultimate investment objectives were and what I desired for my family.

— I left a large, prestigious New York publishing firm to work with Hay House, mainly because everything in the Big Apple was becoming way too complex. My former publisher employed wonderful people, but the company was too big—it had too many tentacles, too many unkept promises, and too many departments that weren't in harmony with each other (or with me). I felt that too often I was being told, "It's not our fault. The fault is over there in finance or over there in marketing or over there in distribution." It was like a 20-headed monster.

I voted once again for tranquility and simplicity, and once again God sent me a gift—this time in the form of the president and CEO of Louise Hay's publishing company, Hay House. When I met Reid Tracy, we clicked almost immediately. This man—who's unafraid to roll up his sleeves and unload trucks, even though he's in an executive position—promised me personal attention, and he delivered. We talked every day about a publishing company that didn't get so big that it forgot to care for its authors. Reid promised me no large conglomerates and said, "If you have a desire, make it known to me, and I'll act on it." I loved the lack of complications, since I didn't wish to be in a large-business labyrinth any longer. *Simplify, simplify, simplify!*

It has been a glorious experience for both Reid (whom I now consider one of my closest friends) and myself. I wanted peace as a writer, and Louise Hay, whom I've long admired, and her fine president have allowed me to create in peace.

As you can see, I've chosen to allow the world of Spirit to send me those individuals who have helped, rather than hindered, me. Without these fine people and their treasured friendship, I wouldn't be able to be here in Maui, playing tennis and walking on the beach. But mostly I'm able to write from my heart and do it in peaceful ease, knowing that the Universe has taken care of all the details in its own Divine way. When *you* desire peace, simplicity, and honesty and send out a matching vibration to those desires, all I can say is, "Start watching. It's on its way!"

### The 12-Step Program to Simplicity

This chapter is going to end a little differently. Rather than giving you some general suggestions for implementing the ideas herein, I'm going to give you 12 very specific tools for simplifying your life. Begin using them today if you're serious about hearing that ultimate call to inspiration.

**1. Unclutter your life.** You'll feel a real rush of inspiration when you clear out stuff that's no longer useful in your life:

- If you haven't worn it in the past year or two, recycle it for others to use.

- Get rid of old files that take up space and are seldom, if ever, needed.

- Donate unused toys, tools, books, bicycles, and dishes to a charitable organization.

Get rid of anything that keeps you mired in acquisitions that contribute to a cluttered life. In the words of Socrates, "He is nearest to God who needs the fewest things." So the less you need to insure, protect, dust, reorganize, and move, the closer you'll be to hearing inspiration's call.

**2. Clear your calendar of unwanted and unnecessary activities and obligations.** If you're unavailable for Spirit, you're unlikely to know the glow of inspiration. Had I not been free enough to go running each day back in the 1970s, no Maya. Had I not moved away from the frenetic rush of New York to Florida (where I longed to be), no John. Had I spent all my time on a demanding board, no Joanna. God will indeed work with you and send you the guidance—and the people—you need, but if you're grossly overscheduled, you're going to miss these life-altering gifts. So practice saying no to excessive demands and don't feel guilty about injecting a dose of leisure time into your daily routine.

**3. Be sure to keep your free time *free*.** Be on the lookout for invitations to functions that may keep you on top of society's pyramid, but that inhibit your access to joyful inspiration. If cocktail parties, social get-togethers, fund-raising events, or even drinking-and-gossiping gatherings with friends aren't really how you want to spend your free time, then don't. Begin declining invitations that don't activate feelings of inspiration.

I find that an evening spent reading or writing letters, watching a movie with a loved one, having dinner with my children, or even exercising alone is far more inspiring than getting dressed to attend a function often filled with small talk. I've learned to be unavailable for such events without apologizing, and consequently have more inspired moments freed up.

**4. Take time for meditation and yoga.** Give yourself at least 20 minutes a day to sit quietly and make conscious contact with God. I've written an entire book on this subject called *Getting in the Gap*, so I won't belabor it here. I will say that I've received thousands of messages (including the one from Gail Beale, which I shared with you in Chapter 5) from people all over the world, who have expressed their appreciation for learning how to simplify their life by taking the time to meditate.

I also encourage you to find a yoga center near you and begin a regular practice. The rewards are so powerful: You'll feel healthier, less stressed, and inspired by what you'll be able to do with and for your body in a very short time.

**5. Return to the simplicity of nature.** There's nothing more awe inspiring than nature itself. The fantasy to return to a less tumultuous life almost always involves living in the splendor of the mountains, the forests, or the tundra; on an island; near the ocean; or beside a lake. These are universal urges, since nature is created by the same Source as we are, and we're made up of the same chemicals as all of nature (we're stardust, remember?).

Your urge to simplify and feel inspired is fueled by the desire to be your natural self—that is, your *nature* self. So give yourself permission to get away to trek or camp in the woods; swim in a river, lake, or ocean; sit by an open fire; ride horseback through trails; or ski down a mountain slope. This doesn't have to mean long, planned vacations that are months away—no matter where you live, you're only a few hours or even moments away from a park, campground, or trail that will allow you to enjoy a feeling of being connected to the entire Universe.

**6. Put distance between you and your critics.** Choose to align yourself with people who are like-minded in their search for simplified inspiration. Give those who find fault or who are confrontational a silent blessing and remove yourself from their energy as quickly as possible. Your life is simplified enormously when you don't have to defend yourself to anyone, and when you receive support rather than criticism. You don't have to endure the criticism with anything other than a polite thank-you and a promise to consider what's been said—anything else is a state of conflict that erases the possibility of your feeling inspired. You never need to defend yourself or your desires to anyone, as those inner feelings are Spirit speaking to you. Those thoughts are sacred, so don't ever let anyone trample on them.

**7. Take some time for your health.** Consider that the number one health problem in America seems to be obesity. How can you feel inspired and live in simplicity if you're gorging on excessive amounts of food and eliminating the exercise that the body craves? Recall that your body is a sacred temple where you reside for this lifetime, so make some time every single day for exercising it. Even if you can only manage a walk around the block, just do it. Similarly, keep the words *portion control* uppermost in your consciousness—your stomach is the size of your fist, not a wheelbarrow! Respect your sacred temple *and* simplify your life by being an exerciser and a sensible eater. I promise that you'll feel inspired if you act on this today!

**8. Play, play, play!** You'll simplify your life and feel inspired if you learn to play rather than work your way through life. I love to be around kids because they inspire me with their laughter and frivolity. In fact, if I've heard it once, I've heard it a thousand times: "Wayne, you've never grown up—you're always playing." I take great pride in this! I play onstage when I speak, and I'm playing now as I write.

Many years ago I was given a tremendous opportunity to appear on *The Tonight Show* with Johnny Carson. The man who took a chance on me, booking me even though I was an unknown at the time, was a talent coordinator named Howard Papush. It was my first big break, and I went on to appear on that show 36 additional times.

Now it's my turn to say thank you to Howard. He's written a wonderful book titled *When's Recess? Playing Your Way Through the Stresses of Life,* which I encourage you to read. (Howard also conducts workshops that teach people how to play and have fun in life.) In the book, Howard shares this great quote from Richard Bach: "You are led through your lifetime by the inner learning creature, the playful spiritual being that is your real self." I couldn't agree more—by all means, get back in touch with your real, playful self, and take every opportunity to play! Notice how it makes everything so sweet, and so simple.

**9. Slow down.** One of Gandhi's most illuminating observations reminds us that "there is more to life than increasing its speed." This is great advice for simplifying your life—in fact, slow everything way down for a few moments right here and now. Slowly read these words. Slow your breathing down so that you're aware of each inhalation and exhalation. . . .

When you're in your car, downshift and relax. Slow down your speech, your inner thoughts, and the frantic pace of everything you do. Take more time to hear others. Notice your inclination to interrupt and get the conversation over with, and then choose to listen instead. Stop to enjoy the stars on a clear night and the cloud formations on a crisp day. Sit down in a mall and just observe how everyone seems in a hurry to get nowhere.

By slowing down, you'll simplify and rejoin the perfect pace at which creation works. Imagine trying to hurry nature up by tugging at an emerging tomato plant—you're as natural as that plant, so let yourself be at peace with the perfection of nature's plan.

**10. Do everything you can to eschew debt.** Remember that you're attempting to simplify your life here, so you don't need to purchase more of what will complicate and clutter your life. If you can't afford it, let it go until you can. By going into debt, you'll just add layers of anxiety onto your life. That anxiety will then take you away from your peace, which is where you are when you're in-Spirit. When you have to work extra hard to pay off debts, the present moments of your life are less enjoyable; consequently, you're further away from the joy and peace that are the trademarks of inspiration. You're far better off to have less and enjoy the days of your life than to take on debt and invite stress and anxiety where peace and tranquility could have reigned. And remember that the money you have in your possession is nothing but energy—so refuse to plug in to an energy system that's not even there.

**11. Forget about the cash value.** I try not to think about money too frequently because it's been my observation that people who do so tend to think about almost nothing else. So do what your heart tells you will bring you joy, rather than determining whether it will be cost-effective. If you'd really enjoy that whale-watching trip, for instance, make the decision to do so—don't deny yourself the pleasures of life because of some monetary detail. Don't base your purchases on getting a discount, and don't rob yourself of a simple joy because you didn't get a break on the price. You can afford a happy, fulfilling life, and if you're busy right now thinking that I have some nerve telling you this because of your bleak financial picture, then you have your own barrier of resistance.

Make an attempt to free yourself from placing a price tag on everything you have and do—after all, in the world of Spirit, there are no price tags. Don't make money the guiding principle for what you have or do; rather, simplify your life and return to Spirit by finding the inherent value in everything. A dollar does not determine worth, even though you live in a world that attempts to convince you otherwise.

**12. Remember *your* spirit.** When life tends to get too complex, too fast, too cluttered, too deadline oriented, or too type A for you, stop and remember your own spirit. You're headed for inspiration, a simple, peaceful place where you're in harmony with the perfect timing of all creation. Go there in your mind, and stop frequently to remember what you really want.

✷ ✷ ✷

A man who personified success at the highest intellectual and social levels would hardly seem one to quote on simplifying our life, yet here's what Albert Einstein offers us on this subject: "Possessions, outward success, publicity, luxury—to me these have always been contemptible. I believe that a simple and unassuming manner of life is best for everyone, best both for the body and the mind."

Wow! I'd say this is pretty good advice, wouldn't you?

# CHAPTER 9

# THERE'S NOTHING MORE POWERFUL THAN AN IDEA WHOSE TIME HAS COME

" . . . *neither does anyone, however many wounds he may have received, die, unless he has run his allotted term of life: nor does any man, though he sits quietly by the fireside under his own roof, escape the more his fated doom.*"

— AESCHYLUS

**INSPIRATION REQUIRES FAITH**—after all, returning to Spirit while in our physical body is unlikely to be successful if we don't believe that it's possible. We may even have to focus on renewing our faith prior to accessing inspiration, since faith allows us to trust and thereby make use of the vast power that's responsible for creating every physical object in the Universe.

Faith is an internal knowing that the All-Creating Spirit provides what we need precisely on schedule. This doesn't mean that we don't have a voice in what happens to us—we do, but the voice only becomes activated when we get our ego out of the way and realign with Spirit. When our spirit works with the Divine Spirit, we can participate in creation and truly know the meaning of this chapter's title, "There's Nothing More Powerful Than an Idea Whose Time Has Come."

There's perfect timing in the Universe, and our arrival on Earth was a part of that synchronicity. In other words, *we* were an idea of God's whose time had come. This chapter introduces the concept of perfect timing and how to believe in it, notice it, tune in to it, and apply it.

### Faith Banishes All Doubt

We know that ego has virtually no control over what happens to us: Our body grows, develops, changes, and declines independent of ego's desires or opinions. We know that eventually we'll shed this garment we've been wearing for a lifetime—not when our ego decides, but when that idea's time has come. Reread the Aeschylus quote at the beginning of this chapter about our "allotted term of life" as an example of what I'm referring to.

Aeschylus was the most famous playwright and scholar of his era, and he claimed direct Divine guidance in his writing. (He was also a contemporary of Socrates, Lao-tzu, Zoroaster, Buddha, and Confucius, who all lived during the 5th century B.C. It's intriguing to note how many visionaries were on the planet simultaneously!) Basically, he tells us that the shape of life must run its allotted course and that we're here to do what Spirit intends. According to Aeschylus, we'll leave Earth and shake off our physical body in concert with Spirit's plan for us. Whether we're ready at age 17, 25, or 105, he advises us to trust in our Source. (I add to this message that at whatever age we read these words, it's the right time to realize that we're in the process of surrendering to Spirit for the remaining portion of our allotment.)

The question now becomes: Can we join with Spirit and play a decisive role in what ideas, happenings, events, or people will show up for us? The answer is a resounding *yes!* Recall once again those words of Patanjali that I shared in the opening chapters: "When you are inspired . . . dormant forces, faculties, and talents become alive." This is where faith becomes critically important.

You see, we must have faith in a Universe that's created and guided by an intelligence greater than our ego—one where there can be no accidents. When an idea's time has come, it can't be stopped—but by raising our vibration to match that of the Universal Source of Being, we can bring about that idea's time. We can raise our level of consciousness from ego and group dominance to what I call "visionary consciousness," in which we reconnect to the mind of God. We banish all doubt by our *knowing*, which is a higher level of consciousness than *believing*. Our vision is God's vision, in a manner of speaking. Let me offer you an example of how this visionary consciousness plays out.

One of my greatest teachers—and a man I now call my friend—is Ram Dass. He lives from the spiritual faith I'm writing about, without doubts or fears. I'd been a long-distance follower and devotee of his for 30 years, always knowing that we'd connect in person. I had this knowing without ever needing to hurry or force what I sensed was a future connection in his and my lifetime. And when that idea's time came, Ram Dass moved to Maui, where I'm writing to you from right now.

Today I have the great pleasure of being in the service of my teacher, helping him in these advanced years of his life. The following self-explanatory letter that I wrote recently is posted on my Website, **www.drwaynedyer.com.** I'm including it here to precisely illustrate how what I'm relating in this chapter can unfold.

One of the truly great men of our time needs our help, and I write these words to encourage your generosity and support. Back in the 1960s a Harvard professor named Richard Alpert left behind the hectic world of academia and traveled to India—there he was to meet his spiritual teacher, who gave him a new purpose to fulfill along with a new name. He, of course, is Ram Dass.

His guru told him to love everyone, feed people, and see God everywhere. Ram Dass became a person who lived out this mandate, doing what so many of us could only dream. He connected to his spirit and devoted his life to serving others.

In 1969 he wrote and published the signature book on spirituality and applied higher awareness, *Be Here Now.* In keeping with his commitment to love everyone and feed people, he donated all of the royalties and profits to foundations that did just that. With millions of dollars at stake, Ram Dass simply chose to live his life as a man of service to God.

After years spent in India in pursuit of a higher, more enlightened consciousness for himself and for our troubled world, he returned to the United States to lecture throughout the country. He spoke to packed venues wherever he went; and, as always, he donated the proceeds to such causes as would keep him in harmony with his mandate to serve. He cofounded the Seva Foundation (**www.seva.org**), and his writing and lecture fees were primary sources for this compassionate and inspired work.

To me, Ram Dass was and is the finest speaker I have ever heard, period! He was my role model onstage; always gentle and kind; always speaking (without notes) from his heart, sharing his inspiring stories; and always with great humor. I tell you this from my own heart: I could listen to his lectures for hours and always felt saddened when they would end. He was the voice for Applied Spirituality—his life was the model. When he was threatened by having his own private sexual preference exposed, in a time when a closet was the only place that was even mildly safe, Ram Dass called a press conference and proudly announced his preference to the world. He paved the way for tolerance and love when no one else would dare to do so.

Most of us could only dream of defying the conventional life and living out our inner callings to promote a cause that was bigger than our own lives—to leave the security of a guaranteed career and a country where comfort was ensured—all to live in a foreign land with few conveniences, traveling and meditating for a more peaceful world. It is what Saint Francis did in the 13th century, and what Ram Dass did in our lifetime.

When Ram Dass's father, who had largely criticized his son's unconventional lifestyle, was close to death, Ram Dass devoted himself to 100 percent service in those final years. He fed his father, he bathed his father, he placed him on and off the toilet until the day he died. Why? Because he felt this was his mandate. He wanted to experience true service on a 24/7 basis and know firsthand the joy that comes from giving one's own life away in the service of others. Always, for over 30 years, Ram Dass was in the service of others.

In 1997 Ram Dass was struck by a semiparalyzing stroke and became wheelchair bound. Still he wrote of his adventure in a powerful book titled *Still Here*. He continued to travel, although he could no longer walk, and continued to speak to audiences, although he spoke from a slowed-down body—but still, he did it to serve others.

Now it is our turn. . . . Ram Dass's body can no longer endure the rigors of travel. He has come to Maui, where I live and write. I speak with him frequently and am often humbled by the tears in his beautiful 73-year-old eyes as he apologizes for not having prepared for his own elderly health care—for what he now perceives as burdensome to others. He still intends to write and teach, however, without the travel—we can now come to him. Maui is healing—Maui is where Ram Dass wishes to stay for now.

He is currently living in a home on Maui, which he doesn't own and is in jeopardy of losing. I am asking all of you to help purchase this home and to set up a financial foundation to take care of this man who has raised so much money to ensure the futures of so many others—to live out what Ram Dass has practiced with his actions. Please be generous and prompt—no one is more deserving of our love and financial support. In the end, these donations will help ensure that Ram Dass and his work will reach another generation or remind a current generation that it is in giving that we receive.

If there has ever been a great spirit who lived in our lifetime, literally devoting his life to the highest principles of Spirit, it has been Ram Dass. I love this man; he has been my inspiration, and the inspiration for millions of us. It is now time to show him how we feel by doing what he has taught all of us to do—just be here for him, now.

Please send your donations to: Ram Dass, c/o Hay House, P. O. Box 5100, Carlsbad, CA 92018-5100.

In love and light,

Wayne W. Dyer

Truly, giving is receiving and vice versa. Ram Dass lived a life of giving; by staying in-Spirit, I was sent to this man who has meant so much to me. I always had a knowing that I'd be involved in his mission and his life—it was an idea that I held in-Spirit for several decades, and now its time has come and cannot be stopped. (If you feel called to help, you can send in any contribution to the address above, and I will see that it goes directly to Ram Dass.)

It was Ram Dass's total belief in what his spiritual teacher told him to do with his life that allowed this all to unfold. When we banish all doubt in favor of faith, there's nothing more powerful on this planet. You must believe, and then you'll see it unfolding right before your eyes.

### *Spirit's Timing at Work*

The power of an idea whose time has come is really the power of Spirit at work. Equality for all is how God is, for instance, and we seek to be like God. When enough of us, along with one or two at visionary consciousness, begin to contemplate these in-Spirit ideas, they can't be stopped. Let's take some time here to note a few such ideas from America's history:

— When it was time for the unspeakably horrid practice of slavery to be abolished, that was an idea whose time had come. This was because a critical mass of individuals with a new vision for humanity began to contemplate something that had been espoused a few generations earlier: "We hold these truths to be self-evident, that all men are created equal." It took more than 85 years after Thomas Jefferson wrote these words, but then the idea couldn't be stopped— even though slaves represented a tiny part of the population and had no voting rights. When a man with visionary consciousness, Abraham Lincoln (along with many others), approached this idea from an inspirational perspective, it was clear that the time had indeed come to end slavery. This new idea of equality for all is the way of Spirit.

— We can see also an idea whose time had come in the granting of voting rights for women in 1920. Despite the opposition of a nonvisionary President (Woodrow Wilson), and over the objection of a majority of men who had voting privileges, the idea couldn't be stopped. Several visionary women, who aligned with many other men and women, believed and made it happen—a right that we take for granted today.

— The racial integration of the United States is another example of an idea whose time had come. When this concept began to surface in the visionary consciousness of a few individuals such as John F. Kennedy; Martin Luther King, Jr.; Lyndon Johnson; and Rosa Parks; it couldn't be stopped—despite the objections of millions of people, many of whom were in positions of political power. Today, in schools that once practiced segregation, we have a multiracial student body. Racial integration is still in the process of manifesting everywhere in our society, and there's much still to be done, but make no mistake about it, this idea cannot be stopped.

— Gay rights is another idea whose time has come. One of the many reasons I admire Ram Dass so much is the stand he took a long time ago on equal rights for people of all sexual orientations. No individual or group can be denied legal or social privileges because we all come from one Source, which excludes no one. An idea whose time has come is always in perfect alignment with our originating Spirit.

— Finally, the shift in consciousness from a collective belief that smoking in public places is permissible to one where it's not tolerated was an idea whose time had come. The idea became unstoppable when one visionary airline banned smoking on their commercial flights—and then the rest fell into spiritual alignment. Since we come from a nontoxic Source of Well-Being, aligning with It is our destiny and can't be stopped.

I could go on and on with examples of such ideas manifesting in our society, but instead I propose that we begin looking around us for evidence of ideas whose time has come. You see, when we're ready, willing, and open to it, the Divine guidance we seek will spring into action on our behalf. It has been that way throughout our life. For example, the people we've had love affairs with—regardless of how long the relationships lasted—are all characters in this dream of ours called "life." They come to us for any number of reasons, such as to help us create a child (or children), to teach us forgiveness, or to assist us in fulfilling some other destiny.

It's difficult for our ego to grasp, but every single person who's drifted in and out of our life is a part of our Divinely chosen life experience—that is, they are ideas whose time had come. As we move into a life of inspiration, we'll find it easy and even necessary to give thanks for all of these individuals, and to take serious note of what they brought us at the time of their arrival and/or departure.

By the same token, when we needed to have a certain vocational experience, it was made available to us. Because we were a vibrational match to what showed up, we took it in and got out of it precisely what we needed. And when we were no longer a vibrational match to that job, those people, that city, that house, or whatever, we left.

We're in a system that's directed by a Supreme Intelligence, and we're a part of that system. *Everything is on purpose.* Our vibrational matchup determines what we attract and what we repel in our life. We needn't focus on what's already happened and what we've gone through; rather, we must shift our vibration upward so that it harmonizes with Spirit, and then—and only then—will spiritually based ideas come knocking on our door. These ideas won't give up or go away because, as we know, there's nothing in this Universe more powerful than an idea whose time has come. Our responsibility is simply to become beings who expect and await inspired ideas that will not and cannot be stopped.

### Manifesting in-Spirit Ideas

Our expectations are virtual ideas that are manifesting right now in our life. Remember that we receive what we match up with energetically, so if we persist in expecting our ideas to work, we'll create an idea whose time has come. It's our job to shift the energy of our thoughts so that they harmonize with what it is that we truly wish to attract.

For example, many years ago I believed in something called "writer's block," those times when ideas simply refused to flow. Today I have a very different point of view: I know that in some way, God writes all the books and builds all the bridges. Now when

I sit down to write, I expect ideas to flow through me and onto the pages. I feel as if I'm a vibrational match to ideas that want to be expressed in the words I write; consequently, I know that these are ideas whose time has come—they're matching up with me right here, right now, and they can't be stopped.

If I ask myself, "Where does what appears on this paper really come from?" I know that I don't own them. The words flow from Spirit to physical manifestation because I allow myself to be a receiving agent who's willing to transcribe them on pieces of paper that will eventually be a book. I expect these ideas to be here and know that they can't be stopped. I sit here awestruck and in a state of love and gratitude for being able to be used in such an inspirational way—while writing about inspiration, no less!

The crucial message here is to *match our desires to our expectations.* We need to see it all arriving and know that it can't be stopped. We must learn to smile inwardly at those who scoff at our optimism and then go on about the business of expecting our in-Spirit ideas to manifest by looking for evidence of their arrival. At the slightest hint of their appearance, we can energize them with gratitude.

Finding even a penny can be a clue that our expectation of abundance is manifesting. That penny is right where it belongs, so we should treat it like a treasure-hunt clue. That is, we should gratefully assume that it was placed there for us to shift our expectations so that they're compatible with the unlimited abundance that we desire. We can say, "Thank you, God, for this symbol of abundance," knowing that we've initiated a new idea that's so powerful that its time has come!

We need to create compatibility with Spirit by changing around our expectations so that they align with the central premise of this chapter: *There's nothing more powerful than an idea whose time has come.* Try these words out as personal affirmations for tuning in to this new expectation: *I desire it. It's on its way. There's nothing for me to worry about.* Whatever "it" is—a job, a promotion, financing, the right person, well-being, the return to health, information, or what have you, tell yourself: *It's an idea that can't be stopped because I'm balanced perfectly with my Source of Being. I am at God-realization, and with God all things are possible, so that leaves nothing out.*

We don't want to ask the Universe to be different so that we can feel better, but we can *choose* to feel better by shifting our expectations so that we're vibrating with the Universe. We don't have to be like anyone else in order to achieve this vibrational harmony because we're individualized expressions of God, unique in what we have and what we desire. After all, when we approach a long food buffet, we don't focus on eliminating the things we don't want; instead, we begin to vibrate in our thoughts to what we *do* want and ignore what we don't.

Keep in mind that our expectations are uniquely our own. They're ideas whose time has come . . . and that have always been coming.

### Oneness and Sameness

I'd like to take a minute here to explain that there's a vast difference between oneness and sameness. We're all one, but we're *not* the same. If this sounds like a conflict, think about the fact that there's only one light, yet there are many colors; there's only one fire, yet there are many bonfires; and there's only one water, yet there are many lakes, rivers, and oceans. Likewise, although we all come from one Source, we are individualized expressions of It, and therefore unique.

We live in a society that often seeks to make us conform and fit in with everybody else, yet Spirit created each of us as a distinct, separate entity that's unique in all of creation. Thus, in order to be inspired, we must maintain our singular individuality while seeing our connection to our Source and to everyone and everything in the Universe. Each of us is an unparalleled idea whose time had come: We didn't manifest to be the same as each other, but to be like God and express ourselves as we agreed to when we merged into physical form.

I've always loved author Leo Buscaglia, and here's a story he often told that perfectly illustrates the point I'm making.

The animals got together in the forest one day and decided to start a school. There was a rabbit, a bird, a squirrel, a fish and an eel, and they formed a Board of Education. The rabbit insisted that running be in the curriculum. The bird insisted that flying be in the curriculum. The fish insisted that swimming be in the curriculum, and the squirrel insisted that perpendicular tree climbing be in the curriculum. They put all of these things together and wrote a Curriculum Guide. Then they insisted that *all* of the animals take *all* of the subjects. Although the rabbit was getting an A in running, perpendicular tree climbing was a real problem for him; he kept falling over backwards. Pretty soon he got to be sort of brain damaged, and he couldn't run anymore. He found that instead of making an A in running, he was making a C and, of course, he always made an F in perpendicular climbing. The bird was really beautiful at flying, but when it came to burrowing in the ground, he couldn't do so well. He kept breaking his beak and wings. Pretty soon he was making a C in flying as well as an F in burrowing, and he had a hellava time with perpendicular tree climbing. The moral of the story is that the person who was valedictorian of the class was a mentally retarded eel who did everything in a halfway fashion. But the educators were all happy because everybody was taking all of the subjects, and it was called a broad-based education.

Respect your oneness and eschew any pressure to be a conformist—be the being you came here to be. After all, *you* are that powerful idea whose time has come.

## Some Suggestions for Putting the Ideas in This Chapter to Work for You

— Become aware of as many things that impinge on your reality as you can, particularly the ones you call "meaningless" or "circumstantial." *Nothing* is meaningless in this Universe, so remind yourself that whatever shows up in your life has been attracted there. For example, an accident isn't any kind of karmic payback or something to feel guilty about—it simply means that you were a match to it. When you stub your toe, bang your elbow, cut your hand, feel a twinge, get a headache, or anything similar, remind yourself that this is energy that has shown up on time. Try to notice what you were thinking at that precise moment, and be open to the idea that it showed up physically to teach you something.

— *You get what you think about, whether you want it or not! So be careful about what you think about.* Memorize this beautiful little homily and post it in a conspicuous place in your home or workplace. Always be mindful of your thoughts about what you expect from the Universe.

— Send a silent blessing to everyone who's ever shown up, or continues to show up, in your life. A surly waiter can trigger a reminder to send love out if that's what you want back. An ex-spouse can be blessed for what he or she offered you, and even for being an ex. A slow driver ahead of you is an idea of God who's shown up on time—bless him for giving you an opportunity to slow down, thus saving you from the speeding ticket you were a vibrational match to before he showed up.

— Resist fitting in: Do it gently, but do it just the same. Every time someone attempts to get you to conform, affirm: *I am an individualized expression of God.* That's all you need to remember. Then be in the place within yourself where you feel one with God, and send love to those who'd push you in the direction of uniformity and conventionality. Refuse to be "a mentally retarded eel who [does] everything in a halfway fashion," or even worse, the way other people want you to.

— Most important, *have faith.* Trust in a Universe that's endless and endlessly creating. Trust that the Creative Source of All knows exactly what It's doing. Trust in the awareness that there can't be accidents in such an intelligent system. Look out at the vastness of the Universe and contemplate the power of its Source—by doing so, you'll shift your energy. Practice this every day.

* * *

Truly, there's absolutely nothing in this Universe, including ourselves, that isn't perfectly timed. There are no wrongful deaths or mistakes—what shows up is ours, and it showed up precisely on schedule. Before we move on to Part III, I'd like you to think about the simple wisdom that the former slave and philosopher Epictetus imparted to us nearly 2,000 years ago: "It is my business to manage carefully and dexterously whatever happens." Now there's a powerful idea whose time has come!

# PART III

# GIVING AND RECEIVING INSPIRATION

*"We ought, so far as it lies within our power,
to aspire to immortality, and do all that we can
to live in conformity with the highest that is within us;
for even if it is small in quantity, in power
and preciousness, it far excels all the rest."*

— ARISTOTLE

CHAPTER 10

# ABSORBING
# THE INSPIRATION
# OF OTHERS

*"A man may have never entered a church or a mosque,
nor performed any ceremony; but if he realizes God
within himself, and is thereby lifted above the vanities
of the world, that man is a holy man, a saint,
call him what you will . . ."*

— VIVEKANANDA

ONE OF THE BEST MEANS AVAILABLE for heeding our
ultimate calling comes from connecting to the saints that the
Indian monk Vivekananda referred to more than 100 years ago.
The holy people mentioned in this context don't necessarily need
to be connected to a religious practice; in fact, it's unlikely that
they'll be dressed in devotional garments or engaged in any theological studies at all. Rather, those we view as inspirational will
be the ones who radiate spiritual energy back to us and fit Vivekananda's brilliant observation. They've reached a higher level of
God-realization than most, suspended their ego, and have lived
from a high-energy perspective. They're spiritual beings having a
human experience, rather than the other way around.

One of the things we absolutely know about energy is that
when higher/faster energy comes in contact with lower vibrations,
they're converted into higher energy. Thus, light introduced into

a dark room not only eliminates the darkness, but converts that darkness to light as well. (If this concept intrigues you, I suggest that you read my books *There's a Spiritual Solution to Every Problem* and *The Power of Intention*.)

The parallel I'm drawing here is that when we enter the energy field of someone who's connected to Spirit, we find ourselves not only forsaking our uninspired ways, but also converting to their higher energy—in other words, we become inspired just by being in their presence. However, identifying those who actually live their lives in-Spirit is often not as simple as it sounds.

### What Inspirational People Are <u>Not</u>

It's possible for someone to achieve at a high level, earn many accolades, be widely admired and respected, but not be living from Spirit. Inspirational people aren't necessarily highly motivated in society's sense of the word; after all, such individuals may just be chasing after more symbols of success, satisfying their desire to dominate and control others by acquiring as much power as possible. People who have motivated *us* are also not necessarily inspirational: We may have been motivated by those who threatened or beat us, or cursed and called us a fool and a wimp for not doing what they thought we should be doing. Clearly, inspiration wasn't part of their motivation!

We also can't assume that all teachers are living their ultimate calling. A good instructor might be very knowledgeable about a given subject and extremely effective at conveying that knowledge to students, but he or she might also be very disconnected from God-realization. Teachers often have such low self-esteem that they lose themselves completely in devotion to something that's far removed from their true calling—especially when great teaching skills can fill a void and seem to be a substitute for that calling. Of course I'm not saying that all teachers are lacking in God-realization, but be wary of assuming that a gifted instructor is automatically living in-Spirit.

A person may have the highest intellectual credentials available and still be detached from his or her Spirit. The ability to cite historical sources, speak with distinction, and earn advanced degrees doesn't automatically mean that someone is capable of inspiring others. (Once again, it doesn't disqualify that individual either.) The smartest people may turn us off with their pomposity and braggadocio, or they may be so cerebral that it's difficult to know what they're talking about. Be on the lookout for mistaking intellectualization for inspiration. The journey to our ultimate calling isn't a scholastic endeavor—there are no written exams, no grades to earn, no report cards, and no advanced degrees.

It's important to understand that any of the traditional measures of success, such as job promotions, wealth, public acclaim, expensive clothing, a commanding presence, verbal adeptness, a voluminous vocabulary, a charismatic appearance, fame, and so forth don't necessarily mean high marks as an inspirational person. In fact, some people who rate very high marks on the ego-based indexes of success are the ones I find most difficult to be around—and totally uninspiring.

While fame in all of its forms seems highly desirable and is focused upon by endless television shows discussing the personal lives of those who are in the news (particularly show business), this does not measure the ability to inspire in the slightest. When one of my daughters once told me that her goal was to become famous, I urged her to shift her sights to living and acting in rapport with her passion and then letting the fame thing take care of itself.

I've met many celebrities in all fields of endeavor, and I can assure you that public notoriety is not in any way an indicator of a person's connection to Spirit. And if I happen to be famous personally, it's not because I chose it or even earned it. Fame is located outside of me—it's in the opinions that others have of me. It's my choice to be inspired, however, and that always involves being independent of the opinions of others.

Inspirational people aren't interested in winning a popularity contest, especially when those who seek praise and recognition often do so to soothe feelings of insecurity. In general, people who doubt their Divinity fear being criticized because they see themselves as fraudulent beings; consequently, they take on the full-time job of trying to be liked by everyone they meet. Despite their obvious popularity, they'd be disastrous in the inspiration department.

I need to add a disclaimer here: I don't in any way want to imply that a person who *has* gained great popularity and notoriety is thereby disqualified from being a source of inspiration. Quite the contrary: Many of the most inspiring people I've come across in my life have achieved worldwide acclaim. I simply urge you not to equate inspiration with recognition.

### *What Inspirational People <u>Are</u>*

Now let's take a look at the qualities we *do* find in inspirational people—that is, those special individuals who've risen above their ego and the vanities of the world—and how our awareness of, and association with, them helps raise our vibrations to the level of Spirit.

Over the years, as a result of teaching at a major university and lecturing to audiences of experts, I've had the distinct pleasure of being in the company of some extremely knowledgeable people. I've also been blessed to associate with a number of very wise individuals who have achieved enlightened mastery in their own lives and as spiritual teachers. My observation is that the more expertise so-called experts appear to have, the less joy they seem to experience, while those who are genuinely wise consistently have an aura of joy that permeates their being and radiates outward, impacting those around them.

We can use this "joy index" as a nonscientific measure of inspiration. When we meet others who we think might be living in-Spirit, we must ask the following questions: Do they seem to have a rapturous heart, sending out signals that they love the world and everyone in it? Are they jubilant about the work they do? Do they see the world as a friendly place? Are they at peace with themselves?

Do they appear to be kind rather than judgmental? Are they confident without being boorish? Do they tend to be cheerful? Do they love to play? Are they elated to be in the company of young children as well as older people? Do they listen rather than lecture? Are they willing to be students as well as teachers? Do they love nature? Are they in awe of the world? Do they express rational humility? Are they approachable? Do they take great pleasure in serving others? Do they seem to have tamed their ego? Do they accept all people as equals? Are they open to new ideas? The answers to these questions will help us ascertain whether another person is potentially an inspiring influence in our life.

Those who have the gift of inspiration exude something that's difficult to pin down intellectually, yet is undeniably recognizable in how we feel in their presence: We can sense that they're aligned with the Source Energy from which we all originate. We perceive a place within them that resonates deeply within ourselves—a vibrational recognition of inspiration—and they have much to offer us. We recognize their high spiritual energy, which longs to be active in our life. When we feel this resonance, it's reflected in a feeling that's similar to a warm, soothing shower that's running deep within us.

When I'm in the presence of an inspiring person, the first thing I notice is this warm shower overtaking me: It's like a wave of energy that slowly moves down my shoulders and spine, and I know something is happening energetically. Even though I can't see, touch, smell, or hear it, I know that I'm experiencing a shift that makes me feel incredibly good (or, as I think of it, *incredibly God*).

### My Experiences with Inspiring People

In this section, I'd like to further illustrate what inspirational people *are* by noting some individuals who have particularly impacted my life with their high energy.

— I vividly recall the days of the Cuban missile crisis more than 40 years ago. I'd recently been discharged from active duty in the Navy after four years and was attending Wayne State University in Detroit. If the U.S. had been drawn into a war with the U.S.S.R., I would have been at the top of the list to be called back to active duty because I had a top-secret job classification. But more than my concern about my own status was what had us collectively biting our fingernails globally—that is, the thought of the consequences of an exchange of nuclear weapons, which would put all of civilization at risk.

I'll never forget the scene that the film *Thirteen Days* reenacted so well. After being besieged by his military advisors to nuke the entire island of Cuba, and encouraged by others to take alternative decisive action that could easily lead to war, President Kennedy retired alone to his chambers in the White House and reminded himself of what he believed the number one duty of the President was: to keep the country out of war. Having already fought in one war that had also taken the life of his older brother, Joseph, JFK knew how damaging such a battle with the Soviet Union would be, so he retreated in solitude and allowed the peace of Spirit to guide him. Ultimately, the idea for a blockade—and a prayer for a peaceful resolution—took hold of him. He went to Spirit in a time of crisis, and his being in-Spirit rather than "in-ego" turned the tide of history.

President Kennedy was a source of inspiration to me, but not because of his political views or any of his Presidential actions; rather, I embraced him as a man who conveyed love, peace, and joy in his demeanor and showed respect for all people by vowing to end segregation in America. As Robert McNamara, Kennedy's Secretary of Defense, once observed, if JFK had lived, there would have been no Vietnam War. That's because he believed that war should be an absolute last resort, and that his primary job as President was to maintain the peace.

I found JFK inspiring back in the early 1960s, and I've continued to be profoundly touched by his spirit throughout my lifetime. He inspired me!

— In 1978 I was invited to go to Vienna to participate in a presentation to a group of young presidents of companies. I was assigned to be on a panel with a man who had been a huge source of inspiration to me: Viktor Frankl. Frankl was a medical doctor who had been herded off to die in a Nazi concentration camp in WWII; while imprisoned, he kept notes that ultimately became a book called *Man's Search for Meaning*. This work, which touched me deeply many years later, illustrated not only how Dr. Frankl survived the horrors of Auschwitz, but also how he helped other camp mates do the same. For example, he taught his fellow human beings how to find meaning and even joy in a fish head floating in the dirty water that masqueraded as soup. He taught them to be with his spirit and infuse it in others who were giving up on life. He even practiced sending love and peace to his captors, and refused to feel hatred and vengeance because he knew that it was foreign to his spirit, which he wouldn't forsake.

So, 33 years after his liberation, I was about to address hundreds of corporate presidents who were all under the age of 50 (as I was at the time). I'd read *Man's Search for Meaning* as a young doctoral student and practiced Frankl's logotherapy, which taught therapists in training to help clients find meaning in their existence regardless of their circumstances. Viktor Frankl had been one of the truly inspirational figures in my life, and being on the same panel—under the pretext of being a colleague of this master teacher—was overwhelming to me. And an afternoon I've never forgotten followed, full of pure exhilaration and inspiration.

Viktor Frankl stayed true to his spiritual origins in the face of horrors that destroyed so many. When I met him, he exuded joy, peace, kindness, and love, and he wasn't bitter. Instead, he felt that his experience taught him lessons he'd never have known otherwise. I spent a good part of that afternoon in Vienna in 1978 listening and being in awe; and now, years later, I'm still greatly impacted by the presence of this man in my life. Yes, indeed, he inspired me.

— In 1994, 24-year-old college student Immaculée Ilibagiza came home to be with her family in Kibuye, Rwanda, for the Easter holidays . . . and inadvertently found herself in the middle of one of the worst genocides in history. As a member of the Tutsi tribe, Immaculée was forced to hide in a tiny bathroom (which was configured in such a way that it appeared to be inaccessible from the house) with seven other women for a total of three terrifying months. As she told me, "By the grace of God, we were never found. How that happened, I do not know. All we could hear was the smoke of hatred coming from the men right outside the door."

After living in this terror for 90 days, trembling in fear every day, knowing that they would be hacked to death if they were discovered, the women were finally released from their entombment into the protection of French soldiers. As Immaculée related: "When we were finally safe, I learned how most of my family had died: My father was shot by soldiers, my mother was killed by machete, and my younger brother was murdered in a stadium while searching for food. My big brother was executed after questioning—they said that they wanted to see the brain of a person who had a master's degree, so they cut him to pieces."

I met this incredible woman in New York after she was granted an asylum visa as a victim of this organized attempt at ethnic cleansing by a band of thugs. (Just about one million men, women, and children were systematically slaughtered with machetes or blunt instruments, and the U.S. didn't intervene—something that former President Clinton publicly acknowledged was the greatest failure of his administration.) Immaculée isn't bitter or filled with rage—she merely wants to be sure that such a tragedy never occurs again. She has love and faith in her heart, and she applied these spiritual gifts to the telling of her story, which has just been published as a remarkable book through Hay House. I felt privileged to have been able to write the Foreword for this amazing work, which is called *Left to Tell: Discovering God Amidst the Rwandan Holocaust.*

I'm honored to join this Divinely inspiring woman by going to Rwanda and helping set up a program to educate and provide for the vast number of orphans who were left behind by this geno-cide. And yes, being in Immaculée's life in the small way that I am inspires me beyond anything that I can convey to you here in words.

— In 1999 I was invited to South Africa to lecture to some public audiences. While in Cape Town, I took the ferry over to Robben Island to visit the prison where Nelson Mandela had been incarcerated for so many years. (I actually visited at the time of the tenth-anniversary celebration of his release.)

Here was a man who spent more than 27 years of his life im-prisoned—he wasn't even allowed visitors because he was a vocal opponent of a system of apartheid, in which an entire race of peo-ple were declared by law to be inferior and unworthy of the same privileges as the remaining citizens of the country. And he worked all day in a limestone quarry, where the burning sunlight glared so against the white rock that his eyes became mere slits due to the squinting that he was forced to practice in order to survive. I spent 30 minutes in that quarry and my eyes stung all day—imagine what years of such exposure would wreak.

Mandela went deep within himself, and when he was finally released, he came out with forgiveness and reconciliation in his heart. His staying in-Spirit was the force behind the dismantling of apartheid and his ultimate election to the presidency of an emerging democracy of South Africa a few years later. As I medi-tated in the prison outside of this great man's cell, I felt the warm inner shower I described earlier in this chapter. Then I was handed an autographed copy of his book *Long Walk to Freedom,* which I treasure.

Nelson Mandela conveyed the spiritual energy of love, peace, kindness, and tolerance during all of his travails, and this spiritual energy provided a blueprint that changed the face of Africa—and the world—forever. Yes, he inspired me!

— Closer to home, I was inspired by Mrs. Olive Fletcher. In 1956 I was taking biology for the second time at Denby High School in

Detroit. I'd failed the class the previous year because of my own stubbornness: I'd refused to complete a leaf collection, which my then-15-year-old self perceived to be an absurd requirement.

At that time, my mother was divorcing my alcoholic stepfather, and I was working in a local grocery store every evening during the week and all day on Saturday and Sunday. My instructor for this second foray into biology was Mrs. Fletcher, and she was the very first teacher I encountered who seemed to care about me personally. For example, she was there for me after school, called my home to see if I was okay during the tumultuousness (including frequent fights and other unpleasantness) taking place at the time, and allowed me to put my head down and sleep during study periods when I'd completed my assignments. She also encouraged me to tutor other students because she recognized something in me that I'd never heard a teacher say before: She told me that I was brilliant and had a mind that could take me wherever I wanted to go.

This incredible person even invited me to go bowling with her and her husband. I'd never imagined that teachers were actually human, let alone went bowling, before I met Mrs. Fletcher! She was also the first "authority figure" who welcomed my questioning and tolerated my sometimes disruptive behavior. By living from Spirit, she showed me that I was worth being loved by someone in a position of authority.

Thanks to Mrs. Fletcher's inspiration, I went from a failing grade the previous year to an A—I wanted to excel just for her because she had so much faith in me. Now, exactly a half century later, Mrs. Olive Fletcher still stands out as the one individual in all of my school years who turned the direction of my life from fighting the system to being able to choose to *fit in* without having to *give in*. Yes, she certainly inspired me!

— Switching gears a bit here, in 1971 Don McLean read a book on the life of the famous artist Vincent van Gogh and was so touched by the painter's fight for his sanity, along with his desire to be loved and understood, that he wrote a song about it.

Called "Vincent (Starry Starry Night)," it was written as he stared at van Gogh's classic painting *The Starry Night*—and every time I hear that song and recall how McLean was so inspired by the life of van Gogh, I'm inspired, too. I'm moved to tears, and I vow to be more understanding and compassionate toward those struggling with sanity as van Gogh did. (It's interesting to note that in the 1970s the Van Gogh Museum in Amsterdam played the song daily, and today a copy of the sheet music, together with a set of van Gogh's paintbrushes, is buried in a time capsule beneath the museum.)

I'm enormously inspired by people who act upon their own moments in-Spirit and create similar opportunities for countless souls as well. Don McLean moved me to read the same biography of van Gogh that he did and to include this example in this book. He inspired me!

I could write many more short descriptions of those who've provided me with life-altering inspiration, but I'd be remiss if I were to omit the one person among all those I've known who has been my greatest source of it.

Back in 1942, when I was two years old, my mother was left to take on the responsibility for raising my two brothers (ages three and five) and me alone. My father, of whom I have absolutely no recollection, literally walked out on his family and never once placed a phone call to see how we were doing. He paid no child support, since he spent a great deal of time in trouble with the law, including some jail time for being a thief. He simply walked away and never looked back.

After I was born, my mother brought me home to their tiny apartment on the east side of Detroit . . . and discovered that my father had left my 16-month-old brother, Dave, in the care of my 4-year-old brother, Jim, and had temporarily moved in with a woman in Ann Arbor, some 40 miles away.

Try to imagine the scene: *It's 1940. A depression has left almost everyone economically bankrupt. There are no government programs to aid the support of three children under the age of four. An alcoholic husband*

403

*refuses to work, steals money from everyone, and regularly chooses the company of other women, leaving his wife to care for their three babies. An anemic infant needs medical assistance, which is largely unavailable to anyone living in poverty. . . .* Yet out of this seemingly hopeless scenario emerged a woman who had a dream that her life could and would get better.

After finally going through the divorce, my mother was totally on her own. She worked first as a candy girl at a five-and-dime store, and then as a secretary for the Chrysler Corporation—and her earnings came to approximately $17 per week. She was forced to place Dave and me in a series of foster homes supported by the Methodist church, while Jim moved in with her parents. Her nightmare was realized: Her family had been split up, and the thought of this being a permanent condition was too devastating for her to contemplate. But she held a vision for herself that she never ever abandoned: *Somehow, someday, I will unite my family and raise my boys under one roof.*

Unfortunately, times were challenging and the years passed. Mother visited Dave and me whenever possible. She didn't have an automobile or even a driver's license, and the distance to Mt. Clemens (where we resided) was approximately 17 miles. But it might as well have been 7,000 miles, since there was no transportation or money to pay for her to get there. But my mom was determined: She even married a man she didn't love as a way to unite her family.

In 1949, our family moved into a tiny, and I mean *tiny,* duplex on the east side of Detroit. Like our father, our new stepfather was also an alcoholic and an irresponsible provider. Drinking became his escape; and frequent, hostile interchanges were the norm. But Mother, who refused to see her boys separated again, continued to work, work, work.

Every morning she was up at 5 A.M., making breakfast and packing lunches for her three growing boys. She took three buses to work and three home every day, standing outside on those endless freezing winter mornings and returning home at 5:45 P.M. in order to prepare an evening meal. My brothers and I all had paper routes or were stock boys, but the hard work fell on the shoulders of this never-complaining, always-cheerful woman. Every weekend looked like this for my mother: washing endless loads of clothes and hanging them on the line to dry; making breakfast, lunch, and dinner; ironing down in the basement on Sundays. The work never ended . . . yet this woman was the most joyful, loving, beautiful soul to be around.

All my brothers' and my friends came to our house to hang out because of my mother. They loved her, and more than that, they loved being in our home because of the energy she brought to it. This woman lived from Spirit and offered all of us inspiration. Not one of us would ever have even considered talking back or being disrespectful in any way—she commanded our respect, but she never demanded it. And with all the responsibilities she had, Mother never left the house with her hair in curlers or her clothes in disarray—she took great pride in herself, and through her example, she taught my brothers and me to do the same.

While going through a second divorce from a now out-of-control alcoholic, she never abandoned her role as a mother to all of us. In later years when her own mother was quite sick, I watched in astonished admiration as she took on the sole responsibility for caring for her mom, despite the fact that she had four siblings. And then wonder of wonders, as my ex-stepfather reached a stage where his alcohol and smoking addictions were taking their final toll, I watched in amazement as she cared for this man who had largely mistreated her throughout their marriage. She went to his home, did his laundry, called for medical help, visited him in the hospital, and extended love where she had received only mistreatment and even abuse.

Today Mother approaches the age of 90 and still bowls twice a week, lives on her own, and never complains. To this day she won't leave home unless she's dressed to her high standards of appropriateness and her hair is beautifully coiffed. She respects herself, and this esteem has trickled down to me, her youngest son, and my two brothers as well. Now she has three boys who are all eligible for Social Security and Medicare, yet still she lives and breathes that loving Spirit.

In a wonderful book written by Michael Murphy called *What I Meant to Say,* he describes saying good-bye to his mother as he leaves her home after a Thanksgiving dinner. It's all small talk as he makes polite excuses for having to leave, which prompts the following tribute that I'm including here. I'd like to say these beautiful words to *my* mother:

> What I meant to say was . . . How can I possibly say good-bye to the person who was the first to hold me, the first to feed me, and the first to make me feel loved?
>
> From a distance I watch you move about, doing the mundane tasks that to everyone else seem so routine. But for me, the tasks you lovingly completed year after year built and reinforced the foundation, the structure that made my world a safe and comfortable place to grow.
>
> All that I am and all that I have can be traced back to you. Whatever accomplishments I have made along the way would not have occurred without first believing in myself. And you, you were the person who always believed in me.
>
> Now with a family of my own, I am amazed at the number of times I hear your words flow from my mouth. This ventriloquistic phenomenon was at first most irritating, but now warms me as I've come to understand that there is a part of you that will live on in me forever.
>
> When time parts us, I pray that you will reach across from the other side to again touch my face and whisper into my ear.
>
> For your warm and gentle presence in my life . . . for this, I will always be most thankful.

Yes, Mother, you inspire me!

# Some Suggestions for Putting the Ideas in This Chapter to Work for You

— Make a deliberate decision to spend more time in the presence of those whom you're most closely aligned to in-Spirit. This means seeking out "higher-vibrational people" and avoiding those who reflect more ego-oriented behavior patterns. Keep in mind that higher spiritual energies nullify your lower tendencies, while also converting you to more in-Spirit frequencies. Use your own inner hunches to determine if you're in the right places with the right people: If you feel good in their presence, meaning that you feel inspired to be a better and more joyful person, then these are right for you. If, on the other hand, you feel more anxious, depressed, and uninspired, and you can't wait to get away because of conflict, then these are not going to be sources of inspiration for you.

— Read biographies of those people who reflect your ideas of high spiritual energy, be they historical or contemporary figures. Just by spending time reading about their lives, you'll feel a great sense of inspiration; moreover, their examples will serve to inspire you to emulate their lives and their greatness.

— Immerse yourself in movies, television shows, plays, and recordings tendered by individuals and organizations that reflect a rapport with Spirit. Simply listening to lectures by great spiritual teachers can increase your daily inspiration level.

Also, notice how you feel during explosion and chase scenes in movies that lead to an inevitable overexposure to violence, hatred, and killing. Check yourself in these moments: Do you feel closer to Spirit or further and further removed from It? Use your own intuition to remind yourself when it's time to change the channel or leave the movie theater. You have more control than you realize over who and what you allow into your mind and the minds of your loved ones, particularly your children. Exercise that control to stay connected to

Spirit. Invite into your heart only those energies that resonate with the desire to obey your ultimate calling to inspiration.

— Be clear about the distinctions between those you admire for their success in the physical world and those who are inspirational. The more you seek out and immerse yourself in ego-dominated energy fields, the more you'll feel disenchanted and lacking in joy. Use the tenets of Spirit to indicate what you desire to emulate, rather than using wealth or success as benchmarks.

Now while a successful person like Bill Gates may be a model for great fortune, it's important to realize that he and his wife have contributed more money and effort to the causes of literacy, healing, and peace than anyone else in the history of our planet. This stands in stark contrast to many of the "super rich" who use their money and status to further bolster their own ego. The Gateses represent high spiritual energy and serve as inspirational models for me, even though my financial picture doesn't even come close to theirs. I've learned from their actions, and I've found great inspiration from their in-Spirit philanthropy.

— Choose some of the most inspirational people in your life and tell them precisely why you've placed them in this category. As you relate your feelings and appreciation, you'll feel inspired merely by the simple act of acknowledgment. Every time I receive a letter or hear a personal testimony from someone who was inspired to pursue their own greatness because of my efforts, I'm touched and inspired myself. But I also know that the recognition and expression of that person's feelings means that they'll perform a similar service for others. And being in the service of others is really being more like God.

* * *

Ramakrishna, a great saint who lived in India and inspired millions of others from his God-realized perspective, once offered this observation: "[Saints] are like big steamships, which not only cross the ocean themselves but carry many passengers to the other shore." May you too be like those big steamships—but if you're not, then by all means allow yourself to be one of those lucky passengers.

Get on board by going on to the next chapter.

# CHAPTER 11

# BEING AN INSPIRATION FOR OTHERS

*"We are all teachers, and what we teach is what we learn, and so we teach it over and over again until we learn . . ."*

— FROM *A COURSE IN MIRACLES*

*"The real purpose of teachers, books, and teachings is to lead us back to the kingdom of God within ourselves."*

— JOEL GOLDSMITH

**JUST AS WE'RE ALL STUDENTS THROUGHOUT LIFE,** we're all teachers. In fact, we learn best by offering what we desire for ourselves to as many individuals as we can, as frequently as we can. And that's one reason I wrote this book: If I instruct enough people for a long enough period of time, I'll teach what *I* most want to learn, which is how to live in-Spirit. Following this line of thinking, it's imperative that we make a deliberate effort to increase our inspirational energy, as this will lead us to being both a spiritual learner and teacher simultaneously.

Spiritual teachers have raised the vibrational frequency of their daily life to a point where they're able to provide inspiration to others merely by their presence, and this is the standard to which we need to aspire. It isn't necessarily a scholarly undertaking—there are no lesson plans or report cards for the kind of teaching I'm writing about in these pages. Rather, I'm talking about the things we can do each and every day to inspire our fellow humans . . . which is what this chapter is all about.

### Kindness Inspires Others

Recently three of my kids and I were seated at the food court of a mall here on Maui. As we were talking and enjoying our meals, a young boy stumbled, and the tray full of hamburgers and French fries he'd just purchased from McDonald's went flying all over the floor. His parents immediately came to his rescue, and the manager of the restaurant good-naturedly replaced all of the food at no cost. The boy was embarrassed, but it all worked out fine . . . except that people were having to dodge what he'd dropped as they lined up for their purchases.

Neither the boy's family nor the people working at the restaurant took any initiative to clean up this mess, which was actually a hazard to the crowd at the food court. I watched for a few moments, and then I took an empty tray and proceeded to pick up all of the food and dispose of it in the trash container. I returned to my seat, saying nothing about the incident.

About ten minutes later, a woman who'd observed this scene without my noticing came over to our table. To my teenagers she said, "You girls have just been given a lesson by your father—he has shown you by his actions what it means to be a caring, helpful citizen. No one else in this entire place thought of doing anything about that mess on the floor, but he did. He inspired me, and I hope that you were inspired by his actions, too." She left, and my girls sort of smiled knowingly, since this is rather a normal thing for them to see.

The point of this story is to illustrate that one simple act of kindness and service that's in alignment with our Source will do more to inspire others than lectures on the virtues of being a thoughtful citizen ever could. All I wanted to do was eliminate the potential peril of greasy burgers and fries on the floor—I wasn't trying to inspire anyone—and that's the crux of this chapter.

When we elevate our consciousness above the level of ego, which says, "I didn't spill that food, so it's not my job to clean it up!" to the level that asks, "How may I serve?" we become an inadvertent source of inspiration to anyone who's in the energy field of our spiritually based actions.

We can also be on the lookout for opportunities to be a source of inspiration. For example, when I board an airplane, I tend to look for the chance to extend some sort of service to "strangers." (I put the word in quotes to emphasize that there aren't actually any strangers anywhere in the Universe.) Helping vertically challenged passengers place their carry-on luggage in the overhead compartment is perfect because others noticing this act of kindness may be inspired, while, at the same time, I'm heeding my own calling to be both inspired and inspiring.

I know that someone who needs my assistance is really a Divine emissary who's right there in front of me, offering an opportunity for me to be in-Spirit. For instance, not long ago I flew from Maui to Los Angeles and then boarded an all-night flight to New York. On the way to L.A., I'd watched the fabulous movie *Chicago;* once on the plane to New York, I noticed one of the stars of that film, Renée Zellweger, getting on. Vertically challenged with heavy luggage, she certainly met all of my criteria for being both a source of inspiration and becoming inspired. I helped her with her baggage and then gave her a copy of my book *10 Secrets for Success and Inner Peace.*

Many people on the plane approached her, including the flight attendants, and I watched and felt inspired by the kindness, patience, and personal concern Renée showed toward everyone she talked to. As we left the plane, she handed me a note that I've reproduced on the next page, exactly as she wrote it, to illustrate how everyday acts of kindness serve as memorable moments of inspiration. Sharing it here with you is a way to express my gratitude for her thoughtfulness—what a bonus!

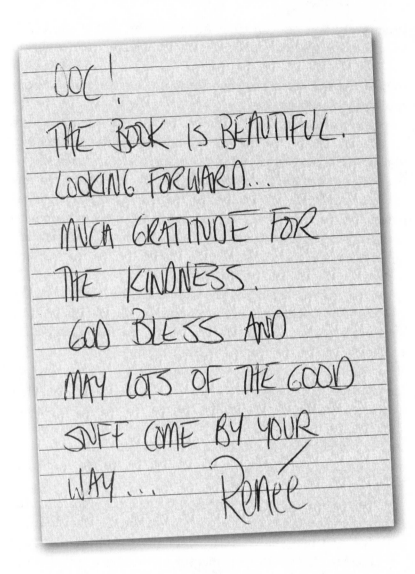

To this day, whenever I see Renée in a movie or an interview, I recall the extraordinary, gentle kindness that she displayed toward everyone who approached her, and it inspires me. My moment or two of extending service to her was a gift to *me,* not because she's a celebrity, but because of that dual reward of being in-Spirit.

### *Gratitude Inspires Others*

Without exception, I begin every day of my life with an expression of gratitude. As I look in the mirror to begin my daily ritual of shaving, I say, "Thank you, God, for life, for my body, for my family and loved ones, for this day, and for the opportunity to be of service. Thank you, thank you, thank you!"

If we practice gratitude as opposed to maintaining an attitude of entitlement, we'll automatically extend inspiration wherever we go. Being grateful helps remove the influence of our ego, which is certain that we're better than everyone else. An attitude of gratitude allows us to adopt what's called "radical humility," a trait that's very persuasive in helping others feel inspired.

Most of the people I've met or observed who are at the top levels in their chosen fields have these attitudes of gratitude and radical humility. After all, when so many high achievers reach for their statuette or championship trophy, they say, "First I'd like to thank God." It's almost as if they can't help themselves—they're so grateful for their accolade, but even more than that, they know that there's a Force in the Universe way bigger than they are that allows them to act, sing, write, compete, or design. And if *we* adopt this kind of an attitude, we'll inspire others. It's that simple.

Pomposity, on the other hand, will never inspire anyone. When we encounter someone who brags and uses the pronoun *I* excessively, we'll find that we want to get away from them as quickly as possible. Vanity, conceit, and boasting are all signs that a person has **e**dged **G**od **o**ut of the picture.

Gratitude and humility, on the other hand, send signals to all who meet and greet us that we're all connected to something larger than life itself. This reminds me of the wisdom I discovered many years ago reading the Kena Upanishad: "At whose bequest does the mind think? Who bids the body live? Who makes the tongue speak? Who is the effulgent Being that directs eye to form and color, and the ear to sound?" When we know the answer to these questions, we not only become inspiring beings to others, we also gain immortality.

### Generosity Inspires Others

It doesn't matter if we call It God, Krishna, Atman, Allah, the Universal Mind, Ra, Yahweh, or even Anna or Fred—I think we'd all agree that the All-Creating Source of Everything is the most generous Being there is. Along with life itself, It offers us unending abundance in the form of air, water, lungs, heart, kidneys, liver, and all we need to sustain life. On just this one tiny planet hurtling through space, Whatever Name We Want to Call It provides the ability to feed all of us and dispose of all of our waste, which then gets used to fertilize new life—and then repeats the process over and over again. . . . And remember, this is only one planet in an endless Universe of heavenly bodies. Talk about benevolence!

Generosity is obviously one of the ways to be more God-like. I know that I'm inspired when I see evidence of it on the part of others. Very often it's manifested during or following times of crisis, almost as if God gets our attention and reminds us to be more like Him when we face devastating circumstances. A tsunami diverts our aircraft carriers away from killing each other and into a zone where food and shelter are offered; an earthquake motivates us to risk our own lives to save strangers who days before were called enemies; and hurricanes bring out the best in us. Such so-called disasters lead us to the inherent God-like generosity that's latent within all of us. However, we don't need a crisis to remind ourselves to give—we only need to be in-Spirit to be reminded of the joy of donating our energy, time, and possessions to others.

For example, my brother Jim and my sister-in-law Marilyn are inspiring because of the time they give to our mother. Days spent going to movies and playing *Scrabble* are more than just entertaining activities—they're inspiration in action because Jim and Marilyn are giving their time to lovingly be with a person who lives alone. While I've been blessed to be able to give to Mother financially, they've been blessed to give of their time.

Generous actions are always inspirational if we just spend a few seconds to notice and appreciate them. The message is that *we must give whatever it is we have that will benefit others*. It's how our Creator conducts Itself—always giving and providing. When we emulate our Creator by giving, we become sources of inspiration to others.

When Oprah Winfrey visited Africa and vowed to give all that she could, including money and time, to help eradicate the poverty and disease of that continent, she inspired me and millions of others. When she said, "Now I know why I have been given so much. Now I know why," I also began saying to myself, "Now I know why *I've* had so many financial blessings. I feel so grateful for all that has come my way that giving back seems to be the only avenue available."

I was inspired by the generosity of a woman I've known for 30 years, who also came from an impoverished background, to set up a scholarship fund at my alma mater, Wayne State University. Oprah's philanthropy inspired me, and I hope that I in turn will inspire young people to do the same with their lives. Think of the incredible good that would come if people who read this book also became inspired to give. Of course we don't have to be wealthy to give, but we might need to remember this: *If we're not generous when it's difficult, we won't be generous when it's easy.*

### Listening Inspires Others

As ironic as it may sound, we're far more inspiring to others when we're willing to listen than when we're giving them advice. That's because conveying to others that we value what they have to say is a way of demonstrating that we care. It's a way of being inspiring, a way of listening like God. People who find it difficult to listen to another person without bringing the conversation back to themselves are convinced by their ego of their self-importance. And as you're well aware by now, that ego is an illusion that's convinced us to pay attention to a false self.

There's no higher compliment than to be told we're a good listener. Everyone loves a good listener largely because it makes them feel loved, cared for, and worthy of being heard. When we leave any encounter where we feel we've been heard, even if we know the listener strongly disagreed with us, we're still inspired. Why? Because for a few moments the listener has emulated what it feels like when we pray. In deep prayer, we're not looking for the resolution of conflict or answers falling from the sky; we just want to feel as if we're in contact with someone who cares enough to hear us out.

This brings to mind something Mohandas Gandhi, one of the truly inspirational beings of our time, once said: "Silence of the sewn up lips is no silence. One may achieve the same result by chopping off one's tongue, but that too would not be silence. He is truly silent who, having the capacity to speak, utters no idle word . . ."

In addition, these words from Ralph Waldo Emerson have always reminded me to be a listener: "I like the silent church, before the service begins, better than the preaching." It's a good idea to keep this in mind if we wish to be a source of inspiration.

### Being at Peace Inspires Others

Lecturing or demanding that others live peacefully is one of the least effective ways to inspire them; however, when we simply demonstrate that we're living peacefully, we offer other people a large dose of inspiration by our mere presence.

During my first encounter with Swami Satchidananda, for instance, he emitted such an aura of peacefulness that I felt inspired by merely standing next to him. It would have been impossible for me to feel anything other than peace in his midst. That day I purchased his wonderful book, *Beyond Words,* and on page 21 was given an inkling as to why I felt so inspired merely by being in his company: "If anybody asks me, 'What is your philosophy of God?' I say, 'Peace is my God.' If they ask, 'Where is He?' I reply, 'He is in me and He is everywhere. He is all peaceful; He is all serenity. He is to be felt and experienced within oneself.'"

Being at peace with ourselves is a way of going through life eschewing conflict and confrontation. When we're in a state of tranquility, we actually send out a vibration of energy that impacts all living creatures, including plants, animals, and all people (even babies). And, of course, the reverse applies as well: Belligerent individuals who live in turmoil and revel in hostile encounters send out nonverbal energy that adversely impacts those around them. The immediate impulse is to remove ourselves from these low-energy, nonpeaceful people because sticking around means tension and a lowering of our energy. Moreover, we become a counterforce to what we're experiencing, meaning that we become angry at their anger and arrogant toward their arrogance.

Practicing a peaceful approach to our life on Earth is a way of returning to where we came from. At the same time, it's a powerful source of inspiration to all living creatures.

### Living Passionately Inspires Others

Did you know that the word *enthusiasm* originated from the Greek language, signifying "the God within us"? By definition, then, living our passion is the way to convey to others how to be in-Spirit. Being excited about life is infectious—it rubs off on others and is wonderfully inspiring. I'm reminded of a recent whale-watching trip I took, where I observed a young woman I know named Beth as she spoke to a group of people about humpback whales. Her enthusiasm was palpable to the entire group aboard the boat, and the more passion she displayed, the more she seemed to inspire her audience. I've been aboard other boats and seen the impact of guides who merely go through the motions: People in this low-energy environment don't leave the experience feeling inspired.

Beth, on the other hand, feels a passion that she conveys to others every single day during the whale-mating season. Every day! You see, she studied marine biology in college and has always been fascinated by humpback whales and their amazing ability to travel between Alaska and Hawaii, to go six months without eating, to give birth in warm waters, and then navigate to cold waters on the return. For Beth, these whales are a part of God's mysterious, miraculous creation. She's living her passion, and she inspires others by her enthusiastic way of being. In fact, everyone in this vicinity knows that expeditions with Beth are almost a guarantee that you'll not only get to see the whales, but that they'll dance and breach and even swim under the boat for you. It's as if the whales themselves are inspired by Beth's excitement!

When we're enthusiastically living our passion, whatever it may be, we transmit spiritual signals to those around us that we're in-Spirit, loving who we are, what we came here to be, and whoever comes into our field of vision.

### *Truth Inspires Others*

Finally, and perhaps most urgently, we need to live and breathe truth because nothing inspires other people more than being in its energy field. Years ago I wrote an article called "Who Do You Trust?" in which I explained that the trust issue rests on who we seek out when we want truth. Are we drawn to those who'll tell us what we want to hear or those who are unafraid to be honest with us, even if it might be unpleasant or difficult for us to hear? The answer is obvious: We prefer to hear the truth.

Honesty is a necessity if we're ever to live in harmony with Spirit and become a source of inspiration for others as well. When we shade the truth, a part of our brain registers this incongruity— it shows up as a disconnect from God, and we're out of balance. Our body reacts by becoming weaker in the face of any falsehood, including our attachment to the false self known as ego. As we practice living and speaking from our truth without being hurtful or arrogant in any way, we reconnect with the energy we emanated from in the first place.

In kinesiology there's a procedure called muscle testing, where the body is used as a veritable lie detector. In other words, if a person isn't telling the truth, their muscles are weaker than when they're answering honestly. They can't hold their arm up or their fingers together against applied pressure when they're thinking a falsehood; yet when they shift to a truthful thought, with the same pressure applied, they're able to withstand the same force. Try it, and you'll be amazed. It turns out that experimenters have discovered that the body, an instrument of God's creation, is stronger when it's directed by honesty. Since Spirit creates only out of truth, a thought of truth is in harmony with God's truth. (The entire procedural blueprint, along with instructions on how to use the body as a "lie detector," is readily explained in *Power vs. Force*, written by David Hawkins and published by Hay House.)

So let's remember truth as a means for inspiring each other. We must be unafraid to live and speak our truth—think how inspiring we'd all be for each other if honesty was a prominent feature of our interactions. By demonstrating 100 percent commitment to truth, with no exceptions, we send out a signal that we're in accord with our Source, and we'll do more to inspire others to live and breathe from their own truth than a thousand readings of the Ten Commandments or any other written document.

Truth and God are one. We don't have to preach it, only *live it*—by doing so, we'll radiate it to everyone we come into contact with. As an ancient Hindu saying reminds us, "The name of God is truth."

## Some Suggestions for Putting the Ideas in This Chapter to Work for You

— Work on becoming more peaceful, and start noticing how you're perceived by others. Practice daily meditation to become more peaceful, and then watch as others who previously engaged you in confrontation are less inclined in that direction. Decide for yourself that you're an emissary of peace and that that's precisely the energy you're going to radiate wherever you go. By lifting your thoughts upward so that they resonate with the peace that divines your origination, you'll automatically become a person who inspires others to do the same, without having to adopt any new strategies and with an absence of "effort" on your part.

— Actively work at reducing your inclinations to interrupt others with an *I* reference in conversations. Just "stifle yourself," as Archie Bunker used to say. Make a concerted effort to be silent when you're about to interrupt. See the words *stifle yourself* flash on your inner screen, and remind yourself at that moment that you inspire by listening and encouraging, not by self-reference or sermonizing.

— Before speaking, consult your inner "truth barometer" and resist the temptation to tell people what they want to hear if that feels untrue to you. People do respect those who are willing to speak their truth, and even more, to *live* the truth they feel. When I write an article, for instance, I know precisely who to show it to for comments if I want a guaranteed set of compliments to come my way—but I also know who's unafraid to come from their truth, and this is where I seek feedback. Not that someone else's truth will automatically match up with mine, but at least I'm hearing from a person who lives and speaks from their own inner fidelity. This kind of person inspires me by being aligned with our place of origin, which is, of course, pure honesty. You can be this inspiring kind of a person by abandoning your need for approval and replacing it with authenticity and integrity.

— Let everyone you meet know that there's one thing about you that isn't up for discussion: You are going to live your passion, and there's absolutely no room for compromise on this point. Carry yourself proudly and show your enthusiasm in all of your waking hours. Be passionate about all of your activities, and keep reminding yourself that you will never elect apathy or ennui. Never! By refusing to concede this point, you'll become a model for others to live out *their* lives in-Spirit.

When I speak to audiences, I'm always aware that by my being in-Spirit and conveying this vibration to them, I'm offering everyone there an opportunity to do the same for themselves. When beginning speakers ask me for advice on how to become an in-demand lecturer, my answer is always the same: "Talk from your heart authentically and be enthusiastic." Passionate, truthful communication is always inspiring.

— Practice being generous as often as you can. Promise yourself to extend some kind of unexpected generosity to someone, preferably a stranger, every single day for two weeks. This will not only help you develop a habit of giving, but you'll also discover how wonderfully inspiring your generous nature feels. The more you practice being charitable, the more you'll impact others in an inspiring way. By letting others know that you're willing to give of your time as well as your possessions, you'll serve as an inspirational model. Who isn't inspired by those who're willing to share their time, money, and possessions? We name cities (San Francisco) for such people and we nominate them (Mother Teresa) for sainthood . . . you too can inspire by being a benevolent soul.

Also practice tithing (giving 10 percent of what you earn in a given period to support teaching that provides you with spiritual uplift) and see if it doesn't return to you tenfold. This has worked for me my entire life, and continues as I practice my natural instinct to be generous.

※ ※ ※

In an exceptionally inspiring book titled *Season of Life,* Jeffrey Marx, a Pulitzer Prize–winning writer, chronicles a high school football team in which a former player with the Baltimore Colts named Joe Ehrmann is on the coaching staff. His coaching philosophy is to "help boys become men within the context of sports"— that is, without threats, screaming, or violence.

"I expect greatness out of you," the team's head coach tells his players, "and the way we measure greatness is the impact you make on other people's lives." As the ten coaches and assistant coaches huddle with the team on game day, one of them asks, "What is our job?" "To love us!" the team yells back in unison. "And what is *your* job?" the coach asks. "To love each other," the team responds. This is the philosophy that these boys were exposed to every day—at practice, on the field, and during and after the games—and so it goes for all of us who wish to inspire others. We must love all others and teach them to love each other. After all, in the Talmud we're told that "God said: you must teach, as I taught, without a fee . . ."

Inspiring others and becoming inspired ourselves involves being more like our Creator, since true teaching is about leading others back to the Spirit that's within everyone.

# CHAPTER 12

# TRANSCENDING COMMONPLACE, UNINSPIRING ENERGY

*"For all our insight, obstinate habits do not disappear until replaced by other habits . . . No amount of confession and no amount of explaining can make the crooked plant grow straight; it must be trained upon the trellis by the gardener's art . . ."*

— CARL JUNG

*"Habit rules the unreflecting herd."*

— WILLIAM WORDSWORTH

**THANKS TO THE WORLD WE LIVE IN,** we've developed many habits that are the direct result of living almost exclusively "in-ego" rather than in-Spirit. This chapter will stress how to gain awareness of these ego habits, how to immediately protect ourselves from these onslaughts, and how to develop alternate strategies to ensure that we remain connected to Spirit—even in the face of a blitzkrieg that's designed to take us away from living an inspired life.

I'm not suggesting that there's a conspiracy to keep us from living in-Spirit. My contention is simply that when a majority of society members are raised and persuaded to believe in the illusion of ego, then that society will develop and evolve firmly committed to that false self. It would then be natural for such a society to put forth messages designed to promote the idea of the importance of ego and all of its inherent ideas—and we're fully immersed in just such a society.

I once heard Swami Satchidananda lecture about this subject of the collective ego and its unceasing impact on all of us. He looked at the two words *heart* and *head,* the symbols for Spirit and ego, respectively, and confirmed that we're in-Spirit when we act from our heart. Swami also observed that the word *heart* contains two words, *he* and *art,* and that leads to the thought that <u>he</u> *and his* <u>art</u> *make up the heart.*

The word *head,* on the other hand, also contains two words—*he* and *ad*—which leads to the thought that <u>he</u> *and his* <u>ad</u> *make up the head.* Swami reminded us that the head is an advertisement—that is, it's the ego looking for recognition. He then asked a question I've never forgotten: "Why is it that lovers call each other sweet-*heart* and not sweet*head*?" And he reminded us not to despise the head or symbolically cut it off, but rather to let our heart (that is, our feelings) lead, and the head will then follow, rather than the other way around. To that end, this chapter provides three steps to help us transcend the ego's uninspiring energy. They are: *becoming aware, cultivating a defense,* and *developing our own alternatives.*

### Ego's Warriors

Let's first take a look at some of the "habits that rule the herd," in the words of William Wordsworth. Following are several omnipresent, lacking-in-inspiration entities that join up with ego to bombard us daily, and that we need to become aware of.

### The Media

A century or so ago, long before the media became such an active force in our lives, the news was almost exclusively received from one's village. Bad news was rare, and tended to only involve accidents or natural disasters, such as fire, flood, drought, or the occasional crime perpetrated by someone in the community. For the most part, one's daily life was consumed by work and family interaction—any kind of news was essentially information about the village and was primarily communicated by word of mouth.

Today, however, it's a very different picture. We've created a society that sends out specially trained people to scour the globe for depressing bulletins that are delivered to us wherever we are. The news is now available at home, at work, in our car, at the gym, on airplanes, standing in line at the bank, in the hospital, and on portable devices wherever we go. We're now able to directly tune in to the reports of those organizations who search for information designed to make us feel bad—that is, removed from Spirit, which is all about feeling good (God).

An explosion on the other side of the planet? We get a continual video loop. A suicide bomber in the Middle East kills 75 people? We get to see it all in grisly detail. A man stabs his wife and children anywhere in the country, and we get to hear about it on our local 11 o'clock news—thanks to an eyewitness reporter who's interviewing every neighbor willing to go on camera. . . .

We're constantly subjected to this army of bad-news collectors who gather and disseminate low-vibrational energy for our consumption. Keeping in mind that being inspired is about feeling good and returning to our Source of love, it's imperative to become aware of what we're allowing into our consciousness. These bad-news assemblers are on a mission to convince us of the inherent evil in the world—they can't possibly believe that we live in a friendly Universe, and they seem determined to convince us that their illusion is truth.

As we become aware that we're paying attention to uninspiring reports that are directed at us in the guise of keeping us informed, we can begin to take the necessary steps to return to Spirit. First, we must be aware that this "news" is more accurately a steady dose of low energy that's addictive. When we watch or listen to such messages, we can simply check in with our heart self and ask, "Is this a match to how I want to feel? If I continue to stay connected to these energies, will I feel good (God) or bad?"

Note that there are hundreds of cable news channels that need to fill 24 hours a day of broadcasting. Consequently, the analysts of these shows must dissect every crime, horrible accident, and bit of conflict they can find, and they must also maintain a confrontational attitude with whomever they're talking—or more likely, arguing—with. Being a match to the originating Spirit of Well-Being and Peace is close to impossible in such situations.

I'm not suggesting that we stay uninformed or in a state of blissful ignorance; rather, I'm saying that awareness is the key to staying in-Spirit when we're force-fed a steady diet of low-energy news. We simply need to become aware of what we've decided to allow into our space when we're online, watching television, or reading a newspaper. By catching ourselves when we're getting worked up, we can then begin to defend against these assaults on our spirituality. And we can start by asking ourselves this question: "Do I feel good right now?"

The defense against a media blitz of uninspiring energies is to remind ourselves that we want to feel good, in the sense that *good* and *God* are synonymous. We can't feel bad enough to change any of the bad news we're exposed to, nor can we eliminate hatred in the world by feeling hateful—we can't do anything positive or loving by joining those who've elected to live in these energies, or even those who broadcast it to us nonstop. However, by feeling good (God), we have an opportunity to be a small force that can transcend and convert lower energies into spiritual ones.

Our alternative to feeling down when we're exposed to a media offense of bad news is to instantly remind ourselves that we refuse to be a vibrational match to anything uninspiring. So, armed with this defense, we can become informed as well as inspired—and we'll ultimately reach a point where we remember that we're not accepting uninspiring energy any longer. Lo and behold, by being more like God (rather than more like ego), we actually will make a dent in all of the negativity that's delivered to us via the various faces of the media. By successfully opting for alternatives to the bad news and the political quarreling, we'll choose to remain in-Spirit and feel good (God), regardless of how many others wish to live as if they're in a pitched battle where conflict and agitation rule.

## The World of Advertising

Everywhere we turn, we're a target of someone wanting to sell us something. There are advertisements on buses, in the backseat of cabs, at the movies, on telephone poles, on our cell phones, after every click of our computers, on the radio and television for more than a third of the airtime, in more than 50 percent of magazine pages (in most cases, anyway), while we're on hold on the telephone, and even in restrooms! It's difficult to escape this assault on our senses and our spirit as well. Behind this huge blitz that's aimed at us during every waking moment of our lives is the idea that we need to purchase something in order to be "fixed" or "complete." Madison Avenue just keeps telling us that we'll overcome our deficiencies and be happier and more fulfilled if we simply buy whatever it is they're selling! The essential message behind this juggernaut is that we need *more* in order to be happy. Coincidentally, the mantra of the ego is just that: *more, more, more.*

Ego insists on believing that we don't have enough, others have more, there's newer and better stuff, we won't be liked unless we purchase that thing, we lack status, and some designer label will make life better. This is the exact opposite of what Spirit gently whispers, which is: "You are complete already, a product of universal abundance, so relax and enjoy life . . . what you desire will show up with less effort and no anxiety."

The first step in transcending the uninspiring messages that besiege us to buy more is to *become aware of what's going on and realize that we don't really need anything else in order to be happy.* After all, there's no way to happiness—happiness *is* the way. We may need to say this to ourselves over and over until it sinks in: "Nothing can make me happy. Happiness and inspiration are what I bring to life, not what I purchase." This awareness diminishes the annoyance of all those commercial messages, and at the same time allows us to enjoy the creativity of the advertising industry, because we've detached from the ego messages and connected to Spirit. Knowing that we don't need any more things in order to have a more complete life means that we can either ignore the pressure to buy or enjoy it. With awareness and a reconnection to Spirit comes the realization that ads aren't directed at our authentic self—and when we choose to stay in-Spirit, this awareness becomes its own defense.

What I'm suggesting is that we can be free from the push to convince us that we need more, while still being able to enjoy the material aspects of the world. In other words, we know that we don't *need* more, and at the same time, we're free to live happily and enjoy our world the way it is. I want this distinction to be clear because it's fun enjoying a new automobile, well-made clothes, dinner in a nice restaurant, an expensive piece of jewelry, or anything else that might be advertised (including this book). What we want to avoid is the inner belief that somehow our true essence is lacking if we don't get the things we're being encouraged to buy. We must also guard against allowing this "stuff" to define our worthiness, which is what advertisers are frequently attempting to convey.

When I allowed my awareness to purchase only what I desired, thus maintaining my sense of true inspiration, I found myself less and less attached to *stuff*. You see, the more I have, the more it becomes almost burdensome to store it, insure it, dust it, decide if it's tax deductible, and ultimately dispose of it. These days I'm almost amused by the advertising I'm subjected to, and when it appears, I press my "spiritual mute button" and feel even happier that I'm immune to the invitations of advertisers to add their brand of status to my life.

Another thing I've noticed that's a considerable impediment to living a life in-Spirit is the content of ads. They're designed to convince us that we're inherently powerless in the face of illness and stress when it shows up in our body. To begin with, our body is the most amazing pharmacy ever created, and it's perfectly capable of manufacturing and distributing whatever healing materials we need. Our body originated from a stream of pure well-being, so when we feel depressed, anxious, fearful, or whatever, our brain can create whatever prescription it needs.

I'm not disparaging the magnificent strides that modern medicine has made in helping us all to live healthier, more fulfilling lives. However, I *am* alarmed by the recent phenomenon of large pharmaceutical companies in bed with the medical profession, inundating our airwaves with messages designed to get us to ask our doctor to prescribe a pill for every real or imagined malady. Almost 50 percent of prime-time television shows are sponsored by drug companies, promoting items that can only be prescribed by a licensed physician. We're being sold the idea that we need a variety of pills to feel better, walk better, breathe better, sleep better, play better, and even make love better! Also appearing as three- and four-page announcements in national magazines, these ads are contrived to put our health and happiness in the profit-motivated hands of drug companies and physicians—at the expense of our living an inspired life. It's a veritable invasion of our spirit.

We're in a body that has a natural tendency toward health and can overcome almost anything if we allow it to perform its own magic, so we must be cautious about the motivations of companies that want us to become hooked on medicine that can conveniently be prescribed for a lifetime. We probably don't need to rely on something manufactured in a laboratory and sold by a huge pharmaceutical conglomerate whose primary objective is skyrocketing profits through advertising; rather, by practicing awareness, we can be in-Spirit and rely on our body's own pharmacy and doctor in one miraculous spiritual package.

## Entertainment

As we progress toward a more inspired life, we'll begin to notice that the activities we've called "entertainment" have actually been leading us away from being in-Spirit. Since everything that we allow into our life represents an energy that impacts us both physically and spiritually, it's imperative to raise our awareness level and defend against the habits that deter us from being in-Spirit.

Reflect on Wordsworth's observation at the opening of this chapter: "Habit rules the unreflecting herd." We certainly don't want to be either unreflecting or part of a herd because as we know, when we follow the herd, we end up stepping in herd poop! Thus, we need to sharpen our awareness of the habits we've developed that camouflage uninspiring activities—it's all too common in our society to believe that nonspiritual energies are an important part of our entertainment package.

It's vital that we're conscious of the following "big four," which are really low-level energies masquerading as entertainment and are obstacles to anyone's ultimate calling to inspiration.

**1. Violence.** On average, children in America see 12,000 simulated murders in their own home on commercial and cable television before their 14th birthday; and virtually all movies made to appeal to a younger audience have grim killings, explosions, and chase scenes built into the story line, which seems to consist of "guns, guns, guns, and kill, kill, kill—the more gruesomely, the better."

These decidedly uninspiring messages continually bombard all of us when we're supposedly experiencing uplifting entertainment, but we can do something about it. If enough of us decide that this is not going to be on our daily menu, then the manufacturers of this kind of recreational material would bring it to a halt. For example, if more of us were aware of the content of the video games that our kids play—many of which simulate rape, torture, and even murder—we wouldn't permit them in our homes.

In addition, sporting events that are supposed to be entertaining to spectators are increasingly being tainted by escalating levels of violence. It's become commonplace for athletes to take steroids to make them bigger and more ferocious, and fans applauding hotheaded cheap shots and encouraging melees to break out is considered entertaining. Even the music being written and performed today often contains messages of violence and profanity. And I could go on and on with an inventory of the violence and bloodthirstiness that's prevalent in the entertainment industry (as you practice being more aware, I'm sure you'll add examples to this list, too).

Yet there are alternatives available to us. First on this list is screening our entertainment options for violence and making a commitment to choose only those pastimes that are free of any energy that doesn't match our desire to be in-Spirit. Our Creator creates out of love, kindness, and peace, so if we clear opposite energies out of our life, we'll almost immediately feel inspiration returning to our life.

What follows is one of the most poignantly inspiring letters I've ever read, written by my dear friend Ram Dass to the parents of a young girl who'd been brutally murdered. Even in such horrific circumstances, Ram Dass was able to provide inspiration. I reproduce this moving letter with Ram Dass's permission in order to help you see how it is possible to transcend violence with inspiring spiritual energy.

> *Dear Steve and Anita,*
>
> *Rachel finished her work on Earth and left the stage in a manner that leaves those of us left behind with a cry of agony in our hearts, as the fragile thread of our faith is dealt with so violently. Is anyone strong enough to stay conscious through such teaching as you are receiving? Probably very few. And even they would only have a whisper of equanimity and peace amidst the screaming trumpets of their rage, grief, horror, and desolation.*
>
> *I can't assuage your pain with any words, nor should I, for your pain is Rachel's legacy to you. Not that she or I would inflict such pain by choice, but there it is. And it must burn its purifying way to completion. For something in you dies when you bear the unbearable, and it is only in that dark night of the soul that you are prepared to see as God sees, and to love as God loves.*
>
> *Now is the time to let your grief find expression—no false strength. Now is the time to sit quietly and speak to Rachel, thank her for being with you these few years, and encourage her to go on with whatever her work is, knowing that you will grow in compassion and wisdom from this experience. In my heart, I know that you and she will meet again and again, and recognize the many ways in which you have known each other.*

*And when you meet you will know, in a flash, what now it is not given to you to know: why this had to be the way it was.*

*Our rational minds can never understand what has happened, but our hearts—if we keep them open to God—will find their own intuitive way. Rachel came through you to do her work on Earth, which includes her manner of death. Now her soul is free, and the love that you can share with her is invulnerable to the winds of changing time and space. In that deep love, include me.*

*In love,*

*Ram Dass*

**2. Hatred.** Much of our entertainment dollar is spent watching malice, hatred, and hostility in some form. Now in my opinion, there's far too much animosity in our world, so I have no desire to sit through a movie or listen to a song that repeatedly describes how one group hates another. Martin Luther King, Jr., one of my personal heroes, said that the only way to convert a perceived enemy into a friend is by love. Since we know that hatred itself breeds more of the same, then being exposed to it—even when it's dressed up as entertainment—is something to be cognizant of when we choose a film, television show, sporting event, play, or book. *Any* hateful message is nonspiritual energy that we're exposing ourselves to . . . and the more we consciously allow, the more we'll be inclined to attract in our life.

The moral of all of this is that entertainment can be uplifting and edifying, or it can be demoralizing and debasing. So where do we want our energy to flow—and, even more important, what kind of energy do we want our children to experience? We must be on guard against any entertainment that uses excessive profanity and seems to support hatred and disrespect in its narrative.

I love this story that the Dalai Lama told in a documentary titled *The Yogis of Tibet*. It seems that one of the most enlightened Tibetan yogis who witnessed the carnage and decimation of the entire Tibetan culture by the Chinese, beginning with the Communist Revolution of Mao Tse-tung in 1949, related a story in which he stated several times, "I was in great danger." This was surprising, since these yogis cared very little about their own safety. When the enlightened yogi was asked about his perceived danger, he responded, "Yes, yes, I *was* in grave danger. That is, I was in danger of losing my compassion for the Chinese."

This is not only a beautiful story, but it also helps us remember to be careful about accepting hatred as normal in our entertainment activities, for they can put us in the same kind of danger that the enlightened yogi recognized. And even more personally significant, enjoying hatred as entertainment can keep us from reconnecting to inspiration.

**3. Fear.** A quick review of today's morning paper reveals that a killer is on the loose, there are new terrorist threats to the U.S. and more terrorist threats in Spain, global warming is melting the polar ice caps, deaths at rail crossings have increased 11 percent in one year, gasoline prices are increasing and automobile sales are declining, OPEC's cutting off the oil supply, frequent-flier miles probably won't be redeemable because the airlines have nine trillion miles they owe us, the expectation of a heavy-duty forest-fire season is high, hurricane devastation will increase in the next ten years . . . and I'm only on page three!

Every day we're inundated with urgent messages to live in fear by our news-gathering agencies, our movies, our television programming, and even our government. Try buying anything to consume without having to remove layer after layer of protective seals to keep out all of the monsters who are trying to poison our foods. As a child I recall slurping from a garden hose—today we fear the toxins in our drinking water. I recall riding my bike all day in my Levi's and a T-shirt—today we fear brain injuries and require helmets and protective gear just to ride a bicycle. I recall talking to strangers and trusting their good intentions—today everyone is a potential predator. I recall being home when the streetlights came on and never having to call home to reassure my mother that I was safe—today every child needs a cell phone and lives in fear of being abducted.

We've become a fear-based society, and this dread has crept into all facets of our lives, including our entertainment. We sit in movie theaters biting our fingernails as we watch the machinations of a serial killer or see someone being decapitated by a chain saw. We're told a thousand times a day to live in fear and worry about one kind of disaster or another: Someone is going to rob us or set our house on fire, a natural disaster is on its way, and the television beseeches us to watch *Fear Factor*. I could go on and on here, but I'm sure you get the point. Yet *I* have a point, too: When we live in fear, inspiration is virtually impossible.

Consider what I'm writing here with an open mind. In fact, let me offer this disclaimer: Every bad thing that's come your way, including any victim status, natural devastation, sickness, or what have you, *is not your fault*. There's no blame—you're not getting targeted for some kind of "karmic payback"—rather, what happened is there and it's yours. Since fear is a vibration, you were a vibrational match to whatever entered your life at the moment of its arrival. Remember that you live in a Universe that operates by the Law of Attraction, so when you live in fear, you actually bring to you what you're afraid of. Thoughts themselves are an energy, and it's vital to realize that you need to work at not holding on to the ones that will weaken you. Keep in mind that *you get what you think about, whether you want it or not!*

There's no fear in our spiritual Source—still we're persuaded to be afraid by continual exposure to the onslaught of fear-based dispatches that arrive on our doorstep. It's possible that our life experiences, which were a vibrational match to our thoughts at the time of their arrival, instilled fear in us. Nevertheless, this doesn't make our dread acceptable if we're dedicated to living in-Spirit. Franklin Delano Roosevelt was right: "The only thing we have to fear is fear itself."

Our Universe is created out of love, kindness, peace, and well-being, so when we're an energetic match to this awareness and refuse to live in fear, we'll attract the protection and guidance we desire. We can absolutely affirm that we won't attract anything that's harmful to us or to our loved ones, we can heighten our awareness that we're never alone, and we can have faith that whatever we need to experience is on its way and God won't send us anything we're incapable of handling.

We can also be aware that the word *fear* is just an acronym for **f**alse **e**vidence **a**ppearing **r**eal! That one phrase can help us remember that the ego is the false self, and identifying with it leads us to believe the false evidence. Even now, after reading all of this, some readers may continue to make fear real with thoughts such as, *He wouldn't be able to say these things if he knew all that I've been through.* But in my heart I know that this is a Universe that's on purpose and supported by a Creator Who is good. I never doubt it, and not only do I refuse to live in fear, but I also refuse to attract to myself the vibrational energetic equivalent of those fear-based thoughts. As an old German proverb proclaims: "Fear makes the wolf bigger than he is."

**4. Sarcasm.** Just about every situation comedy on television has a familiar focus: dialogue that's dedicated to sarcastic, unflattering comments between the supposedly comedic characters. Put-downs are the very bread and butter of almost all prime-time shows today, so in essence we're asking to be amused by children being smart-alecks toward their parents and siblings mouthing off to each other with as many disparaging comments as possible. Oh, and these nasty rejoinders are followed by a laugh track to really drive home that we're being "entertained."

Sarcasm designed to inspire laughter sends a message to viewers that's anything but inspirational. Remember, our ultimate calling is always about being in harmony with our Source of Being—we're all here as the result of a Creator Who has great respect for all of Its creations. Since no one is inferior in our Creator's eyes, no one deserves to be ridiculed for the purpose of gaining an artificial laugh . . . not in life or on TV. When a comment is made in jest and there's a kind of clever banter taking place, that's comedy at its best—but when hostility and disrespect are uttered in almost every verbal exchange, with the express purpose to discredit and mock another person, that's a decidedly uninspiring signal being sent to the audience. Awareness and choice are ours to exercise, so if this tendency toward sarcasm has become a habit, we must begin exploring alternatives to this style of entertainment and family interaction.

You may recall that I wrote earlier in this book about my mother—well, I simply cannot even imagine using her as the butt of a joke to demean or ridicule her. And yet I see this kind of disrespect taking place in nearly every episode of every situation comedy on the air today. Being courteous to others is a matchup to the energy of Spirit. Having fun, telling jokes, and being playful with others are all part of being in-Spirit, but a hostile, sarcastic sense of humor is an energy that moves us away from Spirit and into the realm of hurt and dishonor.

### Cultural and Family Influences

I'd be remiss if I were to leave out this important category in this chapter. After all, we encounter lots of people in our everyday lives who attempt to convince us that we can't live the dream that beckons us. Statements such as, "That's not possible," or "We've never done it that way in our family," characterize our family or community members' attempts to dissuade us from following our calling. I've written about these family and cultural pressures in other chapters of this book, but they bear repeating here.

We need to be on the alert so that we're instantly aware of what others are trying to accomplish with uninspiring pronouncements about what we can or cannot do. Practicing increased awareness when we're around uninspiring family and/or cultural messages concerning our unique inspiration is extremely important: With that awareness, we're gracefully able to smile and politely move away from any energy that isn't encouraging us to follow our inner spiritual convictions to return to Spirit.

Many of our cultural influences are very subtle and aren't actually intended to be a distraction from our calling. Often, though, organized religions will push us in the direction of fearing God and living life in ways that have been prescribed by ancient theological doctrines and customs that have no merit in today's world. And frequently there are rules meant to quell desires that we may have to live out the life that we feel burning deep within us. In these situations we must look within, consult with our Creator, and make a decision to be in-Spirit—even if it conflicts with what we're being told by well-meaning people and institutions whose mission includes keeping us "in the herd."

Institutions of formal education may also want to discourage any attraction we have to listening to our inner guidance. This makes sense, since school is often designed to teach students to unquestioningly accept what's taught and to conform to societal standards. There's little room in this kind of classroom for following our own inner callings—the choice is generally between being like everyone else or being labeled as a troublemaker. Once again, we're forced to contemplate the Shakespearean dilemma of "to be or not to be." The stronger our burning desire to live a life of inspiration, the more we're pushed in the direction of "to be." We can learn to look at social pressures to conform and smile kindly, all the while choosing Spirit rather than the herd.

As I sit here writing, I'm looking at a framed photo of Ralph Waldo Emerson, a powerful man of Spirit and one of my most inspirational teachers and mentors. I'd like to end here by sharing an observation he once made: "Every man takes care that his neighbor shall not cheat him. But a day comes when he begins to care that he does not cheat his neighbor. Then all goes well. He has changed his market-cart into a chariot of the sun." This is a thought well worth pondering as we move in to the next chapter.

## Some Suggestions for Putting the Ideas in This Chapter to Work for You

— When you find yourself being exposed to media onslaughts that are decidedly uninspiring, listen to your very first impulse and *switch off!* Turn off the television or radio, leave the movie theater, put the magazine down, and affirm: *I no longer wish to be in the energy field of anything that isn't a vibrational match with Spirit.*

— Be aware of brazen attempts by pharmaceutical companies to profit off of your presumed maladies, with advertising telling you to consult your doctor for some new medication. Let the ad be a reminder that you're an instrument of health; by doing so, your body will react to the messages being sent by your mind. Remember that your body/mind is the greatest pharmacy ever created. It has an unlimited potential for creating well-being, since that's where it originated from in the first place!

— Say it out loud! By this, I mean, that you shouldn't be afraid to make unusual or provocative affirmations. For example, you might avow: *I won't attract any further illness to my life. I'll never allow myself to feel old, feeble, or frail; and I refuse to allow Alzheimer's, cancer, or any other infirmity into my life. I don't vibrate to frequencies that are designed to keep me from being in-Spirit.*

— Always remember that you're a being who was created out of love. Write this out, place in a conspicuous place, and repeat it to yourself: *I live in a Divinely inspired Universe. I have nothing to fear. I trust in myself, and when I do so, I trust in the very Wisdom that created me.* Convince yourself (as I have) that when you live on purpose and "take care that [you do] not cheat your neighbor," then you're watched over by a "Senior Partner" Who knows that you're both living and vibrating to the same spiritual frequency.

— Work at developing your faith each and every day by taking time to be quietly in conscious contact with the Creative Source of your being. When you take time to meditate and commune with Spirit, not only will you feel revitalized, but you'll adopt a defense system that can't be penetrated by efforts to uninspire you, no matter how frequently others may attempt to do so. Ultimately, you'll find that you won't even bother to invite uninspired energy into your life via the media—or any other source, for that matter.

* * *

On every radio, CD player, and television set there's a wonderfully inspiring little button that says *on/off,* and it's your choice to befriend it. You can literally push it anytime you wish, or you can use an inner off button whenever you're bombarded by anyone or anything whose purpose is to distract you from your ultimate calling to inspiration.

Don't be afraid to use the off button—it works!

# CHAPTER 13

# INSPIRATION
# IN ACTION

*"In our era, the road to holiness necessarily
passes through the world of action."*

— DAG HAMMARSKJOLD

*"Knowing is not enough; we must apply.
Willing is not enough; we must do . . ."*

— JOHANN WOLFGANG VAN GOETHE

**WHEN WE FEEL INSPIRED,** we're on the "road to holiness"
that Dag Hammarskjold refers to above. Yet that road can only be
paved with actions that mirror the intention of our originating
Spirit—actions that we're capable of choosing consciously, if we're
aware of the duality of giving and receiving.

Like two sides of the same coin, giving and receiving are in-
separable. Other examples of our duality abound: Before we can
take a breath, we must give a breath; in order to give anything
away, we must first have been willing to receive it; and our ability to feed others is linked to being able to accept food ourselves.
Who has ever seen a person with a front but no back? How about
an inside without an outside? Or a magnet with a north pole but
no south pole? So, just as the Prayer of St. Francis reminds us that
*it is in giving that we receive,* in order to receive inspiration we must
be willing to give it away, and vice versa.

### *Two Examples of Inspiring Action*

As Goethe instructs, reading a book about inspiration isn't enough, and certainly waiting for it to fall from the heavens into your lap won't work either! Clearly, if you want to be inspired, you must be willing to offer inspiration. You've got to act on a desire to inspire others, thus becoming a person of inspiring action yourself. So in this section I'd like to share two beautiful examples of inspiration in action with you, along with suggestions for applying them to your life.

## Example #1

I was inspired by a short documentary called *Ryan's Well,* about a young Canadian boy whose actions made a huge difference in the lives of some people in Uganda. You see, as a first-grader in the small town of Kemptville, Ontario, Ryan Hreljac learned that there were people in Africa who didn't have clean drinking water—yet it would cost just $70 to build a well that could provide pure, potable water for an entire village. This six-year-old boy began a campaign to earn the necessary money, only to discover that the cost was actually several *thousand* dollars. His reaction was, "I'll do more chores" . . . and he did.

In the film we see Ryan travel to Africa with his parents a few years later. The villagers greet him with enthusiasm and declare a day of commemoration that they call "Ryan's Day," in appreciation of his commitment to helping his fellow human beings on the other side of the world. It turns out that Ryan was instrumental in helping to raise what eventually grew to be more than *a million dollars!* His inspiration had motivated other schools in Canada to get behind his project; after the national news media picked up on the story, the television networks climbed on board, too.

Here was one small boy who decided to act on his strong inner calling to help others. He had no money or other resources at his disposal, but he *did* have a burning desire to reach out and serve people in need. He was willing to do the chores necessary to fulfill his call to be a vibrational match with his Creator and serve others. In turn, his actions created an immense wellspring of inspiration for all who contributed and got involved in Ryan's foundation. He inspired the children in Uganda (and even the government and school officials in that country), who all paid tribute to the spirit within Ryan that did so much good (God) in a remote village far away from his small community in Ontario. Ryan himself was the recipient of even more inspiration than he gave away.

When I watched the film, I was so moved that I insisted that all of my children see it, and they became inspired as well. In fact, I'm writing these words with the admitted intention of inspiring others to take action, too. Ryan's Well Foundation has a Website (**www.ryanswell.ca**), and with some inspired action, everyone reading these words can find their way to it and contribute to making clean drinking water, something most of us take for granted, available for others.

One person's inspiring actions will ultimately lead to many, many others. In the duality of inspired actions, giving and receiving inspiration is a never-ending circle of living more and more in-Spirit.

**Applying this example:** The moral of Ryan Hreljac's story is that none of us has an excuse for not being a person of inspiration. We don't need money or the help of any government or bank—all we need is an internal commitment to be more like God, and then to act on that desire. Everything else that we need will begin to arrive when we're in-Spirit: The right people will show up, the financing will materialize, those around us will be attracted to our enthusiasm and commitment, and we'll be a source of inspiration to others . . . while becoming more inspired ourselves.

Ryan's story represents our true nature, and our ability to be purposefully in-Spirit. He found a way to give to others the inspiration he wanted for himself, and all those who observed this boy in action responded in kind. To that end, whatever *we'd* like in our life that would provide us with inspiration is there—we just need to find a way to offer to others what we desire, and we'll solve the riddle of how to feel inspired and give inspiration away at the same time.

### Example #2

On a recent airing of *Extreme Makeover: Home Edition,* Cassie, a young cancer patient, was given a surprise by the show's producers: They built a beautiful mansion where the tiny bungalow that housed the little girl and her large family once stood. But Cassie hadn't written to the show to ask for a more impressive home for her family; instead, she wanted the producers to consider making over the children's cancer ward in the hospital where she spent a large portion of her young life. She felt that the surroundings were far too dreary—the walls were bare, and the entire place was disheartening—and she felt that a makeover would help uplift and inspire everyone, including her young friends who were also patients. The show agreed to finance and re-create the children's cancer ward, and they also got all the kids involved in the project.

When it was completed, the ward looked like a fairyland that any child would love: Playrooms replaced old storage closets, the walls came alive with creative artwork, and the sleeping facilities were redone so that they no longer even resembled hospital beds. The entire ward turned into a place of inspiration . . . all thanks to the dreams of a very young child who listened to Spirit and took action. But I haven't even gotten to the most inspiring part of the story yet!

Without exception, all of the children in the cancer ward who participated in the renovation had their white cells increase in the direction of well-being and away from the damaging cancer in their bodies. Imagine—by moving more into harmony with Spirit and using this newfound inspiration to take action in the service of other children, the actual process of returning to perfect health was activated. The healing power within these young people somehow miraculously responded to the results and actions of Cassie's inspiration by increasing their white cells!

**Applying this example:** There's so much to ponder in Cassie's story—above all, how taking action to inspire others may activate something that reconnects us (and them) to a stream of well-being and perfect health. Additionally, there's the inspiration that we receive by giving. Consider these powerful words of Robert Frost, one of America's most illustrious poets: "Something we were withholding made us weak. Until we found out that it was ourselves." Our weaknesses, including our illnesses, may come to us because we're withholding something—which could very well be our healthy, conscious connection to Spirit. By taking action to inspire others in any way, we gain the opportunity to convert a weakness to a strength.

If a child of five or six who's living with cancer in a ward with other kids in similar circumstances can find a way to take action that inspires others, then surely *we* can go within and find our way to inspiring action. Little Cassie was acting more like God than ego when she wrote to the *Extreme Makeover: Home Edition* show. And she also behaved in a more God-realized way when she got involved in the cancer-ward renovation to make it a more healing and good-feeling place. As one of my greatest mentors and teachers, Carl Jung, once observed: "Whatever you do, if you do it sincerely, will eventually become a bridge to your wholeness, a good ship that carries you through the darkness." Dr. Jung's key advice centers on the word *sincerely,* which I interpret to mean "in collaboration with our essential spiritual essence." By taking action from that place of Spirit, we become whole again, and all darkness dissolves.

Cassie and Ryan's examples are not out of our range, no matter who we are or what our place in life is. We *all* have the capacity to become inspired, to act in a more God-realized fashion—we just need to take the time to seek out the opportunities to do so.

### *How I've Practiced Inspiration in Action*

In this section, I'd like to present some examples of my own deliberate efforts to put the duality of inspiration in action into practice. I work at this every single day of my life: Every human encounter represents a moment of truth for me, one in which I choose to be reconnected to Spirit and offer to others what I genuinely want for myself. The opportunities present themselves in the form of a smile or a greeting or an extension of kindness, even if it's just a silent blessing to a person begging on a street corner or a prayer said quietly to myself when I hear a siren. (The siren is a reminder to me to offer my thoughts of comfort to whomever is in need of assistance.) These are habits that I've developed over a lifetime.

Then there are the days when I go out on a premeditated odyssey of inspiration, without any fanfare or need for recognition. Here's the result of one such inspiration excursion—and keep in mind that this all happened in one afternoon!

— I reside on west Maui while I'm writing, and on this particular day I decided to make the 20-mile trek to Costco to load up with supplies for two weeks of uninterrupted writing. As usual, someone was standing by the roadside looking for a lift to "the other side." This is a commonplace occurrence here on Maui, and it's my regular practice to pick up whoever's seeking a ride— usually a young person with a surfboard or a couple with luggage needing transportation to the airport. I always view giving rides as an opportunity to serve another person, and I get to feel good as well. If you're thinking about how dangerous this practice might be, I simply don't ever entertain such thoughts, and I never attract people or events into my life that cause me harm. It's just not my way of being in the world.

On this day I picked up a 41-year-old Canadian named Raven (Maui tends to attract people with names like that) who needed to get to the airport. As we talked, it turned out that my passenger hadn't spoken to his father in 17 years, distancing himself out of respect for his mother and sister, who had their own unresolved conflicts with the man. Raven admitted that he felt distressed and incomplete; moreover, he found himself repeating some of the behavioral patterns of his father's that had caused this family rift in the first place.

I brought up the subject of forgiveness, mentioning this quote from *A Course in Miracles:* "Certain it is that all distress does not appear to be but un-forgiveness." I related the story of my experience at my own father's grave in 1974, and how that one single act of forgiveness turned my life around and headed me back in the direction of Spirit.

As I dropped Raven off at the airport, he hugged me. With tears in his eyes, he said, "I can't believe how much this one trip has changed my life. I feel that you were sent here by God to remove this sword that's been hanging over my head. I know what I have to do, and I will do it soon." It was a moment of inspiration for both of us.

It would have been just as easy for me to maintain silence on that 20-mile ride along the ocean, but I knew that on this day, I was on a pilgrimage of inspiration, and Raven was one of my co-conspirators.

— I headed back to Costco for one of my favorite activities. I love the opportunity to purchase large amounts of goodies of all description in the store's open, warehouse atmosphere, among lots of local people doing the same thing.

At the back of the store on this day, a gentleman who recognized me from my PBS appearances approached me and wanted an appointment to discuss a problem he was having. I informed him that I was writing a book, so a scheduled meeting would be impossible. But knowing that some force had brought us together in the midst of all this delightful chaos, I asked, "What's the problem?"

The man told me that he was a diabetic who'd developed a fail-safe method for delivering insulin, in a manner that would leave no one out. "So what's the problem?" I once again asked. "Why not implement your plan?"

He went on to explain how he'd been unable to get the necessary government agencies to meet with him—various layers of bureaucracy were impeding his progress. On and on he went with a litany of obstacles that he felt were being placed before him, until I finally stopped him. "I sense that you know exactly what's needed, since you're a diabetic, too," I said. "And you know exactly what needs to be done to implement your idea."

He lit up like a Christmas tree. Giving me a knowing smile, he said, "Exactly, but I can't—"

I stopped him cold, reminding him that when we focus on what we don't want, then that's what we'll get. We get what we think about, whether we want it or not. I then asked him to consider staying out of the "system of obstacles" altogether; he should go ahead with his plan, forget about what couldn't be done, and just do it without the assistance or resistance of anyone else. "If your plan is viable, then they'll ultimately come along," I reminded him. "Just do it, and stop trying to get the approval of a bureaucracy." And then I asked, "You know what to do and how to do it, don't you?"

"Yes, I do," he replied, "and I will. I feel as if this little meeting was arranged by God just for me today." After getting my second hug from a "stranger" in the past 30 minutes, the man pushed his shopping cart away with a newfound sense of inspiration. He'd returned to Spirit, where the idea of anything being impossible is . . . impossible! And I'd been able to extend some Spirit offerings to another.

— Continuing on my way back to west Maui, I picked up a young fellow named Andy who was on his way to the Hard Rock Café. Fancying himself a Rastafarian rap artist, Andy had long dreadlocks and a strong inclination toward using marijuana as a stimulus for his music. As it turned out, he simply wanted to approach the manager at the Hard Rock to see if he could perform there on weekends. He was out of funds and without a plan—even his upcoming spontaneous audition had been purely a fantasy, since he hadn't contacted anyone at the restaurant for an appointment.

As we talked, I told him a story that my daughter Sommer had recently related to me. She has a little dog named Joey that she takes with her every day as she trains horses and gives riding lessons. Her friend Mimi had told her that Joey was a perfect example of a being at peace with God, and my daughter agreed. "Joey's mantra is: *Breathe in, breathe out, life is good,*" she said. "That's Joey all day, every day: *Breathe in, breathe out, life is good!*" Andy loved this story . . . so I asked him to give me a song using this theme as the primary lyric.

My car was suddenly filled with the sounds of a Rastafarian rapper pounding out a fast-paced lyric. It was sensational, and Andy was in heaven. By the time I dropped him off at the restaurant, he had his audition all planned, and he'd written his very first song: "Breathe In, Breathe Out, Life Is Good."

I handed Andy a $50 bill, which inspired him to cry out in appreciation, and off I drove. It was a double dose of inspiration: Andy was aligned with Spirit by being a creator of his own music and feeling purposeful and confident, and I was experiencing heaven on Earth for being able to extend love and assistance to another person. And it was my third such gift in the past two hours!

— Next I proceeded to a grocery store to pick up a few items in smaller quantities than were available at Costco. As I stood in the check-out line, I struck up a conversation with the woman behind me on the subject of raspberries. I was purchasing two half-pints of these precious little jewels to put on my morning bowl of cereal, and the lady asked about the price, which I hadn't noticed. She went on and on about how much she loved raspberries, but their cost was so outrageous—she'd never spend that kind of money, even for something she loved so much.

I responded by telling her about my happy memories of growing up in Michigan and picking berries as a young boy. To this day, raspberries are one of my very favorite foods, and I buy them whenever they're available. The woman could relate to my memories, since she grew up in Pennsylvania and used to pick the berries herself, coming home with red stains on her fingers and all around her mouth.

At the register, we saw that the baskets of berries came up as $7.99 each. My new friend almost collapsed, but told me to "savor each and every one of those little treasures." As I walked away, I reached into my bag and placed one of the containers in her hands and told her to enjoy them as a gift from me. This lady, who was counting out her change to pay for a single container of yogurt, was stunned. I finally convinced her that if she wouldn't accept them as a gift from me, she'd be depriving me of my own treat in knowing how much pleasure she was going to have relishing and savoring these little gems.

My new friend was obviously inspired by this unexpected expression of kindness to a "stranger." I could see the gratitude and love in her eyes as she tucked the berries in her straw bag. I, of course, was right on track, enjoying my fourth occurrence of inspiration in action on the same afternoon. And much to my surprise, number five was evolving right in front of my eyes. . . .

— In almost every aisle of the grocery store, I'd seen the same woman, dressed in flowery slacks and a bright orange blouse. As I approached the bakery to buy a loaf of olive bread for my daughter Serena's arrival the following day (she loves this bread!), the woman in the colorful outfit talked to me about a multigrain bread that *she* absolutely loved. "It's the best I've ever tasted," she said in a heavy foreign accent. As I approached the cashier, there she was ahead of me, asking if I'd hold her place while she picked up some item she'd forgotten. Then in the parking lot, she stopped her car to allow me to enter the exit ramp. Finally, as I was driving home, I spotted her again! Her car was sitting by the side of a putting green—with the door open and the engine running—and she and a man were hitting golf balls on the green.

To me, this was more that a series of accidental encounters, so I decided to turn around and deliver a present to her. I pulled up behind the car and approached with an autographed copy of *The Power of Intention* in my hand. It turned out that this lady was originally from Poland and was on her honeymoon. She introduced me to her husband, and I gave them the surprise wedding present, for which they were most grateful. I have no idea what took place in their lives after I drove off—I can't tell you why she kept appearing over and over again, or if the book I gave them made any kind of a difference in their lives—all I can say for certain is that these newlyweds were very touched by my gesture, and I had my fifth gift of feeling connected to Spirit in one afternoon!

As you can see, countless opportunities to reach into the lives of others in an inspiring way arise every single day. We can either act on these momentary impulses and feel inspired, or we can ignore them and stay in our ego-dominated world. I choose to act, for it makes me feel creatively alive, connected to good (God) and everyone else in the world.

Taking action is how we increase our connectedness to Spirit. If we're heeding our ultimate calling, we must be willing to act on that mission. We may believe that inspiration is something that arrives in some mysterious way that's beyond our control—or perhaps we're waiting for God to send us motivational signs—but it's clearly best to rely exclusively on our decisions to act in ways that will intensify our awareness of Spirit.

Try this action plan for a few weeks and see if you don't feel more inspired than you've ever felt before.

## Some Suggestions for Putting the Ideas in This Chapter to Work for You

— Before beginning your day, spend a few moments with God during the early morning. When you awaken, remind yourself, "These are my few moments with God." During those precious seconds, ask, reflect, feel the peace, and most important, extend your gratitude. I end my few moments with God every morning with this: "Thank You, thank You, thank You!"

453

— Upon awakening, decide to do something, anything, that will improve the quality of life for someone, without seeking any credit for yourself. (If you can do it before breakfast, great!) A letter, some flowers, a contribution, an unexpected plan to visit someone later in the day—do anything at all that will make someone else feel good (God).

— Overcome your inertia. Since to be inert is to be without action, agree to become a being of movement: Plan to exercise, make that call you've been avoiding, or write that letter. Just as the key to Spirit is movement, the key to health is circulation. Spirit is always in a state of creation, so commit to less lying or sitting around and more movement.

— Listen to your inner voice and promise that you'll take corrective action. For example, if you've been addicted to alcohol or drugs, overeating, or being a doormat, listen to that inner voice that begs you to be big rather than small, and take one corrective step. Just for today, throw the cigarettes away, pass on the sweets, walk around the block, or stand up for yourself. That inner voice is God pleading with you to rejoin Him in-Spirit by being pure, strong, and an instrument of well-being.

— Accept no excuses: Stop with the BS and be truthful with yourself, admit your flaws rather than defending them, and look in the mirror and talk to yourself honestly. Affirm: *I am a creation of God, and I am Divine. I've forgotten this, but now I'm not accepting excuses. I'm going to stop fooling myself and work at being all that I was destined to be.*

— Experience the apprehension and *do it anyway!* It's the doing that brings you to a new level of inspiration, so don't deny your fear. Allow the panic to come, and then move in the direction of facing it. Visualize the fear right in front of you. Stare it down and tell it how you truly feel and what you intend to become: "I'm stronger than you. I have my Creator here with me as a Senior Consultant, so I'm no longer willing to allow you to have dominance in my life. I'm scared, but I'm also taking action."

— Look for opportunities that you're going to create to feel inspired. In my afternoon of inspiration described in this chapter, I made a specific decision to act in-Spirit. It was my choice. I was seeking those situations, and if they hadn't transpired, I would have made them happen. Once you get proficient at manufacturing circumstances that allow you to be inspirational, you'll begin to see these situations materializing all around you every day.

— Finally, don't ever quit. Never give up on yourself or feel shame as a result of not fulfilling your objectives to be a being of inspiration. Every fall that you take is a gift, and every relapse is a glorious opportunity—after all, without them you can't manifest the energy to get to a higher place.

\* \* \*

There it is—a blueprint for taking action to live from inspiration. These strategies, as simple as they may seem, will bring you to a new level of inspiration if they're just adopted one day at a time. But reconnecting to Spirit *can* all happen in one day—this day. As one of my favorite Chinese proverbs reminds us:

*I hear and I forget*
*I see and I remember*
*I do and I understand.*

If you want to understand inspiration, it will require some doing. So remember what the Dalai Lama says: "If you want others to be happy, practice compassion. If you want to be happy, practice compassion."

I close Part III of this book with the simple yet profound words of Shakespeare: "Action is eloquence."

# PART IV

# CONVERSING
# WITH YOUR
# SPIRITUAL
# SOURCE

*"The greater the power*
*that deigns to serve you,*
*the more honor it demands of you."*

— SOCRATES

# CHAPTER 14

# YOUR SPIRITUAL SOURCE CAN ONLY BE WHAT IT IS

*"I cannot imagine a God who rewards and punishes the objects of His creation, whose purposes are modeled after our own—a God, in short, who but is a reflection of human frailty."*

— ALBERT EINSTEIN

*"We are—because God is!"*

— EMANUEL SWEDENBORG

**IMAGINE A WAREHOUSE FILLED,** from floor to ceiling, with coconuts—and one of them believes and acts as if it were a raisin. "Raisin" hasn't a clue that it's a coconut, too, and the other coconuts haven't a clue that Raisin doesn't know it's a coconut. Get the picture? When Raisin wonders why it's all dried up and wrinkled, the coconuts don't respond, because they only see another coconut (albeit a crazy one). In order to get the warehouse coconuts to respond, the raisin will have to communicate as the coconut it really is. All coconuts, just like us, cannot be anything other than what they are.

If we continue our lighthearted coconut/raisin metaphor and apply it to our Creator, we can see that if we (and coconuts) can't be something we're not, then we need to avoid asking our Creator to be or talk as if It's something It's not. Please pay close attention to the words that follow. They're from *The Disappearance of the Universe* by Gary Renard (Hay House, 2004), a special-delivery agent of *A Course in Miracles:* "Because your idea is not of God, He does *not* respond to it. To respond to it would be to give it reality. If God Himself were to acknowledge anything *except* the idea of perfect oneness, then there would no longer *be* perfect oneness."

When we understand these words, it changes the way we approach God, Who can't and doesn't interact with ideas that are false. We can then begin to clarify our knowing that Spirit is true and ego is false by realizing that we must come to God in terms that are *of* God in our prayers and our discourses. We'll know that we need to put ego aside and make a new attempt to speak to our Source in terms of It. This can be a radical shift, especially if we've always approached prayer and making conscious contact with God from the perspective of ego.

### *Five Characteristics of God*

Let's now examine the elements that most of us agree define the essence of our Creator, along with how they can help us sensibly approach Him.

### 1. God Is Love

We came from love, and we desire to return to that heaven while still on Earth. I repeat Emerson's appropriate observation that "love is our highest word and the synonym for God"—in other words, if we dwell in love, we dwell in God. If God is love and cannot be anything other than what God is, and we wish to have a dialogue with Him, then it seems to me that we come to our Source in love or we're wasting our time. God cannot and will not respond to unloving requests.

Unloving prayers, which originate in arrogance, hatred, or fear, are the work of ego, so they won't be answered. In fact, they won't even be *heard.* God's message is to love all people, without exception, so we can be in vibrational harmony with Him. As the Bible reminds us, "[W]e are all members of one body" (Eph. 4:25) and "Let everything you do be done in love" (7 Cor. 16:14).

Now the way to approach God for guidance and help with anything in our life is to do so from the vantage point of forgiveness—for any and all we perceive to have wronged us, and for ourselves. Think about it: How can we expect God to hear our request for help in improving a relationship when we have hatred in our heart because of supposed misdeeds and maltreatment? God, Who only knows love, will have no idea what we're talking about.

No matter what our religion, whenever we want to discourse with our Source of Being, we must do so without malice or hatred in our heart. In this way, we'll shift our vibrational energy to a frequency that harmonizes with the highest vibration in the Universe, which, of course, is that of Spirit. As Saint Francis instructs so simply, "Where there is hatred, let [us] sow love."

Love and forgiveness will then activate the dormant forces I wrote about in the opening chapters of this book—that is, the right people and events will materialize synchronistically. This is because we're in-Spirit, remembering that God simply can't help if we expect Him to hear anything other than love and forgiveness. As Martin Luther King, Jr., once said: "We must develop and maintain the capacity to forgive. He who is devoid of the power to forgive is devoid of the power to love." This seems to say it all.

So in the private, quiet, prayerful moments of asking for God's help, don't ask Him to help defeat others in any way; rather, pray: "Dear God, make me an instrument of Thy love. I want to be like You. I have forgiven them, and I have forgiven myself." And remember that there can be no forgiveness without love—and without love, there can be no way of being heard by our Source.

## 2. God Is Peace

One of the most-quoted verses in the Old Testament (which may also be my favorite biblical offering) is this: "Be still, and know that I am God." So a corollary of this might then be: "Be agitated and turbulent, and you will never know God."

In order to communicate with our Source, it's vital to recall that *It can only be what It is.* And what It is, is peace and stillness. After all, creation doesn't take place in a violent manner—it's actually calm and peaceful. That is, movement from the invisible realm of Spirit into the material world of form isn't a loud, chaotic, explosive process—it's actually done with no fanfare at all. In the time it takes to read this chapter, millions upon millions of new life forms will emerge into this world, all without thunderclaps or fireworks. This is because peace is all that Spirit knows.

Now, if we approach God in a panic or with a frenzied, fearful, overly anxious demeanor, He's not going to help. You see, when we commune with our Source in a way that reflects an absence of peace, we'll have these nonpeaceful beliefs continually reinforced. By holding on to our panic, we'll believe even more in the disorder that our mind and body are accustomed to. Furthermore, we'll leave our prayerful state believing that our petitions aren't being answered, and very likely blame God for creating and allowing war and the other evils that define the world. Yet blaming God for the absence of peace is like the coconut who believes it's a raisin blaming the other coconuts for its wrinkled, dried-up life. The "raisin" is living an illusion, and so are we when we blame God for the absence of peace.

Along with praying or communing with our Source with peace in our heart, we must "be still." This means taking time to get quiet before meditating, and also monitoring our breathing. As we exhale, we can train ourselves to let go of all of our nonpeaceful thoughts, and as we inhale, we can breathe in Spirit.

We can also ask Saint Francis to guide us. He had very little peace in his lifetime, but when he prayed, he knew what his Source was like. Saint Francis wanted to be in-Spirit, so rather than asking

God to deliver him some peace so that he could escape the disorder and chaos he saw all around him, he'd request, "Lord, make me an instrument of thy peace." In other words, Saint Francis knew that God was peace, so in his prayer, he asked to be returned to a state where he'd be like his Creator.

We can keep reminding ourselves that all of the nonpeace that's in the world is not of God, it's of ego . . . then we can ask to be helped back to His peace. This approach will attract the assistance we're requesting—it's all about matching up the vibrational energy of our desire for peace with thoughts and behaviors that are consistently *peaceful* with those desires.

### 3. God Is All-Inclusive

We won't be heard by, or receive assistance from, our Source if we're touting our separateness from our fellow humans. You see, when we seek special individual favors from God, or even when we seek to converse with our Source from this perspective, we're once again living an illusion. If God were to acknowledge our belief in separation, as Gary Renard suggests, perfect oneness wouldn't and couldn't exist. It's impossible for a Source that creates everyone (and therefore is *in* everyone) to even have a dialogue with someone who's harboring ideas of their specialness or separation from everyone else.

We must be in a space of loving everyone—more than that, we've got to see ourselves as *connected to everyone*—in order to get the attention of our Source. So we've got to make every effort to avoid any thought that sets us apart from another being, such as a request to defeat someone, to have more than anyone else, to win a contest, to receive special attention on a job application, or to be considered first among many. These kinds of thoughts simply won't be recognized by a Source that's in all of the people we're asking to be given preferential treatment over.

Similarly, the great folly of war is the incredulous ignorance of the nature of God. When our politicians ask God to bless America, for instance, and to help us kill more of our "enemies" and win, it's analogous to having our body engage in a war in which our legs and lower torso are fighting against our arms and upper torso. Our body consists of all of its parts, so any war between them would surely kill the entire body. The body, just like God, can't process any talk of separation.

In conversing with our Source (as always), we strive to be more like It. So we need to see ourselves as connected to everyone in the Universe as we enter into prayer. Then we can ask for guidance and assistance in summoning that All-Inclusive Spirit: "Make me an instrument of You. Allow me to see You in everyone I encounter. Help me to see myself in others and to extend first to them what I aspire to myself. I've noticed that this is how You are, and I wish to be just like You."

This is the kind of dialogue that activates the dormant forces I've spoken of. The key is getting past our ego-based idea of separation and instead seeing ourselves a part of the oneness of all. As Thomas Aquinas put it so succinctly: "True peace consists in not separating ourselves from the will of God."

### 4. God Is Abundance

Picture this: A group of one-gallon containers has the capacity to speak to each other. One of them wants to discuss its emptiness with one that's always known fullness. "Full Gallon" probably won't be able to relate to the quandary of "Empty Gallon," since no matter how much Empty Gallon experiences lack, Full Gallon won't be able to understand because it can't be anything other than what it is.

While this is a crude example, it nevertheless illustrates our predicament when we attempt to engage in a discourse with God, a Source that's only known abundance, and ask it to relate to and correct our perceived shortages. Trust me, God knows nothing of lack, and there's enough of everything to go around. All of God's gifts, including life itself, are given as freely and abundantly as oxygen, sunlight, and water.

As Saint Paul once said: "God is able to provide you with every blessing in abundance." So why is there so much apparent shortage in the world, including people starving and living in poverty, and millions of folks having the persistent problem of too much month left at the end of the money? Well, what I can say for certain is that God is not to blame—there's more than enough to go around. After all, we came from a place that knows nothing of deprivation, and we arrived on a planet that has the capacity to grow the food and slake the thirst of every one of its inhabitants many times over.

As a species, we human beings have brought the ideas of deficiencies and depletions of God's gifts on ourselves, largely by taking very un-God-like actions. God serves all of us, but our greed has made us forget others and focus only on ourselves. As a people and as individuals, we've brought lack to our lives, and we can only fix this deficiency by becoming more like our Always-Serving, Endlessly Abundant Spiritual Source.

The answers to the resolution of poverty and scarcity are readily available to us, and they'd be resolved tomorrow if we remembered that we're all *one* on this planet: We all share the same origins, and we all end up back in the same nonplace where we began. When we return to Spirit in our heart, our governments will align with this truth, and our leaders will emerge from in-Spirit consciousness.

We need to pray for the elimination of a perceived shortage and approach God in the style of Saint Francis with words that go something like, "Make me an instrument of Thy endless abundance," rather than asking God to fulfill something that's missing. In this way we can summon His energy back to us, rather than staying focused on what we don't have. If we focus our thoughts on lack, we'll only attract more of the same.

We need to start seeing ourselves as a vibrational match to the frequency of God's abundance. If our desire is to attract wealth and prosperity, then we must entertain prosperous thoughts that match our desire and that activate the manifestation process. And the dormant forces of abundance will come to life to help fulfill these desires.

## 5. God Is Well-Being

Spirit never has a fever and knows nothing of illness, so in my humble opinion, it makes no sense to pray or engage in a discourse with God from a perspective of asking to be healed—unless, that is, we have a firm understanding of what we mean by the word *heal*. If we mean "to overcome an illness or infirmity," then I feel that we're again violating the truism that nothing can be what it isn't, including God. As Ernest Holmes once wrote: "The will of God is always good," which means to me that disease, sickness, and suffering are not part of God's energy.

On the other hand, if we use the word *heal* to mean "reconnecting to our Source of Well-Being," then we're open to the potential of receiving assistance to overcome any infirmity. And that's how *I* use the word. I never ask God to help me get over a feeling of sickness. Even when I had a minor heart attack five years ago, I asked to be made an instrument of God's well-being. I acknowledged that my body had taken on non-well-being, be it from my lifestyle, diet, and habits; or the toxins I breathe in and out—whatever—it was not of God. It was of me in this physical world, and I prayed to be reunited to a stream of well-being. I knew that I was a piece of God, and that it was just as easy for Him to heal a cut on my finger as it was to restore my heart to a healthy state. Since I knew that God's healing power was within me, I just needed to help my body remember this.

Similarly, in a time of recent disharmony in my life, I found myself feeling sick to my stomach and unable to sleep—until I remembered that this experience was a gift to me. As I conversed with my Higher Power, I asked for guidance and visualized myself as a magnet, attracting plentiful well-being. And in this way, healing was virtually immediate.

In *The Amazing Laws of Cosmic Mind Power*, Joseph Murphy offers this magnificent advice on conversing with God when we're seeking to be healed:

Know that God loves you and cares for you. As you pray this way, the fear gradually will fade away. If you pray about a heart condition, do not think of the organ as diseased, as this would not be spiritual thinking. To think of a damaged heart or high blood pressure tends to suggest more of what you already have. Cease dwelling on symptoms, organs, or any part of the body. Turn your mind to God and His love. Feel and know that there is only one healing presence and power. . . . Quietly and lovingly affirm that the uplifting, healing, strengthening power of the healing presence is flowing through you, making you every whit whole. Know and feel that the harmony, beauty, and life of God manifest themselves in you as strength, peace, vitality, wholeness, and right action. Get a clear realization of this, and the damaged heart or other diseased organ will be cured in the light of God's love.

These words bear reading repeatedly . . . especially when you take into consideration that my damaged heart of five years ago is now completely healed.

## Some Suggestions for Putting the Ideas in This Chapter to Work for You

— Before beginning any prayerful activity, make a note to keep in mind precisely what your Source is and is not. Ask yourself, "Am I asking God to be something that He is not? Am I expecting my Spiritual Creator to join me in my ego, which has truly edged God out?" This will allow you to stay focused on clearing the channel between you and Spirit, rather than putting out requests to a Source that can't relate to your ego-driven world. Remember, it's you who has left God, not the other way around.

— Begin all your conversations with Spirit with, "Make me an instrument of . . ." Then add "love," "peace," "joy," "kindness,"

THE ESSENTIAL WAYNE DYER COLLECTION

"abundance," "well-being," or any other quality that you know in your heart defines the essence of the Holy Spirit.

— As you put forgiveness to work in your life, study the ideas expressed in the two following observations:

*"If we could read the secret history of our enemies,*
*we should find in each man's life sorrow and suffering*
*enough to disarm all hostility."*

— HENRY WADSWORTH LONGFELLOW

*"Tolerance comes of age.*
*I see no fault committed that I myself could not*
*have committed at some time or other."*

— JOHANN WOLFGANG VON GOETHE

Assimilating these thoughts will help you to practice forgiveness. We all have times in our life when we totally understand the common phrase "there but for the grace of God go I." Attempt to be that grace of God, and extend it to all you believe have wronged you.

— Make it a daily practice to meditate for peace—yours *and* the world's. By going within, you can make conscious contact with God. Then your Spirit energy will radiate to those around you, and to those on the other side of the world as well!

— Remember that the healing power of God is within you. That same power, which made your body, knows how to restore it to its original state of well-being. All you have to do is remove all of the obstacles erected by you and our toxic world, and allow this healing power to flow through you.

\* \* \*

Before we go on to the next chapter, let's go back to the observation made by Emanuel Swedenborg, "We are—because God is!" and add, "Not because of what God isn't."

CHAPTER 15

# YOUR SPIRITUAL
# SOURCE KNOWS

*"It is true that Divine will prevails at all times
and under all circumstances. . . . There is no need
to tell God your requirements. He knows them Himself
and will look after them . . ."*

— RAMANA MAHARSHI

*"The thing we surrender to becomes our power."*

— ERNEST HOLMES

**AS THE FATHER OF EIGHT CHILDREN,** it goes without
saying that I've witnessed many occasions when a two-year-old
made a request that couldn't be accommodated. Often the request became a standoff, with the toddler crying, insisting, and
even throwing a tantrum—but since I was the adult, I'd stand
firm and refuse to grant the child's wishes. Running around
the block unsupervised, racing through the house with a sucker
sticking out of his or her mouth, playing with electrical sockets,
climbing up the stairs alone, and putting his or her fingers in a
younger sibling's eyes were some of the behaviors forbidden by
me, the parent, who simply knew better.

If we put ourselves in the place of toddlers and give our Creator
the very same leeway that we, as parents, took with our children,
the purpose of this metaphor becomes perfectly clear. Just as it's
absurd for a two-year-old to insist on having his or her way, our

Creative Spirit doesn't need to be reminded of what to do for us or how to go about doing it—It already knows. In fact, there's a wonderfully enlightening quote in the Bhagavad Gita that says: "Only the fool whose mind is deluded by egotism considers himself to be the doer . . ."

When we're about to enter into a discourse with our Creator, it's crucial to approach with the understanding that we aren't the doer. It may sound a bit extreme, but this is how Immanuel Kant described our situation: "God is our owner, we are His property; His providence works for our good." (Please don't take the word *owner* as an insult—it's only the ego that's offended by this concept.) In other words, we needn't presume to tell our Source what needs to be done to provide us with a happy, fulfilling life. Instead, it's our job to change our thinking so that it's vibrating to a frequency that matches God's energy. And this begins by understanding that it's impossible for God to forget *anything*. Unlike human parents, God is omnipotent, so it's unnecessary to remind Him of our needs.

### Our Creative Source Never Forgets

When I lived in New York, I had a cat named Schlum. Every October and November I noticed that his coat would get thicker in preparation for the coming winter months—even though the current temperatures might be mild or even warm, Schlum's fur would be in the process of changing. I remember thinking about this fact and being in awe of the great Source of All Creation. There must be millions of cats, dogs, beavers, rabbits, rats, horses, and other fur-bearing animals living in the Northern Hemisphere who go through the same process every year—and our Source never forgets a single one of them.

One August when I visited a dingo farm in Brisbane, Australia, I was told that the wild dogs were shedding their coats for the upcoming spring. *Spring after August?* I thought, before remembering that the seasons follow opposite patterns in the Southern Hemisphere.

Wondering if this would be confusing to God, I asked the farm's curator what would happen if a dingo was shipped on an airplane to New York in August—would its coat go from thinning to thickening, since winter would now be following summer?

"Happens all the time," the curator said. "We fly them up there, and when they arrive, their coats start to thicken up." Amazing, isn't it? Now, if God remembers to adjust the coat on a dingo flying on a 747 from Australia to New York, surely He doesn't forget us!

All of our life experiences—the struggles, the falls, the victories, the lessons, the emerging talents, all of it—is orchestrated by our Source. Be mindful of this fact: Whatever we decided upon with our Creator in advance of our manifestation into form is playing out right now. We must strive to always consciously remember that God hasn't forgotten us—even though we may have edged God out—because He *can't* forget us.

Just as all that composes decomposes, our infinite self is only here for a few moments in eternity. But even though we're on loan for this temporary human experience, we're never ever forgotten by God, the Source that provides us and everything else that lives and breathes with the energy to sustain life. So we need to continually trust that the organizing intelligence of our Source, which is always operating in the Universe, is ever-mindful, and provides us with every blessing in abundance.

### *Trusting and Surrendering*

Now how do we trust a Source that we can't see or touch? Well, we can start by noticing the results that we attribute to It and tell ourselves, "Someone or Something is responsible for all of the ongoing infinite creation that I witness with my senses, and I'm going to trust in It from now on." This is the kind of logic that I hope I've been conveying throughout the pages of this book—that it's possible to reconnect with where we came from, and where we came from isn't physical (as our quantum scientists now inform us). But rather than using blind trust or my attempts at logic to trust in the existence and the assistance of Spirit, I suggest that we ultimately each use our own life experience for our "trust barometer."

Returning to the analogy at the beginning of this chapter, most children are free-spirited little beings who don't think about questioning their parents' judgment. After all, mothers and fathers tend to know what's in their offspring's best interest, including what's required for successful survival. These senior partners look out for their kids' needs and direct their early life activities—and they do this as long as is necessary, which is usually until their children begin to develop the ability to trust their own instincts and apply what they've learned.

As adults, we can look back on our earliest days with a strong sense of appreciation: We learned not to play in traffic, to avoid eating poisonous foods, to get enough rest each day, and so on. Today we feel thankful and appreciative that our parents were there to guide us toward the responsible, self-contained people we are now—we can appreciate that they did what was best for us, and they never forgot us.

I trust that the analogy is clear: Our relationship with God, our All-Knowing, Never-Forgetting Senior Partner, is just like our childhood relationship with our parents. Just as we did with our mothers and fathers, we're now choosing to trust in the wisdom of our Creator. In other words, we don't need to be told by virtual parents what's best for us, and we don't have to rely on so-called religious superiors to keep us in line because we're no longer needy little infants. We now trust our Source because we've matured to a point where doubt has been supplanted by faith. Somewhere between childhood and maturity, we surrendered and trusted our parents, just as we're now surrendering and trusting the All-Knowing, Loving Source of Creation.

## Surrender in Southeast Asia

By beginning the process of turning our life over to a Higher Power and staying connected to Spirit in inspired living, we become more observant and less attached to our ego-driven beliefs and attitudes. A lifesaving example of this came out of the devastating tsunami of 2004, in which 305,000 people either died or were reported missing. This gigantic tidal wave affected people in Indonesia, Southeast Asia, and even as far away as the shores of Africa.

Months after this tragedy, reports came of a nomadic tribe of people who lived on the water, traveling back and forth between a series of remote islands off the coast of Thailand. Their villages and boats had been destroyed, yet they suffered not a single casualty—it seemed like a miracle!

It turned out that these people had a history of orally passing down the wisdom they'd gained while living on boats and on secluded islands that were far removed from modern civilization. They'd lived on the water all of their lives, as had hundreds of generations of their ancestors. Because they lived so closely with nature, they knew the water and how to catch fish with crude wooden spears, but mostly they stayed connected to Spirit. And they relayed what they learned from generation to generation.

Tribal elders had passed down stories of tsunamis in ancient times, so when one of them noticed a sign of the shifting water patterns in 2004, he immediately knew what was coming. As the beneficiary of ancient knowing, he alerted everyone on the boats and in the villages to move to higher ground immediately. No one doubted his wisdom—everyone, without exception, left their boats and villages and moved to higher land. When the tsunami hit, it destroyed every boat and home, yet the entire tribe safely watched from a distance as the water did what they knew it was about to do.

I believe that these nomadic people survived because they lived lives defined by being in-Spirit—there were no words indicating ego consciousness in their language. They lived in God-realization, grateful for all that they were given; consequently, they were able to join in God's knowing and make it their own. I suggest that we can do the same, even while living in a world where so many have chosen to be in-ego rather than in-Spirit.

Just as the tribe in Southeast Asia surrendered to their Spiritual Source and permitted ego to stay out of the picture, we too can become more observant and aware of what we need to do when we're in-Spirit. We just need to stop believing that we're the doer, and instead learn to listen to and trust our inner intuition— which, of course, is guiding us in collaboration with the creative power of the Universe.

### Communing with the All-Knowing

Imagine a camera that can accomplish photographic feats that no camera has performed prior to this time. For instance, it can take pictures through concrete walls, or in the dark without benefit of a flash. But most ingeniously, it can record a person's thoughts, producing an exact pictorial likeness of what any subject is imagining at the moment the shutter snaps. And inside the camera's package is an invitation to talk with the creator of this remarkable device. The printed material states that he'll be happy to discuss how and why his invention works, along with the amazing results that it can produce.

The conversation we'd have with the creator of our new miracle gadget probably wouldn't begin with the things we thought he'd forgotten or should or shouldn't have done. And it's unlikely that we'd complain about the price or how it was marketed, or attempt to convince him that we had more expertise. Instead, we'd probably use the opportunity to maximize our ability to work with our new camera and derive the greatest pleasure possible as it performed the tasks it was designed to accomplish.

It's safe to say that we'd approach the creator of something we can see, touch, and use—but haven't a clue as to how it came into being—with deference, respect, and awe because we'd be so eager to absorb all that he has to offer. If this analogy is unclear, you might want to quit reading at this point and seek an expert to re-move your blinders! Clearly, I believe that we should approach our Creative Source with openness, and the willingness to maximize our ability to be in-Spirit.

When we finally "get" that our Source is all-knowing, we can approach the act of spiritual communication from an entirely egoless perspective. Our discourse must begin with a recognition that it's impossible for us to be ignored. We can link up to all-knowingness by thinking like God—that is, by being an energetic match in our thoughts and actions, by being grateful, and by thinking of others and offering them what we desire.

Since we know that when we ask, it is given, we must next ask God for what we want. I'm not implying that we should beg, or think that we've been overlooked, but rather ask in a way that takes the form of a vibrational shift in energy. So we'd request to be an instrument of God's abundance, for instance, instead of pleading for cash. We'd simply match what we want with the All-Encompassing Abundance that is our Spiritual Source.

Note that any- and everything that keeps us from appreciating our Spiritual Source is an impediment. This particularly includes relying on someone else or some organization without examining the truths that they insist we believe. While this may come as a surprise, Jesus wasn't a Christian, Buddha wasn't a Buddhist, and Mohammed wasn't a Muslim. These were Divine spiritual beings who came here as emissaries of truth . . . yet when their truths were organized, we saw the horrors of inquisitions, mass murders, crusades, holy wars, and jihads, all in the name of "God."

Those who claim to represent these Divine beings of truth fre-quently do so from a decidedly nonspiritual perspective. When an organization includes some, yet excludes others, they're announc-ing that they're not actually preaching or teaching truth. Since God excludes no one, any religious organization that does isn't affiliated with Him. God is all-knowing. *No one else is,* unless they experience pure God-realization . . . and those beings who have ever lived among us belong to a very small club.

No one else can intervene for us in our efforts to commune

with our Source of Being: We shouldn't rely on organizations, gurus, rituals, temples, or any other outside sources as the means to make conscious contact with God. Instead, we must approach the All-Knowing Source in silent communion, and be willing to listen and receive guidance. We must speak in words of our own choosing with statements that tell God: "I know that You are all-knowing and could never forget me. I desire to align with Your all-knowingness, to have the faith that I can attract into my life all the goodness, peace, and abundance that You are. I will stay in this place of trust, for I am here to serve. I am grateful for all that You are, and all that You allow me to be."

### *Co-creating with Spirit*

Keep in mind that we can't co-create with anyone, including our Spiritual Source, unless we're in a place of harmony. To that end, we must suspend our false self (ego) and stop all thoughts of resistance before we can participate in creating the inspired life we desire, in perfect symmetry with Spirit. Whatever we ask of our Source in our prayerful communion will no longer be a wish or a hope—it will become a reality in our mind, just as it is in the mind of God. The how and when of its arrival, which have always troubled ego, are no longer issues.

We maintain our optimism with thoughts such as *I desire it, It's in harmony with my Source,* or *It's on its way—there's nothing to fuss about.* And then we can relax and surrender to our knowing. As Ernest Holmes reminds us: "The thing we surrender to becomes our power." I know that the term *surrender* is generally associated with defeat, but there's no victor or victim when surrendering to God—this isn't about winning or losing.

You see, what we're doing here is giving up our false self in favor of returning to our authentic one. And when we do, we'll meet our Spiritual Creator and become empowered to live in the same vibration with It. We'll become co-creators by surrendering and joining the All-Knowing, All-Creating Force that allows everything to come into existence. Then our knowing replaces our doubts, and "Divine will prevails at all times." Only now, *we* are in harmony with that Divine will.

## Some Suggestions for Putting the Ideas in This Chapter to Work for You

— Put some of the well-known words of the recovery movement to practical use in your life. *Let go and let God* is a wonderful phrase to repeat to yourself when you feel under pressure, overly taxed, frustrated, or just plain angry. By saying these words, you'll free yourself to allow the only real Doer there is to take over, and you'll become an observer rather than feeling the futility of trying to control things. Try it now. Let go and let God . . . relax into the awareness that you have an All-Knowing Partner. Now what's there to worry about?

— When you begin to question God's omniscience, banish that doubt from your mind. Shakespeare reminds us that "Our doubts are traitors / And make us lose the good we oft might win / By fearing to attempt." Notice that he says "lose the good," which is another way of saying "lose the *connection to God*." In other words, your doubts keep you from joining in God's knowing. Think about it: How can you know and doubt at the same time?

God knows, and you want to be like Him in order to be inspired. So when you communicate with God, do so from your own knowing that He is there, listening and ready to spring into action with you.

— When you pray or otherwise communicate with your Creative Spirit, don't assume that just because It's all-knowing, It's going to handle every problem for you. Remind yourself that you're a co-creator, and you have the free will to choose to either be or not be consciously connected to that Creative Spirit. When you consciously surrender to the *co* in co-creator, it will assist you in a zillion mysterious ways.

— Here's a suggestion from one of our great commonsense ancestors, Mark Twain: "Keep away from people who try to belittle your ambitions. Small people always do that, but the really great make you feel that you, too, can become great." Your ambitions are of God, so as you communicate with Him, ask for the strength to ignore those around you who'd malign or otherwise disparage what you and your Source have placed in your heart.

— Remind yourself as frequently as you can that to surrender is a sign of enlightenment and strength. What you're surrendering to is responsible for all of creation—it's to this omniscience and omnipotence that you're surrendering, and it's here that you'll gain your power to live an inspired life.

* * *

Many years ago I copied down this observation by the brilliant Ramesh Balsekar, an enlightened scholar. I still ponder this frequently, and I feel that it concisely sums up what I've written about in this chapter: "Most of the near-perfect actions or performances, and almost all the works of creativity, happen in this state of egolessness, when the tenet 'Thy will be Done' is actually put into practice."

As you pray to the All-Knowing Source, it only makes sense to close your communion with these four words: *Thy will be done.* But keep in mind that *Thy will* also includes you.

CHAPTER 16

# IT'S ALL ABOUT REMEMBERING

*"The memory of God comes to the quiet mind.*
*It cannot come where there is conflict; for a mind*
*at war against itself remembers not eternal gentleness. . . .*
*What you remember is a part of you. For you must be as*
*God created you. . . . Let all this madness be undone for you,*
*and turn in peace to the remembrance of God,*
*still shining in your quiet mind."*

— FROM *A COURSE IN MIRACLES*

**I HOPE YOU'VE GATHERED BY NOW** that becoming inspired isn't achieved by attending workshops, learning new techniques, or by following a master teacher—it can only be accomplished by returning to Spirit, or going back to a place where we experienced bliss. After 15 chapters emphasizing this point, there shouldn't be any doubt that we originated in love and peace from a spiritual Creator.

This chapter is going to focus on our communication with God from a perspective of remembering Him, rather than trying to befriend some spiritual presence we don't know. That is, we need to tune our prayers and discourses to help us recall who we really are and what it was like before we came to this physical world.

Most of us will probably find it difficult or even impossible to recollect what we abandoned so long ago when we adopted ego as our self-definition. But this picture of eight-month-old Tysen Humble (one of my grandchildren) in a bathtub has to inspire anyone looking at it to see the relevance of remembering.

What a joyous creature in rapturous harmony with life! Tysen's expression reveals pure and complete bliss, and just looking at him is enough to make us smile—especially when we think about what *we* surely must have felt when we were his age.

This beautiful baby also communicates something to us about ourselves: As we remember our Spirit, we want to keep in mind Tysen's state of jubilation and absolute contentment. It isn't just a smile and a burst of laughter that's responsible for that blissful expression on my little grandson's face—there's an invisible force coming through what we see in the photo, and that's what we want to return to. If we could see our Spiritual Source with our eyes, we'd witness pure joy, ecstasy, happiness, and peace—the photo you see on the previous page is a personification of that. It's also important to note that we emerged from the same vibrational energy as Tysen, and we had the same inner sensation that's unmistakably evident on that baby's face. It's denied to no one.

If we train ourselves, we can recall feeling the bliss that's on my grandson's face and which inspires his entire persona. *Everything* we've ever experienced is still stored as an invisible memory, and we can access it if we choose. For example, when my grandmother was close to death and doing what some called "involuntary hallucinating," she was pulling out all kinds of facts from her earliest days. Street addresses; the names of neighbors; locations of family outings; relationships with friends of her own mother, who were only there in my grandmother's infancy—all of it was somehow available to her. It turned out that in some mysterious way, Grandma was tapping in to memories that everyone else thought couldn't possibly be recalled because she was only a baby at the time.

I have no idea how she did this—all I know for certain is that we reach into our own personal history and bring to the present thoughts that impact our state of mind as well as our level of inspiration. You see, the mere recollection of something in the past that we call a memory is capable of affecting us either positively or negatively in the present moment; therefore, they're extremely powerful tools for our current state of mind. Obviously there are some negative memories lurking around somewhere in the nethermost regions of our mind, but why access them if they're going to cause us to feel uninspired? Instead, let's think about how to get back to that delirious happiness that's portrayed by the gleeful Tysen, who's only a few months removed from 100 percent immersion in the rhapsodic arms of his original Creator.

What I'm trying to make clear here is that we've got to figure out how to return to where we came from in order to commune with our Spiritual Creator. Therefore, being inspired itself is going to require us to go back and do some major remembering.

### *Remembering Your Spirit*

At the beginning of this chapter, there's a powerful quotation from *A Course in Miracles* that I feel sums up all we need to know to facilitate going "all the way back"—that is, prior to our baby days, our birth, and even our conception. It's about remembering our origination. I committed this passage to memory many years ago, and I use it as a way to remember who I truly am and where I really came from, particularly when I communicate with my Creator to stay on purpose and in-Spirit.

Now I'd like to go through each of the messages in this observation from the *Course* one by one:

**1. "The memory of God comes to the quiet mind."** We came from a quiet, peaceful place that's the very essence of creation, so when our mind is filled with noisy dialogue, we shut out the possibility of remembering our Spirit. Incessant chatter keeps us attached to the physical world and produces anxiety, stress, fear, worry, and so many of the emotional reactions that are decidedly removed from God-realization.

A quiet mind is open to recall because it allows us to open a space within ourselves where we experience a sensation of familiarity with Spirit. Intuition sharpens, we access higher energy, and what we thought of as information about God is supplemented with an unmistakable remembrance. Knowing *about* God is very different from actually knowing God—so a quiet, disciplined mind is needed to be able to remember, and consequently return to, a state of being in-Spirit.

We must minimize distractions when we wish to communicate with God, so being in nature, away from the artificial noises that invade our space, is helpful. But the most important thing to consider is how to keep our mind free from the dizzying, bewildering cascade of thoughts flowing through our head from morning till night, and even on into our dream state. It's been estimated that we have something like 60,000 separate thoughts every day.

The real problem is that we have the *same* 60,000 thoughts today that we had yesterday!

I've made the practice of meditation a part of my daily life because it's one way to quiet the mind so that the memory of God is accessible. So by learning to meditate—or at the very least shutting down the inner dialogue produced, directed, and acted upon by your ego—you can open up a space for remembering and returning to Spirit.

**2. "It cannot come where there is conflict . . ."** In order for conflict to exist, there must be two opposing forces at work; that is, one force—in the form of an idea, a point of view, a desire, or a contribution—directly clashes with another. Conflict defines our lives in many ways, as we oppose our partners, our children, our bosses, our neighbors, and even our countries. In politics, it's always one party versus the other, and the entertainment industry portrays battling points of view that are usually turned into violent scenes. Essentially, conflict requires "two-ness."

However, remembering where we came from involves our returning to the oneness of being in-Spirit. After all, there are no battling powers in the Divine realm of Spirit—there's only perfect oneness, and this is what we want to rejoin. We want to become one again with our Creator, and we can't retrieve this "memory of God" with a mind in conflict in any way.

Imagining oneness is often a difficult process because we're so steeped in our beliefs of two-ness and dichotomies. If God (Who is perfect oneness) was able to acknowledge our beliefs in conflicts and two-ness, then oneness simply could not exist. So we need to leave all conflict out of the picture to succeed in remembering God and achieving oneness. In our mind's eye, this is done by picturing ourselves fully integrated with our Source. Visualizing melting into the oneness of God will lead to a sense of merging until we can no longer make a distinction between ourselves and Him. And this consolidated state is where our memories of God become luminous and unobscured.

**3. ". . . for a mind at war against itself remembers not eternal gentleness."** Conflicting thoughts tend to fill our consciousness with never-ending chatter, including plans for retaliation against those people we label as the source of our discontent. It's not at all uncommon to conduct an imaginary dialogue that goes something like this: "First I'll say this to her. Then when I say that, she's going to respond with this. But she always says that, even though I know she's lying. So this time I'll trip her up by responding this way. She'll have to agree that I'm right—but she never does. I know that I'm right, and I'm going to force her to admit it. I'll tell her that even her own mother agrees with me. . . ." This could go on all day and night, and it frequently does. We conduct this inner combat over and over again—and the only advantage is that we almost always win the argument being waged because it exists only in our mind.

The second part of this teaching from the *Course* reinforces that a combative mind cannot remember where it once resided in eternal gentleness. Obviously you can't wage war and simultaneously focus on peace and gentleness, and it is eternal gentleness that you want to remember and rejoin. It's really quite simple to do this: Just close down the battlefield and surrender. Remove all of the artillery, send the soldiers home, and replace the instruments of war in your mind with thoughts of peace, tranquility, and surrender. Making your mind a place of peace is achieved by your own will, so steadfastly refusing to have thoughts of conflict allows you to activate the glory of remembering your Spirit.

I can recall times in my life when I've cluttered up my mind with that back-and-forth inner dialogue with my children or my wife. I'd literally get to a point of exhaustion by silently repeating my side to their side and back again, until one day I made the decision to abandon this battleground in my head. I began to practice putting the word *cancel* up on my inner screen, and I'd stubbornly refuse to go through those senseless sparring matches in my own mind. After a few days of practice, it became my automatic response to go to eternal gentleness—and peace and Divine guidance were my rewards.

**4. "What *you* remember *is* a part of you."** Every memory I have is me . . . what a glorious feeling it is to know this! We each have the power to retrieve any piece of ourselves that we desire, and to experience it right here, right now, in this present moment. The great Danish theologian Søren Kierkegaard once observed that "life can only be understood backwards, but . . . it must be lived forward." In other words, if we can't go back and remember the spiritual bliss that defined us before the beginning, we've abandoned a part of ourselves.

As we move into communion with God, we must know that our inability to remember our spiritual origins is another way of saying, "I'm unable to know myself because I have no recollection or memory of my Spirit." In fact, the corollary of this line from *A Course in Miracles* that we're processing right now would be, "What you *don't* remember is *not* a part of you." In other words, if we fail to remember Spirit, then obviously it isn't a part of us.

The most effective thing we can do to remember our Source is to affirm unhesitatingly: *I'm first and foremost an eternal spiritual being—I can't be anything but this. I will never doubt it, and I can go within and try to be like God in all of my thoughts and actions.*

When we begin this inspirational practice, the memory of our spiritual origins will emerge from behind the clouds and become unquestionably clear.

**5. "For you must be as God created you."** I've made the following point repeatedly throughout the pages of this book: *We must be what we came from.* Just like that droplet of blood must be like the rest of our blood supply because that's what it came from, we must be of God because that's what we came from. It's only by edging God out that we've come to believe that we are our false self.

As you communicate with your Source of Being, know that you're awakening a part of yourself that's just like God. In fact, you ought to try to approach communication with God by being as closely aligned to the way that you were created as possible—that is, by becoming a vibrational match to the All-Loving Creator. Come to the quiet moments in consultation with God in love, in peace, and without judgment. As the *Course* is saying, you must be as you were created—so why put on a false mask and pretend to be anything or anyone else? In this way, you can open the channel of communication because you've finally remembered to be the way you were created—and that's the key to effective prayer. And, as Gandhi once said: "Prayer is not an old woman's idle amusement. Properly understood and applied, it is the most potent instrument of action."

**6. "Let all this madness be undone for you, and turn in peace to the remembrance of God, still shining in your quiet mind."** Let's take the three suggestions in this teaching one at a time.

— First, the *Course* says to "let all this madness be undone." The madness here is that of living in a state of conflict. In other words, we must make an attempt to transcend the dichotomies of our life because the division creates so much suffering and keeps us from living an inspired life. I remember a Ram Dass lecture in which he said, "I've firmly come to the conclusion that there are no 'thems' for me anymore. I can't be told who to hate, who to fight, who to subdue—I only see an 'us' in my heart."

All those messages to divvy up our world are insane. All our self-centeredness just drives our ego's insatiable appetite for making us special and putting other people down. All our inclinations toward violence—even when it's "acceptable," such as supporting war in the name of patriotism or endorsing hatred in the name of doing our duty—are wrong. The *Course* encourages us to be done with this madness once and for all, both in our mind and in our actions.

— Second, we're told to "turn in peace to the remembrance of God." Once again, we know in our heart that we came from a place of peace, so any discord can't be the result of our Creator's actions. God cannot come to us when we pray from nonpeace, so the solution is to return to the remembrance of Him and ask to be made an instrument of His peace. When I find myself out of sorts, I remember. And what I remember is to turn to peace right now in prayer. I become peace, rather than anguish, and I feel the calmness I long for come over me like a wave of pleasurable relief.

We always have the power within us to shift into a peaceful mode. And when we respect someone, we're able to be in peace in their presence by suspending our inclination to be arrogant. For example, I recall watching John McEnroe behave in boorish ways on the tennis court, slamming his racquet, hurling profanities at the referees, and generally being in a very nonpeaceful state— but he never behaved this way when he played his rival, Björn Borg. Amazingly, McEnroe was almost always able to control his outbursts of negativity whenever he played this cool, easygoing, nonviolent, brilliant tennis player. Because he respected Borg so much, McEnroe came to his presence in peace.

— Finally, the *Course* reminds us that this peaceful remembrance is "still shining in [our] quiet mind." Notice the words *still* and *quiet*—regardless of where we are in life, if we're breathing we're connected to our Source of Being, even though the connection might have gotten a bit corroded. We still have the remembrance of God shining inside of us . . . it can't be otherwise. Our job is to access those memories, and it will help if we keep them in our *quiet* mind. This remembrance doesn't shine in our ego mind, our noisy mind, in our self-important mind; rather, it shines in a quiet, nonviolent, peaceful, loving mind. When we go to the quietness, that shining is a luminous reminder of how to approach our Creative Spirit by remembering.

One of my favorite teachers is the Russian mystic Leo Tolstoy. In his powerful book *The Kingdom of God Is Within You,* I was struck by the words he used to implore his 19th-century readers to heed nonviolence in their war-torn country:

> If you believe that Christ forbade murder, pay no heed to the arguments nor to the commands of those who call on you to bear a hand in it. By such a steadfast refusal to make use of force, you call down on yourselves the blessing promised to those "who hear these sayings and do them," and the time will come when the world will recognize you as having aided in the reformation of mankind.

What Tolstoy is saying is that it is incumbent upon all of us to return to the peace from whence we came. We must refuse to use force, especially in our thoughts—and above all, we must remember our Spirit.

## Some Suggestions for Putting the Ideas in This Chapter to Work for You

— Find a picture of yourself as a very young child in which you were lost in your bliss. Place that photo in a conspicuous spot and let it serve to remind you that the same Spirit you're expressing in the photograph is alive and well within you right now, and that you're going to remember it and consort with it every day.

— Train your memory. By doing so, you'll be able to return to early childhood memories of love, peace, and joy—and back even further to your spiritual origination. Recapturing early events in your life will help you discover that you have more access to your past and your spiritual beginnings than you might have believed. It's all in there, so discipline yourself to become a retriever.

— Pray in solitude. Make peace with silence and remind yourself that it's there that you'll come to remember your Spirit. As Blaise Pascal, the great French scientist and philosopher, once remarked, "All man's miseries derive from not being able to sit quietly in a room alone." When you're able to transcend an aversion to silence, you'll also transcend many other miseries. And it's in this silence that the remembrance of God will be activated.

— Vow to have fewer conflicts in your life. It is your objective in reading this book to become inspired—therefore, you'll want to bring a halt to your feeling that conflict is normal and unavoidable. You came from no conflict, and you can return to that heaven right here on Earth by refusing to have your inner world conflicted by anyone at anytime. Affirm it over and over: *I do not attract conflict to myself.*

— Try this visualization that I replicate here from *The Book of Runes:*

> *Visualize yourself standing before a gateway on a hilltop. Your entire life lies out behind you and below. Before you step through the gateway, pause and review the past: the learning and the joys, the victories and the sorrows—everything it took to bring you here.*

By doing this exercise, you'll be practicing the virtue of re-membering, and it will almost force you to return to Spirit!

✳ ✳ ✳

You don't have to learn a single new thing in order to communicate and make conscious contact with your Source—it's all in you already. All you have to do is remember. . . .

CHAPTER 17

# THE LANGUAGE
# OF SPIRIT

*"When asked where God is, people point towards the sky
or some far and distant region; no wonder then that
He does not manifest Himself! Realize that He is in
you, with you, behind you, and all around you;
and He can be seen and felt everywhere."*

— SATHYA SAI BABA

**IN THE PREVIOUS THREE CHAPTERS** I've tried to stress
that it's our job to take responsibility for opening the channel to
communication to God, rather than viewing Him as a "cosmic
bellboy" whose job it is to listen to our whims and respond just
because we asked. But how can we recognize when our Spiritual
Source is getting in touch with *us?*

Spirit's messages are not necessarily going to be in our native
tongue, since It is in no way restricted by words (either written
or spoken) as the exclusive means for communicating with us.
Remember, the world of Spirit contains the highest and fastest
energy in the Universe—it vibrates so quickly that it manifests the
invisible into particles and then into the forms that we see, touch,
taste, hear, and smell with our senses. All It needs is to activate the
immensely mysterious power of creation and send us guidelines
and assistance via its high-energy vibrations.

As Jesus said in one of my favorite quotes (which I've shared thousands of times in my life): "With man this is impossible, but with God all things are possible" (Matt. 19:26). I'd like you to read through the ideas I'm offering here concerning the language of Spirit with this quote in mind. As weird as some of the communication patterns I talk about may seem, and as much as your ego may be tempted to dismiss them as mere coincidences and devoid of meaning, remember that "with God all things are possible."

We're communicating with a Source Energy that creates worlds, One that knows no restrictions and certainly doesn't use the low-energy, slow-language methods that we do. Spirit communicates instantaneously, tapping in to our higher faculties of intuition, telepathy, insight, psychic awareness, spirit acumen, clairvoyance, the sixth sense, and even beyond.

The brilliant poet Rainer Maria Rilke put this all into perspective when he made this observation: "We must accept our existence *to the greatest extent possible;* everything, the unprecedented also, needs to be accepted. That is basically the only case of courage required of us: to be courageous in the face of the strangest, the most whimsical and unexplainable thing that we could encounter."

### Being Ready for the Teacher

It's been known for millennia that "when the student is ready, the teacher will appear." Well, our teachers are always there because they're gifts from Spirit. The real question is our readiness to tune in to what they have to teach us. The key word here is *readiness*—that is, we must be open to all possibilities and trusting in our intuitive hunches.

Wondering if something might possibly be a message from God is evidence that we're open to our intuiton. Our thoughts are sacred and substantiate our connection to the Divine, so they don't need to be corroborated by anyone or anything else. Our Creator is listening and responding in ways that don't necessarily correspond to the laws of the material world—that is, we won't be hearing from a physical source that's aligned with cause and effect, the laws of physics, or even what we believe is "possible." It's our job to do all that we can to vibrationally match to that spiritual energy.

We were once perfectly together with our Creative Force, and now we're being called to come back to It. It's vitally important to be open to the language of alignment—most of us need to begin the process by recognizing our tendency to discount such messages as mere happenstance. In an infinite Universe, with an organized intelligence supporting it at all moments, there can be no such thing as accidents.

For the rest of this chapter, I'll be offering some of my own hunches about how the All-Knowing Creative Spirit communicates. Some of these ways fall into the category of "inexplicable alignments," which means that there's meaning there, but our ego mind—chained as it is to its belief in the material laws it has always lived by—refuses to see the hidden messages that are staring us right in the face.

### The Four Messages of Alignment

For many years I've felt what I considered to be the language of Spirit speaking to me in ways that often defy my logical mind. These feelings are more than hunches and even go beyond intuition—and I sincerely believe that they've contributed to my living an inspired life.

The following four examples aren't rules or laws that apply to everyone, but if they *do* work for others, I'll be even more inspired because it's my intention to be in a space where I'm able to give to others all that I know. I also offer these ideas with the constant reminder that when one listens to Spirit, all things are possible. (And even though I'm offering them in a numbered sequence, they certainly don't conform to any linear arrangement.)

## 1. Alignment of Feelings

When I feel good (God), I'm aligned with Spirit. As I tell my children, we must rely on how we feel to determine our state of health, rather than seeking our answers in a medical printout full of numbers. Feeling energized, content, excited, and happy are better indicators of our health and well-being than having our bodily functions assessed by a distant laboratory. A positive honest response to the question, "Does this [or will this] make me feel good?" tells us immediately if we're aligned with our Creative Source or not.

For example, I'd been having an uninspired relationship with my cell-phone provider. For weeks I'd been unable to resolve the conflict: Each morning I'd plunge ahead and call the company again, traipse through the endless recorded messages, be on hold for sometimes a half hour, and finally reach a supervisor who'd read this from a company manual: "We're doing our best and apologize for any inconvenience this may be causing you. We can't give you a timetable for when this will be resolved."

Every day I'd hear the same words being read, so it was obvious that I was getting nowhere. But what upset me more than this lack of progress was my unmistakable misalignment. I was so upset I wasn't feeling good that my writing, my exercise program, and even my health were being negatively impacted. And then I remembered to follow my own advice.

The next time I started to go through my morning ritual with the cell-phone company, I stopped and told myself that I intended to feel good on this issue. I then put the phone down, went for a swim in the ocean, and thanked God for a renewed sense of peace. And sure enough, a voice inside me said, "By not being able to receive your calls, you've been given a rare opportunity to be at peace, which is something you've complained about in the past because of so many disturbances. Also, the phone company is doing the best they know how, so surround them with light and let the issue resolve itself." And finally, the most astonishing thing I heard was, "You're being protected from receiving messages that wouldn't serve you well. I have put your incoming calls on temporary hiatus so that you can be free from what will only make you feel bad. So enjoy your peace!"

I've since allowed Spirit to handle the issue, and now when I think about what was such a source of annoyance and inner turmoil for me, I feel good (God). This might seem like a petty example in a book about such a large topic as inspiration; nevertheless, I urge you to ask the question, "Does this make me feel good?" and pay attention to the answer the next time there's a similar "petty" situation in your life. You may be surprised to find yourself realigned!

## 2. Alignments with Nature

Everything in nature is in-Spirit—it isn't spoiled by ego, nor can it ever be. So when nature speaks to us, we should listen intently. When a wild bird touches us, for instance, or a fish brushes by when we're swimming in the ocean or a lake, I believe that it's a direct communication from our Source of Being. Since these creations of God instinctively keep their distance, when they depart from their DNA patterns to actually contact us physically, I think we should pay attention.

A few times in my life, I've had a bird sweep by my body, and on each of these occasions I've felt a deep sense of connection to God. Each time I've stopped and reexamined my thoughts at the precise instant of contact, and I was able to interpret that connection as a message to pay closer attention to my mission of writing.

Just today, as I walked along the ocean and thought about writing this section on nature and spiritual alignment, a bright red cardinal flew within inches of my face and stopped right in front of me. It looked directly at me, nodded its head, and flew off, again very close to my body. At the time of this encounter I was contemplating whether to even include these bird stories, considering that they might be misunderstood or perhaps even criticized by the professional community. In such moments, I always decide to listen to my own inner knowing—let the critics be damned!

I also recall other ways in which nature has gotten my attention and let me know that I was in touch with Spirit. For example,

I remember once being in a fierce wind and having a leaf blow right into my face, almost smacking me as I was thinking a decidedly nonspiritual thought of revenge; on another occasion while I was filled with anger, a tree branch collided with me as I exited my car—and it was a calm day without a breeze, and nothing was visibly disturbing the tree. And I have a piece of driftwood that meandered into my open hand while I was meditating at one of the "Seven Sacred Pools" near Hana (on Maui). When it touched me while my eyes were closed in deep meditation, I was startled— yet I knew that it was saying something to me. This wood, which I've kept for more than 22 years, is a reminder to me that Spirit is alive and working. To this day, when I look at it I think of God . . . and as you know, thinking of God and becoming like Him are precisely what it takes to live a life of inspiration.

Pay attention to episodes in nature that arouse Spirit and kindle an inner spark of awe and admiration for you. You don't have to discuss it with another being—if it has meaning for you, it's valid. (In fact, this is the first time I've shared the story of my sacred piece of driftwood.) Listen to the winds, the critters, the clouds, the rains, and the oceans—listen to it all.

Here's a Chinook Blessing Litany that reveals the Native American awareness of the language of Spirit inherent in all of nature:

We call upon the earth, our planet home, with its beautiful depths
and soaring heights, its vitality and abundance of life,
and together we ask that it:
*Teach us, and show us the way.*

We call upon the mountains, the Cascades and the Olympics,
the high green valleys and meadows filled with wild flowers,
the snows that never melt, the summits of intense silence,
and we ask that they:
*Teach us, and show us the way.*

We call upon the waters that rim the earth, horizon to horizon,
that flow in our rivers and streams, that fall upon our gardens

and fields, and we ask that they:
*Teach us, and show us the way.*

We call upon the land which grows our food, the nurturing soil,
the fertile fields, the abundant gardens and orchards,
and we ask that they:
*Teach us, and show us the way.*

We call upon the forests, the great trees reaching strongly to the sky
with earth in their roots and the heavens in their branches,
the fir and the pine and the cedar, and we ask them to:
*Teach us, and show us the way.*

We call upon the creatures of the fields and forests and the seas,
our brothers and sisters the wolves and deer, the eagle and dove,
the great whales and the dolphin, the beautiful Orca and salmon
who share our Northwest home, and we ask them to:
*Teach us, and show us the way.*

We call upon the moon and the stars and the sun, who govern
the rhythms and seasons of our lives and remind us that we are
part of a great and wondrous universe, and we ask them to:
*Teach us, and show us the way.*

We call upon all those who have lived on this earth,
our ancestors and our friends, who dreamed the best for
future generations, and upon whose lives our lives are built,
and with thanksgiving, we call upon them to:
*Teach us, and show us the way.*

And lastly, we call upon all that we hold most sacred,
the presence and power of the Great Spirit of love and truth
which flows through all the universe . . . to be with us to:
*Teach us, and show us the way.*

Indeed, nature has much to teach us, and it *will* help show the way. All we need to do is align with its perfection and note how it aligns with ours.

### 3. Alignment with Events

Strange occurrences and seemingly inexplicable events may actually be our All-Creating Source lining up "coincidences" to teach us and show us the way. Recently, for instance, I'd been advised to read a particular book that had been on bestseller lists for several months. I looked for it in various stores at the airport, but finally gave up because it was time to board my flight.

The title was still swirling around in my thoughts as I got to my seat. A woman who'd had her seat changed twice ended up sitting next to me, and she was carrying the very book I was seeking. And when I got home and turned on the TV, a guest on a talk show was talking about it. I couldn't help but notice the four alignments within a few hours concerning this book: my friend telling me about it, my search for it in the airport, a fellow passenger reading it, and a talk-show discussion of it.

When I experience these kinds of alignments, I've learned to not dismiss them as accidental. I'm still not totally certain of what was happening here, but I did purchase the book (*The Secret Life of Bees,* by Sue Monk Kidd), and while reading it I happened upon a story that I quoted in *this* one. Perhaps all the aligned events showed up so that the message in that story would be read and shared by someone reading this work, or so I'd have this example—the possibilities are endless!

One of my favorite quotes is from Mark Helprin's *Winter's Tale:* "In the end, or, rather, as things really are, any event, no matter how small, is intimately and sensibly tied to all others." It's exciting to observe the pattern of events appearing repeatedly in our conscious field of experience. We can notice the spine-tingling amazement we feel while reminding ourselves that this could very well be Spirit inviting us in to reconnect with It.

The language of Spirit will proclaim its creativity by producing sequences of repetition to align us with our Source. When we have an idea about taking on a new project and then read about it in a magazine that mysteriously shows up in our hands, and then a stranger in line at the movie theater begins talking to us out of the blue about this same topic—which is mentioned in the movie itself—and during dinner we overhear the people at an adjacent table discussing this same subject, guess what? We're in an "alignment attention-getter," written and carried out by Spirit. In other words, this is not an accident—the teachers are not only showing up, they're practically hitting us over the head!

The reason we begin to notice all of this aligned synchronicity is because we've tuned in to it. The teachers have always been there, but now we notice them. And our noticing indicates a new level of readiness to listen to our ultimate calling. In fact, these alignments can take some really interesting forms. The same numbers showing up—for example, we awaken at precisely 4:44 morning after morning, and then see those numbers appear on the odometer, on the radio, as a checkbook balance, at the deli counter, and as an assigned number for a charity walk—causes us to ask, "What's going on here?" The answer is that the Universe is asking us to be receptive and pay attention. It's not about playing all fours in a casino or the lottery—it's about knowing that these seemingly accidental repetitions are actually invitations from Spirit to join It.

Over the 30 years I've been writing books, I can't tell you how many people have told me, "A book just fell into my hands off of the shelf, and it was exactly what I needed at the time." I'd wager that virtually every person has had a similar experience more than once in his or her lifetime. (I trust in this type of spiritual communication whenever I write a book: I feel guided to pick up a particular item, and I know I'm in alignment with Spirit when these kinds of messages continually materialize throughout the months of preparation and actual writing.) When a book literally falls into our lap or is sent to us by several different people—or even when we keep seeing the title and having it referred to by others over and over—we need to notice, stop our resistance, and surrender. When we end up reading the contents and applying what it offers, we're aligning ourselves and becoming a vibrational match to the same Source that's sending us these signals.

## 4. Alignment with People

We commonly receive alignment when our thoughts become strangely tied to the actions of another human being. For example, we think about somebody we haven't seen for several years; in fact, we can't seem to shake our inner visions of him or her—especially when someone else mentions the same person for no apparent reason, or we run across a picture of that individual. Then the phone rings, and it's the same person whom we haven't been in contact with for years! The language of Spirit works by aligning our thought energy with the vibrational energy of another.

When people line up with our thoughts and mysteriously connect their physical presence with our private inner meanderings, we should take note. We must tell ourselves, "Spirit is aligning my thoughts with events that are happening. I'll stay alert to what I'm being offered here because there may be a reason." That's all—just be cognizant of what might be happening, and by being open to what may be baffling and perhaps indecipherable, we're likely to discover what we're being guided to learn.

A few weeks ago I was reading through a book I'd written 16 years ago. In it, I mentioned a friend, Earlene Rentz, with whom I attended school from fourth grade through high school. I put the book down and went jogging, yet Earlene was still on my mind. I thought, *I'm going to call her the next time I'm in Detroit—after all, we're both having our 65th birthdays this year.*

That very evening, I was scheduled to receive the Martin Luther King/Mohandas Gandhi Peace Award from the Unity Church of Maui, which would be attended by approximately 1,000 people. As I completed my speech and walked to the lobby to sign autographs, I saw the little girl who sat next to me in grade school, who was my first love, and who occupied my thoughts throughout my school years. Believe it or not, as I was thinking of her more than a half century later, Earlene was thousands of miles from home and hugging me in the lobby of a theater in Lahaina! It turns out that she was visiting Maui, had seen the award announcement in the newspaper, and had come to the auditorium to surprise me. It was one of those synchronistic alignments of Spirit at work. Somehow at an unconscious level, I was already reconnecting to Earlene without being aware that she was even in the area.

Noticing the same folks showing up in different settings; running into people we haven't seen in a while after we've just heard their names mentioned; and repeatedly seeing an individual's name in magazines, on television, or at a local bookstore are all also synchronistic alignments. Spirit is lining up these sequential happenings for a reason—we just need to be open to learning the reason, and it most likely will be revealed. Perhaps it will be a dream or a sudden instant of *Eureka!* or maybe it will become clearer when simply allowed—no matter how the message comes, we'll look back on it with a renewed insight and the benefit of no longer being closed off to such possibilities.

It may be helpful to consider that even with all of our sophisticated technology, we can't reproduce an eyeball that can compete with the ones made by our Creator. One little eyeball and we're all baffled! And our Creator's making them at the rate of six million per day—and that only takes *human* eyeballs into account! If a Spiritual Creator can do that, then aligning our thoughts with the people we need as teachers now is a minor task indeed. Again, with God, *all things* are possible.

## Some Suggestions for Putting the Ideas in This Chapter to Work for You

— Always remember that when the student is ready, the teacher will appear. Stay in an attitude of readiness at all times, and the teachers and the teachings will manifest for you. Write or print out these words and place them in a conspicuous place: *I am ready.*

— Once you've declared your readiness, don't scoff at anything or anyone that may have some connection to your return to

Spirit. Even an overheard conversation between four-year-old children can be a message to you—if it registers with you in any small way, then drink it in and allow yourself to process it as a Divine communiqué.

Trust your own intuition—no one else has to agree with you or even understand you. In fact, I'd urge you to resist defending your inner inclinations to anyone who has an attitude of resistance. Remember, you want to feel good (God).

— Now begin the process of actually looking for ways in which Spirit might be communicating with you right now. When these unexpected synchronicities appear (as they will more and more frequently when you're open to them), ask what it is that you're to learn from them. When you peacefully ask your Creator in quiet meditation or prayer, you'll see what it is that's guiding you. There are angels of Spirit surrounding you, so don't be hesitant to ask. And, of course, when you do, you will receive.

— Be prepared to make major changes in your life after you become accustomed to what these alignments you're experiencing are saying to you. I personally received many messages from Spirit that told me over and over that I was to give up my addictive ways—yet for years I ignored them at my own peril. Today I look back at the obvious nature of what I was being encouraged to do, and now I know why I had to ultimately follow those alignments of energy or die.

You may be guided to leave a job, a city, or even a relationship—all of which may sound terrifying at the moment. Nevertheless, if the signals keep coming and they resonate internally with you, take the step—and while doing so, know that you're being guided to a life of inspiration.

— Whenever you seem to be receiving an unexpected jolt from the Universe, make every effort to note precisely what it was that you were thinking at the moment you took in the message. That bird that touches you, that leaf that blows into your face, that toe you stub for the third time—anything at all—note your thoughts at the moment and see if you can detect any connection to what has just happened. Your thoughts are energy, and Spirit communicates by aligning Itself with you by getting your attention, and allowing you to then move on it or ignore it.

＊ ＊ ＊

What I know for certain within my very core is that there's no separation between us and all that we encounter in the Universe. One of my favorite poets is William Butler Yeats, and here he perfectly sums up the ideas in this chapter:

> *O chestnut tree, great rooted blossomer,*
> *Are you the leaf, the blossom or the bole?*
> *O body swayed to music, O brightening glance,*
> *How can we know the dancer from the dance?*

You are the dancer and the dance, just as God is. In other words, those messages from Spirit are you if you feel them—because it's impossible to separate the dance from the dancer, the root from the blossom, and you from God. The only place where separation takes place is in your mind. But since you're now heeding your ultimate calling, you're right on your way to living an inspired life.

# PART V

# A PERSONAL
# LOOK AT
# INSPIRATION

*"There is a way of living in the world
that is not here, although it seems to be.
You do not change appearance, though you smile
more frequently. Your forehead is serene; your eyes
are quiet. . . . You walk this path as others walk,
nor do you seem to be distinct from them,
although you are indeed. Thus can you serve
them while you serve yourself. . . ."*

— FROM *A COURSE IN MIRACLES*

CHAPTER 18

# HOW LIFE LOOKS
# WHEN I AM INSPIRED

*"Give me a man who sings at his work."*

— THOMAS CARLYLE

*"They can because they think they can."*

— VIRGIL

**IN THIS FINAL CHAPTER,** I offer my own very personal view on how the world looks when I feel inspired.

I'd like to acknowledge right from the outset that I don't live at this level of being in-Spirit 100 percent of the time—like most everyone else, I occasionally have lapses and feel uninspired. Yet these moments have become rarer and rarer; in fact, it's difficult for me to recall a day in the past several years when I felt completely uninspired.

What follows is a personal account of both how I feel inside and what seems to take place in the world around me when I feel connected to Spirit in the ways that I've written about in the pages of this book.

## *Jack*

The same day that I completed Chapter 17 and read it over the telephone to my editor, Joanna, on Bainbridge Island, Washington, I had the most profoundly mystical experience of being in-Spirit in all of my 65 years. The photograph on the cover of the book is a re-creation of what happened.

When I finished up with Joanna, I went for my daily hour-long walk along the beach . . . but for some reason I elected to take a slightly different route along a grassy area *adjacent* to the beach. I was recalling my friend Jack Boland, a Unity minister in Detroit, who crossed over about a decade ago. Jack loved monarch butterflies, often telling stories of how he marveled at these paper-thin creatures who migrated thousands of miles in high winds and returned to the same branch on the same tree where they first emerged from their cocoons. Before Jack passed away, I presented him with a beautiful paperweight containing a dead monarch that I'd found in perfect condition. When he died, his wife returned it to me, telling me how much Jack loved that gift and how much he admired these amazing creatures who had such mysterious intelligence built into their brains, which are the size of a pinhead.

Jack always told me to "be in a state of gratitude," and he ended every sermon with this message to God: "Thank You, thank You, thank You." On three occasions since his death, a monarch butterfly has landed on my body. Since these creatures studiously avoid human contact, each time this has happened I've thought of Jack and said to myself, *Thank You, God—thank You, thank You.*

Anyway, as I walked, feeling grateful for having completed the second-to-last chapter of this book, a monarch landed on the ground, not three feet in front of me. I said Jack's magic words to myself *(thank You, thank You, thank You),* and felt deep appreciation for my life and the beauty of the day. The butterfly stayed right there until I approached, then he flapped his wings several times and flew away. Thinking of Jack and feeling a little bewildered and immensely thankful, I watched this creature in flight, now 40 or 50 yards away.

As God is my witness, the butterfly made a U-turn and not only headed in my direction, but landed right smack on my finger! Needless to say, I was shocked—but not totally surprised. I must confess that it seems to me that the more I stay in-Spirit, the more I experience synchronicities similar to this one. But what followed did border on the incredible, even for me.

This little creature became my constant companion for the next two and a half hours—he sat first on one hand and then moved to my other hand, never even coming close to flying away. He seemed to be trying to communicate with me by moving his wings back and forth, and even opening and closing his tiny mouth as if attempting to speak . . . and as crazy as it may sound, I felt a deep affinity for this precious living being. I sat on the ground and simply stayed with my new fragile friend for 30 or so minutes. Then I called Joanna from my cell phone, and she was also stunned by the synchronicity, insisting that I somehow get a picture of this event.

At this point I decided to return to my home, approximately a mile from where I was sitting, with my new companion. I returned along the beach walk, where the winds were brisk—the butterfly's wings were pushed by these high gusts, but he clung to my finger, and even moved to another hand without making any effort to leave. As I walked, I encountered a four-year-old girl with her mother. The girl was sobbing over some perceived tragedy in her young life, and when I showed her my "pet" butterfly, her expression went from sad to blissful in one split second. She smiled from ear to ear and asked me all about the winged creature on my forefinger.

When I got home, I was talking on my cell phone to my friend Reid Tracy as I walked upstairs. He laughed with me as I related the bizarre synchronicity at play in this very moment. I said, "Reid, it's been 90 minutes, and this little guy has adopted me." Reid also encouraged me to get a photograph of this, since it was obviously in complete harmony with what I was writing.

I left my new friend—whom I was now calling "Jack"—sitting on the handwritten Chapter 17 on my lanai, and went downstairs. I found Cindy, a young woman who works nearby, and asked her to run to the store and purchase a disposable camera. She did, and I went back to the patio, put my hand next to Jack, and watched him jump right onto my finger! (The photo on the cover of this book is a re-creation of that magical moment.)

It appeared that my butterfly companion had decided that he was now going to live with me forever. After another hour or so of meditating and communing with this little creature of God—and pondering this event as the most unprecedented and out-of-the-ordinary spiritual episode I'd ever encountered—I gently placed Jack back on my manuscript while I proceeded to take a long, hot shower. When I returned to the patio, I placed my finger near my winged friend as I'd done many times in the previous 150 minutes, but he now seemed like a totally different little critter. He fluttered away, landed on a table, flapped his wings twice, and flew off, straight up toward the heavens. Moments with him were now history, but I still have the photographs, which I treasure.

The next morning, I decided to watch one of my favorite films, *Brother Sun, Sister Moon,* which I hadn't viewed for more than a decade. And sure enough—in the opening scenes of Franco Zeffirelli's interpretation of the life of St. Francis, there he was . . . with a butterfly alighting on his fingers.

### *Inspirational Vibrations*

When I live my life so as to be open to the language of Spirit, I find almost overwhelming rapture overtaking me. For several days after my experience with Jack, people kept telling me that I seemed so peaceful and content, and one woman even suggested that I was "walking grace." This episode with my butterfly friend and the communiqués from Spirit touched me at an unprecedented level. From the perspective of being in-Spirit, I've seen Its hands embrace me and heard It say: "You are not alone. You can count on Me to guide you—and whatever you do, do not doubt My presence."

This makes me feel safe, comforted, and that I'm not alone. I feel good (God) because I'm living in almost perfect harmony with the Source of my being, living on purpose and writing from my heart. The reason I feel inspired isn't because the world looks perfect. Rather, it's the other way around: The reason the world looks perfect to me is because I'm in-Spirit—a person who chooses to live an inspired life. I'm able to stay in a state of gratitude from the moment I awake early in the morning right up until I close my eyes while falling asleep; and throughout each day, I'm reminded that staying in-Spirit is really about staying in vibrational harmony.

I don't find it necessary to change anyone or anything that I encounter or read about in my daily life. Each time that I'm tempted to, I catch myself and return to a mind-set that calls to me to be more like God, right here and right now. I stay inspired by making an energetic shift within myself; when I do, the world looks completely different, and I move inwardly toward peace and kindness. The energetic shift is merely a way of processing people and events from the insight of being unified with the All-Creating Source—that is, by eschewing judgment and allowing the world to be as it *is*, rather than as I think it *should be.*

I stay inspired by encouraging others to live out their destiny and allowing the world to unfold as it will, and I'm much more likely to feel peaceful. In fact, when I'm living my life from this perspective of inspiration, my vibrational energy is more attuned to that of the creative energy of the Universe, and I find that my effect on others is far more spiritually aligned. Furthermore, I know within my own being that I'm doing something very powerful to make this world a more spiritually oriented place for us all.

You see, when I resonate to anger, shame, hatred, or revenge, I add to these decidedly nonspiritual energies by joining in what I find to be so objectionable. But when I remember to bring nonjudgment, love, tolerance, and compassion to these low, ego-dominated energies, I see how different the world looks, and even how different those around me act in the presence of these God-realized energies. I feel optimistic when I'm in-Spirit, with an inner knowing that nothing can interfere with an idea whose time is coming or has already arrived.

I trust that our Creator knows what It's doing, and that good triumphs over what ego believes is bad or evil. I sense that we're all moving toward a world that will no longer know the horrors of war or practice our long-established habits of inhumanity toward our brothers and sisters around the globe, who may have different cultural views and their own unique physical distinctiveness. By staying in-Spirit, I'm truly inspired to see the potential for greatness that's in all of us, as one people, and I turn from anguish to faith that at least I can live from a place of God-realization, and practice being a force for good (God).

Staying in vibrational alignment with Spirit allows me to be more present in all of my life activities. I find myself less concerned with goals, outcomes, winning, and accumulations, and far more involved in the process of enjoying the activities of my life. Arriving seems to replace striving, and being in a state of flow is far more common than my old uninspired state of worry and anguish. I remind myself that Spirit is only here and now—not yesterday, not tomorrow, only *now.* By keeping my vibration aligned spiritually, I see the ecstasy in the present. Everything else that once was a source of worry doesn't come up for me, since the outcomes are already handled for me in my own mind. *What will be, will be,* I remind myself. The world looks so much more peaceful when I approach it this way, and my ego, which once needed to win at all costs, is relegated to a distant seat in a stadium in another galaxy!

### Choosing Inspiration

My experience with Jack, as well as many similar kinds of episodes in my life, taught me the the that the laws of the material world truly do not apply in the presence of God-realization. And I know that I have the choice to live at this level of inspiration. When I do so, it seems that the world changes: Animals behave differently than their biological genetics would seem to allow, people at a distance seem to hear me telepathically and respond to my highest thoughts, objects seem to materialize in defiance of what scientists say is possible, and healing takes place in spite of modern medicine saying otherwise. In other words, miracles seem to be ordinary. The world looks like a place where everything is possible, where restrictions and limitations are nonexistent, and where the power of our Creator seems to roll right up and land at my feet, begging me to hop on board and witness the infinite possibilities it offers. This is how I feel when I align myself to Spirit: cocky inside because I know something that so few ever come to realize, but humble and awestruck on the outside at the miraculousness of it all!

When I remember to stay in-Spirit, I've realized that when one thing appears to be going wrong, I can see clearly that ten things are going right. For example, if my cell phone isn't working, I can note that my health is fine, my family is safe, the ocean is calm for swimming, my bank account has a surplus, my electricity is fully functional, and on and on it goes. From a perspective of being in-Spirit, I automatically shift my attention away from what's going wrong and onto what's right—this then becomes my point of attraction and I attract more of what I'm focused on, whereas at an earlier time in my life, I'd attract more of what was going wrong because that was my point of attraction. How sublimely beautiful the world now looks to me from this magnificent place of inspiration! No longer do I stay focused on and attract more of what's going wrong, for I've learned to place my attention on what's right, what's working, and what's aligned with the All-Creating Spirit.

From this place of inspiration, I ask, "What if I looked deep within myself and found no original sin at all—that is, what if I discovered original *innocence* instead? And what if the same were true for everyone?" I know that our Creative Source is One of good, and I also know that we must be just like what we came from—therefore, everyone, including myself, is a piece of God. We come to this world from innocence and love, not from a place of sin or weakness. When I see Christ consciousness in everyone, even those with whom I differ greatly, I'm able to feel good (God). When I know that there's no original sin in anyone, I'm able to think like Mother Teresa, who told the world, "In each [ill person], I see the face of Christ in one of his more distressing disguises."

When it is goodness that I look for, rather than sin and weakness, that's what I see. I then see goodness in the little old lady driving slowly in front of me, the elderly man fumbling with his change and delaying me at the supermarket, the children squealing loudly as I'm attempting to concentrate on a book, the teenagers shouting along with their earsplitting rap music, or the jackhammer operator whose deafening sounds fill the air with chaos. When I'm inspired, I see God-realization disguised as a minor blip, and the world looks fine, happy, and even peaceful. I remind myself of Rumi's sage advice: "If you are irritated by every rub, how will you be polished?"

When I feel inspired, I notice how much zest I have for life and everything that I do: I play tennis with exuberance and without fatigue, I write from my heart—I feel good (God), and this inner feeling radiates outward in all of my waking moments. Inspiration means doing what I love, and even more significantly, loving what I'm doing. It's my willingness to bring love and passion to the activities of my life, rather than looking for love to emerge from those events and activities. It's an attitude, and knowing this, I remember to pick a good one as often as possible. I know that being enthusiastic feels good (God), and I also know that I have the choice to select these attitudes at any and all times. When I stay in-Spirit, these outlooks on life become second nature to me.

By deciding to live an inspired life, I'm choosing to be in balance with a Creative Force that responds to my in-Spirit thoughts. I'm also believing that I live in a friendly Universe rather than an evil one, and feeling supported by It in a similar manner. Being grateful for all that God sends my way, I'm not surprised when synchronistic events happen in my life. When I have someone on my mind who lives some distance from me, I actually expect that he or she will call me . . . and it occurs over and over.

I know that thoughts are energy and that those harmonizing with Spirit will align to activate the creation process. I love watching all this flow so perfectly and being in harmony with the Force that's responsible for all of creation. I know deep within me that I can participate in the activation of this Force to bring into reality the manifestation of my spiritually aligned desires.

Rather than hoping, wishing, and even praying for an outcome, my inner world aligns with the idea that what I desire is feasible and on its way. This kind of inspired knowing frees me from anxiety and worry. I affirm: *It's on its way; there's absolutely nothing to fuss about.* And I leave the time of its arrival into my life in the hands of the All-Knowing, Always-Creative Spiritual Source. I find that I no longer question the Creator of the Universe because I'm at peace with the timing of everything. I know enough now not to push the river, not to demand that the timetable of my ego be the same as God's.

I know that by staying in-Spirit, I'm actually participating as a co-creator, and that the more I stay in this aligned space, the more it seems to speed up the process. I've noticed that ever since I've become more conscious of staying inspired (and all that this implies), the time between what I think and having it actually show up in my physical life has become shorter and shorter. I'm aware that the ultimate in manifestation is a complete absence of any delay between a thought and its physical manifestation. What's been called the "gift of loaves and fishes" is what true, 100 percent God-realization is. That is, think food and it appears; think well-being for anyone, and disease dissolves. While I know that this Christ consciousness is available for us all, I have many more glimpses of it as I stay more in-Spirit.

### Singing My Song

The major change that's taken place for me in this manifestation of my inspired desires has been the awareness of my own capacity for activating the Creative Force to work with me. Today, as I live consciously in-Spirit, I feel as if I'm more and more able to be an activator of this Divine Synchronistic Force and have it work *with* me, rather than *to* me. I view these mystical moments as holy

517

instants when my ego is suspended, and Spirit (in conjunction with my own Divine desires) has become the teacher.

As my sense of inspiration grows within me, I find myself wanting to do more for others and focusing less upon myself. What I desire is realized through the paradoxical means of desiring it for others even more than I want it for myself. By reaching out in this way and deliberately looking for ways to inspire others, I feel closer and closer to Spirit—and, ironically, I sense that more of what I desire seems to be flowing back to me as a result of this sharing.

At this point in my life I feel that staying in this glorious state of inspiration practically requires me to avoid condemning others. I look at the behaviors of others, even those whose actions are anathema to an inspired world, and I send them love. I know deep within me that declaring war on the problems of violence, poverty, cancer, AIDS, and drug addiction isn't the solution. I'm uninterested in increasing those problems with violent, angry, or hateful thoughts or behavior. I know that I can't get sick enough to make one person better, or angry enough to end violence anywhere. I also sense very strongly that by staying in-Spirit and bringing a higher mental energy to the presence of these lower, ego-based energies, I'm a force for change, one that helps move the world closer to Spirit.

I anticipate a planet at peace—along with health, abundance, and love in my life and in the lives of all others—and I know that it's moving in this direction. I know that for every act of apparent evil, there are a million acts of kindness. That's where I place my attention, and that's what I choose to give away. By doing so for the larger percentage of my days, my reward is a feeling of being in harmony with purpose. I watch the myna birds singing every morning, and I know they're not doing it because they have the answers to all of life's problems—they have a song inside of them that they obviously feel compelled to let come out. I too have a song to sing, and by staying in-Spirit I'm able to sing it all day, every day.

I know that the answer to "What should I be doing?" is to see the word *yes* on my inner screen: "Yes, I am listening"; "Yes,

I am paying attention"; and most important, "Yes, I am willing." I notice that those around me who feel uninspired are unwilling to say yes to the feeling at the core of their being. By doing so to every hunch, burning desire, and thought that won't go away, I feel the hand of a guiding Spirit that's with me simply because I've been willing to say yes. By saying yes to life, I see the world and all of its inhabitants in a completely new way.

As a result of being more and more inspired, I see Spirit in virtually everyone I meet. And I feel much more connected to everyone as a result of sensing *their* spirit instead of noticing all of the accumulations of success that they've amassed. I call this "seeing with my mind and not my eyes." It now seems that my identity is associated with experiences that are not exclusively of this world. And I love what my mind sees—possibilities and openings for miracles! It looks past the limitations of my eyes, and it knows that we're all one in an infinite world. My mind no longer views death as something to fear; rather, it lives in an infinite place and is able to step back from this corporeal world and be an observer. With each passing day, I feel what my mind knows to be true, and I look for this all-encompassing loving essence everywhere.

\* \* \*

Adequately conveying how I feel when I'm inspired is probably impossible. What I so sincerely want to share here is that the feeling of being completely in harmony with our Source generates miracles everywhere. I have the delicious spine-tingling sensation of bliss as I observe and interact in this world from the wondrous vista of being inspired. These words from *A Course in Miracles* ring true for me: "All that must be recognized, however, is that birth was not the beginning, and death is not the end." This is the knowing that I have from this infinite in-Spirit perspective.

There are no conflicts—all is as it should be. The things I wish to improve aren't going to be accomplished by fighting, but by placing my attention on staying connected to Spirit. In 1 Corinthians, Saint Paul says, "The very fact that you have lawsuits among you means you have been completely defeated already." As I live from a place of inspiration, I see that conflict is no longer possible for me, and I understand what Paul was attempting to say to the people of Corinth in that letter. I will not be defeated—I can't, because for me, there's no *they* any longer, there's only *us*. I've turned my mind to Spirit. I know that God created me to be like Him, and I must be what I came from. This idea, more than any other, inspires me beyond what I can share on these pages.

It's my intention to continue to stay inspired and live what my mind knows, rather than only what my eyes see. And my mind knows that we're all in a Universe that has a creative, organizing intelligence supporting it. I know that it flows through me, and God willing, I'll stay in-Spirit and assist you to live that life of inspiration that you came here to live. There can be no greater blessing!

I send you love, I surround you with light, and I invite you to live with me in-Spirit.

# EXCUSES BEGONE!

For Tiffany Saia.
The light from which
I *Shine On* . . .

# INTRODUCTION

I spent the year 2006 immersed in the ancient teachings of Lao-tzu, studying his monumental tome, the Tao Te Ching. I read, meditated, lived, and then wrote an essay on each of the 81 verses of the Tao, which many have called the wisest book ever written. That collection of essays is titled *Change Your Thoughts—Change Your Life: Living the Wisdom of the Tao*. I learned, and to this day, practice, *what* to think, although all that Lao-tzu taught me in that year is beyond my abilities to describe completely.

I find I now choose thoughts that are flexible, not rigid; soft, not hard. I think with humility, not arrogance; with detachment, not attachment. I practice thinking small and accomplishing big things, as well as thinking in harmony with nature, rather than with my ego. The idea of not interfering replaces meddling and advising. I prefer peaceful solutions over the notion of fighting to solve disputes. I opt for contentment, rather than ambition; arriving, not striving. And most significantly, I choose thoughts that are congruous with the Great Tao (God), rather than the illusions of self-importance conjured up by ego.

*Excuses Begone!*—the book you're presently reading—was also influenced by that eminent master Lao-tzu. Since the Tao Te Ching taught me *what* kind of thinking harmonized with my higher self, I asked Lao-tzu for advice on *how to change* long-established habits of thought. I realized that knowing what to think does not necessarily clarify how to go about changing a lifetime of habitual thinking. Thus, I've drawn on Lao-tzu's wisdom by contemplating his teachings and asking for his guidance on what it takes to bring about a change in the long-held habits of thought that manifest as excuses. Through a process of writing that felt as though I were being directed by a force larger than myself, the *Excuses Begone!* paradigm evolved with what appears to be the cooperation of this man named Lao-tzu, who lived some 2,500 years ago.

This paradigm works! I've taken many people through the seven questions that constitute this exciting new paradigm, and I've seen powerful changes take place to my—and their—delighted amazement. (I've even worked the paradigm on myself and turned some habits of thought around almost magically.) By examining the support system that individuals have erected over a long period of time, often going back to early childhood, and putting these timeworn thoughts through the seven steps in this paradigm, I find that excuses begin to fade away. They become replaced with thoughts that speak fervently, almost shouting, *Yes, you can change any excuse pattern, no matter how long or pervasive the conditioning process has been!*

I've seen men and women give up a lifetime of being overweight or addicted to all manner of substances by simply applying the principles that are inherent in the *Excuses Begone!* approach to life. If you're truly serious about changing any long-established habits of thought that have led you to use excuses as your rationale for staying the same, then I encourage you to follow the practices presented in these pages.

The great poet Rainer Maria Rilke once observed:

Behind the world our names enclose is
the nameless: our true archetype and home.

I would like to add, "Behind the world your excuses describe is the Great Tao; let yourself be lived by it, and all of those excuses will fade away so that you finally come home once and for all."

I would like to acknowledge my friend and colleague Byron Katie, particularly in the formation of some of the questions in the paradigm in Part III of this book. I encourage you to become familiar with *Loving What Is,* and the program we produced together titled *Making Your Thoughts Work for You,* and to also visit: **www.thework.com**.

— **Wayne W. Dyer**
Maui, Hawaii

*Don't believe
everything you
think!*

# PART I

# IDENTIFYING
# AND REMOVING
# HABITUAL
# THINKING

*"Every human being's essential nature is perfect and faultless, but after years of immersion in the world we easily forget our roots and take on a counterfeit nature."*

— Lao-tzu

# CHAPTER 1

# YES, YOU CAN CHANGE OLD HABITS

*"I wasn't kissing her. I was whispering in her mouth."*
— Chico Marx
(Response to his wife when she caught him kissing a chorus girl)

*"An excuse is worse and more terrible than a lie . . ."*
— Alexander Pope

It's been said that old habits die hard, implying that it's next to impossible to change long-standing thought patterns. Yet the book you hold in your hands was created out of a belief that entrenched ways of thinking and acting can indeed be eradicated. Furthermore, the most effective means for eliminating habitual thoughts is to go to work on the very system that created, and continues to support, these thinking habits. This system is made up of a long list of explanations and defenses that can be summed up in one word: *excuses*. Hence, the title of this book is really a statement to yourself, as well as to that system of explanations you've created. It is my intention that *all* excuses be . . . gone!

*Can I make dramatic changes in the way I live? Is it possible to change self-defeating thoughts and behaviors that have been my constant companions for as long as I can remember? Can I really do a U-turn and deprogram myself when I've never known any other way to think and act? I've been depressed [or stubborn, overweight, scared, clumsy, unlucky, or any other descriptor you choose to insert here] my entire life. Is it even feasible or practical for me to contemplate removing these old and familiar ways of being and open myself up to a brand-new me?*

This book is my answer to those questions. Yes, there *is* a way available to you, right here and right now. You can relinquish any unwanted-but-long-held thoughts that have become your self-definition. *Excuses Begone!* presents a powerful and easy method for removing deeply embedded thinking habits that are preventing you from being the person you want to be.

The power of your beliefs to keep you stuck is enormous. Those deeply ingrained notions act as chains restricting you from experiencing your unique destiny. You have the capacity to loosen these chains and make them work for, rather than against, you, to the point that you can alter what you thought were scientific explanations for your human limitations and characteristics. I'm referring to things such as your genetic makeup, your DNA, or the early conditioning imposed upon you when you were an embryo, infant, and young child. Yes, you read that correctly. *Your beliefs, all of those formless energy patterns that you've adopted as your self-image, have the ability to change dramatically and give you the power to conquer unwanted traits, or what you unhappily presume to be your fate.*

The implacable sciences of genetics, medicine, psychology, and sociology may cause you to feel helpless about overcoming "proven" facts that are said to determine virtually everything about you. "I can't help the way I think . . . I've always been this way. It's my nature and it can't be changed. This is all I've ever known. After all, you take what's handed to you, and you make the best of it." All of these are the laments of those who opt to use excuses to explain their lives away. (**Note:** I will be using the word *excuses* for what many call *conditioned ways of being.*)

Every self-limiting thought that you employ to explain why you're not living life to the absolute fullest—so you're feeling purposeful, content, and fully alive—is something you can challenge and reverse, regardless of how long you've held that belief and no matter how rooted in tradition, science, or life experience it may be. Even if it seems like an insurmountable obstacle, you can overcome these thoughts, and you can begin by noticing how they've been working to hold you back. Then you can embark on a deprogramming effort that allows you to live an excuse-free life, one day at a time, one miracle at a time, one new belief at a time!

### The New Word on Beliefs

Have you ever wanted to change some facet of your personality, but another part of you insisted that this is impossible because your genetic programming is responsible for how you think, feel, and behave? That latter part of you believes in biologically determined unhappy genes, shy genes, fat genes, and bad-luck genes, among many others. Due to your luck of the draw, it will tell you, you have a set of misery genes, along with a sizable cache of weight-gaining genes, if those are the aspects you want to change. This part means to be helpful—but while it probably wants to protect you from the disappointment of failure, it keeps you stuck in an excuse-driven life. Using the excuse of genetic programming *not* to do anything about the personal characteristics that you dislike is popular and clearly acceptable in today's culture.

So, using the aforementioned genetic predisposition as a rationalization, living in constant or unnecessary terror might be explained as your having an overabundance of fear cells, which you're stuck with. Thus, a formidable excuse is formulated. No wonder a part of you gets indignant when you attempt to be brave, since it believes, *I can't change my biology.* A sense of powerlessness ensues when it comes to altering anything about yourself that has become so established that it feels like who you are. This is particularly true when you observe traits and characteristics that have been with you for as long as you can recall. As if to further cement the idea that you've "always been this way" into your total worldview, the limiting part of you asserts: *There's nothing that can be done about it; after all, I can't change my basic biology.*

Excuse me—thanks to the principles I share in this book, you most certainly can!

The belief that we cannot change our biology is beginning to be challenged by scientific scholars engaged in cell-biology research. It seems that humans *do* have the ability to change and even reverse some of their genetic blueprints. Openness and curiosity, along with a desire to be free from excuses, are the basic prerequisites for learning about the exciting evidence concerning genetic predisposition.

One of the pioneers of the new way of understanding DNA, Bruce Lipton, Ph.D., is a cell biologist who taught medical students before resigning to do research and lecture full-time. In a groundbreaking book called *The Biology of Belief,* Lipton writes that life is not controlled by genes—in fact, his research led him to the conclusion that they're strictly blueprints. The invisible, formless energy that constitutes the genes' environment is the architect that turns the blueprint into this mystery we call life. Listing hundreds of research results, he concludes that the old medical model depicting life's essential building blocks as physical particles is misleading; incomplete; and, in most cases, false. Treating illness more or less exclusively with drugs or surgery to facilitate a healing begs to be reexamined.

Lipton's conclusions led to his resignation from the University of Wisconsin's School of Medicine because he discovered that what he'd been teaching (the model of physical particles as the controlling force in life) was incorrect. He realized that both the human body and the universe itself are mental and spiritual in nature. There's a field of invisible energy with a total absence of physical properties that creates the particles that we call "cells," and this invisible field is the sole governing function of the body. So, since the body is not exclusively a physical machine, we can all find out how to control and impact our health.

Even more astonishing is Lipton's understanding that our personal belief systems, including our perceptions, have the capacity to trump our genetic inheritance and our cellular DNA. It's possible to influence the infinitesimally tiny particles we've come to believe are the ultimate determiners of our lives. That is, when we change the way we think, and learn new ways of perceiving, we can actually change our DNA!

In other words, you can impact and alter your genetic structure by modifying how you see yourself and your place in this glorious mystery called life. *Your perceptions have the power to change your genetic makeup—your beliefs can and do control your biology.* This may sound radical or even impossible, yet it is this awareness that will lead you to say good-bye to the excuses you've unwittingly adopted.

I encourage you to immerse yourself in *The Biology of Belief.* You'll be inspired to reset your mind to the possibility that your beliefs carry far more weight than you realized in determining what you can do, what you'll undertake, and how far you're capable of going. Let's take a look now at another piece of research that will help you realize what you're capable of achieving.

### *The Placebo Effect*

That the mind controls the body is hardly up for dispute. You've probably heard of documented studies where sugar pills given to a control group believing that they're a remedy for, say, arthritis, turn out to be as effective as the drug being administered for the arthritis. This placebo effect apparently occurs due to a belief in the effectiveness of the pill. But consider how powerful the mind is when it goes beyond administering a sugar pill to the world of surgery:

A Baylor School of Medicine study, published in 2002 in the *New England Journal of Medicine* evaluated surgery for patients with severe, debilitating knee pain. (Moseley, et al, 2002) The lead author of the study, Dr. Bruce Moseley, "knew" that knee surgery helped his patients. "All good surgeons know there is no placebo effect in surgery." But Moseley was trying to figure out which part of the surgery was giving his patients relief. The patients in the study were divided into three groups. Moseley shaved the damaged cartilage in the knee of one group. For another group, he flushed out the knee joint, removing material thought to be causing the inflammatory effect. Both of these constitute standard treatment for arthritic knees. The third group got "fake" surgery. The patient was sedated, Moseley made three standard incisions and then talked and acted just as he would have during a real surgery—he even splashed salt water to simulate the sound of the knee-washing procedure. After 40 minutes, Moseley sewed up the incisions as if he had done the surgery. All three groups were prescribed the same postoperative care, which included an exercise program.

The results were shocking. Yes, the groups who received surgery, as expected, improved. But the placebo group improved just as much as the other two groups! Despite the fact that there are 650,000 surgeries yearly for arthritic knees, at a cost of about $5,000 each, the results were clear to Moseley: "My skill as a surgeon had no benefit on these patients. The entire benefit of surgery for osteoarthritis of the knee was the placebo effect." Television news programs graphically illustrated the stunning results. Footage showed members of the placebo group walking and playing basketball, in short doing things they reported they could not do before their "surgery." The placebo patients didn't find out for two years that they had gotten fake surgery. One member of the placebo group, Tim Perez, who had to walk with a cane before the surgery, is now able to play basketball with his grandchildren. He summed up the theme of this book when he told the Discovery Health Channel: "In this world anything is possible when you put your mind to it. I know that your mind can work miracles." (Lipton, *The Biology of Belief*)

I believe that this kind of research offers motivating evidence for making a commitment to the *Excuses Begone!* paradigm.

Another recent procedure may completely reverse an old medical model. It seems that a man's forefinger was accidentally sliced off at the top knuckle, and by altering genetic instructions, a team succeeded in regrowing a new half-inch top to his finger in four weeks. Fingers are genetically programmed to stave off infection when an injury like this occurs, so the medical team replaced his sliced-off stub with stem cells programmed to grow a finger—the subsequent new growth included the nail, cuticle, and flesh. This man's DNA was overturned by introducing newly programmed instructions.

In a variety of studies on severe depression, heart disease, rheumatoid arthritis, ulcers, and even cancer, the power of the mind to overcome these maladies trumps the conventional medical wisdom of treating the cells rather than the environment in which they reside. The new biology is clearly indicating that beliefs—some of which are conscious and most of which are subconscious (or habitual)—determine our physical and mental health, along with our level of happiness and success.

Author James Allen observed: "We do not attract that which we *want* but that which we *are*." I've contemplated this idea for a long time. Until recently, I accepted the idea that what we are is pretty much formulated by complex genetic input and strands of DNA inherited from our parents and other relatives. But I've changed my mind. My new personal philosophy is that who I am is first and foremost determined by what I believe—and that leads me to consciously focus on the fact that limitations or traits inherited from my ancestors are absolutely not the final word. For me there's now a surprise tucked into James Allen's quote: *by changing my beliefs, I change who I am.* As a result of this shift in my beliefs, I've attracted some new and wondrous features into my life, including being prompted to write this book and share its insights with you.

As you work your way through these pages, remember that *what you are is what you believe, not what you were handed genetically.*

If you stay focused on what you are as a set of beliefs, you will align with the same kinds of energy. As you read on, remind yourself that you attract what you are, not what you want; and what you are is your beliefs, not your cells. As *The Biology of Belief* establishes, your mental activity is strong enough to overcome material particles *and* the influences of early conditioning and programming that you unwittingly adopted through your formative years.

### Your Lingering Early Programming

In addition to our genetic makeup, the other big excuse that most of us use to justify unhappiness, poor health, and lack of success is the family and cultural conditioning we've been programmed with. To that end, there's a fascinating area of inquiry known as *memetics,* which deals with the mind and is analogous to the relationship of genetics to the body. So as the basic unit of genetics is the gene, the basic unit of memetics is the meme (rhymes with "team"). Yet unlike an atom or an electron, the meme has no physical properties. According to Richard Brodie, in his work *Virus of the Mind,* it's "a thought, belief, or attitude in your mind that can spread to and from other people's minds."

Richard Dawkins, the Oxford biologist who coined the word *meme,* describes the process in his book *The Selfish Gene.* My understanding is that memetics originates from the word *mimic,* meaning to observe and copy behavior. This behavior is repeated and passed on to others, and on and on the mimicking process goes. The key point is this: *transferring an idea, attitude, or belief to others is done mentally.* We won't find memes by turning up the magnification on any microscope—they pass from mind to mind via hundreds of thousands of imitations. By the age of six or seven, we've all been programmed with an endless inventory of memes that act very much like a virus. They aren't necessarily good or bad; they simply spread easily throughout the population.

Once a meme is in your mind, it can and will subtly influence your behavior. This is one of the ways you acquire a huge category of excuses that keep you in a rut. For example: "My memes made me do it! I can't help it! These ideas [beliefs, attitudes] have been passed on to me from one mind to another for generations, and there's nothing I can do about the way I think. These memes have been the building blocks of my mind, and I can't deprogram myself from these viruses of the mind that just keep replicating and spreading. These ideas [memes] are so much a part of me that it's impossible to 'disinfect' myself from the results of all of these mind viruses." Every excuse you read about in this book is, in reality, a meme that was once planted in your mind.

Richard Brodie uses the word *virus* to describe what happens in the mind through mimicking and imitating. The core purpose of a virus is to make as many copies of itself as possible by penetrating wherever an opening occurs and spreading itself to as many hosts as possible. Similarly, you're a host for countless memes; they're the entrenched thoughts and behavioral characteristics of your personality. You've spent years repeating and replicating ideas that were traveling from one mind to another, spreading these ideas and beliefs to many others.

Memes die hard because they've become who you think you are; shedding them is like trying to discard one of your vital organs, and it taps your life energy. Many memes, in fact, were firmly implanted by your parents during your early family history—it will come as no surprise that they were easily transferred to you from your parents or grandparents. Since ideas get fixed in your mind by spreading from other minds, they become your reality, often for your entire life.

Personally, I find it fascinating that there are invisible little units that I allowed to be implanted in my mind, which continue to impact how I think and behave today. Moreover, I've acted on these mind viruses and have passed them on to my children . . . unwittingly, I've become a carrier.

Here are some examples that continue to crop up in my life:

I grew up with a Depression mentality. Even though I was born in 1940 at the tail end of the Great Depression, my parents and grandparents lived through hard economic times and shared a lot of their scarcity messages with me. *Don't spend recklessly; save for the future because things will only get worse; there are shortages everywhere; food is in minimal supply; don't waste anything; eat everything on your plate; you don't have enough money* . . . these ideas were invisibly passed on to me as I grew up in the Midwest in the 1940s. I mimicked or imitated these ideas and allowed myself to become an instrument of these mind viruses. They grew in me, and I spread them wherever I went, until they became fully ensconced in my mind and many of my actions.

Although I'm now in my 60s, these memes are very much alive today and are still attempting to replicate and spread. To some extent they serve a purpose, although they occasionally work overtime. My world isn't endangered by poverty, for instance, but I'm still a financially cautious person who likes to save rather than dispose of items retaining some usefulness. I respect those attitudes, and they no doubt originated in my childhood by being programmed into my habitual subconscious mind. But do I really need to retrieve used-up toothpaste tubes discarded by my children in wastepaper baskets, and strenuously squeeze out another two weeks' worth of product . . . when I've earned enough to buy the toothpaste factory?!

Here's another mind virus I've noticed lately: I must have imitated sulking when I didn't get my way as the youngest of three boys, or as a child in a series of foster homes, because I remember my adult forms of sulking (pouting and even yelling) when I was in my 30s and 40s. Recently I was alone in my office, feeling frustrated because I couldn't locate something I needed. As my frustration mounted, I became increasingly irrational: I raised my voice, loudly protested (although there was no one else there), used profanity, and stomped through the house until I was distraught and had given myself an upset stomach. This incident lasted one or two minutes, and then I finally calmed down and found the book I thought was the culprit in my private drama.

Why am I admitting to this silly scene, given my desire to be seen as a rational spiritual teacher? Because it illustrates a point

I'm making in this opening chapter. As an embryo, an infant, and a young boy, I must have seen this kind of behavior and mimicked it—the meme infected me, replicating and spreading from a relative or friend's mind to mine. And now, some 60 years later, I could have a built-in excuse for behaving irrationally enough to feel embarrassed by my infantile behavior and for making myself sick. The excuse is right there for me to use: *I've always overreacted to frustration; it's just a part of me. I don't have any control over stomping around and blaming who knows what, using mild profanity, and being immobilized because I cannot tolerate my frustration.* The possibilities are inexhaustible for excusing this behavior, but the question I must ask myself is: *Do I really want to hold on to these habitual behaviors that are ultimately capable of making me sick?*

Just like me, you have thousands of imitated thoughts and actions that were absorbed through contact with individuals in your childhood environment. When mind viruses serve you, it's a pleasure to observe them and express silent gratitude. But when they continue to plague your life, inhibiting you from achieving your desires, then you're on notice to start shedding them. The point is that these mind viruses, or memes, can work against you in myriad ways today, but you can also change them. (I hasten to add here that by becoming aware of my own inclinations to use old, no-longer-sensible-or-practical responses to my frustrations, and by being willing to do the deprogramming work on my long-held thoughts, I now notice those infantile temptations and choose a healthier way. The bonus is that I'm more effective at locating the missing items that used to perplex me!)

Thinking that you'll always be poor, unlucky, overweight, or underweight; that you'll always have an addictive personality; that you'll never attract your soul mate; that you'll continue to have angry outbursts; that you'll always lack musical, artistic, or athletic ability; or that you'll forever be shy because you've always felt that way . . . are *excuses.* And when you see them for what they are, you can eliminate them. On the other hand, if you find them to be firmly entrenched personality traits and habits of thinking that can't be challenged, you'll symbolically suck your thumb and cry when life doesn't appear to cooperate. Believe me, though, it's far more energizing and fulfilling to practice the *Excuses Begone!* paradigm. Using a new set of thinking habits will enhance your life and help you attract all that you really are. At the same time, you'll be modeling a new and better way to live for the people in your environment who are unwitting victims of the excuse virus.

You've been a memetic superstar since birth, mimicking beliefs and behaviors from other influences beyond your family and social structure. Influences from your religious training, ethnic culture, television programming and advertising, and the like have become a fixed part of your habitual mind. It isn't my purpose to examine all the ways you've acquired beliefs, since that's something only *you* can do. I'm writing this book to help you gain awareness of the excuses you use for behaving in ways that don't help you to achieve the level of health, happiness, and success you desire. I agree with the Roman Emperor Marcus Aurelius, known for his brilliance as a leader of men and a spiritually conscious being. He is reported to have said, "Our life is what our thoughts make it."

Your behaviors are supported by your thinking patterns; that is, your thoughts truly make or break your life. While some of them are operating on a conscious level and are easy to recognize, others are deeply embedded within your subconscious. However, I prefer to call this deeply programmed or almost automatic second-nature part of you, "the habitual mind."

For me, *subconscious* implies being below the level of creative awareness, a sort of mysterious entity that can't be known. Since the central theme of this book is that anything used to explain thinking and acting in the same self-sabotaging ways is an excuse, it seems to me that calling it "subconscious" is really underscoring this notion: *I can't help it, I can't talk about it, and I certainly can't change it; because it is, after all, below my conscious level, where I do all of my living.*

I personally find it hard to work with a part of myself that's not within my conscious life. Therefore, I choose to call this huge reservoir of emptiness—a reservoir that pushes us all away from our Divine dharma as well as our optimal level of health, happiness, and success—"the habitual mind." And while these types of thoughts might seem to be unreachable, I assure you that they'll come to the surface with an *Excuses Begone!* attitude.

### Kissing the Big Excuses Good-bye

This opening chapter has introduced you to recent research and observations that are increasing our understanding of human nature. My purpose is to help you use this information to alter the parts of your life that are hampered by old science and old thinking. In summary, there are basically two big excuses we all utilize:

— The first one is: *I can't really help the way I am; after all, people can't change their DNA. My genetic makeup is the culprit.* The new biology says that there's an energy field surrounding, and contained within, all of your cells, and this field is influenced by your beliefs. Moreover, it is out of this field that all particles are created —it's the sole governing entity of the body. Something like 95 percent of us do *not* have genetic reasons for illness, depression, fear, or any other condition.

Here in the 21st century, science invites you to stop believing that you're a victim of your genetic makeup, because a large body of evidence demonstrates empirically that your beliefs can change your genes. I encourage you to examine this mind-bending idea at greater depth than I'm able to offer here. There's an invisible part of you that you can call intelligence, higher function, Tao, thought, belief, Spirit, God . . . you choose.

— The second big excuse is rooted in your early history and family conditioning. It impacts you in so many ways that you probably feel it's an impossible-to-be-free-of aspect of your life.

Kiss this one good-bye as well. Just because you've been infected with a tradition meme and programmed to repeat it and pass it on to future generations doesn't mean you're unable to disinfect yourself and reprogram your inner world.

These funny little non-things called memes are thoughts that you allow to become your master—and make no mistake about it, every excuse you've ever used is really a meme disguised as an explanation. Yet you can deprogram yourself from these mind viruses. A virus isn't concerned with whether it's contributing to your well-being or your ill-being because it only wants to penetrate, replicate, and spread. But you don't have to be a victim of anything that was transferred from another mind to yours. Your beliefs have made these memes seem like second nature to you. While excuses are just thoughts or beliefs, you are the decider of what you ultimately store away as your guide to life.

A short discourse from the Dhammapada gives a sense of the route individuals travel as they advance toward their own inherent perfection and self-realization. Savor this ancient wisdom and incorporate its message with the modern understanding of genetics and memetics: "All that we are is the result of what we have thought. It is founded on our thoughts. It is made up of our thoughts. If one speaks or acts with a pure thought, happiness follows one, like a shadow that never leaves."

# CHAPTER 2

# YOUR TWO MINDS

*"The hell to be endured hereafter, of which theology tells,*
*is no worse than the hell we make for ourselves in this world*
*by habitually fashioning our characters in the wrong way. . . .*
*We are spinning our own fates, good or evil . . ."*

— from *The Principles of Psychology,* by William James

Sometime ago I challenged myself to study the process of making dramatic thought transitions, using attitudes and behaviors that had been with me for a lifetime. For several years I scrutinized precisely what I did to undo old patterns in myself. This activity led me to question basic beliefs about the legitimacy of environmental and genetic authority in determining who I am and what I can change. Due to my success in modifying my thoughts and, subsequently, my actions, I developed a new paradigm for eliminating unwanted, lifelong thinking habits. At first glance, much of what I'm sharing here may seem radical and inconsistent with established psychological and sociological academic tenets. So be it. Here is what I believe—this is how I see it!

In a brilliant one-act play by Jean-Paul Sartre titled *No Exit,* the central character states emphatically: "A man is what he wills himself to be." This idea of willpower is a core theme in much of my earlier writing, and I still strongly subscribe to the belief that we all have within us an invisible force that we recognize as *will.* But I also know that there are many facets of our lives that seem to be beyond the pale of the will—for example, it often isn't enough to eliminate lifelong habits. Identifying and changing some thoughts, particularly those that have been with us for what seems like forever, requires a brand-new perceptual process.

In contrast to Sartre's observation, Ralph Waldo Emerson offers this: "Man is a stream whose source is hidden. Our being is descending into us from we know not whence." In the 1600s, Benedict de Spinoza made a similar observation about the human mind, which I read in my college days and have never forgotten: "[T]he human mind is part of the infinite intellect of God." I still apply this to myself whenever I question how or why I got myself into one of the many predicaments I've brought upon myself throughout my adult life.

The mind that Spinoza is referring to has no form or substance; is always working—even while you're sleeping—and, most significantly, is your connection to Source. Viewed in this light, it is your personal God component, always with you and always ready to serve you in fulfilling another of Spinoza's observations: "The mind's highest good is the knowledge of God." Yes, your mind is largely responsible for who and what you've become, but there's also a beingness buried within you, in a place where your thoughts originate. Emerson suggests that it's a mystery, "descending into us from we know not whence."

These two ideas about human nature combine in you to form what I call *two minds:* The one that's frequently referred to as your "conscious mind" is what I call "creative consciousness"; and the other is your "habitual mind," which, as I explained in the last chapter, is what I call the subconscious mind. Yet whether they originate in creative consciousness or the habitual mind, I believe that any thought patterns that don't enhance and expand your joyous development are *excuses*. As you'll see, this means that you have far more influence than you've probably been led to believe to rearrange and change ineffectual and harmful beliefs or ideas.

### Creative Consciousness

In this paradigm, the conscious mind is more accurately described as the *creative* conscious mind. This close-to-the-surface, nonhabitual mind makes endless decisions about what you wear, what you eat, what appointments you keep, what time you go to bed, and thousands of other daily choices in your life. This invisible and "placeless place" is the part of your brain that makes and cancels plans, adds new ones, and thinks continuously. This creative consciousness is always there, to the point that even when you want to shut it down, it can be extremely difficult to do so . . . the thoughts just keep coming. What an immeasurable benefit to consider that this vast, mysterious mind is really part of the Source that creates everything, as Spinoza suggests.

So if your mind is a creator, just as God's mind is a creator of the universe, then it can perform at the absolutely highest level imaginable. The creative force asks for nothing and has no ego—it's simply an instrument of giving, providing and offering at all times with no consideration for itself. Put another way, the highest calling of your conscious creative mind is to be the human equivalent of God's mind. Yet you'll probably agree that most of your thoughts focus on the relatively tiny universe of your human self!

Rest assured that you can choose to learn how to shift your everyday thoughts away from *What am I doing? What can I get?* and *How quickly can I get it?* to Spinoza's concept of discovering the highest-functioning, all-knowing part of yourself. This may sound like a tall order, but I guarantee that reprogramming your creative conscious mind is really a simple matter. The endless thoughts of *me, me, me* are close to the surface and highly susceptible to change. (You'll have the opportunity to practice this when you study the paradigm for eliminating excuses in the third part of this book.)

The creative conscious mind can do almost anything you instruct it to do: It can change thoughts at your bidding, practice affirmations you create, wander in blissful meditation at your invitation, and learn almost any new skill at your insistence. It can think of everything you direct it to. Through discipline, effort, and continual practice, it can also accomplish almost anything you focus your thoughts on.

The problem with creative consciousness is that its constant shifts and changes can overwhelm/flood you. It's often referred to as "the monkey mind" because it keeps flitting about almost continuously, first having one thought, then another, and then still another. Most of this close-to-the-surface mental activity is the ego's attempt to dance to the beat of rhythms and influences that are outside of you, which are probably unwanted and unnecessary, and running your life without your permission. Your creative consciousness has developed a weak connection that's full of static, so its signals from a part of the infinite intellect of God are silenced by an ego-based accompaniment that broadcasts: *What's in it for me? How do I look? How much money can I make? How can I get ahead? Whom do I have to please? Why are there so many demands on me?* On and on these thoughts come, then go, then come right back.

There's statistical evidence that the conscious mind occupies approximately 5 percent of the total workings of the brain, leaving 95 percent to the realm of the subconscious. Percentages interest me less than the ability to sense your mind as not some amorphous component of your being that's constantly changing from one ego-based thought to another, but rather as evidence of your nature, or your connection to the infinite intellect of creation. This style of magnificent respect alerts you to your ability to access the highest function of your mind.

### The Habitual (Subconscious) Mind

According to Tor Nørretranders, the author of *The User Illusion,* the subconscious mind has been calculated to process millions of environmental stimuli per second versus only a few dozen environmental stimuli per second that the conscious mind can process. Conventional psychological wisdom says that much of what you believe about yourself, along with almost all of your daily actions, is programmed into your subconscious or habitual mind. You spend a great deal of your time operating on automatic pilot, so to speak. In fact, you could visualize your two minds as co-pilots: the conscious mind is aware of its thoughts but is a minor player, like a real pilot in training; while the subconscious takes care of virtually everything you need to think, say, or do.

I take exception to this assertion that the habitual mind runs the show, doing everything that the creative mind isn't paying attention to. According to this view, the habitual mind is like a computer running a downloaded program that will play throughout your life—it's been permanently programmed from the moment of conception, and it's next to impossible to get new software to rewrite existing programs. I simply cannot agree that a part of your mind was nourished by ideas, images, and input that continue to be necessary for your sustainability today. It's my contention that this is a false belief that's easily revealed as an excuse. I don't believe that anyone has to live with the belief that they have programming in their subconscious mind that can't be rewritten. I'll explain my perspective on this issue.

If you're the way you are because of something that's subconscious—that is, below your level of waking consciousness—then it's clearly something you can do nothing about. You can't even talk about it, since it's beyond your conscious mind. For the same reason, you can't understand it; you can't challenge it; and, most egregiously, you can't change or fix it. How can you fix something that's totally inaccessible? It would be like attempting to repair a broken watch that was sealed away in a vault: obviously, you'd need the combination to enter into that previously inaccessible space.

If something is subconscious and thus automatic, it's believed that you don't have a choice in the matter. And to me, that's the most regrettable thing about this subconscious model: believing that you don't have a choice. The truth, as I see it, is that everything you think, say, and do is a choice—and you don't need to think, speak, or act as you've done for your entire life. When you abandon making choices, you enter the vast world of excuses.

Right now, while reading this book, decide to begin *choosing* instead of *excusing*. You can instantly decide to reprogram and direct your life toward the level of happiness, success, and health that you prefer.

I've had a downloaded pattern since childhood, and it concerns my stroke in my daily swim. Some people who have observed me making my way through the ocean have said that I swim as though I've *had* a stroke. I never paid much attention to what others said until I discovered that the way I kicked my feet (using only my right leg, while my left leg stayed motionless) was putting undue pressure on my back and throwing me out of alignment as I practiced yoga and simply got older.

When I was advised to change the way I swam by kicking both legs simultaneously, my first reaction was to think, *I can't change my swimming style—I've been doing it this way for almost 60 years! I even swam competitively with this "Dyer stroke." This is something I've downloaded into me from thousands of hours of swimming and is a subconscious habit.* Yet after putting to the test the ideas I'm writing about in this book, I was able to rather easily adopt a brand-new swimming stroke, even though I was 65 years of age at the time.

Just like my being able to rather quickly change a 60-year-old habit, you can access the program you're operating with by examining your thoughts. Your habitual mind takes over when you choose to ignore your conscious beliefs, and you just continue to act in ways you've been programmed to. But you *can* shift to your creative mind and explore your options. You don't have to buy the old argument that a part of you is inaccessible, unreachable, or buried so deep down inside that undoing early programming is impossible. You'll never successfully reprogram your computer, or your mind, by telling it to stop spewing out the same garbage. You're stuck until you change to a new operating system or download some new files . . . but first you have to know that this is an option.

Think of the many ways in which you identify yourself, particularly in the gray area of deeply entrenched thoughts. Identify the programs in your habitual mind that are so outdated that they're hampering your system. Those attitudes, beliefs, and thoughts that don't serve you are excuses, ultimately destined to be sent to the trash bin.

Mark Twain had this wonderful observation about how we change old, unwanted ways of thinking and behaving: "Habit is habit, and not to be flung out of the window by any man, but coaxed downstairs a step at a time." My objective is to help you coax down the stairs those ways of thinking that keep you from living your life at the optimal level. Should this seem daunting, know that it doesn't have to be a lengthy, winding staircase that takes years to traverse. Or, to use the computer metaphor, your internal system is as capable of change as contemporary operating systems are. Freedom from long-established habits, whether they originated genetically or memetically, is attainable with the *Excuses Begone!* paradigm presented in Part III.

Reaching into the part of your mind that works on automatic pilot as a result of early programming and conditioning isn't nearly as troublesome as allowing it to continue to run your life. It's actually quite uncomplicated and won't take a great deal of time to shift from old habits to new choices. You are a part of the same intelligence that creates worlds; in fact, your mind *is* that intelligence. Knowing this, how could you consider a part of you to be unreachable or unprogrammable? *No* part of you is unreachable, no matter how automatic or habitual it may have become.

Certain aspects of your life may seem to be governed by a force that you're unaware of, and you can feel that there's no possibility of choice and that you're imprisoned by your excuse inventory: *I can't really help it; it's just my nature; I've always been this way.* Talk about futility! However, anytime you choose, you can access your habitual mind and begin to reprogram it, changing patterns that may have been useful once but no longer work for you.

### See Yourself Through a New Lens

The quote at the beginning of this chapter was written almost 120 years ago by the father of modern psychology, William James, who urges us to be aware of the danger of living as if there are no choices. I am personally convinced that everyone has a capacity for greatness that transcends anything they've been taught to believe, that every being who's ever existed is in fact a portion of the all-creating power of intention. Since we're all pieces of the infinite creative Source, we should continually be telling ourselves, "I came from God, and since I must be like what I came from, I am a piece of the Divine." Trying to imagine the all-creating spiritual force coming up with excuses for anything is impossible, because it is creating from its own consciousness.

Now put *yourself* in this picture. While your mind is part of the unlimited Source, it becomes limited when you believe it to be *fallible, weak, impotent,* or any other adjective that misidentifies with creative energy. When you edge God out in this manner, you invite ego—which is known as the "false self" by spiritual teachers of all persuasions—in.

I invite you to try on a new lens that lets you access your false self with its ton of excuses (many of which I've detailed in the following chapter) and its belief in limitations. As it edges God out, your false self forces you to part with ideas that prove you're a spiritual being having a temporary human experience. Ego gives you a rationale for creating the rationalizations and justifications that eventually go on to direct your life. They become so embedded in what social scientists call the subconscious that your habitual mind turns into an excuse machine.

Allow yourself to look through your new lens by acquiring a set of beliefs that includes your spiritual or God-realized nature. It may feel a little unfamiliar, or even mysterious, at first, but be willing to allow your senses to adjust to this new way of seeing. Transcend the idea that your genetic makeup is static. With your new ability to perceive ego, you'll become a wizard who easily dethrones the dictator of your false self, bypassing early conditioning imposed by people in your environment who have edged God out.

As you get comfortable with this new way of seeing yourself, ask yourself the following question: *If no one told me who I was, who would I be?* Quietly meditate on this by spending some time in the spaciousness of *not knowing.* Imagine that your subconscious mind is nonexistent and there is no storage receptacle for excuses during your life. There's just an open and inviting clear space inside of you—a tabula rasa, or blank slate, with a magical surface that nothing adheres to. You might imagine that your everyday conscious mind simply doesn't absorb the opinions of the folks you grew up with. In this little fantasy, there's never been anyone telling you who you are. So who are you?

When I did this exercise, I found that my answer to the above question was quite simply: *I would be anything that I, and only I, decided to be in this moment and all future moments.* As the song goes, "I've gotta be me," and that means jettisoning all of the excuses I've accumulated. My habitual life wouldn't be based upon anyone's early programming, since there wouldn't be anyone who ever told me who I am. Or, as the Tao teaches:

> *Look to nature for your sustenance.*
> *Look to the great mysterious Tao [God] that*
> *does nothing and leaves nothing undone.*
> *Observe how the entire universe and all of*
> *these beautiful Tao-centered creatures work.*[1]

Tao-centered creatures allow. They trust. They live here in the present moment and, most assuredly, they have no need for any excuses.

*Applying Your Fresh Perspective*
*to Common Excuse Categories*

Now I'd like to show you how you can take the fresh perspective you've gained by looking through your new lens. The excuse categories of genetics, memetics, and consciousness are about to be shown the door.

## Your New Outlook on Genetic Programming

I'm sure you're familiar with some variation of this popular excuse: "I can't help it; it runs in my family." New biology, however, has proven that beliefs can override DNA, so move what you thought was a fact to the "excuse file" by altering how you view its authenticity. You can change what you perceive as immutable and beyond your reach by eliminating excuses such as the ones in the genetic excuse category.

As Gregg Braden writes in his astonishing book *The Spontaneous Healing of Belief:*

> Paradigm-shattering experiments published in leading-edge, peer-reviewed journals reveal that we're bathed in a field of intelligent energy that fills what used to be thought of as empty space. Additional discoveries show beyond any reasonable doubt that this field responds to us—*it rearranges itself*—in the presence of our heart-based feelings and beliefs. And this is the revolution that changes everything.

Here are two exercises to practice applying these ideas to your genetic program:

1. Be open to the scientifically verified idea that your beliefs have the power to rearrange and change the material world. Start by making this particularly pertinent for you in your physical and personal destiny by contemplating that more things of this nature are possible than you've previously experienced. Allow these new

thoughts about your biology to gently enter your belief system. Encourage yourself to consider your beliefs as things that affect you, perhaps even more than physical particles do. If it suits you, you may even see beliefs as nonparticles in the nonmaterial or spiritual world.

2. Create an affirmation that attests to this new no-excuses philosophy for genetics. Something from the following list would work fine, but feel free to come up with your own:

- *I can change my body's infirmities by shifting my beliefs.*

- *I have the power to undo old thoughts about my genetic destiny.*

- *If I stay with them and live from my heart, my beliefs can inspire new talents if I so desire.*

- *I can heal anything by healing my beliefs first.*

- *I intend to keep my beliefs uppermost, and I refuse to blame anything in the material world for any deficiencies in my life.*

### Your New Outlook on Memetic Programming

Again, this is an excuse category that you've probably depended on to justify why life isn't what you really want it to be. These are the big mind-virus excuses: *My family made me the way I am, and I can't change it. My early childhood experience and all of the unfair criticism I received explain why I have low self-esteem. I'm stuck in this place because I've been infected by a multitude of mind viruses and environmental facts that have left me shortchanged when it comes to fulfilling a higher destiny. How can I change what I've imitated and mimicked for so many years? I've been infected by mind viruses, and it's impossible to change.*

What follows are two exercises to practice applying to your memetic program:

1. Affirm: *I believe that I am perfectly capable of overcoming any early conditioning I have adopted as a part of my personality and my current life experience.* Know that research is demonstrating that the power of thought is aligned with the universal mind, which many call "the Tao" or "God." Just hang on to this idea for now—it will become clearer as you progress through this course in *Excuses Begone!*

2. Assert that anything that's been programmed into you and acts like a virus is perfectly capable of being *de*programmed if you decide it's worth the effort. Remind yourself that since you're not presently a victim of beliefs that were modeled for you when you were much younger, using these as excuses is no longer your method. At this point you don't even have to know how to deprogram or disinfect yourself. All you need to believe is that you have the ability and will begin now.

Here's an affirmation that will guide you to awareness and answers: *I am much more powerful today than the old programs and mind viruses that I absorbed in my childhood.* Telling yourself this will make your inner teacher appear!

### Your New Outlook on Creative Consciousness

The everyday activity of your creative consciousness also proliferates excuses. You might think that you have no control over the thoughts that just keep popping into your head, but consider this radical idea: *Your thoughts are not located in your head.* Thought is an energy system that isn't found anywhere in the physical world. The universe itself and everything in it is both mental and spiritual in nature. You create a field of energy with your thoughts, and the field creates all of the particles, or what Lao-tzu called "the world of the 10,000 things." This energy field is an important function of the body; your conscious mind is always working and connecting to this field from which everything is intended.

Apply these two exercises:

1. Quiet the mind by practicing daily meditation. As Sogyal Rinpoche wrote in *The Tibetan Book of Living and Dying:* "The gift of learning to meditate is the greatest gift you can give yourself in this life. For it is only through meditation that you can undertake the journey to discover your true nature, and so find the stability and confidence you will need to live, and die, well." Find a way to give yourself that gift and access your conscious creative mind by eliminating unnecessary, unwanted, superfluous thoughts through meditation.

2. Use positive proclamations daily that are life enhancing and align you with the loving Source of everything. Rather than allowing your thoughts to insist that something is wrong or missing, retrain your conscious creative mind with beliefs such as these: *What I desire is already here; I just haven't connected to it yet. It can't be stopped because my thoughts are aligned with the mind or intellect of God.*

### Your New Outlook on Habitual Consciousness

In this category you'll find excuses such as: *I can't help the way I am because I've had so many limiting ideas programmed into me. It's my subconscious, so I can't even reach in there and examine it, let alone deprogram myself.* If you believe that your mind is below your level of conscious awareness, you've created a ready excuse to use whenever it's difficult to change your thinking. And if the self-limiting thoughts have been with you for years, it seems like a perfect excuse. So rename the subconscious mind the *habitual* mind.

555

*Habit* implies that you've made the same choices over time, and your thoughts and behaviors are simply accustomed to a certain way of being. It also suggests that there's room to make your thoughts less automatic and more aligned with the realm of choice. Later you'll read about awareness as one of the keys to bringing these thoughts into your daily experience; but for now, practice the following as you start to eliminate excuses from your habitual mind:

1. Begin noticing what you're thinking as a way to weaken your reliance on the excuse of your subconscious. Repeating these quotes can be helpful: "Every extension of knowledge arises from making conscious the unconscious" (Friedrich Nietzsche), and "The unconscious . . . is dangerous only when our conscious attitude towards it becomes hopelessly false" (from *Modern Man in Search of a Soul,* by Carl Jung). Two of the world's greatest teachers state that you can change previously unconscious thinking habits and bring them to your conscious mind. Relying upon the excuse of a subconscious mind is both false and dangerous.

Why not create your version of those quotes as well? Try something like: "I am perfectly capable of reaching into my own mind and changing anything about myself that is supported by my habitual thinking patterns, even if they seem to be automatic at this point in time." Speak your truth in a way that assists your choice to rid yourself of those excuses.

2. Make this a motto for your thoughts: *Do good things, and don't do bad things!* Bad thoughts prompt you to engage in self-limiting behaviors; good thoughts, on the other hand, support your desire and capacity to live at high levels of joy, success, and health.

Here's some advice from ancient China, attributed to a fictional character named Birdsnest:

> Long ago in China, there lived a monk who perched in a
> certain tree every day to meditate. No matter if the tree swayed

556

in fierce winds and rain, the monk settled himself comfortably, high up in the branches. Because of this, he was nicknamed "Birdsnest" by the village folk nearby.

Many of these villagers passed beneath the monk while hunting or while gathering wood in the forest, and after a time, they grew used to him. Some began to stop and talk of their concerns with Birdsnest. They liked the things he had to say, and soon Birdsnest became known for his kind and thoughtful words.

After some years, the monk's wise reputation spread throughout the province. Visitors from distant cities hiked to the remote forest for advice. Even the governor of the province decided that he too would like to visit Birdsnest to discuss matters of importance. So one spring morning, the governor set off to find him. After traveling for several days, he at last located Birdsnest's tree in the dense forest. The monk sat calmly, high in the topmost branches, enjoying the warmth and the birdsong of spring.

Looking up, the governor shouted, "Birdsnest! I am the governor of this province, and I have come a great distance to speak with you! I have a most important question!" The governor waited for a reply but heard only the pleasant sounds of leaves stirring in the breeze. The governor continued, "This is my question: tell me, Birdsnest, what is it that all the wise ones have taught? Can you tell me the most important thing the Buddha ever said?" There was a long pause—just the soft rustle of leaves again.

Finally, the monk called down from the tree: "This is your answer, Governor: Don't do bad things. Always do good things. That's what all the Buddhas taught."

But the governor thought this answer far too simple to have walked two days for! Irritated and annoyed, he stammered, "Don't do bad things; always do good things! I knew that when I was three years old, monk!"

Looking down at the governor, Birdsnest replied with a wry smile, "Yes, the three-year-old knows it, but the eighty-year-old still finds it very difficult to do!"

When it feels difficult to do good things, remember to seek the three-year-old within that Birdsnest referred to. Give yourself the gift of hearing thoughts from a time before conditioning was deeply embedded.

CHAPTER 3

# YOUR EXCUSE CATALOG

*"I know of no more encouraging fact than the unquestionable
ability of man to elevate his life by a conscious endeavor."*

— from *Walden,* by Henry David Thoreau


I have an undeniable affinity for Henry David Thoreau's experience while communing with nature at Walden Pond in Massa-
chusetts. I've visited his home in Concord on many occasions,
meditated at his desk, and rested on his bed to enhance this magical connection. The quote above is so meaningful to me that it
actually influenced my writing of this book!

I've occasionally been accused of being a Pollyanna, offering
hope to the hopeless. Some see my philosophy concerning the
human ability to elevate life to higher levels of peace, love, and
joy to be naïve. Being compared to Pollyanna isn't a source of discomfort for me, however. After all, here was a little girl who arrived
in a town where the people were miserable and pessimistic, with
doom and gloom dominating the horizon. Within a short while,

the energy of Pollyanna permeated the community—her enthusiasm was infectious; and people began to feel hope, passion, and love replacing their despair and futility. So if I'm to be compared to anyone, I find it an honor to be viewed in Pollyannish terms. I think that many of Mr. Thoreau's contemporaries might have applied a similar label to him as well.

Thoreau left the corrupt world of humankind to live in the natural world, with trees, animals, and the weather as his teachers. He discovered an ecstatic awareness of a current of life coursing through the entire planet, which led to his optimism about human potential. His message is essentially this: *Realize the existence of the unknowable and ecstatic aspect of your existence. Know that this Divine element is an intrinsic part of yourself. Begin trusting your underlying nature by becoming conscious.* In other words, excuses be . . . gone!

There are four words in this chapter's opening quote that I want to highlight—*encouraging, unquestionable, elevate,* and *conscious:*

1. This book is *encouraging* you to challenge patterns and feel inspired by a newfound awareness of the life hidden beneath your excuses. Invite yourself to move out of established thought patterns, and realize that there is nothing standing in your way of living at your highest levels.

2. You have an *unquestionable* ability to eliminate excuses—they'll get up and go when they're revealed as the false beliefs that they are. There's simply no question about this!

3. You *elevate* your life by taking responsibility for who you are and what you're choosing to become. You can transcend the ordinary, mundane, and average with thoughts of greater joy and meaning; you can decide to elevate your life, rather than have it stagnate or deteriorate with excuses. Go beyond where you presently are.

4. You can bring your desires to consciousness by disconnecting the power from your subconscious so that it can't continue to run your life. Your subconscious (habitual) mind is accessible, so unearth the excuses buried deep within you. Become *conscious!*

Be *encouraged* by the *unquestionable* ability you have to *elevate* your life by a *conscious* endeavor. Remember these four words as you review the following list of some of the most common excuses that you'd probably like to free yourself from.

### *A Catalog of Some Common Excuses*

In my role as a counselor, teacher, and parent, I've heard many reasons that people use to explain an unhappy existence . . . and almost all of them inevitably fall into one huge category, which I call "excuses." The rest of the chapter will introduce you to 18 of the most commonly used ones, along with a brief commentary about each of them. This will give you a primer before you go on to learn the *Excuses Begone!* method that's detailed in the rest of the book.

Here they are, in no particular order:

### 1. It Will Be Difficult

While this may seem like a supportable reason, it's clearly an excuse designed to discourage you. If you're honest with yourself about the difficulty you're experiencing with addiction, obesity, depression, shyness, low self-esteem, loneliness, or any other life aspect, you'll recognize the *useless suffering* you're hanging on to. If it's going to be difficult anyway, why not opt for some use*ful* suffering? Still, the fact is that you have absolutely no incontrovertible evidence that what you'd like to change is actually going to be challenging. It's just as likely to be easy for you to change your thinking as it is to be hard.

Decades ago when I decided to give up smoking, for example, I used *Excuses Begone!* beliefs. It was encouraging for me to realize how much more difficult it was to smoke than not to smoke. The smoker part of me always had to have a pack of cigarettes and an ashtray within easy reach, carry matches or lighters, dispose of ashes, deal with smelly fingers and stained teeth, earn money to pay for this disgusting habit, be careful exhaling noxious fumes, cough up nicotine residue from my lungs, buy lighter fluid and flints, and on and on. The truth was that continuing to smoke was the real difficulty, and changing my habit involved one simple thing: not smoking.

This is true for virtually all of your habits. The belief that they're going to be hard to change is only a belief! Making something difficult in your mind before you even undertake the effort is an excuse. *Nothing in the world is difficult for those who set their mind to it,* as an ancient Taoist master concluded.

## 2. It's Going to Be Risky

Again, this may seem like a good reason, but if you convince yourself that something involves more risk than you're capable of assuming or have the strength for, this is a poor excuse for not taking action. What is unquestionable here is your ability to choose your belief about the drawbacks of this endeavor.

Over the years, countless people have thanked me for taking so many risks in speaking out about what I believe so fervently. I'm always taken aback by such expressions of gratitude—I've never assumed that I was being courageous by speaking my mind. Even if my opinions and statements were certain to be perceived as offensive by large numbers of people, the idea that being myself and also being willing to express my own truth involved taking a chance never occurred to me.

I don't believe you can ever be 100 percent certain that something will be risk free. Holding back in silence out of fear of retribution or criticism could actually be the more hazardous behavior.

Speaking from the heart doesn't always mean critical fallout; after all, about 99 percent of the time, the feedback I receive is positive and heartwarming.

The fear involved in anticipating a risk simply serves to keep you from taking action. When you convince yourself that it's your job to avoid taking chances, you can continue your familiar habits. If you're accustomed to playing it safe by attempting to please everyone you encounter, then you're a victim of your own excuse making.

The point is that if you fear the opinions of others—or if you fear failure or success—then anything that you think or do will involve some risk. But if you're willing to live from *your* convictions and fulfill *your* destiny, then what others perceive as taking chances are simply the ways you choose to elevate your life. Even if you do believe that changing the way you think will involve risks, so what? The peace that you feel because you ignored the worry of a risk is far greater than staying stuck in a belief that is really only an excuse.

As writer Logan Pearsall Smith once noted: "What is more mortifying than to feel that you have missed the plum for want of courage to shake the tree?"

### 3. It Will Take a Long Time

Is this a valid reason, or an excuse not to proceed? If you wish to elevate your life, it really doesn't matter how long it takes, does it? And this is particularly true when you're conscious that *you live your life, every single bit of it, in the present moment and only in the present moment.* All you ever get is now. Every thought occurs in the present moment, and every change has a defining moment. Often it takes something or someone outside of you to help you realize that.

An entertaining psychiatrist named Dr. Murray Banks does just that with the following little exchange between himself and a woman who has decided not to return to school because she'd be too old when she finished.

"How old would you be in five years if you got that degree by starting now?" he asks her.

"Forty-nine," she replies.

"And how old will you be in five years if you don't go back to school?"

"Forty-nine," she answers, seemingly confused . . . but with the look of one who's become conscious of the excuses she created for not elevating her life.

However long it took you to create any self-defeating habit, you did it all one day, one moment at a time. There's absolutely no proof that anything will take a long time, since even the idea of "a long time" is an illusion—there is only now. Make this awareness a part of your consciousness. The Tao Te Ching reinforces this in perhaps the most famous line in that masterful work: "A journey of a thousand miles begins with a single step." Elevate or move on in your life, not by thinking big and in long time periods, but with consciousness focused on the present moment.

### 4. There Will Be Family Drama

After spending many years as a family therapist, I've seen how people often become stuck in their habituated modes of thinking because they fear the criticism that could result if they change. And I receive so many phone calls on my weekly radio show (on **HayHouseRadio.com**®) from individuals who insist on remaining stuck because of this excuse. When I encourage a shift in thinking, I regularly hear things like, "I'd love to try what you suggest, but it would kill my parents," or "My family would disown me if I did that! It's too big a price to pay." I've heard more than a few admit that if their spouse died, it would be an easier solution than making changes!

Now let me be very clear here: *I believe in family.* I have eight beautiful children, a mother in her 90s whom I adore, and two brothers whom I love dearly; and I treasure my immediate and extended families.

However—and this is a crucial point—living a life of your own choosing involves the unquestionable willingness to endure the slings and arrows that could come your way when you respond to your inner knowing rather than to the opinions of your family. Samuel Butler was probably feeling something similar when, toward the end of his life in 1902, he wrote: "I believe more unhappiness comes from this source than from any other—I mean the attempt to prolong family connection unduly, and to make people hang together artificially who would never naturally do so."

You don't belong to your immediate family; you're a member of the *human* family. You don't own your children, nor are you a possession of your parents. You're not obliged to fulfill the wishes or a destiny dictated by kin. It's important to consciously know that you're here to create your music, and that you don't have to die with your music still in you. Granted, this can trigger some family drama, but then again, that might just be your excuse for not following your own path. It's been my experience that I earn far more respect than reproach from my family whenever I encourage myself to live the life I want.

To that end, these types of excuses need to disappear: "I can't disappoint my grandparents or my parents. Why should I be the only one rebelling and wanting to move out of town? Or take up a new occupation? Or marry outside of our faith [or whatever else may incur disapproval and censure from relatives]?" These are thoughts or memes based on fears that were originally internalized in childhood, when they seemed the only way to secure a place in your "tribe." Yet what were reasons to the child you were then need to be recognized as excuses by the adult you are today. Don't let fear of family dramas keep you from changing outmoded, unnecessary, and unwanted thought patterns.

## 5. I Don't Deserve It

In *Revolution from Within: A Book of Self-Esteem,* Gloria Steinem writes that "self-esteem isn't everything; it's just that there's nothing without it." I believe that lack of self-esteem is the basis for the "I don't deserve it" excuse. I hear it in sentences such as these: "Nothing seems to work for me," "I try, but nothing ever comes my way . . . I must not be worthy of it," and "Other people can get ahead, but I guess I'm not good enough to succeed."

These excuses are based on a belief in the validity of your unworthiness. It's as if a part of you wants to protect you from (what's assumed to be) the unbearable pain of feeling that *maybe they're right, and I don't deserve it.* If you ask that part of you why it's doing this, it will have good reasons. But those reasons are, in effect, lies, and functioning by their edict means that you're *living* a lie. You don't earn worthiness—you're equally as deserving of all that this glorious world offers as anyone else is.

Believing that you're not good enough to have unlimited happiness, success, and health is a colossal fabrication that bears no resemblance to the truth of your life today. It keeps you discouraged, with a well-intentioned excuse to protect you from taking action. But it isn't *protecting* you; it's *preventing* you from becoming conscious of your unquestionable worthiness. In the presence of now, this excuse has no place in your life.

## 6. It's Not My Nature

The sentences cropping up in this category sound something like this: "I've always been this way; I can't help it," "I was born with these personality traits," "I've never known any other way to think," and "Yep, it's my nature, so I'll have to accept it." Earlier in this book, I explained my understanding of new research demonstrating that your genetic and memetic heredities are capable of being altered. If you're willing to consciously endeavor to change the beliefs that support what you call your nature, you'll discover that the "it's not my nature" excuse is gone.

I firmly believe that your intrinsic self is well equipped to help you fulfill your unique destiny. Just because you have no recollection of ever having been other than you are today, this isn't proof that your nature is unchangeable. To once again quote Henry David Thoreau: "It is surprising how much room there is in nature, if a man will follow his proper path." I take this to mean that nature itself will shift to accommodate you when you begin to know your unquestionable ability to elevate your life. Incorporate Thoreau's advice and begin to follow your own path. Recognize excuse logic that sounds like this: "I've always been this way; it's just who I am. I'd like to change, but how can I change my own nature? It's all I've ever known, so I guess I'll just have to stay the way I am."

Can you see how this kind of logic keeps you stuck in a life-long thinking habit? The very fact that you've been a certain way throughout your life is a perfect reason for encouraging yourself with thoughts such as: *I'm fed up with being frightened, shy, poor, unhappy, used by others, condescending, fat, or out of shape. It's all I've ever known, and it stems from the way I think and the beliefs I've come to accept as defining my nature. If this is my nature, then I'm going to change it, beginning right now.* Now these are notions that the philosopher Bertrand Russell could get behind. He wrote: "If human nature were unchangeable, as ignorant people still suppose it to be, the situation would indeed be hopeless . . . what passes as 'human nature' is at most one-tenth nature, the other nine-tenths being nurture."

So whatever you believe is your nature, allow it to be nurtured the way you'd like it to be, starting with *Excuses Begone!* Nine-tenths of your nature has been learned and adopted as a habit, and you can coax those old habits down the stairs, one step at a time.

### 7. I Can't Afford It

It's a rare day when I don't hear some variation of this excuse, including: "I didn't go to college because it was too expensive," "I haven't been able to travel because I never had the funds," and "I couldn't go into the business I wanted because I had to stay where I was and earn money to pay the bills." I call this belief lame and a cop-out, yet there seems to be almost universal agreement for its existence.

You originated in a world of abundance, which you unquestionably have the ability to access. Whenever you discourage yourself with thoughts that your financial situation is preventing anything from appearing, that's an excuse. If you instead decide to bring abundance awareness into your consciousness, you'll shift your thoughts from *I can't afford it* to *Whatever I need in the form of assistance to guide me in the direction of my life is not only available, but is on its way.* You'll then consciously watch for the necessary funding to show up, but you'll also be reminding yourself to believe that you have the ability to use abundance to elevate your life.

Encourage yourself by realizing that you have the capacity to create a space within you that's filled with peace and joy, an inner island of contentment that has nothing to do with money. Practice gratitude for the essentials of life, which are yours to enjoy virtually free of charge. These include air, water, fire, the sun, and the moon; the very ground you walk on; the continuous beating of your heart; the inhaling and exhaling of your lungs; your food digesting; your eyes and ears; and so on. Be utterly grateful for all that you have naturally, which is beyond the scope of what's "affordable." As that endeavor strengthens, assess what you'd truly like to do, where you'd like to live, and what creature comforts you desire.

When I made the decision to attend college after spending four years in the military, for instance, I knew in my heart that money wasn't going to be the thing that prevented me from reaching my goals. I understood the costs involved, and I didn't act on my fear of shortage or what I couldn't afford—I acted on my internal knowing that I indeed was going to attend a university. This knowing prompted me to investigate financial assistance from the government as a veteran, open a savings account designated for tuition and books, talk with the financial-aid people at the university I was interested in, and make alternative plans to attend community college, if plan A were not to materialize. I had a certainty inside of me that the "I can't afford it" reasoning is an excuse that many people who aren't considered wealthy employ as a means for exonerating themselves when they need a rationalization for why they're stuck where they are in life.

Oscar Wilde made this wry observation in 1891: "There is only one class in the community that thinks more about money than the rich, and that is the poor. The poor can think of nothing else." I'd add that such thinking includes lamenting the fact that they'll *never* have money. I advise tossing out this meme, and instead rewiring thoughts to connect with what's *intended* to manifest, regardless of your current financial status.

Whatever you feel is your *dharma,* and no matter how hard that calling seems to be pulling you, if you maintain the belief that you can't manage to pull it off, I can assure you that you're right. To paraphrase Henry Ford, whether you believe you can afford to do a thing or not, you're right.

### 8. No One Will Help Me

This excuse really saddens me because there's no truth in it whatsoever. The fact is that the world is filled with people who would jump at the chance to help you with whatever you'd like to create. But if you hold on to a false notion that no one will be there to help you, your experiences will match that belief.

If you've spent way too much of your life overweight, seriously addicted, lost in poverty, or what have you, then you need to realize that the ball is in *your* court—no more excuses! Once that belief begins changing, you'll see help arriving, but the initial movement is completely in your thoughts. It begins with this new belief: *I can access help.*

Begin encouraging yourself with affirmations that support and elevate your beliefs, such as: *I have the capacity to create by myself if necessary, I know the right people to help me are here at the right time,* and *The world is full of people who would love to assist me.* These will help to align you with the source of energy that's always available to your intuitive self. Elevate your confidence further with this journal entry made in November 1843 by Ralph Waldo Emerson: "[I]f I have lost confidence in myself I have the Universe against me." *You* are the universe; you originated from the invisible world of Spirit. When you doubt yourself, you doubt the universal intelligence that you are, and it seems there's no one to help you.

As an example from my own life, I repeat this thought from *A Course in Miracles* when I'm about to give a speech: "If you knew who walked beside you at all times on this path that you have chosen, you could never experience fear or doubt again." As I approach the microphone/podium, I remember that I'm an instrument for the words and ideas. My confidence trusts the wisdom that created me. In other words, I know that I am never alone. *No one will help me* becomes an invalid excuse.

I affirm that all that is needed or required will be there, and I consciously encourage myself with this unquestionable certainty. And help seems to come from all directions: The money I need somehow shows up, the right people emerge, and circumstances occur that are unexpectedly helpful—almost as if some synchronistic force steps in and bewilders me with the beauty of it all! I'm encouraged by my unquestionable power to elevate myself in any situation.

### 9. It Has Never Happened Before

"Be not the slave of your own past," my literary soul mate, Ralph Waldo Emerson, wrote in his journal. Just because you've "always" been a particular way, this isn't a rational explanation for your present state of affairs. In fact, it's an excuse attempting to explain away what you feel are shortcomings.

The past is a trail you leave behind, much like the wake of a speedboat. That is, it's a vanishing trail temporarily showing you where you were. The wake of a boat doesn't affect its course—obviously it can't, since it's only appears *behind* the boat. So consider this image when you exclaim that your past is the reason you aren't moving forward.

The logic of *It's never happened before* or its equally debilitating corollary, *It's always been that way for me,* stems from these beliefs: *My past is over, and what's over can't be changed. What happened before will happen again, so I'm being guided today by what can't be changed; therefore, it's impossible for me to change. It's over for me. What I want has never happened before, and that means it will never, ever happen.* This is what happens when you live in the trail you've left behind: convinced that your past is the reason why you can't change, you hang on to it to excuse yourself from thinking differently.

Consciously choose a new set of affirmations that encourage you to believe in your ability to elevate your life above past levels. Try: *I can accomplish anything I put my mind to here in the present moment. My past has no bearing on what I can and will create. If it has never happened before, that is all the more reason for me to make it happen now. I will cease being a slave to my past.* Inventory the mental excuses you have for avoiding risk, failure, criticism, ridicule, or the negative opinions of others. See how you're creating them as the formation of your current excuse memes. Yes, I said memes—those ideas placed in your head from mimicking the ideas of others until they've become a set of mind viruses. When they're put to the seven-part *Excuses Begone!* paradigm in Part III of this book, they'll simply crumble right before your eyes because they have no substance.

I doubt this point could be better summarized than in the last lines of Carl Sandburg's poem "Prairie":

> *I tell you the past is a bucket of ashes.*
> *I tell you yesterday is a wind gone down,*
> *a sun dropped in the west.*
> *I tell you there is nothing in the world*
> *only an ocean of tomorrows,*
> *a sky of tomorrows.*

Give up hanging on to that bucket of ashes.

Recently I spent an afternoon swimming with the dolphins in the Mexican Riviera. I'd never done such a thing in all of my 68 years. But rather than telling myself that I couldn't undertake such an outing because *it's never happened before,* I reversed the logic and instead thought, *Since I've never done this before, I want to add this to my repertoire and have this unique experience right now.* And it was sensational!

Adopt this kind of thinking regarding everything you've "never done" before. Open up to vistas that bring you to a new way of being where you create wealth, health, and happiness in the present moment.

## 10. I'm Not Strong Enough

The "I'm not strong enough" excuse unquestionably keeps you locked into a habituated way of thinking. Years spent believing in your weakness actually strengthens the belief that you aren't an emotionally, spiritually, or physically capable individual. It only takes a little bit of criticism to discourage you and activate this belief: *I'm not a strong person, so I'll resort to my true self, who is weak.* The idea that you aren't tough enough to hold a certain job, stand up to a bully or victimizer, take care of yourself, face life alone, or travel by yourself are all mind viruses that are ready excuses when life gets tough. This is true on a collective level as well.

I spent a couple of years teaching American history, with a special interest in colonial America. I was always intrigued by how the United States broke free from the small island on the other side of the ocean that had ruled it with an iron fist for so many years. The message that the British had always sent was: "We are strong, and you, fledgling wannabes, are weak." The result was a kind of servitude that had kept the colonists in excuse mode but was ultimately brought to a halt once and for all.

The transformation required a paradigm shift, which ulti- mately resulted in new thinking habits. It began with that great assortment of Founding Fathers from north to south, who challenged the mind virus that they were weak and the British were strong. When enough of these courageous leaders shared their beliefs about American might, the new meme began to replicate, infiltrate, and spread throughout the 13 colonies. In that vein, here's a portion of a speech delivered by Patrick Henry before the Second Revolutionary Convention of Virginia in 1775: "[W]e are not weak if we make a proper use of those means which the God of nature has placed in our power. . . . The battle, sir, is not to the strong alone; it is to the vigilant, the active, the brave."

Shift out of the mental belief that you're too weak. Become vigilant and active, and demonstrate a new kind of bravery. Affirm that you're breaking free of thinking habits that have convinced you you're not a strong person. Here are some affirmations: *I shall never see myself as lacking in strength again. What you think of me is none of my business. My strength is my connection to Source; it does not know weakness.*

Become conscious of the fact that seeing this belief as an excuse illuminates its weakness, but it also strengthens your ability to encourage yourself. You possess all the fortitude of character, mind, and body to live at the highest levels of happiness, health, and prosperity. Let these words of Mohandas K. Gandhi inspire you: "Strength does not come from physical capacity. It comes from an indomitable will."

### 11. I'm Not Smart Enough

Your vast intelligence isn't measurable by an IQ test, nor is it susceptible to the analysis of school transcripts. Your ideas or beliefs about what you'd like to be, accomplish, or attract are evidence of your genius. If you're capable of conceiving it, then that act of visual conception, combined with your passion for manifesting your idea into reality, is all you need to activate your genius. If you think that it's impossible to categorize yourself as a genius, I emphatically ask: *Why not?* You originated in the same infinite field of intention as everyone else who's ever lived. Your mind is a component of the mind of God or the universal Tao, so how could it be other than the brilliance of the Creator? Were you not created out of this vast sea of invisible intelligence? Are your ideas somehow inferior, or incapable of being transformed into this material world? Even as a part of you hangs on to the "I'm not smart enough" excuse, another part recognizes this truth.

When you state, "I've never been smart enough," you're really saying, "I've bought into a definition of intelligence that's measured by what family members or educators provided me with earlier in life." You can give yourself encouraging input instead of the discouraging messages from your past by knowing that intelligence can never be measured, nor can it in any way be limited. So if you're willing to put your passion and perseverance into your ideas, you'll meet the genius part of you. Even if you subscribe to the idea that this excuse is warranted because your brain is somehow not up to par, consider the conclusions that Sharon Begley offers in her book *Train Your Mind, Change Your Brain*. Here's what she says about the power of the brain to change, not through prescription drugs, but through the will: "The conscious act of thinking about one's thoughts in a different way changes the very brain circuits that do that thinking . . ." and "The ability of thought and attention to physically alter the brain echoes one of Buddhism's more remarkable hypotheses: that will is a real, physical force that can change the brain."

So even if you want to hang on to the excuse that your brain is chemically deficient, you have within you the power to change its material makeup—you can rearrange your old thinking system so that it conforms with the genius model. Why not think that the ideas in your head are by-products of your genius instead of a limited intelligence? Let what Oscar Wilde is said to have remarked to a New York City customs official encourage you. When asked if he had anything to declare, he responded, "I have nothing to declare but my genius," and in many ways, he was absolutely correct.

When you trust in yourself, you trust in the very wisdom that created you. Make a conscious effort not to second-guess that originating wisdom. Like Oscar Wilde, have only your genius to declare. Trust your elevated thoughts, especially those that stir up passion, and then act on them as if they were unquestionable.

### 12. I'm Too Old (or Not Old Enough)

The age of your body can seem to be quite an obstacle on the road to changing long-held thinking habits, particularly since you received an extensive list of memes concerning age very early on. Depending on where you grew up, you heard statements such as: "You can't ride your bicycle until you're seven," "You can't sleep over until you're ten," "You can't drive a car until you're 16," and "You can't have sex until you're married." Then at some point you discovered that you went from being not old enough to being too old! Then you started to hear: "You can't get a new job after age 35," "You can't change occupations because you're past your prime," "You can't fall in love again at your age," "It's too late to write the book or compose the symphony you've always dreamed about," and, of course, "You can't teach an old dog new tricks." And all of these memes became your reality.

The age excuse comes from an inclination to identify yourself with the number of trips you've made around the sun rather than from the unlimited side of you that lives independent of the age of your body. Part of you has an ageless mind and is quite oblivious to the physical aging process—and it's available to you if you'll just encourage it with conscious invitations to participate in your life.

As a young child, you had daydreams about what you might invent, draw, write, or design. Mind viruses came your way routinely, which made age your reality. "Wait until you're bigger to do those kinds of things" seemed to be a never-ending pronouncement, all too quickly turning into: "You're too old; act your age; it's too late." Somewhere between the two, your private destiny wasn't elevated to a primary position in your life.

You are the age you are—period. Yet those thoughts swirling around inside and outside of your head are ageless. They have no form. No boundaries. No beginnings. No endings. When you speak of age, you speak of your body, this finite thing that houses your invisible essence. This excuse is all about your physical self, and it is unquestionably influenced by your mind. You're the perfect age right here in this moment, and your body can be no other age than what it is. Identify yourself in what Lao-tzu calls "the subtle realm," or the invisible domain of Spirit, with thoughts like these: *I am ageless, and I can train my body to work with me in achieving anything I can conceive of in my mind. There's nothing about my age today that prohibits me from fulfilling my dreams. My mind is free, and I can train it to do my bidding rather than acquiescing to an excuse pattern.*

I've had two very persuasive callings in my life. One occurred when I knew I'd be pursuing a college education regardless of being the oldest freshman on campus. Age was of no consequence to me. In fact, the eight years I spent as a student on several college campuses to earn my three academic degrees were accomplished in part because I was so unconcerned about my age. I was living my passion, and everything else took a backseat to that vision.

My second huge calling came at the age of 65 years and one day. Compelled to detach myself from worldly possessions accumulated over many decades, I disposed of clothes, furniture, books, records, awards, photographs, and memorabilia of all description. Studying and living the Tao Te Ching, I wrote an essay on each of the 81 verses in a book titled *Change Your Thoughts—Change Your Life*. That I might be too old simply never occurred to me.

As I look back on my life, I realize that I've made many smaller decisions where I refused to consider age as a factor. At the age of 42, I decided to become a long-distance runner and ran the original Greek marathon. At the age of 17, I decided to write my first novel; and at the age of 9, I faked my age to get a paper route (10 was the "required" age). At the age of 68, I can't conceive of thinking that I'm too old to do what I love. Without that excuse, I continue to live life by activating my particular dharma or destiny. In fact, I just completed a brand-new career undertaking as an actor and a filmmaker—I encourage you to view *The Shift* and tell me if you think I was too old for such a project.

## 13. The Rules Won't Let Me

Perhaps the most famous of Henry David Thoreau's observations is this one from the conclusion of *Walden*: "If a man does not keep pace with his companions, perhaps it is because he hears a different drummer." Thoreau is referring to the unlikelihood of being able to always march to the same beat as everyone else. There are times in your life when you have to listen to the rhythm of rules that are beating within you, and only you, instead. But perhaps you've latched on to a belief that the rules of society are so sacrosanct that bending them would be crossing a line that you (or anyone) should never cross. The words that follow the above sentence in *Walden* are even more compelling for living an *Excuses Begone!* life: "Let him step to the music which he hears, however measured or far away." I'm not making a case for being a lawbreaker just for the sake of nonconformity—I *am* encouraging you to give up habituated behavior that demands following the rules and obeying laws when this keeps you from fulfilling your destiny.

Bertrand Russell observed that "from childhood upward, everything is done to make the minds of men and women conventional and sterile." This includes many of the edicts, both written and spoken, that you've been taught to observe as you move through life. Many of these rules are simply the *shoulds:* "You *should* do things the way we've always done things in this family," "You *should* keep quiet and do as you're told," "You *should* fit in and take the courses that the school offers," "You *should* take the advice of authorities, rather than have a different opinion," "You *should* want to continue living near family, instead of moving across, or out of, the country," and so on. All of these *shoulds* are designed to keep you from hearing a certain drumbeat, which, if further ignored, may lead to disastrous results.

Thoughtless obedience to rules and laws is both dangerous to society as a whole and an impenetrable obstacle in the way of your health and happiness. You see, your subconscious mind may be so programmed that you allow all of these memes or mind viruses to dictate your options in life. If you recognize that you're a spokesperson for always obeying rules and laws and doing as you're told, you need to also recognize that you pass on mind viruses to others similar to the ones that are curtailing your own life. Some of the most heinous acts in human history have been performed under the umbrella of "the law" and "the rules." And many beliefs and opinions are merely excuses defended as rules or laws.

Listen to your own heart, and obey whatever is consistent with what you know to be the highest law of all. Subscribe to edicts that encourage you and others to be all that you're capable of becoming without interfering in any way with anyone else's God-given rights. In this *Excuses Begone!* attitude you'll never be limited by laws, rules, or *shoulds*. As the 18th verse of the Tao Te Ching states:

> *When the greatness of the Tao [God] is present,*
> *action arises from one's own heart.*
> *When the greatness of the Tao [God] is absent,*
> *action comes from the rules*
> *of "kindness and justice."*

Let the greatness of the Tao live in your heart and encourage you to act from that elevated place.

## 14. It's Too Big

The "It's too big" excuse is *so* big that it seems to plop on top of people and totally immobilize them. Perhaps surprisingly, this belief only needs to be reversed. If you believe that people are successful because they think big, for instance, I'm here to tell you that success demands small thinking! Bring this realization into your consciousness and you will have accessed the ability to think small and act on what once seemed to be big issues. Some of these include: being overweight, battling an addiction to legal or illegal substances, having an unwanted self-image, earning your Ph.D., building your new house, getting out of debt, fixing your relationship with your mother, or becoming more self-reliant.

Verse 63 of the Tao clearly and gently explains what I'm talking about:

> *Take on difficulties while they are still easy;*
> *do great things while they are still small.*
> *The sage does not attempt anything very big,*
> *and thus achieves greatness.*

These words may appear to be paradoxical, but they're the unquestionable response to this particular excuse.

As I write this, there's a 12-story structure being erected next door to my condo building. Admittedly, there had to be some big thinking on the part of those who imagined and designed this project. However, the actual creation of this beautiful new edifice is being accomplished in terms of what can be done right here, right now—one step, one brick, and one shovelful of dirt at a time. What a great metaphor to touch base with when you feel overwhelmed by the sheer scope of something. You cannot lose 50 pounds or quit smoking *in a single day,* get your Ph.D. *tomorrow,* or eliminate all debt from your life *forever* . . . such goals *are* too big when approached that way, and this makes it too easy to fall back into habituated ways.

The *Excuses Begone!* method invites you to challenge your thought patterns and encourage your own success. So acknowledge that you can't get the humongous things done today, but you *can* take that first step. While you can't receive your Ph.D. today, you can register for a course that begins next week, and that's all you can do regarding that lofty goal for now. Think small and accomplish what you can in the here-and-now. You can't quit drinking alcohol or smoking cigarettes for the next ten years, but you can refuse to give in to your addictions today, or even smaller, in this moment. That you *can* do. And that is precisely how all habituated thinking habits get changed: by thinking and acting small in the now moment and living the only way that anyone really does live—one minute, one hour, one day at a time. With this new consciousness, you can begin thinking in terms that encourage you to eliminate excuses and elevate success.

### 15. I Don't Have the Energy

Not having the vitality to fulfill your life purpose is part of a learned response. *I'm tired, I'm exhausted, I'm worn out,* and *I'm too weary* are just a few varieties of mind viruses that have infected you, consciously or not. They're generally an unintended excuse as opposed to a legitimate explanation for not doing the things you want to do. Accept the belief that you're lacking the energy to make significant changes in your life and you latch on to a flimsy, albeit very effective, strategy for maintaining some pretty slovenly habits.

You can hang on to any old and comfortable behavior patterns by using the tiredness excuse. *I'd love to get into shape, but I'm simply too exhausted to do what's required.* Or, *I want to become qualified for that new position, but I'm just too fatigued to go to school at night.* The belief in your "non-energy" becomes self-fulfilling until you have to rest again, because coming up with excuses is a very tiring practice!

The low-energy excuse is simply what I've seen myself and many others employ when we don't know how to overcome our own inertia, and I've found that when we really put it to the test, it doesn't hold up. I've witnessed an absence of energy turn into an avalanche of high energy in just an instant. When my children used to complain about being bored or too tired to move, for instance, all it took was a suggestion that we visit the water park, go shopping for a new bicycle, or do anything that they perceived to be fun, and they'd miraculously convert from weary to excited in a split second. And so it goes with all of us. We use the "I don't have the energy" excuse as a reason to hold on to an inert and pathetic way of being.

The antidote to this is to find a way to inject energetic thoughts into your everyday thinking. One of John F. Kennedy's biographers, Arthur M. Schlesinger, Jr., quoted the former President as saying: "I suppose if you had to choose just one quality to have, that would be it: vitality." Vitality isn't simply the amount of high-energy atoms you have swirling around inside of you; I consider it a way of thinking. You can learn to overcome the ennui of low-energy thinking and replace it with a way of processing the world that serves you in a positive, life-fulfilling way.

Low energy is by and large not a problem of body chemistry—it's a function of a long history of habituated thinking that needs excuses to stay the same. You can learn to practice more satisfying and vibrant thinking that will elevate your enthusiasm, and ultimately produce an energetic lifestyle filled with purpose. No matter what your chronological age is, you have the power to use your thoughts to elevate yourself to new levels of success, happiness, and health. *Excuses Begone!* thinking encourages you to spend your daily moments in aliveness, free of the old tiredness routine.

Refuse to cater to low-energy mental activity. Be determined to unquestionably place your thoughts not on what you can't do, but on what you intend to create. Stay in this mind-set and you'll never want to use the low-energy excuse again. Maintain your high-energy consciousness for what you want to accomplish, and watch it filter down to everyone you communicate with. High energy is infectious, and it originates with vital thinking that replaces those old mind viruses.

### 16. It's My Personal Family History

You've always had a place in your family, and regardless of your opinion about it, there's nothing you can do to change that. If you were the youngest and always ordered around, that's simply the condition of your early life. The fact is that your birth order (that is, being an only, oldest, middle, or youngest child) or any other familial sequencing—including being part of a blended family, having divorced or single parents, being adopted, having alcoholic parents, being of a low socioeconomic status, being racially mixed, or any of an endless combination of factors in your situation—is all in the past, and it's all over! Your relatives did what they did, given the circumstances of their lives. Acknowledge this, and then move into the present moments of life. Look at your family history as a blessing. Yes, a blessing! It's precisely what you had to go through to arrive where you are today.

The manner in which you were treated or even mistreated provided you with an opportunity to be a stronger, more self-reliant person. Early experiences aren't meant to be hidden behind when life isn't working out the way you want it to—they aren't reasons for staying stuck! But the family-history excuse has a huge following, so you have lots of company if you're using it to explain to yourself and others why you aren't who or what you want to be today.

The divorce that took place when you were a young child may have taught you many important life lessons, but more likely, you caught the cultural mind virus that goes something like this: *Coming from a broken family is a traumatic experience that causes irreparable damage to children.* A part of you believes and promotes this meme because it seems easier than exploring the pain that leads to a healthier and stronger mind-set. This part of you probably thinks that it's protecting you from that extremely painful childhood experience. Thus, you readily believe: *Chances are almost zero that I'll have a happy relationship after seeing how miserably my parents failed at marriage.*

You can change all of this by reminding yourself that you absolutely have the power to elevate your attitude and beliefs. Consciously take time to reimagine the family experiences you had in the early years of your life, regardless of how traumatic or troublesome they were at the time. You didn't have the ability as a child to make peace with them, but you do now. Be in a state of appreciation and gratitude for the parts of you that survived and still want to grow. Encourage them by refusing to settle for the "easy out" of excuses.

For example, the years I spent in foster homes gave me life experiences that helped me to teach self-reliance to millions of people. Watching my stepfather drink himself to death, along with living with the effects that alcoholism has on a family, was (and still is) a great lesson that keeps me on the path of sobriety today. The presence of scarcity and food shortages as a child gave me an appreciation for all that has come to me, and I can now assure the poverty-conscious part of me: *That was then, and this is now.*

*Excuses Begone!* encourages you to make peace with everything that transpired in your life, including the painful experiences of abuse, abandonment, and disrespect. By hanging on to these life-long, self-defeating thinking habits, you do yourself the following major disservices:

— **You get weaker and sicker.** Your biography can become your biology; that is, by clinging to old hurts or remembrances, you keep yourself in a place of attracting disease (or *dis-ease*) into your body. All of that anger, hatred, and anxiety is a vibrational match to the presence of serious illnesses . . . it's the Law of Attraction at work. If you think about what's missing or what you disliked about your early life, the universe will offer experiences that match what you're thinking. More of what was missing and what you disliked will continue to flow into your life in the form of disease.

— **You remain stuck in the past.** If you can't elevate the thoughts about your past that are causing you to remain unhappy, unsuccessful, and unhealthy, you stay stuck where you are. Keeping unfortunate memories from the past alive with remnants of the originating anger, hate, and sadness becomes a habituated way of processing life. For example, if you hated how your father didn't pay enough attention to you, and you use this to explain your adult self-consciousness, you're stuck in that long-held belief pattern.

You have the unquestionable ability today to elevate your consciousness to explore ways to relieve self-consciousness and attract people you want to be with, rather than continuing to explain to yourself that you can't attract those people because your father didn't pay enough attention to you. Remember, your life is happening *now*, in the present moment.

### 17. I'm Too Busy

Prior to writing this excuse catalog, I invited visitors to my Website to e-mail me their excuses for not living at the highest levels. In essence, I was interested in the excuses *they* have used in their lives. "I'm too busy" easily topped the list.

If you're overextended, know that you've chosen to be in this position. All of the activities of your life, including those that take up huge portions of your time, are simply the result of the choices you make. If your family responsibilities are problematic, you've opted to prioritize your life in this way. If your calendar is crammed, you've decided to live with a full schedule. If there are way too many small details that only you can handle, then this, again, is a choice you've made.

Surely, one of the major purposes of life is to be happy. If you're using the excuse that you're too busy to be happy, you've made a choice to be busy, and in the process, you've copped out on living your life on purpose. If you've substituted being busy for actively and happily fulfilling your destiny, you need to reexamine your priorities. Here is my mentor, Thoreau, on unexamined priorities: "Most men [or women] are engaged in business the greater part of their lives, because the soul abhors a vacuum, and they have not discovered any continuous employment for man's nobler faculties."

Don't let your soul languish unfulfilled in a vacuum. Instead, begin to examine just how you prioritize your life. All the details that occupy it keep you from a destiny that you're aware wants your attention. Contemplate these encouraging ideas to counter the "I'm too busy" excuse:

- *I know that I'm not a bad parent if I don't arrange my life to be available to chauffeur the children every day until they're adults.*

- *I'm allowed to say no to requests that keep me from having time to pursue my life purpose.*

- *There's no such thing as "a place for everything and everything in its place."*

- *There's no right way to do anything.*

- *I can have it my way because there are no absolute universal rules.*

It isn't my purpose to delineate all of the ways in which you can unload this excuse category. Practicing delegating, getting others to help out, and taking time for yourself are all possibilities as well. Thoreau is right in that there are nobler faculties you need to pay attention to, in addition to all of those other details that occupy your life. If you fear the part of your soul that's calling you to a higher place, then you'll probably continue to haul out this particular excuse.

Change this pattern by never saying or implying that you're too busy. Just drop it, and replace it with the following affirmation: *I intend to take time for myself to live the life that I came here to live, and to do it without ignoring my responsibilities as a parent, spouse, or employee.*

I learned this valuable technique from the great Vietnamese spiritual bodhisattva Thich Nhat Hanh in his book *Peace Is Every Step.* Recite these two lines anytime you can steal a few minutes from your daily schedule: "Breathing in, I calm my body. Breathing out, I smile." As Hanh writes: "'Breathing in, I calm my body.' Reciting this line is like drinking a glass of cool lemonade on a hot day—you can feel the coolness permeate your body. . . . 'Breathing out, I smile.'. . . Wearing a smile on your face is a sign that you are master of yourself." This simple exercise helps you prioritize your life with a sense of peace. Then you can look at precisely what it is you need to do in order to discard the busyness excuse.

There's a wonderful cartoon posted on the bulletin board of the yoga studio I frequent that summarizes the importance of saying "Begone!" to this popular excuse. Underneath the depiction of a doctor talking to an overweight patient, the caption reads: "What fits your busy schedule better, exercising 1 hour a day or being dead 24 hours a day?" That sums up my approach to this particular excuse. Practice elevating your thoughts every day, no matter how busy and important you are. Rather than insisting that you're too busy to exercise, for instance, think, *I exercise because I'm way too busy to take time for being sick.*

### 18. I'm Too Scared

Again, turning to my e-mail correspondents, here's what else they've told me: "I've always been afraid of being alone," "I'm scared of failing and I've been this way since I was a child," "It's a scary world and someone could hurt me," "I'm afraid something bad will happen to me or my family," "I'm afraid that someone will yell at me, and I can't handle criticism," and "I'm scared about being poor or losing my job and not being able to get another one." Clearly, fear is a biggie in the excuse catalog.

A way out of the "I'm too scared" thought pattern is offered in *A Course in Miracles.* I have a special love for this weighty tome that tells us there are only two emotions we can experience: *love* and *fear.* Anything that is love cannot be fear, and anything that is fear cannot be love. If we can find our way to stay in a space of love, particularly for ourselves, then fear is an impossibility.

I believe that fear is a mind virus that insists you're either a success or a failure, and it's passed from one mind to another until it becomes a habit. From an early age, you're taught to feel: *If I don't succeed at everything I attempt, then I'm a failure as a person— and I'm scared to death of having to live with such an awful label.* This virus is passed on to you from other minds who bought into the same logic . . . and it keeps on replicating, infiltrating, and spreading, until it becomes a habitual way of responding. You think fearful thoughts, and then you use those same thoughts to explain the deficiencies of your life. You act as if they're really true, when, in fact, they're nothing more than excuses.

Franklin D. Roosevelt's famous refrain from his first inaugural address, "The only thing we have to fear is fear itself," was crafted from Thoreau's observation that "nothing is so much to be feared as fear." These Tao men had it right—there really is nothing to be afraid of. When you begin applying the *Excuses Begone!* paradigm you'll find in Part III of this book, neither "I'm too scared" nor any of the other excuses in this chapter will hold up.

Here's a personal example: In the practice of Bikram yoga, which is a regular part of my life, there are two postures that require the practitioner to bend all the way over backward and hold the posture for a period of 30 seconds or so. When I first started this practice, I'd feel fear welling up in me as I attempted to grab my heels from a kneeling position. I remember saying to my instructor, "I just can't bend over backward; I feel as if I'm out of control. In fact, I've never even been able to do a backward dive into a swimming pool in my entire life." I had a great meme going here, which told me, *Going backward is scary—you'll lose control, you won't be able to see where you're going, you could fall, you could really hurt yourself,* and so forth. Each of these explanations was an excuse that kept me from mastering these new poses.

My fear was rooted in my absence of trust in myself based on a lifetime of mind viruses. When I shifted my mind from fear to love, however, a remarkable thing happened that freed me from the chains of that habituated thinking: I saw myself cradled in the arms of a loving presence. I then said something to myself that I'd never uttered before: "Wayne, you can do these two exercises; you are a Divine piece of the all-knowing intelligence. First, love yourself and trust in this wisdom, and then let go and let God." By moving to love, fear was impossible, and 60-plus years of excuse making went out the window.

Today, I enjoy demonstrating both the Camel and Fixed Firm postures for new students. Out of all 26 postures, these 2 give me the greatest sense of joy and accomplishment. As the saying goes: "Fear knocked on the door. Love answered, and no one was there."

Here's a recap an affirmation for each of the 18 most commonly used excuses. The affirmations will assist you in making a conscious effort to encourage yourself to elevate your beliefs, unquestionably!

1.  **It will be difficult:** *I have the ability to accomplish any task I set my mind to with ease and comfort.*

2.  **It's going to be risky:** *Being myself involves no risks. It is my ultimate truth, and I live it fearlessly.*

3.  **It will take a long time:** *I have infinite patience when it comes to fulfilling my destiny.*

4.  **There will be family drama:** *I would rather be loathed for who I am than loved for who I am not.*

5.  **I don't deserve it:** *I am a Divine creation, a piece of God. Therefore, I cannot be undeserving.*

6.  **It's not my nature:** *My essential nature is perfect and faultless. It is to this nature that I return.*

7.  **I can't afford it:** *I am connected to an unlimited source of abundance.*

8.  **No one will help me:** *The right circumstances and the right people are already here and will show up on time.*

9. **It has never happened before:** *I am willing to attract all that I desire, beginning here and now.*

10. **I'm not strong enough:** *I have access to unlimited assistance. My strength comes from my connection to my Source of being.*

11. **I'm not smart enough:** *I am a creation of the Divine mind; all is perfect, and I am a genius in my own right.*

12. **I'm too old (or not old enough):** *I am an infinite being. The age of my body has no bearing on what I do or who I am.*

13. **The rules won't let me:** *I live my life according to Divine rules.*

14. **It's too big:** *I think only about what I can do now. By thinking small, I accomplish great things.*

15. **I don't have the energy:** *I feel passionately about my life, and this passion fills me with excitement and energy.*

16. **It's my personal family history:** *I live in the present moment by being grateful for all of my life experiences as a child.*

17. **I'm too busy:** *As I unclutter my life, I free myself to answer the callings of my soul.*

18. **I'm too scared:** *I can accomplish anything I put my mind to, because I know that I am never alone.*

This concludes Part I. You've identified 18 of the most common excuses and have been introduced to reasons for removing habituated thoughts that have been holding you back from living life at the highest levels of success, happiness, and health. Now, in Part II, you'll find the seven principles that lead to a lifetime of no excuses!

# PART II

# THE KEY
# *EXCUSES BEGONE!*
# PRINCIPLES

*"Every mind must know the whole lesson for itself—
must go over the whole ground. What it does not
see, what it does not live, it will not know."*

— Ralph Waldo Emerson

# INTRODUCTION TO PART II

Each chapter in Part II illustrates one of the seven principles of *Excuses Begone!* that I've personally explored and applied to my own life. Yet I'm leaving out any remnants of my scholarly research persona, and instead expressing my unbridled enthusiasm about what it feels like to live in this new way. While I'll share my discoveries with you, it's my hope that you'll share my excitement through your own experience. (I've included exercises at the end of every chapter that will help you put these life-changing principles into practice.)

# CHAPTER 4

# THE FIRST PRINCIPLE: *AWARENESS*

*"Thinking without awareness is the main dilemma of human existence."*

— Eckhart Tolle

*"It's the awareness . . . of how you are stuck, that makes you recover."*

— Fritz Perls

Lifelong, set-in-stone thinking keeps you stuck . . . often without your even realizing that you're stuck! Since this type of mental activity can't lead you in a new direction, becoming aware must be the first step to getting rid of your excuses forever.

Cultivating awareness is indeed the preliminary activity in the "I-opening" experience of meeting your *authentic self*. Living your life oblivious to your thinking patterns and beliefs, day after day, year after year, is a habit that encourages and elevates your ego or *false self.* Eckhart Tolle states that "awareness and ego cannot co-exist" because awareness encourages and elevates your authentic self to be the center of your life experience. Although the false and authentic selves are mutually exclusive, I believe that knowledge of both is valuable. The way I see it, if you're going to practice an *Excuses Begone!* life, your primary relationship needs to be 100 percent with your authentic self.

Who you truly are originated in a formless, invisible world. Scientists acknowledge that all particles (including you) emerge from an energy field of *no-thing-ness*. It's Spirit that gives life, and it's to Spirit that all life returns. There's very little room for ego here, since it clings to the false belief that you are your possessions and achievements. Becoming mindful of your true essence leads to awareness of your magnificence, your Divinity, and your unique power to create for yourself whatever you feel is your destiny here on this planet, beyond any and all excuses.

When awareness is your reality, you don't need to explain your shortcomings or missed opportunities. Instead, you transcend the pull of ego and move into a totally new dimension of higher consciousness. To put it simply and bluntly: if you don't realize that you no longer have to be stuck in your old thinking habits, then the habits will prevail and persist.

This chapter introduces you to what awareness of the elevated experience of life feels like.

### From Excuses to Awareness

Breaking old habits requires noticing that you're creating impediments in your life, and that these impediments have become excuses for so-called limitations. For example, if you're averse to risk taking and tend to choose the safe or easy path, this has caused you to erect mental barriers. Such barriers are what I'm calling "excuses," and they give you a way out. So when it's time to try something new—or to take a step that might result in failing, becoming the butt of criticism, losing a contest or competition, or anything at all that puts you on the path toward becoming a stronger and more self-reliant person—you come up with the same old excuse and avoid the risk. This is all an exercise that starts and ends in your mind: it's habituated thinking you rationalize by saying that it was inherited, or foisted on you by well-meaning (albeit cautious) parents.

Simply being cognizant of your excuse making will open you up to vast arenas of new possibilities. You can begin this process by paying attention to the false part of yourself that *believes* in limitations. Simply observe the thoughts in your mind and the feelings in your body and note when they don't resonate with your authentic self. Yet you don't have to change or fix those thoughts and feelings. By becoming aware of your true being, you only need to pay uncritical attention to the ego self, and it will recede gradually and naturally in the light of your awareness. Remember, you're not just the temporary shell that you call your "body"— you're a Divine essence who is limitless, formless, and infinite.

When you notice your ego's chatter, you discover the ability to overcome long-established habits, and you begin to see all that you've been blinded to by excuse making. Awareness leads to your highest self; ego leads to your earthbound self. When you let the Divine grow within you, awareness will be what you bring to all aspects of your life.

As a Hindu devotee was once told: "The blossom vanishes of itself as the fruit grows, so will your lower self vanish as the Divine grows in you." Letting the Divine grow within you involves sincerity, service to others, kindness, and reverence for all of life. Endeavoring to become aware encourages authentic thoughts to grow and appear in your inner world, and so will your lower self vanish as the Divine grows within you.

Let me share with you how awareness has been such a boon for me personally as I've changed some long-held thinking patterns. In the opening chapters of this book, I described two big excuses (genetic and memetic) that many of us use to explain away what appears to be our failure to change the habits that plague us. As I read *The Biology of Belief*, the phrase *perception controls genes* kept attracting me. It triggered something in me that I hadn't considered before: the idea that the way I think about and perceive my world can overcome my DNA and my genetic inheritance.

This means that I can rewire my internal circuitry and process physical or health problems from an entirely new perspective. If I were to stay unaware of my built-in ability to influence my genetic programming, I'd be stuck believing that those things were outside of my control. So I've become increasingly aware that my mind has power over my environment—which means that when my body is off track, it's because my beliefs are off track. All my life I've heard that the one thing you can't change is your DNA, and I've always nodded in agreement. With my current awareness of the power of perception, however, a whole new world has opened up for me.

For example, I have a history of infection and discomfort in my chest and bronchial area, and I've tended to feel that this is an area of weakness to be concerned about. A minor sore throat appears, which proceeds to some coughing that then produces green phlegm, followed by some difficulty breathing, and I head out to purchase some antibiotics and go through the same old process until the infection and discomfort ultimately disappear. Yet since doing the research for this book, part of which involves putting into practice what I'm learning and writing about, I've moved into a new mental state. I now encourage myself to apply awareness rather than my old routine, and I seem to skip over those days of discomfort and the annoying antibiotics.

In fact, I'm approaching everything about my body with a new awareness. Rather than first reverting to ways I've used in the past to process early signs of a physical malady, these days I shift to a level that allows me to mentally suspend my ego and even my body. Then I tell myself something along these lines: "My perceptions [beliefs] control my environment [my body, which is the environment for all illness], my genetic structure, and my DNA. I have the power to see this situation differently than I used to. Inherent within me is the power to create an inner environment that isn't susceptible to illness or disease." When I know that I have an option of awareness, I'm able to send away a possibly painful episode.

I'm using all of the power that this approach holds to talk differently to my body, and not only with respect to potential bronchial infections. I'm also employing it with sore joints, muscle pulls, cramping in my calves, stiffness, and any of the multitude of physical inconveniences that crop up in a 60-something body that loves exercising—particularly swimming, running, walking, and doing yoga—on a daily basis. The key is to be aware that awareness itself is available rather than that same tired old ego-dominated approach. The reason why "awareness of awareness" is so powerful is that it immediately puts me in touch with a dimension of myself that knows: *here in awareness, all things are possible.* That statement leaves nothing out, including the ability to realign with Source and introduce my genes to a new set of beliefs.

Reading about and processing these cutting-edge scientific ideas triggered my entry into awareness. But it was my willingness to work on *applying* it where only old thinking habits previously resided that brought me to this new level where I feel as if I have an all-knowing friend with me at all times. This friend is awareness.

Here's another example of the power of awareness to alter some long-running thinking habits:

> Just being conscious of the fact that you are exercising can lead to better fitness. A recent Harvard University study, published in a February 2007 issue of *Psychological Science,* tracked the health of 84 female room attendants working in seven different hotels and found that those who recognized their work as exercise experienced significant health benefits.
>
> The women were separated into two groups: One learned how their work fulfilled the recommendations for daily activity

599

levels, while the other (the control group) went about work as usual. Although neither group changed its behavior, the women who were conscious of their activity level experienced a significant drop in weight, blood pressure, body fat, waist-to-hip ratio and body-mass index in just four weeks. The control group experienced no improvements, despite engaging in the same physical activities.

The study illustrates how profoundly a person's attitude can affect her physical well-being. So, if your daily routine keeps you on the move, start thinking of it as exercise. It may be enough to move you toward your fitness goals. (*Experience Life* magazine, May 2008)

Notice the opening line of this article: "Just being conscious of the fact that you are exercising can lead to better fitness." Awareness takes you out of your customary thinking.

As for me, since rewiring my thoughts to influence my body and even my DNA, my reality has changed significantly. Today when I feel a heaviness in my chest or get a sore throat, a pain in my joints, or even a headache, I first begin noticing without judgment. I simply pay attention by observing uncritically and allowing myself to focus in a curious, gentle manner. By turning toward my higher self, all of ego's fear begins fading in its light. By becoming aware—without falling into ego thoughts of pain, disruption, annoyance, or creating other mental barriers—the symptoms move on through my system, which is in a state of higher consciousness.

Where I once had a lifelong thinking habit that I didn't have the ability to adapt my genes to my perception or to rewrite my genetic codes with my beliefs, I now live in a new way. I gently notice my old ego-based beliefs whenever I note any kind of bodily malfunction. Awareness leads me to think totally differently, and it, sans ego, has put me into an instantaneous healing place on many occasions.

### The Many Paths of Awareness

Awareness doesn't come to you exclusively from your intellect. Hafiz, a Persian poet in the Middle Ages, explains it this way: "Oh, thou who art trying to learn the marvel of love from the copybook of reason, I am very much afraid that you will never really see the point." In other words, studying these pages and memorizing the components of awareness will never replace experiencing it. So encourage yourself by spending time *noticing* where and what you're feeling in your physical body. This is the initial step toward achieving the consciousness that Lao-tzu speaks of: "The mystical techniques for achieving immortality are revealed only to those who have dissolved all ties to the gross worldly realm of duality, conflict, and dogma."

This is a telling message. I know that I see myself as an immortal being who receives guidance on awareness specifically because I let go and dissolve most of my ties to the world of duality, conflict, and dogma. The excitement of living from this perspective is beyond anything I can describe. It reminds me that I do exist in a place of *all things are possible,* and I apply this consciousness to all of my old thinking habits. I encourage you to do the same.

Know that you are a soul with a body rather than the reverse, and understand that this knowledge is your ticket to changing beliefs that keep you stuck in what Lao-tzu calls "your shallow worldly ambitions." Awareness will remind you of who you are capable of becoming. All that you need will appear when you're vigilant about replacing old thinking habits with it.

These days, the words *infinite possibilities* flash on my inner screen almost every waking hour. This phrase continually assures me that nothing is impossible if I can conceive of it, and if I'm willing to apply awareness rather than excuses. Awareness allows me to perceive possibilities rather than difficulties, to feel connected to my Source of being and see the outcome as working rather than failing. I feel a dazzling rush of excitement when I think about no longer employing all the tired excuses that were handed down to me from my family, my schooling, my religious training, my government, ad infinitum. The messages were similar: "These are your limitations," "This is what you can and can't do," "This is the real world of competition and pain and violence and fear and hatred," and so on. These ideas strongly influenced me, but I'm here to tell you that I now have a new and welcome outlook on the world of infinite possibilities.

When you simply become aware, you cease being a victim to endless mind viruses that seemingly prevent you from accessing your complete fulfillment. You no longer find it difficult to change those familiar thought patterns that prevent you from living at optimal levels of success, happiness, and health. You consciously enjoy the knowledge that memes or genes or anything else in the material world don't have absolute control over you . . . and who you can become is unlimited. Your first response to any troublesome life situation isn't one of the 18 excuse categories from the last chapter; rather, you shift to your awareness of awareness and tell yourself, "Hold on here. There's something beyond what I'm noticing, and I'm going to tap into it first."

Madame Blavatsky, who was instrumental in introducing Eastern religions to the West, encouraged this kind of thinking. Here's what she said on this subject: "Have patience, Candidate, as one who fears no failure, courts no success. Fix thy Soul's gaze upon the star whose ray thou art, the flaming star that shines within the lightless depths of ever-being."

### Suggestions for Implementing an Awareness of Awareness

— Develop a mind-set that stays open to all possibilities. Refuse to rule out the ability to use awareness as your primary tool for combatting long-held thinking habits. By being open to it, you invite higher awareness in. As I've said throughout this chapter, with this new approach, *all things are possible, and that leaves nothing out.*

— Practice using awareness at your own pace, in your own way, in circumstances that crop up throughout your daily life. Practice *giving* rather than *asking* for more; practice *being nonjudgmental* and *offering help* where you previously offered criticism. Want what you want for yourself even more for someone else, and observe how much better you are at eliminating those old "me first" thoughts that have demanded your attention in the past.

— In childhood, repetition was something you most likely used to reinforce things you were mastering. (You can probably recall insisting on someone reading and rereading a book or story until you knew it by heart.) In that spirit, repeat this affirmation over and over to have it solidify; and move from your subconscious, habitual mind to the forefront of your conscious mind: *I let go of old ways of thinking, and I access awareness.*

— When you feel compelled to use an excuse, become aware that you no longer need to. Simply become aware of this new awareness.

# CHAPTER 5

# THE SECOND PRINCIPLE: ALIGNMENT

*"[I]t is only by becoming Godlike that we
can know God—and to become Godlike
is to identify ourselves with the divine element
which in fact constitutes our essential nature,
but of which, in our mainly voluntary
ignorance, we choose to remain unaware."*

— from *The Perennial Philosophy,* by Aldous Huxley

Ego-dominated excuses wouldn't exist if we were able to adopt Huxley's advice above, which paraphrases Plato, and perfectly sums up the value of this second *Excuses Begone!* principle. Were we to "become Godlike" and be steadfast in thinking in harmony with the universal Source of being (which is our essential nature), then we simply wouldn't need to employ ego-dominated excuses.

Alignment is a basic truth that functions as your personal code, unlocking the mystery of manifesting anything into your life. You can learn how to readjust your thinking so that it aligns with your essential nature and puts you in harmony with Source energy . . . this symmetry will allow whatever you'd like to flow to you. Stay aligned with Source, and enjoy exploring an excuse-free life.

At this very moment, you can begin to practice alignment. First, notice your thoughts, and watch out for any of those habitually misaligned ones. Then just implement a different way of thinking that replaces the old habit. When you shift your thinking to align with an awareness of your essential nature, the energy is actually measurable.

It turns out that we live in a universe that is all energy. Everything vibrates, and the frequency of those vibrations determines how everything appears, including our body, which senses our thoughts and has energy components that can be measured. Our physical universe and everything in it is a vibrating machine. The act of creation itself, bringing nonbeing into being, is a vibrational frequency. Personally, this realization has been an awesome awakening for me, leading to my knowing in my heart that I have the power to harmonize with the vibrational Source and can activate whatever I focus on. And I believe that this ability is within every being.

There's an invisible energy field from which everything originates. Through the first *Excuses Begone!* principle of awareness, you can realign with the same vibrational frequency of that energy field and access what I call "Divine guidance." Why? Because of what seems to be a law of the universe, two frequencies that are alike are attracted to each other, and those that are unalike *don't even recognize* each other. Staying vigilant and continuously monitoring all thoughts causes you to notice what frequency you're transmitting and receiving. When you perceive that a thought is out of alignment, you can correct it; by doing so, you activate Divine guidance because you're now thinking at the same frequency as Source energy.

In the words of Lao-tzu some 2,500 years ago: "Relinquish the notion that you are separated from the all-knowing mind of the universe. Then you can recover your original pure insight and see through all illusions. . . . The breath of the Tao speaks, and those who are in harmony with it hear quite clearly." Note that Lao-tzu urges us to see that this is a *recovering* project—that is, the rediscovery of our original nature—and that our goal is to simply harmonize with the Tao (God source) in our thinking. So how does the Tao think?

If you could measure such a thing, you'd see that Source energy is a creating, giving, abundant, loving, joyful, nonjudgmental, all-things-are-possible, invisible mechanism. It is always giving, always serving, always in endless supply. It isn't really doing anything, yet nothing is left undone. It manifests being from non-being at a certain frequency—your job is to align with this frequency while simultaneously disabling the old, slower, ego-dominated thought frequencies. Being stuck in lack, busyness, lost opportunities, bad luck, and so on is a misalignment with the frequencies of your original nature. I'm sure that you'd prefer being in a state of rapport with the all-creating Divine mind, as opposed to being stuck in the muck of excuses.

### Excuses Are All Misalignments

Look back at Chapter 3 and consider what those 18 excuses I delineated say to you. Go down the list and you'll see that they all focus on what "can't" be done or why it has "never" happened. The only thing an excuse gives you is an option out of the life that you'd like to live. Words like *difficult, risky, can't, not strong, not smart, rules, too big,* and *too complicated* excuse you from being the kind of person you'd like to be and were destined to become. Now consider how Source energy seems to operate. Does it really seem that it's possible for God or Divine mind to think in "it can't be done" ways? Of course not.

The logic seems abundantly clear to me: *harmonize with energy that can do anything and everything, for this is your original nature.* Excuses are evidence that you've discarded a way of thinking that's all-powerful for one that's all-limiting. In other words, it's imperative that you decrease ego-dominated thinking (which offers you mostly excuses) in favor of thinking that's aligned with "all things are possible" ideas.

One of the most common kinds of habituated self-debilitating ideas concerns money. *I don't have enough money* is a misaligned thought because money is in inexhaustible supply in the world. There is so much of it, in fact, that it would be impossible to create a calculator large enough to even count it!

Now, in order to receive what's being transmitted, frequencies of thought have to match up. Thought energy is picked up by a receiver tuned to the same frequency, so if Source energy is transmitting at 95.1 FM, tuning in to 610 AM isn't going to bring you what you want to hear. Likewise, it's impossible to pick up on what universal Source energy is transmitting if you stay misaligned and don't change frequencies to tune in to it. Just sit for a moment and let these thoughts be received right now: *You came from a Source that has unlimited abundance. It is still generating that same idea today—you merely left it behind. But when you return to those frequencies of your Source, you'll start to recognize them again. They'll begin to sound familiar to you. And ultimately you'll be back in harmony, singing the music that you sang long before you acquired an ego and began your journey of misalignment.*

While I'm using the example of money here, this logic applies to all the habitual thoughts or excuses you use to explain why your life isn't the way you claim to envision it. Therefore, *I need to be healed* is a vibrational match to *I don't have access to perfect health, and God is withholding His healing power from me.* You are a physical extension of the Source of life, and that Source is nothing but well-being. But you can't access this well-being when you vibrate to a different frequency!

*I need someone to live up to my expectations and to love me in the way I want to be loved in order to be happy* is another common misaligned thought. Yet Source energy is only about love. As Meister

Eckhart wrote in the 13th century: "All God wants of thee is for thee to go out of thyself . . . and let God be God in thee." So come on, wake up! Just let Source energy *be* Source energy in you. And Source energy has no excuses built into it. It simply says that you are love and you are loved, and all you have to do to get this is to be a vibrational match to love. Or as the Prayer of Saint Francis puts it: "Where there is hatred [or anything else that is not of Source], let me sow love." When you become that vibrational match and align yourself in this way, you'll see your desires begin to manifest for you immediately.

### Alignment Is Awareness in Action

You may recall from the previous chapter that awareness is a representation of your highest self, the self that truly knows that it is a physical extension of the Divine, the invisible Source of all. Alignment represents movement into this state of awareness. *Alignment* is a verb—it connotes action, be it the action of literally changing old thinking habits so that they match up to your awareness, or the actual shifting of behavior so that you think and act as a God-realized *Excuses Begone!* being.

When you become aligned, your thoughts are no longer focused on what you don't want but rather on what you intend to manifest as a co-creator with Source. The best way to begin retraining your mind is to consciously think in aligned ways, so consider the following:

- Your universal Source of being never thinks in terms of what is missing. *Do you?*

- It never thinks in terms of what it can't have or do. *Do you?*

- It never thinks in terms of what has never happened before. *Do you?*

- It never thinks in terms of what others will think, say, or do. *Do you?*

- It never thinks in terms of bad luck or the way things have always been. *Do you?*

Every time you have a thought that extends to a conversation with others about what is missing, what shortages you have, your bad luck, what always has been, how others don't understand you, and so forth, you're practicing a misaligned/excuses mentality. But remember that your mission is to shift into the action state of realigning.

That reminds me of a story I was told by a minister on Maui. It seems that there was a family who had a very rambunctious five-year-old, and the parents were deeply concerned that he might inadvertently cause harm to his new baby brother. One night while they looked into the nursery to ensure the safety of their sleeping infant, they overheard their eldest son ask his brother, "Would you please tell me what God is really like? I think I'm forgetting." Indeed, most of us have forgotten what our Source of being is like, and it's particularly noticeable in the excuses we habitually make.

It's my contention that the universe not only will, but *must* provide you with what you conceive of. So if you complain about what's missing from your life—including the money that you believe to be in short supply—you'll be offered experiences that match that energy. When you say, "I love my job, but I'll never get rich at it," you're aligning with a frequency that will give you what you think. This is why, I believe, the rich often get richer . . . it's certainly been true for me since I left poverty behind me some 60 years ago.

By staying focused on what I intend to create, by believing that the universe is all-providing, and by knowing that I'm worthy of the unlimited beneficence of the Source of being, I just keep attracting prosperity to me. And by being unattached to what shows up, which means that I have no desire for more and more, I'm able to let it go easily. What remains a mystery to so many remains a simple truth to me.

Stay in a state of gratitude, and let the awesome yet unexplainable Tao proceed to do nothing and yet leave nothing undone. Rather than asking for more—which implies shortages and, therefore, creates a vibrational match to more shortages—focus on what you have and how thankful you are for everything that has shown up in your life.

To that end, keep in mind a "happiness index" that was recently taken for different countries around the world. It turns out that Nigeria, which is one of the poorest of nations, with the least modern of conveniences, came in at number one for reports of happiness among the people there. The U.S. ranked 46 out of 50, despite having one of the highest standards of living in the world. Apparently, the emphasis in Nigeria isn't on the mantra of the ego, which demands more, more, more. Emphasizing needing *more* has built within it the idea of shortage, lack, and *I don't have enough.* Consequently, when you think *more,* you become a vibrational match to experiencing more shortage in your life . . . like it or not!

### Thinking Alignment at All Times

When you're thinking about the principle of alignment, keep in mind that Source energy is ever present, and that you always have the power to bring yourself into harmony with who you really are. And who you really are is a higher awareness than your earthbound form. Just this simple idea—that you're not an ego-based self but rather Divine energy in physical form—will help readjust your energy. Once you recognize your Divinity, you'll shift out of misaligned thought patterns. Such thinking focuses on what's wrong or missing, what others have told you are your limitations, what always has been, what used to be, and so on.

Since everything comes in response to the vibration of energy, shift out of the lowered vibrations and into the vibration of Source. *It's already here; I just need to connect to it. Nothing can stop my creative ideas from materializing. I've banished all doubt. I'll soon be seeing evidence of my manifestations everywhere . . .* now this is a new kind of thinking. While it may sound too simplistic and naïve for you, I'm encouraging you as strongly as I know how to give this retraining of your mind a chance.

Note that the strength of nonphysical energy is flowing everywhere. It's in you; but it's also in every tree, every flower, every bug, every planet, and in everything that you want to attract to your life. The nonphysical energy is pure positive oneness, which only your thoughts can disconnect from or misalign with. It flows everywhere at once; and it's always creating, always loving, and always animating life. The only thing that keeps it from working for you is a belief that it can't, it won't, or it never has before—in other words, your excuses.

The tremendous value of noticing the alignment of your thoughts will rapidly appear in your awareness. You can summon Source energy whenever you slip into a misalignment: just return to possibilities, manifestations, and your own sense of feeling good (which is just another way of feeling the presence of God).

When you find it difficult to move into this alignment attitude, put more attention on your *feeling-self* concerning your desires. For example, if that same old shortage of money surfaces, you may find that you can't stop yourself from being upset about the fact that you still believe that more cash would be your proof that this is working. Try something different, and let the energy of what you're feeling reveal what's blocking your alignment. Even if you have to borrow a few hundred dollars just to carry around with you and get the sensation of abundance, feeling prosperous, safe, secure, and positive concerning the flow of money will gradually align you with an abundant Source. This has been my way since I was a little boy.

I've attracted money into my life because I always felt prosperous and deserving. That feeling motivated me to act, and I loved carrying groceries or collecting soda-pop bottles or mowing lawns. My little bank account was growing while my brothers and friends spoke so often about not having enough cash. Today, I'm still mowing lawns and collecting soda-pop bottles, only on a much larger stage, and prosperity has never failed to flow into my life. I know in my heart of hearts that the journey from despair to hope and on to prosperity and abundance can be achieved with realigned thinking. I know because I've done it for a lifetime, and I trusted this under circumstances where it never could have been predicted that I'd emerge with unlimited prosperity as my calling card.

No one else can do this realignment exercise for you. You must decide to stay in the feeling of love, prosperity, wellness, or whatever you desire, and let that feeling just flow through you. And remember that you get what you think about, whether you want it or not. Remain thoughtfully in the field of infinite possibilities rather than your negative emotions—fear, worry, hate, and shame are indicators of separation from your authentic self in the present moment. When you come back to your authentic self, it will work full-time to deliver to you whatever you think about.

Silently repeat the following: "I get what I think about, and I am choosing from here on in to think in harmony with my Source of being until it is habitual!" This is alignment.

## Suggestions for Implementing a Realigned Way of Being

— Test your ability to access Divine guidance. Think in harmony with Source energy by taking on a small project. Choose any subject—bumblebees, lightbulbs, feathers, pennies, anything at all—and do nothing but keep it in your mind. Generate pure positive energy around this topic: See the feather or the penny showing up, and feel good about this occurrence. Let your mind be at living peace with this item, and then become an observer rather than a demander and notice what happens.

By aligning with a field of possibilities in a nonjudging, non-demanding, yet totally accepting way, you'll notice the manifestation into your life space of that which you're aligned with in your thoughts. Release any ideas that you're impotent when it come to co-creating your life.

— Practice catching yourself when you're engaged in the habit of negative thinking. Monitor any thought that expresses, *It can't, It won't,* or *It's not my luck;* and change it to an aligned thought such as, *It will, It must,* or *It's already here and I know it will arrive on schedule with Divine timing.* Change these misaligned thoughts (excuses) one minute, one hour, one day at a time.

— Affirm: *I am aligned with my Source in all of my thoughts, and with God, all things are possible,* continuously as many times as you can in a five-minute period. The act of repetition helps the thought become a habituated method of alignment. Soon you'll emphatically say, "Excuses, be . . . gone!"

CHAPTER 6

# THE THIRD PRINCIPLE:
# *NOW*

*"Memories of the past and anticipation of the future
exist only now, and thus to try to live completely in
the present is to strive for what already is the case."*

— Alan Watts

You've heard it many times, so often in fact that it has become
a cliché: *Live in the present. The now is all there is. Forget about the
past; it's over. Don't worry about the future; there is only today.* While
these are familiar refrains, the truth is that living in the now is an
elusive activity for virtually everyone. It may be easy to say, but
it's very tricky to do day in and day out. And yet, Alan Watts is
absolutely correct in the above quotation when he states that it
"already is the case." This is why living in the present moment is
so baffling.

Think about the past and you're not living in the now . . . but
the now is the only time available for thinking about the past! Live
in anticipation of the future and you're admonished for not being

here now . . . but now is all you have for engaging in that delicious "futurizing." Thus, as Alan Watts reminds you, you strive for what *already is*. To be in the now is really your only option. But the real question isn't how to *live* in the now, it's how to *use* the now by being present—rather than wasting it on reflections of the past or concerns about the future. And if you carefully examine the 18 categories of excuses detailed in Chapter 3, you'll discover that none of them applies if you master the art of being present.

### *Ego, Excuse Making, and the Elusive Now*

After spending several days preparing to write this chapter, I was trying to focus on its significance when I decided to go for a long swim in the ocean. As I walked toward the water, I noted that I felt some tension in my solar-plexus region. It wasn't anything serious—it was just the discomfort I often feel when I have many things to do or decisions to make. At the moment I was about to dive in, my thoughts went back to the reading I'd just finished on the psychology of the now. I decided to see if I could totally immerse myself in the moment (which, of course, meant that I was in fact striving for what "already is the case," since I have no other moment than this one), only this time, I'd be fully present, letting everything just be. I wouldn't worry about the ache in my chest, think about how cold the water would be or which direction the current was flowing, or rehash all the things I had on my current to-do list. I'd simply be in the now.

I indeed let everything else go and stayed focused on the instant, the place, and the surroundings. And something strange and wonderful happened: My chest stopped hurting, I loosened up, all of my anxiety dissolved, and I felt totally energized. For the next 60 minutes or so, I moved through the water staying 100 percent present. The moment I decided to just be there completely, with all other thoughts pushed aside, the discomfort I was experiencing disappeared. Moreover, I had the most peaceful swim I've ever had, and I emerged from the water fully refreshed.

My conclusion is that the present moment is an antidote for the pain and difficulties we experience, which we habitually try to soothe with rationales and explanations. When we plunge ourselves 100 percent into the now, experiencing it and nothing else, we're on an *Excuses Begone!* journey, with no need for all of those old habituated thinking patterns.

In fact, excuses are simply what you've developed to explain *now* moments that are tangled in the past or future. If you're truly in that blissful presence of the now, there's no desire to alter what is. When your sentences express that "it's going to be difficult . . . it will take a long time . . . I'm not smart enough . . . I'm too old," you're wasting a present moment with excuses from a not-now moment! And when are you having these thoughts? You guessed it—the only time you have a thought is in the now. So if your present moment is being used up replaying why present-moment thinking is incorrect (making excuses), is it available for you to do something constructive? Obviously not!

All excuses are avoidance techniques to keep you from taking charge and changing your thinking habits. If you weren't rehashing your excuses but were instead immersed in the now, you'd be experiencing your own form of the bliss and healing that took place for me during my magical swim. You see, when I removed ego from the moment, I stopped thinking about myself and focused on being fully present—and then I was able to be truly *here* without ego's excuses. I had plenty of explanations for the tension in my chest, but when I moved totally into the now with no other thoughts, the excuses disappeared along with the pain.

The ego is a false self that believes in its separation. It strives to acquire and to achieve, and it's constantly in search of more. Just as it can't coexist with awareness and alignment, it can't survive in the now. When you luxuriate in the moment, it's impossible to ask for anything else, let alone more. The essence of living in the present is total acceptance of precisely what is here. Your mind doesn't wander to what used to be, what ought to be, or what's missing; and you don't conjure up excuses. Rather, you have a heightened awareness of experiencing your highest self.

You also feel a deep sense of connection to God, Who isn't doing anything differently than God was doing an hour or a century ago, or will be doing a millennium from now. Your Source energy is always only here and now. It doesn't know how to be any other way. It has no plans, no regrets, no worries about the future, no guilt over the past. It simply is. And what is God doing? Nothing. And what does God leave undone? Nothing.

By staying in the now and in a state of gratitude for all that is and all that you are, you tame the ego and enter a state where excuses cannot even be considered. What excuse do you need when you're fully present? None. Of what use is ego, that false self, when you're with your Source in the moment? Don't use up the now with thoughts of regret or worry; the experience of higher awareness is your reward. When the ego's in control, virtually every thought is making an excuse, focusing on what always has been or what you fear always will be. But when you befriend the present moment, you say good-bye to that troublesome ego.

The issue isn't whether you choose to live in the now or not, because the basic truth is that it's the only thing that's ever available to live in. The past all occurred in the now. The future, which never comes except as a present moment, is all that's available. *The real issue is how you choose to use up the precious moments of your life.* You can choose higher awareness and suspend ego-dominated past/future thoughts, eliminating your reliance on excuses. Full immersion into the essence of the now is when you truly come face-to-face with your Source of being. This is the great value of learning to become fully present.

### Befriending the Now

Often, the now is seen by ego as simply a means to an end, something to be endured to get to a future point. This means never getting to be fully here in the moment, since you're using it up anticipating where you'll be in the future. Of course the future is endlessly always just ahead of you—as thoughts in your head—setting you up for a life of striving rather than arriving.

However, this particular course in *Excuses Begone!* takes quite a different stance. Rather than wasting time being annoyed because there's so much planning to do for the future, stop and remind yourself to *Be Here Now,* as my friend Ram Dass suggested in the title of his famous book. To do so, *befriend* the now. See it as your ally—the only place you've ever been, or ever will be, and do a brief meditation reminding yourself what this life experience is all about.

One of my favorite techniques to bring me squarely into alignment with the present is to imagine what all of God's beautiful creatures do in every moment of their existence. They're not concerned with their demise; they bask in the exhilaration of the now. Every moment is fully experienced. I don't see any creatures seemingly hating what they're doing, cursing their lot in life, or arguing with themselves or each other over what is. They don't make life an enemy and use up their precious moments in a state of anxiety or depression.

Years ago I was privileged to take part in a safari in the northern region of South Africa. The other members of the group and I were gathering for dinner one evening when we noticed six or seven zebras grazing outside our tent. As we got a closer look, I noticed something that I've used ever since to remind me to maintain a friendly relationship with the now rather than treating it as an obstacle to endure on the way to somewhere else.

One of the zebras had been attacked during the night, and its right hindquarter and leg looked as if it had been chewed on by a lion looking for a meal. This beautiful animal seemed to be peacefully grazing, completely in the moment, even though one of its legs had almost been chewed off the night before. I thought that if that animal was capable of being fully present under such conditions, how could I suffer anxiety over what might or might not happen in the future, or be upset about what took place in the past? That zebra seemed to be saying, "This is the only moment

I have. This is what is, and I'm going to live fully in each instant until I leave this plane of existence."

While this is an extreme example, it always serves to help me—particularly whenever I'm leaning toward those excuses that I've often employed when I slip into making the present moment an enemy rather than a constant companion. I think of that astonishingly beautiful yet maimed zebra, and I get myself right back to the now. And I'm there in such a way that I don't use it up by being upset over a past event or worrying about what's coming up.

Our relationship to the present moment defines our relationship to life itself. One of the greatest insights I've ever had concerns my experience of time as the ultimate illusion. I think about it in this way: Whatever has happened in the past—no matter how many years, centuries, or millennia ago—all took place in the now. Just now. There's no way to experience anything other than in the precious present. Thus, the idea that it happened in the past must be an illusion, since everything only gets experienced now. The "time thing" is a grand illusion.

The same logic applies equally to the future—whatever we fantasize about happening then will also only take place in the now. All we get is *now-now-now*. Time is what we seem to be measuring with wristwatches, clocks, and calendars; but in fact it's nothing more than a series of present moments.

The message, then, in this *Excuses Begone!* paradigm is that being in the now will help you overcome all of your explanations for why you aren't living at your highest level. Your relationship to life itself reflects your relationship to the present moment, so if your head is filled with frustrating or angry thoughts about what isn't happening or the way the world looks to you, you're not going to have a very good relationship with life. Yet a dysfunctional relationship with life is really nothing more than a dysfunctional relationship with the present moment. Again, *life only gets lived in the now.*

Rather than seeing your present moment as an obstacle, see it as the supreme miracle. "Wayne, this is the only moment you have," is a sentence I often say to myself to keep me on friendly terms with the now. Think about that: *the only moment you have*. When you realize the significance of this, you'll immediately want to shift into a state of awe and gratitude for it, regardless of what is transpiring. I do this frequently in my yoga practice, particularly when I'm challenged by a difficult posture. Balancing on one leg and holding the other one straight out with my hands cupped beneath the ball of my foot is a challenge that leads me to murmur, "Be here now, Wayne. There's a time for being exhausted, and there will be a time for resting, but it's not here yet, so just stay in the present moment." And of course it always passes, but the next moment that shows up, amazingly, also shows up as a now . . . and the next. And so it goes with every experience of life.

### Removing Judgment

I've discovered that I have greater success with being fully present when I remove judgment from what I'm experiencing. Rather than making an event a bad or a good experience, I find myself simply being in the "isness" of the moment; that is, what I'm feeling is much more helpful than why it isn't what I think it should be. This is called *allowing* rather than *resisting* what is. Even if I wish to change the moment, it's far more useful to allow it without any judgment and then notice everything I can about it.

The more I stay out of my good-thought/bad-thought routine, the more I'm able to just be with it. I love to observe the instant without any judgment. Birds simply allow whatever comes their way, no matter if the wind picks up or the rain falls, and I work at being like one of those fabulous creatures. The way I do so is to ask myself this question: "What's happening right here and right now, independent of my opinion about it?" Then I notice all that I can take in—the sky, the wind, the sounds, the light, the insects, the temperature, the people, the judgments . . . everything. I stay free of opinions and just let myself be. In these moments, I don't need an excuse for anything.

Even while I sit here and write, I'm practicing being present and simply allowing the words to flow through my heart to my hand and onto the page with a total absence of judgment. And when I eat my lunch, I work at just being present in a state of gratitude for my food and the experience of eating, rather than using those moments to think about all that I have to do in the evening or passing judgment on the taste, color, or smell of my lunch experience. I try to keep in mind that whenever I react against any form that life takes in the present moment, I'm treating the now as some kind of impediment or even as my enemy.

As a child you knew how to be totally present. I encourage you to become an observer of little children. Notice how they don't react to every single disturbance in their world and how they're in the moment, and then in the next moment, and so on. You can use this kind of nonjudgment to practice your new explanation-free identity. Total immersion in the present, without judging—that is, simply allowing yourself to be—is a great way to rid yourself of these long-held thinking habits that I'm calling "excuses."

Be without judgment and you'll never feel the need for some tiresome excuse to use up your precious seconds, such as *It's never happened before . . . I'm too old . . .* or *It will take a long time.* Instead, you'll be in the now, welcoming your constant present-moment companion, your Source of being, which knows nothing of excuses and doesn't know how to be anywhere but here, now. As one of my spiritual predecessors, Dale Carnegie, once wrote: "One of the most tragic things I know about human nature is that all of us tend to put off living. We are all dreaming of some magical rose garden over the horizon—instead of enjoying the roses that are blooming outside our windows today."

Become one in the present with all of the roses that show up in your life.

## Suggestions for Implementing
## Present-Moment Awareness

— Practice becoming aware of your reactions when someone introduces any kind of mental disturbance into your life. Where do your thoughts take you? What do you think about in that instant? You'll probably find that your thoughts are projections into the past or the future, so bring yourself back to the now. As you're receiving the disrupting information, ask, *How am I feeling right now?* instead of *How am I going to feel later?* or *How did I feel back then?* By giving yourself a gentle reminder in the moment of your discomfort, you'll bring yourself back to what you're experiencing now. Watch as your discomfort dissolves when you return to the present. Just keep practicing bringing yourself back to the here-and-now, and remember as you do so that this is your relationship to life. Accept the present moment and find the perfection that's untouched by time itself.

— Give yourself the luxury of learning present-moment living by adopting the following two practices, making them a regular part of your daily life:

1.  *Meditation.* Get rid of the excuses you've used that it's too difficult, you don't have the time or energy, and so forth. Begin today, practicing any form of meditation that appeals to you. You'll discover that you become adept at allowing interfering thoughts to flow through in the now, rather than trying to stop or change them.

2.  *Yoga.* Find a studio and give yourself the opportunity to experience this ancient practice. The word *yoga* means "union," and the practice helps you rejoin your Source and free yourself from many of your use-less, habitual thoughts. Yoga helps you look into your soul and be present. You'll experience the oneness of everything . . . you'll find peace rather than excuses.

— Repeat this affirmation: *I choose to stay fully present in the now, and this is the only place that I will come to know God.* By repeating this to yourself in silence for a five-minute period, you reinforce the importance of being a present-moment person. Repetition is crucial! Make this a regular practice and it will ultimately become your way of being.

— Stay present: every second, every minute, and every hour. Every day of your life is full of present moments of infinite value. You won't find God yesterday or tomorrow—your Source is always only here, now.

# CHAPTER 7

# THE FOURTH PRINCIPLE: CONTEMPLATION

*"Contemplation is the highest form of activity."*
— Aristotle

Every discovery of something new involves the crucial concept of contemplation. Think about airplanes weighing hundreds of tons flying around the world in relatively short periods of time. A century or so ago they didn't exist, but then the mechanics of flight were discovered. By generating a high rate of speed and designing wings that forced the air to push upward, lo and behold, heavier-than-air objects were staying aloft. When the Wright brothers arrived at Kitty Hawk, they hadn't been focusing on how things stayed on the ground; rather, they'd been contemplating the elevation of things moving in the air. So because they and others like them were willing to seriously think about something that didn't yet exist, air travel was brought into our reality system.

Contemplation is the mental activity behind all inventions—indeed, behind all of creation. Consequently, I urge you to become fully conscious of how you choose to use your mind as you study this fourth *Excuses Begone!* principle and its relationship to action. It's important that you understand that you can create the life you desire by concentrating on what you wish to attract. Once you master the ideas surrounding this concept, you won't want to use your mind for the purpose of excuse making. Instead, you'll prefer to use it to really consider what you want to manifest into your life and then visualize it as coming true.

The principle of contemplation is also what motivates human progress in cultural, political, and social contexts. For example, the idea of slavery being a horrible stain on the spiritual nature of humankind was realized by one person first, and then another, until the practice was finally abolished. The idea of women having the same right to vote as men was also conceived in a few minds before becoming a reality. These notions were *contemplated* first, and their destiny fits this sentiment from Victor Hugo: "There is nothing more powerful than an idea whose time has come."

### Contemplation and Attraction

The excuses you tend to rely on probably include some ideas that you've contemplated throughout your life to date. Yes, even thinking *It will be difficult . . . I can't afford it . . .* or *I don't deserve it . . .* is engaging in what Aristotle called "the highest form of activity." The more you ponder the impossibility of having your desires show up, complain about life's unfairness, and get upset about what continues to manifest, the more those very things define your reality. That's because whatever you focus on invariably shows up in your life—be it what you want or what you *don't* want. So if you're always thinking or talking about what's wrong with your life, then you're attracting exactly what you don't desire.

Choosing an *Excuses Begone!* approach means that you absolutely refuse to participate in the self-defeating rhythm that I just touched on. You learn to move into a new realm where your thoughts are viewed as potential realities, and it's your sacred duty to contemplate only that which originates from your authentic self. This is something you can begin to work on right away.

I learned a long time ago from one of my mentors, Abraham Maslow, that self-actualizing people never use their minds to think about what they don't wish to attract. They don't worry about an illness getting worse, an absence of funding, a downturn in the economy affecting them, a negative outcome in a business venture, their children getting into trouble, and so on. Their minds focus on the conditions they wish to produce—then the lucky break, the right people or circumstances, or the synchronistic opportunity somehow presents itself as a result of their contemplation. We all become what we think about, so it's pretty important to pay attention to those thoughts.

And keep in mind what Aldous Huxley once noted: "Contemplation is that condition of alert passivity, in which the soul lays itself open to the divine Ground within and without, the immanent and transcendent Godhead." It's as if by thinking about what you desire, you release a zillion little invisible yet alert worker bees who guide you in the act of creation. Rather than being focused on a lame excuse, you use your mind to align with the all-knowing "transcendent Godhead." And when you use your mind in this way, miracles begin to show up.

This makes me think about something that recently happened to my daughter Serena. After graduating from the University of Miami, she and her friend Lauren were excited about creating a television show focusing on healthy eating, cooking, and general living geared toward their age group. We could all easily imagine Serena and Lauren hosting the show, and they went so far as to write a proposal and practice presenting the idea in a TV format. Unfortunately, they didn't seem to be able to find the right person or agency to represent them.

I asked Serena to contemplate herself surrounded by what she and Lauren wanted to attract, and to discard excuses such as, *It will be difficult . . . It's never happened before . . . It's too big . . .* or *I'm too young.* I reminded her to just keep contemplating, because that's the highest form of activity. Neither of us anticipated the way this would work out. But to understand, you first need a bit of history.

About 15 years ago, my daughter's best friend, Jesse Gold, and her family spent an evening with us in our summer apartment on Maui. That night, seven-year-old Serena had the entire gathering in tears one moment and laughing hysterically the next as she entertained us with her natural acting ability. Jesse's father, Harry, even wrote an agreement saying in effect that when Serena came to Los Angeles to become an actress, he'd like to represent her. He signed this spirit-of-the-moment contract and gave it to my wife, who kept it—unbeknownst to Serena—all these years.

Back to the present. A decade and a half had passed, and I was running late for a meeting in Burbank to discuss a television show with some producers. The traffic was heavy, I had difficulty finding a parking spot, and it felt as if nothing was going right with respect to the timing of this appointment. As I finally entered the lobby of the building where the meeting was to take place, the elevator door began to close as I approached. Thankfully, however, someone held it open.

I breathed a sigh of relief as I headed to my meeting on the 14th floor. And that's when I noticed that Harry Gold, who happens to be one of the top talent agents on the West Coast, was the person who was holding the elevator door open for me! Although we hadn't seen each other in years, Harry insisted that I stop to say hello to Jesse, who was working part-time in a restaurant in that same building while she pursued her career. We all hugged, laughed, and marveled at the set of circumstances that brought Harry and me together at that moment, in that elevator. And when I called Serena's mom later, she pulled out that little contract written in jest some 15 years ago.

By contemplating herself surrounded by the conditions she wished to attract, I believe that my daughter created an alignment that caused me to arrive late for that appointment at precisely the right moment that Harry could hold the elevator for me. Coincidence? Maybe. But what a beautiful coincidence. So many things had to appear to go wrong in order for all of this to manifest. Serena has now been able to welcome an opportunity for producing her television show, with representation for her idea by someone who agreed to do so in writing when she was a seven-year-old . . . someone who was as close to her as her own family was when she was a little girl.

I'm not the least bit concerned about the outcome of Serena's adventure. The point is that when you engage in the act of active contemplation, you set in motion a powerful force—you allow yourself to be lived by the great universal mind or Tao. I have no doubt that as my daughter continues her contemplative inner work, eschewing any excuse patterns and keeping all of her mental activity on what she intends to manifest, she'll see this kind of occurrence showing up regularly. What she does with it and where it will go are all wrapped up in what she continues to contemplate.

### The Mechanics of Contemplation

Both Aristotle and Aldous Huxley offer us wonderful insights regarding the principle of contemplation. They both explain how the very act of reflecting on an idea, any idea, sets the process of creation into action—this is an integral component of living an *Excuses Begone!* life. As we know, Aristotle wrote: "Contemplation is the highest form of activity." And Huxley hit it on the head when he reminded us that the very process allows our soul to open to the Divine guidance that operates within us and everywhere in the universe simultaneously.

I've also been greatly influenced on this subject by a brilliant scholar named Thomas Troward. In 1910 he delivered a series of lectures that became books, which forever changed the way we look at the process of creation and manifestation. His writings can help us understand the power of contemplation, particularly in relationship to creation itself. I urge you to read his remarkable treatise, *The Creative Process in the Individual.*

In the Foreword, Troward writes: "In the present volume I have endeavored to set before the reader the conception of a sequence of creative action commencing with the formation of the globe and culminating in a vista of infinite possibilities attainable by every one who follows up the right line for their unfoldment." In the subsequent pages, he relates that the entire cosmos was created by self-contemplation, and infinite possibilities are available if you follow a pertinent sequence of creative action. This is all attainable for whoever is willing to follow "up the right line."

Troward asks you to get the steps of the creative process clearly into your mind as they relate to contemplation, and then watch excuses melt away and see the results of your efforts. Here is a summary of the four-part sequencing, or right line, for your consideration:

**1. Spirit is created by self-contemplation.** The process of moving from nonbeing to being involves an invisible Source, which we call "Spirit," deciding to expand into the world of form. This is God expressing Himself/Herself in all material things. Thus, coming from their originating nature, everything and everyone is a result of Spirit contemplating itself and expressing its inherent life, love, light, power, peace, beauty, and joy as a part of the material world.

**2. So what it contemplates itself as being, it becomes.** Contemplation by Spirit results in the manifestation of what is being contemplated. Troward goes to great lengths in his book to explain the Divine ideal and how the very cosmos had to come into being as a result of how the originating Spirit (Tao or God) engaged in self-contemplation for the purpose of expressing life.

**3. You are individualized Spirit.** Here's where you once again are urged to recognize your own Divinity. You too were materialized from nonbeing (Spirit) to being (form) by the self-contemplation of Spirit itself. And Spirit itself is oneness, indivisible. Since you are a piece of God, so to speak, the following conclusion is offered by Troward:

**4. "Therefore, what you contemplate as the law of your being becomes the law of your being."** And he goes on to state that you must use your creative power of thought to maintain your unity with Spirit rather than to create a separate sense of self that is cut off from Spirit and suffers from poverty and limitation. That is to say, as long as you're able to use your power of contemplation and stay in harmony with how Spirit contemplates itself, you have precisely the same powers of manifestation. After all, in the truest sense of the word, you are the same as your originating Spirit—the separate sense of self that Troward refers to comes from that troublesome ego.

To understand the power of contemplation, you must strive to understand the law of your being as one that allows you to use your thought processes to remain aligned with Spirit or Source energy.

While I recognize that the information in this section may seem a bit too esoteric for your tastes, if you carefully digest the works of Thomas Troward—and the creative process in you as a self-actualizing individual—you'll clearly see that contemplation is a powerful tool that may have escaped you up until now. That's because of your focus on your ego and the excuses you've employed to explain away your deficiencies.

Try imagining that everything and everyone originates in formless energy that you agree to call "Spirit," and then envision Spirit as a creative force that uses contemplation to express itself in a material form. You are an individualized expression of that same contemplation, so you have the possibility of doing precisely the same thing. The only requirement is that you don't dismiss your spiritual nature and replace it with a false self. The false self contemplates from a position of excuses, because it cannot manifest the creative energy necessary for the life it desires.

The mechanics of contemplation boil down to this:

- Contemplation is the *continual* use of your thought process.

- Your thoughts are actually like things that act to begin the process of materialization.

- If you contemplate with thoughts that *match* originating Spirit, you have the same power as originating Spirit.

- When contemplation is a vibrational match to originating Spirit, you gain the cooperation of Divine mind, attracting and fulfilling your desires.

- Contemplation is therefore a kind of action in and of itself, which sets into motion all of the creative forces of the universe.

- When you rely on excuses, you allow your false self (ego) to concentrate on what you *don't* want or why you can't create it for yourself.

- The presence of excuses in your life is evidence that you focus on what you can't do or have, rather than the infinite possibilities that are inherent in your Divine creative self.

- To rid yourself of excuses, you must learn to practice contemplating what you intend to manifest, and simultaneously detach from the outcome.

- Contemplate like God does, with thoughts of *How may I serve?* rather than *What's in it for me?*

- Remember Troward's famous observation: "The law of floatation was not discovered by contemplating the sinking of things . . ." In other words, when you see what you contemplate as if it's already here, the universe will ultimately offer you experiences that match what you're contemplating.

### Suggestions for Implementing a New Way of Contemplating

— Thomas Troward urges us to grasp the idea that the contemplation of Spirit as power is the way for the individual to generate that same power within him- or herself. "We all have it in us," he says, and "it depends upon us to get it out into expression."

Your mind is always contemplating something, mulling this or that over and over again. Take some time each day (or even several times each day) to contemplate Spirit as power, rather than continuing the inner dialogue that generally results in your latching on to the same old excuse patterns. Try something like this: *The creative and intelligent power manifests perfectly as the universe. I am a result of this power. I feel connected to it, and I know it will work with me in creating the life I desire.* See your mind as a powerful force that's in harmony with the same power that's behind all of creation. Contemplate just this one idea, and you'll activate an *Excuses Begone!* cosmology for yourself.

— Begin the practice of viewing contemplation as action, rather than as passive mental meandering. Treasure your mind as a grand gift from your Creator, a gift so wondrous that it has the Creator's mind inside of it as well. View your contemplative moments the same way you view your practice time for improving your skills at any endeavor. An hour a day throwing a bowling ball is action that leads to a higher bowling average; a few moments several times a day musing about what you intend to manifest in some area of your life will have precisely the same effect on your *manifesting* average. Contemplation is action. It's necessary mind training for the implementation of anything you desire.

— Repeat the following mantra to yourself for a minimum of five straight minutes each day: *I contemplate myself surrounded by the conditions I wish to attract into my life.* Say it quickly and repeatedly, even if it sounds ludicrous to do so. The repetition will help you begin to imagine the right people or circumstances, the necessary funding, or whatever it is you desire. Stay detached and allow the universe to take care of the details. Stop focusing on those ancient excuses of yours and instead cooperate with the all-creating universal mind that can do anything and is part and parcel of your Divine self.

— I'm closing this chapter with one of Thomas Troward's pieces of advice, which has served me flawlessly since I was first made aware of his contribution to the art of mental science. This is the practice I've employed in manifesting my own desires for several decades now. Allow Troward's words on manifesting your heart's desire to resonate with you, even if his wording may appear to be convoluted and unusual:

> Simply [use] the one method of Creative Process, that is, the self-contemplation of Spirit. We now know ourselves to be Reciprocals of the Divine Spirit, centers in which It finds a fresh standpoint for Self-contemplation; and so the way to rise to the heights of this Great Pattern is by contemplating [and/or appreciating] it as the Normal Standard of our own Personality [individuality].

Allow yourself to reflect upon the above paragraph until it registers. You gain the power of creation by contemplating yourself as you are already!

# CHAPTER 8

# THE FIFTH PRINCIPLE: *WILLINGNESS*

*"If you are willing to be lived by it, you will see it everywhere, even in the most ordinary things."*

— Lao-tzu

The word *willingness* describes a sizable concept. You might immediately think, *Of course I'm willing . . . willing to think or do anything at all in order to live a life of success, happiness, and super health.* Yet my experience as a helping professional for more than 40 years—as well as my being a man who attempts to help himself live what he writes about—has led me to a different conclusion. Most of us actually just give lip service to a life of higher awareness; we don't always want to undertake the necessary steps to create the life we desire. For this reason I've chosen to explore with you the fifth *Excuses Begone!* principle: willingness, an essential element in the approach toward living your life fully.

*Four Key Questions about Willingness*

Habituated thinking is largely the result of the memes you've allowed into your brain. The sole function of these mind viruses is to make umpteen copies of themselves and then infiltrate and spread wherever possible. While you might have been unaware that you were able to choose to reject those memes, the choice was nevertheless available. Although it may have been very difficult for you to overcome early influences—perhaps you believed it to be way too burdensome and exhausting an undertaking—you were still unwilling to do so.

Right now, declare yourself on the side of willingness rather then unwillingness. Begin in this present moment to kick those old excuse patterns down the stairs, one step at a time.

Ask yourself the following four questions, which will reinforce your willingness thoughts:

### 1. Am I Willing to Take Total Responsibility for All of the Conditions of My Life?

Examine how much you fault other people and circumstances for keeping you from achieving the level of success, happiness, and health you'd like to be enjoying—are you willing to stop doing this? Blaming others for deficiencies or any of the conditions of your life keeps you from fulfilling your own highest destiny.

Everyone in life does exactly what they know how to do given the conditions of their lives. That's the way I've chosen to look at the factors that made up the story of my life. For example, my mother had three small children under the age of four; and an alcoholic, thieving husband who walked away without ever providing any support. She placed one of my brothers and me in a series of foster homes, while my other brother lived with my grandmother until I was ten years old. This is not a story of pity or blame; it's precisely what had to take place in order for me to learn about self-reliance firsthand. Because I've lived self-reliance, and then gone on to teach it to millions of people, I don't find fault with anyone for any of the conditions of my life.

I see all of my early-childhood experiences as necessary gifts, even the ones laced with pain and sadness. Of course my past wasn't all roses, but then again, *no one's* past is all roses. There are times when life presents challenges, when good fortune turns into bad, when your roses die . . . that's just the way things go. There's no need for blame, since that only serves to provide a host of excuses.

Be willing to accept total responsibility for every facet of your own life. You didn't inherit your personality traits from anyone in your past—you've repeatedly chosen them, even though you may be unaware of how or why. If you're shy, loud, fearful, assertive, loving, hateful, kind, cruel, passive, or aggressive, learn to assert: *This is what I have chosen for myself up until now.* Similarly, if you find yourself mired in debt, languishing in poverty, wasting away in an unfulfilling career, wilting in an unsatisfying partnership, in pain over someone's poor business decisions, or even bored out of your mind because your parents made you pursue a career not of your liking—whatever the current conditions of your life, ask yourself if you're willing to take sole and total responsibility for them.

Begin by focusing on the following subjects:

— **The current status of your body.** Are you overweight, out of shape, plagued by annoying discomforts, constantly fatigued, or susceptible to many disease patterns from the polluted environment you live in? You do yourself a huge disservice if you're unwilling to say, with conviction, "In some way that I don't fully understand, I've made myself a vibrational match to all of the conditions of my life, and I'm willing to take all of the responsibility for these conditions. It's no one's fault; I bear full responsibility."

— **All that you are, all that you have (or don't have), and all that has come your way.** Yes, it's easier to cast blame someplace else. But when you choose an *Excuses Begone!* life, you put the steering wheel of your life back in your hands where it belongs. I'm aware that taking responsibility often appears difficult—accidents, mistreatment, abandonment, and dreary circumstances can certainly make life challenging. Being willing doesn't mean feeling a sense of personal shame or guilt over wrongdoings that may have been perpetrated upon you, nor does it mean believing that you've been punished because of some karmic payback. You indeed may have suffered at the hands of uneducated, poorly informed, badly addicted people. It was *not* your fault.

Even as we recognize this, I still urge you to accept, without guilt, that everything that has shown up in your life has value equal to your assuming responsibility for its existence. At the very least, be willing to accept it as you would an unwanted, uninvited child whom you've come to care for through unforeseen circumstances.

There's something for you to learn in any difficulty. Be willing to say, "Thank You, God, for the experiences I've lived through" on a daily basis. Look for the blessing in all situations, and remind yourself that you're no longer a child, but a fully functioning adult who's ready to accept responsibility.

In the 1st century A.D., slave-turned-philosopher Epictetus offered this wisdom: "It is the act of an ill-instructed man to blame others for his own bad condition; it is the act of one who has begun to be instructed, to lay the blame on himself; and of one whose instruction is completed, neither to blame another, nor himself."

Your own instruction can be completed by successfully following an *Excuses Begone!* way of life. Blame must be supplanted by a willingness to look at everything that occurs in your life and choosing to think, *I attracted and created it all, and I am happy to take full and sole responsibility for all of it.* As an ancient Hindu proverb reminds us: "He who cannot dance claims the floor is uneven." If you can't dance, that's your choice. But if you want to get out there and enjoy yourself, there's nothing holding you back . . . except your excuses.

## 2. Am I Willing to Surrender?

Ridding yourself of excuses involves receptivity to turning yourself over to something greater than your own little ego. In order to live the life that's waiting to materialize for you, you simply must be willing to let go of the one you may have been planning for years. As Lao-tzu puts it so succinctly: "If you want to be given everything, give everything up." While it may sound strange to you now, the thing you surrender to becomes your power.

In the first question in this section, you asked yourself if you were willing to take full responsibility for all of the conditions of your life. Now you must discover whether you're able to let go to the point that it becomes almost second nature. By surrendering to a higher power, you become intimately familiar with the highest place within you: your true, infinite, co-creating self.

If you're immersed in the workings of the ego, you may not even have the faintest idea of what is meant by subordinating yourself to a higher principle. If this is the case for you, then your false self is the beginning and the end, the sum of all your existence. Abandoning excuses is not a likely outcome in that scenario, so simply recite this sentence to yourself: "I'm willing to surrender to that all-creating force responsible for all of life coming into form, and to allow myself to be lived by it, rather than my living it."

I love the words of Ramana Maharshi, who sees this subject as applying not to some external higher being, but rather to the highest part of yourself: "Surrender is giving oneself up to the original cause of one's being. Do not delude yourself by imagining this source to be some God outside you. One's source is within oneself. Give yourself up to it."

The secret is to let yourself be lived by that highest part of yourself. As Lao-tzu's observation at the beginning of this chapter states: "If you are willing to be lived by it, you will see it everywhere, even in the most ordinary things." While the pesky ego keeps telling you to run the show, that wise spiritual teacher from ancient China and I encourage you to do the reverse. Why not give in to this notion and let yourself be lived by the creative spirit that is always within you? Just let go . . . recognize that you own nothing, that you're doing nothing, and that it is all being done right before your eyes. Surrender and become less attached to the ego-dominated idea that the world is giving you a raw deal. This *is* the deal, period.

You came here when you were supposed to, and you will leave on time, independent of your opinion about it. If you watch your body aging, you know that you aren't making the changes to it— they're just being made. Your body is being lived by the great Tao, the all-creating Source. If your ego were truly in charge, you would never wrinkle, see age spots, get gray hair, or die. Like it or not, something greater than ego is in charge of everything.

Now extend this same thinking to all of your life, beyond your body, and release yourself to this great energy source. As my teacher Nisargadatta Maharaj once put it: "Spiritual maturity lies in the readiness to let go of everything. The giving up is the first step. But the real giving up is in realizing that there is nothing to give up, for nothing is your own." As hard as it may be for you to realize, when you relinquish, you produce riches. Willingness to surrender means never needing excuses again. In the end, it's all just the way it is. God doesn't need excuses—and since you and God are one, you don't need them either.

### 3. Am I Willing to Hold the Vision?

It's one thing to make a pronouncement in a moment of inspiration about what you intend to manifest in your life or what kind of a person you intend to become. It's quite another to make a commitment to holding that vision regardless of what difficulties or obstacles may surface. Holding the vision involves an unwillingness to compromise what you're visualizing for yourself.

It means being willing to suffer through criticism and what appears to be an uncooperative universe.

To get to this level, you have to be willing to release some mighty powerful images that you've carried with you since you were a young child . . . images that are very likely entrenched in that 18-item excuse catalog I wrote about in Chapter 3. Excuses aren't just words explaining the lack of success in various areas of your life—they also show up as pictures or visions that you carry around with you, a series of photos that you see projected on your inner screen.

These visuals are strong because they've appeared on your screen so many times in so many varied circumstances that they've become reality. Even though they're excuse-based images that define your imagined self with all of its shortcomings, they've become your guides. They've stood the test of time and have been reinforced by many well-meaning friends and family members. They're like trusted confidants, giving you the same advice and encouragement about dealing with life from a perspective of what you can't accomplish, how unlucky you are, or how unfortunate you are to have the life experiences you've had. They're quite adept at showing you how to compromise and settle for less than you might have hoped for.

Your old pictures don't fade or disintegrate quickly, and the screen they appear on can't seem to display anything else. These images of your destiny have ultimately become the definition of you—you've looked at them for so long and become so accustomed to them that you've forgotten that they're actually false. So if you see yourself as undeserving of financial success, you act on that "unworthy" image. The fact that this is a mind virus caught from many other minds is of no consequence. It's still defining *your* reality and hindering *you* from projecting alternative pictures for yourself.

You can readjust your willingness meter to avow that you're open to seeing an alternative vision by affirming: *I am worthy of attracting unlimited abundance and prosperity into my life, regardless of what life experiences have gone before me. I only reinforce and contemplate images that are in harmony with this vision.* After all, it's your inner screen and yours alone. No one from your past has exclusive rights to what plays on your screen—you can display whatever you deem appropriate and can delete anything you choose.

Now let's go back to the third question in this section. Even if you're not convinced that you can change or make something happen that has never happened before, are you in fact willing to hold a new vision? If your response isn't a wholehearted "Yes!" see if there's an old picture on your inner screen; if so, allow it to disintegrate as you watch. Eventually, you'll be willing to hold the vision of yourself as smart, energetic, and deserving of the best that life has to offer. When that happens, you'll be a vibrational match to the Source of all, and this new receptivity will become your *Excuses Begone!* way of life.

As the Bible warns: "Where there is no vision, the people perish" (Proverbs 29:18). I'd add that when you have a *faulty* vision based on excuses and memes, you'll also perish. Not in the literal sense of course—but if you insist on remaining a being who's living an unfulfilled life, then the authentic you destined for greatness, happiness, success, and health will die.

Hold a vision that asserts: "I'm entitled to be respected, loved, and happy; to feel fulfilled and prosperous; to exercise; and to enjoy all the moments of my life! This is my vision, and I'm more than willing—I'm absolutely *determined* that this is what will come my way." When anything crops up that's inconsistent with this vision, take the advice of Lao-tzu: "In order to eliminate the negative influences, simply ignore them." Such words are so simple, yet so profound.

### 4. Am I Willing to Shed All Unwillingness?

The concept of unwillingness might be even more significant than willingness when it comes to adopting the *Excuses Begone!* way. So what are *you* reluctant to do in order to make your dreams and desires become your reality?

Are you unwilling to change locations and move to another city? To leave your parents or your grown children in order to start a life that you've dreamed about? To quit your current job because of all the benefits you'd lose? To end a long-term relationship that you know is wrong for you because of the discomfort it would cause in others? To spend the money that you've saved for emergencies to invest in a dream of your own today? To overcome your fear of beginning a new exercise regimen that you know would benefit you? To enroll in a college course because you feel that you're too old to learn something new? To get the help you need to overcome an addiction that continues to wreak havoc in your life? To stand up to family members or co-workers who continue to treat you unfairly? As you can see, this list of examples could go on forever.

Develop your own list of things you're unwilling to do in order to re-create your life. Then find a big eraser and rub out those excuses on your list. After adding the header ALL THE THINGS I'M UNWILLING TO DO IN ORDER TO LIVE THE LIFE THAT I INTEND TO LIVE—THE LIFE I SIGNED UP FOR EVEN BEFORE I CAME INTO THIS BODY IN THIS WORLD, keep this smudged and perhaps tattered sheet of paper in a prominent place. Use it as your reminder to erase the concept of unwillingness from your consciousness.

In 1975 when I'd written my first book for public consumption, I recall my agent Artie Pine asking me, "Is there anything that you're unwilling to do in order to create the kind of excitement in the country that will make this book a big success?" The answer was no, I was willing to do anything: pay my own expenses; travel the entire country; stay up all night, night after night, talking on call-in radio; do 12 to 14 interviews a day; take my family with me on this adventure; and buy up the first two printings of the book to distribute myself. All the while, I was having the time of my life living what I considered to be my purpose, telling anyone who would listen about the commonsense ideas that filled the pages of *Your Erroneous Zones*.

Similarly, when I first began to record lectures for public television, I made up my mind that there would be nothing on my unwillingness list. I visited more than 170 TV stations to talk about the ideas and raise money for PBS throughout the country—there were no stations too small for me to visit. I was willing to do this for seven days a week during entire pledge periods, flying from city to city, staying up late and getting up in the middle of the night to go on to the next place, most of the time paying my own expenses, yet always living my passion.

And even though I'm now in my 68th year, I still have nothing on my unwillingness list. When it comes to my film, *The Shift,* I love it so much that nothing will hold me back from telling the world about it. I know that if enough people view it, it's capable of changing not only individual lives, but the entire planet as well.

The payoffs for having a blank unwillingness sheet are monumental. The biggest and most basic one is that you have no excuses to fall back on when you're explaining what's missing in your life; there's nothing to find fault with and no one to blame. You simply do whatever you need to do to fulfill your dreams, and you have the luxury of not needing to explain your actions to anyone. (You may want to include some items on your own list such as being unwilling to lie, steal, cheat, be immoral, break the law, and so on. I didn't write about these because I'm assuming that such behaviors are inconsistent with who you are as a being aligned with your Source.)

Now let me ask you this: what is it that you've been loath to think or do in order to create the life that you're desirous of living? Anything that crops up in your mind is likely to be in that catalog from Chapter 3. *It would have taken too long, so I didn't sign up for the training. It would have caused too much of a disruption to my family, so I didn't follow my intuition. I'm too old to make such changes, so I was unwilling to begin an entirely new endeavor. The money wasn't there, and I couldn't justify the expense at the time.* These and many more like them sound like legitimate reasons for not fulfilling that inner calling that your heart knows is your true dharma, your ultimate purpose.

There's nothing rational about what I'm asking you to consider here, nor is this an intellectual exercise I'm imploring you to contemplate—this is your *heart* I'm speaking to, not your head. When you feel that there's something for you to do, and that inner voice will not be silenced, I urge you to look at that sheet of paper that represents what you will not do to fulfill your destiny. By all means, stay aligned with your Source and live from a God-realized perspective, but remind yourself, *There's nothing I'm unwilling to think or do (as long as it is aligned with my Source) in order to bring my dreams into reality.* When you discard unwillingness from your life, you'll be guided to a place where any and all excuses will definitely be . . . gone!

### Suggestions for Applying a Willingness Mind-set to Your Life

— End the blame game once and for all. Begin to see all of your personal traits and the conditions you experience as choices rather than factors that came about because of some external circumstances. Refer to everything in your life with statements such as, "I chose to listen to what my parents said when I was a child, and I'm still under their influence in some ways today," rather than "I can't help the way I am; I've always been this way, and it's largely the fault of my early training." Similarly, state: "I've always been fearful about leaving this job or city because I've made other people's opinions more important than my own," rather than "I can't help being fearful—I was trained by my parents, who have always been afraid to try something new themselves."

Be willing to say these words and mean them: "I'm the product of all of the choices I've made in my life. I have no one to blame for anything that isn't going the way I'd like it to go, including myself."

— Practice being willing to hold the vision by rehearsing scenes in your mind that deal with others who aren't in agreement with your new stance. Don't argue with family members or partners who think you're foolish to have a vision for yourself that's incompatible with the one they have of you. Instead, simply respond with, "Thank you for sharing your vision; your opinions are always helpful to me." And then—and this is important—*hold on to your vision even tighter* and make every effort to act on it without being confrontational.

If you're determined to get a college degree or complete some kind of specialized training that you've always wanted, and others around you think that such ambitions are preposterous, silently note: *What you think of me is none of my business.* Then hold the vision. Your vision of yourself and your willingness to hold on to it through resistance from others is crucial to your *Excuses Begone!* life.

— Create an inventory of the things you're unwilling to do in order to manifest your destiny. Then erase everything on it but this title: WHAT I AM UNWILLING TO THINK OR DO IN ORDER TO BECOME ALL THAT I DESIRE FOR MYSELF. Leave this sheet of paper in a prominent spot, where you can look at it every day to remind you of your commitment to shed all unwillingness. When you're challenged and find yourself reverting to old habits, look at your empty sheet, and then affirm the following for at least five minutes: *There is nothing that I am unwilling to think or do in order to become all that I am destined to become.* Repeating this inner mantra will serve as an energy shifter for you, and it will put you on the path of greatness.

Virginia Woolf once offered a single line that has guided me throughout my adult life: "Arrange whatever pieces come your way." I pass it along to you with this caveat: you must be willing to take whatever pieces of life come your way and arrange them so that they work *with* and *for* you rather than *against* you. The key is to be willing. The pieces will show up—they always have, and they always will. Your willingness to arrange rather than complain or make excuses will pay off.

# CHAPTER 9

# THE SIXTH PRINCIPLE: *PASSION*

*"When a man's willing and eager, God joins in."*

— Aeschylus

Memorize these four words: *passion always trumps excuses!* However, keep in mind that when I use the word *passion,* I'm not referring to the romantic notions that this concept conjures. Instead, I'm equating it to a vigorous kind of enthusiasm that you feel deep within you and that isn't easy to explain or define. This kind of passion propels you in a direction that seems motivated by a force beyond your control. It's the inner excitement of being on the right path, doing what feels good to you and what you know you were meant to do.

It's my contention that the mere *presence* of passion within you—and the enthusiasm that comes with it—is all you need to fulfill your dreams. And let's take a brief look at the word *enthusiasm.* As the novelist and woman of letters Madame de Staël noted in 1810: "The sense of this word among the Greeks affords the noblest definition of it; enthusiasm signifies God in us."

Earlier I wrote that God is in no need of excuses, ever. The creative Divine Spirit is able to manifest anything it contemplates, and you and I are the results of its contemplating itself into material form. Thus, when we have an emotional reaction that feels like overwhelming passion for what *we're* contemplating, we're experiencing the God within us . . . and nothing can hold us back. Enthusiasm becomes our co-creator.

I take you back to those four words that I opened this chapter with: *passion always trumps excuses.* Stay with your passion, and excuses will most assuredly be . . . gone!

### Enthusiasm Overcomes Excuses

Passion is a feeling that tells you: *This is the right thing to do. Nothing can stand in my way. It doesn't matter what anyone else says. This feeling is so good that it cannot be ignored. I'm going to follow my bliss and act upon this glorious sensation of joy.*

Excuses, on the other hand, communicate the opposite message: *I don't necessarily have to follow through—look at how dull all of this is anyway. This isn't very important; if it was, I'd be excited about it. I'll drop it for now; I can always do it later. This isn't really for me; I'll just finish it quickly and get it over with.*

Think of Madame de Staël's definition of *enthusiasm,* that it signifies God in you. If you can imagine God at work creating beingness (form) out of nonbeingness (Spirit), you'll begin to understand the assertion of Jesus that "with God all things are possible." So if all things are possible with God, and God is within you in the form of your passionate enthusiasm, why would you ever need to employ an excuse of any kind?

When you're enthusiastic, nothing seems difficult. When you have passion, there are no risks: family dramas become meaningless, money isn't an issue, you know that you have the strength and the smarts, and the rules laid down by others have no bearing on you whatsoever. That's because you're answering your calling— and the you who is doing the answering is the highest part of you, or the God within.

The presence of passion within you is the greatest gift you can receive. And when it's aligned with Spirit, treat it as a miracle, doing everything you can to hold on to it. I feel this way about the creation of my books. I've learned over the years that when I go to that place of passion within me, there's no force in the universe that can interfere with my completing a project. I live and breathe it, keeping notepads close at hand when I eat, drive, practice yoga, and even sleep. My life is consumed by the passion I feel for what I'm doing—yet I know that as long as I feel this, I'm experiencing the God within.

My enthusiasm seems to cause my world to endlessly offer me cooperative, co-creating experiences. Ideas come to me in my sleep, and I awaken and jot them down. Ideas flow to me in yoga class, and I make a mental note to record them when I've finished exercising. I'm willing and I'm eager, and not just about my writing—I feel the same way about staying in shape, enjoying my family, preparing to do a film, giving a lecture, or whatever it may be. As the famed Greek dramatist Aeschylus suggested in the quote that opens this chapter, when willingness and eagerness are present, "God joins in." This is why I say that the presence of passion is so critical. It doesn't just help us emulate the all-creating Divine mind; it allows us to become one with it again.

If you have passion, there is no need for excuses, because your enthusiasm will trump any reasoning you might come up with. Your excitement will propel you toward acting on what you've been imagining with such gusto that you won't need an explanation for what is holding you back. While this doesn't guarantee that your venture will be financially successful or well received, it *does* guarantee that you'll follow it through to completion, since the force behind it is God within you.

Enthusiasm makes excuses a nonissue. When you seek the presence of your creative Spirit and are filled with passion about virtually everything you undertake, you'll successfully remove the roadblocks from your life and enjoy the active presence of Spirit.

## Activating Passion in Your Life

Comfort and luxury are usually the chief requirements of life for your ego—its top priorities tend to be accumulations, achievements, and the approval of others. Consider a new alternative for what makes you happy, one that soars beyond the superficial demands of the ego. The only thing that you need for this state of joy is something to be passionate about. Something that speaks only to you . . . that gets you tingling inside with excitement . . . that will not go away . . . that radiates within you . . . that sends you into a frenzy of good feeling because it makes you feel purposeful and connected to your Source of being. It doesn't matter what it is. The only requirement is that you feel intensely about it and are willing to act with enthusiasm, awakening the sleeping God within you.

As Abraham Maslow once observed about self-actualizing people: "They must be what they can be." Take a moment now to think about what you can be, and contrast that with what you've chosen to be up until now. So what *can* you be? You might decide to become passionate about getting yourself in optimal physical shape. Are you able to walk up a few flights of stairs without gasping for air? Are you capable of running ten miles without being totally exhausted? Are you carrying excessive weight? Are you in that high percentage of people who fall into the obesity range? Do you treat your body as a temple, attending to its highest needs? Can you become zealous about living a healthy life?

Perhaps you have an idea that you've been carrying around with you for decades, such as a book that you know needs to be written, which only *you* have the wisdom to create. Can you get so passionate about realizing your vision that you activate the presence of God to assist you in co-creating your dreams? Remember, the mere presence of that passion, nothing more, is evidence that the energy of the Divine creating spirit is alive and well in you. That's all you need—just the willingness to allow your passion to speak up and awaken from its dormant status. You don't have to know *how* to activate your long-buried enthusiasm or precisely *what* to focus on. What you need is the willingness to say yes to signals from within you, the God within you who wants to be active.

I've always treasured the observations of the famous Greek scholar Nikos Kazantzakis, who is one of my favorite authors. In page after page of his wonderful novel *Zorba the Greek,* Kazantzakis details what a truly passionate man looks, sounds, and feels like, as the title character simply lives his bliss and feels the presence of God in every waking moment. And I've had these words by Kazantzakis posted in my home for more than a decade now, yet I still read and contemplate them every day: "By believing passionately in something that does not yet exist we create it. The nonexistent is whatever we have not sufficiently desired." The "something that does not yet exist" for you has very likely been explained away repeatedly with any number of excuses, and what's "not sufficiently desired" describes the absence of passion to a tee.

Returning for a moment to the ideas I brought up in the last chapter, practice both holding the vision for your life and surrendering it to a power greater than yourself—one that you're also connected to at all times. As I always respond whenever I'm asked what my secret is for having overcome a mountain of various addictions in my life: "I turned the entire matter over to a higher power, and I began to passionately believe in something that did not yet exist." I've come to see passion as synonymous with God. When I began to fervently hold on to my vision for myself, I accessed the Divine guidance that steered my life away from harmful substances and behaviors: suddenly I'd find new circumstances that were addiction free, the right people started showing up, and the wrong people became "mysteriously" unable to contact me.

Give this new enthusiastic vision a try. Believe in its ability to not only kindle the fire inside of you, but keep it alive as well. Draw it, smell it, sense it, smile about it, and see it coming to you on the wings of angels right into your life. Let go of those tedious, worn-out justifications for what you haven't been able to produce, and take comfort in Zorba's model of a passionate person. Begin to believe in the nonexistent you rather than in a part of you that's stuck in place and full of excuses. Get excited about your vision and know that when you change the way you look at things, the things you look at change. Revisit passion within yourself and see how the world not only looks different, but acts differently *toward* you.

### Enthusiasm Is Inspiring

Enthusiasm enables you to stay "in-Spirit" or inspired. And just like anything else (including excuses), the more you access and hold on to enthusiasm, the more it becomes a habit. The best thing about this particular habit, however, is that it's always accompanied by joy and happiness. To that end, James Baldwin once wrote that "fires can't be made with dead embers, nor can enthusiasm be stirred by spiritless men."

The best way to keep your passion alive is to make your number one relationship in the world be that between you and your Source of being. Stay in a state of wonderment and bewilderment over everything and everyone you encounter. Go through life being continuously grateful and appreciative—give thanks for all of nature and the multitude of miracles you see appearing before your eyes each and every day. This is a daily practice for me, and it's the most prominent factor I can identify for keeping my zest for life alive and well.

I'm in awe of this entire business that we call life. I sit here writing, yet not having a clue about how it all takes place. Words appear on the page from *no where* and suddenly they are *now here.* Where did they come from? Is someone guiding me? And what about those trees outside my window, or that tiny little creature crawling across the page of the book I just opened, which have the same life force in them that I have in me? And those stars and galaxies out there . . . are we alone in this vast, endless universe?

I could go on and on writing about the gazillion things there are to be passionate about. The point is that there's no shortage of things to inspire us. And by staying in this space of wonderment, bewilderment, and especially gratitude, we feel the excitement of being alive. This is a far different stance from the one that exists when we rely on excuses to explain our life's deficiencies away.

The longer I live, the more I'm content to allow unseen powers work their magic with and around me, and the less I question any of it. I have relinquished the notion that I'm ever separate from the all-knowing mind of the universe. In this state of awe, I feel passion all the time. I don't need to do anything—I feel it in every face I look into and in every star-filled night and blossoming flower I observe. My greatest moments of enthusiasm occur while trying to think and act like the all-knowing, benevolent Source of everything does; when I let go of ego, I'm most able to maintain my passion.

Lao-tzu once observed: "If your willingness to give blessings is limited, so also is your ability to receive them. This is the subtle operation of the Tao." Your own willingness to give blessings can be totally unrestricted. By staying aligned with the way the all-creating Tao works, you maintain an exceptionally high level of enthusiasm, and it all seems to make so much sense. When you stay aligned with God and think like God thinks, you act as God seems to act. You live in-Spirit—and with enthusiasm.

### Nurturing Your Passion

Experiencing that thrill of passion in your body is an indication that you're fulfilling a destiny you may have signed up for even before you merged into the world of being from nonbeing. The opening lines of the Old Testament convey that "God" and "good" are essentially synonymous, so know that when you feel good, that's akin to saying that you feel *God*.

The presence of passion (feeling good) is also the same as having God awakened within yourself. Think of this awakened presence as something you need to continuously pay attention to and nurture in order to prevent it from either going back to sleep or disappearing entirely. In other words, you must keep this passion ever-present on the front burner of your life.

I encourage you to spend as much energy as you can reaching out and helping other people. Recall Lao-tzu's message that your willingness to *receive* blessings is related to your ability to *give* them. I know that I feel the greatest passion when I'm in the process of serving others. Giving money to individuals to finance dreams that otherwise would go unfulfilled or sending books and CDs to hospitals, prisons, libraries, and schools is always a thrill for me. Even taking my 92-year-old mom out for dinner, just the two of us, sends waves of pleasure down my spine.

Giving to others is a great first step in finding your passion. Recently, for instance, I had the opportunity to spend a morning in a first-grade classroom (I was invited to read *Unstoppable Me!* one of the four children's books I've co-authored with Kristina Tracy). Interacting with the children and hearing the questions they asked filled me with enthusiasm, but what I saw in their teacher, Ms. Wimmer, was equally thrilling. Here's a woman living her passion every day through serving those first graders—she radiates her joy in nurturing the love of learning in all of her students, and she glows with excitement as she talks about each of the boys and girls whom she feels honored to teach.

Her students simply adore this wonderful educator, and who can blame them? She takes them on after-school field trips, has them write their own illustrated books, plans elaborate graduation ceremonies, and gets down on the floor with them to instruct from a hands-on perspective. Every subject is taught from a creative point of view.

Ms. Wimmer is also more than willing to spend her own money to provide experiences for the kids in her classroom who wouldn't otherwise have the opportunity due to budgetary considerations. There simply are no limits to what she'll do to give her students an ideal first-grade experience. This is passionate nurturing!

Rather than using our days to just go through the motions and feel a sense of ennui, we all need to go through life as enthusiastically as Ms. Wimmer does. After all, how can we be expected to find any passion if we're seemingly stuck in a dull world that typifies our daily existence? We must discover the joy and satisfaction that comes from feeding our passion—it's a much better idea than hauling out that tiresome excuse that "life is boring."

It may be helpful to think of your passion as the presence of the creative Source inside you. Talk to this invisible yet tangible presence within and thank it for never abandoning you. Go for walks with it and even imagine holding hands with it. Ask it questions and listen to what it has to say, making mental notes of how it is directing you. Feel enormous gratitude for the reality of this presence, and allow it to guide you in any way it wishes.

Always remember that your passion is evidence of God within, and you can make it your own very private experience. You don't need to share your inner stirring with anyone you feel might rain on your parade. Rather, make a promise to yourself that you'll pay attention to your passion, that you'll do at least one small thing daily to make it your reality. Even if you only do a silent meditation on keeping your dream alive, write one paragraph of the book you've been envisioning, make one phone call exploring how to get into that business you've fantasized about running, or put a few dollars aside to finance your future endeavor, do it. Pay attention to your passion—*never ignore it.* Talk to it so that you don't have to drag out excuses to explain why it was always impossible for you to see and follow your own bliss.

Keep in mind that your passion must be fed in order to survive; it will never let you down if you nurture it. How could it? It is God within you. And with God all things are possible . . . and no excuses are necessary.

### Suggestions for Living a Passion-Filled Life

— Do something every day to keep the awakened God within from falling back asleep. Remember that your feelings of excitement are the result of the way you think, and when your thoughts harmonize with Source energy, you begin to feel your passion. Therefore, you must keep a constant watch on your mental activity. Maintain a journal to record what fires you up—the more you write, the more you invite passion to live within you.

Go on the Internet and view sites that talk about and promote ideas you feel enthusiastic about. Telephone or e-mail someone out there who shares the same vision as you. Open a private bank account that contains seed money to fund a passion. Whatever you do, remind yourself that this is *your passion* and you're feeding and nurturing it every day. As this becomes your habituated way of being, you'll see the universe cooperating and offering experiences that match your desires.

— Develop a sense of awe that then leads to the creation of passion by beginning to look at everything as though you're seeing it for the first time. Don't let the concept of boredom even creep into your thoughts.

I've participated in thousands of interviews of all types over the past four decades. Frequently I've been asked, "Don't you find it boring to be asked the same questions over and over?" My response, which comes from my heart, is: "I've never been interviewed by this person, at this time, on this subject, under these circumstances before." Thus, every interview is a brand-new joyful endeavor, and this keeps my passion alive. I employ the same kind of thinking when I'm about to give a lecture for the tenth time in two weeks—each presentation before a live audience is a novel experience.

Look at your entire life in this way: Make love to your spouse like it's the first time. Read to your children like it's the first time. Go for your daily run like it's the first time. Every new moment is a gift from the all-knowing Tao, so when you act as if each experience and moment is a fresh one, you'll feel the passion I'm attempting to convey in this book.

— Take a five-minute time-out today to repeat the following affirmation: *I invite the presence of God to be with me in the form of my passion.* This reminds you that every moment of excitement you feel is evidence that you have Divine guidance in the moment. By holding on to it, you'll enter the *Excuses Begone!* zone.

As Thomas Aquinas observed: "True peace consists in not separating ourselves from the will of God." All of your moments of excitement, enthusiasm, and passion are moments of connection. They bring true peace. Excuses, on the other hand, are what you employ when you separate yourself from your passion, or the will of God. Excuses are lifelong thinking habits that take you away from peace. You always have the choice: passion, peace, and alignment with God; or excuses, excuses, and more excuses.

# CHAPTER 10

# THE SEVENTH PRINCIPLE: COMPASSION

*"True compassion is more than flinging a coin to a beggar . . . it under-stands that an edifice which produces beggars needs restructuring."*

— Martin Luther King, Jr.

There is a widely told story that speaks to the value of compassion. It seems that a woman who lived a Tao-centered life came upon a precious stone while sitting by the banks of a running stream in the mountains, and she placed this highly valued item in her bag.

The next day, a hungry traveler approached the woman and asked for something to eat. As she reached into her bag for a crust of bread, the traveler saw the precious stone and imagined how it would provide him with financial security for the remainder of his life. He asked the woman to give the treasure to him, and she did, along with some food. He left, ecstatic over his good fortune and the knowledge that he was now secure.

A few days later the traveler returned and handed back the stone to the wise woman. "I've been thinking," he told her. "Although

I know how valuable this is, I'm returning it to you in the hopes that you could give me something even more precious."

"What would that be?" the woman inquired.

"Please give me what you have within yourself that enabled you to give me that stone."

The woman in this story was living her life from a sacred place of compassion . . . which is the seventh and last principle for an *Excuses Begone!* life.


### Compassion and Excuses

It is impossible to need excuses when the focus of life shifts to *How may I serve?* Thinking of others first—reaching out to them despite how it might inconvenience you—causes you to feel joy, which is what the hungry traveler was actually seeking. This gift of feeling good (or feeling God) within comes from serving and surrendering rather than asking and demanding.

There's no room for blame in your life as long as you live with kindness. And excuses, regardless of their form, are all about blame. Blaming your past. Blaming the economy. Blaming your perceived personal flaws. Blaming God. Blaming your parents. Blaming your children or your spouse. Blaming your DNA. There's no shortage of circumstances, people, and events to blame—and there's no shortage of blame itself.

When you shift to compassion, all blame disappears. So no matter what you may want for yourself, discover how you can want it more for someone else, and then make that shift. In that contemplative moment, compassion will eradicate finger-pointing and trump excuse making. And you'll begin to think like God thinks: serving, offering, giving, and loving freely.

The wise woman in the mountains who gave the precious stone to a stranger had no need to think about poverty or unhappiness, to hold a cynical view toward the greedy masses, or to explain the way she lived her life. Why? Because her ego was out of the picture, and love and service reigned supreme.

I've certainly found that when I remember to nurture kindness and courtesy, everything in my life seems to move toward more harmony and peace, to say nothing of how much better I feel when I'm giving rather than wanting.

I heard the Dalai Lama speak on compassion some years back, and the essence of his message contained these two points:

**1. Compassion is the single most important quality that humanity needs to learn.** This is the way to find happiness and health and to feel successful.

**2. War and violence would become extinct in one generation if, beginning at the age of five, children were taught to meditate on compassion for an hour a week for the rest of their lives.** Such is the power of a compassionate approach to life, which is truly thinking of others and living by the ancient Golden Rule.

The very second you feel yourself retreating to excuses, repeat the mantra *How may I serve?* Then act upon the answers you receive. You'll become aligned with the universal mind, which is always giving, and the bonus is that you'll notice the universe asking you back, "How may I serve *you?*" As your compassion for others flows back to you, remember the truth I've written about many times in this book: *You do not attract what you want; you attract what you are.* So make compassion be what you are.

### Three Questions

For the past several years I've celebrated Father's Day in a way that reflects what this chapter is about: I give special gifts to my eight children, rather than receiving presents from them. Being a father is one of the greatest privileges that I've enjoyed for more than 40 years. I consider it an incredible honor as well as a sacred undertaking to parent my six beautiful girls and two handsome sons, so it's my wish to thank them for choosing me as their dad and for allowing me to play this glorious role in their lives.

I think of the responsibility of raising and supporting a child as an amazing gift, because to be able to fully support another human being is as close to being in a place of God realization as there is. After all, when God contemplates us into existence, doesn't He/She support us, and allow the free will to choose a compassionate existence?

This past Father's Day, my gift to my children was a copy of Leo Tolstoy's short story *Three Questions*. Tolstoy tells of a king who was certain that if he just knew the best time to act; the right people to listen to; and, above all, the most important thing to do at all times, he'd never fail in anything he might undertake.

So he proclaimed that he would bountifully reward anyone in his kingdom who would teach him the answers to these three questions. Many learned men came to see the king, but since they all responded differently—and he didn't agree with any of them— none of these men were rewarded. But the king still greatly desired to have his three questions answered, so he decided to consult a hermit who was widely renowned for his wisdom.

The reclusive old man received only common folk, so the king put on simple clothes, left his bodyguards, dismounted from his horse, and went to see him alone. When the disguised king reached the hermit, he asked him his three questions, but the elder fellow didn't answer. Noting that the hermit was very frail and attempting to dig some flower beds, the king took over, shoveling earth for hours. When he attempted his questions again, the hermit noticed a bearded man running out of the woods, holding his hands over a profusely bleeding wound in his abdomen.

The hermit and the king took the bearded man inside and tended to him. The next morning, the man asked the king to forgive him, even though the ruler was certain he'd never seen this individual before.

The injured man explained:

> You do not know me, but I know you. I am that enemy of yours who swore to revenge himself on you, because you executed his brother and seized his property. I knew you had gone

alone to see the hermit, and I resolved to kill you on your way back. But the day passed and you did not return. So I came out from my ambush to find you, and I came upon your bodyguards, and they recognized me, and wounded me. I escaped from them, but should have bled to death had you not dressed my wound. I wished to kill you, and you have saved my life. Now, if I live, and if you wish it, I will serve you as your most faithful slave, and will bid my sons do the same. Forgive me!

The king not only forgave him, but he also said that he'd send his servants and his own physician to attend to the man, and he promised to give him back the property that had been taken from him.

At that point, the king went outside and saw the hermit placing seeds in the beds he'd dug the day before. He decided to ask the old sage his three questions one final time, and was surprised when the elderly fellow responded that his queries had already been answered:

"How answered? What do you mean?" asked the king.

"Do you not see," replied the hermit. "If you had not pitied my weakness yesterday, and had not dug these beds for me, but had gone your way, that man would have attacked you, and you would have repented of not having stayed with me. So the most important time was when you were digging the beds; and I was the most important man; and to do me good was your most important business. Afterwards when that man ran to us, the most important time was when you were attending to him, for if you had not bound up his wounds he would have died without having made peace with you. So he was the most important man, and what you did for him was your most important business. Remember then: there is only one time that is important—Now! It is the most important time because it is the only time when we have any power. The most necessary man is he with whom you are, for no man knows whether he will ever have dealings with anyone else: and the most important affair is, to do him good, because for that purpose alone was man sent into this life!"

Let's go over the three questions as they pertain to your living from a place of compassion. As you read this section, think about the lessons that the king learned from his wise teacher, the hermit; as well as what can be taken from the example of the wise woman who gave away her precious stone to a traveler.

### 1. When Is the Best Time to Do Each Thing?

Both the hermit and the wise woman understood what Tolstoy meant when he wrote: "Remember then: there is only one time that is important—Now! It is the most important time because it is the only time when we have any power." You may recall that the third *Excuses Begone!* principle explained that compassion can only be experienced in this current moment. *Now* is where everything takes place. So your relationship to life is truly your relationship to the present.

I love the definition of compassion offered by historian Arnold Toynbee: "Compassion is the desire that moves the individual self to widen the scope of its self-concern to embrace the whole of the universal self."

In any given moment of your life, when you embrace another beyond any concern for yourself, you are living compassion . . . you're also making it impossible to employ excuses. Thus, you now know the secret that Tolstoy's king sought and the wise woman knew instinctively: *This is the time to widen your scope beyond self-concern and embrace a universal self that includes everyone, especially the person who is before you.*

Can you imagine that compassionate woman or wise hermit coming up with an excuse for life not working at the level they liked? Be like them and recognize that this moment is your power—seize it and extend compassion without regard for yourself. And remember that your appointment with life is always in the present.

## 2. Who Are the Most Important People to Work With?

We often hear about, and respond to, the importance of offering assistance to others in drastic need in faraway places. As we try to work toward bringing about world peace, we join organizations dedicated to improving the lives of those who are most needy. Yet this doesn't answer this second question adequately.

Whoever is in your immediate space is the most important person for you to work with, be it friend, family member, co-worker, or total stranger. Therefore, extend kindness to whomever you see before you. As Tolstoy reminds you, you can't know that you'll ever have dealings with anyone else. *This* is your moment, and the person to work with is right there. The wise woman understood this well—she wasn't saving the precious stone for herself, for someone more deserving, or for a relative. She gave her gift, which came from her compassionate heart, to a person she'd never met before. So the lesson is: Don't look beyond the moment. Now is a perfect opportunity. Whoever is in your presence is the one who is available for your compassion.

As the Vietnamese master Thich Nhat Hanh once observed:

> If you cannot make your own child happy, how do you expect to be able to make anyone else happy? If all our friends in the peace movement or of service communities of any kind do not love and help one another, whom can we love and help? Are we working for other humans, or are we just working for the name of an organization?

## 3. What Is the Most Important Thing to Do at All Times?

The compassionate actions of the hermit and the wise woman show that they both knew the answer to this question very well. Tolstoy concludes *Three Questions* by explaining why compassionate action toward the person in the moment is so highly esteemed: "because for that purpose alone was man sent into this life!" As we learned in the last chapter, doing *good* is the equivalent of doing *God*. We're not here to conquer others, wage war, build towering temples to our deities, become number one, win anything, or defeat anyone. No, we are here to be like God, or to be good—to serve, reach out, allow, not interfere, and be humble wherever we go.

Give your ego a rest and live compassionately by being a decent human being. The king learned this when he let go of his importance—by simply doing good, he saved his own life. And the woman in the mountains was able to teach an ego-driven man how to be happy by a simple demonstration of goodness.

Allow me to conclude this chapter by telling you another story, this one concerning my daughter Sommer and me. As I was driving her to the airport for her return to college after a long weekend home, she was admiring my new watch. Now this was the first new timepiece I'd had in at least a decade. I really enjoyed looking at its shiny steel-and-black face, and as I did, I'd think about how this was my favorite watch of all time. Yet I knew in my heart that Sommer would love to wear it, since men's watches seemed to be the current craze for young women.

As I dropped my daughter off at the curb and assisted her with her luggage, I was prompted to remove the watch and give it to her, even though it was my most prized possession (particularly since I have almost no possessions any longer that I even care about, let alone prize).

Sommer's response was, "No, Dad, you love this watch!"

I insisted, telling her that I'd feel greater joy by giving it to her and knowing she'd treasure it. I also said that I felt it would symbolize our staying together in time, even though we'd be thousands of miles apart. She boarded her plane glowing, and I left feeling that I had grown immeasurably as a person, since such a compassionate act would have been very difficult, if not impossible, for me several years ago.

Sommer called me in Maui a few months later to tell me that she was sending me a present for Father's Day, stressing that it was a very, *very* special gift. It turned out to be her all-time favorite painting that she'd created and had hung in her apartment for a long time. As she told me later: "I really learned something the day you gave me your beloved watch, and I wanted to give you something that's *my* single most precious item. I'm giving it to you, Dad, even though it's difficult to part with, because I want you to have a piece of me with you."

The painting hangs proudly on my wall as a symbol of the beauty and perfection of reaching out compassionately in response to a felt moment. This personal story epitomizes and personalizes the response to Tolstoy's three questions: (1) do it now, the only moment available; (2) do it with the person you're with in the moment; and (3) do good, because that is why you're here.

By being and living compassion, you invite and encourage others, just by your example, to choose to do the same.

### Suggestions for Living from Compassion

— Upon awakening, let the words *Thank you* flow from your lips, for this will remind you to begin your day with gratitude and compassion. Make it a practice to begin each day by thinking first of someone else and then making a decision to actively do something, anything, that will bring a smile to his or her face. When you become conscious of wanting to do something kind for another human being, you move into a higher way of being. It takes your thoughts off yourself and *What's in it for me?* and puts them on *How may I serve?* which is precisely how the universal mind we call the Tao or God is always operating. When you're aligned with a compassionate outlook, your entire day will reflect this kind of awareness.

Here are some suggestions to get you started: e-mail a note of appreciation, say a kind word to one of your children with whom you've been having harsh words, apologize to an individual you've needed to make amends with, pick a few wildflowers and hand them to someone, give away some personal items such as books or jewelry, or send a smile toward someone that might brighten his or her moment. The point is that it doesn't have to cost money; what you're doing is aligning with compassion and thereby setting up your day to work in this way.

Whenever you find yourself employing one of your personally familiar excuses, you can stop yourself in midthought and immediately shift to the person you showed such humanity toward. Note how excuses disintegrate when your thoughts are on being kind toward others.

You needn't restrict your opening act of compassion to a person. All acts of kindness toward any of God's creatures, even if it's just picking up some trash that was carelessly discarded, impact our planet. The point is to set your mind on serving, and off of your ego's demands.

— In the quote that opens this chapter, Martin Luther King, Jr., suggests that our culture needs restructuring and that compassion is the way. I urge you to work toward electing people to public office—at all levels—who relate sensitivity and kindness in their messages to the public. Attitudes of compassion take into consideration men and women who are involved in concerns of immigration, torture, sexual orientation, religious persuasion, and socioeconomic status. There can be no exceptions here. Look for the compassionate heart, rather than the one that excludes, punishes, seeks revenge, or manipulates with government power. The more our institutions reflect this humane attitude, the fewer collective excuses we will call upon to explain why we haven't been able to create the heaven on earth that is our true calling.

— As I've stated in each of the seven principles in this part of the book, the active repetition of an inner mantra reinforces and creates exactly what you're saying to yourself. Therefore, repeat the following to yourself for at least five minutes: *I am a being of compassion. I extend love outward everywhere because this is my nature.* Affirm this to yourself continually, and post it in a prominent place in your home, your office, or even your car.

In the Sermon on the Mount, Jesus gives us the ultimate words of compassion. If our world today would put them into practice, we'd all be living in peace. But even if the rest of the world hasn't yet caught on, you can. I urge you to put these words to work in your life today; if you do, all excuses will most certainly vanish:

*Ye have heard that it hath been said, Thou shalt love thy neighbor, and hate thine enemy.*

*But I say unto you, Love your enemies, bless them that curse you, do good to them that hate you, and pray for them which despitefully use you, and persecute you* (Matthew 5:43–44).

This is compassion in action!

PART III

# THE *EXCUSES BEGONE!* PARADIGM SHIFT

*"If you correct your mind, the rest
of your life will fall into place."*

— Lao-tzu

CHAPTER 11

# A NEW WAY OF LOOKING AT CHANGING OLD THINKING HABITS

*"Never underestimate your power to change yourself.*
*Never overestimate your power to change others."*

— H. Jackson Brown, Jr.

By now, you surely understand that you have the power to fundamentally change how your brain works, altering aspects of its chemistry to eradicate old mind viruses. You know that you can become a person who no longer relies upon excuses.

I've learned that what's true in nature is true for all humans in understanding ourselves. Just as the blossoms on a fruit tree fall away as the fruit grows, so does our need for a bouquet of rationalizations vanish as the Divine produces the authentic self. The more we allow ourselves to be guided by the principles that identify us as spiritual, the less we have any desire or inclination to use excuses. As Carl Jung put it: "Our most important problems cannot be solved; they must be outgrown."

Outgrow your need to ever use an excuse again. Even before you start putting the paradigm in this part of the book to work,

673

do what you can to move beyond problems that are related to your old thinking habits. The principles I wrote about in Part II are designed to help you grow from a human being having a spiritual experience to the reverse: a spiritual being having a temporary human experience. This is what Jung meant by *outgrow*—something nature always does with its problems.

An acorn is just a tiny seed, a little nut that can't produce anything, yet as I'm fond of saying, "An infinity of forests lies dormant within the dreams of one acorn." An infinity of manifestations lies dormant within *you*, but you must get past the dormancy of your old thinking. So to aid you in doing this, here's a brief review of the seven *Excuses Begone!* principles I went through in Part II:

- Become *aware* of your potential for greatness and the power of your mind.

- *Align* yourself by thinking like God thinks.

- Live here and *now* in your mind as well as in your body.

- *Contemplate* what you are, rather that what you want to become.

- Be *willing* to allow health, happiness, and success to flow into your life.

- Be *passionate* about everyone and everything that enters your life.

- Want more for others than you do for yourself; that is, be *compassionate*.

These seven tools will help you outgrow your reliance on excuses and help you "correct your mind." When you're able to do this, as Lao-tzu reminded you a few pages ago, "the rest of your life will fall into place."

### *Yes, You Can Correct Your Mind!*

In the first two chapters of this book, I described how a lot of time and effort has gone into convincing you to fit in and be like everybody else. That programming requires some effort on your part to overcome. As poet E. E. Cummings explains: "To be nobody-but-myself—in a world which is doing its best, night and day, to make you like everybody else—means to fight the hardest battle which any human being can fight, and never stop fighting."

You can accomplish being nobody-but-yourself without the actual fighting, although you may feel that you're battling something within yourself. As you let the Divine grow within you, however, you'll shift to a feeling of joy as the old discomfort retreats.

As a young person, you were inundated by a whole slew of "No you can't!" messages. These were subsequently internalized by you as *I can't* thoughts, which were buttressed by well-intentioned excuses. You internalized the notion that *I can't* because you were repeatedly told the following:

- "You'll never amount to anything."

- "You're worthless."

- "You're not smart enough."

- "You can never be good enough."

- "Money is hard to come by."

- "You don't deserve to succeed."

- "You'll never find someone to love you."

- "You'll probably get sick like your mother did; it's in your genes."

- "You'll never get ahead if you don't follow the rules."

- "You're just like your father, and he never amounted to anything."

These and thousands of variations on the same theme(s) seem to have erected permanent barriers within you. Excuses feel like they protect you from such awful sentiments, as well as the present disappointment with your life. Even though you've become an adult with no rational reason to hang on to such memes, they still produce a familiar reaction when it seems necessary to defend why your life isn't at the optimal level you'd prefer. And while you probably had no idea that these messages had infiltrated your brain, they nevertheless have a very strong pull on you.

Don't underestimate your power to change yourself, as the quote at the beginning of this chapter advises. You can absolutely overcome the internalized conviction of *I can't* so that it quickly becomes *I can* by affirming the following:

- *I can accomplish anything I choose.*

- *I am a worthy and valuable person.*

- *I am intellectually capable.*

- *I deserve the best because I am good.*

- *I attract abundance in all areas of my life.*

- *I deserve health, happiness, and success.*

- *I am loved by others, and I love myself.*

- *I am guided by my desire to serve others rather than following the rules.*

- *I am unique and independent of the good
opinions of others.*

If you look closely at the preceding affirmations, you may note that they all represent a movement away from your old excuse-making mentality and toward thinking like God must think.

### Seven Core Ideas for Eliminating Excuses

Before I explain the *Excuses Begone!* paradigm, I'd like to share with you a set of beliefs that I've adopted for myself. I encourage you to be receptive to these ideas, even if they initially seem inapplicable to your life at this time, because I feel strongly that they'll assist you in beginning the process of moving away from justification and defensiveness.

Here are the seven tips I've personally found to be very helpful in eradicating excuses from my life:

### 1. Remove Any and All Labels

Old habits of thinking stick around, often for an entire lifetime, largely because you create internal reasons to reinforce and maintain them. These reasons, which I'm calling "excuses," can become permanently lodged in your subconscious—they're labels you place on yourself that ultimately become your self-definition. In the words of Søren Kierkegaard, the famed Danish theologian: "Once you label me you negate me." As you enter the *Excuses Begone!* paradigm, make a promise to yourself that you won't be labeling *or* negating yourself anymore.

My daughter Serena grew up labeling herself as "not athletic" or even "frail," a self-definition that morphed into a comfortable excuse whenever physical activity came up. My daughter's labels negated the real Serena, who could become anything or anyone she chose. By consciously making a decision to remove those labels, and nothing more, Serena has gradually become a young woman who enjoys participating in athletic events and who loves the positive changes in her body as a result of daily exercise.

Rather than saddling yourself with self-limiting labels, affirm: *I am capable of accomplishing anything I place my attention upon.* Make it clear to yourself that you can never negate the real you; you're an infinite being, and with God all things are possible. The corollary of this would be: with labels, most things are negated!

## 2. Converse with Your Subconscious Mind

I refuse to accept the idea that we have an unconscious mind that defies us by being completely inaccessible. To me, this is a prescription for believing that for the major portion of our lives, we're controlled by unseen and unavailable forces residing within us. I recognize that we're often totally unaware of why we're behaving in certain ways, but this implies that we have no choice in the matter. *Awareness* is the simple key for alleviating this condition.

Have regular conversations with your subconscious—remind it that you don't want to go through life on automatic pilot. Discuss your unwillingness to be a victim of the whims of that "ghost in the machine" of your body, whose orders originate in the mind viruses and thinking habits that were programmed into it by people who are either long dead or no longer play a role in your adult life.

I usually tell my own habitual mind things like this: "I know that I have some really silly leftover habits that were instilled in me a long time ago, and I want you to know that I'm no longer interested in having my actions dictated by you. I'm bringing all of those old habits of thought to the surface, and I'm going to make a conscious effort to be more aware of all aspects of my life."

I had a conversation like this recently regarding my inclination to misplace my keys. I treated the ghost inside of me that always seemed to place my car keys in difficult-to-find locations as if it were a real person. While this may seem like an insignificant little habit, for me, changing it was huge. To this day I rarely misplace my keys.

Initiate a conversation with your subconscious mind in which you make it clear that you're not going to let part of your life be run by an invisible stranger who acts and reacts on the basis of memetic or genetic programming. Instead, decide that you're no longer going to allow (or excuse) behavior from an unconscious part of yourself.

### 3. Begin the Practice of Mindfulness

As you head into the seven chapters that identify a new paradigm for ridding yourself of excuses permanently, I encourage you to begin a practice of being more mindful. This is in fact what I did to end my lifetime habit of being forgetful, particularly when it came to where I placed my car keys.

At one time, I simply excused my can't-find-my-keys behavior with this label: "I'm forgetful." I can recall both my mother and my wife often exclaiming, "Oh, that's Wayne, our absentminded professor!" Memes buried within my subconscious became useful excuses for explaining my habit of being forgetful . . . but then I discovered how to be mindful. I began to practice being conscious of what I used to do unconsciously, and it worked!

Each time I came into the house, I made a decision to be aware of my keys in my hand—to feel the texture and shape of each one of them, to hold them with awareness, to listen to the jingle-jangle sound—and then place them in a special spot reserved just for them. And lo and behold, an old unconscious habit had been brought to the surface and into my conscious mind, causing that old excuse of being forgetful to be eradicated. (On the rare day when I can't find my keys now, it only serves to reinforce my commitment to stay mindful.)

By the same token, there was a time when my yoga practice could deteriorate into a boring routine and I'd become frustrated with myself; or while swimming in the ocean, running along the beach, or even sitting and writing, I could get lost in my old forgetfulness and lose sight of the glorious feeling that's available in all human activity. I found that practicing mindfulness in many ways throughout my day helped immensely.

In his book *The Miracle of Mindfulness,* Thich Nhat Hanh advises us on this practice:

> The Sutra of Mindfulness says, "When walking, the practitioner must be conscious that he is walking. When sitting, the practitioner must be conscious that he is sitting. When lying down, the practitioner must be conscious that he is lying down. . . ." The mindfulness of the positions of one's body is not enough, however. We must be conscious of each breath, each movement, every thought and feeling, everything which has any relation to ourselves.

These days when I swim, I experience my arms moving, my legs kicking, my shoulders stretching, the feel and taste of the salt water, my fingers cupped and moving the water, my breathing, my heart rate . . . all of it. Practicing mindfulness has taught me how to be in the moment and find my *self* as well as my keys!

That makes me think of a story Mobi Ho, a Vietnamese scholar who translated Hanh's book, tells:

> As I sat down to translate *The Miracle of Mindfulness,* I remembered the episodes during the past years that had nurtured my own practice of mindfulness. There was the time I was cooking furiously and could not find a spoon I'd set down amid a scattered pile of pans and ingredients. As I searched here and there, Thay [Hanh] entered the kitchen and smiled. He asked, "What is Mobi looking for?" Of course, I answered, "The spoon! I'm looking for a spoon!" Thay answered, again with a smile, "No, Mobi is looking for Mobi."

### 4. Commit to Overcoming Your Inertia

The excuses you frequently employ have taken up residence in your mind, which is dominated by your ego or false self; consequently, they won't simply pack up and leave without putting up a fight. Those excuses have become familiar companions with your ego, and they're always ready and willing to leap to your defense.

What I've found very useful in overcoming these ego-enriched justifications is to have a conversation with myself about who I intend to be and what I'm willing to do in order to bring this about. I call this my "commitment to overcoming inertia" conversation. I'm aware of my instinctive impulse to stay with the familiar, be inactive, and use the convenient excuses I delineated in Chapter 3. When it comes to fulfilling my commitment to complete a book at a certain time, for instance, I can always haul out, *I'm too busy . . . It's too big . . . It will take a long time . . . I really don't have the energy . . .* or what have you. Yet my inertia conversation helps me organize a few techniques to eliminate those excuses.

The first thing I do is draw up a contractual agreement with myself that I look at each day. After conversing with myself about overcoming inertia, I put a hand-drawn model of the book's jacket on my desk, so I'm writing from the perspective of acting as if what I want to complete is already here. I then continually remind myself that my word to my highest self (God) is sacred. This alone can push me in the direction of my writing space. Once I'm seated, all that procrastination—supported by excuses—disappears.

Before beginning the paradigm I explain in the next several chapters, I encourage you to make a commitment to give up inertia. Have a private conversation with your highest self and be willing to hold on to its vision for you, even if the old excuses come trotting back hoping for a sign of weakness on your part. The written agreement helps you recollect that you're in the process of redefining yourself. You are now practicing an *Excuses Begone!* philosophy for organizing and running your life.

## 5. Use the Power of Affirmations

You can make your entire living space an affirmation by having it reflect the energy you wish to utilize in fulfilling your personal destiny.

My own living space reflects what I wish to have in my life, and I've found this extraordinarily beneficial in underscoring my desire to cease using excuses of any kind. I affirm everything I am; all that I wish to become; and all that I treasure with written, photographic, artistic, and natural symbols of what I believe to be high energy sources.

I stay in alignment with this kind of energy by surrounding myself with what I wish to attract. For example, I want love in my life, so I place symbols of it around as affirmations that I'm aligned with what I want to receive. These include photographs that inspire thoughts of love, fresh flowers that are God's gifts of love in the form of natural beauty, books about love, and written statements such as these that I'm looking at as I write: "Love . . . binds everything together in perfect harmony" (Saint Paul); "He whom love touches not walks in darkness" (Plato); and "He who does not love does not know God, for God is love" (1 John 4:8).

Not only do you become what you think about all day long, you become what you avow to the universe as well. So before you start the *Excuses Begone!* paradigm in the following chapters, I urge you to make your home and working space living testimonials to your highest desires. Affirm that you're deserving of all the abundance that the universe has to offer. Affirm your love for yourself. Affirm that you're a Divine creation, and thus willing and open to that Divine Source working on your behalf.

Never underestimate the power affirmations hold in helping you eradicate the excuses you use to defend the shortcomings of your life.

## 6. Live in a Helpful, Supportive Universe

One of the most important decisions you'll ever make is choosing the kind of universe you exist in: is it helpful and supportive or hostile and unsupportive? Your answer to this question will make all the difference in terms of how you live your life and what kind of Divine assistance you attract.

Remember that you get what you think about, whether you want it or not. So if you're sure that this is an unfriendly universe, you'll look for examples to support this point of view. You'll anticipate people attempting to cheat, judge, take advantage of, and otherwise harm you. You'll blame the antagonistic, inhospitable cosmos for not cooperating with you in the fulfillment of your desires. You'll point the finger at belligerent folks and bad luck for the kind of world we all live in. Since this worldview trickles down into every thought you have, you become a person persistently looking for occasions to be offended, and therefore in possession of a whole slew of excuses.

I implore you to see the universe as a warm and supportive one before you begin to apply the *Excuses Begone!* paradigm, because you'll look for evidence to support this view. When you believe that the universe is friendly, you see friendly people. You look for circumstances to work in your favor. You expect good fortune flowing into your life. In other words, you aren't looking for excuses!

My favorite affirmation when I feel stuck or out of sorts is: *Whatever I need is already here, and it is all for my highest good.* Jot this down and post it conspicuously throughout your home, on the dashboard of your car, at your office, on your microwave oven, and even in front of your toilet! Remind yourself: *I live in a friendly universe that will support any thing or desire that is aligned with the universal Source of all.* Such a stance will be a giant step toward living an *Excuses Begone!* life.

Affirming that what you want is already here and all you have to do is connect to it causes you to remember that what you attract is for your highest good, so you can then let go of the timing issue altogether. Just know that it is here and will arrive on God's schedule—as does everything that makes the journey from nonbe-ing to being.

I've found that by shifting my belief about the nature of the universe, I attract whatever I desire into my life. I desire love. I desire peace. I desire health. I desire happiness. I desire prosper-ity. Why would I want to hold the view that our universe is un-supportive, evil, and unfriendly? How could I expect the Divine realm to hear me if I'm asking it to be something other than what it is? Thus, I see my desires in perfect rapport with how the uni-verse works.

When I pray, I do so in the spirit of Saint Francis. Rather than ask God to grant him peace, this inspiring man beseeched God to "make me an instrument of Thy peace." In other words, "Let me be like the Source from which I originated, and then I will rest in the knowing that it must be here, on its way, and for my high-est good." As you can see, there's no room for excuses when you apply this model to your everyday life.

As I've written and said many times, "When you change the way you look at things, the things you look at change." And this applies to the entire universe.

### 7. Don't Complain—Don't Explain!

Complaining and explaining are the two huge allies of excuse making. Generally speaking, when you resort to complaining you employ an excuse of one kind or another, placing the responsibil-ity for what's upsetting you on something or someone external to yourself. Complaining about the way somebody has performed (or failed to perform) is another way of making an excuse for why you're dissatisfied or unhappy. "It's their fault that my blood pres-sure is up—look at how miserably they've performed" or, "How can I enjoy myself at dinner when everyone here at this restaurant is behaving so incompetently?" are prime examples. Finding fault with circumstances, the weather, the economy, other people, or anything else outside yourself is a way to hang on to excuses.

In addition to putting an end to complaints, I recommend that you never attempt to explain. As I've pursued a no-excuses mentality, I've made it my policy to keep the things that I wish to accomplish a private matter. By doing so, I'm never forced into a stance of having to explain myself. I'm well aware that many of my personal life missions sound strange and outrageous to others. Consequently, I've learned to avoid sharing my intentions with anyone, outside of a select few whom I know and trust at a spiritual level. (Anything I might say to these individuals wouldn't require me to explain myself in any way.)

The problem with having to explain yourself is that in doing so, you inevitably invoke the ego to do your bidding. You have a tendency to make yourself right, sensible, and understood; while at the same time dealing with the doubts and antagonisms of those who don't share your views or your optimism. When you keep things to yourself, you stay connected to your spiritual side, or the place within you that has no need to be right or to make anyone else wrong.

Since all of creation comes from the world of nonbeing, if you want to give life to your dreams and desires—if you wish to manifest your own destiny—then you must rely on the great Source of all creation, Spirit. The moment you inject ego into the picture, you invite excuses; and the moment you invoke those familiar excuses, you stop the creative and the creation process from manifesting.

As Lao-tzu put it:

*The Tao gives rise to all forms, yet it has no form of its own . . .*
*Stop striving after admiration.*
*Place your esteem on the Tao.*
*Live in accord with it,*
*share with others the teachings that lead to it,*
*and you will be immersed in the blessings that flow from it.*[2]

In more modern language, stop complaining and explaining—your excuses will soon cease.

These, then, are my seven favorite ideas for you to contemplate as you prepare to study the *Excuses Begone!* paradigm.

### How to Use the Paradigm

I created the *Excuses Begone!* paradigm because of my strong belief in the spirit of the quote at the beginning of this chapter: "Never underestimate your power to change yourself. Never overestimate your power to change others." The key word in this quotation is *power*. I know there's a power within you that's capable of making dramatic changes in relatively short periods of time.

The problem I've discovered is that most people feel disempowered when it comes to overcoming a lifetime of self-defeating thinking. It's actually quite easy to change the way we think and act, regardless of how long we've done it or how much reinforcement we've received that's solidified a way of being. I've put myself to this test on many occasions, and I've always found that making these changes is much simpler than others would have me think. I believe that in the same way our body knows how to maintain an optimal state of health without any outside interference, so too is our mind programmed by Source energy to know how and what to think in order to optimize our emotional and spiritual development.

I have stopped underestimating the power we contain within us to make apparently radical shifts and have applied the *Excuses Begone!* paradigm to overcome addictions of all stripes in my life. I've also used it to help me attract the right people, the right circumstances, the right jobs, the funding I needed, the healing I desired, and so on. I've seen many individuals leave old thinking and behavior behind with very little time or hard effort devoted to the outcome. The impact of early imprinting and conditioning is felt throughout life until a change is initiated, but I've never bought into the idea that our early-childhood programming is insurmountable. Nor do I accept that we have an unconscious mind that cannot be accessed. And you know that I even reject the idea that our genes and DNA are excuses for all manner of thinking and behaving. Rather, I've chosen to believe in the innate power within each of us to change.

Each chapter that follows in this last part of this book is presented as a question to ask yourself. Take some time before you answer, and read through the chapters with a mind that's open to everything and attached to nothing. Consider the examples I present, examine both sides, and stay neutral in your assessment of how they apply to you today. In other words, simply let it all come in—particularly the parts that you immediately think don't apply to you!

There are no exercises to do, lists to make, rules to follow, or complicated instructions to memorize. All you need to do as you read the following pages is keep in mind the words of Lao-tzu: "If you correct your mind, the rest of your life will fall into place." This paradigm for changing habituated thinking is all about helping you to correct your mind. Enjoy, as everything else just falls into place.

CHAPTER 12

# THE FIRST QUESTION: *IS IT TRUE?*

*"I shall try to correct errors when shown to be errors, and I shall adopt new views so fast as they shall appear to be true views."*

— Abraham Lincoln

I've heard estimates, from those who engage in such accounting practices, that the average adult has approximately 60,000 separate thoughts in a 24-hour period. Even more startling is that we think the *same* 60,000 thoughts today that we had yesterday and will have tomorrow. Thus, many of us go through our daily lives in a habituated pattern, endlessly repeating the same thoughts over and over again!

Now let me add a bit of fuel to this firestorm. I suggest that the vast majority of those continually reiterated notions, particularly those that fall into the excuse category, are very likely untrue. It then follows that we use our incomparably brilliant minds to obliviously process false thoughts on a daily basis. *Is it true?* has to be the first challenge to this repetitious, habitual, and unconscious activity of making excuses.

This first question in the *Excuses Begone!* paradigm will lead you to an awareness of the personal nature of your justifications. When you discover how your mind selects untrue thoughts to guide you, you'll also reveal a major impetus to ending that habit that has held you back from so much in life.

### Finding the Truth in Four Popular Excuses

If you were to discover that a thought you use to define who you are to yourself and others is false, would you want to continue using it? Obviously I've posed this as a rhetorical question, since readers of a book titled *Excuses Begone!* probably don't want to hang on to anything that is preventing them from improving their quality of life. It's far more beneficial and desirable to be guided by the simple teaching that the truth shall set you free. So be open to the truth as you read this chapter—your honest answers will assist you enormously in unearthing your thought patterns.

The question *Is it true?* demands that you determine whether or not you can be absolutely certain that those mental crutches you've been relying on are indeed accurate. If they're not, then you must decide right away to invalidate them—using these excuses to hold you back from what you're drawn to do or be is akin to running your life on the basis of a lie.

In the earliest days of our democracy, Thomas Paine wrote: "But such is the irresistible nature of truth that all it asks, and all it wants, is the liberty of appearing." This suggests that the truth only wants to show up; it doesn't wish to overwhelm or rule us. So let's allow "the irresistible nature of truth" to make its appearance right now.

Under close scrutiny, the old familiar explanations almost always turn out to be false, so it's important to test their truth. Here, I'll use 4 of the 18 excuse categories I detailed in Chapter 3 to illustrate working with the first question in our new paradigm:

## 1. It Will Be Difficult

This is certainly one of the most common excuses. Such a meme keeps you from fulfilling your highest vision, but is it even correct? Are you 100 percent certain that what you wish to accomplish is going to be a challenge? Is it plausible that what you desire isn't actually difficult but might in fact require very little effort? While you may feel that isn't likely, you have to admit that the *possibility* of its being easy rather than hard is real.

Keep in mind that all of the seemingly impossible happenings that occur under the guise of what Carl Jung called "synchronicity" do so with a kind of ease and an inexplicably bizarre twist of fate, in which little or no effort is expended. This happens to us all quite frequently, particularly when we're more aligned with Spirit than the material world. There seems to be a collaboration with destiny, and a magical connection takes place making what was perceived to be hard rather easy.

If the thought *It's going to be difficult* might not be true, then something could very well occur to make it not be difficult, which means that the habituated meme is false. So now you have a choice with this excuse: (a) you can believe a thought *(It's going to be difficult)* that is very likely false and most assuredly preventing you from accomplishing what you want; or (b) you can believe an opposite thought *(It will be easy)* that could also be false yet still assists you in fulfilling your desire. When there's a choice, the notion that something is possible or easy is hands down more inviting than the one that insists it's impossible or difficult. So which thought do you wish to hold?

I recall the advice that I received concerning getting my first textbook published a year or so after completing my doctoral studies. This is what I kept hearing: "It's sure going to be hard," "Getting published is impossible," "You're unknown—who would want to publish what you, a 30-year-old novice, has to say?" and the like. Yet I never bought into that logic; consequently, I didn't adopt the *It's going to be difficult* excuse meme. I sent out 100 copies of my manuscript, and within a week I had 99 rejection letters

. . . but I also had an offer from a small publisher in New Jersey. Essentially, what others thought of as a challenge didn't strike me as such. I knew instinctively that someone somewhere would be interested in what I had to say, and it all came about with relative ease.

I also recall quite clearly my experience getting national publicity for *Your Erroneous Zones,* my first book written for the general public, in 1976. The experts all proclaimed that it was next to impossible to get booked on *The Tonight Show, The Phil Donahue Show,* the *Today* show, and so on; this ready-made excuse would have been as good a reason as any to give up.

As it turned out, Howard Papush, a talent coordinator on *The Tonight Show,* read *Your Erroneous Zones* on a flight from New York to Los Angeles. He called me to come out for a preinterview, and I was booked on the program a week later. Over the next three years, I made 37 appearances on *The Tonight Show,* and I was a guest on virtually every other national talk show as well. It turns out that this first excuse didn't apply at all—it was actually quite easy to get national media coverage. I only had to answer the phone!

So once again, if the belief that *It will be difficult* isn't 100 percent true, why would you choose to support that notion? Not once in 1976 did I say that getting on a national TV show would be hard. I trusted that the universe would provide experiences that matched my desires, and that it would all work out for my highest good. The most important point is that by staying aligned with this thinking, I had no need to fall back on a tired old (and untrue) excuse.

## 2. There Will Be Family Drama

This is one of those rationales people employ all the time to explain why they feel stuck or otherwise precluded from living the life they desire. On and on go the reasons for staying put and doing the bidding of family members: "My parents would have a fit," "Everyone would be so upset with me," "No one in my entire family has ever done such a thing," "I'd be labeled a troublemaker or a rebel," "No one has ever stood up to my father before—it would be a nightmare," and so forth.

If you tend to use this excuse, ask yourself: *Can I be 100 percent certain that there will be family drama if I take the action I'm contemplating? Does the possibility exist that I could do the thing I desire and not generate any outbursts?* If the potential exists that there won't be any problems, then this excuse has to go into the "not true" category.

The opposite thought of *There will be family drama* is *There will be no family drama if I carry out my plans as I would like them to unfold.* You may think that without this excuse, you'd automatically be placed on the risky path of doing something that you've been avoiding. But think again! You have a choice to believe that there will either be a family disruption or there won't. Since either one has the potential to be true, why not opt for the thought that could bring about your desired result?

By staying aligned with the idea of loved ones who will both understand and support you in your desire, you may very well see that happen. Or your relatives could indeed react in the disconcerting way that your excuse predicted. But which thought do you think is more likely to produce the kind of results you'd like to have? The point is that you cannot be absolutely certain of what this excuse predicts, so I urge you not to select an explanation for your habituated behavior that's most assuredly untrue.

I can tell you with some degree of certainty that by not expecting to be impacted in a negative or fearful way, you have a much better chance of eliciting the reaction you want. You have a higher chance of your family members being supportive when you support your own desires and intentions. And do be willing to endure any disapproval you might face by asserting your strong beliefs about your purpose in life—that disapproval will most assuredly morph into respect, gratitude, and even awe.

In my own life, I know that if I fail to show up for a cousin's wedding, an uncle's funeral, a grandchild's birthday party, or any other family occasion, there will be no drama for me to withstand.

693

I've shown my relatives that I'm uninterested in dealing with censure or nagging, so I never have to use this second excuse.

You can bid adieu to this excuse yourself by simply asking: *Is it 100 percent true that my loved ones will disapprove if I _____?* Since you can't guarantee family drama all of the time, revise your thoughts to reflect that there won't be any, period. Now, you can't be certain that *some* turbulent or emotional episodes won't occur, but at least you've set your mind on what you desire, and you're aligned with the idea of a peaceful family response. Cement your new reality by affirming: *What I desire is already present and on its way.*

When you eliminate the belief that *There will be family drama* from your life entirely, you'll once again be reminded of what happens when you stay aligned with an expectation of the higher energy of peace, tranquility, and love. You'll be so much more likely to see this peaceful attitude emerge than if you're angry, frustrated, and hurt because "no one ever understands" you in your family.

### 3. I Can't Afford It

I've always held a different concept about my ability to create the necessary financing for anything I've wanted or needed. As you're probably aware, my background is foster homes, scarcities, economic depression, and having to work for everything I've ever had from the age of nine with my first paper route; yet I've never allowed myself to use this third excuse.

Let's examine this very common meme to see if it's true. Can you be 100 percent certain that you're unable to afford whatever it is that you would like to accomplish or purchase? If there's any doubt in your mind, no matter how unlikely prosperity may seem to you now, then you must reject this excuse. The opposite of *I can't afford it* is *I can afford it, even if I don't know at the moment how I can make it all come true financially.*

Once again, the importance of this question regarding your ability to raise money becomes evident. If the thought *I can afford it* is true or false, and the same can be said of *I can't afford it,* then why opt for the idea that's almost guaranteed to keep you from reaching your goal?

Perhaps you're convinced that you're in a position of being insolvent and unable to attract the financing for your dreams. One of the basic tenets of an *Excuses Begone!* mentality is that you get what you think about, whether you want it or not. Therefore, thinking about a dearth of cash aligns you with the concept of shortage and lack. The more you focus on what you don't have and can't get, the more you provide the universe with opportunities to offer up experiences that reflect those beliefs. By claiming that you can't afford something, you confirm this expectation (which, by the way, is just as likely to be untrue as it is to be true). The belief itself becomes the source of what you attract—it serves as an obstacle to a universe of unlimited abundance.

I'm sorry to tell you that there's no solution for scarcity-focused thought processes. Rather, you have to *outgrow* this kind of immature thinking by reminding yourself that it makes much more sense to assert that you're prosperous instead of focusing on *I can't afford it.* Attract the universal guidance that will help rather than the kind that hinders. Right here, right now, state: "I can never be absolutely certain that the financing I need or desire is not on its way. Thus, the belief *I can't afford it* is false, and I refuse to let myself use this excuse."

This is not about helping you manifest more money, although that's certainly a possibility. It's about helping you eliminate the excuse of *I can't afford it* from your life, because using it keeps you aligned with lack, shortages, and pain. Loving what you have and being in a continuous state of contentment is the key to having what you want. Also, be willing to contemplate that whatever assistance you need is on its way, even when you can't predict where it's coming from. This helps you live in alignment with the laws of the universe. Since this is a universe of unlimited abundance, why have thoughts contrary to that truth?

I've always said that what I need financially is not only on its way, but will arrive on time and is always for my highest good.

In fact, it already exists—all I have to do is connect myself to it. Call me crazy if you will, but this kind of thinking has served me unfailingly. The falsity of *I can't afford it* is even more pronounced now in my 60s as I stay unattached to what comes my way and offer it to others in as generous a fashion as I can. This doesn't mean that I simply open the windows and money flies in; rather, it allows me to act on thoughts that have no room for scarcity. I act on what I believe, and I refuse to believe that money is a reason not to do anything.

Throughout my life, I've been surprised on many occasions when financing for a project of mine just seemed to manifest out of nowhere. When I was a young sailor who desperately wanted to attend college after my enlistment, for instance, the funding wasn't immediately available. Nevertheless, I acted upon my strong intention to attend a major university by putting 90 percent of my savings into a special bank account on Guam. Upon my honorable discharge from a four-year tour of duty, I had enough money in the bank to pay for my four years of college.

The point is that making the choice to take advantage of thinking *I can afford it* allows the following two things to happen: (1) universal cooperation is activated by aligning with a universe that has no limits or shortages; and (2) you begin to act on what you're thinking about.

### 4. No One Will Help Me

This excuse belongs in the blame category. Is it always someone else's fault that you're unable to manifest the happiness, success, and health you'd like? Do other people keep letting you down? Does it seem as if it's next to impossible to get things done because you can't find anybody to lend you a hand? I'm not suggesting that you're unable to accomplish your dreams without the assistance of others; rather, I'd like you to consider the validity of the premise that there's no one there to help you.

Put this fourth excuse to the truth test. Ask yourself if you can be 100 percent certain that there won't be anyone out there to help you or that you're in this all alone. If any possibility at all exists that there *are* people to help you, then you must reject this belief as a falsehood that you've chosen to use as a guidepost for your life. The fact is that there's a limitless number of potential helpers out there, but they may be kept away from you because you keep trying to validate an incorrect belief. Revise this excuse by affirming: *Whatever help I require will show up when I need it, and I trust that it is already here and on its way to help me fulfill my highest good.* This kind of thinking is just as likely to be true or false as your original excuse is, so why not go with it? Such a favorable notion aligns you with how the universe truly works.

There are billions of human beings on this planet, so why conclude that there's no one to help you accomplish what you feel called upon to create? The answer lies in the blame game, which is a meme planted in your mind by others who have been plagued by mind viruses, too. It's just as likely that aid will be there when you need it as it is that it won't be there. So what's the point of using precious mental energy on an excuse that's much more likely to produce an undesirable outcome? You have the option of using that same energy to produce a *desirable* outcome.

Shift your focus off of yourself and your ego desires and on to *How may I serve?* When you want for others what you'd like to have for yourself, you'll find that there's never a shortage of helpful, friendly, kind, understanding folks who can't seem to do enough for you. For every act of evil, anger, hatred, or indifference in the world, there are a million acts of kindness, assistance, and love. Choose to place your attention on all that is good and be done with this falsehood: *No one will help me.* If you're looking for "no one" to support you, I can guarantee you that the universe will present you with experiences mirroring your low expectations. On the other hand, if you believe that you're aligned with supportive energy, that's what will show up.

Let go of this excuse by recognizing and reminding yourself that the belief that no one will be there for you does not hold up to the test of truth: there's no one to blame, and there are thousands of people out there who would love to offer you the aid and guidance you desire. Choose instead to know that you live in a universe that supports you at all times.

Thomas Merton once wrote: "We cannot possess the truth fully until it has entered into the very substance of our life by good habits . . ." And that is precisely what the first question of the *Excuses Begone!* paradigm is designed to do. That is, it aims to help you eliminate counterproductive habits of thinking that are untrue but have become the substance of your life. The truth really will set you free. You no longer need excuse making, because the explanations you've been using for why your life isn't working simply don't hold up to the truth test.

If you go through the 18 excuses in Chapter 3 (you just reviewed 4 of them) and examine each of them closely, you'll find that you can't give an unqualified yes to the question that's the topic of this chapter: *Is it true?*

If you have a choice to use an excuse that may or may not be false and will keep you stuck in place, or to use a different explanation that still may or may not be false but leads you out of self-defeating thinking habits, which choice should you make? To me, the answer is obvious. Your goal is to develop habits that serve you and enhance your opportunity to maximize your success, happiness, and health—and that means eschewing those old excuses, which are just plain lies.

### Suggestions for Applying the First Paradigm Question

— Whenever you're tempted to use an excuse to explain some deficiency in your life (or even after you've noticed that you just relied on a long-standing alibi), silently put the excuse to the truth test. Simply and honestly answer these two questions: (1) *Is it true?* and (2) *Can I be 100 percent certain that it's true?* As you do, you'll discover that no excuse pattern holds up to this scrutiny.

Even if you don't fully understand how you're going to accomplish this, tell yourself that you don't wish to continue vindicating yourself with false notions. This simple truth test will lead to further exploration of what else you can do to eliminate excuses.

— Create an explanation that reverses the excuse you're using. It should be just as capable of being either true or untrue as your mental crutch, but the difference is that this explanation leads you away from self-defeat.

Here's an example of what I mean:

**Excuse:**    *I'm too old to pursue my college degree.*

**Question:** *Is it true?*

**Answer:**    *It may be true, but it also may not be true. I can't be 100 percent certain that such a statement is rock-solid, guaranteed truth.*

In order to demolish this excuse that's been keeping you from pursuing a college degree, create the opposite thought of *I am the perfect age to pursue my college degree.* By holding on to this new belief, which indeed may or may not be 100 percent true, you open a world of possibilities. The bonus is that you align yourself with the field of all possibilities and invite reinforcements to help you.

Since neither your old excuse nor your new belief can be 100 percent guaranteed, and you're free to hold either of these two visions for yourself, why not select the one that will work *for* the highest aspirations you hold, rather than against them? The creative Source that birthed you from nonbeing to being supports you in this endeavor. As it says in the Bible: "Trust in the Lord with all your heart, and lean not on your own understanding; in all your ways acknowledge Him, and He shall direct your paths" (Proverbs 3:5–6).

Your insight has led you to all of the excuses you've relied on for a good part of your life. The "Him" in Proverbs is God (or the eternal Tao), which is the ultimate truth. Be receptive to revising your excuse formula; it may indeed be God calling you to His truth.

Henry Ward Beecher offers heady advice on distinguishing what's true from what's false: "Pushing any truth out very far, you are met by a counter truth." I recommend giving just as much attention to the "counter truth" as you have to the excuses you've been treating as truth.

# THE SECOND QUESTION: *WHERE DID THE EXCUSES COME FROM?*

*"Nor deem the irrevocable Past*
*As wholly wasted, wholly vain,*
*If, rising on its wrecks, at last*
*To something nobler we attain."*

— Henry Wadsworth Longfellow

When you go to your doctor with a medical problem, you're prepared to answer questions designed to help him or her determine what's going on and what treatment plan to initiate. One important function of this inquiry is to assist your physician in understanding what brought about the illness, infection, or trauma. I'm going to use this medical model as a metaphor to explore the question *Where did the excuses come from?* in relation to making them vanish from your life.

## *Getting to the Bottom of Your Excuses*

When it comes to those mental crutches you've relied upon for so many years, it will help you to become your own doctor and to learn the origin and duration of your "condition" before you implement treatment. Just like physical problems, habituated thinking patterns that keep you from attaining the life of your dreams can be remedied by knowing how and why they occurred, and a program of prevention can then be instituted.

Using the same model of an "intake interview" that your medical doctor would conduct, here are five questions that will help you understand where your excuses come from:

### 1. What Are Your Symptoms?

Imagine the excuses you've employed as symptoms that have been keeping you from maximizing your potential for happiness, success, and health—even if they may not be as obvious as a fever, a runny nose, a sore throat, or any other physical symptom that would cause you to seek out medical attention.

Describe what you're feeling when you know you've got the excuse bug, and be as specific as you can. Common symptoms include: frequent episodes of blame and faultfinding, when just about anyone or anything that you think of is held responsible for your unhappiness; shame that sneakily attacks you; anger at yourself and others, which erupts at the tiniest irritation; envy that breaks out when you compare yourself to others; and laziness, inactivity, and complaining. As the excuse bug takes hold, you notice that you spend a lot of time looking for occasions to be offended—anyone else's success, happiness, and good health just serve to intensify your symptoms. Self-doubt, resentment, anxiety, worry, hopelessness, sadness, unworthiness, and more may also occur.

## 2. When Did Your Symptoms First Appear?

Your symptoms could very well stem from childhood memories that still persist in adult versions. For example, the rationalization *I'm too old* may have appeared as *I'm too young* when you were a teenager; and the adult excuse *I'm too busy* might have originated as *I can't play with my friends because I have to do my chores, study, and get to bed* when you were in school. Perhaps you also admired family members who modeled seemingly successful excuse-making behavior.

These lifelong thinking habits have become so incorporated into your being that only now are you beginning to see them as symptomatic of a disease process. While there's no remedy for the conditions you were exposed to that contributed to the presence of your "excuses disease" today, you can now see how you were infected at an early age. And the best medicine for this situation may just be found in humor like actress Tallulah Bankhead's, particularly in the observation she was said to have made that "the only thing I regret about my past is the length of it. If I had to live my life again I'd make the same mistakes, only sooner."

## 3. Whom Were You With?

Simply knowing whom you were with when you came down with your excuses disease unfortunately won't change it. You'll gain a modicum of insight, but the conclusion remains the same: your past is always going to be the way it was, and there's no way to alter it.

Those people you were with when you caught so many self-defeating thinking habits should be pretty obvious to you by now. They include members of your immediate and extended family, especially your parents and grandparents; teachers, classmates, and friends; members of religious organizations; and even folks who appeared on the televison programs you watched, in the magazines and newspapers you read, and in the music you listened to.

I could go on and on listing all of the ways you were exposed to mind viruses. The only purpose those viruses had was to replicate, infiltrate, and spread wherever possible—and your inquisitive, open, and willing mind surely was an inviting place for them to take up residence.

So when you ask whom you were with when you caught the excuses disease, you can realistically answer that it was most everyone and everything you came into regular contact with from the earliest moments of your life.

### 4. Did the People You Were Around Have Similar Symptoms? Were They Contagious?

If you were being medically treated for a disease, it would be important to curtail its spread—not only would you need to be treated accordingly, but whomever you caught it from would need to be, too. In addition, you'd be told how to minimize endangering others, and you might even be isolated to stop the epidemic from growing.

The people with whom you had close contact throughout your life carried the illness of excuse making. Obviously, medication or isolation aren't called for here, but you *do* need to make the decision to rehabilitate yourself if you are to overcome lifelong habituated thinking habits.

While you were growing up and being exposed to the excuses disease, you were unaware of what was happening. The means for transferring the mind viruses you caught was through the magic of memetics, which I discussed in the opening chapters of this book. Remember that *mimic* is the root word of *memetics,* and you certainly did mimic the infected people around you. You were a ready, willing, and gullible little package for the memes to take root, replicate, and spread in. If your environment hadn't been so fertile, you wouldn't be dealing with the effects of those excuses today.

This isn't a reason to blame anyone—there were lots of opportunities, particularly as you grew into your teen years and beyond, when you had a choice in allowing the excuses to take hold or not. Rather, this is all about seeing that in your earliest years, you were a magnet for the energy that was directed at you. And as you got older, you didn't exactly stop pulling excuses toward you and start attracting and nourishing the ways that would have allowed you to outgrow them.

## 5. Were You Exposed?

The short answer here is *yes*. Of course you were exposed, because you had daily contact with carriers of mind viruses. However, the *Excuses Begone!* paradigm is designed to strengthen your natural immune system so that you can deal with any similar disease processes that may come your way, now and in the future.

### *Accepting Total Responsibility*

In spite of your history, the one and only place that your excuses originated is in you. Regardless of the age you were when these ideas were implanted; how contagious your early family conditioning was; how frequently you were exposed; and how potent the diseases were in your home, school, church, and culture, the responsibility is yours. To live a totally excuse-free life, you must be willing to state: "I adopted these behaviors—I chose all of it. I may have been a child, and I may not have had the skills or natural abilities to resist early influences, but it was still my choice. I take full responsibility for any and all excuse making that I've engaged in."

The reason I took you through the five questions in the last section wasn't so you could find new explanations for your habit, but rather so you could see just how prevalent mind viruses were during the formative years of your life. Now, at each stage of exposure to these mind viruses, there was always you. You may have been vulnerable, gullible, fearful, wanting to fit in, or just going along with the program, but there was still *you*. You're not a chair that's been redesigned and reupholstered or a robot that was created in a laboratory and oiled to perfection by its owners . . . no, you're a live human being with a mind of your own. After all, other members of your family—perhaps even some of your siblings—weren't fooled like you were, and you probably saw some of your friends resist the efforts of others to enculturate them in this manner.

I encourage you to accept complete responsibility for all of your excuse-making tendencies. You are capable of making choices to cease self-sabotaging thinking habits now, and you were just as capable when you were a child. Yet please don't take responsibility with any sense of shame or self-reproach. Know that throughout your life, you always did what you knew how to do; you're also not currently being punished or attracting these inclinations because of some past-life karmic debt. I elaborated the excuse-building symptoms and the contagious effect of those early memes so that you can understand them, give them a fond embrace, and bid them all farewell! Think about what Saint Paul said in his Letter to the Corinthians: "When I was a child . . . I thought like a child" (1 Cor. 13:11). Look back at those early childlike mimicking behaviors and remind yourself: *I no longer need to hang on to anything I adopted as a young person, regardless of how powerful the influences may have been.*

When you ask *Where did these excuses come from?* the answer is that they came from you, an individual who was once willing to listen to that kind of thinking. But avow that you now intend to say good-bye and good riddance to excuses that keep you from experiencing the highest, most glorious levels of happiness, success, and health.

The key concept to grasp here is that once you start understanding, you can stop rationalizing and justifying. Your past isn't another reason to explain your deficiencies—don't tell yourself that old influences are your excuse for making excuses! Take responsibility for your life, and discontinue the use of blame and faultfinding.

Let's take a look at 4 of the 18 excuses from Chapter 3 to illustrate how your excuse-making habit has been shaped:

## 1. I Don't Deserve It

How is it possible for a Divine creation to be unworthy? You are and always have been a piece of God. And you know by now that all beings come from nonbeing; the Bible itself reminds you that it's Spirit that gives life. So where on earth did you learn to use this excuse?

As a developing child, you were weaned on ideas that your worthiness is based on ego-dominated formulations making you what you do, what you have, and what others think of you. Your worth became intertwined with these ego constructs: *If I do well, I'm worthy; if I don't, I'm unworthy. If I accumulate more valuable stuff and make more money, I'm worthy; if I don't, I'm unworthy. If I gain the approval of others, I'm worthy; if I'm unpopular, I'm unworthy.*

Like most of us, you were immersed in a culture that taught and reinforced these ideas, which are the work of the false self. Consequently, as an adult, when you see others who are more successful than you are, have more toys than you do, and enjoy reputations far greater than yours, your first impulse is to make a disconnect between your status in life and your worthiness as a human being. Years of solid training in ego development have caused you to retreat into an *I don't deserve it/I'm not worthy* mind-set. Since these excuses come from the false self, they'll stay with you until you leave the planet, unless you're willing to tell your-self: "Okay, I understand where this kind of egotistic reasoning originated—and I can see that I still use it—but I'm practicing the *Excuses Begone!* way of life from now on."

For every one of these excuse categories, I urge you to decide to start thinking something along the lines of this: *Everyone in my life did what they knew how to do, and I chose to buy into it at that time. But today I'm going to stop this insidious kind of absurd thinking and remind myself that I'm a Divine being, an individualized expression of God. Therefore, I will no longer entertain thoughts of my being unworthy—I've lived with them long enough, and they've never served my highest good.*

## 2. It's Not My Nature

Have you been allowed to develop as if your Creator were in charge of the process? Of course your physical shell was permitted to take the course nature dictated: you developed the height; body type and shape; hair, eye, and skin color; and facial features that nature called for. But what about your personality, your emotional and intellectual development, your aspirations, your self-concept, or your spiritual awareness—were those aspects of you encouraged to unfold naturally?

The excuse *It's not my nature* came directly from the list of what you were taught you couldn't do or be that I elaborated earlier in this book. You were formulated and then crafted into the finished product that your family and culture desired. When you're told "You can't do this; you can only do that" enough times, and you're willing to become the product the people around you want you to be, then you believe that your nature is what you've been told. You act on the pronouncements about yourself that you've absorbed. So if you hear that you're lazy, undeserving, or uncoordinated often enough, it ultimately leads you to adopt this as your self-portrait. If you're told over and over again that you're just like your father and he never amounted to anything, then you'll ultimately view your nature the way that others viewed your dad.

Go back to the question I asked you earlier in this book: *Who would you be if you didn't have anyone to tell you who you are?* Take total responsibility for whatever you believe constitutes your nature, reminding yourself to think in a fresh way about where this excuse originated. Try something like: *I chose to allow the opinions of others to be more important than my fledgling opinions of who I was and what I intended to become. Yes, I was small and vulnerable, but it was still my choice.* This kicks the old excuse down the stairs and helps you love the person you were then, causing you to tenderly undo what you (not someone else) have done. While you can never change the actions of others, taking responsibility for your own life will help you make the shift to an *Excuses Begone!* existence.

### 3. I'm Not Smart Enough

Where do you think you learned that you were somewhat shortchanged in the brains department? Well, you were enrolled in an educational system that assigned numbers to your intellectual capacity. A test gave you an IQ number to carry around for life. You learned to listen to a teacher whose lesson plan wasn't designed for the variety of learning modes in the classroom, so all of the students were being exposed to the same instruction. At the end of the week, an exam gave you a grade that measured you against the performances of all of your classmates; you all had your place on a bell-shaped curve depending on your aptitudes that day, in that week, and on that particular subject area. You developed a self-image based on what teachers, test scores, and academic performance indicated—you learned that you were average at spelling, above average in art, but mentally challenged in mathematics. Soon you had the makings of a great excuse (*I'm not smart enough*) that you hauled out whenever it was convenient.

What you failed to learn is that intelligence tests only measure how well you take intelligence tests! It turns out that academic performance has nothing to do with your potential for intellectual mastery. Nonetheless, your young mind hung on to those school experiences and added them to the messages you'd already absorbed about how you're not as smart as your siblings, you've never been good at figuring out numerical problems, or you're not as talented as the kids next door. This cascade of criticism directed at your intellectual capacities can easily lead you to defend yourself from these jabs with excuses.

The fact is that since you're a creation who originated in the world of Spirit, you have exactly the right amount of smarts to accomplish all that you will do while you're here. It's all perfect . . . and so are you!

To me, a person like my son-in-law Joe, who can lay a beautiful hardwood floor and have it come out flawlessly, is a genius. Whether or not he performed well in some aptitude test, Joe's genius is displayed in his artistic sense—in that magnificent mind

709

that arranges and positions the grain of the wood, leveling and sealing, with endless measurements and computations. You too have all the intelligence you need for anything that ignites your creative and problem-solving passion. Believe this about yourself and you'll never want or need to trot out the excuse of *I'm not smart enough* again.

## 4. The Rules Won't Let Me

Always obeying the rules is a meme, or a mind virus that's become an acceptable indicator of your honesty and integrity. But note this sentence in a letter that Martin Luther King, Jr., wrote from the Birmingham city jail on April 16, 1963: "We can never forget that everything Hitler did in Germany was 'legal' and everything the Hungarian freedom fighters did in Hungary was 'illegal.'" I also love this observation from Ralph Waldo Emerson: "No law can be sacred to me but that of my nature."

I'm not making a case for being lawless and indifferent to edicts that govern a civilized society. I *am* encouraging you to recognize what some of our finest minds say about running your life by rules. I include here what my great teacher Lao-tzu wrote in the Tao Te Ching:

> *When the greatness of the Tao is present,*
> *action arises from one's own heart.*
> *When the greatness of the Tao is absent,*
> *action comes from the rules . . .*

Live your life in accordance with a Tao-centered or God-realized point of view. You know what is right, what your heart tells you. You know that you don't need cumbersome rules laid down by others, some of which make no sense to obey at all, to guide you. This fourth excuse is a huge cop-out in every sense of the word.

I want to cite one more famous American who was adamant about the need for feeling a sense of independence as a criterion for living a full, happy, successful, and healthy life. Read his words carefully: "The care of every man's soul belongs to himself. But what if he neglect[s] the care of it? Well, what if he neglect[s] the care of his health or estate . . . will the magistrate make a law that he shall not be poor or sick? Laws provide against injury from others; but not from ourselves. God himself will not save men against their wills." The person who wrote those words was none other than Thomas Jefferson.

So there you have some of history's most admired teachers reminding you that the rules should never be a final factor in determining anything about yourself. Instead, these wise men ask you to go within and be guided by what your passion dictates (as long as it doesn't hurt anyone else, of course).

If you have a tendency to employ the excuse *The rules won't let me,* know that it was handed down and enforced by those who wished to control your behavior. Yet here again, it's important to take full responsibility for your own actions. You're no longer a child who needs rules to make sure that you're safe, healthy, and functional within a family or a classroom. Be willing to consult your adult sense of what's right *for you.* Assertively pursue that vision, keeping a silent vigil on your inner passion. Overlook the pressures to do things by following instructions and edicts that are simply no longer applicable to you.

As you can see, all of these excuses originated in the earliest years of your life. But even as you take responsibility for your role in excuse making, always be kind to yourself. Remember that you only did what you knew how to do when you were a child. So go visit those "wrecks" Longfellow talks about in the quotation that begins this chapter—discover where they came from and why they've persisted for so long as your habituated ways of thinking. Do as the poet suggests and move on to an *Excuses Begone!* life, which is far more noble than an existence full of self-sabotaging explanations.

### Suggestions for Applying the
### Second Paradigm Question

— The most helpful suggestion I can offer you regarding the question of *Where did these excuses come from?* is to answer it with the following four words: *they came from me.* Take total responsibility for your thoughts in the form of the words that come out of your mouth today. By all means study the proliferation of mind viruses and early-childhood conditioning practices that were directed your way. But also practice thinking and saying this: *I chose to use excuses as a child. I didn't realize at the time that I had other choices available. I realize I've continued to choose those excuses until now.*

Be solely responsible—you have no one to blame. You don't need to wait for anyone to come around and undo what he or she did, since you can't become an excuse maker without giving your consent. And if you have given your consent, the *Excuses Begone!* paradigm revokes it now.

— Forgive everyone, including yourself. All those individuals who proliferated mind viruses and conditioning were only doing what they knew how to do given the circumstances of their lives, and those meme dispensers are only one generation removed from receiving the same kind of habituated thinking. Keep in mind the line from the Prayer of Saint Francis: "It is in pardoning that we are pardoned." Eschew blame and free yourself from anything that's been plaguing your life and holding you back from activating your highest calling. By forgiving everyone, you pardon them . . . and yourself. And remember, if you'd never blamed anyone for your tendencies toward being an excuse maker, you'd have no one to forgive!

# CHAPTER 14

# THE THIRD QUESTION:
## *WHAT'S THE PAYOFF?*

*"[W]e lie to ourselves, in order that we may still have the*
*excuse of ignorance, the alibi of stupidity and incomprehension,*
*possessing which we can continue with a good conscience*
*to commit and tolerate the most monstrous crimes."*

— Aldous Huxley

In the quotation above, from Huxley's essay "Words and Behavior," the "monstrous crimes" are committed by *and* against yourself, allowing you to continue habituated—and detrimental—thought patterns through dishonesty. This third question will help you clarify the psychological system that supports such lying.

Why maintain a thinking habit that impedes your highest vision for yourself? The solution seems easy enough: Simply stop using the excuses! But it obviously takes more than this to eliminate your mental crutches, otherwise you'd have abandoned them by now. It's similar to the alcoholic or drug addict who knows that his reasons for not quitting are holding him back, yet his behavior continues unabated. In some way you must feel that you're benefiting from your self-sabotaging thoughts, even when the facts indicate otherwise.

Your answer to *What's the payoff?* will give you insight into the reward system you've carefully constructed. It's the reason you can reach into your bag of excuses and pull out some real gems whenever it's convenient. And the fact that these thought patterns have been with you for most of your life makes them almost automatic responses.

Take a moment now to reflect on why your thoughts might sustain behaviors that don't serve your highest ideals. William Wordsworth, the insightful English poet, once remarked: "Habits rule the unreflecting herd," with *herd* being used as a pejorative term for thinking like everyone else. Your goal is to disrupt those habits that have led you to act like just one more member of the obedient pack, and that requires a new kind of understanding. Such understanding may be more accessible now than in the first part of your life, which was when you tended to form and accumulate your habits. Thoreau's words encourage you to make this second part of your life work for you by changing your path:

> As a single footstep will not make a path on the earth, so a single thought will not make a single pathway in the mind. To make a deep physical path, we walk again and again. To make a deep mental path, we must think over and over the kind of thoughts we wish to dominate our lives.

The *Excuses Begone!* paradigm invites you to explore the same kinds of reasoning that created your habit of excuse making, and then develop a new set of beliefs. Just as an elephant can be tethered by a thread if it believes that it's being held captive, if you believe that you're chained to your excuses, you're in bondage. Asking *What's the payoff?* allows you to gain insight into the nature of your servitude to old thought processes, and helps you form a new path in your mind that will soon become well worn.

For example, there was a time in my life when I consumed eight or more artificially sweetened soft drinks a day. My excuse was that I'd always done this, so it would be way too difficult to break the habit. Then I happened to read Epictetus's *Handbook of Conscious Living* (written by students from his oral teachings more than 2,000 years ago), and this passage jumped out at me: "Nothing is in reality either pleasant or unpleasant by nature; but all things become so by habit." This was a great insight for me. The junk I was drinking daily wasn't pleasurable because of what it was or how it tasted; it was simply something I'd done for so long that I'd worn a path in my brain from which I thought there was no escape.

In 1986, armed with this new insight and nothing more, I began to create a *new* path. I kept reminding myself that this artificially sweetened brown water wasn't pleasurable in and of itself—it was only my habit that made it so. To this day, I haven't even had a sip of any kind of soda. So as you can see, getting to the bottom of why we tread the same path day after day can be very helpful and life changing.

### *Common Hidden Payoffs for Excuse Making*

I've used the word *hidden* to alert you to the fact that you're often totally unaware of the reasons why you continue to walk down the same path and rely on the same old excuses. Many behaviors and thought patterns persist because of perceived rewards . . . which may not be that good for you. In fact, most of the psychological benefits you receive from your excuse-making habit are actually quite self-destructive.

The most prevalent psychological payoffs used to support your nasty habits are discussed in the following pages. Apply the insights you acquire from reading about them to create a new excuse-free path within your own mind:

## 1. Avoidance

When you grab on to a self-sabotaging belief, it only serves to keep you marching in place. *It's going to be very difficult . . . It's going to take up way too much of my time . . . What I want is too big . . . I don't have the money . . .* and so on merely justify your inaction with an explanation. And once you've done so, you're free to enjoy the avoidance payoff.

I was a doctoral-student advisor at a major university for six years in the 1970s. I found that with very few exceptions, most doctoral students were able to complete the course work—but when it came time to write their dissertation (which is a very involved research project that's generally the length of a book and must be completed to earn a Ph.D.) and then defend it before a committee of faculty members, many of them fell short. They'd justify their behavior with *I'm too busy . . . I'm not smart enough to write and defend a book . . . It will take a long time . . . I don't have the energy . . .* and many more from the catalog of excuses. Such explanations were absolutely vital for those who were trying to avoid something.

Avoidance is a common and easily identifiable payoff, or the psychological reward that allows you to be somewhat at peace with yourself when you make self-thwarting decisions. The excuse becomes your ally, even though it's an ally that doesn't have your best interests at heart.

## 2. Safety

None of us like to feel unsafe, so excuses become what we use to avoid potentially dangerous situations. Rather than wandering off into uncharted territory where we might face the risk of low performance, failure, criticism, exhaustion, the unknown, appearing foolish, getting hurt, and the like, it's more convenient to retreat into a haven of familiarity. The problem is that the excuse habit only brings us a false sense of security, in the same way a "blanky" comforts a frightened child.

Inside you there's a powerful calling that's urging you to fulfill the destiny you feel churning through your veins, yet taking the safest route is causing you to avoid that calling. On the one hand, you feel pulled toward your purpose; and on the other, any number of convenient excuses sing to you like sirens. *It will be risky . . . It's not my nature . . . I'm too scared . . . There will be family drama . . . I'm too old . . . It's too big . . .* and statements like them can be very difficult to ignore.

This brings to mind my daughter Tracy, who ignored her own calling for years. She had a secure job as an executive, with good benefits, excellent pay, nice people to work with, a great location, and lots of other reasons that could have kept her there until she retired at some point down the road. Yet burning inside her was a strong desire to be her own boss, to use her design and marketing skills to create her own products. But when she talked about leaving her safe position with all of the benefits, she couldn't make the move, and her excuses provided her with the rationale she required.

After years of talking about why she couldn't follow her dream, my daughter finally decided to put the *Excuses Begone!* paradigm to work for her. Today she's the CEO of her own company, called Urban Junket. She designs high-quality women's handbags and laptop bags, traveling the world to procure the very best materials. While she hasn't attained her previous salary and benefits level yet, she's happy, fulfilled, and very pleased with what she has created. Tracy is no longer a slave to the payoff her excuses offered her. Check out her beautiful creations online (**www.urbanjunket .com**) and send her a note of appreciation if her story of leaving excuses behind inspires you—as it does me, her very proud father.

### 3. The Easy Way Out

Any excuse at all offers the bountiful reward of *the easy way out*. Let's face it, when you're confronted with a choice between doing something requiring effort and something that's effortless and easy, you're apt to pick the latter, even if it's not the choice that will actually lead to your objectives.

Your highest self wants you to fulfill your destiny, which often involves some type of sacrifice, expenditure of time, mental and physical energy, and material resources. Ego is frequently in conflict with what your highest self desires—your false self pushes and cajoles you into staying put, threatened by anything that disrupts its mission of keeping you nice and comfortable by avoiding difficult choices. Thus, there's a big payoff for using excuses that allow you to take the easy road.

I know the effort and daily struggle I'm in for when I opt to sit and write, day in and day out, often for an entire year, until I complete a book. I've done it long enough to know with sweet certainty that the project's completion is fully aligned with my life's purpose. I recognize that sitting here in solitude and doing the work keeps me in balance, or aligned with the highest callings of my soul. Even so, over the years I've noticed the intense temptation to allow excuses to keep me from doing what my heart tells me I must. They insist: *It's too big a project, and you don't have the energy. You don't have anything else to prove, so just relax. You're tired—let up on yourself. Writing takes you away from your family, and you're already overcommitted.*

These statements and others like them would give me an easy payoff if I allowed them to. I could then avoid the anxiety, struggle, loneliness, and nose-to-the-grindstone actions that are a necessary part of the creative process. But there's far more joy when I see the results of my labors, along with all the good such efforts seem to be doing in the world, than any temporary pleasure I might gain by taking the easy way out and avoiding what I know I need to do.

## 4. Manipulation

One of the great payoffs that so many of these excuses provide is the opportunity to manipulate others into doing your bidding.

While this may not be seen as the most positive of things, that's nevertheless just what happens. When you make the choice to use an excuse such as *I don't have the energy . . . I'm too busy . . . I'm not strong enough or smart enough . . .* or the like, you place the responsibility on some other person. After you've given that person your explanations for why you can't do something, you can then sit back comfortably and watch how they spur him or her into action.

As the father of eight children, I've seen this strategy thousands of times. For example:

— *I'm too tired* translates to: *Have someone else do the chore.* The payoff? *I get to sleep while another person takes over my responsibilities.*

— *I can't afford it* or *I spent all my money* translates to: *You buy what I want or need.* The payoff? *I've manipulated you with my generic excuse.*

— *I don't deserve it* translates to: *Feel sorry for me.* The payoff? *You're going to give me what I want because you can't stand to see me feeling unworthy.*

Of course you don't have to be a child in a family to benefit from virtually all of these excuses that, in one way or another, allow you to manipulate others into doing your bidding.

### 5. Being Right

There's nothing that the false self loves more than being right—and making someone else wrong—and excuses are tailor-made for this. When you use an excuse, you get to feel superior and put someone else in the position of being a loser . . . and ego loves feeling like a winner, especially at the expense of others.

Excuses are simply explanations you make to yourself that have no necessary bearing on the truth—yet even though they're lies, they do bring you some sort of reward. So while your only evidence may be a habitual thought, if you convince yourself that you're right, you get to retreat into the illusion of winning. In this case, the excuse is a deception that props up your low self-esteem. You've substituted an excuse in place of authentic self-worth, and the payoff is that your reasoning helps you live with yourself without acknowledging your self-deceit.

So:

— *No one will ever help me* translates to: *I'm not deserving or lucky enough to get others to help me, just like I've always said. So there you have it—I'm right again.*

— *The rules won't let me* translates to: *See how smart I am? I've always said that you can't get ahead, and anyone who disagrees with me is a loser.*

— *There will be family drama* translates to: *I'm right about this family, and I've always been right. All the rest of you just don't know as much as I do.*

On and on goes this convoluted logic. When you're an excuse maker, you need to be right and haul out anything you can think of to prove to the world how wrong it is. And, conversely, how right you are!

### 6. Blame

When you resort to using an excuse, the ultimate payoff is that you remove responsibility for your own shortcomings and place responsibility for them on the shoulders of someone else. I've written about this blame game throughout this book: once again, this is the work of the ego, that false self that doesn't believe in your infinite Divine nature but does keep track of how well you stack up against the people and events of this material world.

If you're not doing well, the ego says that it's someone else's fault. If you're *unhappy, unhealthy, indigent, unlucky, fearful,* or any other negative descriptor that you can come up with, this is all the fault of something or someone external to yourself. While your highest self happily thrives on humility, the ego is exceptionally proud. Thus, when anything goes wrong, the ego's inclination is to blame someone else and maintain its pride.

Blame pays a colossal dividend, so the ego constructs something to bring it about whenever possible. That's why when you blame the economy, the political party in power, the oil-rich sheiks in Saudi Arabia, or anyone else you can think of, your false self receives a reward. Unable to save money, get investors for your pet project, pay your bills, or justify your bankruptcy? Not only does the blame game provide you with a convenient scapegoat, but it also delivers a rich payoff for continuing to use all of the excuses that have become a way of life.

### 7. Protection

When you were a child, you were most likely offered the protection of your family. You were small; they were big. You didn't have much; they controlled just about everything. You had to ask permission; they doled out their authority. In other words, you were protected. As you grew into adulthood, these leftover behaviors were convenient to hang on to, even though being grown meant no longer seeking permission from parents or getting the sustenance you had when you were little. A host of excuses evolved that had the feeling of being protected as their primary payoff, so you may still be thinking and acting like a kid.

To maintain the benefits of childhood without appearing childish, you've created excuses that allow you to retreat into the familiar territory of feeling taken care of. Reasons why you're not manifesting the life you desire provide you with the reward of being able to retreat to the feeling of being a little boy or girl again. This is a powerful payoff indeed, even though it doesn't serve you very well as an adult.

As a parent, I've felt that my job isn't to be someone my children can lean on, but rather to help them realize that leaning is unnecessary. As some of my kids reached adulthood, however, I noted that they were obviously reluctant to take on the full mantle of self-responsibility. As excuses surfaced, I saw that they were seeking the protection of having everything decided for them. *I'm not strong enough* translated to: *You do it for me, Daddy, and then I can feel protected again.* And *I can't afford it* translated to: *You pay for it, and then I'm off the hook.*

Similarly, so many of the excuses you may be using have that built-in dividend of allowing you to explain away your deficiencies and feel like a protected youngster again. While regressing back to childhood may let you feel temporarily protected, it's obviously going to keep you stuck in place—after all, reality dictates that Mommy and Daddy cannot shield you ad infinitum.

## 8. Escaping the Present Moment

The now is all there is. It is all that has ever been and all that will ever be. Yet just as there are many ways to live gloriously and happily in the present moment, there are also many ways to attempt to escape from living fully in the now. And that's where excuses come in.

Like all other mental activities, excuse making takes place totally in the here-and-now. When you engage in this practice, that's how you use up the present. If you're devoting the moment to justification and defensiveness, then it isn't possible to use it to do something constructive, work at changing, make love, marvel at your children, enjoy each breath you take, and so forth. The payoff is that you get something to do with your time. Even though it may be neurotic in nature, it's nevertheless a convenient escape mechanism to keep you stuck in your old habits.

The present is all you'll ever have, and every excuse you use keeps you from being here now. While you can never avoid the now, excuse making makes certain that you won't change old habits, since you'll be too busy filling up your precious seconds with excuses.

### *Suggestions for Reversing These Payoffs*

Now let's turn the eight payoffs around and see how they can work for you rather than against you. Read these suggestions with the intention of outgrowing old thinking habits, as well as discovering the harmony of living from your highest vision:

## 1. Avoidance

Make the decision that you'll no longer use excuses to keep you from what you know is in your best interest. Today, act on something you've always avoided and explained away with a convenient excuse. Make that phone call you've been putting off, write a letter to a distant friend or relative, put on a pair of walking shoes and go on a one-mile jaunt, clean out one section of your closet—do anything at all, as long as it's something you've been justifying not doing with excuses.

Affirm: *I have a free will, and there is nothing I need to avoid. I will refrain from using any excuses to justify my avoidance behavior.*

## 2. Safety

Plan to take a vacation without any guarantees—just go, and let yourself be guided by your instincts rather than a detailed itinerary. Eat at a restaurant that serves food you're unfamiliar with, attend a symphony or a soccer game, visit a mosque, take a yoga class, go on a nature hike, or do anything else that you may have been afraid of. Decide to outgrow the excuses you've employed, and adopt a philosophy of having a mind that's open to everything and attached to nothing.

Affirm: *I choose the less-traveled path and resist seeking out familiarity and an illusion of security.*

### 3. The Easy Way Out

Have a conversation with your subconscious mind, which has grown accustomed to choosing the familiar path, and explain that you're no longer interested in living in this way. Then go into reversal mode: rather than congratulating yourself for avoiding something difficult, cheer yourself on for having the courage and the determination to move in a new and possibly uncomfortable direction.

At one time, my payoff system for a self-defeating smoking habit was the belief that *I receive pleasure from this activity, so I'm not going to quit.* Clearly, my mind felt that continuing this filthy habit was far easier than quitting. But after many conversations with my subconscious mind, the day came when I reversed my reward system. Instead of using my old payoff procedure, I began to congratulate myself for having the internal strength to make the difficult choice rather than the familiar and easy one.

Affirm: *I am open to making difficult choices when they happen to be in harmony with my highest good.*

### 4. Manipulation

Have a conversation with yourself *before* you speak or act in a way that's likely to cause you to manipulate others. A private inner dialogue is crucial in eliminating this old psychological payoff system that you've inadvertently created. When it comes to your family members and close friends, also have these silent conversations—no one need know what you're doing. With your children, for instance, practice noninterference and remind yourself that in most cases, they already know what to do.

Weigh what the consequence is likely to be if you were to say a particular thing. Anticipate how others in the room might react, how you'd respond, and what might flare up. (All of this will only take a second or two.) The end result may be that you simply stay silent and allow your ego to take a well-deserved break, rather than doling out advice that is really a form of manipulation.

Affirm: *I am content within myself. I have no need to control or manipulate anyone so that they will think and act as I prefer.*

## 5. Being Right

The ego spends a lot of time practicing always being right. In order to remove this item from your psychological portfolio, begin letting *others* be right. When someone says something that you'd normally disagree with for the purpose of making them wrong, try saying, "You're right about that." This will immediately put a reverse spin on the ego's need to be right.

If someone tells you, "You always ignore my point of view, and we end up doing what you want," try this reply on for size: "You know, that's really a good point that I've never considered before. The more I think about what you're saying to me, the more I realize that you're right about that." *Voilà*—the cycle of arguing stops, the psychological support system for using excuses is reversed, and you begin a conflict-free life!

Make these words the cornerstone of your new policy by repeating them to others as often as possible: *You're right about that.* While the ego will loudly protest, this strategy can only bring you peace and happiness. So would you rather be right or happy?

Affirm: *I release the inclination to make anyone else wrong.*

## 6. Blame

Remind yourself that no one can ever make you feel anything without your consent. Therefore, there's no one to blame for whatever is taking place in your life. With this simple concept, you permanently eliminate the payoff system of blaming others for your shortcomings, and eradicate a tendency toward excuse making.

Tell yourself: *I am the sum total of all of the choices I've made in my life, even those I made as a small child.* When your ego launches into its blame game with *It's not my fault . . . I couldn't help it . . . They made me do it . . .* and so on, stay firm about your choice to begin abolishing payoffs with the *Excuses Begone!* guide.

Affirm: *I practice self-responsibility rather than faultfinding, and I am willing to forgo the inclination to blame others for anything in my life.*

## 7. Protection

The words of Johann von Goethe may help you release the desire to seek the protection of childhood: "If children grew up according to early indications, we should have nothing but geniuses." And, from the great Indian poet Rabindranath Tagore: "Every child comes with the message that God is not yet discouraged of man." Goethe and Tagore are saying that you're someone who came here to fulfill a personal dharma, so let that genius gift from God finally be active in your life.

Everything you need to fulfill your destiny was with you at the moment before, during, and after your conception—so retreat to that knowledge now. Your payoff system of feeling fragile and needy and wanting to be protected dissolves as you begin to trust yourself. At the same time, you're trusting in the infinite wisdom that created you.

Affirm: *I am a grown-up, and I arrived here from nonbeing equipped with everything I need to fulfill my greatness.*

## 8. Escaping the Present Moment

When you feel dejected or out of sorts, ask yourself: *Do I wish to use the present moment—the precious currency of my life—in this manner?* This will help you to become conscious of the importance of being here now—not just in your body, but in your thinking as well. I urge you to think of the present as just that: a wondrous present from your Source. Anytime you're filling the now with thoughts about how you used to be, concerns about what someone has done to harm you, or worries about the future, you're saying "No, thank you" to your Source for this precious gift.

As I've pointed out throughout this book, everything that has ever happened did so not in the past, but in the now—so your relationship to life is your relationship to the now. Become conscious of just how valuable this present is, and obliterate that old tendency to use excuses for the purpose of escaping the moment.

Affirm: *I refuse to use my precious present moments in any way that takes me away from the Divine love from which I originated.*

This concludes the third question of the *Excuses Begone!* paradigm. Do you see the folly of your self-paralyzing excuses mentality? As you close out this chapter and move on to the next one, ponder these poetic words from Walt Whitman's *Leaves of Grass:*

> *There was a child went forth every day,*
> *And the first object he looked upon and received with*
> *wonder or pity or love or dread, that object he became,*
> *And that object became part of him for the*
> *day or a certain part of the day . . .*
> *or for many years or stretching cycles of years.*

So watch what you look upon. Even more significantly, don't create a reward system of excuses to defend, pity, or dread. This is a great time to remember this thought, which I frequently repeat: *When you change the way you look at things, the things you look at change.*

# THE FOURTH QUESTION: *WHAT WOULD MY LIFE LOOK LIKE IF I COULDN'T USE THESE EXCUSES?*

*"What is now proved was once only imagin'd."*

— William Blake

In the fourth question of the *Excuses Begone!* paradigm, you switch into the powerful world of your own imagination. The observation above, from the English poet William Blake, reveals an important truth: the things that you take for granted and treat as gospel were initially imagined. Just as the cell phone had to first be an idea before it became a reality, the same is true of everything you encounter in life.

Imagination is crucial in order to bring things from the world of nonbeing into the world of being. Jesus of Nazareth said that it's the Spirit that gives life, and Lao-tzu said that all being comes from nonbeing. What was good enough for these two spiritual giants to embrace has immeasurable importance for you as well.

This pathway from nonbeing or Spirit to the world of an *Excuses Begone!* existence originates in your imagination. I love to remind myself of this mind-blowing idea that I touched upon in Chapter 11: *An infinity of forests lies dormant within the dreams of one acorn.* Even a forest needs a vision, a dream, an idea; indeed, a fertile imagination.

This chapter is designed to help you do the same kind of work as one little acorn, which has an entire forest to create. You have within you the power to create a series of ideas for yourself that will erase obstacles to your highest calling. When you imagine that you're free of any need to use excuses, you'll ultimately act on what you're imagining. So practice the process of envisioning precisely what your life would look and feel like if it were impossible to enlist your excuse patterns. A good way to begin is by getting accustomed to visualizing exactly who you are, *as if you've already arrived.*

### Seeing Who You Want to Be as Already Here

Let's look further at the quote that opens this chapter, along with the implications of breaking our excuse-making habit. Our poet friend Mr. Blake is saying that we imagined these self-limiting ideas before they became facts in our life. Memetics, genetics, early-childhood reinforcements, cultural conditioning, and years of thinking limiting thoughts joined forces to become the excuses that have come to feel like reality.

If Blake's observation is true for you, its corollary applies as well. In other words, if you make the *Excuses Begone!* shift and hold fast to its ideas, then you prove to yourself just how powerful your imagination is. This is why I included the words *already here* concerning the way you want to see yourself. For all intents and purposes, what you actively imagine is authentically and undeniably already here, so you can absolutely change from self-defeating excuses to self-enhancing actions. Once your new thinking habits are truly in place, it's the same as saying that you're already actualizing what you want.

When I was in my early 20s, I used the imagination practice on the excuse *I'm too tired.* I'd heard this so frequently that it finally became a mind virus I mimicked and employed regularly. It was a convenient but debilitating excuse, because thinking and talking about how tired I was made me more fatigued than I actually was. The more I said the words *I'm tired,* the more my energy seemed to be depleted, even when there were no physical reasons behind this.

One morning after listening to a friend tell me that he was too exhausted to carry out a planned weekend retreat, I decided to end my use of this excuse permanently. I pledged to never again tell others (or myself) how tired I was, and I began to imagine myself in possession of unlimited energy. I didn't change my sleep habits, take energy supplements, or change my lifestyle—all I did was imagine myself as a high-energy person. I was able to change the way I viewed myself in relationship to fatigue and started to see myself as a never-tired person. This all started with a new thought, which was placed first in my imagination. And to this day, some 40 years later, I've steadfastly refused to even think *I'm tired.*

One of Ralph Waldo Emerson's essays includes a line that has always made an impact on me: "Imagination is a very high sort of seeing." To me, this is seeing with a capital *S.* Seeing myself with boundless energy all those years ago allowed me to eliminate the obstacles of fatigue and energy depletion, and I created a new me in those imaginative moments.

### *Imagining Your Way to a Life Without Excuses*

I encourage you to actively examine the question *What would my life look like if I couldn't use these excuses?* by giving yourself permission to let your imagination run wild. Envision something like a magical potion that doesn't permit you to think thoughts that have anything to do with excuses, and pay attention to what this visualization provokes within you. What would life look like? How would you feel? What alternative thoughts would you have?

I'll take you through this exercise now, using several of the excuses from the 18-item catalog I detailed in Chapter 3:

## 1. It Will Be Difficult/It Will Take a Long Time

These two similar excuses are frequently substituted for action. Now, imagine that you're incapable of creating these thoughts. In the same way that you can't imagine the mental activity of a jellyfish without ears or eyes that lives in the middle of the sea, neither can you conceive of a task as being difficult or taking a long time. So if it were absolutely impossible for you to think this way, what would your life be like?

Whatever it is that you'd like to accomplish, be it becoming an artist, creating your own musical composition, starting a new business, repairing your relationship with your parents or spouse or anyone else, building a new home, getting into physical shape—anything at all—how would your world change if you couldn't even conceive of the idea that it would be difficult and/or take a long time?

— **Without these excuses, what would life look like?** It's a safe bet that you'd immediately initiate action propelling you in the direction of the fulfillment of your dreams. You'd talk to others who had similar kinds of dreams and then emerged successfully. You'd have a lot of energy, and you'd be actively engaged in the process of living the life you imagine. You'd attract synchronistic assistance and notice the right people, the right events, and the right circumstances persistently showing up. Why? Because you'd be acting just like the Source of all creation does. You'd be aligned with a universe that says, "Yes, you can!" and gives you the tools to prove it. You'd have no hesitation or fear that something would be difficult or take too long . . . you'd happily *do* rather than explain or complain.

— **Without these excuses, how would you feel?** With these limitations completely out of the way, let me hazard a guess that you'd feel ecstatic and finally, completely on purpose. A sense of freedom would delight you, because avoidance of your true dharma would no longer exist. You'd feel enormous contentment rather than worrying about what you're avoiding or where you're going. There would be no focus on your destination since *too long* would no longer exist for you, and the *now* of the journey would provide the success and happiness you desire. You'd experience a great deal of bliss because you'd be guided by your creativity and initiative rather than fear of disappointment, and joy would rule your life.

— **Without these excuses, what alternative thoughts would you have?** Rather than focusing on what you can't do because it's difficult and takes a long time, you'd think like this: *This is definitely something that I can and will create for myself. I know I can do anything I put my mind to. I anticipate that this is within my ability to readily accomplish. I have no fear, because I recognize that whatever guidance and assistance I require is available. I'm excited, thrilled, and elated about fulfilling this dream. I realize that the thoughts I have are meshed with enthusiasm and passion, and that nothing can stop me. In fact, I'm certain that whatever I need to actualize my dreams is already on its way. I contentedly watch for what the universe sends me.*

### 2. There Will Be Family Drama

Again, I'm suggesting that you see yourself as utterly incapable of coming up with this excuse. Imagine that you can't conjure up even a single thought that forecasts any kind of familial disruption. Thinking in this way is equivalent to anticipating that your relatives are fine with whatever decision you make—you absolutely will not experience resistance, criticism, hostility, or rejection. Your family is, at the very least, neutral and perhaps even indifferent. There are no hassles or antagonisms, and no drama for you to deal with.

— **Without this excuse, what would life look like?** Since you'd no longer have to consider the ramifications of your family knowing the authentic you, your life would be exactly how you always wanted it to be. You'd never have to consult anyone whose opinion you didn't value: you'd choose the kind of work you prefer, study the subjects you wished to, live where you pleased, and come and go as you determined—without a single moment of conflict or disapproval from your relatives. Disproving the popular saying that "friends are God's way of apologizing for our relatives," your family members would even become your close friends!

   **— Without this excuse, how would you feel?** You'd feel free, because now drama could never be a consequence of following your bliss.

Take a second now to imagine your family enthusiastically encouraging every decision that you make concerning your life . . . this is how you'd feel every day if it was impossible to entertain the thoughts that are the basis of this excuse. With everyone around you at peace, you'd feel the soothing effect of a harmonious and supportive environment. Anxiety and worry would disappear, and you'd feel in charge of your inner world, perhaps for the first time. Feeling safe would replace all the fear of potential condemnation that forced you to behave like such a good little family member.

   **— Without this excuse, what alternative thoughts would you have?** Your new thoughts would be based exclusively on the best way to conduct your life, since you wouldn't be able to employ the family-drama excuse. You'd think: *I'm in a position to ask anyone I love for his or her opinion, and I can accept or reject that advice without any negative repercussions coming my way. I'm free to practice any religion I choose, or none at all. I'm free to date, marry, or cohabit with whomever I choose. I'm free to pursue any line of work, live in any location, and just plain live my life, and all of my family members love me and support my choices.*

This doesn't need to be a fantasy—it's your mind, and you have the freedom to fill it with the thoughts you choose. This new way of thinking is immediately available to you, just as soon as you do an *Excuses Begone!* makeover on this old belief.

### 3. I'm Not Strong Enough/I'm Not Smart Enough

What if you couldn't have these excuses? If you were incapable of believing that you're deficient physically and intellectually, you'd focus on the opposite idea. You'd think thoughts like the following, which reflect a new mind-set: *I'm as strong as I need to be to accomplish anything I place my attention on. I'm a creative genius, a piece of the Divine creator; therefore, I have in my possession all of the brainpower that I'll ever need to fulfill any desires of my choosing.*

Before you object to these lofty self-pronouncements, remind yourself that the point of this exercise is to help you imagine a new existence without your old mental crutches.

— **Without these excuses, what would life look like?** Here again, you'd bask in the exquisite belief that you possess all of the physical and intellectual abilities you could ever need. Your life would flow naturally from a position of supreme confidence in yourself and all of your God-given, natural abilities. You'd take risks and be capable of trying anything, content with whatever results were to ensue. You'd exude courage because you'd be unable to manufacture doubtful thoughts that manifested as excuses. You'd never compare yourself to others or evaluate your abilities on the basis of what others do—how you measure up to the performance levels of others would have no bearing on you or what you attempt. You'd know that God doesn't make mistakes, so whatever levels of personal strength and intellectual proficiency you possess are absolutely perfect. In short, you'd be content, grateful for who you are and all that you'd been given, in both the physical and perceptual realms.

— **Without these excuses, how would you feel?** The most noticeable feelings you'd experience would be self-assurance and personal pride. You'd have a sense of bliss stemming from being completely satisfied with who you are. You'd feel awe and pleasure about the miracle of your mind and body. You'd no longer cast your gaze outward and feel inadequate by comparison; instead, you'd look inward and feel peaceful and blessed, independent of the opinion of others.

**— Without these excuses, what alternative thoughts would you have?** With no more excuses about mental and physical inadequacies, you'd engage in all kinds of new and nourishing beliefs. Your first one might be something like this: *I have all the mental and physical tools I need to actualize any dream I've ever had. All I need to do is maintain my passion, and all of the assistance I need will come to me.*

Without excuses, there wouldn't be any way of creating obstacles for yourself. But just thinking *I am strong* or *I am smart* begins to stop the excuse-making modes in their tracks. With the positive attitude of *I can do it; I have all that I need right here and right now,* you're on the way to fulfilling the destiny that was in that tiny little embryo that became *you.* That little embryo knew nothing of limitations, weaknesses, stupidity, and the like. It had a Divine nature; it was perfect; and it had everything it needed in the way of mental and material strength to fulfill the destiny that it signed up to accomplish.

Once the excuses are gone, there will be nothing to stop you from thinking and acting in harmony with the gifts that you were given at the moment of your transition from nonbeing to being, from Spirit to form, from *no where* to *now here.*


### 4. I Don't Have the Energy/I'm Too Busy

Once again, remember to play with your imagination. You're imagining that your brain is constructed in such a way that there's no excuse-making apparatus. So the moment you contemplate pursuing something you've always wanted to accomplish, your thoughts center around the idea that you possess boundless energy to do anything you put your mind to, and that you have plenty of time to pursue these activities.

— **Without these excuses, what would life look like?** Life would have a high-energy appearance, and you'd enjoy thinking about accomplishing the things you've dreamed about. You might tell yourself: *I'm a vigorous person and possess all the vitality and liveliness to accomplish anything I set my mind to.* And with only this type of sentiment available, that's precisely the kind of action you'd take. Such an attitude would spur you on, giving you un- limited vim and vigor. You'd find joy in doing the kinds of things you always wanted to do but couldn't when you used to claim that you didn't have any energy or you were too busy.

Without those lame excuses, your life would shift from un- motivated to engaged in the daily activities that bring you a sense of well-being. Although you'd be busier than you ever were before, you wouldn't be thinking about business and crammed schedules as excuses for not living life totally on your own terms. You'd revel in knowing that your activities serve you in the best way because they're aligned with your highest aspirations for yourself.

— **Without these excuses, how would you feel?** You'd feel fully *alive, joyful, blissful,* and other similar happiness descriptors. But more than this, you'd notice a significant decline in the bodily sensations of fatigue, headaches, cramps, high blood pressure, coughing, congestion, fever, being overweight and out of breath, and other symptoms. That's because when you engage in activities that make you feel good, your body reacts with sensations of well- being—since you can't use an excuse to escape or explain away your desire to live your life on purpose, you enjoy optimal health. This is the equivalent of feeling the presence of your Source energy, which knows exactly why you're here and cooperates as soon as you become aligned with the energy that intended you here in the first place.

— **Without these excuses, what alternative thoughts would you have?** Imagine not being able to come up with the ideas that make up the foundation for these excuses. What would this leave as an alternative? You'd think: *I have all the juice and vitality I need* *for fulfilling my own dharma; I am highly energized. I trust in the wisdom of the Source in which I originated to provide me with all I need to match the grand design I have for my life. The very fact that I possess the passion for what I wish to accomplish means that I have the necessary high energy that is required.*

As you know, your actions flow directly from your thoughts. So if you couldn't come up with excuses to explain a lack of energy or an overly busy life, your thoughts would focus on what *is* possible rather than what *is not*. You'd muse about whatever brought you joy and kept you in harmony with your highest vision for yourself. You'd love having a full life, yet you'd happily eliminate activities that came under the heading of "busywork"—you wouldn't fill your days with drudgery or meaningless activities.

This is the way you think when you're unable to conjure up excuses.

Victor Hugo once made an observation that succinctly and emphatically sums up the message that I've attempted to convey in this fourth question of the *Excuses Begone!* paradigm: "One can resist the invasion of armies; one cannot resist the invasion of ideas." To that end, treat this exercise on imagination as the welcome arrival of a new idea. I've found it to be so powerful that in just a few brief applications, I've been able to permanently banish many excuses I once relied on.

If you're about to blame someone else for why your life isn't unfolding in the way you prefer, I encourage you to think about how your world would change if you didn't have the capacity to blame. Ask yourself the questions brought up in this chapter: *What would my life look like? How would I feel? What alternative thinking would I engage in, since my brain couldn't process any kind of excuse making, which lays the blame on anyone other than myself?*

Yes, that's it: you'd immediately turn to yourself. You wouldn't solve your problem; you'd simply outgrow it. That's the purpose of this paradigm, this chapter, and this entire book—grow up and live an *Excuses Begone!* life. When you integrate this concept, you welcome these new ideas into your life.

CHAPTER 16

# THE FIFTH QUESTION: *CAN I CREATE A RATIONAL REASON TO CHANGE?*

*"[N]either believe nor reject any thing because any other person, or description of persons have rejected or believed it. Your own reason is the only oracle given you by heaven . . ."*

— Thomas Jefferson

My 21-year-old son, Sands, has a long-standing habit of being unable to wake up for his morning classes, and on weekends often sleeps until two in the afternoon. I've had countless discussions with him about breaking this habit, because he's continually dealing with tardiness issues in school, rushing around in the morning in a state of anxiety, driving fast because he's late, and being tired all day because of an insufficient amount of the precious sleep that his body seems to crave. His habit gets in the way of his schoolwork, his happiness, and his health, since he feels fatigued throughout any day in which he has to wake up before noon.

Whenever we discuss breaking this habit, my son's answers go like this: "I can't just change and jump up in the morning," "I've always been this way; it's my nature," "I don't have energy in the morning," "I'm young, and this is the way all my friends live," "I've tried, but it's never been something I can do," and "It's just too difficult." Sound familiar? Like most of us, my son has allowed his life to be ruled by excuses.

### Four Criteria for Creating a Rational Reason to Change

The previous four questions in the *Excuses Begone!* paradigm urged you to examine whether your excuses are true, to look at their origins, to review the payoff system, and then to imagine what your life would look like if you were unable to even come up with these limiting thought patterns. What's needed now is to understand the necessity of using logic as you make a portentous shift in your life, which brings us to the fifth question: *Can I create a rational reason to change?*

If your desire to break any habit isn't matched by a reasoning process that *registers with you,* then your work in this new paradigm will be weakened to the point of ineffectiveness. So when you intellectually accept the four criteria below, your ability to undermine and undercut your old habituated patterns will have a solid base from which to proceed, and you'll graduate with honors from this complete course in *Excuses Begone!*

### Criterion #1: It Must Make Sense

Eliminating lifelong thinking habits cannot and will not happen if it doesn't strike you as a sensible thing to do. It doesn't really matter that everyone you know tells you how important it is to change—if it doesn't make sense to you, then you'll retreat to your old ways and continue to explain them away with your convenient laundry list of excuses. If the answer to *Do I really want to bring about this change?* is yes, then that's all you need in order to proceed and succeed. But if you have any doubts whatsoever, your old excuse making will surface, and you'll revert back to your long-held habits.

For example, when I was in my 30s, I made the decision that I was no longer going to allow myself to continue the unhealthy habits that had dominated my life up until that point. I could see myself gaining weight around the middle, eating and drinking things that weren't good for me, and generally not paying the proper attention to the well-being of this temple that temporarily houses my soul. I remember thinking: *I'm going to change. I don't know how, but I do know that I can't rely on anyone else but myself. I'm not going to enter the afternoon of my life as an obese, out-of-breath, toxic man. It makes sense to me to make this shift, so that's what I'm going to stick with.*

One day in 1976, I began a regimen that included exercise, drinking lots of water, taking supplements, and improving my diet. Although no one around me fully understood my drive to stay in shape, it made sense to me. Consequently, I was able to begin a new strategy for living that resulted in eliminating all of those tired excuses I'd been using to explain my retreat from well-being.

Whenever anyone has told me over the years that they just don't understand why I'm so "compulsive" about my health habits, I always think: *If I didn't have a healthy body, I wouldn't have anywhere to live.* Because my lifestyle makes sense to me, I'm immune to others' perplexed questioning, and I'm never tempted to reverse my decision to live as healthful an existence as I possibly can. My rational determination to pursue optimal wellness makes self-defeating choices unappealing.

Today, I enjoy noticing the long-term effects of that decision I made more than three decades ago. Simply resolving to become more health conscious led me to run daily, which led me to eliminate red meat from my diet, which led me to drink water instead of alcohol, which led me to give up all soft drinks, which led me to swim regularly, which led me to eat more and more raw vegetables, which led me to practice Bikram yoga four to five times a week, which led me to study and live the Tao Te Ching . . . and on and on it goes.

743

Most obese persons know that their self-destructive patterns have brought them to more poor choices (explained away by excuses), until the final result is out of their control. And while all addicts started out small and gained one ruinous habit after another, *you* can choose to be someone who breaks free of limitations right now. This one basic thought: *This makes sense to me—even if no one else understands me and I don't know how to make it happen—and that's what I'm going to stick with,* will lead you to a new path to walk upon. Each step from that new position leads to another and then another, until you finally have the freedom that comes from living without the hindrance of excuses.

### Criterion #2: It Must Be Doable

Within you is a private space where "no visitors are allowed." This is where you meet yourself in total honesty, where you know what you're willing to dream, desire, and ultimately do. It's also where you find your answer to this question: *Am I willing and able to do what it takes to overcome these long-held habits of thought and action?*

If the answer is that you just can't make a change—you know yourself well enough to predict that you won't do the work that's necessary to accomplish it—then you're wise to heed that response. Forget about changing those old habits, at least for now. However, if you don't know how you'll do it but you still feel that it's doable, then proceed. You'll find the answers coming to you because of your willingness to view these changes as a real possibility.

Here are a couple of examples from my life that occurred recently, at my tender age of 68:

— I attended a meeting with several television executives to discuss the possibility of hosting my own national show. The idea of spreading the word of higher consciousness and promoting a loving, compassionate approach to helping people appealed to me. I've been doing precisely that on my radio show each

Monday on **HayHouseRadio.com**® for the past few years, so the thought of expanding this to a much larger audience was indeed tempting.

But in that honest place within me, where the No Visitors Allowed sign hangs, I found hosting a national TV show to simply not be doable. It's not about having excuses; it's about the fact that I'm just not willing to give up my writing, yoga practice, ocean swimming, long walks, hikes in the woods, or time with those I love. Because it's not going to happen and I know this, I simply let it go, with no excuses necessary for my decision. It's not doable, period. No complaining; no explaining.

— The second example involved a totally new experience that would take me all the way out of my comfort zone. It would be an opportunity to test myself in such a way that would be highly challenging, requiring me to have the mettle to overcome some old habits that had been supported by excuses. I was asked to be in a full-length motion picture based on the teachings that I've been associated with throughout my professional career.

Even though I was to play myself in a script that included professional actors, this endeavor would still require me to take direction from a well-established film director, learn lines, shoot scenes over and over and over from every conceivable angle, and work on a movie set for a month. It would entail 12-hour days; often staying up all night and working outdoors; and always being told what to do, where to sit, how to react, where to go next, what to wear, and on and on. These experiences were certainly foreign to all that I've done in the past three-plus decades . . . but it was doable for me. In that quiet, private place within me, I was thrilled at the idea of learning to become an actor in a movie based upon my teachings.

Once I knew that this project had an inner *go,* I totally surrendered to the process. I knew that the greater good would be served by the film, and I let go of all of my reasons (excuses) for not taking it on: *I know it will be difficult. It's a real risk. I've never acted before. I don't take direction. I do what I want, when I want, and*

*I say what I'm guided to say. It's not my nature to be an actor. No one will help me; I'll be hopelessly lost. I've never done such a thing before— what if I look stupid? I'm too old to learn a new profession, let alone master it, at the age of 68. A movie is too big a project. I'm too busy with my writing and overly full schedule. I'm scared—I don't like being put in a position where I might look bad, or even worse, fail!*

And so I arrived on the set to meet the director, actors, sound and lighting people, and rehearsal folks with a new attitude. I came ready to listen, learn, and master whatever skills I needed to create this full-length movie. Once I knew that it made sense and was definitely doable (even though I didn't have a clue as to how I'd accomplish it), all that I needed (and much more) began to show up right on time. The moment I stowed my skepticism, every excuse for not being involved in the project disappeared.

I must add here that I met some of the most intriguing people I've ever known, all of whom have become close friends. I loved the entire experience, and there's now a beautiful motion picture thanks to the accomplished actors, director, editors, and film crew. Titled *The Shift*, it brings me more pride and joy than I can describe.

### Criterion #3: It Must Allow You to Feel Good

Your left brain deals with the details of your life—this is where you analyze, compute, figure, and get all of your ducks in a row— and the first two criteria detailed above speak right to it. When you ask yourself the question *Can I create a rational reason to change?* your intellect responds: *Yes, indeed, that does make sense, and I really believe that I can do this thing and bring about the desired changes.*

Your right brain, on the other hand, deals with things like your emotions, your intuition, your enthusiasm, your awareness, and even your consciousness. So let's examine the creation of a rational reason to change from the right brain's point of view and discover how this change *feels*.

When I did this exercise in connection with the possibility of having my own daily TV program, I didn't feel good at all. I felt tense, rushed, tight in my stomach, and nervous about all of the time I'd have to devote to the show. I actually began to feel sick, and that was enough for me. My emotions, which show up in my body as a result of my thoughts, were giving me the answer. Contrast this with what happened when I visualized how I'd feel after taking up the movie/acting challenge: I felt dizzy with excitement about learning a completely new craft—not to mention strong, content, and proud. My emotions actually empowered me.

If you want to shed old habits and excuses, take some time to visit that private place within you. Close your eyes and visualize yourself as being completely free of these limitations . . . how does your body react? If you feel good, that's all the evidence you need to prove to yourself that you have a rational reason to change.

If you're hanging on to a whole bunch of habits that have been reinforced by excuses, note that these will make you feel bad. Your old mental crutches only serve to keep you from having an experience within your body that registers as "good," so you may even be accustomed to being emotionally bankrupt.

Pain, anxiety, fear, anger, and the like make themselves known in your body as rashes, eczema, heart palpitations, arthritis, backaches, headaches, stomachaches, diarrhea, eyestrain, cramps, and many more ailments too numerous to mention here. The point is that these emotional reactions that show up in the body can become your way of life, to the point that they define your reality. And when you're questioning why that is, that's when the excuse *I've always been this way* tends to rear its ugly head.

You can feel better: You can feel healthy. You can feel strong. You can feel blessed. You can feel joy. In short, you can feel great! If the idea of eliminating an incapacitating thinking habit that you've had for a long time resonates with you, then imagine it being gone. Does its disappearance register in your body as a positive, healthy, and happy sensation? If so, then that alone is reason enough to plunge into the *Excuses Begone!* formulations presented here.

### Criterion #4: It Must Be Aligned
### with the Callings of Your Soul

How do you determine that you're aligned with your soul's purpose? You know by the way the rational reason speaks directly to you in that personal place within. The thoughts and feelings that surface tend to go like this: *This is truly who I am. By making these changes and eradicating these excuses, I will be living my life on purpose, fulfilling a destiny I came here to accomplish.*

I could go on and on here detailing the benefits that accrue when you connect to the callings of your soul. However, I'm going to suspend my desire to write and just let you know that in the next chapter, the sixth question in the *Excuses Begone!* paradigm takes off from this point. It takes you on a journey in which you will see how the universe itself begins to cooperate with you through the Law of Attraction, when your habits detach from the world of ego and align, excuse free, with your Source of being.

I'd like to switch gears here by returning to the story of my son Sands, which opened this chapter. As I already mentioned, this young man has had a lifelong problem with waking up in the morning, but he was ultimately able to create a rational reason to change his old self-sabotaging thoughts and eliminate the excuses that supported his bad habit.

Sands loves nothing more in this world than to surf in the ocean. He was given a surfboard at the age of four, and he immediately paddled out to where the waves were breaking, jumped up on his board, and surfed all the way to shore. All of us stood there dumbfounded as we watched that little boy ride his first wave like an expert. As for Sands, he was hooked—he's lived and breathed surfing ever since. It's like he connected to his purpose the moment he jumped on that board.

My son has an entire library of videos on the subject and regularly checks the surf reports all over the world. He dons a wet suit and goes into the water with one of his many boards, regardless of his location on the planet or any consideration of the temperature of the air or water. He studies waves like an ornithologist studies birds. It truly is his great passion. In fact, he just returned from a 16-day trip throughout the islands of Indonesia, on a boat that specializes in taking surfers to some of the greatest waves available on planet Earth.

Now, for the 16 days that he lived in cramped quarters on a boat with eight other surfers, Sands was able to wake up every morning before dawn. He'd be out in the water all day, well past dusk; stay up at night to talk with the other surfers about the waves they caught that day; sleep soundly until 5 A.M.; and repeat the same routine for more than two consecutive weeks . . . and he never felt tired. The same is true when my son visits me on Maui—if the waves are good, he no longer has a sleeping-in-all-day habit.

For my son, a rational reason to change is the notion that he's able to live in harmony with his passion. So let's review the four criteria for eliminating the excuses that travel the same path as the habit itself:

1. Sands has a rational reason for changing his habit that definitely **makes sense.** Maybe you or I would perceive riding waves all day in freezing water as absurd, but to my son, this means that he's able to be in a place where his strongest desires are in rapport with his actions. The waves are there, he is there, and he loves riding on those waves—so it all makes perfect sense.

2. Sands has a rational reason for changing his old habits that's also positively **doable.** When he's near the water and is free to surf, without any real responsibilities, he never says, "I can't get up," "It's too difficult," "It's not my nature to rise early," "I don't have the energy," or any of the other excuses he likes to break out when he's away from the ocean. When his friends call to confirm that they're going to pick him up at 4:30 A.M., his first response is, "Great!" Regardless of what time he goes to bed the night before,

he can be found in the kitchen at the appointed time, fixing a bagel and drinking his juice, excited and ready to go on an early-morning surfing expedition.

3. There's no doubt that being in the water and riding those waves allows Sands to **feel good**, and I equate this with God. As I wrote in Chapter 9, whenever we're enthusiastic about something, that means we're tapping into the God within—feeling *good* is akin to feeling *God*. And when we're doing what we love and experiencing the passion that accompanies such moments, we're truly being guided by our Source.

I watch my son as he paddles out, as he rides his board, as he tells me his stories of the barrel that he rode, and as he watches his videos—there's a kind of seeing with a capital *S* that isn't with him at any other time. His concentration in studying the waves and knowing exactly when to pounce is like observing a cat concentrate on potential prey . . . pure poetry in motion. It's his nature, and watching him in these moments allows me to see him in a totally new light. It is the same excitement I feel within myself when I speak before an audience or as I sit here in my sacred space writing these words that I hope will touch you and unborn generations as well.

4. All of what I've written above (as well as what follows in Chapter 17) leads me to conclude that for Sands, a rational reason to change a long-held bad habit is that his early-morning journeys to the sea are moments when he's being called by Spirit to get up and be in harmony with the **callings of his soul.** I have no doubts whatsoever about this conclusion.

### Suggestions for Applying the
### Fifth Paradigm Question

— Do a unique inventory within yourself, an honest assessment of what lifelong thinking patterns you'd like to change, even if you haven't a clue as to how you could possibly bring this about. The more firmly entrenched the path in your mind, the better.

Now, without even considering how you're going to put this change into effect, ask yourself the first three criteria in this chapter and eliminate any that don't measure up:

1. If it doesn't make sense to you but everyone around you is telling you that it's the right thing to do, erase it from your inventory.

2. By being brutally honest with yourself, determine if, given the conditions of your life and how well you know yourself, this thing is truly doable. You may not know *how* to do it, but you can still assess if it is in fact something that's possible for you. If it isn't, then discard it.

3. Picture yourself as being free of your habituated way of being, totally disconnected from the habit. If that idea doesn't make you feel good—and I mean *really* good—then it's not for you.

Clean out the inventory of habits you'd like to break, and excuses you'd like to see vanish, based upon the criteria for having a rational reason to change. You'll be left with several lifetime thinking habits that make sense, are doable, and leave you feeling good.

Try putting one of the habits from your inventory to the test of the *Excuses Begone!* paradigm. After doing so, you might not even recognize the person you used to be. I know that when I think of some of the old habits I've freed myself from—such as drinking diet sodas, eating greasy foods, not exercising, procrastinating on deadlines, always being rushed, speaking out and talking over others rather than listening, not taking health supplements, being right rather than kind, and so on—I've noticed how much I've changed . . . and that those old tiresome excuses never seem to crop up anymore.

— Really examine your habits, along with all of the excuses you've adopted to explain yourself, and then ask yourself a simple question: *Do these make me feel good?* If the answer is no, then it's incumbent upon you to begin the process of making decisions that do in fact make you feel good. It's the same as aligning with the callings of your soul—because feeling good does indeed lift you into alignment with the callings of your soul.

Say this aloud: "I intend to feel good, and anything that I think or do that interferes with this intention must, out of necessity, be shelved permanently." You are allowed to feel good; it is your birthright. You emerged from the total bliss of oneness—God, if you will—into this human experience.

According to the Tao Te Ching, all being comes from non-being. I urge you to feel your innate goodness by eliminating the limitations that have kept you from experiencing the good feelings you had before beingness, and what you will have after being-ness as well. Just stating, "I intend to feel good" is a powerful and rational reason for living an excuse-free life.

Use reason in eradicating excuses and habituated behavior. As Benjamin Franklin wrote in *Poor Richard's Almanac* in 1753: "When Reason preaches, if you don't hear her she'll box your Ears." Listen up or cover your ears!

# THE SIXTH QUESTION: *CAN I ACCESS UNIVERSAL COOPERATION IN SHEDDING OLD HABITS?*

*"The mystical techniques for achieving immortality
are revealed only to those who have dissolved all ties to
the gross worldly realm of duality, conflict, and dogma.*

*"As long as your shallow worldly
ambitions exist, the door will not open."*[3]

— Lao-tzu

As we move to conquer limitations, we're now going to switch from an intellectual approach to a spiritual one. Why? Because self-defeating habits, and their accompanying excuses, are the province of the ego, the part of us that has edged God out. Convinced that our identity is only of this earth, most of us are controlled and manipulated by ego's false interpretation of who we are. And as Lao-tzu reminds us in the quote above, as long as we're tied to shallow ambitions in the material world, we're going to continue to be slavishly tied to old habits.

When you ask yourself this sixth question: *Can I access universal cooperation in shedding old habits?* you begin to apply the mystical principles of higher consciousness to your life. Step-by-step, you dissolve the belief that you're exclusively tied to this material world. Even taking hesitant little baby steps will allow you to open the door to an amazing new existence.

Take a moment to review what your intellect has learned from the *Excuses Begone!* paradigm, and then trust that any help you need is forthcoming. When you completely relinquish the notion that you're separate from the mind of the universe—when you're in a God-realized or Tao-centered place—this is the point where you bid farewell to excuses.

### *Accessing Universal Cooperation*

The moment has come for you to recover your original pure insight, the clarity and light that are within you now, as they always have been. *Enlightenment* means that you access that light within you, which is where you find Divine guidance. Now is the time to surrender your worldly ambitions and turn yourself over to that guidance.

The Source of all creation is pure energy, completely devoid of material form. You came from this Source, and you will return to it, as I've written frequently in this book. You don't have to physically die in order to access its unlimited power; you only need to become more like it. Your Source of being recognizes only that which it is, so when you're unlike your Source (or God, the Tao, the universal mind, or Spirit), that's when you're dominated by ego and think that you need all of its excuses. Yet Lao-tzu warns you at the beginning of this chapter that the mystical techniques for accessing Divine guidance cannot and will not be revealed when you edge God out.

Imagine a fish that lives five miles below the surface of the ocean: it has never seen light, has no experience of what air is, has no eyes, and thrives in an atmosphere so pressurized that it would squash any creature who lives above the surface. Now imagine that deep-sea fish communicating with a bird that's flying five miles above this creature's place of residence. You can see how unlikely this would be, since the sea creature can't recognize something that's in a separate reality system.

Likewise, your Source of being knows nothing of struggle, hatred, revenge, frustration, fear, tension, or excuses—these are all inventions of the ego. When you behave in ways that are separate and distinct from your Source, it can't communicate with you. Since conflict and excuses require duality, you can't access a Source that only knows oneness when you come to it in conflict or with excuses about why you aren't all that it intended you to be. In order to access the infinite power of the Tao, you must become more and more like God. In other words, you must move into the space where you experiment with thinking and acting like you imagine God does, and suspend your intellect.

The Law of Attraction proclaims that *like is attracted to like*. So when you think like the universal mind thinks, it will join you; when you think in ways that are antithetical to this Divine mind, you'll attract more of what you're thinking about. That means that if your thoughts are all focused on what's wrong, what's missing, what you can't do, or what you've never done before—that is, on *excuses*—you'll access more of what you're thinking about.

Use the Law of Attraction to say good-bye to excuses. When you do, the universe will recognize you, and help and guidance will show up in a synchronistic way. As you align with your authentic original self, rather than your ego, you'll start to feel as though you're collaborating with destiny.

### Aligning with Source in Your Thoughts and Actions

If you attempt to figure out how your Source of being thinks, the first thing you need to do is get rid of the ego. When you observe how creation takes place, you see that Source energy is all about *giving,* while your ego is all about *getting.* So aligning with

Source energy means taking the focus off of *What's in it for me?* and shifting to *How may I serve?*

When you say, "Gimme, gimme, gimme" to the universe, it uses the Law of Attraction to say, "Gimme, gimme, gimme" to *you.* You subsequently feel pressured, put-upon, and out of sorts because so many demands are being made of you. It is out of this vortex that you create excuses that only serve to keep you stuck and striving to meet the ego's demands: *I'm not strong enough . . . I don't deserve it . . . I don't have the energy . . . I'm scared . . . It's too big . . .* and on and on. All of this stems from identifying with the false self that edged God out of your deliberations.

Shift to a new alignment now, one that puts you in rapport with the creative universal mind. You can begin by thinking like God, and follow up by acting like God. Take the focus off of *Gimme, gimme, gimme* and place it on *How may I serve? What may I offer? How can I help?* When you do, the universe will respond similarly, asking, *How may I serve you? What may I offer you? How can I help you?*

This is when the ego's old habits fall away and are replaced by unexpected meaningful events, with the right people, circumstances, and funding appearing. Lao-tzu comments on the magic of this practice:

> If you wish to become a divine immortal angel, then restore the angelic qualities of your being through virtue and service.
>
> This is the only way to gain the attention of the immortals who teach the methods of energy enhancement and integration that are necessary to reach the divine realm. . . . These angelic teachers cannot be sought out, it is they who seek out the student.[4]

The way to get to the point where you've abolished old habits and excuses is to petition the Divine realm and restore the angelic qualities of your being. Restoring is crucial, for when you begin to think like God thinks, you're actually returning to your Source of being without having to die.

I can't emphasize enough here that *you don't attract what you desire; you attract what you are.* Once again, I turn to Lao-tzu, who concludes the passage quoted on the previous page with:

> When you succeed in connecting your energy with the divine realm through high awareness and the practice of undiscriminating virtue, the transmission of the ultimate subtle truths will follow. This is the path that all angels take to the divine realm.[5]

That is to say that you can't just wish for a change, or simply think about what you want, and expect it to appear. To see the old habits fall away and access Divine guidance in making your life work at the highest levels of happiness, success, and health, you must *forget about what's in it for you.* Start practicing higher awareness by serving and wanting even more for others than you want for yourself. Otherwise, you'll never experience the subtle joy of a blissful, fulfilled life.

As Lao-tzu says, this is the only way. You can't demand guidance; it will come when you align as your Source is aligned. Then—and only then—as you live and practice the virtues, you'll gain the attention of the immortals. Otherwise, I repeat that the door absolutely will not open.

### Living the Virtues

Some 2,500 years ago, Lao-tzu spoke of "the four cardinal virtues" and noted that when we practice them as a way of life, we come to know and access the truth of the universe. These four virtues don't represent external dogma, but a part of our original nature—by practicing them, we realign with Source and access the powers that Source energy has to offer.

According to the teachings of Lao-tzu, the four cardinal virtues represent the surest way to leave habits and excuses behind and reconnect to your original nature. That is, the way you were before acquiring physical form, and the way you will be when you leave your physical self. The more your life is harmonized with the four virtues, the less you're controlled by the uncompromising ego. And when your ego is tamed, you discover how easy it is to access Divine guidance—you and the Divine begin to operate on the same frequency. As you contemplate your life without excuses, you leave the ego part of you in the dust!

Below are the four virtues and how they manifest, along with a brief description of how they relate to your commitment to live an *Excuses Begone!* life:

### The First Cardinal Virtue:
### Reverence for All Life

This is number one because it is the key to diminishing the ego. The Source of being is the Source of *all* beings, including our planet and our universe, and it doesn't create that for which it has no reverence. Since the Tao or God is in the business of creating and allowing, why would it create anything that is unlike itself, or even worse, something that it despises?

To that end, the first cardinal virtue manifests in your daily life as unconditional love and respect for all beings in creation. This includes making a conscious effort to love and respect *yourself,* as well as to remove all of the judgments and criticisms from those early memes and mind viruses. Understand that you are a piece of God, and since you must be like what you came from, you are lovable, worthy, and Godlike. Affirm this as often as you can, for when you see yourself in a loving way, you have nothing but love to extend outward. And the more you love others, the less you need old excuse patterns, particularly those relating to blame. Excuses originate in a false belief that the universe and its inhabitants aren't there for you. The notion that they're obstacles—inhibiting you from living at your highest levels of success, happiness, and health—is based on an inauthentic premise.

As you adopt this first cardinal virtue, allow yourself to see others as willing to assist you in maximizing your human potential. The more reverence you have for yourself, and for all of life, the more you see everyone and everything as willing assistants, rather than inhibitors to your highest life. As Patanjali put it so succinctly several thousand years ago: "When you are steadfast in your abstention of thoughts of harm directed toward others, all living creatures will cease to feel enmity in your presence." The key here is to stay so steadfast that you seldom, if ever, slip from this first cardinal virtue.

## The Second Cardinal Virtue:
## Natural Sincerity

This virtue manifests itself as honesty, simplicity, and faithfulness; and it's summed up by the popular reminder to be true to yourself. Using an excuse to explain why your life isn't working at the level you prefer isn't being true to yourself—when you're completely honest and sincere, excuses don't even enter into the picture.

The second virtue involves living a life that reflects choices that come from respect and affection for your own nature. Ralph Waldo Emerson described the significance of sincerity in an 1841 essay, *The Over-Soul:* "Deal so plainly with man and woman, as to constrain the utmost sincerity, and destroy all hope of trifling with you. It is the highest compliment you pay." And the great humanitarian Albert Schweitzer once observed that "sincerity is the foundation of the spiritual life."

Make truth your most important attribute. Walk your talk; that is, become sincere and honest in all that you say and do. If you find this to be a challenge, take a moment to affirm: *I no longer need to be insincere or dishonest. This is who I am, and this is how I feel.* From now on, when you make a commitment, do everything in your power to live up to what you've promised. Remember that when you're living your life from the perspective of your truest nature, you connect to Source. And as Schweitzer said, this is the very foundation of the spiritual life. As you work at being totally honest with yourself and others, those old self-defeating habits no longer crop up.

When you know and trust yourself, you also know and trust the Divinity that created you. That means if you want to live in the mountains or by the ocean, so be it—you know it's your soul calling you to live harmoniously within your true nature. If you love sculpting and no one else gets it, so be it. If you want to become a triathlete, a ballet dancer, a hockey player, or a trapeze artist, so be it. If you live from honesty, sincerity, and faithfulness to the callings of your spirit, you'll never have occasion to use excuses. This is the significance of the second cardinal virtue offered by Lao-tzu, a mighty tool that you can employ as you work your way through the *Excuses Begone!* paradigm.

### The Third Cardinal Virtue:
### Gentleness

This virtue personifies one of my favorite and most frequently employed maxims: "When you have the choice to be right or to be kind, always pick kind." So many of your old thinking habits and their attendant excuses come out of a need to make yourself right and others wrong. When you practice this third virtue, you eliminate conflicts that result in your need to explain why you're right. This virtue manifests as kindness, consideration for others, and sensitivity to spiritual truth.

Gentleness generally implies that you no longer have a strong ego-inspired desire to dominate or control others, which allows you to move into a rhythm with the universe. You cooperate with it, much like a surfer who rides with the waves instead of trying to overpower them. I recommend that you look very closely at your relationships and find out how much of your energy is directed toward dominating and controlling, rather than accepting and allowing.

As you develop this virtue, the pronoun *I* ceases to be the center of your communication. Instead of insisting, "*I've* told you so many times how to deal with these frustrating and rude people," you're more likely to say, "*You're* really having a tough day. Is there anything I can do to help?" Beginning a sentence with "I" implies the need to control; beginning a sentence with "You," on the other hand, expresses kindness and consideration for the other person.

The more kindness and sensitivity you extend to everyone in your life, the less likely you are to blame others for not living up to your expectations. Gentleness means accepting life and people as they are, rather than insisting that they be as *you* are. As you practice living this way, blame disappears and you enjoy a peaceful world—not because the world has changed, but because you adopted this third cardinal virtue of gentleness.

## The Fourth Cardinal Virtue:
## Supportiveness

This virtue manifests in your life as service to others without any expectation of reward. Once again, when you extend yourself in a spirit of giving, helping, or loving, you act as God acts. As you consider the many excuses that have dominated your life, look carefully at them—you'll see that they're all focused on the ego: *I can't do this. I'm too busy or too scared. I'm unworthy. No one will help me. I'm too old. I'm too tired.* It's all *me, me, me.* Now imagine shifting your attention off of yourself and asking the universal mind *How may I serve?* When you do so, the message you're sending is: *I'm not thinking about myself and what I can or can't have.* Your attention is on making someone else feel better.

Anytime you're supportive of others, you automatically remove ego from the picture. And with no ego, you go from edging God out to being more like God. When you think and act this way, the need for excuses evaporates. Practice giving and serving without expectation of reward (or even a thank-you)—let your reward be spiritual fulfillment. This is what Kahlil Gibran meant when he wrote in *The Prophet:* "There are those who give with joy, and that joy is their reward."

The greatest joy comes from giving and serving, so replace your habit of focusing exclusively on yourself and what's in it for you. When you make the shift to supporting others in your life, without expecting anything in return, you'll think less about what you want and find comfort and joy in the act of giving and serving. It's so simple: no focus on yourself equals no excuses.

The four cardinal virtues are a road map to the simple truth of the universe. Remember what Lao-tzu offered you 500 hundred years before the birth of Jesus: "These four virtues are not an external dogma but a part of your original nature." To revere all of life, to live with natural sincerity, to practice gentleness, and to be in service to others is to replicate the energy field from which you originated.

Starting on the following page, I'm going to take you back through the list of the 18 excuse categories to see how they evaporate if you live the four virtues and consequently access universal cooperation:

| Excuse | Accessing Universal Cooperation |
|---|---|
| 1. It will be difficult. | With God, all things are possible. |
| 2. It's going to be risky. | I cannot fail when I trust in the wisdom that created me. |
| 3. It will take a long time. | There is only now. I live fully in the present. |
| 4. There will be family drama. | My inner callings are the voice of God. I must follow what I feel so deeply. |
| 5. I don't deserve it. | Everyone deserves the grace of the Tao. |
| 6. It's not my nature. | My nature is to have reverence for all of life—to be sincere, gentle, and supportive to all. |
| 7. I can't afford it. | If I stay in God realization, all that I need will be provided. |
| 8. No one will help me. | How may I serve others so that they may have what I desire? |
| 9. It has never happened before. | I am content with all that has shown up in my life. |
| 10. I'm not strong enough. | I know that I am never alone. I will reach out to others who are not as strong as I am. |
| 11. I'm not smart enough. | I trust in the Divine, omniscient intelligence to which I am always connected. |
| 12. I'm too old (or not old enough). | In an infinite universe, age is an illusion—there is only now. |
| 13. The rules won't let me. | I live by the four cardinal virtues. |
| 14. It's too big. | If I can conceive of it, passion and the abilities to create it will be given. |
| 15. I don't have the energy. | There is an energy in the universe greater than me, and that energy is always available. |
| 16. It's my personal family history. | Everything that has ever happened to me was perfect, and I can learn and grow from it. |
| 17. I'm too busy. | With infinite patience, I produce immediate results. |
| 18. I'm too scared. | There is nothing to fear. I am an infinite expression of God (the Tao). |

This sixth question in the *Excuses Begone!* paradigm is designed to assist you into a Tao-centered, God-realized pattern. As you've seen in this chapter, old thinking habits die quite readily when you get your ego out of the way and live by the four cardinal virtues. Without even trying, a need for defensiveness and justification disappears as soon as you reach out to others and take responsibility for everything that occurs in your life.

### Suggestions for Applying the Sixth Paradigm Question

— Practice one of the virtues daily and take note of how it decreases your tendency to focus only on yourself. When you find yourself slipping back into an old, habitual way of being, use the moment to concentrate on unconditionally loving someone else. Then notice that the old thinking habits and excuses are no longer present.

Keep in mind that these four cardinal virtues represent the real you, the being you were prior to developing the false self (ego). Notice how naturally good you feel when you're demonstrating reverence for everyone, natural sincerity, gentleness, and supportiveness—that's because you're in harmony with your Source of being. All that it takes to remove an old self-defeating habit is returning to your original nature in the moment.

— Dissolve as many ties to the gross worldly realm of conflict and dogma as you can. Recall how Lao-tzu suggests that by doing so, you'll see the door open to universal cooperation. Stop identifying yourself on the basis of what you have, whom you're superior to, what position you've attained, and how others view you. See yourself as a piece of God, willing to act as close to that consciousness as possible. When you desire something, try wanting it more for someone else than you do for yourself; in fact, act to make it happen for them before you even think about yourself. Or if you're about to be critical or unkind to anyone, remind yourself that your original nature is gentle. Imagine yourself in a formless world about to transform into a material being—that state of nonbeing is who you were before you cultivated ego and began the process of edging God out.

The way to access universal cooperation in shedding old habits is to realign with your original nature in all of your thoughts. Think like God thinks, practice the virtues in all of your thoughts and behaviors, and devote yourself to living a selfless life. It cannot fail you. Your habits will dissolve and your excuses will surely be . . . gone!

# THE SEVENTH QUESTION: *HOW DO I CONTINUOUSLY REINFORCE THIS NEW WAY OF BEING?*

*"The mind is indeed restless, Arjuna: it is indeed
hard to train. But by constant practice . . . the mind in
truth can be trained. When the mind is not in harmony,
this divine communion is hard to attain, but the man whose
mind is in harmony attains it, if he knows, and if he strives."*

— Lord Krishna, from the Bhagavad Gita

When they're next to each other, the number 1 and the number 8, which is the symbol of infinity, signify one infinite Source. I invite the symbolic nature of the number 18 to inspire this final chapter of *Excuses Begone!* along with the last question of our paradigm shift.

In Hebrew, the number 18 signifies life. There are also 18 holes on a golf course, which can't simply be an accident, can it? The Tao Te Ching contains 81 chapters, and many believe that it was contemporaneously written with the Bhagavad Gita, the ancient Hindu holy book that just happens to contain 18 chapters.

The Bhagavad Gita details the conversation between Krishna, an avatar of the god Vishnu, and the spiritual warrior Prince Arjuna. The quote that opens this chapter comes when Krishna, who is disguised as a charioteer, gives advice to Arjuna as he's preparing to go into another huge battle. Elsewhere in this iconic volume, Krishna instructs: "Give not your love to this transient world of suffering, but give all your love to me. Give me your mind, your heart, all your worship. Long for me always, live for me always, and you shall be united with me." This is the essential message of *Excuses Begone!*

Unite with God, the Tao, universal mind, or Source; and trust in this wisdom, which is your original nature. Know your original nature so that you can intuitively turn your awareness away from this transient world when necessary. Then you don't need or want self-defeating habits or excuses.

Krishna reminds you that with constant practice, your mind can be trained to overcome any habits of thought. The key is *with constant practice,* and that's the affirmative answer to this seventh and final question: *How do I continuously reinforce this new way of being?*

Practice the essence of *Excuses Begone!* daily or even hourly, particularly the seven questions comprising the paradigm. When you do, before long you'll find yourself running those seven questions through your mind in a matter of moments—and you'll come out on the other side of an old habit with a new way of thinking, acting, and being. Learning to overcome excuses involves training your mind to become harmonious, or at one, with your Source. As Krishna says: "When the mind is not in harmony, this divine communion is hard to attain, but the man whose mind is in harmony attains it, if he knows, and if he strives."

The remainder of this chapter focuses on suggestions for staying in harmony with your Source of being. Thinking like God thinks is essential for all of your practice—not so much to learn new techniques for overcoming excuses, but to keep you consciously connected to Source and detached from the material world as much as possible. In this way, you'll let the angelic realm guide you through all of the doors that will now be opening for you.

*Nine Ways to Reinforce Your New Way of Being*

Throughout these pages, you've had the opportunity to examine the many ways your mind has learned self-sabotaging thoughts. You learned how those bad habits became a familiar reality system for you, with a catalog of excuses explaining why you abandoned your original nature in favor of edging God out. Now, however, you're freeing yourself of those excuses by training your mind to welcome and cultivate your original spiritual nature.

Each of the seven principles for living an excuse-free life, as well as the seven components of the new paradigm, are directed toward the message Krishna imparts to Arjuna: *When you get your mind into harmony with Source, there will never be a need for bad habits or excuses again.* As he states in the Bhagavad Gita:

*Even the worst sinner becomes a saint*
*When he loves me with all his heart. This love*
*Will soon transform his personality*
*And fill his heart with peace profound.*
*O son of Kunti, this is my promise:*
*Those who love me, they shall never perish . . .*

*Still your mind in me, still yourself in me,*
*And without doubt you shall be united with me . . .*

Here are nine suggestions for uniting with your Source, and living from that place:

### 1. Know It

As Krishna tells Arjuna, your mind can be trained if you *know* that you and your Source cannot be separated. This knowledge is so close—it's only a thought away.

Knowing is like having a private room that contains all of the answers you need, and only *you* have the entrance key. Since it's in you, you can go there at any time, and no one can prevent you from accessing what it contains. The moment your sense of knowing dissolves, however, old habits and a ton of excuses inundate you. When you're aligned with your Source, you're guided by the greatest good; without that alignment, your Source and guidance don't tend to get involved with the way you choose to live your life. Create your own space where you're aligned with Source, and then ego and doubt can't enter.

Always keep in mind that no single person, place, or thing can force you to believe or disbelieve anything. Perhaps that was true when you were a child, but not now. Now you have the independence to choose what you believe. Your knowing is *yours*.

Here's how I speak to myself about my own knowing:

> A sacred space is within me that contains a knowing. I go there frequently, and I don't allow doubt into that Divine inner dwelling. It is mine alone, and I share it with my Source of being. It is to this knowing that I retreat whenever I find myself slipping into excuse habits. In this knowing space within, I have no doubt about the guidance that's available to me when I'm unified with my Source. I know that the doors will remain closed and the angelic teachers will not seek me if I'm only attached to this corporeal world of conflict, material things, and judgment. I keep this knowing space sacred for the moments when old habits and excuses attempt to influence my life.

Be aware of how significant this doubtless knowing is for living an excuse-free life.

## 2. Act as Your Source Would in Every Instant

From this place of inner knowing where doubt is banished, ask: *What would God do right now?* (Or, if you conceptualize God as love, ask: *What would love do now?*) If you're ever perplexed by your habitual thoughts, asking this question will serve as a way to reinforce that there's an alternative. When you ask what God or love would do, you attract the Source energy that was lost in your voyage from childhood ego development to the present.

A few hours ago, the sound of a chain saw cutting a cement pole in half permeated my writing space, and my habituated way of thinking began to surface. I felt so resentful toward the noise pollution that I thought about quitting for the rest of the day, with the built-in excuse: *How can I write with all of this racket? It's their fault, not mine.* But I decided to reinforce the *Excuses Begone!* way of being by asking: *What would God do?* Then I sat down, dismissed my judgmental notions, and let myself be in peace. Within a few moments I chose to ignore the sound and write anyway, imagining the chain-saw noise as music to accompany me. Five minutes later, the noise was gone—and I'd sent an excuse packing by being in a God-realized space instead of continuing with an ego-dominated inner dialogue.

### 3. Initiate a Conversation with Your Habitual Mind

As you work to overcome your self-created limitations, talk to your subconscious, telling it that instead of *reacting,* you're now going to *respond* with conscious choices. This will work rather quickly for you if you're serious about breaking a pattern— awareness of feeling locked into automatic reactions, along with a serious commitment to change, will allow you to choose a new response.

This is what happened with my 30-year habit of drinking caffeinated diet soda. Until that day in 1985 when I chose to break this habit, I drank six to eight cans of carbonated brown water every day. I'd certainly been living at what I call the "reaction level," with excuses to explain and fortify why I did this, so I made a commitment to myself to change. I knew I wanted freedom from the chemicals that dominated my life so much that I was seldom without a can of them in my hand, and this became much more important to me than continuing down my well-trod path.

I became vigilant about noticing my subconscious pattern: as soon as I caught myself reaching for a soda, I'd stop myself and substitute a conscious response that aligned with my commitment. By the same token, if *you w*ant to break a pattern, you need to truly commit, and then start conversing with your habitual mind. You'll be amazed at how fast the excuses disappear!

### 4. Get Quiet

Decide to reduce the noise level of your life. Noise is a distraction to your highest self because it keeps your ego on red alert. Ways to discard habits along with their attendant excuses are often found in silence, in the void that's the creative Source of all form. I've always loved Blaise Pascal's observation on this subject: "I have discovered that all the unhappiness of men arises from one single fact, that they cannot stay quietly in their own chamber." And *this* from a scientist!

Another scientist, Albert Einstein, reminds us of the importance of noise reduction as we become more adept at outgrowing the habits of childhood: "I live in the solitude which is painful in youth, but delicious in the years of maturity." Adopting a similar attitude will help you reinforce your *Excuses Begone!* life. So learn to take time each and every day for quiet contemplation: For example, when you're driving alone, turn off the constant chatter bombarding your inner world. Then when you arrive at your destination, honor the OFF button on the TV remote—and honor the ON button for your highest self!

Try to make meditation a daily practice as well, even if it's only for a few moments. (If you're unsure of how to begin, I've written a book called *Getting in the Gap* that comes with a CD to guide you in learning the meditation technique of Japa, which has been so extraordinarily helpful to me.) This is how Carl Jung described what he felt in deep meditation: "Those inner states were so fantastically beautiful that by comparison this world appeared downright ridiculous. . . . It is impossible to convey the beauty and intensity of emotion during those visions. They were the most tremendous things I have ever experienced."

Finally, while you're in that inner bliss-filled silence, let yourself be willing to simply ask. *A Course in Miracles* points out that you do not ask too much; in fact, you ask too little. And of course the Bible says: "Ask, and it will be given to you" (Mark 7:7). All creation stems from the void, the great silence—this includes the creation of a new you devoid of self-defeating thinking habits and accompanying excuses. As Swami Sivananda reminded his devotees: "Silence is the language of God." Ask in silence, listen in silence, and let silence be the jumping-off point for becoming one with the creative force of the universe.

### 5. Reenergize Your Surroundings

The Law of Attraction works when you surround yourself with people who are on a spiritual path similar to your own. Remember, this law states that like is attracted to like, so you attract Source energy to you by being like it. Similarly, when you're continually in the company of low-energy, angry, depressed, shaming, hateful people, you'll probably find life a little more challenging.

It was said of Jesus that when he entered a village, the population would be elevated just by his presence; no one could bring him down. Become more Christlike yourself by remembering that no one can bring *you* down because of his or her low energy. If people around you are angry or depressed and you feel drained emotionally, it's your responsibility to yourself to create the right energy for you—you don't have to join them in their negativity. Stay in your place of peace, regardless of how tempting it may be to lash out or argue.

Practice Lao-tzu's four cardinal virtues, and keep your environment as pure and free from negativity as you possibly can: Literally and metaphorically turn off any medium that broadcasts a litany of reasons to be depressed and frightened. Make your home a temple of kindness and love. Stay away from places that thrive on loud noise, alcohol consumption, smoking, and insensitivity. Pay attention to the music you listen to, the art you view, even the arrangement of your furniture and flowers—all of it! The more peaceful and loving your environment (and the people in it), the more you're in a serene place where excuses aren't on the agenda. This is the environment in which self-defeating habits are most likely to fade from your consciousness.

Further reinforce your new way of being by having your surroundings reflect the design of what you want your life to look like. In this energy, like-minded people will appear. Choose to be in the company of those who hold a space for you to achieve the joy of maximizing, rather then minimizing, your highest human potential.

### 6. Get Back to Nature

When I'm on Maui writing, I make it a weekly practice to drive halfway around the island to a lush spot with a stunning waterfall that empties into a refreshing pool, where I spend several hours swimming and meditating while the water cascades down on me. In those moments it feels as if God has entered my consciousness, and a rapturous feeling of contentment overwhelms me. This is a ritual I do just before beginning a new chapter, and it reconnects me to my Source of inspiration. There's no confusion, no worry, no fear . . . nothing but pure ecstasy and a lightness of being. In these moments, which I cherish deeply, I receive the answers I seek, not only for the writing I know I'll be doing in the next several days, but for my personal life as well.

This setting that showcases nature's beauty is pure God in action. As I get quiet and listen, any self-limiting thoughts are simply impossible. I understand what my spiritual friend Thoreau meant when he wrote these words in 1854, explaining why he chose to live in nature at Walden pond: "I went to the woods because I wished to live deliberately, to front only the essential facts of life, and see if I could not learn what it had to teach, and not, when I came to die, discover that I had not lived."

You will also find your answers in nature, because God *is* nature: unspoiled, untended, alive in stillness, and teeming with life. When you're there, you'll begin to see the miraculousness of every cubic inch of space. You'll feel the presence of an energy that you may have lost touch with in your daily life, and that energy is in you, just as it is in all of the flora and fauna. The creative spirit of God or Tao is so easy to align with when you're in a natural, unpretentious setting.

A week before writing this chapter, I trekked to the waterfall and natural pool with someone I love, stood in the cool flowing water, and ate guava fruit hanging from a branch above the surface. In those moments everything I needed to say here solidified. Excuses were out of the question, and I understood what Einstein wrote in his later years: "I lived in solitude in the country and noticed how the monotony of a quiet life stimulates the creative mind."

### 7. Practice Yoga

As I mentioned earlier in the book, the meaning of the word *yoga* translates to "union." The ancient *rishis* who gave us yoga considered stretching, balancing, and flexible exercising an opportunity to experience union with God. Such a union with the Source of being wasn't a painful experience, since God was viewed as natural, peaceful, and gentle.

In our Western world, the most popular exercise regimens involve some degree of harsh, vigorous, punishing, no-pain/no-gain activity. These include: running or jogging; bicycling; aerobics; and weight lifting, particularly on complicated machines, to add muscle tone. Yoga, on the other hand, has no harshness to it. Yet even as you stay in a space the size of a small mat, you attain the same kind of benefit those other physical pursuits give you, without the pain or exertion.

Yoga is a great workout for the entire body—particularly the joints, muscles, and even internal organs—but especially for the mind. I've practiced it just about every day for four years, and it's been a great healing factor in overcoming the aches and pains I inherited from three decades of daily running and weight lifting, along with the endless stopping and starting that accompanied years of competitive tennis. I lived with chronic back pain for many years before I began my practice of a daily 90-minute class of Bikram hot yoga, and I'm happy to say that I've been pain free now for almost four full years.

One of the most appealing features of yoga is that it's done in silence. The mind gets to stop all of its chatter and concentrate on union with God through specific *asanas* that are designed to align the body, mind, and spirit with the Source of being. And that's why I included this little pitch for yoga in a book on eliminating excuses and bad thinking habits—this entire work has been about finding a way to reconnect to the Tao in all of our thoughts and actions.

When you experience union, let go of your ego and no longer rely on excuses. In the 2nd century B.C., Patanjali, who is often called the father of yoga, defined it this way: "Yoga is the ability to direct the mind exclusively toward an object and sustain that direction without any distractions. . . . Yoga is the control of the ideas in the mind." Now this is precisely what an *Excuses Begone!* approach to life teaches. Control your mind, and everything will fall into place.

Give yoga an honest 30-day trial. Notice how your body feels better all over, and your inclination toward excuses dissipates as well!

### 8. Make Sure Your Number One Relationship Is with Your Senior Partner

I know that you have many significant and important relationships: certainly the ones you enjoy with your children, parents, spouse/lover/significant other, co-workers, and best friends rate very high in your life. Here in the *Excuses Begone!* paradigm, however, I ask you to place your relationship to your Source of being at the very top of this list. When this becomes your reality, you intuitively go to the silence within and remember to send your ego to a place where it doesn't interfere with your deliberations.

Make your relationship to Source your priority even if you declare yourself an atheist. When you go to this place within yourself, you don't need any religious orientation or belief in the supernatural. You needn't see God as a bearded old white man floating around in heaven awaiting your requests. You needn't believe in talking snakes; whales swallowing people and then spitting them out; God's only son being sacrificed by his Father in order to save us; or boats with all creatures on board, including insects and dinosaurs, to assuage God's wrath with a flood that covers the earth. While these stories are fine, I have my own opinions on religious tales, as I'm sure you do.

Rather, I ask you to think of God—or the Tao, Divine mind, Krishna, Source, or any of the thousand names for God—as love. Even the Bible itself states that "God is love" (1 John 4:8). And when Carl Jung was asked in an interview if he believed in God, he said these words, which reflect what I want to convey: "I could not say I believe. I know! I have had the experience of being gripped by something stronger than myself, something that people call God" ("The Old Wise Man," *Time,* February 14, 1955).

There's a loving energy in the universe that allows for the creation of all beings. It is a nonbeing without form or boundaries, and it does nothing while leaving nothing undone! Make this energy your primary relationship, above all others in your life, consulting it before anyone else. Retreat there in silence, and listen and know that this force is outside of you and within you. It's here that you will be guided to change self-defeating excuse patterns.

By all means, love your family (and everyone else on this planet). Treasure all of your relationships, but first and foremost make your relationship to your highest self your priority. When you see God simply as love, there will be no room left for excuses and bad habits. You will only be able to give away the love that is your creative essence.

I vividly recall reading an essay published in *Time* magazine that was written by Patti Davis, the daughter of former President Ronald Reagan, describing her long battle with cocaine addiction. She wrote that after she'd been clean for five years, the desire to take up the old habit was still very pronounced within her. She concluded her commentary by saying that although the desire was still there, and the memory of the euphoric feeling in her brain when she was on the drug was still enticing, she continued to stay away from this debilitating habit because she didn't want to disappoint God by returning to those old ways.

This is what it means to make your relationship to God the supreme relationship. It seems that Patti could handle disappointing her parents, her friends, and even herself, since she had done so many times. But she just couldn't go back to a state of being that was antithetical to Source energy, because her primary relationship in life was now to God. And in all honesty, I must say that this is the reason I personally have never gone back to alcohol.

As you can see, old habits disappear much more readily when you make your Senior Partner number one in your life. That's because your Senior Partner is pure love, and when you go there first, all that you could ever need is provided for you.

### 9. Work the Paradigm

I close this chapter with a reminder to work the *Excuses Begone!* paradigm whenever you find yourself stuck in self-defeating thought patterns or behaviors. The paradigm can be applied at any time, to any long-standing limitation that you want to change. When you notice that you've employed an excuse, just say these three words: *Work the paradigm.* In a matter of moments, the old mental crutches will vanish.

You can easily work the paradigm by quickly going through each of the seven questions and silently responding with short answers. When you notice that any question in the paradigm elicits a response that keeps the old excuse pattern activated, shift your answer so that it aligns with the highest vision that you have for yourself. This is a powerful act of changing the way you've allowed yourself to be conditioned to think, but it only works as long as you are honest and keep what you're doing a private matter between you and the highest part of yourself.

I don't feel that there's any need for me to elaborate on the seven questions we've already looked at in such detail. However, I would like to leave you with a brief summation of the essence of the *Excuses Begone!* paradigm, with a short response to each of the seven questions:

1. Is it true? *Probably not.*

2. Where did the excuses come from? *I allowed them.*

3. What's the payoff? *I get to avoid risks and stay the same.*

4. What would my life look like if I couldn't use these excuses? *I'd be free to be myself.*

5. Can I create a rational reason to change? *Easily.*

6. Can I access universal cooperation in shedding old habits? *Yes, by simply aligning with my Source of being.*

7. How can I continuously reinforce this new way of being? *By being vigilant.*

If you work the paradigm several times, you'll soon see where you're guiding your life with thoughts that aren't necessarily true. You'll be able to discern where those thoughts came from and what your life would look like without them, and then you'll create a rational reason to change them by accessing Divine guidance through perfect union with your Source of being. To be consciously merged into that perfect union with God is a feeling that's difficult to explain, but ego does take a backseat. You know that you're allowing yourself to be guided by a force that's bigger than you are, yet if you so choose, you can stay infinitely connected to it. In this state of knowingness, excuses become a thing of the past.

In 1851, Thoreau described his boyhood ecstasies in his journal, and his words take me back to my *own* boyhood ecstasies. I'm ending this very personal book with his observation because it is to those kinds of moments that I urge you to return as well:

> There comes into my mind such an indescribable, infinite, all-absorbing, divine, heavenly pleasure, a sense of elevation and expansion, and [I] have nought to do with it. I perceive that I am dealt with by superior powers. This is a pleasure, a joy, an existence which I have not procured myself. I speak as a witness on the stand, and tell what I have perceived.

I too perceive that I'm being dealt with by superior powers. I too speak to you as a witness telling you what I have perceived. I too have felt the all-absorbing, Divine sense of elevation that comes from living my life with a minimum of excuses. And as I conclude this labor of love, I wish for you to come to know the heavenly pleasure of living each and every day aligned with your Source of being in such a way that you can shout out: "Excuses, I no longer need you in my life, so be . . . gone!"

# ENDNOTES

[1]From *Hua Hu Ching: The Unknown Teachings of Lao Tzu,* translated by Brian Walker (Harper San Francisco, 1992).

[2]Ibid.

[3]Ibid.

[4]Ibid.

[5]Ibid.

# ABOUT THE AUTHOR

**Dr. Wayne W. Dyer** is an internationally renowned author and speaker in the field of self-development. He's the author of more than 40 books, has created many audio programs and videos, and has appeared on thousands of television and radio shows. His books *Manifest Your Destiny, Wisdom of the Ages, There's a Spiritual Solution to Every Problem,* and *The New York Times* bestsellers *10 Secrets for Success and Inner Peace, The Power of Intention, Inspiration, Change Your Thoughts—Change Your Life, Excuses Begone!* and *Wishes Fulfilled* have all been featured as National Public Television specials.

Wayne holds a doctorate in educational counseling from Wayne State University and was an associate professor at St. John's University in New York.

Website: **www.DrWayneDyer.com**

# Hay House Titles of Related Interest

*YOU CAN HEAL YOUR LIFE, the movie,*
starring Louise L. Hay & Friends
(available as a 1-DVD program and an expanded 2-DVD set)
Watch the trailer at: www.LouiseHayMovie.com

*THE SHIFT, the movie,*
starring Dr. Wayne W. Dyer
(available as a 1-DVD program and an expanded 2-DVD set)
Watch the trailer at: www.DyerMovie.com

▲▼▲

*THE ESSENTIAL DOREEN VIRTUE COLLECTION,* by Doreen Virtue

*THE ESSENTIAL LAW OF ATTRACTION COLLECTION,*
by Esther and Jerry Hicks (The Teachings of Abraham®)

*THE ESSENTIAL LOUISE HAY COLLECTION,* by Louise Hay

All of the above are available at your local bookstore,
or may be ordered by contacting Hay House (see next page).

▲▼▲

We hope you enjoyed this Hay House book. If you'd like to receive our online catalog featuring additional information on Hay House books and products, or if you'd like to find out more about the Hay Foundation, please contact:

Hay House, Inc., P.O. Box 5100, Carlsbad, CA 92018-5100
(760) 431-7695 or (800) 654-5126
(760) 431-6948 (fax) or (800) 650-5115 (fax)
www.hayhouse.com® • www.hayfoundation.org

▲▼▲

*Published and distributed in Australia by:* Hay House Australia Pty. Ltd., 18/36 Ralph St., Alexandria NSW 2015 • *Phone:* 612-9669-4299 *Fax:* 612-9669-4144 • www.hayhouse.com.au

*Published and distributed in the United Kingdom by:* Hay House UK, Ltd., Astley House, 33 Notting Hill Gate, London W11 3JQ • *Phone:* 44-20-3675-2450 *Fax:* 44-20-3675-2451 • www.hayhouse.co.uk

*Published and distributed in the Republic of South Africa by:* Hay House SA (Pty), Ltd., P.O. Box 990, Witkoppen 2068 • *Phone/Fax:* 27-11-467-8904 www.hayhouse.co.za

*Published in India by:* Hay House Publishers India, Muskaan Complex, Plot No. 3, B-2, Vasant Kunj, New Delhi 110 070 • *Phone:* 91-11-4176-1620 *Fax:* 91-11-4176-1630 • www.hayhouse.co.in

*Distributed in Canada by:* Raincoast, 9050 Shaughnessy St., Vancouver, B.C. V6P 6E5 • *Phone:* (604) 323-7100 • *Fax:* (604) 323-2600 www.raincoast.com

▲▼▲

Take Your Soul on a Vacation

Visit www.HealYourLife.com® to regroup, recharge, and reconnect with your own magnificence. Featuring blogs, mind-body-spirit news, and life-changing wisdom from Louise Hay and friends.

Visit www.HealYourLife.com today!

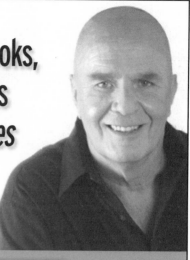

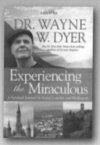

# Free e-newsletters from Hay House, the Ultimate Resource for Inspiration

Be the first to know about Hay House's dollar deals, free downloads, special offers, affirmation cards, giveaways, contests, and more!

 Get exclusive excerpts from our latest releases and videos from *Hay House Present Moments*.

 Enjoy uplifting personal stories, how-to articles, and healing advice, along with videos and empowering quotes, within *Heal Your Life*.

 Have an inspirational story to tell and a passion for writing? Sharpen your writing skills with insider tips from *Your Writing Life*.

## Sign Up Now!

*Get inspired, educate yourself, get a complimentary gift, and share the wisdom!*

http://www.hayhouse.com/newsletters.php

Visit www.hayhouse.com to sign up today!

 HAY HOUSE

 radio for your soul®

HealYourLife.com ❤

# Heal Your Life One Thought at a Time . . . on Louise's All-New Website!

*"Life is bringing me everything I need and more."*

— Louise Hay

**Come to HEALYOURLIFE.COM today** and meet the world's best-selling self-help authors; the most popular leading in-tuitive, health, and success experts; up-and-coming inspi-rational writers; and new like-minded friends who will share their insights, experiences, personal stories, and wisdom so you can heal your life and the world around you . . . one thought at a time.

## Here are just some of the things you'll get at HealYourLife.com:

- DAILY AFFIRMATIONS
- CAPTIVATING VIDEO CLIPS
- EXCLUSIVE BOOK REVIEWS
- AUTHOR BLOGS
- LIVE TWITTER AND FACEBOOK FEEDS
- BEHIND-THE-SCENES SCOOPS
- LIVE STREAMING RADIO
- "MY LIFE" COMMUNITY OF FRIENDS

**PLUS:**
FREE Monthly Contests and Polls
FREE BONUS gifts, discounts, and newsletters

## Make It Your Home Page Today!

### www.HealYourLife.com®

HEAL YOUR LIFE®